LITURGIES OF
THE PAST

Stave Church, Gol. Now in the Bygdøy Museum, Oslo

Liturgies of the Past

ARCHDALE A. KING

LONGMANS

LONGMANS, GREEN AND CO LTD
6 & 7 CLIFFORD STREET, LONDON W I

THIBAULT HOUSE, THIBAULT SQUARE, CAPETOWN
605–611 LONSDALE STREET, MELBOURNE C I
443 LOCKHART ROAD, HONG KONG
ACCRA, AUCKLAND, IBADAN
KINGSTON (JAMAICA), KUALA LUMPUR
LAHORE, NAIROBI, SALISBURY (RHODESIA)

LONGMANS, GREEN AND CO INC
119 WEST 40TH STREET, NEW YORK 18

LONGMANS, GREEN AND CO
20 CRANFIELD ROAD, TORONTO 16

ORIENT LONGMANS PRIVATE LTD
CALCUTTA, BOMBAY, MADRAS
DELHI, HYDERABAD, DACCA

© A. A. King 1959

First published 1959

PRINTED IN GREAT BRITAIN BY RICHARD CLAY AND COMPANY,
LTD., BUNGAY, SUFFOLK. NIHIL OBSTAT JOANNES M. T. BARTON,
S.T.D., L.S.S., CENSOR DEPUTATUS. IMPRIMATUR E. MORROGH
BERNARD, VIC. GEN. WESTMONASTERII, DIE 19A NOVEMBRIS, 1958

PREFACE

THE fourth and final volume of the 'Rites of Western Christendom' has been called, for want of a more apposite title: 'Liturgies of the Past'.

The terms 'rite' and 'use' have been employed interchangeably despite the obvious fact that variants of a rite are, strictly speaking, no more than 'uses'.

Liturgies are described which have long since disappeared without hope of recall, although, in the case of the primitive rites of Aquileia and Benevento, and to a lesser degree that of the Celtic Churches, their very framework is open to considerable doubt. We have, however, no reason to suppose that the service-books of the Celts, before the infiltration of Roman texts, were other than augmented and embellished early Gallican books.

It has been thought that a description of the mediaeval rites of the British Isles would be of especial interest to English-speaking peoples; while the Norwegian rite of Nidaros (Trondheim) has been included at the suggestion of Mr. Christopher Hohler, since it was used at one time in the Isle of Man, Shetlands and Orkneys.

In the belief that 'composition of place' is of considerable interest and importance in a book of this kind, it has been the endeavour of the writer to visit personally, as far as possible, all the places which have been in any way connected with the various liturgies concerned.

Buildings erected for the worship of God according to the several rites and uses are described.

The primitive rite of Aquileia is little more than conjecture, and the so-called 'Patriarchal' rite was a late mediaeval Roman variant. Work on this *Ritus Patriarchinus* was, however, facilitated by the kindness of the acting librarian of the archiepiscopal library at Udine, who placed at the disposal of the writer such

v

liturgical MSS. as pertained to Friuli. Udine was the last of the residences of the patriarchs of Aquileia, but it was found possible to visit also the one-time patriarchal seats at Aquileia, Grado and Cividale.

Knowledge of the rite of Benevento is scant indeed, and in fact limited to a series of texts belonging to the old repertory, which found their way into later Roman MSS.

Much of the chapter on the Gallican liturgy was written on the island of Lérins: 'foyer of the Gallican rite'. The island is now occupied by the Cistercians, and the use of books from the library was facilitated by the kindly offices of the spiritual director, Fr. Paul. Visits were entailed also to Marseilles, the home of Cassian; Arles, from whence in all probability the embellished Gallican liturgy was diffused throughout France; Poitiers, a Merovingian centre; and Tours, the city of Martin and Gregory.

A study of the Celtic rite included a journey to Ireland, as well as to the foundations of St. Colomban at Luxeuil and Bobbio.

The description of the rites and ceremonies followed in the churches of the British Isles in the Middle Ages owes much to the help afforded by Mr. Christopher Hohler of the Courtauld Institute of Art in the University of London. Mr. Hohler's reputation for scholarship respecting the sacrementaries and missals of this country will serve as a passport for accuracy.

The use of Nidaros or Trondheim, as it is sometimes called, is virtually a *terra incognita*, as far as this country is concerned, although a very useful book on the Norwegian *Ordo Missae* was produced a few years ago by a Lutheran pastor of Oslo.[1] The author, Dr. Helge Faehn, proved 'guide, philosopher and friend' when the writer was in Oslo, and made it possible to study the three MS. manuals of the rite, which by a stroke of good fortune were on loan from Copenhagen at the time. Very heartfelt thanks are due also to Mr. Per Bang, who has been good enough to translate long articles on the rite, which, with a total ignorance of the language, would have been otherwise unavailable.

The photographs of the ambones in the cathedral church of Ravello were taken by the Rev. Bruno Scott James, to whom, as

---

[1] *Fire Norske Messeordninger fra Middelalderen.* Oslo, 1953.

for so much else, I would like to express my gratitude. The courtesy of the Irish Travel Office has permitted the reproduction of many of the Celtic subjects.

Finally, thanks are due to the Norwegian Travel Office, which has supplied photographs of *stave* churches.

ARCHDALE A. KING

Westminster
St. Olaf, 29 *July* 1957

CONTENTS

PLATES

xi

Chapter One

RITE OF AQUILEIA

Historical Background

THE small decayed village in the Gulf of Trieste, to the north of the Adriatic and at the extremity of the delta formed by the river Isonzo, shows but little of its one-time importance. It is indeed difficult to realise that it was an important naval station and frontier fortress, the point of departure for the imperial legions in their campaigns against Illyria and the districts watered by the Danube. Aquileia at the beginning of the 2nd century was *Roma secunda, maxima Italiae urbs, Italiae emporium, frequentissima, praedives*:[1] the residence of the emperors from Augustus (*ob.* 14) to Theodosius (*ob.* 395). Its position as a frontier station between Eastern and Western Europe supplied a trading centre of considerable commercial worth. Christianity must have reached Aquileia at an early date, but there is no historical foundation for the tradition that 'St. Mark founded the Church and wrote the Gospel there'.[2] A chapel was erected near Morsano di Belvedere in 1747, in order, so it is said, to mark the spot where the Evangelist landed, but unfortunately the legend of his apostolate dates only from the 7th century. The story was probably invented for the purpose of enhancing the importance of the new patriarchate. Thus it was affirmed that St. Mark was sent from Rome by St. Peter to be the apostle of Aquileia (46–50), prior to his journey to Alexandria.[3] Then, before leaving for Egypt, the Saint is said to have chosen as his successor an 'elegant

---

[1] Henri Leclercq, *Aquilée (archéologie)*, *Dict. d'Archéol. Chrét. et de Lit.*, t. I, part II, cols. 2660–61.

[2] Gaetano Moroni Romano, *Dizionario di Erudizione Storico-Ecclesiastica*, vol. II (Venice, 1840), art. *Aquileia*, p. 257.

[3] The calendar of the missal of Aquileia (1519) gives the Translation of St. Mark as an additional feast on 31 January (nine lessons).

I

person' named Hermagoras, who had been consecrated bishop by St. Peter. Hermagoras is venerated in Istria and the surrounding districts as patron saint and first bishop of Aquileia, and, according to the same tradition, he is said to have preached the Gospel in Belluno, Como and Ceneda, accompanied by a deacon of the name of Fortunatus.[1] Late and quite untrustworthy *acta* say that the two Saints were martyred at Aquileia in the persecution of Nero, who had sent a certain Sebastius to carry out the edict against the Christians. It may well be that there was a bishop called Hermagoras, who was put to death and subsequently venerated by the inhabitants of those parts, and that there was a deacon of the name of Fortunatus who also suffered for the faith, but there is no reliable information about either of them, and absolutely nothing to connect St. Fortunatus with any Hermagoras or with this date.[2] A recent history of Friuli speaks of St. Hermagoras as the 'first bishop of Aquileia of whom there is any record', but his episcopate is placed in the first half of the 3rd century, when the city had become a centre of Christian influence in Venetia and Norica.[3] The two Saints were already invoked in litanies in the time of the Patriarch Pellegrinus I (*c.* 1150), and by the middle of the 13th century their feast was celebrated solemnly.[4] The missal of 1519 provides two feasts: 12 July as a *duplex majus* (nine lessons) with an octave, and 27 August (Translation) as *cum pleno officio*. The collect of the Saints was prescribed by the Patriarch Pertold (*ob.* 1251) to be recited daily at Mass.[5] An annual visit to the tomb of the martyrs was incumbent upon the bishops of the province and those abbots whose houses depended from the patriarchal see.[6] In the middle of the 9th century we find Pavia placing herself under the protection of St. Hermagoras, as part of that 'break away' from Milan which had

---

[1] Tradition also describes St. Hermagoras as the 'Apostle of Como'.

[2] *Acta SS.*, July, t. III, pp. 249-51; Delahaye, *Les Origines du Culte des Martyrs*, p. 377; Thurston, *Lives of the Saints* (London, 1932), vol. VII, July, pp. 156-7.

[3] P. S. Leicht, *Breve Storia del Friuli*, chap. I, p. 36. Udine, 1930.

[4] From a ritual note of the time. De Rubeis, *Differt. citat. de Ritibus*, cap. XII, num. III, p. 252. The feast was celebrated throughout the province in the time of the Patriarch Raymond della Torre (1273-99).

[5] Rubeis, *Monum. Eccl. Aquil.*, cap. LXXI, num. I.

[6] Francesco Florio, *Vita del Beato Beltrando* (Venice, 1759), pp. 100-1.

begun at the beginning of the previous century.[1] The Saint is honoured today as the patron of the archdiocese of Udine, which has been for many centuries the successor of the deserted Aquileia.

Chroniclers mention the existence of a baptistery at Aquileia in the time of the emperor Aurelian (270), and there is little doubt that the city was already an episcopal see. The many Eastern martyrs in the Friulian martyrology suggest that Christianity came to Aquileia from the East. Tradition recalls St. Hellarus (Hilarius) as a bishop who was martyred in 285, and the calendar of the missal of 1519 says: 16 March, 'Hellarus, bishop, and Dacian, deacon, martyrs' (in Aquileia *duplex*).[2] In the 4th century Aquileia was the principal ecclesiastical centre for the region at the head of the Adriatic (Venetia and Istria), and its bishop was created metropolitan in 360. The city was the ninth in size in the Roman Empire, and Decimus Ausonius (*c.* 310–*c.* 395) has described it as *moenibus et portu celeberrima*, surpassed only by Rome, Capua and Milan.[3] The number of Christians in Aquileia was very considerable, but it is difficult to estimate their number in the smaller towns of the province. Concordia and Giulio Carnico may have had bishops in the 4th century, but we know nothing in this respect about Cividale (*Forum Julii*) until later.

Theodore, bishop of Aquileia, who erected the great church which served as the metropolitan cathedral, assisted at the council of Arles in 314. The clergy of his time seem to have been extolled for their unswerving orthodoxy, and praised for the splendour of their worship.[4] The bishop Fortunatianus (347–60) is said to have built a *templum magnificum*.

At a council held at Rome in 347, the bishop of Aquileia occupied a place second only to that of the Pope. Lebrun, in commenting on this pre-eminence, says that it was customary for the Pontiff to have the metropolitan of Aquileia on his right hand and

---

[1] Achille Ratti, *La Chiesa ambrosiana, Conferenze di Storia Milanese* (Milan, 1897), p. 170.

[2] The bodies of St. Hilary and Companions, martyrs of Aquileia, were translated in 1342.

[3] Ausonius, *Ordo urb. nob.*, V, 65.

[4] Leicht, *op. cit.* p. 37.

the bishop of Ravenna on his left, although such precedence must surely have been in the absence of the bishop of Milan, as it would have been unbecoming for this prelate to have held a lower place than his brother of Aquileia.[1]

In 381, an important council was held at Aquileia for the purpose of combating the Arian heresy. St. Ambrose (*ob.* 397) presided, with the assistance of thirty-two (? twenty-four) bishops, among whom was the Aquileian bishop of Torcello (Altinum), St. Eliodorus, the friend of St. Jerome and Rufinus.[2] The Balkan bishops Palladius and Secundianus were condemned on a charge of Arianism, but their supporters complained bitterly of the alleged high-handedness of the 'haughty' bishop of Milan and the bishop of Aquileia.

St. Valerian was succeeded in the see of Aquileia by St. Chromatius (*ob.* 407), who had baptised Rufinus and was also a friend of St. Jerome, as well as a supporter of St. John Chrysostom. He was well known as a commentator of Holy Scripture, and seventeen of his treatises on the gospel of St. Matthew and a homily on the Beatitudes are extant.

The purity of the chant in the cathedral church at this time was commented on by St. Jerome (*ob.* 420), who likened the singing to a 'choir of angels'.[3]

Western Illyrica, Norica and Rhaetia were in the ecclesiastical jurisdiction of Aquileia, but it was not until the time of the emperor Honorius (*ob.* 423), following the reign of Theodosius (379–95), that paganism came to be finally vanquished.

For more than a century, Aquileia served as a *scutum saldissimum et antemurale Christianitatis* against barbarian invaders,[4] but in 410 the city was sacked and burned by the Goths; while in 452 it was so completely devastated by Attila and his Huns that its very site was said to have been hardly recognisable. The metropolitan Secundinus and most of the inhabitants fled to the neigh-

---

[1] Lebrun, *Explication de la Messe* (Paris, 1726), t. II, p. 222, n. 24.

[2] St. Eliodorus is held by many to have been the first bishop of the Roman city of Altinum, which changed its name later to Torcello. Others, however, have considered St. Teonistus, the martyr, as the first bishop.

[3] Leicht, *op. cit.*, p. 37.

[4] Pope Leo X (1513–21) so described Croatia as a bulwark against the Turks.

bouring island of Grado,[1] but his successor, Nicetas, returned to Aquileia, where he set about restoring the ruined churches.

The city, however, never regained its former prosperity: diminished cultivation and loss of commerce were succeeded by malaria.

In 489, Aquileia was invaded by the Arian Ostrogoths under Odoacer, who held the city until the coming of the Lombards in 568.

Grado was more fortunately situated, and the island served as a base for the Byzantine fleet.

The council, held under Macedonius at Aquileia in 553, decided to go into schism over the controversy concerning the 'Three Chapters', and it was not before the 8th century that the patriarchate, as it had then become, was restored to Catholic unity.[2]

St. Columban, who died at Bobbio in 615, although not personally implicated in the schism, wrote a letter to Pope Boniface IV (608-15), in which he referred to the supporters of the 'Three Chapters' as 'victims of the impudent Vigilius', and said that a reversal of the decision of his predecessor would be to the honour of the Apostolic See, and the extinction of a deplorable schism. The letter, however, failed to give any reason for such a revision of policy, and confined itself to affirmations, apostrophes, protestations and reproaches.[3]

The title of patriarch was assumed by the metropolitans of

---

[1] The 'island' is now joined to the mainland by a causeway, and it must have been similarly joined in 662, if it is true that Grado was invaded by the Lombard duke Lupo and his cavalry.

[2] *Schism of the Three Chapters;* Three Nestorian documents—(*a*) Writings of Theodore of Mopsuestia; (*b*) Writings of Theodoret of Cyrus against the council of Ephesus; (*c*) A letter of a certain Ibas to Maris. They had been condemned by the emperor Justinian and the Eastern patriarchs, in the hope of a reconciliation with the Monophysites, in 544. The bishops of Africa, North Italy and Dalmatia opposed the condemnation, as it was thought to compromise the council of Chalcedon. In 548, Pope Vigilius (537-55) condemned the Chapters, and then retracted, but in 554 he was bullied by the emperor into confirming the acts of the council at Constantinople which had again condemned the writings. Several of the Western archbishops went into schism, including the metropolitan of Illyria, whose province was not recognised until 700—hence arose the patriarchate of Aquileia. The dispute, which concerned the expediency and implications of the condemnation, was in no way connected with a definition of faith.

[3] Eugène Martin (Ital. trans. Giuseppe Monteverde), *Vita di S. Columbano* (Bobbio, 1923), part II, chap. III, pp. 166-73.

Aquileia in 560, but, eight years later (568), Paulinus, the first to bear the title, fled to Grado, with the relics and treasures of his Church, on the approach of the Lombards, mindful of the horrors that had attended the invasion of the Huns in 452. Paulinus (557–69) took it for granted that residence in Aquileia was for the future impossible, and his successor, a Greek of the name of Elias (571–86), obtained a decree from Pope Pelagius II (579–90) transferring the see and title of patriarch to the Church of Grado, 'New Aquileia' (*Nova Aquileia*). The decision of the Pope was approved by a synod of suffragan bishops which met at Grado in 579, and the misfortunes of Old Aquileia were recounted: *Jam pridem ab Attila funditus est destructa, et postea Gothorum incursu et caeterorum barbarorum quassata vix respirat etiam nunc Langobardorum nefandae gentis flagella sustinere valens.* Grado became henceforth *Venetae orae Istriaeque Ecclesiarum caput et mater et Aquileja nova.* Memorials of the patriarchate of Elias are still to be seen at Grado in the cathedral church of S. Eufemia, its baptistery, and the basilica of S. Maria delle Grazie.

The Lombards at Aquileia seem to have been on the most cordial terms with the Catholics, and about the year 670 renounced their Arianism. The patriarchate was divided on the death of Severus, the successor of Elias, in 610, as the Lombards considered it to be in conformity with the dignity and interests of their kingdom that Aquileia should be the seat of a patriarch. A division was duly effected: the Lombard king Aygulf and Gisulf, duke of Friuli, nominated John; while the clergy of Grado, with the consent of Pope Boniface IV (608–15), elected Candidian. The patriarch of Aquileia had jurisdiction over the bishops in Lombard territory, and the patriarch of Grado over the bishops of the seacoast and Istria, who were subjects of the Byzantine Empire. Grado thus succeeded to the Roman heritage of Aquileia, and flourished from the 6th to the 10th century, finally transmitting its power and influence to Venice. It had joined the Venetian naval league in 697, and was the ecclesiastical centre for all seafaring places, but its isolation from the hinterland heavily handicapped it in the race with Venice.

The election of Candidian to the see of Grado in 606 (607)

terminated the schism of the 'Three Chapters' for those sees which lay within the limits of the Byzantine Empire, but Old Aquileia, despite the efforts of Popes and exarchs (Ravenna), persisted in its isolation. It was not before the year 700 that a synod at Aquileia submitted to Pope Sergius I (687–701), and the schism came to an end. The pallium was not granted to the patriarchs of Aquileia until 769, as it was considered that Grado was too close, but in that year Rome, at the request of the Lombard king Luitprand, formally recognised the two patriarchates, on the condition that the rights of the Church of Grado were respected.

In 803 we read of Fortunatus, patriarch of Grado, visiting France, and taking with him as a present 'two doors of ivory magnificently carved'.[1] It would be of interest to know whether these 'doors' were the two leaves of a diptych, such as we find today in the treasury of the cathedral church at Monza.

The extent of the patriarchate of Aquileia was considerable, and in the 5th and 6th centuries it had obtained jurisdiction over *Rhaetia Secunda* (Augsburg, Seben), *Noricum* (Tiburnia) and *Pannonia Prima*.[2]

In a council convoked at Frankfurt in 794 for the condemnation of the heresy of Adoptionism,[3] the patriarch had sat in the first place, before the archbishop of Milan.

The creation of a metropolitan see at Salzburg in the latter part of the 8th century deprived Aquileia of a part of its territory, and Ursus of Aquileia (*ob.* 811), at the behest of Charlemagne, was compelled to relinquish the Carinthian district north of the river Drave to Arno of Salzburg. On the other hand, St. Leo III (795–816) subjected the see of Mantua to the jurisdiction of Aquileia in 804, and we find no less than three Popes—Leo VIII (963–65), John XIX (? XX; 1024–32), Alexander II (1061–73)—referring to its patriarch as the 'first metropolitan in all Italy'.[4] Not-

---

[1] D. T. Rice, *Byzantine Art* (London, 1954), chap. XVII, p. 248.

[2] Duchesne, *Christian Worship* (London, 1904), chap. I, 4, p. 31.

[3] *Adoptionism* taught a double sonship in Christ: one by generation and nature; the other by adoption and grace. The man Christ is therefore the adoptive and not the natural Son of God.

[4] Moroni, *op. cit.*, vol. II, p. 258.

withstanding this, however, a decree of Clement II (1046–47) assigned the first place to Ravenna, the second to Aquileia and the third to Milan.[1]

The following sees were at some time or other within the patriarchate of Aquileia: Udine, Trieste, Capodistria, Cittanova, Eraclea, Pedena, Parenzo, Pola, Concordia, Oderzo, Marianum, Ceneda, Belluno, Feltre, Asolo, Zuglio, Treviso, Padua, Vicenza, Verona, Mantua, Como, Trent, Laibach (Lubliana).

Aquileia, as we have seen, never recovered from the barbarian invasions, and the decadence of the city was further hastened by a change in the current of the river Isonzo.

The residences of the temporal and ecclesiastical rulers were in course of time moved to Cividale (*Forum Julii*), which thus became the capital of the Lombard dukedom, and it was here that Paul the Deacon, monk of Monte Cassino and author of *Historia gentis Langobardorum*, was born in about 720.

In 627, the patriarch Fortunatus had fixed his place of residence at Cormons, but in 737 this was changed to Cividale, the capital of the duchy, as Callixtus, the patriarch, resented the bishop Amatore, a mere suffragan, living in close proximity to the duke, while he remained in a small unimportant town. The duke, Rachis (737–44), was a lover of culture and art, and under him Cividale became a centre of learning.[2]

The 8th century saw more than one invasion of the patriarchate by the Avars, but the final dissolution of the duchy was hastened by the discords and general indiscipline of the Lombards themselves. The country became a part of the Frankish Empire of Charlemagne. In 787, Timothy, a former teacher of the imperial palace school, was nominated patriarch with the name of Paulinus. St. Paulinus II (*ob.* 802), who was a Friulian by birth, took a prominent position in the affairs of his day, and presided at a provincial council in his cathedral city in 796. He showed the greatest prudence and pastoral zeal in his dealings with the Churches of Istria, as well as with the patriarch of Grado, the representative of

---

[1] Ratti, *op. cit.*, p. 171.

[2] Paschini, *San Paolino patriarca e la Chiesa Aquileiese alla fine del secolo VIII* (Udine, 1906), cap. II, p. 13.

Byzantine interests, obtaining, among other privileges, a diploma guaranteeing the free election of future patriarchs of Aquileia. The destruction of Aquileia by the Avars in 788 called forth a poetic lament from Paulinus: [1]

> *Quomodo jaces despecta, inutilis*
> *pressa ruinis; nunquam reparabilis*
> *tempus in omne.*

His successor, Maxentius, appealed to Charlemagne for permission to rebuild the city: *cum nostro adjutorio construere atque reparare ad pristinum honorem.* This was effected in 811.[2] Commerce once again began to flourish, and the Emperor granted special privileges to the ship owned by Fortunatus, the patriarch of Grado. Lack of documents makes it impossible to determine with any certitude how many monasteries were directly dependent upon the patriarchate of Aquileia at this time. We know, however, of the monastery of S. Maria in Valle (with the hospital of S. Giovanni) at Cividale and that of S. Maria in Organo at Verona; also the monastery on the Timavo. The houses at Rosazzo and Moggio were not yet founded. On the confines of the diocese of Aquileia with Concordia we find Sesto, but it is doubtful which diocese it depended from. The monasteries in the territories of Treviso and Verona were directly under the jurisdiction of their own bishops.[3]

St. Paulinus took a leading part in the struggle against the Adoptionist heresy, and he is known as a writer of considerable ability. He composed eight rhythms or hymns to be sung in his church at Christmas, Purification, Lent, Easter, St. Mark, SS. Peter and Paul and the Dedication, as well as the *Versus de Lazaro*. The rhythms are interesting, as they furnish the origins of proses in North Italy.[4] According to Walafrid Strabo (*ob.* 849), they were employed by the Saint 'in private Masses at the offering of

---

[1] Paschini, *San Paolino patriarca e la Chiesa Aquileiese alla fine del secolo VIII* (Udine, 1906), cap. I, p. 12.

[2] *Ibid.,* cap. VII, p. 139.

[3] *Ibid.,* cap. I, p. 12, no. 2.

[4] J. de Ghillinck, *Littérature latine au moyen âge*, vol. I, chap. II, i, p. 92.

B

the Sacrifice'.[1] What, says Dom Cabrol, does the vague expression *hymnos* imply? Poetry in the form of hymns and proses, or rather more liturgical elements, such as collects, or even the prayers of the Canon, as the phrase *circa immolationem sacramentorum* might suppose? It is not easy to say.[2] Ebner has published a very curious and important variant of the *Hanc igitur* in litany form, which he attributes to Paulinus.[3] The works of the Saint are to be found in volume ninety-nine of the *Patrologia Latina*.

The first appearance of the name of Paulinus in the liturgy occurs in the 9th-century *Litaniae* of Charles the Bald. His feast was observed on 11 January until the 16th century, but, as the day fell in the octave of the Epiphany, the commemoration was transferred to 9 February at the beginning of the following century.[4] The relics of St. Paulinus lie under the altar in the crypt of the cathedral church of Cividale, where the feast is celebrated on 2 March. A figure of the Saint is represented on the silver antependium of the high altar, which dates from the end of the 12th century.

Relations between Aquileia and Grado were unfortunately not always in the happy condition that we find in the time of Paulinus, and the rival patriarchs repeatedly appealed to Popes and councils, each claiming jurisdiction over the whole of the territory formerly subject to Old Aquileia. The synod of Mantua in 827 had decided in favour of Maxentius, patriarch of Aquileia, but the rivalry nevertheless persisted. Matters came to a head two centuries later in the patriarchate of Poppo (1019–42), who dreamed of a renaissance of his cathedral city, and envied the flourishing sea-borne trade of Grado. In 1024, Poppo, taking advantage of an insurrection at Venice, attacked the island: churches were dese-

---

[1] *Traditur siquidem, Paulinum Foriuliensem Patriarcham, saepius et maxime in privatis Missis, circa immolationem Sacramentorum, hymnos vel ab aliis, vel a se compositos celebrasse. Ego vero crederim tantum tantequae scientiae virum, hoc nec sine auctoritate, nec sine rationis ponderatione fecisse.* Walafrid Strabo, *De Exord. Increm. Rer. Eccles.*, lib. I, cap. XXV; Hittorp, *De Div. Cath. Eccles. Offic.* (Paris, 1610), col. 688.

[2] Cabrol, *Aquilée (Liturgie), Dict. d'Archéol. Chrét. et de Lit.*, t. I, part II, col. 2684. Cf. Baumstark, *Lit. Rom. e Lit. dell'Esarcato*, cap. IV, pp. 176–7.

[3] Ebner, *Iter Italicum* (Freiburg, 1896), pp. 416–17.

[4] The feast appears in the missal of 1519 on 11 January: 'Nine Lessons'.

crated, relics stolen and nuns were violated.[1] The patriarch was
forced later by the doge Otto Orseolo to restore the stolen treasure, but shortly before the death of Poppo in 1042 Grado was
again attacked. There was, however, a constructive side to this
bellicose prelate, who was in many ways a great ecclesiastic and an
able temporal ruler. The patriarch of Aquileia was at this time the
Lord of Friuli, as a result of the Hungarian invasions, which had
decimated the ranks of the nobility.[2]

The transfer of government to the Church had been largely due
to the patriarch Frederick (921), but the change of rule was favoured by kings and emperors alike. A diploma of Otto III (1001)
to the patriarch John IV granted to the Church of Aquileia jurisdiction over all the towns it had rebuilt. Poppo reconstructed his
cathedral church, which had been restored by Maxentius in the
time of Charlemagne. In addition to this he built a palace, con-
solidated the city walls, revived commerce by establishing the sea-
port of Piro, endowed the canons of his basilica and certain of the
Benedictine monasteries and obtained permission from the emperor Conrad to coin his own money. The figure of Poppo may
be seen today in the apse of the cathedral alongside the emperors
Conrad the Salic and Henry III, and in company with the saint-
protectors of the patriarchate. The church was consecrated in
honour of the Blessed Virgin and Saints Hermagoras and Fortunatus on 13 July 1031, and the 'Dedication of the Mother Church
of Aquileia' is found in the missal of 1519 as a *duplex majus*. The
predecessor of Poppo, John IV, had consecrated the cathedral
church of Bamberg in Germany, assisted by no less than thirty
bishops. The privilege of wearing a pallium and a rationale at one
and the same time was accorded to Poppo by Pope John XIX
(1024–32) in 1027, although the use of the former was restricted
to the more solemn feasts. The great patriarch lies buried in the
centre of the basilica on which he lavished so much care and devotion, but no memorial has been erected to mark the site. The
Roman synod of 1047, at which the German patriarch Eberhard
assisted, declared Aquileia to rank next in importance to Rome,

---

[1] H. Leclercq, *Aquilée (archéologie)*, *D.A.C.L.*, t. I, part II, col. 2656.
[2] The Hungarians had invaded the country in 899, 904, 923 and 942.

Ravenna and Milan, although, as we have seen, several of its suffragans were transferred later to other metropolitan sees. The centuries-old dispute between the rival patriarchates of Aquileia and Grado was finally settled in 1160, with the recognition of a Metropolitan jurisdiction of Aquileia over the dioceses of Venetia, Istria, Como and Mantua.

The patriarchate of Grado came to an end in 1451, when that of Venice was established, with the seat of the patriarch in the church of S. Pietro in the island of Castello. The patriarchs of Grado, however, had resided in Venice since 1156, owing to the serious floods caused by the scirocco which had engulfed much of Grado. The *Casa Petraca* (Venice) occupies the site of the palace in which the patriarchs of Grado resided from 1156 to 1451. Here in 1177, after the preliminary truce of Chioggia (*Trattato Clodiano*), the final terms of peace between emperor Frederick I Barbarossa and Pope Alexander III were arranged by the mediation of the doge, Seb. Ziani, and Ulric II, patriarch of Aquileia. In 1815, Grado passed to Austria: to be recovered by the Italians exactly a century later.

Aquileia remained under the temporal jurisdiction of its patriarchs until the 15th century: from the 11th to the 13th century they seem to have been always Germans, with strong Ghibelline sympathies. Pellegrin was one of the chief members of the synod of Pavia (1160), which recognised the claims of the antipope Victor IV. His successor, Ulric II, espoused the cause of the Pope and the Communes, but the change of policy was unpopular in Aquileia, and a writer of the time relates how on Holy Saturday 1163, when the patriarch wished the name of Alexander III, the lawful Pope, to be introduced into the *Exsultet*, he could not find any cleric willing to recite it. When at length a canon was induced to do so, the clergy and faithful caused a riot in the basilica: *il clamore ed il tumulto saliriono fino al cielo*.[1] The duchy of Friuli was altogether subject to the temporal jurisdiction of the patriarchs from 1077 till 1420, and was known by that name. The great nobles, however, and the counts of Gorizia in particular, were far

---

[1] Leicht, *op. cit.*, chap. II, p. 78.

from acquiescing in their rule, and the sword was no less necessary than the crozier.

In 1238, Udine came to be the normal patriarchal residence, and from 1348, when Aquileia suffered severely from earthquake, the patriarch, while retaining the ecclesiastical title of Aquileia, was to all intents and purposes metropolitan of Udine. The seat of civil jurisdiction remained at Cividale. The need of money from the Florentine bankers after the council of Lyons (1245) caused a change in political alignment, and Friuli became almost entirely Guelf in sympathy. The year 1334 has been considered one of the most important dates in the history of Friuli, as in that year Blessed Bertrand of Saint Geniès was elected patriarch, a prelate remarkable for sanctity and pastoral zeal no less than for ability in the administration of the temporalities.[1] The actual cathedral church of Udine was consecrated in 1335, and dedicated under the title of the Annunciation. The care of Blessed Bertrand for liturgical worship is evidenced by the increase in the number of canons, and by the summoning of four diocesan synods and two provincial councils. The first council, which was held at Udine in 1335, made provision for the safe keeping of the Eucharist and the holy oils,[2] and at the same time directed that the Divine Office should be recited with care and devotion.[3] A chalice presented by the *Beatus* is preserved at Cividale, and a gradual of his time may be seen at Gemona. A terrible dearth that afflicted the country, possibly in 1348, saw Bertrand, following in the footsteps of so many of the saints, selling church treasures in order to feed the poor. The patriarch ruled in the midst of an archipelago of independent feudal jurisdictions, with the nobles ever ready to encroach on the rights and property of the Church, and it was in defence of these rights that the Aquileian Thomas Becket laid down his life. He was murdered at the age of ninety on 6 June 1350 at Richinvelda, as he was returning from a council at Padua. Blessed Bertrand was buried in the cathedral church of Udine in a tomb which had probably been constructed to receive the relics of SS. Hermagoras and Fortunatus, which the patriarch had intended to translate

---

[1] Leicht, *op. cit.*, chap. II, p. 116.   [2] Can. 16.   [3] Can. 17.

from Aquileia.[1] At first in a chapel to the right of the high altar, the tomb was moved to the east end of the building in 1706, when the cathedral church was transformed from Gothic to Baroque. Udine and Gemona have Blessed Bertrand for their protector. His cult was approved by Clement VIII in 1599, and a Mass of thanksgiving was directed to be said on his feast. Benedict XIV confirmed the cultus in 1756, prescribing a Mass of the Holy Spirit with a commemoration of the *Beatus*; while Clement XIII extended a Mass and Office of a confessor bishop to the diocese of Udine. Solemn centenary celebrations were held on 1 October 1950, at which Cardinal Schuster, archbishop of Milan, pontificated and preached.

Nicholas of Luxemburg, the successor of Blessed Bertrand, requested Pope Innocent VI in 1354 to transfer the chapter and title of the patriarchate to Udine, as the earthquake of 1348 had so grievously devastated Aquileia, but the Pope declined to change the *status quo*. Cividale had been recognised as a *studium generale* in 1353, but by the time of the patriarch Markward (1365–81) it had already ceased to be more than a school for notaries. Markward of Randek, a former imperial chancellor, was a promoter of the arts, and reconstructed the basilica at Aquileia after the damage caused by the earthquake. In 1420, the patriarch, after three and a half centuries of temporal jurisdiction, was reduced to a purely ecclesiastical status. Venice had long cast covetous eyes on the duchy, and its moment of success arrived when Louis of Teck (1412–39) compromised himself in the war between Venice and Hungary. The Republic seized the lands which the Empire had ceded to the patriarch, and, although Louis refused to accept the situation, the *Friuliani* declined to support his efforts to regain the duchy. His successor, Louis Patavino, signed a peace with Venice in 1445, by which the patriarch was accorded full sovereignty over Aquileia, S. Vito and S. Daniele. The treaty was approved by the three Cathedral chapters of Aquileia, Cividale and Udine. Venetians came to be the exclusive holders of the office of patriarch, but Gorizia was taken by Austria in 1500, and Aquileia in 1509, so

---

[1] The relics of the alleged apostles of Aquileia are said to lie under the high altar of the cathedral church of Aquileia.

that ecclesiastical jurisdiction extended to imperial territory. Aquileia itself, now more than ever *Donna di tristezza, sovrana di dolore*,[1] was left desolate, and, although still the cathedral city of the patriarchate, no patriarch from 1509 till 1751 ever set foot in it. *Roma secunda, maxima Italiae urbs* was reduced to an impoverished village infested by rogues and malaria. Austria bitterly resented the claim of Venice to nominate the patriarch, but it was not until the 18th century that anything was done to solve the difficulty. In 1749, Benedict XIV (1740–58), who had been appointed arbiter, nominated an independent vicar apostolic with residence at Gorizia for the Austrian dioceses in the patriarchate. The arrangement, however, was not satisfactory to Venice, and in 1751 the Pope suppressed the patriarchate and created two archdioceses. Daniel Dolfin, the 109th and last patriarch of Aquileia, was permitted to retain his title, with jurisdiction over the lands of S. Vito at Tagliamento and S. Daniele. Bartholomew Gradenigo was appointed archbishop of Udine for Venetian Friuli and Count Charles Attems, archbishop of Gorizia, for Austrian Friuli. The basilica of Aquileia was made immediately subject to the Holy See, and its archpriest, as a reminder of its one-time patriarchal dignity, was permitted to use *pontificalia* seven times in the year. The archpriest of the former patriarchal basilica of Grado was accorded a similar privilege.

The successor of Charles Attems, Rudolf Eling, refused to publish the so-called reforms of the emperor Joseph II in his archdiocese, thereby causing a quarrel between Rome and Vienna. Gorizia was suppressed as a see in 1788, and Gradisca was chosen to take its place. The arrangement, however, was not of long duration, and Gorizia was again created a cathedral city, although it was not restored to archiepiscopal rank until 1830.

CHURCH ARCHITECTURE

In the first quarter of the 4th century, Theodore, bishop of Aquileia, erected two parallel basilicas with magnificent mosaic pavements. The churches have long since disappeared: the one

---

[1] Giovanni Brusin, *Aquileia e Grado* (Udine, 1947), p. 12.

destroyed without a successor, and the other many times rebuilt to serve as the cathedral church of the patriarch. Happily, however, the pavements of the two original buildings have for the most part survived. The very mosaics on which St. Ambrose walked, when he presided at the council in 381, were discovered by chance in 1909. One of these mosaics of Bishop Theodore, still to be seen on the floor of the basilica, is of particular interest: a representation of the *canistrum* or wicker basket in which the Eucharist in these early days was probably reserved and carried to the sick.[1]

The two churches were destroyed by Attila in 452, but a letter of Pope St. Leo the Great (440–61) to Bishop Nicetas shows that at least one of them was immediately rebuilt.

The small basilica discovered at Giulio Carnico is believed to have been the cathedral church erected in the 5th century, and destroyed two centuries later.

The foundations of yet another basilica have been uncovered close to the road leading from Aquileia to Belvedere. It would seem to date from the early years of the 6th century, and is known as *Basilica del Fondo alla Beligna di Aquileia*.

Grado has preserved much of architectural interest.

Excavations in the Piazza della Vittoria have brought to light the remains of two early Christian churches. One of these, which may well have been the cathedral church of Nicetas (454–85), has vestiges of the episcopal throne and the benches for the presbyters behind the altar;[2] while a little way to the north-west are the scanty remains of a baptistery. The second church, in which two nave aisles were added, dates from the time of the patriarch Fortunatus (803–30), who was a friend of Charlemagne and the Franks.

The foundations of a 5th-century church have been discovered under the existing patriarchal church of S. Eufemia, and the remains of a large hexagonal font are to be seen beneath the floor.

---

[1] Cf. Two 2nd-century frescoes in the Catacombs of St. Calixtus, Rome.

[2] The inclusion of a throne at the end of the apse, for the use of the bishop, was a pagan feature, taken over along with the basilican plan; it was, in the original basilicas, the seat of the *Judex*.

The cathedral church of S. Eufemia, a magnificent example of a late 6th-century basilica, has great nobility and charm. It was the work of the patriarch Elias (571–86), to whom also we owe the neighbouring octagonal baptistery [1] and the graceful little basilica of S. Maria delle Grazie. The church, which is without an atrium, is an aisled basilica, terminating in a single apse. The interior walls are severely plain: one original fretted window has survived, constructed in a kind of concrete and cast from a mould for repetition throughout the church. The capitals of the columns are for the most part classical Roman, and would appear to have been taken from a pagan temple. Originally, each of the aisles terminated in a small square room: that on the north serving for the preparation of the matter for the Eucharist, as well as for the reserved Sacrament (*prothesis*); while the room on the south was a vesting chamber or sacristy (*diaconikon*). Such an arrangement is only to be met with in the East or in countries influenced by the Orient. The church of St. Peter in Vienne, as we shall see, has retained the 'prothesis', but the 'diaconikon' has disappeared.[2] The Byzantine rite requires both *prothesis* and *diaconikon*. A screen has been reconstructed in recent times from fragments of the original screen found during the restoration of the church.[3] The Romanesque ambo, which still serves its original purpose, has a canopy in the Venetian–Byzantine style, presenting a distinctively Moorish appearance. The old patriarchal throne was removed to Venice when the see was transferred there. The mosaic pavement of the 6th century, extending over the greater part of the nave, is of especial interest. An inscription informs us that its construction was paid for by a number of donors—'Friends of the Cathedral', as they would be called today. An epigraph of the patriarch Elias testifies to the date of the work. The composition is very different from that of the *Opus Alexandrinum* which we find in the churches of Rome, being composed entirely of small tesserae of different colours which form inscriptions in Greek and Latin.

---

[1] Cf. Aquileia and Parenzo.   [2] The church is now used as a museum.
[3] Cf. Torcello, where we find the original low marble parapet, carved with animals and birds of a purely Byzantine character. The 'pig-faced' lions are particularly intriguing!

The octagonal baptistery on the north side of the church is connected by a passage.[1]

S. Maria delle Grazie, on the other side of the baptistery, is a late 6th-century aisled basilica, with the episcopal throne and benches for the presbyters *in situ* along the east wall. The nave has preserved its 6th-century mosaic pavement, and in the south aisle we may see some of the original 5th-century pavement, showing signs of the fire that destroyed the church.

Torcello, a solitary island in the Venetian lagoon, was formerly in the patriarchate of Grado. The old cathedral, an aisled basilica in the early-Christian style, was founded in the 7th century and rebuilt in 864: the present nave and campanile date from 1008.[2] A special point of interest is the ancient arrangement of the seats for the presbyters in the apse, rising in tiers with the lofty episcopal throne in the centre.[3] The neighbouring basilica of S. Fosca, formerly used as a baptistery and dedicated to St. John the Baptist, dates in its present form from the 12th century.

The basilica of Aquileia was in all probability rebuilt by Maxentius in the time of Charlemagne. It was devastated by the Huns in the 9th century, and again by an earthquake in 993. Legend connects the crypt with the prison of the early martyrs, but the actual structure seems to date from the Carolingian period, and shows Byzantine inspiration. The frescoes, depicting the legendary passion of St. Hermogaras and St. Fortunatus, are of the 13th century. The restoration of the patriarchal church after the earthquake of 993 was effected by John, who figures as the solitary Italian of his time to occupy the metro-

---

[1] Baptisteries of octagonal form are met with also at Ravenna and Parenzo. At Aquileia, the square structure of the lower part becomes octagonal in its upper part. Torcello, which was in the patriarchate of Grado, has a baptistery of circular construction before the central door: a type unique among contemporary baptisteries within the zone of Ravennese influence. It would seem that Torcello has retained the classical Roman construction, adding a single Byzantine characteristic in the two deep niches which received light from a small window.

[2] The cathedral was first erected in 639, on the authority of the exarch of Ravenna, Isaac. On 1 May 1818 the bishopric was definitely suppressed, and united to the Patriarchate of Venice.

[3] An arrangement of the 9th century. The stoup of the 9th–10th century, which we find by the sacristy door, would probably have been introduced at about the same time as the ceremony of the Asperges before the Sunday Mass.

politan see. It was, however, almost totally reconstructed by Poppo (1019–42), who erected a bell-tower out of the ruins of the amphitheatre. A final restoration was undertaken by the patriarch Markward (1365–81), as a result of the earthquake of 1348. The untenanted patriarchal throne is still to be seen behind the high altar, against the east wall of the basilica. A Renaissance sacrament house (1498), long since disused, is found in the wall above the altar to the right of the apse.

The cathedral church of Cividale is an early Renaissance building, but an annexe on the south side of the nave contains the remains of an 8th-century Lombardic baptistery decorated with interesting reliefs. One of these depicts a cross standing on a *mensa* between two candles, which, if it is Eucharistic in purport, is one of the very earliest examples of the use of altar ornaments. The annexe houses also the ancient episcopal throne.

The *Tempietto*, a chapel in the former Benedictine convent at Cividale, is an 8th-century Lombardic structure, which has a 12th-century Romanesque stucco relief.

The cathedral church of Udine is largely the result of 18th-century restoration, and the patriarchal palace, now occupied by the archbishop, is of the same period.

San Pietro di Castello, a domed church in the suburbs of Venice, was the cathedral church of the patriarchs of Grado from the 12th century, and it was not before 1451 that the title was finally transferred. The building has few features earlier than the late 16th and 17th centuries. The first patriarch of Venice, St. Laurence Justinian (*ob.* 1455), lies under the high altar. Between the second and third altars on the right is a marble throne from Antioch, with Arabic ornamentation and verses from the Koran in Cufic characters. In 1807, the patriarchal palace was converted into barracks by Napoleon, and the seat of the archbishop was transferred to S. Marco, the state church of the Venetian republic.

MONZA

The adoption of the liturgy of Aquileia by the diocese of Monza is generally thought to have been the result of the adhesion of the Lombard queen Theodolinda and her court to the schism of the 'Three Chapters'. Anton Frisi, however, the author of *Historical Memorials of Monza and its Court*, suggests a much later date for its introduction. He maintains that the queen, at the behest of St. Gregory (590–604), adopted the Roman rite, and that this was studiously followed for several centuries. Then, says Frisi, the 'spirit of novelty', which is always ready to hand, produced a mixture of rites, so numerous that it would be far simpler to name those not appropriated by Monza than to attempt to give a list of those incorporated in the diocesan rite! [1] Amid this welter of rites, that which was dominant would seem to have been the so-called Patriarchal rite of Aquileia, probably introduced by the archpriest Raimondo della Torre, who became bishop of Como in 1262, and patriarch of Aquileia in 1274. [2] A 13th-century ceremonial is extant *per circulum anni observatur in Ecclesia Modoetiensi.* [3]

The importance of the Church of Monza was due to 'Theodolinda, that passionately Catholic Lombard queen, who was able to lead her Lombards into the fold of the Roman Church, and who in her son Adalwald by her second husband Agilulf, whom she had raised to the throne, presented the Lombard kingdom with its first Catholic king, and had thus done her part to secure the future'. [4]

The foundation stone of the basilica of St. John Baptist was laid on 5 July 593. [5] The church was placed directly under the jurisdiction of Rome by Pope Calixtus II (1119–24), and was given the title of 'royal' by the emperor Lothair III (1125–37). The present building dates from the 14th century, but the treasury contains a number of objects reputed to have been the gifts of the royal foundress, of whom Paulinus the Deacon says: *Multisque ornamentis auri et argenti mirifice decoravit.* [6] The collection includes a silver-gilt hen with seven chickens (on a modern copper

---

[1] A. F. Frisi, *Memorie Storiche de Monza e sua Corte* (Milan, 1794), t. I, p. 65.
[2] *Ibid.*, p. 66.
[3] *Ibid.*
[4] Edward Hutton, *The Story of Ravenna* (London, 1926), chap. IX, p. 140.
[5] Ughelli, *Italia Sacra*, t. IV, col. 60: in the reference to Constantius, bishop of Milan. Paulinus the Deacon gives the date as 595.
[6] Paul the Deacon, *Rer. Ital. Script.*, lib. IV, cap. XXI.

base), perhaps representing Lombardy and its seven provinces, which was executed by order of the queen; a crown, fan and comb; and a richly adorned book-cover with an inscription of Theodolinda. The most important exhibits from a liturgical point of view are the three ivory diptychs, one of which is said to have been given to the queen by St. Gregory the Great (*ob.* 604). Frisi, however, considers that it dates rather from the latter part of the 9th century.[1] The diptych has been curiously altered in order to make it more serviceable for liturgical purposes. Over the figure of a Roman consul we find the words *David rex*, and over the figure on the other leaf, *Sanctus Gregorius*. The *toga picta* in which the figures are clothed has been retouched in such a way that it may simulate a *paenula*; while the symbol of authority has been changed into a cross, and a tonsure traced on the heads.[2] The chapel to the left of the choir contains the plain sarcophagus (14th century) of Queen Theodolinda, and frescoes (1444) of scenes from her life; while on the altar of the chapel is preserved the famous 'Iron Crown of Lombardy': a broad hoop of gold adorned with precious stones, round the interior of which is a thin strip of iron, said to have been made from a nail of the true Cross brought from Jerusalem by the Empress Helena.

The archpriest of Monza assumed civil jurisdiction in the city and was invested with quasi-pontifical powers. In the absence of the archbishop of Milan he was permitted to crown the 'King of Italy' with the 'Iron Crown'.[3] The bishop of Ostia and Apostolic legate, Cardinal Guido da Somma, gave the archpriests the right to ordain clerics in 1149,[4] and we find the text of such an ordination in the missal and sacramentary of the church, preserved in the chapter library, together with the forms for consecrating chalices and patens, and blessing the swords destined for newly created knights.[5] The canon in the missal contains the

---

[1] Frisi, *Memorie Storiche di Monza . . .*, t. III, p. 9.

[2] Righetti, *Manuale di Storia Liturgica*, t. I, part III, cap. II, p. 240.

[3] Frisi, *op. cit.*, t. I, cap. V, pp. 40–1.

[4] *Ibid., Libere habeat potestatem titulandi, et ordinandi Clericos in Ecclesia sua Archipresbyter sicut usque hodie habuit . . . . Ibid.*, p. 39.

[5] *Ibid.*

phrase: *et mihi famulo tuo . . .* and *pro salute plebiumque commis-sarum mihi.*[1] The archpriests are said to have been permitted the use of *pontificalia* 'from time immemorial'. A calendar under 16 June mentions legacies left to the basilica in 1196 by its archpriest Oberto de Terzago, later archbishop of Milan: *Sandalia IIII, mitras III, balteum I, Episcopales cirotecas IIII, anulum optimum cum smeragdo.*[2] A brief of Alexander IV (1256) to the archpriest Raimondo della Torre, later patriarch of Aquileia, conceded the use of an episcopal ring, to him and his successors in perpetuity. Two inventories in the treasury, dated 1275 and 1353 respectively, refer to dalmatics, sandals, gremials, mitres, rings, croziers and pectoral crosses for the use of the archpriests.[3] Even outside the basilica they were permitted the use of a faldstool (*sella plica-tile*), crozier (*sceptrum*) and pectoral cross (*crux sceptri*).[3] At a solemn Mass the archpriest was assisted by two deacons, two sub-deacons and an assistant priest, but, says Frisi, this is now permit-ted only on the titular feast of the Nativity of St. John Baptist.[3] A MS. of the Church of Monza, describing the ceremonies for St. John the Evangelist, speaks of the episcopal cross carried before the archpriest: *Al vespro si usciva dalla sacristia in processione, e si portava avanti a Monsignore Arciprete la crocetta sopra di un'asta piccola al modo episcopale, ed un sagrista lo seguiva con la mitra.*[3] Many of these privileges were withdrawn from the archpriest in 'turbulent times', but they were restored by Pope Sixtus V, at the mediation of St. Charles Borromeo, on 28 September 1585. They were confirmed by a decree of Clement XI in 1712, who approved also of the use of a baldachino.[4] A complete list of archpriests exists from 768. In 1748, Benedict XIV granted the use of a rochet and violet *cappa magna* to the canons of Monza, with permission to wear them outside, as well as inside, the church.[5]

EXTINCTION OF THE RITE OF AQUILEIA

The distinctive rite of Aquileia, which came to be called *Ritus Patriarchinus*, was abandoned some two centuries before the sup-pression of the patriarchate. In order therefore to complete the

---

[1] Frisi, *op. cit.*, t. I, p. 39.   [2] *Ibid.*, pp. 38-9.   [3] *Ibid.*, p. 39.
[4] *Ibid.*, p. 41.   [5] *Ibid.*, p. 53.

historical background, something must be said in respect to its disappearance, before attempting to describe what little we know of the rite. The Aquileian use was followed both at Monza and Como.

The Church of Aquileia in 1589 petitioned Rome for the clergy to be permitted to say the Roman Office when not in choir, owing to the scarcity of breviaries. The letter of the Roman Congregation approving the request, addressed to Paul Bisanti, auxiliary of the Patriarch, is extant: *E cosa santa e conveniente, che si serva il rito di quella chiesa* (Aquileia) *tanto antico, é approvato, e tutti si confrontino nell'officio stesso. Pero il capitolo si provvederà di breviarii di quel rito: il che potrà fare commodamente, sendo poco fa stampato in Como. E quando no si possi far altrimenti, monsignore Patriarca procuri, che à sue spese tra due anni sia stampato: e intanto sia lecito extra chorum solamente dir l'Officio Romano.*[1] The decision of the Congregation was made known to the clergy in a pastoral letter dated 10 September 1589. The new impression of the Aquileian breviary, however, never materialised, and the Roman books, once introduced, took root. Ten years later there was no vestige of the mediaeval use, even in the patriarchal church itself.

The final abandonment of the distinctive liturgy[2] was the work of the patriarch Francesco Barbaro in the provincial council of Udine (Aquileia) in 1596, although, for some years past, the Pian books had probably been in very general use. The council admitted the antiquity of the 'patriarchal' usages,[3] but made it clear that in future none of the clergy could fulfil their obligation by making use of a breviary other than the Roman: *minime satisfacere nisi de Breviario Romano recitaverint.* Dr. Wickham Legg seems rather unfair when he says that 'the liturgy of Aquileia went in 1594 under a patriarch rightly named Barbaro'.[4] The learned doctor speaks as if a primitive and indigenous rite had

---

[1] Madrisius, ap. append. II ad *Opera S. Paulini Patriarch. Aquil.*

[2] In actual fact, the missal differed in next to nothing from the ordinary Roman rite.

[3] *In nostra metropolitana Ecclesiae Aquileiae de proprio breviario canebantur superioribus annis canonicae horae, et erat proprium etiam missale, atque alii proprii adhibebantur in diocese nostra quidam ritus antiquissimo usu recepti.* Labbe, *Concil.,* t. XV, col. 1481; *Dict. d'Archéol. Chrét. et de Lit.,* t. I, part II, col. 2684.

[4] Wickham Legg, *Ecclesiological Essays,* vol. VII, no. V, 3, p. 135. London, 1905.

been wantonly abolished merely for a caprice of 'Romanising',
whereas, to tell the truth, the 'liturgy of Aquileia' was no more
than the Roman liturgy with a small number of variants, added to
which there was a serious shortage of 'patriarchal' books.

The Aquileian rite had been used in the Middle Ages in the
Armenian monastery of St. Cosmas at Milan, which depended
from a house at Genoa, and had no connection with Armenia.
The Order was suppressed in 1650.[1]

Monza abandoned the 'Patriarchal' liturgy at the behest of St.
Charles Borromeo in 1578. The clergy and people, however, re-
solutely refused to accept the Ambrosian rite, and, after an appeal
to Rome, were permitted to use the Roman books of the Pian
reform.[2]

Aquileian usages persisted at Como until the end of the century, and a few ceremonial survivals were found in the Doge's
church at Venice (S. Marco) for another hundred years.

Tradition, as we have seen, claims St. Hermagoras (*c.* 70) as
the apostle of Como, but the first bishop for whom there is any
historical evidence was a certain Felix, consecrated by St. Ambrose in 379. Como was certainly in the ecclesiastical province of
Aquileia at the end of the 9th century, but, as Achille Ratti pointed
out, it had previously belonged to Milan,[3] and returned to that
province in 1528. St. Abundius (*ob. c.* 462), the patron saint of
the city, was sent by St. Leo the Great (*ob.* 461) to the council of
Chalcedon in 451.[4] A remarkably fine Romanesque church, formerly Benedictine, is dedicated in his honour. The present cathedral church was begun in 1396 and completed in 1595, so that it
was just finished as the last vestiges of the old 'Patriarchal' rite
were disappearing.[5]

So late as 1565 and 1579, we find diocesan synods approving of

---

[1] Benigni, *Milan, Archdiocese of, Catholic Encyclopedia*, vol. X, p. 301.

[2] Similar opposition to an acceptance of the Ambrosian rite was met with in the Swiss
canton of Ticino, when Cardinal Gaisruck (1818–46) attempted to introduce it in those
districts which followed the Roman liturgy. The people declared that they would be
Roman or Lutheran, but never Milanese!

[3] Ratti, *La chiesa ambrosiana, Conferenze di Storia Milanese* (Milan, 1897), p. 170.

[4] Abundius was a Greek from Thessalonica. *Acta SS.*, April, t. I, p. 90. His feast is
celebrated on 2 April. Ughelli, *Italia Sacra*, t. V, col. 260.

[5] The cupola and some small chapels were added in 1730–44.

the old 'rite'.[1] The synod of 1565 directed the clergy to recite the Office 'according to the use of the Church of Como': *Beneficiati, vel alias in sacris Ordinibus constituti quamvis non Beneficiati, quotidie legant Officium, sive Horas Canonicas, secundum morem Ecclesiae Comensis.*

Fourteen years later, the synod, held under the aegis of the bishop, John Antony Volpi, permitted the clergy, if they were unable to obtain Como books, to use (exclusively) those of the Pian reform: *Utantur sacerdotes in Missa ritibus hujus Ecclesiae consuetis, quibus si ejusmodi missalium copia non adsit, alios ritus, caeremonias, et ordinem omnino non sequantur, praeterquam contentos in missali et rituali romano novissimo.* And again: *Recitent Horas Canonicas quotidie, sub poena alias per nos, et postea per Pium V Fel. Record. praescripta, easque secundum Ritum, et Usum Ecclesiae Comensis: qui Ritus in Missis celebrandis pariter observetur. Hi vero quibus librorum Comensium non fuerit copia, Missali et Breviario Romano novissimo utantur, donec reformandi Comensis ratio ineatur.* In the same year (1579), in virtue of a commission of Pope Gregory XIII (1572–85), Francis Bonomio, bishop of Vercelli, made an apostolic visitation in Como. The visitor, while recognising the right of the Church of Como to its own distinctive liturgy, advised the canons of the cathedral church either to correct and reprint their books or, better still, to 'go Roman', assuring them that their rite was practically identical with that of Rome, 'except in the order of some Sundays, and in the feast of the Holy Trinity, which is transferred to another time'. Aquileian missals, moreover, were scarce, and they were in any case in manuscript, so that the canons would find little difficulty in passing to the exclusive use of the liturgical books of the Pian reform: *Cum autem missalia Patriarchino ritu quam paucissima inventa sint, eaque manuscripta, quae praeterea a missali romano nulla ferme alia re differunt, nisi dierum aliquorum Dominicorum ordine, et sanctissimae Trinitatis festo die, qui in aliud tempus translatus est; ideo ritu romano missas passim celebrari, et a plerisque etiam sacerdotibus pro libito fieri animadvertimus, ex antiqui missalis*

---

[1] The statutes were printed in 1588.

C

instituto, in quo quamplurima correctione digna fuisse, novissima ostendit editio.[1] The breviary, continued the visitor, was not wanting in apocryphal stories: *Breviarium, quo Ecclesia Comensis ad ritus, ut vocant Patriarchinum praescriptum, in horariis divinarum precum officiis utitur mandis sane, et apocryphis historiis non caret; quamobrem canonici non tanti illud facere debent, quia satisfaciant potius reverendissimi episcopi sui voluntati qui romanum officium ad ecclesiae comensis cultum introducere studuit.*[2]

Ughelli, in commenting on this visitation, maintains the legend of the apostolate of St. Hermagoras, and says that the *ritus patriarchinus* was not finally discarded till 1598: *Quod Comensis Ecclesia usque ad a 1598 proprio canendi ritu, ut vocant, honoris gratia Patriarchinum, quem postea Clemens VIII sustulit romano inducto, usa est. Quae omnia videntur testari a sancto Hermagora Comenses fuisse institutos in fide, illorumque pastorem Aquileiensi tanquam metropolitano fuisse subjectum.*[3]

There was, as we have seen, a scarcity of books of the rite, which was to a great extent the reason for the adoption of the Roman liturgy, and by the beginning of the 18th century Aquileian liturgical MSS. were almost unobtainable. Lebrun had little success in finding exemplars: *Je n'ai rien oublié pour tâcher d'avoir les livres de ce Rit Patriarchin.*[4] He does, however, refer to a MS. breviary of Como in the archives of the cathedral church: *Breviarium Patriarchinum nuncupatum secundum usum Ecclesiae Comensis correctum, et auctoritate Apostolica probatum.*[5] This was a breviary corrected on the lines of the Pian book by Nicholas Lucinius, a canon of the cathedral. It bore the attestation of Cardinal Sirleto (21 October 1583), who approved it in the name of Gregory XIII (1572–85).[6] Lebrun repeats the verdict of the Apostolic visitor in respect to the Aquileian missal, but he thinks it possible that the breviary may have been somewhat different

---

[1] *Acta Visitationis Comi* (1618), p. 9; J. F. Bonhomii, *Visita Apostolica, Decreta generalia in Visita Comensi* (Como, 1618), pp. 94 seq.; Lebrun, *op. cit.*, t. II, p. 227.

[2] Bonhomii, *op. cit.*, p. 94; Lebrun, *op. cit.*, pp. 225–6.

[3] Ughelli, *op. cit.*, t. V, 24, 235.

[4] Lebrun, *op. cit.*, t. II, p. 222.

[5] *Ibid.*, p. 223.

[6] The approbation would seem to have been withdrawn by Clement VIII (1595–1605).

from that of the Roman Church, in much the same way as we find a distinctive Benedictine Office, whereas the Order adopts either the Roman missal or that of one of the dioceses in which there is a house.[1]

RITE OF AQUILEIA

'It is not easy', says Dom Cabrol, 'to say what was the primitive rite.'[2] This is undoubtedly true, although somewhat of an understatement, as there is no existing document that can satisfactorily settle the question. The *Ritus Patriarchinus* of the Middle Ages was no more than one of the Roman variants so numerous in mediaeval times. It was certainly not the primitive rite of Aquileia.[3]

In the 9th and 10th centuries the liturgy is said to have been specifically Roman, and the *Componimento elegiaco* of Amelli represents St. Paulinus as a protagonist for the Roman rite as against the Ambrosian, *ma moderato e transigente*.

Carolingian influence towards the end of the 8th century may well have effected a virtual change of rite.[4]

The marginal notes of the *Codex Forojulensis* of the Gospels represent a North Italian type, which Canon Borella considers to have been probably Aquileian prior to Roman infiltrations. Three pericopes are given for the Rogation days, with the rubric: *In triduanas*.[5]

The earliest and most instructive document extant is perhaps the 7th- or 8th-century Gospel lectionary (*Capitulare Evangeliorum*), which has a text anterior to that used by St. Jerome. It was added to the *Codex Richdigeranus* (6th century) by a Lombard hand, and, if Dom Germain Morin[6] and H. F. Haase[7] are correct, represents the ancient use of Aquileia. The MS., however, is

---

[1] Lebrun, *op. cit.*, t. II, p. 227.

[2] Cabrol, *Aquilée (Liturgie)*, *Dict. d'Archéol. Chrét. et de Lit.*, t. I, part II, cols. 2683–84.

[3] A description of the 'Patriarchal' rite is given by A de Rubeis in *De antiquis Forojuliensium ritibus, dissertatio*. Venice, 1754.

[4] Paschini, *San Paolino patriarca e la Chiesa Aquileise alla fine del secolo VIII* (Udine, 1906), cap. II, pp. 15–16, n. 1.

[5] Borella, *excursus* II, ap Righetti, *op. cit.*, t. II, p. 399.

[6] Morin, *Rev. bénéd.*, t. XIX (1902), pp. 1 seq.

[7] Haase, edit. Codex, Breslau, 1865.

defective, and the calendar comprises no more than from Advent to June. There are many divergences from Roman usage, and its characteristics resemble those of Milan rather than of Rome.

Advent has been provided with five Sundays, the last of which has the gospel *Missus est*, and is evidently the feast of the Annunciation, as in the Ambrosian rite. St. Stephen is observed on 27 December, following the rites of Jerusalem, Antioch and their derivatives. The Holy Innocents appears as *Efantorum* (*Infantum*), as we find in the Gallican, Mozarabic and Carthusian liturgies; while St. James the Less is on 29 December, as originally at Milan. A further resemblance to Ambrosian usage is found in the two Sundays before Lent, which existed also at Capua in the 6th century and probably also at Naples.

There are three scrutinies, as in the ancient Roman[1] and Ambrosian rites: the *Traditio Symboli* on the Sunday before Easter, as in Gaul, which is followed by a provision for two Masses on the Sunday and Holy Thursday respectively. Finally, it may be noted that *Vigesima* is the fourth Sunday after Easter, although it is found in some lectionaries on the third Sunday: the numbering is inexact. A mid-Pentecost feast follows a usage existing in many of the Eastern rites.

The prayers of the canon in the *De Sacramentis* of St. Ambrose are believed by Dr. Rudolf Buchwald to have originated at Aquileia, so far as the West is concerned. He considers that they were borrowed by that Church from Alexandria, and later adopted by Milan, which was in the 4th century influenced by Aquileia.[2] The unchanging prayers make Dr. Buchwald confident that they are Eastern in origin, and in support of his theory that they emanated from Alexandria he cites a letter from the council held at Aquileia in 381: 'In all things we always hold the order and arrangement of the Church of Alexandria.'[3] In addition to this, he considers that Rome received her canon from Aquileia at about the same time, which, if such was the case, would make the influence of that

---

[1] Rome had eight scrutinies in the 7th–8th century.

[2] *Weidenauer Studien*, no. 1, Weidenau and Vienna, 1906; Adrian Fortescue, *The Mass*, chap. III, pp. 151–2.

[3] *Weid. Stud.*, I, p. 47; Labbe, *op. cit.*, t. II (Epist. II, Council. Aquil. to Emp. Theodosius), col. 1000.

Church of the greatest importance to the history of the Western liturgy. Aquileia would thus be the gate through which our Roman canon came to Europe. The theory, however, plausible as it is, remains untenable, particularly now that the *De Sacramentis* has come to be regarded by the majority of scholars as a genuine work of St. Ambrose. Baumstark, who rejects the Ambrosian authorship out of hand,[1] ascribes the Canon to the Church of Ravenna, while considering its text to have been no less borrowed from Alexandria by the Church of Aquileia.[2]

A lengthy formula of the *Hanc igitur*, attributed to St. Paulinus of Aquileia (*ob.* 802) and found in a sacramentary emanating from the Benedictine convent of S. Salvatore (? S. Giulia), Brescia, has been considered by Baumstark to be a vestige of the old Aquileian rite.[3] In the 9th century—and the MS. is mid-9th century—the monastery of S. Salvatore was directly subject to the patriarchate of Aquileia. In reference to the *Hanc igitur*, the sacramentary says: *Hanc Domnus Paulinus in canone addidit.* The formula, however is not unique to the Brescia sacramentary, and it is found also in two codices originating from St. Denis, in one of which, formerly preserved in the Cistercian abbey of Vauclair, we find it styled as a 'prayer of St. Ambrose': *Infra actionem quotidianum S. Ambrosii Mediolanensis archiepiscopi.*[4] A 10th-century codex in the Library at Rouen has a similar text.[5] Ebner, who is convinced of the Paulinian authorship, says that the *Hanc igitur* is important because it shows that Paulinus was known and used beyond the confines of Aquileia, and also because the text shows an old form.[6]

The Rouen MS. says: *Hanc igitur oblationem servitutis nostrae, sed et cunctae familiae tuae, quaesumus Domine, placatus accipias, quam tibi devoto offerimus corde pro pace et caritate et unitate s. Dei ecclesiae, pro fide catholica, ut eam inviolatam in meo pectore et in*

---

[1] *L'autore non meno ignoto del De Sacramentis che a torto reca il nome di S. Ambrogio.* Baumstark, *Lit. Rom. e lit. dell'Esercato* (Rome, 1904), cap. I, p. 54.

[2] *Ibid.*, cap. IV, pp. 168–73.

[3] A. Ebner, *Iter Italicum* (Freiburg im Breisgau, 1896), pp. 22–3. The MS. is found today in the *Biblioteca Queriniana*, Brescia.

[4] Martène, *Voy. Lit.*, p. 40; Baumstark, *op. cit.*, cap. IV, p. 159.

[5] *Bibl. Rouen*, Cod. A. 566.

[6] Ebner, *op. cit.*, p. 416.

omnium fidelium tuorum jubeas conservari; pro sacerdotibus Restoldo, Albuino, Tedo', Val. et omnium fidelium tuorum et omni gradu ecclesiae, pro regibus et ducibus et omnibus, qui in sublimitate sunt constituti, pro familiaribus et consanguineis et omnibus nobis commendatis, pro omnibus viventibus ac defunctis famulis et famulabus tuis, qui mihi propter nomẹn tuum bona fecerunt et mihi in tuo nomine confessi fuerunt; propitius sis illis Deus; pro pauperibus, orfanis, viduis, captivis, it (in) erantibus, languidis, defunctis Frostero, Mai', Angelboldo, Clantiae (?), Ermengradi, Gerelmo, Fulconi, Rodulfo, Tetb., Osolti, Varnero, qui de hac luce in recta fide et in tuo nomine confitentes migraverunt. . . .[1]

The text in the Brescia MS. is very similar.[2] Among the features of the Brescia codex it may be noted: In fo. 41, a list of the Lombard kings, followed by a mention of the abbess Amelperge [3] (fo. 42). The members of the community are included in a subsequent *Liber vitae.* The Passion according to St. Mark is found on fo. 53 and on the succeeding page the Passion of St. John (incomplete). The names of Hilary, Martin, Augustine, Gregory, Jerome, Benedict, Faustina and Jovita appear in the *Communicantes. Pax Domini sit semper vobiscum* terminates the Ordinary of the Mass, and, as we have seen, mention is made of the *Hanc igitur* which Paulinus added. A number of votive Masses are found in the codex.

Baumstark thus regards Ravenna, rather than Aquileia, as a source for the liturgy. In support of this hypothesis, he cites Agnellus, abbot of *S. Maria ad Blachernas* [4] (first half of the 9th century), who said that the service books compiled by St. Maximian, archbishop of Ravenna (c. 546–56), in the 6th century were

---

[1] Ebner, *op. cit.*, p. 417.

[2] *Ibid.*, pp. 22–3.

[3] Cottineau (*Répertoire Topo-Bibliographique des Abbayes et Prieurés* (Mâcon, 1939), vol. I, col. 488) gives SS. Cosmas and Damian as the title of the Benedictine convent in Brescia of which Amalberga (*sic*) was abbess.

[4] The church at Blachernae, situated at the north-western extremity of the walls of Constantinople, was the 'head and metropolis' of the countless churches and oratories dedicated to the Mother of God. It enshrined the alleged robe of the Blessed Virgin: its most cherished possession. Under the impression that this church was especially dear to the *Theotokos*, Byzantine Christians came to call churches by the title of *Blachernae* in other places. Thus it came about that a monastery at Ravenna, formerly known as *Pinetum* or *De palatiolo*, received this name.

still in use in his time.[1] There is, however, no trace of the great
Eucharistic prayer employed at Ravenna before the acceptance of
the Gregorian canon, but 'stones speak'.[2] The mosaics in the
nave of the basilica of S. Apollinare Nuovo at Ravenna witness to
a non-Roman *Nobis quoque*;[3] while *Supra quae* is depicted in the
same church, as well as in that of S. Vitale.[4]

The political importance of Ravenna under the Byzantine exarchs inclines Baumstark to consider that church as the source of
the 'Patriarchal' rite.[5] Lack of data, however, makes it impossible
to know with any certainty either the source or the specific characteristics of the ancient rite of Aquileia.

Mgr. Duchesne and Dom Morin are probably correct in thinking that Aquileia approximated to Milan rather than to Rome, but,
says Duchesne, 'We have no documentary evidence for the uses
followed in Aquileia, in the Danubian provinces and in Dalmatia.
It is probable that the use observed in Aquileia and the Danubian
provinces resembled the Milanese rather than the Roman
liturgy.'[6] We must, however, dissociate ourselves from the
further hypothesis that the Ambrosian rite was the starting-point
of the Gallican rite, and it is an over simplification to 'consider the
local Aquileian use as one more variant of the widespread Gallican
family'.[7]

There have not been wanting also those who have maintained
that the primitive rite of Aquileia was Roman, and De Rubeis
says that the liturgical books of the patriarchate passed through
the successive stages of Leonine, Gelasian and Gregorian.[8]

A 7th-century *Ordo scrutiniorum*, attributed to the Church of
Grado, has been cited by Dom Morin as exhibiting the Milanese
arrangement of the collects and blessing before the dismissal
of the catechumens. Aquileia agreed also with Milan in the

---

[1] Baumstark, *op. cit.*, cap. IV, p. 164.
[2] *Ibid.*, p. 165.
[3] *Ibid.*, pp. 165–6.
[4] *Ibid.*, pp. 166–8.
[5] *Si cerchi se Ravenna non sia il centro della propagazione d'un terzo o quarto tipo di questa
specie, dal quale derivi il rito patriarchino pressochè obliato. Ibid.*, p. 178.
[6] Duchesne, *Christian Worship* (London, 1904), chap. III, p. 88, n. I.
[7] Adrian Fortescue, *Aquileian Rite, Catholic Encyclopedia*, vol. XVI, p. 3.
[8] Rubeis, *De antiq. Forojul. ritibus, dissertatio*. Venice, 1754.

announcement on the Sundays in Lent of the forthcoming
Baptism: *Qui vult nomina sua dare, jam offerat.*[1]

The ritual for the scrutinies has been given by De Rubeis,[2] who
establishes the ceremony of the *Traditio Symboli* on the Sunday
next before Easter.[3]

The *Traditio symboli* or imparting of the Creed to the candi-
dates for Baptism on Palm Sunday had a special place in popular
affection in North Italy. For centuries the ceremony was commonly retained, in part at least, even after the Roman liturgy had
displaced all other vestiges of the old indigenous rites. It was
often, in fact, the only really ancient formulary that had survived.
The non-Roman ceremony, customary in Spain, Gaul and North
Italy, was very different from the analogous Roman rite, which
under the name of *Aurium aperitio* appears in the Gelasian and
8th-century Gelasian sacramentaries.[4]

The solemn formula for the exclusion of the 'unworthy' is
given before the offertory on this Sunday, but the Aquileian text
would seem to have been uninfluenced by that of Milan. Aquileia
employs the word *secedat* rather than *procedat*: a peculiarity
shared by a North Italian *ordo* of the 11th century: [5]

> *Si quis arianus est, secedat.*
> *Si quis sabellianus est, secedat.*
> *Si quis nestorianus est, secedat.*
> *Si quis theodocianus, secedat.*
> *Si quis macedonianus, secedat.*
> *Si quis pelagianus, secedat.*
> *Si quis priscillianus, secedat.*
> *Si quis eutycianus, secedat.*
> *Si quis fotinianus, secedat.*
> *Si quis haereticus est, secedat.*[6]

This Aquileian dismissal is to be found in a set of catechetical
rites taken from a MS. in the library at Frideli, and not identified

---

[1] Rubeis, *op. cit.*, p. 285.   [2] *Ibid.*, pp. 230–46.   [3] *Ibid.*, p. 236.
[4] *Lib. Sacram. Rom. Eccles.*, edit. H. A. Wilson (Oxford, 1894), pp. 50–9.
[5] *North Italian Services of the 11th Century*, Henry Bradshaw Society, vol. LXVII
(1931), p. 24. *Ordo Romanus* VII has both *recedat* and *secedat* (*Pat. Lat.*, LXXVIII,
cols. 996, 998, 999).   [6] De Rubeis, *op. cit.*, p. 245.

since. The editor gives no indication as to the age of the MS., but a rubric supplies a clue in respect to the compiler of the ritual: *Et huic mysteria (Traditio Symboli) pontifex interesse debet, sicut mihi Luponi visum est ecclesiae sanctae Aquiliensis pontifici.*[1] There were, however, two patriarchs of Aquileia with the name of Lupo: (1) The successor of Teutimarus (*post* 855) in the reign of the emperor Lewis II; and (2) the patriarch who was living in 994 in the time of King Hugh and his son Lothair. There is nothing to indicate which of the two patriarchs is designated.

The document shows traces of extensive and disordered alterations, and the editor has modified the local liturgy, in order to change it as far as possible in a Romeward direction. The ritual of the scrutinies has, in fact, much in common with *Ordo Romanus* VII,[2] although we find native material interjected in the Roman order. The Roman scrutinies have been adopted, and the *Traditio Symboli* moved from Palm Sunday to the preceding Saturday, but the priest and deacon are directed to lead the choir in reciting the archaic Aquileian version of the Creed,[3] which was similar, although far from identical, to that used by Rufinus.[4]

An earlier document, the 8th-century gospel-list published by Morin, twice designates Palm Sunday as *In Symbolo*, thus indicating that the Creed was imparted on this day.[5]

A third source, dating some time between these two, is the baptismal treatise *De significatu* of the Patriarch Maxentius (*c.* 811–33). It seems to have been written by way of a reply to the questionnaire of Charlemagne, who was examining the metropolitans of his Empire as to their understanding of the various rites of Christian initiation.[6] The prelates, in their answers, avoided any references to distinctive local usages, basing their comments on the *Gelasianum* or the allegedly Roman *ordo scrutiniorum*. Maxentius at first sight would seem to follow simply the Roman order,

---

[1] De Rubies, *op. cit.*, p. 229.
[2] *O.R. VII: Pat. Lat.*, t. LXXVIII, cols. 993–1,000.
[3] Rubeis, *op. cit.*, pp. 229–30.
[4] Rufinus, *Pat. Lat.*, t. XXI, cols. 340–73.
[5] Morin, *Rev. bénéd.*, vol. XIX (1902), p. 6.
[6] H. Boone Porter, *Maxentius of Aquileia and the North Italian Baptismal Rites*, *Ephem. Liturg.*, vol. LXIX (1955), fasc. I, p. 5.

without the slightest regard for the ancient liturgical heritage of his own local Church, yet a closer study of the document shows that he was cognisant of a formulation of the *Traditio Symboli* substantially like that used in the time of the Patriarch Lupo. In fact, he seems to quote from both the *Gelasianum* and the native material included in the Aquileian order of Lupo.[1] Unlike most of the other archbishops, Maxentius says nothing of any separate rite of episcopal Confirmation. He seems, rather, to find the gift of the Holy Ghost in a single post-baptismal chrismation. If this be his real meaning, his testimony harmonises with that of other North Italian sources.[2]

An old *ordo* of Aquileia is found in a codex of Cividale, which is a 13th-century copy of a much older manuscript. It would seem to have been originally transcribed at a time when the 'discipline of the secret' and the catechumenate were already things of the past, as the long formula of dismissal is given *after* the *traditio*, despite the monition of St. Ambrose: *cave ne incaute symboli vel dominicae orationis divulges mysteria*.[3] The position of the dismissal in the Mass must have been a matter of indifference at the time the *ordo* was compiled.[4] The *traditio* appears after the lessons and before the offertory.[5] A 13th-century ceremonial of Monza, where, as we have seen, the rite of Aquileia was used, has a ritual of scrutinies after Mass, with both Milanese and Roman elements in a Milanese framework.[6] The codex provides three scrutinies, as originally at Rome, and the dismissal of the *competentes*, without a blessing,[7] takes place after the gospel: *Dicto Evangelio, in Missa majori, diaconus statim dicit alte: Procedant competentes; et puer respondit similiter ante altare, et tunc pueri portantur extra ecclesiam, et morantur extra usque ad finem missae.*[8] The document, which has been edited in part by Frisi, begins with

---

[1] H. Boone Porter, *op. cit.*, pp. 6–7.
[2] *Ibid.*, p. 7. *Pat. Lat.*, t. LVII, cols. 777–9.
[3] St. Ambr., *Epist.* XX, 4; *Pat. Lat.*, t. XVI, col. 994.
[4] Pietro Borella, *La 'Missa' o 'Dimissio Catechumenorum' nelle Liturgie Occidentali*, ap. *Ephem. Liturg.* (1939), p. 105.
[5] *Ibid.*, p. 104.
[6] Milan, *Bibl. Capit.*, B. 43.
[7] This was also customary at Rome.
[8] Frisi, *Memorie storiche di Monza e sua Corte* (Milan, 1794), t. III, p. 192.

the introduction: *Incipit ordo ministerii, quod per circulum anni, observatur in Ecclesia Modotiensi.*[1] Monza[2] and Como,[3] following the mother-church of Aquileia, observed the ceremony of the *Traditio Symboli* on the Sunday before Easter.

An interesting ceremony is described in the ceremonial of Monza, which has affinities with Milanese practice: A ball of cotton (*bambagia, pharus*), known as *corona lampadarum*, was lighted on certain feasts at the top of the processional cross: *Et cum intramus chorum, custos levata cruce aurea cum candelis accensis desuper, ponit ignem in corona lampadarum tota circumdata et cooperta bombice, quod dicitur pharum.*[4] In Ambrosian churches it was customary on the titular and patronal feasts of martyrs for a ball of cotton (*bambagia, pharus*) to be hung up and lighted before the altar at the beginning of the solemn Mass, when the stational procession met the incoming priests. Beroldus recalls the Milanese practice of fixing candles on the arms and at the top of processional crosses, and of lighting the *pharus* with the candle fixed at the summit of the cross of the *decumani*.[5] A *corona* attached to the *pharus* is mentioned in a document from Cremona of the year 666.

Stations for the three Masses of Christmas, as well as for St. Stephen, St. John, Holy Innocents and the ferias of Easter, are found in an old missal of Aquileia.[6]

It is interesting to note that the earliest known Italian reference to the observance of a feast of the Conception of our Lady comes from an early 13th-century missal of Aquileia.[7] The collect, which is found also in a missal of Fécamp of the end of the 12th century,[8] expresses the belief that with the conception of Mary, the Mother of the Redeemer is conceived: the beginning of

---

[1] Frisi, *op. cit.*, p. 71.

[2] *Ibid.*, p. 193.

[3] De Puniet, *Dict. d'Archéol. Chrét. et de Lit.*, t. II, col. 2616.

[4] Frisi, *op. cit.*, t. III, p. 196.

[5] *Beroldus sive Ecclesiae Ambrosianae Mediolanensis Kalendarium et Ordines, saec. XII* (edit. Magistretti, Milan, 1894), pp. 61, 65.

[6] De Rubeis, *op. cit.*, cap. XVIII, cap. XXIV.

[7] Cod. 31, *Bibl. arcivescovile*, Udine. Andrea M. Cecchin, *L'Immacolata nella Liturgia Occidentale anteriore al secolo XIII* (Rome, 1943), p. 35.

[8] MS. A 313 (290), *Bibl.*, Rouen.

the work of our salvation: *Deus ineffabilis misericordie, qui prime piacula mulieris per virginem expianda sanxisti, da nobis quaesumus conceptionis solemnia venerari quae unigenitum tuum Virgo peperit Dominum nostrum Jesum Christum. . . .*[1]

The patriarch of Aquileia, as we have seen, exercised temporal as well as spiritual jurisdiction, and the chronicles relate how Blessed Bertrand celebrated the office of Christmas night (1341) at Gorizia, not only in sacred vestments, but also *in armi materiale*, assisted by Guibert, Benedictine abbot of Moggio, in a cuirass.[2] A relic of this practice persisted in the Church of Aquileia until the suppression of the patriarchate in 1751, and Lebrun says that on the feast of the Epiphany in the 'collegiate church of Friuli' the deacon wore a helmet and held a drawn sword at the gospel: *In signum temporalis jurisdictionis et meri et mixti imperii die Epiphaniae diaconum galea et stricto ense canere Evangelium jubent.*[3] At the end of the Middle Ages it was customary for the emperor to sing the gospel (*Exiit edictum a Caesare Augusto*) at the midnight Mass of Christmas, vested as a deacon with royal and military insignia. The *Ordines Romani* (XIV, XV) only assign this right for the lesson in the office of matins,[4] but it would seem to have been exercised also at the gospel of the Mass, as we read, in this connection, of Charles IV (*ob.* 1378) at Basle, Sigismund (*ob.* 1437) at Constance and Frederick III (*ob.* 1493) at Rome.[5] Frederick, before beginning the gospel in 1468, is said to have drawn his sword and brandished it three times, in token of his readiness to defend the faith.[6]

Henry VIII of England, after he had received the title of *Defensor Fidei* (1521), and prior to his repudiation of that faith in 1534, appears to have unsheathed his sword at the beginning of the gospel, and to have held it aloft in his right hand until its conclusion. This, we learn, was done at La Trappe by King

[1] Cecchin, *op. cit.*, p. 54.

[2] Anon., *Leoben Chron.* ad ann. 1340; *Script. Rer. Austr.*, t. I, p. 959; Francesco Florio, *Vita del Beato Beltrando* (Venice, 1759), p. 89.

[3] Lebrun, *op. cit.*, t. II, p. 221; Ughelli, *Italia Sacra*, t. V, p. 24.

[4] *O.R.* XIV, 67 (*Pat. Lat.*, t. LXXVIII, col. 1182); *O.R.* XV, 9 (*Ibid.*, col. 1278).

[5] Florio, *op. cit.*, p. 89.

[6] Jungmann, *Missarum Sollemnia*, t. II, part III, chap. II, 6, p. 213, n. 9.

James II, when, fresh from the disaster of the Boyne, he assisted at Mass in the abbey church on 25 November 1690.[1]

The mediaeval rite of Aquileia was known from the dignity of that Church as the 'Patriarchal Rite', and Dom Guéranger has described it as 'the most venerable of the mixed rites in Italy in the 16th century'.[2] It is, however, difficult to see why such praise should have been accorded to it, if the extant exemplar of the missal of 1519 is any criterion. Perhaps it was because this missal differed in next to nothing from the contemporary missal of the Church of Rome!

The liturgy of Aquileia, says Baumstark, was always the loser in the unequal struggle with Rome, and always in ever-increasing decadence.[3] When the liturgical books of the Pian reform were finally adopted there remained but little of any distinctive *Ritus Patriarchinus*.

As early as 1250, we hear of Peter IV Pino, bishop of Castello, wishing to follow the Roman rite,[4] and a regulation prior to the time of Blessed Bertrand (*ob.* 1350) counselled the adoption of a liturgy which was that of the 'Mother and Mistress of all the Churches'.[5] A synod held by Bertrand prescribed the exclusive use of the ten Roman prefaces,[6] and in 1347 we hear of Guido de'Guisi, bishop of Concordia and vicar-general of Udine, ordering liturgical books for the choir and altar, as those in use failed to conform to the rite of the Roman Curia, which the Church of Udine then followed. Primicerio thinks that it may possibly have been the Patriarch Bertrand who had prevailed upon the Church of Udine to adopt the Roman rite.[7] However, despite continual and extensive 'Romanising', the *Ritus Patriarchinus* was maintained, at least in theory, until the end of the 16th century. Venice would seem to have made two attempts to maintain its own

---

[1] Ailbe Luddy, *The Real De Rancé* (London, 1931), chap. XIX, p. 252.

[2] Guéranger, *Instit. Liturg.*, t. I, chap. XV, p. 430.

[3] Baumstark, *Lit. Rom. e Lit. Esarcato* (Rome, 1904), cap. IV, p. 170.

[4] *Ibid.* Castello, in the island of Olivola (S. Pietro) near Venice, was founded in the time of Pope Adrian I (772–95). The bishop was consecrated by the patriarch of Grado. In 1451 (till 1807), Castello became the cathedral church of the patriarch, with the title changed to Venice.

[5] Florio, *op. cit.*, p. 116.   [6] *Ibid.*, pp. 115–16.

[7] *Ibid.*, p. 115.

distinctive rite. Thus in 1308 we hear of a decree in the hands of
a certain Donadeo, parish priest of St. Luke, which recommended
the *primicerius* Venier to restore the rite to its original purity in
the basilica of St. Mark.[1] Again in 1418, the bishop Lando insisted on retaining the 'Patriarchal' rite in defiance of the wishes
of Rome.[1] A successor, however, was not of the same mind, and
in 1456 Maffio Giovanni Matteo Contarino, Patriarch of Grado–
Venice, with the approval of his canons, demanded the use of the
Roman rite in Divine Service. Permission was accorded by Pope
Calixtus III (1455–8) in the brief *Ex ingenti* of 12 December of
the same year.[1]

After the promulgation of the bull *Quo primum tempore* in
1570, the several dioceses of the patriarchate successively abandoned their traditional usages: Monza in 1578, Trieste in 1586,
Udine in 1596. It was left to Como to make some sort of attempt
to retain its old use, but here too the Pian liturgy was enforced by
Pope Clement VIII in 1597–98. A solitary survival at Como is
recorded in a mémoire which Cardinal Cusani, archbishop of
Milan, sent to Pierre Lebrun (*ob.* 1729): *On excepta l'Office de la
sainte Vierge, qu'on récite certains jours dans la cathédrale selon le
Rite Patriarchin.*[2]

The basilica of St. Mark and the chapel of the Doges in Venice
retained certain peculiarities of ceremonial derived from the old
'Patriarchal' rite until the fall of the Venetian Republic on 19
October 1807. Still today on great feasts the very distinctive
chant employed for the epistle and gospel is in all probability a
relic of the mediaeval rite of Aquileia.

It is unfortunate that the liturgical MSS. and books of Aquileia
that have survived date only from the time when the rite was little
more than a Roman variant. Many of these codices have been
edited by Giuseppe Vale, canon, archivist and librarian of the
cathedral church of Udine (1877–1950). A number of melodies
for the epistle and gospel, which are sung today on great solemnities in Friuli, were in fact recovered by him from unedited documents of the 'Patriarchal' rite. The canon was also the author of

---

[1] Baumstark, *Lit. Rom. e Lit. dell'Esarcato*, cap. IV, p. 170.
[2] Lebrun, *op. cit.*, t. II, p. 224.

no less than eighteen publications respecting the ancient usages of the Church of Aquileia.

An early 11th-century fused Gregorian sacramentary, written and illuminated in the scriptorium of Reichenau, but used at Aquileia from the second quarter of the century, is in the Bodleian Library at Oxford.[1] It had probably been given to Aquileia by Eberhard, a religious of Reichenau, who became Patriarch in succession to Poppo in 1042.

An 11th–12th-century breviary with musical notation, and a 13th-century processional are preserved in the municipal museum at Cividale. The processional contains a commemoration of the *Planctus Mariae*.

The library of the archiepiscopal palace at Udine, the former residence of the patriarchs, contains a number of liturgical MSS. Three of these, which the 18th-century catalogue (1785) describes as *codices membranacei*, are of especial interest, and came from the Benedictine abbey of St. Gall, which the Patriarch Poppo (1019–42) founded at Moggio Udinese.[2] The MSS., however, would seem to be monastic rather than 'patriarchal'. The title-pages are missing. The first of these, codex LXXIII, which dates from the 11th century, has several folios of the calendar torn out. The following additions have been added later to the calendar: *Non Jul.* William, abbot, ob.: *IV Id.* Hermagoras and Fortunatus, in place of St. Margaret, whose name has been erased; *III Id. Aug.* Gerald, abbot, ob.; *Non. Aug.* Oswald, king and martyr, and M. Dominii (*sic*), confessor; *IV Non. Oct.* Francis, levite and confessor, *funtatoris* (*sic*); *XVII Kal. Nov.* Wecel., abbot, and Hermanus, p.; *Id Nov.* Homobonus, confessor; *IV Kal. Dec.* Dedication of the church of St. Benedict, and altar of St. Nicholas; *VII Id. Dec.* Ordination of St. Ambrose; *VI Id. Dec.* Conception of St. Mary; *IV. Kal. Jan.* Thomas, archbishop. The Greater Litanies contain the names of Benedictine saints, as well as those of SS. Hermagoras and Fortunatus. The name of Leonard was a later addition.

---

[1] Oxford, Bodl. Lib., MS. *Canon liturg.* 319 (19408).

[2] Moggio was a house of the Congregation of Hirsau in the diocese of Spires, as an ordinal of the abbey, written about 1256 and preserved in the Bodleian, attests (*secundum Hirsiacenses*). Oxford, Bodl. Lib., MS. *Canon liturg.* 325 (19414).

The second MS., codex LXXV, dates from *c.* 1199, and, although somewhat mutilated, is of importance as showing similarities with the early Gregorian sacramentary. The calendar includes the Conception of our Lady and St. Zeno on 8 December, and St. Thomas of Canterbury on 29 December. The final clause of the creed is the same as in the Carthusian rite: *vitam futuri seculi.* Folio 90 contains the collects from the Vigil of Christmas till St. Thomas the Apostle. Collects follow *pro Missa generali,* in which intercession is made *Pro cuncta Congregatione et Familia S. Galli;* and *Pro Missa communi,* in which the officiant commends to God: *Domnum Apostolicum, Episcopos et Abbates nostros et cum omni Congregatione et Familia Sanctae Mariae et S. Galli,* at the same time praying: *ut Symoniacam heresim destruat.* The final collect, *Pro defunctis,* contains the petition: *Pro animabus omnium Catholicorum Orthodoxorum, quorum commemorationem agimus, et quorum corpora in hoc monasterio requiescunt vel quorum nomina super sanctum Altare tuum scripta esse videntur.* The 'names' are read by the celebrant himself from a book or tablets placed on the altar. Two folios are missing at fo. 119. There is a lectionary for votive Masses, *temporale* and *sanctorale.* Proses are found for the Conversion of St. Paul, Octave of Easter, St. Benedict, St. Michael, St. Gall and St. Nicholas with notation; also for the Apostles, Common of the Blessed Virgin, St. John the Evangelist and St. John Baptist. The Gregorian canon contains: *pro quibus tibi offerimus vel qui. . . . Memento etiam Domine famulorum, famularumque tuarum N.N.* The response: *Et cum spiritu tuo* occurs after *Pax Domini,* etc. The codex has the following: *IV Kal. Jun. ob. Atto, Abbs., Anima cujus per misericordiam Dei omnipotentis requescat (sic) in pace. III Kal. Jul. ob. Albertus presbyter et monachus nostre congregationis.*

The third MS., codex LXXII, dates from the end of the 13th century, with *tabellae* added in 1352. The calendar begins in March, and another hand has added local (Aquileian) saints. Entries include: *V Idus Jun. Dedicatio Eccles. Mosacensis* (Moggio) *MCXVIIII et ad XIII Kal. Sept. MCCCLXXXIIII terremotus.* The Greater Litanies have invocations to Benedictine and Aquileian saints, as well as to confessors of the Mendicant Orders.

Cathedral Church,
Torcello

Left:

Patriarchal Basilica,
Aquileia (*top*)

S. Fosca, Torcello
(*centre*)

S. Pietro in Castello,
Venice (*bottom*)

Baptistery, Basilica of
Aquileia (post 452)

Basilica of S. Eufemia,
Grado

Baptistery of Basilica of
Grado (sixth century)

Above:

Left: Basilica of S. Maria delle
Grazie, Grado (sixth century)

Right: Cathedral Church,
Cividale in Friuli

San Marco, Venice

Missals of 1304 (three exemplars), 1387 and 1403 are found in the Municipal Museum at Cividale in Friuli, with the names of Hermagoras and Fortunatus inserted in the *Communicantes* of the canon.

A *Missale pro s. Aquileyensis ecclesie ritu* appeared at Augsburg in 1494.

The Archiepiscopal Library at Udine has a missal from Aquileia, dating from the 12th–13th century, with additions of the 14th century.[1] There are eleven prefaces. A Mass is included for the feast of SS. Hermagoras and Fortunatus. The missal ends defectively.

Another missal from the patriarchate, of the 14th–15th century, is found in the *Biblioteca Marciana*, Venice.[2] It was at one time in the library of Bernard Maria de Rubeis and then in that of the Jesuits at Venice. It would seem to have been used in the diocese of Verona, which was a suffragan of Aquileia.[3] Thus we find in this missal, not only a commemoration of St. Zeno, the patron saint of Verona, but also a sequence proper to his feast: *Sidus fulget.*[4] The beginning of the book is defective. Folio 2 has the form for the *Benedictio agni paschalis*, and, among other items, the rubric: *Postea* (after the Blessing) *dicat evangelium In principio*. The names of Hermagoras and Fortunatus appear in the *Communicantes*, and at each memento we find the rubric: *Hic recitantur nomina vivorum* (*mortuorum*). A Mass is given for Daniel the Prophet, and also for St. Joseph (15th century).

A *Missale Aquileyensis Ecclesiae*, printed at Venice in 1519, is in the Victoria and Albert Museum, London. The Mass, of which the following is a summary, shows the so-called *Ritus Patriarchinus* as it appeared at the time of its suppression.

Rank of feasts. Majus duplex, duplex, cum pleno officio, novem lectionum, trium lectionum.

---

[1] *Bibl. arciv.*, Udine, cod. fo. 17. It is described in the *Iter Italicum* of Adalbert Ebner (Freiburg in Breisgau, 1896), p. 269.

[2] *Bibl. Marciana*, Venice, cod. lat. III, CXXV. *Ibid.*, pp. 279–80.

[3] Verona was suffragan to Udine, after the seat of the patriarchate had been moved there. It came under the metropolitan jurisdiction of Venice in 1818.

[4] St. Zeno is commemorated in the Roman martyrology on 12 April, with two additional festivals in Verona: 21 May (Translation) and 6 December (Consecration as bishop).

D

Calendar. January: ii, Paulinus, pat. (9 less.); 29, Julian *de bono albergo* (9 less.); 31, Transl. St. Mark, evang. (9 less.).
February: 6, Dorothy, virg., mart. (3 less.); 13, Fusca, virg., mart. (3 less.); 16, Juliana, v., m. (*cum pleno officio*); 17, Crisantianus & Comp. (in Aquil., d.); 25, Walpurgis, virg. (3 less.).
March: 16, Hellarus, bp. & Dacian, mart. (in Aquil., d.); 27, Rudbert, bp. St. Thomas Aquinas was canonised while B. Bertrand was at Avignon (1323), and his name was inserted in the calendar of Aquileia with double rite after the *Beatus* had become patriarch: *Necrologium Aquilejense ad diem VII Martii.*
April: 5, Agape, Ciconie (Chionia) & Irene, v.m. (in Aquil., d.); 13, Finding of the bodies of Cantian, Crisogonus & Prothus (in Aquil., f.).
May: 2, Sigismund, k. (in Aquil., d.); 4, Florian, m. (3 less.); 13, Gangolfus, m.; 15, Sophia, v.; 19, Potentiana, v.; 31, Cancius, Cancianus & Cancianilla, mart. (double).
June: 4, Quirinus,[1] b.m. (in Aquil., d.); 14, Prothus, m. (in Aquil., d.); 15, Vitus, Modestus & Crescentia, mart. (9 less.); 17, Cyria & Musca, v.m. (in Aquil., d.); 18, Mark & Marcellinus, mart. (3 less.); 22, Achacius & Comp., mart. (9 less.).
July: 4, Udalric, b. (9 less.); 10, Seven Brothers, mart. (in Aquil., d.); 12, Hermachorus & Fortunatus, mart., with oct. (in Aquil., gr.d.); 13, Dedication of Mother Church of Aquileia (gr.d.); 15, Division of the Apostles (*cum pleno officio*); 17, Alexius, conf. (9 less.); 19, Oct. of Hermachorus & Comp. (9 less.).
August: 7, Afra & Comp., mart. (3 less.); 14, Felix & Fortunatus, mart. (in Aquil., d.); 15, Assumption B.V. (gr.d.); 23, Hermogenes & Fortunatus, mart. (in Aquil., d.); 27, Trans. Hermachorus & Fortunatus, mart. (*cum pleno officio*).
September: 11, Prothus & Jacintus, mart. (3 less.); 13, Seven Sleepers (9 less.); 16, Eufemia, Lucy & Geminian, virg. mart. (3 less.); 17, Lambert, b.m. (3 less.; in Aquil., d.); 19, Eufemia, Dorothy, Thecla & Erasma, virg. mart., with oct. (in Aquil., d.);[2] 24, Rudbert, b.; 26, Oct. of four Virgins (3 less.).

---

[1] St. Quirinus (*ob.* 308) was bishop of Sisak in Croatia.
[2] September 3 in the modern proper of Udine (*duplex*). St. Daniel the Prophet (*duplex*) is commemorated on September 6.

October: 6, Faith, virg. (9 less.); 7, Mark, pope (in Aquil., d.); 10, Gereon & Comp., mart. (in Aquil., d.); 16, Gall, ab. (9 less.); Wolfgang, bp.

November: 11, Martin, b., with oct., & Menas, m. (in Aquil., d.); 13, Briccius, b. (3 less.); 16, Othmar, ab. (3 less.); 18, Oct. St. Martin (3 less.); 21, Maurus, m. (3 less.); 23, Felicity & Sons, mart. (3 less.); 24, Crisogonus, m. (in Aquil., d.).

December: 8, Conception of Mary (d.); 9, Syrus, b. (9 less.); 27, John (d.) & Zoilus, conf. (in Aquil., d.).[1]

The feast of the Holy Trinity is given (with octave) for the first Sunday after Pentecost, as in the Roman rite, but the traditional commemoration at Aquileia was on the last Sunday after Pentecost. The original day was retained at Como until the suppression of the rite, and, as we have seen, the peculiarity was commented on by the Apostolic visitor in 1579.[2]

A synodical decree of the patriarch Pertold (*ob.* 1251), which his successor, Gregory, confirmed, forbade the singing of two Masses *col canone* on the same day, unless it was the Nativity of our Lord, or if either a death had occurred after Mass had been already said or some person of importance (*sublime personaggio*) should have arrived who was desirous of hearing Mass.[3] Blessed Bertrand (*ob.* 1350) was accustomed to celebrate several 'dry Masses' (*Missae siccae*), and we read in his 'Life' that after the Mass of the day he was wont to 'recite the prayers of one or two other Masses'.[4]

The *Ordinarium Missae* was inserted in the missal of 1519 after the feast of Corpus Christi. Preparatory prayers before the altar are wanting, but the folios on which they were written in the exemplar preserved in London have probably disappeared, and we find a note on the fly-leaf at the beginning of the book directing the priest 'after the confession' (*post confessionem*) to go up to

---

[1] December 2 in the proper of Udine: St. Chromatius, bishop of Aquileia (*ob. c.* 407), *duplex.*

[2] *Acta Visitationis Comi*, 1618. In the 18th century, the Churches of Narbonne, Clermont and St. Julien de Brioude observed the feast of the Holy Trinity on the last Sunday after Pentecost; while at Sens, Auxerre, Mans, Angers, Avranches, Beauvais and Chartres a commemoration was made on both the first and the last Sundays. Lebrun, *op. cit.*, t. II, p. 227.

[3] Florio, *op. cit.*, pp. 120–1.   [4] *Ibid.*, p. 120.

the altar, and say the prayers: *Aufer a nobis* and *Oramus te Domine*. The additional words: *Et Sancte Spiritus* are found at the end of the *Gloria*.[1] A farced *Gloria in excelsis*, of the type general in the Middle Ages, is given for use on feasts of the Blessed Virgin.

The offertory is styled *Canon minor*, but the prayers are the same as in the Roman rite.[2] The text of the missal provides no response to *Orate fratres*, but *Suscipiat Dominus*, etc., has been written in the lower margin.[3] The prefaces are identical with those in the Pian missal, but the first part of the canon (until the consecration) is missing in the London exemplar. The canon has but few rubrics, although several have been added in the margin. The formula for the kiss of peace combines the actual Roman formula with a very general mediaeval text: *Pax tecum* (*tibi* has been written above) *et ecclesie: Vade in pace. Habete vinculum pacis et charitatis ut apti sitis sacrosanctis mysteriis Christi*.[4] The Communion prayers comprise: *Domine Jesu Christe, qui ex voluntate Patris; Perceptio Corporis* (written in the margin); *Panem celestem*; and *Domine non sum dignus*. The last named is a variant of the customary form, less directly applicable than the ordinary *Domine non sum dignus*, and influenced by *Jeremias* XVII, 14: *Domine non sum dignus: (sed) salvum me fac et salvus ero, quoniam laus mea tu es*.[5] In other respects, the *Ordinarium* is very similar to the Pian missal.

Ash Wednesday. The ceremony begins in the cathedral church with the recitation of four prayers, after which a procession is made to another church, in which the penitential psalms are said. Then, at the conclusion of the psalms, the clergy and ministers return to the cathedral chanting litanies.[6]

Old usages tend to survive in the ceremonies of the *Triduum Sacrum*. This is true, though to a limited degree, of Aquileia.

---

[1] Jungmann, *Missarum Sollemnia*, t. II (Paris, 1952), chap. I, 10, p. 107, n. 16.

[2] *Missal.* 1519, fo. 174.

[3] *Ibid.*, fo. 175.

[4] *Ibid.*, fo. 156.

[5] Jungmann, *op. cit.*, t. III, part IV, chap. III, 10, p. 286, n. 35. A similar form is found in the Missals of Salzburg (12th–13th century), Styria (15th century), Passau (14th century), Augsburg (1386), and Amiens (15th century). Cf. Missal of Sens (13th century), ap. Leroquais, *Sacram. et Missels . . .*, t. II, p. 81.

[6] *Missal.* 1519, fols. 32–3.

A study of the missal of 1519 is disappointing, and the liturgy for these days is predominantly the same as in our missal, before the introduction of the new order for Holy Week.

Palm Sunday. Clergy and people, carrying palms or other kinds of branches, go in procession, after terce, to the choir of the cathedral church. Then, singing *Fratres mei* and other responsaries, they proceed to the church in which the ceremony of blessing is to take place. Here the bishop, when he has blessed the salt and water, says the prayer: *Deus, quem diligere et amare justitia est.*[1] The subdeacon, as directed in the Pian missal, recites a lesson from Exodus: *Venerunt filii Israel in Elim,* but, in place of the responsary *Collegerunt* (or *In Monte Oliveti*), the tract *Saepe expugnaverunt* is sung. This is followed by a gospel taken from St. Mark: *Cum appropinquarent.*[2] A rubric enjoins the blessing of the palms, but the actual text is not given in the missal: *Tunc imediate benedicat pontifex ramos supradictos arborum hoc modo: Exorciso te omnis creatura florium, frondium, vel palmae seu olivae. In nomine Patris . . . (sicut in Pontificali).* The cross occupies a central position in the rite, as we find also at Bayeux[3] and Besançon.[4] It is laid on a carpet at the foot of the altar, and collectively honoured by all. Then the celebrant raises it up, as he chants: *O Crux, ave, spes unica.* Once again the cross is venerated, with the cantors, clergy and celebrant prostrate on the ground, while one of the ministers lightly strikes his shoulder with a palm, intoning the antiphon *Percutiam pastorem.* The celebrant, having received the cross, then triumphantly carries it in procession to the cathedral church, where Mass is celebrated.[5] The introit of the Mass is the same as in our existing missal: *Domine ne facias auxilium.*[6]

Holy Thursday. At the conclusion of the little hours, the bishop, vested in black dalmatic and cope, goes with the crucifer, taperers and thurifer to the narthex of the basilica, where, with the penitents prostrate before him, he begins the office for their

---

[1] *Missal.* 1519, fols. 71v–72.

[2] *Cum appropinquassent* from St. Matthew (XXI) in the Pian missal.

[3] U. Chevalier, *Ordin. de l'Eglise de Bayeux* (Paris, 1902), p. 118.

[4] Martène, *De Ant. Eccl. Rit.*, 6, 20. Ordo III.

[5] *Agenda dioecesis sanctae Aquilegiensis* (Venice, 1575), pp. 92 seq. Elements of the Aquileian rite were found at Venice, where they were adapted for the city.

[6] Fo. 72v.

reconciliation. Then, in the middle of the nave and before the altar of the Holy Cross, the prelate gives a formal absolution. Bishops and sacred ministers vest in white for the Mass. The *Gloria in excelsis* is directed to be said, without any rubric restricting its use to the occasions on which the holy oils are blessed. The missal prescribes a procession of the oils to be made round the cathedral church before their benediction: two crosses may be carried, one at the head of the procession, the other immediately before the oils. The hymn *O Redemptor summe carmine* (*sic*) is sung during the procession.[1] A rubric directs *miserere nobis* to be said after the third *Agnus*, in place of the customary *dona nobis pacem*, as the *pax* is not given on this day.[2] Vespers are recited after the *communio*, not at the conclusion of the procession to the altar of repose.[3] The missal orders the celebrant, at the end of Mass, to take two Hosts to the *sacrarium*, where they are to be kept *in loco mundo*.[4]

Good Friday. The liturgy, as in the Roman rite, begins with lessons from Hosea (*In tribulatione*) and Exodus (*Dixit Dominus ad Moysen*), and the tract *Eripe me*. The Passion of St. John follows, and a rubric orders two deacons, at the words *Partiti sunt vestimenta*, to remove the two cloths (*paniculos*) from the altar. The reproaches (*improperia*) and trisagion are sung after the solemn prayers, and four priests in chasubles carry the covered cross to the altar. There are three 'unveilings' of the cross, as in the Roman liturgy, but, during the adoration, the choir sings the psalm *Beati immaculati in via*, farced with *Ecce lignum crucis*, etc., followed by the antiphon *Dum fabricator mundi* and the hymn *Crux fidelis*. The two Hosts are brought to the altar for the Mass of the Presanctified, but only one of them is consumed, and the other, together with the cross, is taken to the 'sepulchre'. The responsary *Ecce quomodo moritur justus* is sung meanwhile, *suppressa voce*, and, as the procession returns, *Sepulto Domino*, *submissa voce*. The celebrant then removes his vestments, and ves-

---

[1] Fo. 85.

[2] Fo. 85. The restored order of Holy Week in the Roman rite gives a similar direction.

[3] Vespers are no longer said on this day in the Roman rite by those taking part in the solemn evening liturgy.

[4] Fo. 90v. Cf. Rite of Braga.

pers are recited. The ceremonial for this rite of 'burial' (*depositio*) is found in a ritual of Aquileia (with notes) which appeared at Venice in 1575: *Agenda Dioecesensis Sanctae Ecclesiae Aquilejensis*. It may be noted that the 'burial' of the cross and the Host are equally prominent. The deacon and subdeacon carry the *Imago Crucifixi* in the procession, and the celebrant carries the Host. The cross and Host are placed in those parts of the 'sepulchre' specially prepared for them. The ministers cover the crucifix with linen cloths and a sudary. Then, having censed and sprinkled the cross, the 'sepulchre' is sealed. The most informing detail of the 'resurrection' (*elevatio*) ceremony at Aquileia is the leaving of the *lintheamina* and *sudarium* in the 'sepulchre' for dramatic use in the *visitatio* (Three Maries) which is to follow,[1] but no reference is made in the missal (1519) to the *elevatio* itself.

Holy Saturday. The fire is blessed with the prayer: *Deus mundi conditor, auctor luminis, siderum fabricator*, 'with the other prayers as in the pontifical'. *Inventor rutili dux bone luminis* is sung as the procession returns to the choir. Then, before the altar, the deacon raises the tripartite candle, and says in a loud voice (*alta voce*) *Lumen Christi*, to which the choir respond: *Deo gratias*. There are four lessons, as in the Gregorian sacramentary of Hadrian and certain of the monastic rites: (1) *In principio creavit Deus*; (2) *Factum est in vigilia matutina*; (3) *Apprehendent*; (4) *Haec est hereditas*. *Sicut cervus* is sung as the procession goes to the font, and then *Rex sanctorum et angelorum totum mundum adjuva*. . . . The litany follows, during which the clergy and ministers go seven times round the font.[2] When the font has been blessed and the litany concluded,[3] bells are rung for Easter, and the choir sing the *Kyrie: Facta benedictione fontis et finita letania, pulsent omnes campane. Chorarii incipiant pro missa Kyrie eleison paschale*.[4]

The Mass of the *Assumption* has for the introit *Vultum tuum*, with the collect *Famulorum tuorum*.[5] A somewhat strange votive Mass is found on fo. 296v of the missal: *Missa de beato Job contra morbum gallicum*.

---

[1] *Agenda*, pp. 120–3.   [2] Fo. 98.
[3] This is presumably a second litany, sung as the procession returns to the altar.
[4] Fo. 98.   [5] Fo. 233.

Rites and Ceremonies Observed at Monza

An antiphoner of the 10th century provides versicles to be sung after the epistle. Proses appear only at the end of the codex, as if they had just been introduced.[1] A trope in hexameters is found before the introit on the feast of St. Stephen.[2]

An antiphoner of the following century has tropes for the *Kyrie* on certain days; 2 February is called *Natale S. Simeonis*; and the Canticle of the Three Children, called *Benedictio*, is sung on the vigil and the feast of St. John Baptist, the titular of the church.[3]

A sacramentary of the 10th century in the library of the basilica has a codex for the blessing of the new fire, which has a strong similarity to a codex of the Church of Rheims.[4] The 13th-century Monza ceremonial, now in the chapter library at Milan,[5] presents the following features:

Holy Thursday. After *matutinas de laudibus* (*tenebrae*), the lights are extinguished, and antiphons are recited, with one canon in the nave, another near the altar of the Blessed Virgin and a third near the altar of St. Vitus.[6]

Good Friday. At the conclusion of the solemn prayers, three ministers receive an 'ark' (*archa*) covered with a cloth, on which lie a book of the gospels, a large paten and a cross adorned with gems. The ark, preceded by a subdeacon carrying a large golden cross, is taken to the step of the altar, while the antiphon *Vadis propitiator* is sung. Then, raising the Lenten veil, the procession goes to the corner of the altar, and *Popule meus* is begun. When this is finished, the ark is taken behind the altar, and two clerics sing *Agyos*, to which the choir respond *Sanctus*. The 'ark' is taken to another part of the altar, and the Trisagion is repeated. At its conclusion, the veil is raised, and the procession goes into the choir, while *Ecce lignum Crucis* is sung. The 'ark' is placed on a carpet, and the choir sing an antiphon and the psalm *Beati imma-*

---

[1] Frisi, *op. cit.*, t. III, p. 40.
[2] *Ibid.*, p. 41.   [3] *Ibid.*, pp. 44–5.
[4] Martène, *De Antiq. Eccles. Rit.*, t. III, cols. 271–2; Frisi, *op. cit.*, p. 75.
[5] Milan, *Bibl. Capit.*, B 43.
[6] Frisi, *op. cit.*, t. III, p. 194. Cf. Premonstratensian rite.

culati. Then, having said the *Confiteor*, the hebdomadary or archpriest, together with the deacon and subdeacon, kiss the cross. The rite of the Presanctified follows.

Holy Saturday. The litanies directed to be sung before the blessing of the font are said to be *sicuti per quadragesimam*. At the conclusion of the blessing, the bells are rung. The officiant retires to vest, after which he returns to the font and, to the chant of further litanies, goes to the altar for Mass.

Easter. The faithful receive Holy Communion after the *Missa Minor*. After terce, the archpriest goes in procession to the church of St. Michael, preceded by a crucifer with a golden cross, a crozier-bearer and two deacons in *cappas*.[1] Here the ministers vest for Mass, and the procession returns to the basilica, with four taperers, two deacons and two subdeacons, while antiphons are sung. Then the *pharus*[2] is lighted at the entrance to the choir. A dramatic representation of the events on the first Easter morning takes place before the Mass: The faldstool serves as the sepulchre (*quod est in loco sepulchri*), while two clerics in copes take the part of the angels at the tomb, and two others that of the holy women.[3] During vespers a procession is made to the centre of the church.[4]

Candlemas (2 February). The candles are blessed in the church of St. Michael, and the Mass follows at the altar of the Blessed Virgin in the basilica.[5]

The *Rogation Days* were observed in the week before Pentecost, as in the Ambrosian rite.[6] A canon in a green dalmatic and stole sings the gospel.[7]

St. John the Evangelist (27 December). First vespers were sung by the archpriest, who at the words *deposuit potentes de sede* in the *Magnificat* took off his cope and, *con gran segno d'humiltà*, put it round the shoulders of the chaplain or priest sacristan. At the

---

[1] Until 1584 the canons had a black *cappa*, but in that year, at the request of St. Charles Borromeo, Rome sanctioned the almuce and *cappa paonazza* for the archpriest. The violet *cappa magna* was conceded to the canons by Benedict XIV in 1748.

[2] Cf. Ritual of Soissons for Easter. Martène, *op. cit.*, t. III, lib. IV, cap. XXV, col. 500. Cf. Ambrosian rite on feasts of martyrs.

[3] Frisi, *op. cit.*, t. III, pp. 196–7. Cf. Ritual of Strasburg, Martène, *op. cit.*, t. III, lib. IV, cap. XXV, col. 507.

[4] Frisi, *op. cit.*, p. 197. The procession was originally to the baptistery.

[5] *Ibid.*, p. 198.   [6] *Ibid.*, p. 199.   [7] *Ibid.*, p. 249.

same time also, the canons gave their copes to clerics. On the following day, the high Mass was celebrated by the chaplain or sacristan, while the canons served private Masses. All went back to normal at second vespers.[1]

BIBLIOGRAPHY

1. *Agenda Dioecesis Sanctae Ecclesiae Aquilegensis.* Venice, 1495, 1575.
2. De *Antiquis Forojuliensium ritibus,* dissertatio. A. *De Rubeis.* Venice, 1754.
3. *Aquileia e Grado.* Giovanni *Brusin.* Udine, 1947.
4. *Aquilée (Archéologie).* H. *Leclercq. Dict. d'Archéol. Chrét. et de Lit.* T. I, part I.
5. *Aquilée (Liturgie).* F. *Cabrol. D.A.C.L.* T. I, part II.
6. *Aquileia.* Gaetano *Moroni Romano. Dizionario di Erudizione Storico-Ecclesiastica.* Vol. II. Venice, 1840.
7. *Aquileia.* Thomas *Shahan. Catholic Encyclopedia.* Vol. I.
8. *Aquileian Rite.* Adrian *Fortescue. Catholic Encyclopedia.* Vol. I.
9. La *Basilica del Fondo Tullio alla Beligna di Aquileia.* Giovanni *Brusin.* Associazione Nazionale per Aquileia, 1948.
10. Vita del *Beato Beltrando,* Patriarca d'Aquileja. Francesco *Florio.* Venice, 1759.
11. *Beato Bertrando di Saint-Geniès,* Patriarca d'Aquileia (Pastorale e Spada). Udine, 1943.
12. *Breviarium* secundum ritum et consuetudinem *Ecclesiae Aquileiensis.* Venice, 1481 and 1486.
13. *Breviarium* secundum ritum patriarchalem *Comenis Ecclesiae.* Como-Milan, 1585.
14. *Christian Worship*: Its Origin and Evolution. Louis *Duchesne.* 2nd Eng. edit. London, 1904.
15. *Como, Diocese of.* U. *Benigni. Catholic Encyclopedia.* Vol. IV.
16. *Ecclesiological Essays.* J. *Wickham Legg.* Vol. VII, V, 3. London, 1905.
17. *Explication de la Messe.* Pierre *Lebrun.* T. II. Paris, 1726.
18. SS. *Hermagoras and Fortunatus.* H. *Thurston. Butler's Lives of the Saints.* Vol. VII (July). London, 1932.
19. *L'Immacolata nella Liturgia Occidentale anteriore al secolo XIII.* Andrea M. *Cecchin.* Rome, 1943.
20. *Italia Sacra.* Ferdinand *Ughelli.* Tt. I–V. Rome, 1652.
21. *Littérature latine au moyen* âge depuis les origines jusqu' à la fin de la Renaissance Carolingienne. J. *de Ghellinck.* Brussels, 1939.
22. *Liturgia Romana e Liturgia dell 'Esarcato*: Il Rito detto in seguito Patriarchino e le Origini del Canon Missae Romano. Anton *Baumstark.* Rome, 1904.
23. The *Mass*: A study of the Roman Liturgy. Adrian *Fortescue.* London, 1912.

[1] Frisi, *op. cit.,* p. 250.

24. *Maxentius of Aquileia and the North Italian Baptismal Rites.* H. Boone Porter. *Éphemerides Liturgicae.* Vol. LXIX (1955), fasc. I.
25. *Memorie storiche di Monza e sua Corte.* Anton Francesco *Frisi.* Milan, 1794.
26. *Milan, Archdiocese of.* U. *Benigni. Catholic Encyclopedia.* Vol. X.
27. *Missale pro S. Aquileyensis Ecclesiae ritu.* Augsburg, 1494.
28. *Missale Aquileyensis Ecclesie.* Venice: G. de Gregoriis, 1517, 1519.
29. *Officium Hebdomadae Sanctae* secundum consuetudinem *S. Marci Venetiarum,* 1596.
30. San *Paolina patriarca e la Chiesa Aquileise al fine del secolo VIII.* Pio *Paschini.* Udine, 1906.
31. *Paulinus II, Patriarch of Aquileia.* Aluigi *Cossio. Catholic Encyclopedia.* Vol. XI.
32. *Revue Bénédictine* (Maredsous). T. XIX, 1902.
33. *Sacerdotale.* O. P. Alberto *Castellano.* Venice, 1537.
34. *Sacramentarium patriarchale* secundum morem *S. Comensis Ecclesiae.* Milan, 1537.
35. Breve *Storia del Friuli.* P. S. *Leicht.* Udine, 1930.

Chapter Two

RITE OF BENEVENTO

Historical Background

THE orbit of the ancient rite of Benevento may be said to
have embraced the territory comprised in the lines,
Terracina–Chieti and Salerno–Bari. Thus it was the
liturgy of the Lombard duchy of Benevento, which, isolated from
North Italy by the gigantic rampart of the Abruzzi, included such
centres as Naples, Salerno, Capua, Gaeta, Trani and Monte Cassino. The northern frontier did not change appreciably in the
Middle Ages, but the southern frontier varied between the middle
of the 9th and the 13th century. Salerno, for example, became the
capital of a new and independent duchy in 849.

Benevento received its name—'Place of good fortune'—on be-
coming a Roman colony in 268 B.C. The capture and destruction
of Beneventum by the Goths under Totila in 545 were succeeded
by a Byzantine occupation, but in 570 the city was taken by the
Lombards, who founded a duchy which was to endure for many
centuries.[1] The greatest prosperity would seem to have been
attained under two dukes of the name of Arechis, although they
were separated in time by more than a century and a half.[2] The
Lombards on their arrival were Arians, but some time between
the 6th and 8th century they were converted to Catholicism and,
like their kindred of Aquileia, became fervent champions of the
Faith.

During this period, at least three of the bishops of Benevento
were accepted as saints: Marcianus (533), Zenoe (543) and Barbatus (*ob.* 682). St. Barbatus, whose feast is observed on 19 Feb-

---

[1] The duchy of Benevento, in course of time, came to be divided into three principalities: Benevento, Capua and Salerno.
[2] Arechis I rebuilt his capital in 589.

52

ruary, is said to have melted down a golden serpent which had been an object of worship to many of the Lombards. The gold was made into a chalice which was preserved in the city until the invasion of the French in 1799.[1] The Saint assisted at the council of Rome, held under Pope Agatho (678–81) in 680, and in the following year he attended the sixth general council at Constantinople.

Lombard pride reawakened in the time of Arechis II, who for sixteen years governed South Italy as duke, and then in 758 assumed the title of prince (758–87) and, in token of his sovereign right, was consecrated. In 787, Charlemagne, acting on the advice of Pope Hadrian I (772–95), decided to attach the principality to the Frankish monarchy, but Arechis had no intention of tamely submitting to the loss of his possessions, and sought Byzantine protection. The distant βασιλεύς was a far less dangerous opponent to Lombard autonomy. Arechis promised the empress Irene that he would recognise imperial supremacy in exchange for the title and dignity of 'prince'. The empress agreed, and the duchy of Benevento came into the Byzantine orbit.

It would seem that Arechis in his preoccupation with ecclesiastical affairs rivalled the Frankish sovereign. Many of the religious houses in the city owed their foundation to his generosity, and it may well have been in his time that the Roman liturgy supplanted the local 'Beneventan' use. However this may be, Byzantium held a great attraction for him, and it seems to have been the intention of Arechis to rival Justinian.

In 788, a victory of the Franks united South Italy to the Frankish monarchy, but the supremacy of Charlemagne remained very illusory. Benevento retained contact with the Byzantine empire, especially from the end of the 8th to the middle of the 9th century.

The incursions of the Saracens afforded a new occasion for the Greeks to intervene (851–52). Apulia and Calabria had been ravaged, and Benevento and Salerno threatened. The Franks and Lombards made common cause against the infidels, and succeeded in defeating them. War broke out again in 866, and on the Christian victory in 871 the Western emperor made a further bid for the

---

[1] Paten, ap. U. Benigni, *Benevento, Catholic Encyclopedia*, vol. II, p. 478.

submission of the Lombard prince. The Lombards revolted, and in 873 Prince Radelchis turned to Byzantium, with the promise of ruling as the suzerain of the βασιλεύς. It was clear, however, that Radelchis had little or no intention of honouring his word, preferring to negotiate with the Saracens. Pope John VIII (872–82) obtained from the Frankish emperor, Charles the Bald, a right of sovereignty over the Lombard states of the South, transforming into vassals the princes of Benevento and Salerno and the count of Capua.

In 882, an alliance was made between the Roman Church and the Byzantine empire against the Saracens. The Eastern emperor sent an army, which *c.* 885 was commanded by Nicephoras Phocas, who restored Byzantine power in South Italy. Profiting by the general discord, Benevento had been in the throes of civil war since 881, and Prince Aion expelled the Byzantine garrison at Bari. The Lombards were not masters of the situation for long, and by 888 the Greeks were again masters of Apulia. Benevento came more directly under the sway of Byzantium, and in 891 the *strategos* moved his place of residence from Bari to Benevento.

For two years the city remained under the vigilant eye of the direct representative of the βασιλεύς, but at the end of that time a lesser functionary was appointed, and, with the aid of the duke of Spoleto, the Byzantines were chased from Benevento. The duke, instead of re-establishing the ancient dynasty, now represented by a child, retained the power for himself (895–97). In 897, Radelchis, who had already governed the Lombard duchy (881–84), was recognised as prince,[1] but two years later a conspiracy brought about his fall, and Atenolf, count of Capua, founded a new dynasty which was to govern both Capua and Benevento until the end of the 11th century. Capua now became the capital and Benevento passed to second place. To maintain the struggle against the Saracens, Atenolf is forced to seek Greek protection, but, although after the victory of Carigliano (915) the Byzantines had the supremacy from Gaeta to Monte Gargano,

---

[1] The family of Radelchis had governed Benevento from 840–99, except for the years 891–97, when the city had been occupied successively by Byzantines and Franks from Spoleto.

their rule was very superficial. From 926 we find the Lombard princes abandoning Eastern titles and showing open hostility to the emperor. They again became independent sovereigns whose prestige and authority were strengthened in the middle of the century. It was an era of peace for South Italy, marked by the revival of the great Benedictine abbeys of Monte Cassino and S. Vincenzo di Volturno. A new power now comes on the scene in the person of Otto I, who restored the Empire of the West, assuming royal authority at Pavia and imperial authority at Rome. The Carolingian tradition is resumed, with a claim to authority over all Italy. The Lombard principality is indeed the most independent in the Peninsula, although Benevento had been shorn of Salerno in 849. Metropolitan status was accorded to Benevento in 929.

In 967 a common animosity to Pope John XIII (965–72) united the Western empire and the principality of Capua–Benevento, which in fact strengthened the influence of the latter, and under the rule of Padolf the unity of the southern Lombards was reconstituted. It was, however, a fragile unity which did not survive the death of the prince (981). Benevento was forced to recognise imperial suzerainty, but the authority of the emperor was always very tenuous, and in fact the Lombard principalities formed a neutral zone whose rulers enjoyed the fullest independence. The story of Otto III (983–1002) claiming from Benevento the relics of St. Bartholomew will be told in another place. The theoretical overlordship of the emperor counted for but little, and when the German armies, sent to quell revolts, were removed, the Lombard princes continued to govern independently. They succeeded for four hundred years in holding in check the various powers that tried to 'enslave' them. Benevento was taken by the Normans in 1047, but six years later (1053) they were forced by the emperor Henry III to relinquish it. The city, however, had in 1051 accepted the suzerainty of Pope Leo IX (1049–54), a relative of the emperor Henry III, in payment by the Church of Bamberg of the annual tribute to the Apostolic See. Shortly afterwards, Benevento was again occupied by the Normans, but, although the Pope was defeated in the war that followed, the conquerors restored the city to the Pope. It became henceforward Pontifical

territory, but it was not until the death of Landolf nearly twenty
years later (1077) that the Apostolic See was in full possession of
its rights. The duchy remained an appanage of the Roman Pon-
tiffs until the end of the 18th century, and, after a short-lived
French principality (1806–15), again from 1815 to 1860, when it
was finally incorporated in the kingdom of Italy.

Eleven councils met in Benevento during the period 1059–
1545: that of 1091 under Urban II (1088–99) prescribed the imposition of ashes for the faithful on Ash Wednesday: *Omnes tam
clerici, quam laici, tam viri, quam mulieres die illo (in capite jejunii)
cinerem supra capita sua accipiant.*[1]

The title of 'Second Founder of Benevento' has been conferred
on the Dominican Pietro Francesco Orsini, who occupied the see
from 1686 till 1725, in which latter year he ascended the Chair of
Peter as Benedict XIII. The reconstruction of Benevento was the
result of the damage effected by the earthquakes of 1688 and 1702.

Churches

Byzantium, as we have seen, was looked upon with especial
favour by the Lombard rulers of the 8th and 9th centuries. The
Princes of Benevento, despite their promises, would never seem
to have had any intention of submitting to the rule of the
βασιλεύς, but they regarded the culture and refinements of the
Eastern Empire as something to be striven for in their own principality.

Arechis II in fact had it in mind to become a Western Justinian.
High-sounding Byzantine titles were given to the nobles, and a
basilica was erected, which, with its purple hangings and draperies
from Asia Minor, and its vessels of gold and silver set with precious stones, was designed to rival on a small scale the 'Great
Church' on the shores of the Bosphorus. This costly and magnificent building was dedicated to Agia Sophia, 'the Holy Wisdom
of the Word'.[2] The very title expresses a programme: *Arechis
igitur princeps illustris, perfecta jam sancte Sophie basilica, quam ad*

---

[1] Counc. Benevento, 1091, can. 4; Labbe, *Concil.*, t. X, col. 484.
[2] Erchempert, *Hist. Long. Benev.*, n. 3 (*Mon. Germ. Hist. Script. rer. Long. et Ital.*
p. 236); Leo of Ostia, *Chron. Mont. Casin.*, lib. I, n. 8 (Mon. Germ., t. VII, p. 586).

Baptistery of the Arians,
Ravenna

Canons in Centenary Procession of Blessed Bertrand of Saint-Giniès, Udine, October 1st, 1950

Cathedral Church, Como

Cathedral Church, Monza

Detail of Ambo (Jonas and the Whale), Cathedral Church, Ravello (1131)

Ambo, Cathedral Church, Ravello

exemplar illius condidit Justiniane.[1] The church was probably
built on the site of a Roman temple, from which the six granite
and two marble columns supporting the spherical vaulting were
taken (732–74). This circular 8th-century edifice is happily intact, although somewhat damaged in the Second World War
(1939–45). The tympanum on the façade shows a seated figure of
Christ between the Blessed Virgin and St. Mercurius.[2] Arechis
gave the house adjoining this national Lombard sanctuary to
Benedictine nuns, who in about the year 960 were replaced by
monks, and in 1590 by the Canons Regular of S. Salvatore,
Bologna.[3] A handsome MS. of the martyrology and Holy Rule
of St. Benedict was executed for the religious of St. Sophia by the
scribe Eustasius and decorated by a monk from Sipontum about
the end of the 12th century.[4]

The Benedictine convent of St. Mary and St. Peter outside the
town was an earlier foundation, which came under the jurisdiction of S. Vincenzo del Volturno in 674. An 11th–12th-century
missal formerly belonging to the house has been acquired of
recent years by the British Museum.

The piety and generosity of the Lombard dukes and princes
filled the city with churches and religious houses, but they have
for the most part disappeared. The basilica of St. Bartholomew,
built by Prince Sicard in the early years of the 9th century to
house the lately acquired relics of the Saint, was entirely re-
fashioned in the Baroque period, but a small carving from the old
church may be seen in the west wall.

The cathedral church, which had been erected by Bishop David
in the 7th century, was rebuilt in the 9th, and again in 1200. The
building was almost completely destroyed in 1943 in the course of
the Second World War, with the exception of the Apulian
Romanesque façade and the bell-tower (1279). The magnificent

---

[1] *Translatio Sancti Mercurii: Mon. Germ.*, pp. 576–7.

[2] St. Mercurius, greatly revered in the East as a 'warrior-saint', is said to have been a
Scythian officer in the Roman army, who was beheaded at Caesarea in Cappadocia in
c. 250. His icon is popular in Coptic churches: represented as slaying the emperor Julian
the Apostate in battle, having retrieved his sword for the purpose from the church at
Caesarea in which it was venerated as a relic.

[3] The beautiful little 12th-century cloisters date from the time of the monks.

[4] Vat. Lib., MS. lat. 5959.

E

bronze doors with sixty-eight reliefs, mostly of New Testament subjects, were seriously damaged, the ambones reduced to fragments, and the paschal candlestick of the closing years of the 13th century lost to posterity.

The year 1943 was an unfortunate one for South Italian art, and the cathedral churches of Capua and Gaeta suffered a fate similar to that of Benevento. In both places, however, the campaniles were happily spared: that of Capua dating from the 9th century, and Gaeta from 1180.

There is an intimate connection between the history of art and the history of liturgy, and it is no mere coincidence that the ambones on which we find representations of Jonas and the whale are precisely in Campania, Abruzzi and Apulia: those districts which were for the most part in the ancient duchy of Benevento. It is from here that those MSS.—which have for a rubric on Holy Thursday or Holy Saturday: *Lectio Jonae prophetae cum cantico*—emanate. The lesson from Jonas was directed to be read in the *Missale Antiquum* of Benevento and the *Ordo* of Lucca on Holy Thursday, as we find today in the Ambrosian rite; whereas in other MSS. it was normally appointed for Holy Saturday.

The former Lombard Duchy of Benevento is especially rich in highly decorative ambones and paschal candlesticks, chiefly dating from the 12th and 13th centuries, when the Roman rite had already superseded the local use for some centuries, save for certain of the chants which had been retained from the old Beneventan rite. Their type, however, is considerably more ancient, as may be seen in miniatures of the *Exsultet* from these regions. Fragments of earlier work, of the 8th and 9th centuries, are to be found at Minturno and Tuscania (*S. Maria Maggiore*). The following list of ambone, although by no means exhaustive, may be of interest: Canosa, Fondi (*S. Pietro*), Troia (cathedral, removed from *S. Basilio*), Terracina, Minturno, Sessa Aurunca, Tuscania (*S. Maria Maggiore*), Castel S. Elia, Caserta Vecchia, Salerno, Ravello (Cathedral, S. Giovanni del Toro), Scala, Amalfi, S. Angelo in Formis, Cava and Bitonto. The customary form of these ambone is simple and massive: two slabs of a triangular shape, often decorated with cosmati mosaic work, on either side of the steps which lead up to the platform, serve as a balustrade. It is here in this triangular space that we often find a bas-relief representing one or more scenes from the life of the prophet Jonas. The most perfect example is probably in the cathedral church of Ravello (1130), where the whale, in the form of a winged dragon, is represented twice: first in the act of swallowing Jonas, whose legs have not yet disappeared; then throwing out Jonas alive, with the body emerging from the mouth of the monster. A somewhat similar theme is to be found at Minturno; S. Maria in Valle Porclaneta in the Abruzzi (1150); and S. Maria de Lago near Moscufo (1159). At Gaeta, where the ambo has been destroyed, the two representations have been built into the wall on either side of the steps leading through the bell-tower into the cathedral; while at Sessa Aurunca, Jonas emerging from the belly of the whale is depicted on a slab built into the south wall of the choir.[1]

Fine examples of sculptured paschal candlesticks may be seen at Gaeta, Terracina, Cori, Minturno, Sessa Aurunca, Cava and Salerno.

RITE OF BENEVENTO

Dom Benozzi, a monk of Monte Cassino who had become arch-bishop of Benevento, would seem to have been the first to realise that his see had at one time possessed a complete distinctive rite.[2] Unfortunately lack of MSS. makes it impossible to reproduce the full ancient text, and we have no more than a series of pieces taken from the old Beneventan repertory, and retained in later Roman MSS. The most ancient of the noted MSS. of the Beneventan school, however, are not earlier than the end of the 10th century, when the local rite had been superseded by that of Rome for some considerable time.[3] All that remains are mixed documents in a

---

[1] It is interesting to note the marked resemblance between the southern Italian ambone and the pulpits in the old Coptic churches of Abu Sergeh and El-Moallaka in Old Cairo. The example at El-Moallaka has been ascribed to the 11th century.

[2] Dix, *Shape of the Liturgy*, chap. XV, p. 568, n. 3.

[3] R. J. Hesbert, *La Tradition bénéventaine dans la tradition manuscrite*, *Paléograph. Musicale* XIV, chap. II, p. 94.

Gregorian framework, sometimes with corresponding Roman texts. Certain of these, it would appear, survived until the 12th century or even the 13th. Perhaps, says Dom Hesbert, the most characteristic note of the Beneventan tradition is 'archaism'.[1] 'Briefly, the history of the rite seems to be that all the local propers are older than about A.D. 800, when local composition ceased; after that new Masses were taken over from the Roman rite when required. The old collection of local propers, which dropped out of use in the 13th century, was replaced by the corresponding texts from the Western missal then coming into general use in South Italy.' [2] At the very latest, we may say that the Roman chant and liturgy came to South Italy in the first years of the 9th century, and when, on the order of Prince Sicard, the relics of St. Bartholomew arrived in Benevento in 808, the Roman use was sufficiently established there for the new Mass composed in his honour to have all its parts Gregorian. No purely Beneventan Mass of St. Bartholomew existed. One of the many occasions on which the emperor waged war on the principality of Benevento was the result of a hoax which was played upon him in respect to the Saint's relics. The emperor Otto III (983–1002) went on a pilgrimage to the sanctuary of the Archangel Michael on Monte Gargano. On his return he stopped at Benevento, and claimed the body of St. Bartholomew. The citizens, torn between a fear of offending the emperor and grief at depriving the town of so precious a relic, handed over some bones of little importance in place of those of the Apostle. The emperor continued his journey to Rome persuaded that he had with him the remains of St. Bartholomew. A little time later the pious fraud is discovered,[3] and the deceived emperor vows vengeance against the perfidious Beneventans.[4] Finally, the genuine bones, or what purported to be such, arrived in Rome, and were deposited in the church of St. Adalbert on the Isola Tiberina.[5] The journeys of the relics,

---

[1] R. J. Hesbert, *op. cit.*, p. 97.

[2] Dix, *op. cit.*, chap. XV, p. 568, n. 3.

[3] Fraud and even theft in respect to relics are often to be met with in mediaeval history.

[4] Cf. Leo of Ostia, *Chron. Monast. Casin.* II, 24 (*Mon. Germ.* . . ., t. VII, pp. 642–3). According to another text, the expedition against Benevento was due to a Lombard revolt. J. Gay, *L'Italie Mériodionale et l'Empire Byzantin* (Paris, 1904), pp. 373–4.

[5] The church was known later as S. Bartholomew.

says Fr. Thurston, 'are even more bewildering than those of his living body'.[1]

Beneventan Manuscripts. Manuscripts emanating from the ancient principality of Benevento which have retained at least some texts and chants from the old local use include:

(1) A gradual from the private library of Pius VI, now in the Vatican (MS. lat. 10673), probably of the middle of the 11th century.

(2) *Liber typicus* of the 12th century in the Chapter library at Benevento: 1st part, MS. V, 19; 2nd part, MS. V, 20.

(3) Plenary missal of the 13th century, with some rare pieces of chant, noted for the most important Masses and special functions. Benev. *Capit. Bibl.*, MS. VI, 30.

(4) *Missale Antiquum* of the end of the 10th or the beginning of the 11th century. Benev. *Capit. Bibl.*, MS. VI, 33.

(5) Gradual-Tropary of the end of the 11th or the beginning of the 12th century. Benev. *Capit. Bibl.* VI, 34.

(6) Gradual-Tropary of the 12th century. Benev. *Capit. Bibl.*, MS. VI, 35.

(7) Gradual-Tropary of the 11th century. Benev. *Capit. Bibl.*, MS. VI, 38.

(8) Gradual-Tropary of the 11th century. Benev. *Capit. Bibl.*, MS. VI, 39.

(9) Gradual-Tropary of the 11th century. Benev. *Capit. Bibl.*, MS. VI, 40.

(10) Plenary missal of the end of the 11th century, Monte Cassino, MS. 127.

(11) Noted plenary missal of the end of the 11th or beginning of the 12th century. Monte Cassino, MS. 540.

(12) First part of a gradual of the end of the 12th or beginning of the 13th century, Monte Cassino, MS. 546.

Beneventan Script. The script distinctive of the principality would seem to have evolved in four stages: (1) A tentative period from the end of the 8th to the end of the 9th century; (2) a period of formation from the end of the 9th and throughout the 10th

---

[1] Thurston, *Butler's Lives of the Saints*, vol. VIII, August (London, 1933), p. 290.

century; (3) a period of maturity in the 11th and 12th centuries; and (4) the period of decline from the end of the 12th till the end of the 13th century.[1] These periods have been identified with epochs in the history of Monte Cassino: (1) corresponds roughly speaking to the pre-Capuan epoch; (2) to the Capuan epoch; (3) to the century which opens with the abbots Atenolf (1011–22) and Theobald (1022–35), and closes with Desiderius (1058–87) and Oderisius (1087–1105); while (4) corresponds to the age of Abbot Bernard I (1264–82) and his immediate predecessors. In the period of maturity the Desiderian epoch is the most important, as it marks the highest point of development reached.[1]

Desiderius, the future Pope Victor III (1086–87), was a man of great accomplishments, and it is difficult to say whether this cultured Benedictine found the greater satisfaction in buildings or in books: *Non solum in aedificiis, verum etiam in libris discribendis operam Desiderius dare permaximam studuit.*[2]

The oldest dated example of a minuscule MS. written in South Italy falls at the end of the 8th century (779–97):[3] the latest dated example of an entire MS. is 1295.[4] It is unlikely that the script was used to any great extent before or after the limits furnished by the dated examples.

Beneventan script had profound roots in South Italy, which neither the invasion of the Normans nor the hostility of the emperor was able to check.[5] It was not, however, confined to the ancient Duchy of Benevento. It was used in places north of the duchy, as Gaeta, Fondi, Veroli and Sulmona, as well as on the Tremiti Islands in the Adriatic and all along the opposite shores of Dalmatia from Ossero to Ragusa.[6]

It was due in no small measure to such monasteries as Monte Cassino, Cava and Benevento that the script remained vigorous

---

[1] E. A. Loew, *Beneventan Script; History of South Italian Minuscule* (Oxford, 1914), chap. VII, p. 122.

[2] Cf. Leo of Ostia; *Pat. Lat.*, t. CLXXIII, cols. 799–800.

[3] *Bibl. Nat.*, Paris, Lat. 7530; Cava, MS. 2: both from Monte Cassino.

[4] Cava, MS. 24: written in Cava.

[5] Frederick II issued a decree against Beneventan script in 1220 and again in 1231. Loew, *op. cit.*, p. 45, n. 1.

[6] Examples of Beneventan script are found at Ossero, Ragusa, Spalato (Split) and Trau.

for so many centuries, and they were in fact the last strongholds of the *littera Beneventana*.[1]

The script is known also by the name of 'Lombardic', 'Longo-bardic' and 'Cassinese', but 'Beneventan' is the more usual term. Beneventan MSS. are quite clearly not of universal tradition, and they are of a type altogether distinctive.[2]

Liturgical Year. The only feasts, apart from the great solemni-ties of the liturgical cycle, that are known to have been observed in the old rite of Benevento are those of St. Michael, by reason of the proximity of Monte Gargano; SS. Simon and Jude; The Twelve Brothers, especially venerated at Benevento; and All Saints. The feast of All Saints may well have been the last com-memoration to be added to the old Beneventan calendar, if one may take into consideration the late character of the feast.[3]

Beneventan Chant. Dom Hesbert speaks of the chant with its moving accents, suppliant and often pathetic, which does not seem to accord with the Roman genius.[4] Many of these chants are ecclesiastical compositions, and similar to those found in the Ambrosian rite. On the other hand, the term 'Ambrosian' is sometimes used to express no more than 'non-Roman', and the chant in question is not in the Milanese repertory. There is no further trace of the ancient Beneventan chants after the 13th century: the Church of Benevento and those which depended from it had by that time become entirely Romanised.[5] MSS. of the 11th, 12th and even 13th century show the persistence of certain pieces of the ancient chant, but there is no doubt that the success of the Roman chant in these regions was very rapid.[5] There were, however, local variations within the Beneventan use itself, and we find that MSS. from Bari were not always identical with those from Benevento. Complete local traditions of the proper, which included distinctive chants as well as texts, were found both at Benevento and Milan. Some of the melodies are in

---

[1] Loew, *op. cit.*, chap. III, p. 46. The Beneventan script gave place to the more usual form of minuscule, familiar to the Normans and French.

[2] Hesbert, *op. cit.*, chap. II, 2, p. 124.

[3] November 1 was observed in the time of Gregory IV (827–844), with the approval of Louis the Pious and the Frankish episcopate.

[4] Hesbert, *op. cit.*, p. 452. [5] *Ibid.*, p. 448.

substance the same as the corresponding Roman ones, but in each of these Churches the borrowed melodies have been rewritten. Elsewhere, we sometimes find that the text or the music, or both, have been borrowed by Benevento from Milan (or vice versa), and these borrowings too have been freely adapted.

The bilingual chants—Greek and Latin—in the Beneventan graduals are a legacy from the Byzantine occupation of the city, when, in addition to the native Latin clergy, there must have been a number of Greek priests for the garrison. As at Rome in the 8th century and later at Naples, the Latins and Greeks would unite in worship on certain great feasts, and both tongues would be heard.[1] Thus it came about that certain pieces dear to the Greeks would have been incorporated in the local liturgy of Benevento after the Byzantine occupation had ceased.[2] In addition to the trisagion, Greek texts are explicitly attested by Beneventan MSS., and on Good Friday and Holy Saturday we find six texts, accompanied by Latin translations, regularly adapted in the same melody, and several accompanied by a psalm in one or other language. The *Vita Athanasii* says: 'All together, clerics and laity, in a common prayer, assiduously sing the psalms in Greek and Latin, thus rendering a worthy office of praise to God';[3] while the *Translatio S. Severini* speaks of a procession 'with alternate chant of two choirs, Greek and Latin'.[4]

Beneventan Texts. The propers of Benevento and Milan have much that is peculiar to one or other of them, either the product of local talent or borrowed from yet other sources no longer extant.[5] Benevento certainly borrowed from Milan, as did Milan from Rome, which points to a similar origin prior to the differentiation of the Latin liturgies. Thus we have examples of Milan and Benevento as against Rome; Rome and Milan as against Benevento; and Rome and Benevento as against Milan. An indubitable proof of the respective independence of the three traditions, all from the same original trunk common to the Latin liturgies.[6]

---

[1] The bilingual antiphon and psalm came to be very general by the beginning of the 9th century.　　　　　　　　　　[2] Hesbert, *op. cit.*, chap. III, p. 460.
[3] *Mon. Germ. Hist.* . . . , p. 440; cf. *Ibid.*, p. 451.　　[4] *Ibid.*, p. 456.
[5] Dix, *op. cit.*, chap. XV, p. 569.　　　　　　　　[6] Hesbert, *op. cit.*, p. 456.

We find an undoubted rapport between the Beneventan and Ambrosian rites, as, for example, the series of Lenten gospels; the lesson from Jonas on Holy Thursday; and the Good Friday tenebrae responsaries and lesson from Daniel, with the *Tunc hi tres* introducing the *Benedictiones* followed by the two versicles: *Quoniam eripuit* and *Confitemini Domino*. It is clear, however, that Benevento would have copied Milan, and not vice versa.

It has been suggested that the Ambrosian rite was at one time in use in parts of South Italy, and Monte Cassino is cited as an example of this. In the Vatican Library a folio from an Ambrosian MS., copied at Monte Cassino in Beneventan writing and notation, serves as a protecting leaf to a Cassinese martyrology. The MS. dates from the beginning of the 12th or even the 11th century.[1] In addition to this, the Chronicle of Leo of Ostia says that Pope Stephen X (1057–58) forbade the use of the Ambrosian chant at Monte Cassino: *Ambrosianum cantum in ecclesia ista cantari penitus interdixit.*[2] We know, however, that the term 'Ambrosian' in the Beneventan liturgy has no connection with Milan, and in fact the pieces so described are often not be found there. Its significance is no more than 'non-Roman'.[3] The vestiges of the old rite sheltered under the name of the illustrious Milanese bishop, although the liturgy of Benevento, despite a number of similarities, was as distinct from Milan as it was from Rome. There is the possibility of the use of the Ambrosian rite at Monte Cassino, as we know that Petronax, who restored the abbey in 717–20, was a native of Brescia, but it would be rash to assert categorically that he introduced the liturgy of Milan. The evidence cited above is far from conclusive.

From a literary point of view, the liturgical repertory of Benevento is certainly more similar to Milan than it is to Rome. We find, for example, in addition to what has been said already, a whole series of pieces common to the two liturgies: The two communions for St. Michael (8 May), *Multos infirmos curasti* and *Caelestis militiae princeps*, are found as *psallendae* for the

[1] Vat. MS. Ottob. lat 3.
[2] Leo of Ostia, *Chron. Monast. Casin.*, II, 94; *Mon. Germ. Hist. Script.*, t. VII, p. 693.
[3] Hesbert, *op. cit.*, p. 455.

Dedication of St. Michael in Monte Gargano (29 September) in the Ambrosian rite. The Beneventan *ingressa* for St. John Baptist: *Lumen quod animus cernit* and the offertory: *Inter natos mulierum*, are found also as *psallendae* at Milan, as are the *ingressa* of Benevento for the feast of St. Peter: *Petrus dormiebat inter duos milites*, and the communion for the same day: *Ut agnosceres me*. Benevento, Milan and Rome all have *Gaudeamus*: Benevento as the *ingressa* for All Saints; Milan (a slight variant) as the *ingressa* for St. Agatha, Assumption and All Saints; Rome (verbatim as Benevento) as the introit for St. Agatha, Assumption and All Saints. The three traditions show mutual independence, but they are all from the same trunk, common to the Latin liturgies.[1]

No MS. of the complete Beneventan Mass has survived, and the codices that have been preserved show a liturgy indistinguishable from the Roman, save for here and there a chant or rubric which has been retained from the old rite. The British Museum has acquired recently a missal of the 11th–12th century, formerly belonging to the Benedictine convent of St. Peter outside the city, but it is entirely Roman, although it provides for the feast of the Transfiguration (6 August), a solemnity popularised by Peter the Venerable (*ob.* 1156) and the Cluniacs, although it did not become a feast of the Universal Church until 1456.

Some twenty Masses for great feasts, containing texts and chants from the old local use, can be reconstructed from three of the graduals: VI, 35; VI, 38; VI, 40. They are for Christmas, St. Stephen, Palm Sunday, Holy Thursday, Holy Saturday, Easter, St. Michael (8 May), Ascension, Pentecost, St. John Baptist, SS. Peter and Paul, St. Laurence, Assumption, Twelve Brothers (1 September), Exaltation of the Holy Cross, SS. Simon and Jude, All Saints, St. Martin and St. Andrew. Such a reconstruction verifies a law of liturgical evolution maintained by Baumstark, according to which the most unchangeable forms are those for the great feasts of our Lord and for Holy Week. This is especially true in the case of the *Triduum Sacrum*, as may be seen by a glance at almost any of the Western liturgies. Here at Benevento we have some special functions, which, without belonging in the strict

---

[1] Hesbert, *op. cit.*, p. 456.

sense to the liturgy of the Mass, are, however, normally joined to
it: Blessing and Procession of Palms, *Mandatum*, Adoration of
the Cross, and the Blessing of the candle and font. There was
thus produced a series of doubles, which could not last indefi-
nitely. It was necessary in practice to choose between the two
formularies, and by the 13th century the last of the Beneventan
chants had disappeared. The Roman rite, however, had prevailed
from at least the 8th century, and it was no more than some few
texts and chants of the old liturgy that for several centuries continued to appear in the missals of Benevento.

The long series of processional antiphons, which we find in
Beneventan notation of the 11th and 12th centuries in the codex
Vaticanus Reginensis, presents an interesting problem, as it includes a paraphrased trisagion of the type known only to Mozarabic Spain.[1] The MS. is said by Dom Wilmart to have come from
the Benedictine monastery of Sora in the Italian province of
Frosinone.[2] The type of trisagion is unknown to the Byzantine
liturgy, and seems to have been a borrowing from the West rather
than from the East.

The introit in the Beneventan MSS. is termed *ingressa*, as at
Milan, and we find it unaccompanied by psalmody. All the
ingressae of Passion Week and Holy Week (except Holy Tuesday)
are provided with *Glorias*. Besides the three normal indications
of psalm, tone and *Gloria*, a fourth element is sometimes added: a
verse not found in Scripture, whose place is not very clearly indicated. Thus, for example, the Thursday after Ash Wednesday:
*Int. Dum clamarem: Psl. Exaudi Deus orationem meam et ne
despexeris deprecationem, o i a seculorum amen. T. IIII. Conditor
pacis et fons luminis, qui liberavit nos de manu mortis, et vocavit nos
ad premia regni ad quem ego.* A verse of this kind accompanies the
ingressa of Palm Sunday, but it is indicated immediately after the
psalm.

The *Pater noster* was followed by the diaconal monition for the
kiss of peace and the response of the choir. The monition is found

---

[1] *Bibl. Vat., MS. Regin.*, lat. 334, fo. 87r–v.

[2] Wilmart, *Rev. bénéd.* (1929), p. 370, n. 4. Sora (*S. Maria*, later *S. Domenico*) was
founded in 1030, and united to the Cistercian abbey of Casamari in 1222. Janauschek,
Orig. Cist., pp. lxxviii–lxxix.

in MSS. VI, 34 and VI, 38, with a slight variation of rubrics in
the latter codex. The deacon says: *Afferte nobis pacem*, and the
choir answer: *In nomine Christi*; whereas in MS. VI, 38 it is the
clergy and people who respond. Both text and melody have a
certain similarity to the Ambrosian monition, but *Deo gratias*
appears as the Milanese response. It is not possible to say when
such a monition was introduced into the Beneventan liturgy, but
it was clearly a well-established usage in the 11th century. Undoubtedly, however, the custom goes back to a much earlier
period. A glance at the liturgies of the East, as well as of the
West, will show that in quite early days some such invitation of
the deacon was a prelude to an exchange of the kiss of peace. St.
John Chrysostom (*ob.* 407) speaks of the monition εἰρήνη πᾶσι,
which is found today in the liturgy that bears his name. An
invitation to the *pax* may be seen also in the rites of Milan, Gaul
and Spain, although it seems to have been wanting in Rome and
Africa.

The communions in the Beneventan MSS. are without verses,
psalmodic or otherwise.

A Vatican MS., with the Bari type of Beneventan script, provides a Mass: *In Assumptione Sancti Helie*, in which the lessons
are indicated by references to other Masses: *Lectio require, retro in
Ebdomada, retro in Ebdomada de Samaritana in feria III. Evangelium require in quatuor Parabole, in feria secunda.*[1]

The gospels for the Sundays after Pentecost appear to have
varied considerably from the corresponding Roman series.

The distribution of the hymn *Benedictus es* among the four
Ember Saturdays of the year is peculiar to Benevento.

Lent. The arrangement of the Lenten Sunday gospels is similar to Ambrosian usage, which in its turn was probably pre-
Gregorian Roman. The Saturday after Ash Wednesday was at
first *Sabbato vacat*, and the *ingressa* of the later Mass: *Converte nos
Deus, salutaris noster*, is proper to the Beneventan graduals, VI,
35; VI, 38. The communion for the first Monday: *Voce mea*, is
taken from Psalm III, but at Rome, since the 11th century, we
find: *Amen dico vobis*. The *Missale Antiquum* of Benevento and

---

[1] Vat. codex, lat. 10645, fo. 6v.

the Vatican gradual (lat. 10673) are faithful to the older text, while the gradual VI, 38 gives the two communions. The beginning of the proper communion for the Second Sunday in Lent recalls the Roman introit for the Vigil of St. Andrew: *Dominus secus mare.* We find a similar text in the Mozarabic liturgy under the form of a verse of the antiphon *Ad accedentes: Gustate et videte.*[1] The antiphon *Ad Scrutinium* is peculiar to the codex VI, 38, in which the Mass of the day is preceded by the insertion: *Feria II ad sanctum Marcum. Antiphona ad scrutinium: Dum sanctificatus fuero in vobis coram eis tollam quippe vos de gentibus, et congregabo vos, dicit Dominus.* It is interesting to note that we have here an antiphon of scrutiny on the very day fixed by Frankish documents three centuries earlier. The Beneventan text and melody, however, are specifically local, and the MS. seems to be unique in an insertion of the kind.[2]

The *ingressa* for the Wednesday in the fourth week of Lent was drawn from Ezechiel XXXVI, 23–6. A similar borrowing is met with in the Sacramentary of Gellone, but with a different text. The two graduals on the Saturday before the fifth Sunday in Lent (*Sitientes*) show that there were originally three lessons.[3] We find this attested in the Micrologus (1100).[4] The Saturday before Palm Sunday has the rubric: *Sabbato ad helemosyna vacat,* although the *Traditio Symboli* was apparently given on that day.[5]

A Mass peculiar to the local use: *Domine exaudi,* occurs in a Beneventan MS.

Palm Sunday. The responsary *Ante sex dies Paschae,* with the verse *Magister,* is unknown elsewhere. The Beneventan responsaries are analogous to those in the Gregorian repertory, while clearly independent of it. The *ingressa* (*Testificata est turba*) is found in a single MS., but the text appears also as the third *psalmellus* of the day in the Ambrosian rite. The two texts depend from a common original.

A number of Beneventan MSS. have two graduals for the first

[1] *Liber Ordinum* (edit. Férotin), cols. 241–2.
[2] Hesbert, *op. cit.*, chap. III, p. 247.
[3] *Missal. Antiq. Benev.*; Cod. VI, 34.
[4] *Microl.*, cap. LII; Hittorp, *op. cit.*, col. 762.
[5] Ebner, *Iter Italicum*, p. 202.

two days of Holy Week, as for *Sitientes*, showing the primitive Roman arrangement of three lessons for these Masses.[1]

Holy Thursday. The book of the prophet Jonas was read in its entirety on this day, as well as on Holy Saturday, as we find at Milan.[2] Two Masses are given in the Beneventan MSS.: one Roman–Beneventan and the other altogether peculiar to the local use. The first of these is purely Gregorian in style, although it is not found in other codices.[3] It would seem to have been a relatively late introduction, at a time when the ancient use had been already supplanted by the Roman liturgy. The second Mass has an *ingressa* borrowed from the text of St. John, recording the *Mandatum: Postquam surrexit Dominus*. Its gradual: *Vadit propitiator*, is found also in the Roman, Ambrosian and Greek liturgies, taken from compositions of the 6th-century poet Romanos. The offertory and communion are common to Palm Sunday. A distinctive local feature appears in the *Mandatum*.

Good Friday. The liturgy of this day has a truly hybrid character,[4] with a 'telescoping' of the Beneventan and Roman liturgies. The *Missale Antiquum* gives a rubric to the effect that the 'Ambrosian' rite is to be followed on Good Friday: *In Parasceve secundum ambrosianum*.[5] This was certainly the case in respect to the Passion, and, as in the actual Milanese use, it was according to St. Matthew, beginning with the words *Mane facto*. The same passion was prescribed at Benevento for the night (*in nocte*) of Palm Sunday. The MSS. left the Mass for the day (*Ad missam*) blank. There were two distinct ceremonies of the Adoration of the Cross, differing from each other and from the corresponding Roman function.[6] Both have a form of 'ante-communion'. The first of these comprises a series of antiphons with psalmody in the role of an introit; lesson from Wisdom; the responsary *Amicus meus*; and a small excerpt from the Passion according to St.

---

[1] *Bibl. Capit. Benev.*, cod. VI, 34; VI, 35; VI, 38; VI, 39; VI, 40.

[2] *Sequenti die lectus est de more liber Jonae . . . . Erat autem dies quo sese Dominus pro nobis tradidit quo in Ecclesia poenitentia relaxatur.* Ambr., *Epist.* XX, *ad Marcel.*, cap. XXV–XXVI; *Pat. Lat.*, t. XVI, col. 1002.

[3] Benev. *Bibl. Capit.*, VI, 40. *Ingressa; Dixit Jesus discipulis suis; Omnes vos scandalum.*

[4] Hesbert, *op. cit.*, chap. III, p. 290.

[5] *Ibid.*, p. 309, n. 2. [6] *Ibid.*, p. 298.

Matthew. The second contains a number of chants; lesson from Daniel; the responsary *Tenebrae*; and a further reading from the Passion. The Beneventan arrangement of the function is similar to the Roman, but the Presanctified rite follows the second 'ante-communion'. We find, however, that the order of the texts vary in the different MSS. The first of the functions took place at the hour of terce; the second at the hour of sext. The triple antiphon: *Ante crucem*, with which the first office began, is found also in the Ambrosian rite. A Beneventan rubric says: *sicut in Ambrosiano scriptae sunt*. It was chanted successively in Greek and Latin, each with a psalm in the appropriate language. The second office opened with three Greek and Latin antiphons, with corresponding psalms, and was followed by yet another antiphon of a similar type. The gradual *Tenebrae factae sunt*, which was in the Roman tradition, is found in the Ambrosian rite between the second lesson and the Passion, and also in the Roman rite at matins (*Tenebrae*) of Good Friday. The first of the three antiphons at the adoration of the Cross is a Greco-Latin tropary which appears almost exclusively in MSS. of South Italy: ὅταν τῷ σταυρῷ προσήλωσαν, *O quando in cruce confixerant iniqui Dominum gloriae!*[1] It is found today in the Byzantine *triodion*. In the 12th century we find it in the *typicon* of Jerusalem (1122) and in the first half of the 7th century in the *kanonarion* of the Georgians. This *kanonarion* was a Georgian version of the *ordo* of the Church of Jerusalem, which would seem to date from the time of the Patriarch Modestus (631–34). Some writers, however, attribute its authorship to his successor, the hymnographer Sophronius (634–38), as it contains the twelve antiphonal troparies of the Office of the 'Holy Hours of the Passion', which are sung on Good Friday evening.

The three antiphons which were sung during the adoration of the Cross are to be found in an 11th-century Beneventan gradual. The last of these served as the processional antiphon accompanying the return of the cross to the sacristy. All three are in the actual Ambrosian rite, but in a shorter form, and the third Beneventan antiphon is the second in the Milanese series. The two

---

[1] Hesbert, *op. cit.*, p. 305.

rites have altogether different melodies for *Crucem tuam* and *Laudamus te, Christe*, and the third melody, although presenting the same melodic theme, shows considerable variation. Part of the same text was found also at Subiaco and Nonantola, and part at Ravenna and Nursia. The solemn prayers were recited after the adoration of the cross, as they are today at Milan. The deacon was directed to say both *Flectamus genua* and *Erigamus nos*. In short, the Beneventan liturgy for Good Friday was virtually the same as that in use in the Church of Milan.

Vespers, which followed the rite of the Presanctified, consisted of three psalms and the *Magnificat* with its antiphon.

The vestiges of the old rite of Benevento disappeared, as we have seen, after the 12th and 13th centuries, but the vespers of Good Friday are found in a Roman setting in a breviary of Salerno, printed at Naples in 1542.

Holy Saturday. The liturgy began with the litanies and the antiphon *Ad Vesperum*, accompanied by Psalm XXIX.

The Beneventan ceremonial for the blessing of the candle is found in two of the MSS.: *Missale Antiquum*, MS. VI, 33, and the Vatican gradual, MS. lat. 1063. From these, it would appear that the blessing of the fire and the candle took place after the eleventh lesson and the chant of the *Benedictiones*. The lessons, which followed the antiphon and psalm, were twelve in number, as in the Gelasian books, but the fifth was not *Haec est hereditas*, but *Dixit Jeremias: Surgite*. This choice of lesson was a characteristic of Central and Southern Italy.[1] The Vatican gradual (lat. 1063) has a rubric, partially effaced: *Haec est hereditas, que quinta est ordinata, secundum romanum legatur hic; secundum ambrosianum legatur post Benedictionem Cerei*. Thus the twelfth and last lesson at Benevento was *Haec est hereditas*, not *Nabuchodonosor rex*, as in the Roman rite. Eleven tracts and the *Benedictiones* were sung between the lessons. Some of the MSS. qualify certain of the tracts as 'Ambrosian', but the term is wholly unjustifiable. They are in fact doubles with corresponding Roman tracts, although their melodies are specifically different.

The blessing of the fire, as we have said, took place after the

---

[1] South Italy, unlike Central Italy, has no lesson: *Audi Israel*.

eleventh lesson. It was directed to be produced *ex ignario vel alio quolibet modo*. There was a single prayer: *Deus qui per Filium tuum angularem scilicet lapidem*. A candle was then lit from the fire and taken to the ambo 'as discreetly as possible': *quasi ex occulto proferatur in puplicum*. Here the paschal candle was lit, and anointed ('touched') with chrism in the form of a cross, after which the deacon, holding the candle, chanted *Lumen Christi* three times, and the people responded: *Deo gratias*. The Vatican gradual speaks also of a blessing of candles (or of the *Agnus Dei*), which the context seems to show took place after the *Exsultet*.

The blessing of the fire, etc., was not performed by the bishop or even by the celebrant, who only appears later. The rubric refers to the officiant in an altogether impersonal manner.[1]

The *Exsultet* was sung also between the *Benedictiones* and the prayer: *Deus qui tribus pueris*, but such a dislocation could hardly have been primitive. The ambo from which the *Exsultet* was normally sung has been already described in treating of the churches of the rite. South Italy, from the 11th to the 13th century, produced a special class of MSS.: the text of the *Benedictio Cerei* or *Exsultet* inscribed on a long roll of parchment enriched with miniatures. A number of these rolls, emanating from the 'Beneventan' area, have been preserved. The most important and most ancient of these is that of the basilica of St. Nicholas at Bari.[2] The date of this remarkable and richly illuminated document is determined by the portraits of the emperors Basil II (*ob.* 1025) and Constantine VIII (*ob.* 1028); while in the second half of the century the names of certain Popes, archbishops and rulers were added.[3] The Bari text is found also on a roll originating from the collegiate church of Mirabella Eclano near Avellino. The roll of the abbey of St. Peter at Benevento, written before 1050, is now in the Vatican Library,[4] and a similar roll of the same century is preserved in the archives at Capua. The cathedral church of Gaeta has three of the same type: two of the 11th century and one

---

[1] Hesbert, *op. cit.*, chap. III, p. 418.
[2] Bari has preserved also a roll for the Blessing of the font.
[3] The text has been edited by Duchesne: *Christian Worship* (London, 1904), append. VII, pp. 543–5.
[4] *Bibl. Vat.*, MS. lat. 9820.

F

of the 11th–12th century; while a fragment, written for the church of S. Pietro at Fondi in about the year 1115 may be seen in the *Bibliothèque Nationale* at Paris.[1]

The custom of transcribing the *Exsultet* on a band of parchment, which the deacon unrolled as he proceeded with the chant, is peculiar to South Italy.[2] Out of the twenty-eight rolls that exist, either whole or in part, no less than twenty-five were written in South Italy; while of the three others, one is from the hand of a French artist at Velletri with a roll authentically Beneventan, and two from Pisa with rolls displaying a similar origin. Two types of *Exsultet* are to be found in South Italy, known respectively as the Vulgate and Bari texts.

Sometimes we find the two transcribed in the same document. The *Vulgate text*, which appears today in the Roman missal, is the most ancient, as well as the most common in manuscript tradition: hence the name. It figures in the 8th-century Gelasian books and the supplement to the Gregorian sacramentary, from whence it passed into all later tradition, though not without a certain amount of retouching. The eulogy of the bee, for example, which appears in the primitive text, was suppressed, as its Virgilian flavour offended later scribes. Apart from the sacramentaries properly so-called, the Vulgate text is found in four of the Beneventan MSS. The *Bari text*, sometimes described as 'Beneventan' or '*Vetus Itala*', figures in a series of MSS. found throughout the Beneventan region. It is composed on the same themes as the Vulgate, and the prologue is nearly identical, but the preface is altogether different. A fragment from the abbey of Farfa [3] gives the two texts with a single prologue.[4] So late as the 15th century, the Bari text is transcribed in two missals of Salerno, but it would seem to have been very generally discarded at about the same time as the other Beneventan peculiarities.

Blessing of the Font and Baptisms. The chant *Omnes sitientes*

---

[1] Paris, *Bibl. Nat.*, MS. lat. 710.

[2] The miniatures were 'upside down', so that the people could look at them, as the deacon unfolded the roll over the side of the ambo.

[3] Farfa, founded in the 6th century; restored by Benedictines after destruction by barbarians; adopted Cluniac usages *c.* 1000.

[4] Hesbert, *op. cit.*, chap. III, pp. 387–8.

was sung processionally on the way to the font, with a text borrowed from the twelfth and last lesson: *Haec est hereditas.* A
similar chant is found also in the Mozarabic rite,[1] but it was not
apparently primitive. The litanies followed, after which the deacon gave a series of monitions, directing those who were neither
of the faithful nor yet of the *competentes* to leave the church: [2]

> *Si quis catecuminus est, procedat.*
> *Si quis haereticus est, procedat.*
> *Si quis judaeus est, procedat.*
> *Si quis paganus est, procedat.*
> *Si quis arrianus est, procedat.*
> *Cujus curam non est.*

A connection between the Beneventan and Milanese series is obvious, but there is no reference to Arians at Milan, where we find
also a slightly different order. A 'recessional' in the form of a
Greco-Latin tropary is given in two of the Beneventan MSS.: [3]
Δόξα ἐν ὑψίστοις θεῷ .... *Gloria in excelsis Deo, et in terra
pax, alleluia, alleluia, alleluia.* A rubric in MS. Benevento, VI, 38
says *Peractis omnibus, redeunt a fonte.* The double text occurs
also in the Farfa fragment, but at the beginning of the Mass in
the place of the normal *Gloria*, and a litany is sung in the procession from the font to the altar.

Mass. The antiphon *Transivimus per ignem et aquam* was sung
as the celebrant reached the altar. This was followed immediately
by the *Gloria in excelsis*, chanted in Greek and Latin.

The Mass, save for some unimportant elements of the ancient
liturgy in four of the chants, was inserted in an *ordo* specifically
Roman. One MS. supplies a bilingual gradual, which is an incorrect transcription of a Greek *sticherion*, still sung in the Byzantine
liturgy at Easter: πάσχα ἱερον ἡμῖν σήμερον ἀναδέδεικται ...
Pascha sacrum nobis demonstratur.[4]

The prose *Lux de luce*, which was sung on this day at Benevento, is note for note an adaptation of the alleluia which precedes

---

[1] *Liber Ordinum* (edit. Férotin, Paris, 1904), col. 217.
[2] Subdeacon according to the Beneventan *Missale Antiquum.*
[3] Benev. Grad. VI, 38; VI, 40.
[4] Benev. MS. VI, 40.

each syllable of the text. It depends, however, from the ancient Gregorian collection, and was not a feature of the local use. Two different versions appear under the same title: one attested by a single Beneventan MS. (VI, 38); while the other is found, not only in the MSS. of Benevento, but also in several of those of North Italy. The offertory of the Mass, which serves as the communion for Saturday *in albis* in the Roman rite, alludes to the first Communion of the newly baptised: *Omnes qui in Christo baptizati estis, Christum induistis, alleluia. Ymnum canite*, the chant at communion in the Beneventan rite, is the *transitorium* for Easter Thursday at Milan, but with an altogether different melody. The formula probably originated in a common source, from which it was received in a free and independent fashion by the two liturgies.[1]

Easter. Distinctive melodies are provided for the *ingressa*, responsary, offertory and communion, as well as for the Paschal announcement: *Jam Christus Dominus resurrexit*, embolism (*Libera nos*) and diaconal monition before the kiss of peace.

The embolism was certainly sung on Easter Sunday, and it was in all probability the normal practice, as we find today at Milan. The Easter recitative is noted after the *Pater noster* in the MS.[2]

BIBLIOGRAPHY

1. L'*Ancienne Liturgie de Bénévent*. Dom *Andoyer*. *Revue du Chant Grégorien*, 1912–14; 1919–21.
2. The *Beneventan Script*: History of South Italian Minuscule. E. A. *Loew*. Oxford, 1914.
3. *Benevento*. U. *Benigni*. *Catholic Encyclopedia*, vol. II.
4. *Shape of the Liturgy*. Gregory *Dix*. London, 1943.
5. La *Tradition Bénéventaine dans la tradition manuscrite*. R. J. *Hesbert*. *Paléographie Musicale*, XIV. Tournai, 1931.

---

[1] *Hymnum canite Agni mundi, lavacro fontis renati, satiati corpore Christi. Hallelujah. Hallelujah.*

[2] Benev. MS. VI, 40.

Chapter Three

GALLICAN RITE

NOMENCLATURE

THE term 'Gallican' has been used in no less than five different senses, with reference to as many liturgical variations, and it is important therefore to make it clear in what sense it is used in this chapter.

(1) The rite existing in Gaul before the reforms of Pepin and Charlemagne; (2) the Roman rite as altered and enriched in Gaul and Germany by the Carolingian school of liturgists; (3) a French use introduced by the Normans into Apulia and Sicily; (4) the Franco-Roman rite, which, at the instigation of Pope St. Gregory VII (1073–85), supplanted the Mozarabic rite in Spain at the end of the 11th century. The supporters of the traditional Spanish liturgy referred to that which had been imported by the Cluniac monks and bishops as *Liturgia Gallicana*; (5) the liturgical books in many of the dioceses of France in the 18th century, which, in defiance of the Tridentine regulations, had been altered by the bishops, were known as 'Gallican' or 'neo-Gallican'.

The correct use of the term 'Gallican' is unquestionably in relation to the rite existing in Gaul before the 9th century, and it is used in this chapter exclusively in this sense.

REMOTE ORIGIN OF THE RITE

Amid the uncertainties attending the origin of the Gallican rite, we can at least agree that from the end of the 5th century the Churches of Gaul, Spain, Britain, Ireland and, perhaps, North Italy followed a usage for the celebration of Mass other than the Roman, and that these churches formed a more or less homogeneous group that bore witness to a common origin.[1] Righetti

---

[1] Netzer, *Introd. de la Messe Romaine en France sous les Carolingiens*, chap. I, p. 2.

claims for the liturgy an affinity with the East, especially Antioch,[1] but it is impossible to endorse the categorical statement of Thibaut, who maintains, as an 'established fact', that the Gallican Mass shows an Oriental character in its arrangement which clearly differentiates it from the Roman Mass.[2] Such a hypothesis, as we shall see, is by no means 'established'.

Gaul, however, was no conservative backwater in the 4th and 5th centuries. New influences were pouring in from the East, political, cultural and religious, which must have affected the liturgy. 'The popular movement of the native population of Coptic Egypt . . . is already making itself felt in Aquitaine in the polished and charming writings of Sulpicius Severus. The reputation of the Desert Fathers of Egypt and the hermits of the Cyrenaic coasts has reached Italy and southern Gaul before the close of the 4th century, and is arousing a spirit of emulation. . . . The vogue of the Greek novel . . . is believed to have stimulated the growth of stories of miracles; while in the rise of ecclesiastical biographies we may trace the influence of Alexandria.'[3]

An exact reconstruction of the Gallican Mass is by no means easy, and the liturgy would not appear to have been identical in the various churches of the country.

An outline of the Mass is to be found in the two letters of Pseudo-Germanus, although the second of these gives us but little information, and both of them are so encumbered with mystical interpretations that it is often difficult to disentangle the actual from the fanciful.[4] Details concerning the rite are to be met with also in the decrees of local councils; while five or six liturgical MSS. have survived, although these are unfortunately either mutilated or intermingled with Roman elements.

Three main theories have been put forward as to the origin of the Gallican rite: Ephesine, Oriental and Roman.

1. *Ephesine.* In its original form, the Ephesine theory, as we

---

[1] Righetti, *Storia Liturgica*, t. I (1945), part 2, cap. III, p. 113.

[2] Thibaut, *L'Ancienne Liturgie Gallicane* (Paris, 1929), chap. III, p. 76.

[3] N. K. Chadwick, *Poetry and Letters in Early Christian Gaul* (London, 1955), chap. I, pp. 13–14.

[4] Pseudo-Germ.; *Expositio brevis antiquae liturgiae gallicanae*, Autun, *Lib. Sem.*, MS. G. 3; *Pat. Lat.*, t. LXXII, cols. 83–98.

have shown in discussing the Lyons rite in a former volume, has but little to commend it beyond anti-Catholic prejudice. *Une théorie anglaise*, as Dom Leclercq says, *être apostolique sans être romain, c'est bien séduisant, mais bien fragile.*[1] The initiators of the Gallican liturgy, according to this hypothesis, would have been the early bishops of Lyons, Pothinus and Irenaeus, who were in all probability Orientals themselves. It is, however, manifestly impossible that a fixed rite such as the Gallican, with its elaborate ceremonial, could have been evolved in the 2nd or 3rd century, when the Mass was still to a great extent improvised. In the dispute concerning the correct computation of Easter, Lyons, the supposed disseminator of the Ephesine liturgy, agreed with Rome, not Ephesus. The Ephesine hypothesis was maintained by Lebrun,[2] and later by the Anglican writers, Sir William Palmer[3] and Dr. Neale.[4] Palmer cites Abbot Hildwin (*ob.* 840) as saying of the Gallican *Ordo Missae: ab initio receptae fidei usu in hac Occidentali plaga habitus, usque quo tenorem, quo nunc utitur, Romanum susceperat.*[5] It would be difficult to subscribe to the theory that the Gallican liturgy had prevailed in Gaul from the introduction of Christianity, and we may indeed ask 'Did all Christianity in Gaul radiate from Lyons?'[6]

Another and, perhaps, more tenable 'Ephesine' theory, without any association with Pothinus and Irenaeus, has been suggested by Fr. Thibaut. 'The principal compiler and true father of the Gallican liturgy', says this writer, was rather St. Cassian (*ob. c.* 435), who consciously borrowed from the rites of the East with which he was familiar.[7]

It is conceded that the Mass in Gaul was in all probability very similar to the Roman–African liturgy in the 4th and 5th centuries, and that it was only in the first half of the 6th century that the

---

[1] Leclercq, *Gallicane (Liturgie), Dict. d'Archéol. Chrét, et de Lit.* fasc. LVIII-LIX, col. 477.

[2] Lebrun, *Explication . . . de la Messe*, t. II, p. 233 Paris, 1726).

[3] Palmer, *Orig. Liturg.*, vol. I, p. 153 (London, 1839).

[4] Neale-Forbes, *Ancient Liturgies of the Gallican Church* (Burntisland, 1855), pref., p. V.

[5] Hildwin, *Epist. ad Ludovicum Pium*, no. 5; *Pat. Lat.*, t CVI, col. 17; Palmer, *op. cit.* vol. I, p. 157.

[6] Lucás, *Early Gallican Liturgy, Dublin Review*, July 1893, p. 145.

[7] Thibaut, *op. cit.*, III, p. 96.

Gallican liturgy, which was largely monastic in origin, came to be developed and brought to a state of perfection by the archbishops of Arles, who had themselves received their formation in the monastery of Lérins.[1] Then, with the metropolitan Church of Arles as a starting-point, borrowing freely from Marseilles (St. Victor) and Lérins, the Gallican liturgy soon radiated throughout Gaul, on the other side of the Channel, and across the Pyrenees.[1]

The liturgy, says Thibaut, despite contrary appearances, was not imported directly from the East into Gaul by Asiatic missionaries, but it was rather the result of successive imitations of the Church of Ephesus, as adopted by the Chaldean Churches, and also of the usages of the Church of Jerusalem. The fact of the late appearance of such rites was considered by Pope Innocent I (401–17) to be an intrusion of foreign usages into the Roman patriarchate, which, says Thibaut, is a certain indication of the recent formation of the Gallican liturgy.[1]

St. Cassian, according to this hypothesis, is regarded as the initiator and father of the rite. He would have been familiar with the liturgy of Jerusalem through residence at Bethlehem, with that of St. Mark from his sojourn in Egypt, and with the rite of Constantinople from the fact that it was in that Church that Cassian probably received the diaconate from the hands of St. John Chrysostom. In addition to this, intercourse between Marseilles and Ephesus would seem to have been constant in the 5th century, as may be seen from the translation of the Seven Sleepers of Ephesus to the monastery of St. Victor in the time of Theodosius the Younger (c. 449). Who, then, was Cassian, from whence did he originate? Fr. Thibaut maintains that he was a native of Serta (Seert) in Gordyena, a province north-west of Mesopotamia.[2] It was therefore due to him that East Syrian elements are apparent in the Gallican Mass of the catechumens. Cassian became the founder of the monastery of St. Victor at

---

[1] Chief among these archbishops of Arles was St. Caesarius (*ob.* 542), the 'Preceptor of the Frankish Church'. Thibaut, *op. cit.*, p. 100.

[2] *Cassianus natus Serta.* Gennadius, *De vir. illust.*, LXI, written in 467–80. Also, *Cassianus natione Scytha*—coming neither from Palestine I (Scythopolis), nor the Roman province of Gaul (Provence), nor yet from Little Scythia (Dobrudja). Thibaut, *op. cit.*, append., pp. 103–7.

Marseilles, the experimental legislator of coenobitic life in the West, and the friend and counsellor of the archbishop of Arles, St. Honoratus, who had himself initiated the religious life on the island of Lérins.[1] In his Institutes and *Conferences*, Cassian gives us precious, though scant, information concerning the liturgy: the introduction of the *cursus* of the canonical hours and the ordering of the Sunday synaxis in the monasteries of Southern Gaul. We learn also that the Mass of the catechumens consisted of psalmody with prayers and lessons interspersed, and that the *Pater noster* at the conclusion of the Canon was recited by all the faithful.[1]

The hypothesis is ingenious and in many ways attractive, but it has met with but few supporters. Canon Cristiani rejects it out of hand: *bien que totalement invraisemblable*, and favours the view that Cassian was by birth a Provençal;[2] while a recent English writer says: 'We may conclude that Cassian was probably born in one of the Roman provinces of the Balkans'.[3] Such very diverse opinions make it clear that the birth-place of Cassian, as that of St. Patrick, is in fact unknown. The alleged Oriental background of his liturgy has been criticised by Chadwick: 'It is *prima facie* exceedingly improbable that Cassian should have acquired his liturgical knowledge and habits from the place of his birth, where he was young and untrained, rather than from his monastic experience which would no doubt make a far greater impression upon him. There is more reason for supposing that certain Oriental customs were in use at his monastery in Bethlehem than for regarding such customs as an indication of an Oriental birth-place.' Indeed, Thibaut himself was later driven to recognise this improbability when he postulated, without evidence, a journey by the adult Cassian into Mesopotamia between 400 and 403, in order to account for further liturgical knowledge.[4]

2. *Oriental.* The Oriental hypothesis has also been called the Milanese, as its supporters look to Milan, with the East as the *fons et origo*. There were, it is said, many Greek bishops of Milan, and several Eastern Arian bishops resided in the West. Alternatively,

---

[1] Thibaut, *op. cit.*, p. 100.
[2] Cristiani, *Jean Cassien* (St. Wandrille, 1946), vol. I, chap. I, p. 58, n. 33.
[3] Chadwick, *John Cassian* (Cambridge, 1950), append. B, p. 198.
[4] *Ibid.*, pp. 194–5.

we find Western Catholic bishops, for one reason or another, in the East. Pilgrimages to the Holy Land were frequent in the 4th and 5th centuries; while the Ostrogoths, who invaded Italy, had come from the Orient.[1]

An Eastern origin for the Gallican liturgy was claimed by Lebrun, without, however, disclosing its exact provenance. The learned Oratorian judged that many parts of the Gallican Mass conformed to Eastern models, and a number of the first bishops in Gaul were themselves of Eastern origin.[2] A similar view was maintained by Dom Gúeranger [3] and Dom Leclercq.[4] The latter had been largely influenced by Mgr. Duchesne, who held that the Gallican rite, with all its various national ramifications, was in the first place disseminated by Milan, whose bishop towards the end of the 4th century was to all intents and purposes the virtual 'patriarch' of the Gauls, and an authority of the first order in all matters of dispute.[5] Dacius, the exiled bishop of Milan, is reported to have said while at Constantinople: *Ecce ego et pars omnium sacerdotum inter quos ecclesia mea constituta est, id est Galliae Burgundiae.*[6] Baumstark, who looked upon North Italy as the central point of a movement which was felt equally towards Rome and towards Gaul,[7] considers that the Gallican Mass was substantially that of Constantinople.[8]

The metropolitan system seems to have been established in Gaul about the end of the 4th century, at a time when both Duchesne and Leclercq maintain that the Gallican liturgy was already in existence, for, as they say, worship has always been an affair of discipline.[9] The Churches of Gaul, however, unlike those of North Italy and Spain, had no centre of liturgical unity, and Arles, which had once been of considerable importance, later lost much of its prestige. The metropolitan became the sole liturgical

---

[1] Righetti, *op. cit.*, t. I, p. 114.

[2] Lebrun, *op. cit.*, t. II, pp. 132-3.

[3] Guéranger, *Instit. Liturg.* (2nd edit.), t. I, p. 193.

[4] Leclercq, *Dict. d'Archéol. Chrét. et de Lit.*, fasc. LVIII–LIX, col. 486.

[5] Duchesne, *Christian Worship* (end Eng. edit., 1904), chap. I, pp. 32–37.

[6] Leclercq, *op. cit.*, cols. 481–6.

[7] Baumstark, *Lit. Rom. e Lit. dell'Esarcato*, cap. IV, p. 159.

[8] *Ibid.*, p. 161.

[9] Leclercq, *D.A.C.L.*, fasc. LVIII–LIX, col. 477.

arbiter in his province, and, since national councils were rare, the details of the liturgy differed from province to province.

3. *Roman*. There is no reason to doubt that prior to the end of the 4th century the liturgy was very similar to that which was followed in Rome and North Africa, while making allowance for improvisation. In the 4th century, says Probst, the Roman rite was substantially altered by Pope Damasus (366–82).[1] The liturgical changes, however, did not affect either North Italy or Gaul, which maintained their traditional usages. The hypothesis is upheld by Cagin, Cabrol and a group of Milanese liturgists. In addition to these, Mercati[2] and Dom Morin[3] consider that at the basis of the Gallican liturgy there lies a common substratum with the Roman liturgy. Are we, then, to look upon those features in the Mass of Gaul, which differ from those of Rome, as archaic and discarded Roman elements? Gregory Dix would seem to hold this theory when he says that the liturgical usages condemned by Pope Innocent I (401–17) in his letter to Decentius, bishop of Gubbio, were none other than the 'old ways once common to Rome and themselves'.[4] Thibaut, on the other hand, says that the rites disapproved of by the Pope already constituted particularities distinctive of the liturgical order of an Eastern Church, namely Ephesus.

If a reform of this magnitude really took place at Rome in the 4th century it is, to say the least, exceedingly strange that it has not left any trace in history.

Probst would have it that not only was the position of the great Intercession and the *Pax* changed, but also that the variable *Post sanctus*, *Post pridie*, etc., were discarded in favour of a fixed Canon.[5] The reform was adopted in Milan, possibly through St. Ambrose, but not in Gaul and Spain.[6] Should such a hypothesis prove to be correct, though we have not any evidence in its

---

[1] Probst, *Die abendlaendische Messe vom fünften bis zum achten Jahrhundert* (Münster, 1896), pp. 264 seq.

[2] Mercati, *Sull'origine della liturgia gallicana*, Studi e Testi, VII, p. 72.

[3] Morin, *Depuis quand un Canon fixe à Milan*, Rev. bénéd. (1939), pp. 10 seq.

[4] Dix, *Shape of the Liturgy*, chap. V, p. 109, n. 1.

[5] Probst, *op. cit.*, pp. 264 seq.

[6] The later reforms of Leo, Gelasius and Gregory, on the other hand, were not received at Milan.

support, the Latin or Western liturgy passed through three phases, which may be not improperly termed Gallican, Ambrosian and Roman, although the lines of demarcation between them are extremely vague, and the changes were in many respects gradual.[1]

A Roman origin for the Gallican rite has been maintained by the Benedictines of Solesmes[2] and a Jesuit writer, Fr. Herbert Lucas.[3] 'Six of the Gallican variables', says Fr. Lucas, 'fall into pairs, the first member of each pair having been an introductory bidding-prayer, and when further found that these three pairs of prayers answer respectively to the Roman collect, secret and post-communion, the bidding-prayer being represented in the first and third cases by the simple Roman *Oremus*, and in the second case by the *Orate fratres*, it becomes evident that the relation between the two rites is closer than at first sight might appear'.[4] *Qui pridie*, as the introductory words of the recital of the Institution, is a further indication of a Roman origin for the Gallican liturgy.

A Roman origin, however, does not preclude a development along distinctive lines, and it is clear that between the 4th and 8th century the rite assumed its own peculiar characteristics. Gallican love of novelty and ceremonial pomp could not remain satisfied with Roman sobriety and austerity.

The first allusion to liturgical usage in Gaul different from that of Rome is found in the *Vita S. Martini* of Sulpicius Severus towards the end of the 4th century.[5] It is obvious that formulas and ceremonies were not all introduced at the same time, but, as truly ancient liturgical MSS. are lacking, it is impossible to say with any exactitude what is of the 4th, 5th or 6th century.

Two features would seem to be of Frankish origin: the *Benedictus* and the *Benedicite*, introduced in commemoration of the Baptism of Clovis (496), an ever-memorable event which consecrated the beginnings of French national history.[6]

---

[1] Jenner, *Gallican Rite, Catholic Encyclopedia*, vol. VI, pp. 357-8.
[2] Cf. *Paléographie Musicale*, V, pp. 69 seq.
[3] Lucas, *Early Gallican Liturgy, Dublin Review*, July 1893 and January 1894.
[4] *Ibid.*, January 1894, p. 113.
[5] Sulp. Sever., *Vita S. Martini*, cap. IX; *Dial.* II, 2.
[6] Thibaut, *op. cit.*, chap. III, pp. 99-100.

PROXIMATE ORIGIN OF THE RITE

The occupation of Aquitaine by the Visigoths in the 5th century caused the more cultivated elements to move into Provence, which now became the only truly Roman area and a centre of literary activity. There must, however, have been a more or less continuous active intellectual life in southern Provence, owing first to its history as a Greek colony, and later to its active intercourse with North Africa and Rome.[1]

There can be little doubt therefore that the Gallican rite not only originated in Provence, but was also embellished and diffused from that province. The late flowering of Greek learning in and around Marseilles; the intellectual activity of the cities of south-eastern Gaul on the eve of the withdrawal of the Roman civil service and the completion of the barbarian occupation have been justly called 'the Little Renaissance'.[2] *Nous sommes donc*, says Morin, in speaking of Marseilles, *dans un des principaux foyers où s' est élaborée la liturgie gallicane.*

The liturgical collections, of which Gennadius writes, were compiled by a priest of Marseilles of the name of Musaeus; while St. Cassian, the founder of the monastery of St. Victor, resided in the city.

Mabillon considers Musaeus, Hilary and Sidonius Apollinaris as representatives of a type likely to produce the Gallican rite.[3] The island monastery of Lérins also must surely have played a part in the development of the liturgy.

The earliest usages in Gaul, which would seem to have been those adopted in Britain, were in many respects different from what we find at the end of the 5th or the beginning of the 6th century, when, under the influence of Arles, the liturgy came to be augmented and embellished, often with a Romeward trend. A

---

[1] N. K. Chadwick, *Poetry and Letters in Early Christian Gaul* (London, 1955), chap. VI, p. 142.

[2] *Ibid.*, chap. VII, p. 211.

[3] *Tales auctores, id est Hilarium, Musaeum, et Sidonium, habuisse videtur Ordo Missae Gallicanus, quem a Romano diversum exeunte saeculo sexto fuisse constat ex epistola Gregorii M. ad Augustinum.* Mabillon, *De Lit. Gallic.*, lib. I, cap. IV, 7. *Pat. Lat.* t. LXXII, col. 127.

letter of Faustus of Riez [1] (*ob.* between 490 and 495) to Rusticus, bishop of Narbonne, for instance, gives a list of the seven orders of the hierarchy, in which we find *fossarii* and *ostiarii*, but no mention of either acolytes or exorcists. The list corresponds in general with the *Chronicon antiquissimum*, composed in Britain, which ends with the emperor Justin in 578. The *Statuta Ecclesiae Antiqua*, however, which seem to have been formulated under the aegis of the Church of Arles, conform rather to Roman usage. If, then, says Miss Chadwick, the *Statuta* represent 'Gallican' practice, as Duchesne [2] says, it is evidently a later document than that which is indicated in the letter to Rusticus and the *British Chronicle*, a consideration which suggests the early progress of Roman influence on the more ancient ritual of southern Gaul, of which Faustus's letter and the *British Chronicle* furnish early evidence. Rusticus seems to have belonged to the Church of Marseilles, for he is associated in the famous inscription of Narbonne with both Bishop Venerius and the Church of Marseilles: *Episcopi Venerii socius in monasterio; compresbyter ecclesiae Massiliensis.*[3]

Arles, as we have seen, was the probable centre for the embellishment of the Gallican liturgy, the likelihood of which is enhanced when we come to consider the ecclesiastical prominence of the see in the 5th and 6th centuries. It is noteworthy that nearly all the *libri canonum* in use during the Merovingian period came from that Church.[4] Duchesne considers that the Gallican rite was derived from Milan, but,[5] with the exception of the prophetical lesson, which was very general in early liturgies, we find but few Gallican characteristics in the Ambrosian rite.[6]

Many of the local councils of Gaul issued canons dealing with liturgical questions, and it is worthy of note that out of sixteen

---

[1] Sidonius Apollinaris speaks of Faustus as *Dominus Faustus Papa.* Sid. Apoll., lib. IX, epist. III. N. Chadwick, *op. cit.*, chap. VII, p. 196.

[2] Duchesne, *op. cit.*, chap. V, p. 132.

[3] N. Chadwick, *op. cit.*, chap. VII, pp. 205–6.

[4] Duchesne, *Fast. Episc.*, t. I, p. 141.

[5] Duchesne, *Christian Worship*, chap. III, 2, pp. 91–5.

[6] e.g. Psalmody with psalms interspersed; Prophetical lesson; Prayer for the faithful before the offertory; Recital of the Names; *Pax* before the Eucharistic canon. The formula *Pacem habete* before the offertory would seem to indicate that Milan originally gave the kiss of peace in this place.

councils held in the 4th–6th century, no less than eleven were in the primatial jurisdiction of Arles.[1]

Arles became the residence of the prefecture, formerly at Trier, and the chief Roman administration beyond the Alps. The emperor Constantine (*ob.* 337) built himself a palace there,[2] and several of the imperial rescripts speak of the city as *Mater omnium Galliarum.*[3] Arles was captured by the Visigoths in 480, and remained in their hands until 589, when it was taken by Childebert, the Frankish king of Paris. For our purpose, however, the importance of Arles lies in its episcopate and its Church, grouped under the bishops, which Pope Hilary (462) referred to as an 'ecclesiastical monarchy'.[4] The primacy had been conferred on Patrocles by Pope Zosimus (417–18) in 417, an honour which brought with it the right to summon and preside at the councils of the bishops of Gaul, and to consecrate all bishops within his jurisdiction.[5]

The primate, moreover, as apostolic vicar was the official representative of the Pope in Gaul, and in 513 Symmachus (498–514) granted St. Caesarius the use of the pallium, although the bishops of Vienne and Lyons had about the same time asked for it, and had been refused.[6] The bishop of Arles and his Church, after the bishop and Church of Rome, were virtually the first in Christendom.[7] The significance of the see was further enhanced by the Pope (Symmachus), who permitted the deacons of Arles to wear dalmatics, a privilege which had been hitherto reserved to the deacons of Rome. St. Gregory (590–601), on sending the pallium to Virgilius, and at the same time appointing him apostolic vicar,

---

[1] I Arles (314), I Valence (374), Turin (401), Riez (439), Orange (441), I Vaison (442), II Arles (443), Vannes (465), Agde (506), I Orleans (511), Epaone (517), III Arles (524), Carpentras (527), II Vaison (529), II Orleans (533), Auvergne (533; ? Clermont).

[2] The ruins of the baths erected by Constantine may be seen today.

[3] e.g. Constantine, Gratian, Valentinian II, Honorius.

[4] J. A. Joyeux, *La merveilleuse vie de Saint Césaire d'Arles* (Aix en Provence, 1942), IV, pp. 33–4.

[5] Pope Leo the Great (440–61) revoked the primacy in the time of Bishop Hilary (429–49), but it was virtually restored to his successor Ravennius.

[6] It is possible that Arles was the first Church to which the privilege of the pallium was granted, unless it had been accorded shortly before to the bishop of Ostia, as the consecrator of the Pope, and to the bishop of Ravenna, since the *de facto* master of the Empire had his capital in that city.

[7] J. A. Joyeux, *op. cit.*, IV, p. 43.

suggested that the pre-eminence of Arles was in some measure
due to the apostolate of St. Trophimus, but the historical value of
the tradition is meagre, although possibly dating from the 5th
century.[1] In any case, the apostolate [2] could have no possible
bearing on the formation of the Gallican rite, whereas the later
pre-eminence of Arles in the 5th and 6th centuries provided a
likely centre for the diffusion of the rite.

If such was the case, as it may well have been, the contributions
of the important Provençal monasteries of Marseilles (St. Victor)
and Lérins must be taken into account.

St. Cassian (*ob. c.* 435), the founder of the abbey of St. Victor
at Marseilles,[3] is, as we have seen, credited by Thibaut as having
been a native of Serta, and on this hypothesis to have introduced
a liturgy, which in its pre-anaphoral section followed the East
Syrian arrangement.[4] Thus, he says, the Chaldean and Gallican
rites, apart from the trisagion and the creed, which were adopted
in the 6th century, both comprised the psalmodic chants with the
role of three psalms; Scriptural lessons preceded and followed by
a prayer (blessing); a secret prayer for the people, with an inclination; dismissal of the catechumens; presentation of offerings on
the altar; diptychs of the saints, the living and the dead; and the
pax.

St. Cassian, moreover, was the legislator *par excellence* of the
coenobitic life in the Gallo-Roman Church of southern Gaul.[5]
He was the author of the twelve books of the *Institutes*, which
were written at the request of Castor, bishop of Apt (419–26),
who was anxious to introduce Eastern discipline, with St. Victor
as the model, into the monastery which he had lately founded in
his diocese.[6] The books were intended to offer guidance respect-

---

[1] 'We know, as no one can deny, that the faith was disseminated in Gaul by Trophimus, first bishop of Arles.' St. Greg., *Epist.*

[2] According to the legend, St. Trophimus had been sent to Gaul by St. Peter.

[3] St. Cassian founded also the Convent of St. Saviour for women.

[4] The Gallican rite, from the canon onwards, looks rather to the liturgy of Jerusalem–
Antioch.

[5] *Monasticae perfectionis perfectissimus magister.* Bona, *De Divina Psalmodia* (Paris,
1678, p. 24.

[6] *Pat. Lat.*, t. XLIX, col. 1087. Cassian, in the preface of the *Institutes*, speaks of
Castor *as beatissime papa.*

ing the conduct of life for both individual and community in a *coenobium*. The first book lays down minute instructions as to the dress of the monks; the second and third relate to the canonical system of the prayers and psalms, the discipline associated with their observance, and with the order of monastic life generally; while the fourth describes monastic rules.[1]

The *Conferences*, which were written later, were especially intended for the use of anchorites. The spiritual ideal of Cassian is the ideal of the ascetics (Origenist) of Egypt, tempered by his association with St. John Chrysostom, and formulated by his own practical experience in the Western world.[2]

Provence, from 414 to 435, was a haven amid the falling debris of Western civilisation: 'the one retreat that still lived in a dead Roman commonwealth'.[3] Monasticism existed in Gaul before the time of Cassian,[4] but the great abbot of Marseilles holds an important place in Christian history. Not only did he set Western monasticism upon sane lines, but he is the first guide to spirituality in the spiritual tradition of the Western Church.[5] Subsequent guides were in fact his direct descendents.[6] Cassian complained in the preface to the *Institutes* that monastic founders were making their own rules: *pro arbitrio uniuscujusque instituentis monasterium.* He for his part preferred to imitate the religious of Egypt, as far as was reasonably possible, taking into account the climate, as well as the manners and customs of Gaul. Cassian made a definite contribution to the history of liturgy, but the offices which he introduced into Gaul present a curious amalgam of the usages of Palestine and Egypt. The Palestinian offices of terce, sext and none were adopted, as the weakness of human nature, outside Egypt, demanded fixed hours of prayer during the day. Prime (*novella sollemnitas*), which Cassian often calls matins, he had himself seen introduced during the novitiate at Bethlehem in *c.* 338.

---

[1] N. Chadwick, *op. cit.*, chap. VIII, p. 217.

[2] Owen Chadwick, *John Cassian* (Cambridge, 1950), chap. I, p. 33.

[3] Cf. Salvian, *De Gub.* IV, 30 (paraphrased).

[4] St. Martin (*ob.* 397) founded groups of solitaries on the Eastern model at Ligugé and Marmoutiers near Tours; while St. Abraham, a monk from the banks of the Euphrates (*c.* 470), established a community at St. Cyr, Clermont.

[5] O. Chadwick, *op. cit.*, chap. VI, 3, p. 183.   [6] *Ibid.*, p. 186.

The 'little hours' were adopted at Arles by St. Caesarius (*ob.* 543). 'O God make speed to save us', with which the Church to-day begins her offices, was commended, in the singular, by Cassian. It would seem, however, that the Offices and even the Eucharist were regarded by the abbot as 'aids' in the lone pursuit of contemplative perfection.[1]

No definite provision is made for the Eucharist, with little more than a brief mention. The *Institutes* refer to the Egyptian custom of bi-weekly synaxes [2]—Saturday and Sunday—with uncertain traces of the primitive practice of private Communion from the reserved Sacrament in cells on other days.[3] Terce and sext formed a part of the liturgy when there was a synaxis: psalmody inter-spersed with prayers and lessons. Cassian seems to recommend weekly Communion, but we find indications in his writings that it was the custom at Marseilles to receive every day: 'It is neces-sary for us to eat the holy flesh of the lamb every day.' [4] And again, 'The Body and Blood of Christ, whom every day we receive.' [5] To those, also, afflicted with evil spirits, he says: *Communionem vero eis sacrosanctam numquam meminimus inter-dictam: quin immo si possibile esset etiam cotidie eis impertiti eam debere censebat.*[6] It is possible, however, that Cassian's *cotidie* may be figurative, and in his *Conferences* he implies the existence of a particular day for preparation: *Praecavendum est, ne carnis integritas praecedente tempore custodita in ea praecipue in qua nos ad communionem Salvatoris convivii praeparamus nocte fraudetur.*[7] A story in the same work would also lose its entire point if daily Communion was the normal practice.[8] The evidence of Genna-dius, if he was in fact the author of the work that goes by his name, is important as testifying to the contemporary practice in the neighbourhood of Marseilles: *Quotidie eucharistiae communio-nem percipere nec laudo nec vitupero. Omnibus tamen dominicis diebus communicandum suadeo et hortor, si tamen mens sine affectu*

---

[1] O. Chadwick, *op. cit.*, pp. 181–2.
[2] Anchorites normally returned to the *coenobium* for the synaxes.
[3] O. Chadwick, *op. cit.*, chap. II, 4, p. 65.
[4] *Necesse est cotidie sacrosanctis agni carnibus vesci. Instit.*, VI, 8.
[5] *Corporis et sanguinis Christi quem cotidie sumimus. Coll.* XIV, 8, 5.
[6] *Coll.* VII, 30, 2.   [7] *Coll.* XXII, 5, 1.   [8] *Coll.* XXII, 6.

peccandi sit.[1] Cassian, in spite of one striking passage in the *Conferences*, lays surprisingly little emphasis upon Holy Communion, either in relation to the common life or to spiritual progress. It is regarded as a vehicle for individual reception, rather than as a corporate offering, but the hermits, who from a false humility refrained from Communion, were roundly condemned by Cassian, who had little sympathy with this early form of 'Jansenism'. They were told to receive with a greater eagerness, in order to find there a health of soul and purity of mind: *propter animae medicinam ac purificationem spiritus.*[2] If we wait to be worthy we shall not receive Communion even once a year. 'It is much more reasonable to receive the sacred mysteries every Sunday, as a remedy for our maladies, in keeping ourselves humble of heart, believing and acknowledging that we do not merit this grace . . .'[3] Gennadius (end 5th century) cites Cassian as the originator of the 'monastic habit' and the 'canonical method of reciting prayers and psalms', according to the daily and nightly use of the monasteries of Egypt.[4] The *Institutes* and *Conferences* appear to have been written some time between 425 and 429. They dominated the spiritual horizon of Lérins, from which the tempered Egyptian ethos spread northwards to the monasteries of central Gaul.[5]

Lérins, the island *par excellence* of saints and scholars, as well as a seminary of bishops and savants, probably exercised an important influence on the Gallican rite, serving as a bridge-head from whence, by means of the Rhône, Christian philosophy, theology and liturgy penetrated to the Continent.[6] The monastery had been founded in the first decade of the 5th century or possibly even a few years earlier by St. Honoratus. It has been generally considered that the earliest influence on the founder of Lérins was the Egyptian monasticism of the lauras of the Thebaid, but recent

---

[1] Gennadius, *De eccl. dogm.* XXIII; *Pat. Lat.*, t. XLII, col. 1217.

[2] Cassian, *Coll.* II, 5; Palladius, *Historia Lausiaca*, XVII, 9; XXV, 5; XXVII, 2; LIX, 2.

[3] *Coll.* XXIII, 21; cf. Cristiani, *Jean Cassien*, vol. II, chap. XII, pp. 168-9.

[4] Gennadius, *De viris illustribus*, cap. LXII; *Pat. Lat.*, t. LVIII, cols. 1094 seq.

[5] Chadwick, *op. cit.*, chap. VI, I, p. 168. Cf. *Greg. Turon. Hist. Franc.*, X, 29. *Pat. Lat.*, t. LXXI, cols. 560-1, and *Vitae Patr.* XX, 3. *Pat. Lat.*, t. LXXI, cols. 1094-5.

[6] Lerins claimed nearly 70 saints, including 12 bishops and 10 abbots.

scholarship inclines rather to the view that it was Greek of the 'Basilian' type.[1] Later, St. Cassian may well have influenced the monastery in such a way that customs and usages from Marseilles were blended with those introduced by Honoratus himself. Sidonius Apollinaris tells us that the *Statuta Lirinensium Patrum* were adopted by the Monastery of St. Cyr at Clermont,[2] and the third council of Arles (554) directs that the 'rule' of Lérins shall be minutely carried out in that house.[3] It would, however, be unwise to suppose that the term 'rule' implied more than a general carrying out of the island's discipline. In 501, we read that St. Caesarius adopted the 'Lerinensian' manner of singing the Office in his convent at Arles: *secundum regulam monasterii Lyrinensis*.[4] 'Lérins, partly from the intellectual quality of its foundation and partly owing to its proximity to Marseilles, rapidly became a famous literary centre, and almost at once developed as the principal school of religious thought and spiritual activity in western Europe.'[5]

The episcopal sees of southern Gaul were filled with monks from Lérins: St. Eucher (Lyons), St. Lupus (Troyes), Maguncius (Vienne), Sedastus (Vienne), Valerian (Cimiez), St. Maximus (Riez), Faustus (Riez), St. Honoratus (Arles), St. Hilary (Arles), St. Caesarius (Arles), St. Virgilius (Arles).

St. Eucher spoke of St. Honoratus as a 'master of bishops': a title which Gennadius used later of Salvian.

In the time of St. Gregory (590–604), Lérins would seem to have exchanged its primitive customs for those of St. Colomban. The Pope wrote to the abbot, Conan (601–11), complaining of the abuses which a feeble predecessor had failed to check. Conan thereupon hastened to Luxeuil, in order that he might study the rule observed there.[6] As a result, Lérins adopted the Columbanian way of life, but, about fifty years later, this was abandoned

---

[1] N. K. Chadwick, *op. cit.*, chap. VI, p. 149.

[2] *Gallia Christiana*, t. II, col. 320; *Epist.*, lib. VII, *epist.* XVII *ad Volusianum*.

[3] *Regula quae a fundatore ipsius monasterii dudum constituta est in omnibus custodita.* Counc. III Arles, 524; Labbe, *op. cit.*, t. IV, col. 2055.

[4] *Reg. Monast. S. Caesar., Acta SS.*, Jan. 12, t. I, p. 735.

[5] N. Chadwick, *op. cit.*, chap. VI, p. 150.

[6] *L'Ile et l'Abbaye de Lérins* (Lérins, 1929), chap. IV, p. 51.

by St. Aygulf (*ob. c.* 660), who introduced the Holy Rule of St. Benedict and the Roman rite.

Lérins, in imitation of the Egyptian monastic plan, erected seven small chapels on the island, four of which, with the ruins of the three others, may be seen today.[1] Two of these chapels, of more than usual interest, will be described later in the chapter.

The monastery of Lérins may be regarded, in a very real sense, as a foyer of the Gallican rite,[2] and it would be inconceivable to suppose that the many religious who crossed to the mainland to become bishops would have altogether discarded the liturgical usages to which they had been accustomed. The bishops of Arles in particular—St. Honoratus (426–29), St. Caesarius (502–43), St. Virgilius (*ob. c.* 610)—must certainly have had a hand in regulating the formulas and ceremonies of the rite, both in provincial councils and elsewhere.

Arles may well have served as a boulevard through which the Gallican liturgy passed to the other Churches of France. It would be unwise, however, to claim the rite, as we find it in the last centuries of its existence, as beholden only to the Church of Arles. Among the scanty fragments of the existing MSS. we find a marked absence of verbal uniformity, although the main outlines show a similar type. Provincial councils, and notably those in the province of Arles, attempted from time to time to introduce some measure of uniformity, but it is unlikely that the several liturgies were ever identical in their formularies. The ecclesiastical, no less than the political, importance of Arles diminished with the centuries. At the same time, also, it must not be forgotten that the 5th century saw many of the sees occupied by men of the highest intelligence and integrity. As Miss Chadwick says: 'Undoubtedly the greatness of the ecclesiastics of Gaul in this period (5th century) lies in the fact that they were able to combine great deeds with a high standard of intellectual culture'.[3] Sidonius Apollinaris refers to St. Lupus, bishop of Troyes, as 'easily the foremost

---

[1] e.g. St. Saviour, Holy Trinity, St. Porcarius, SS. Cyprian and Justina, St. Caprasius, St. Peter, St. Michael. Cf. Monastic churches at Glendalough and elsewhere in Ireland.

[2] Lérins is claimed to be the first place in which the *Magnificat* was used liturgically. Henri Moris, *L'Abbaye de Lérins* (Paris, 1909), chap. VIII, p. 331, n. 2.

[3] N. Chadwick, *op. cit.*, chap. X, p. 294.

among our Gaulish bishops'[1] and to St. Patiens, bishop of Lyons, as 'a man of whom no praise could be excessive'.[2] Many of these bishops were responsible for the erection of basilicas and churches,[3] and, with the absence of anything approaching a Congregation of Rites, it is not impossible that on such an occasion the local liturgy would have been augmented or embellished.

At an early period also we find an infiltration of Roman prayers and usages, which grew with the centuries.

In the 7th century, a further cause of disunity was introduced by the Irish monks of St. Colomban, who had brought with them their own Celtic way of doing things.

Councils and Episcopal Regulations

St. Hilary (429–49), a former monk of Lérins, presided at the councils of Riez (439), I Orange (441), I Vaison (442) and II Arles (443). He founded a school of art and letters in his cathedral city, and is said to have replaced many of the gold and silver ornaments of the church with substitutes of glass, in order that he might obtain money for the redemption of captives, a procedure followed later by St. Eon and his successor St. Caesarius.[4] Hilary was well known for the length of his sermons, which on occasions lasted for four hours. It was therefore understandable that he should introduce seats into the churches. In the second half of the 5th century we find the council of Vannes in Brittany (465) demanding a unity of liturgy within the province (Tours) as a corollary to unity of faith: *Rectum quoque duximus, ut vel intra provinciam nostram sacrorum ordo et psallendi una sit consuetudo: et sicut unam cum Trinitatis confessione fidem tenemus unam et officiorum regulam teneamus, ne variata observatione in aliquo devotio nostra discrepare credatur.*[5] The nearest approach to liturgical unity in Gaul was effected in the time of St. Caesarius, bishop of Arles (502–43), who augmented the number of provincial coun-

---

[1] Sidon. Apollin., *Epist.* VII, 13; *Pat. Lat.*, t. LVIII, col. 583.

[2] *Ibid., Epist.* IV, 25; *Pat. Lat.*, LVIII, 532.

[3] e.g. St. Patiens at Lyons, St. Euphronius at Autun (St. Symphorian).

[4] *Non credo contrarium esse Deo de ministerio suo redemptionem dari, qui seipsum pro hominis redemptione tradidit. Vita S. Caesar.*, I, 3, 23–4.

[5] Counc. Vannes (465), can. 15; Labbe, *op. cit.*, t. IV, col. 1057.

cils, and bound his Church still closer to the Chair of Peter. It may well have been the influence of Caesarius that enabled the Roman liturgy to obtain a foothold in the country,[1] although there was no concerted movement to supplant the Gallican rite, despite the adoption of certain details, as, for example, at the second council of Vaison (529). St. Caesarius presided at five councils: Agde (506), III Arles (524), Carpentras (527), II Orange (529), and II Vaison (529), of which the first and last were the most important for the liturgy. Agde (506), which was convoked from the six ecclesiastical provinces of the kingdom of Alaric, probably adopted the nine canons formulated at the council of Vannes in the previous century, and a decree was issued in the interests of liturgical unity: *Et quia convenit ordinem ecclesiae ab omnibus aequaliter custodiri, studendum est ut, sicut ubique fit et post antiphonas collectiones, per ordinem ab episcopis vel presbyteris dicantur.*[2] Those of the faithful who failed to receive Holy Communion at Easter, Christmas and Pentecost were excommunicated.[3] The forty-seventh canon forbade anyone to leave the church before the blessing, which was given before the administration of Holy Communion: *Missas die dominico a saecularibus totas teneri speciali ordinatione praecipimus, ita ut ante benedictionem sacerdotis egredi populus non praesumat. Qui si fecerint ab episcopo publice confundantur.*[4] St. Caesarius directed that the doors of the church were to be closed after the gospel: *Ob hoc saepissime ostia post evangelia claudi fecit, donec Deo volente gratularentur cohertione et profectu, qui fuerant ante fugitivi.*[5] The practice of hearing only a part of the Mass seems to have continued nevertheless, and St. Caesarius reverts to the subject: 'Again and again I beg you not to leave the church before the conclusion of the divine mysteries'.[6] Those who were not

---

[1] Suitbert Bäumer, *Ueber das sogen. Sacr. Gelas.*; *Historiches Jahrbuch, Görres-Gesellschaft* (Munich, 1893), XIV, pp. 292–3.

[2] Counc. Agde (506), can. 30; Labbe, *op. cit.*, t. IV, col. 1388.

[3] *Ibid.*, can. 63; *ibid.*, col. 1393.

[4] *Ibid.*, can. 47; *ibid.*, col. 1391. The practice was condemned also by canon 26 of I Orleans (511) and canon 29 of III Orleans (538). Labbe, *op. cit.*, t. IV, col. 1408; t. V, col. 302. Cf. *Codex juris canonici*, Bened. XV, can. 1248.

[5] *Vita*, lib. I, n. 27; edit. Br. Krusch, *M. G. rer. merov.* III, pp. 466 seq.

[6] *Iterum atque iterum rogo ut nullus ex vobis de ecclesia discedat, nisi cum divina mysteria ad integrum fuerint celebrata.*

receiving Holy Communion were permitted to leave the church
after the *Pater noster*, or, if the bishop was present, the blessing,[1]
when, as St. Augustine says, 'Mass was finished'.[2]

The second council of Vaison (529) directed parishes to provide schools for cantors and lectors, thus contributing to the
marked superiority of the clergy of the province of Arles which
was so noticeable in the first half of the 6th century.[3] The council
also instructed priests to preach in country districts, as well as in
towns, and, if infirmity should prevent this, a deacon was to read
a homily from one of the Fathers, for if deacons are worthy to
read the gospel, why should they be unworthy to read the expositions of the Fathers?[4] It would seem that *Kyrie eleison* was not
very general in Gaul before this council, and the third canon prescribes its frequent repetition at both Mass and Office, citing the
example of the Church of Rome, as well as of the Eastern and
Italian Churches.[5] The recitation of the Sanctus (*Aius*), also, was
made obligatory for private and solemn Masses alike;[6] while the
name of the Pope was directed to be inserted in the canon.[7] As a
protest against Arianism, *Sicut erat*, etc., was added to the *Gloria
Patri*.[8] The hundred and two articles of canons and statutes,
known as the *Statuta Ecclesiae Antiqua*, contain valuable information respecting the primitive liturgy. The Arlesian origin of the
collection is considered indisputable, and, if St. Caesarius was not
its author, he was at least responsible for its dissemination.[9]
Rome, in later centuries, borrowed many things from the *Statuta*
for her Ordination offices. Thus the admonition or instruction
in the actual pontifical had its first beginnings in this Gallican
compilation, and here also we find the porrection of the instruments.[10] Gaul, at a time when Rome still employed the strictest

[1] St. Caesar., *Serm.* LXXIII.

[2] *Orationes, cum benedicitur et sanctificetur, et ad distribuendum comminuitur: quam totam petitionem fere omnis ecclesia dominica oratione concludit . . . . Postulationes fiunt, cum populus benedicitur?* St. August., *Epist.* CXLIX, n. 6.

[3] Counc. Vaison (529), can. 1; Labbe, *op. cit.*, t. IV, cols. 1679–80.

[4] *Ibid.*, can. 2; *ibid.*, col. 1680.   [5] *Ibid.*, can. 3; *ibid.*, col. 1680.

[6] *Ibid.*, can. 3; *ibid.*, col. 1680.   [7] *Ibid.*, can. 4; *ibid.*, col. 1680.

[8] *Ibid.*, can. 5; *ibid.*, col. 1680. In the East, it was customary to say a prayer at the conclusion of each psalm, with an ascription to the Holy Trinity after the final antiphon.
Cassian, *Instit.*, II, 8.

[9] Joyeux, *op. cit.*, p. 63.   [10] Righetti, *op. cit.*, t. IV, pp. 280–2.

sobriety in her Ordination liturgy, had already a full and elaborate development of ceremonies and formulas.

A Greek colony existed at Arles in the 6th century, and St. Caesarius not only preached in Greek, but also compiled a popular manual of chants, which appeared in two editions (Greek and Latin). We know also that the Saint was accustomed to introduce Greek formulas into the liturgy, and that he encouraged the faithful to sing, *ut non haberent spatium in ecclesia fabulis occupari*.[1] Great store was set by the bishop on sermons, and on occasions he preached at Prime, Mass and Vespers. A book of homilies composed by him became a popular manual for preachers, and was still in demand a century later. The sermons of Caesarius are in fact an important source for our knowledge of the Gallican rite, and it is from them that we learn that Mass was normally celebrated after terce, and that it lasted for about two hours.[2] We are told also that the Baptismal rites were concluded with a washing of feet. The ceremony is mentioned in the *Missale Gothicum*,[3] but St. Avitus (*ob. c.* 519) and St. Gregory of Tours (*ob.* 594) make no reference to it.

The Church of Arles adopted a number of hymns from the monastery of Lérins,[4] and, in all probability, liturgical usages.

The vestments of the clergy were similar to those worn in civil life, albeit of richer material, and we read of St. Caesarius bequeathing to his successor *indumenta paschalia*, which were sold later for the redemption of a captive.[5]

The short rule for monks, compiled by Caesarius, may have been the first authentic one of its kind, but the most complete work was the rule written for the convent of nuns which the Saint had founded.[6] A 9th-century MS. of this rule (*S. Caesarii Regula*

---

[1] *Vita Caesarii, Mon. Germ. Hist. Script. Rer. Merov.*, t. III, p. 463. On the other hand, it would appear that neither Gregory of Tours nor Fortunatus knew any Greek, beyond some terms of rhetoric to be found in all treatises. René Aigrain, *Ste. Radegonde* (Poitiers, 1952), chap. II, pp. 35–6.

[2] *Caesar. Arel., Serm.* CCLXXXII, 2.

[3] *Missal. Goth.*, edit. Bannister, vol. I (*Henry Bradshaw Society*, vol. LII, 1917), no. 262, p. 77.

[4] Joyeux, *op. cit.*, p. 29.   [5] *Ibid.*, p. 24.

[6] The Rule of St. Caesarius was composed from a letter of St. Augustine (so-called Rule), the usages of Lérins and the Institutes of Cassian: codified by the experience of the bishop of Arles.

sanctarum virginum), preserved in the State Library at Munich, contains six formulas *super defunctae corpus* (two invitatories and four collects), which may very possibly derive from the ancient Gelasian sacramentary.[1] The convent of St. John, known later by the name of its founder, was consecrated on 26 August 512, and Caesaria, the sister of the bishop, who had come from Cassian's foundation at Marseilles, was appointed superior. It had been originally intended to establish the house in the 'cemetery quarter' of Alyscamps outside the walls of the city, where a 'burial' church dedicated to the Blessed Virgin came to be built. A similar arrangement was adopted by St. Radegunde (*ob.* 587) at Poitiers, where the Rule of St. Caesarius was adopted in *c.* 570. St. Caesarius (*ob.* 543) obtained permission from Pope Symmachus (498–514) to profess his nuns as 'consecrated virgins'.

The practice prescribed in the Apostolic Tradition of Hippolytus in respect to the blessing of the holy oils was followed at Arles in the time of St. Caesarius. The blessing took place in the baptistery on Holy Saturday, not on Holy Thursday, as in Rome, nor on the Sunday before Easter, as in certain parts of Gaul. The bishop, at the conclusion of the baptism, administered confirmation in an adjacent room, which from its name was apparently circular in shape: *cocumula*, from *cucumis*, 'cucumber'. It is possible that this custom was peculiar to the Church of Arles.

A final appeal for liturgical unity was made in the council of Epaone (517), after which time councils seem to have been content to regulate details.

Suffragan bishops, says Epaone, must follow the rite observed in the metropolitan church: *Ad celebranda divina officia ordinem quem metropolitani tenent provinciales eorum observare debebunt.*[2] A somewhat similar form of liturgical unity was demanded in Spain before the complete unification in 633, but the story belongs to the Mozarabic rather than to the Gallican rite.

The second council of Tours (567) was concerned with the precise order in which the particles were placed at the fraction:

---

[1] Munich, *Stat. Bibl.*, MS. 28118. Emmanuel Bourque, *Etude sur les Sacramentaires Romains; Les Textes Primitifs* (Rome, 1948), p. 182.

[2] Counc. Epaone, 517, can. 27. Labbe, *op. cit.*, t. IV, col. 1579.

Ut corpus Domini in altari non in imaginario ordine, sed sub crucis titulo componatur.[1] A certain amount of superstition would seem to have attended the arrangement of the particles in the Gallican rite. The canon was framed in order to prohibit the practice of arranging them in the form of a human figure. A letter of Pope Pelagius I (556–61) to Sapaudus, bishop of Arles (*c.* 585), speaks of the strange abuse of distributing a 'figure of flour' to the people, in such a way that each one received a member according to his merits: *Quis etiam illius non excessus, sed sceleris dicam, redditurus est rationem, quod apud vos idolum ex similagine, vel iniquitatibus nostris patienter fieri audivimus, et ex ipso idolo fideli populo, quasi unicuique pro merito, aures, oculos, manus ac diversa singulis membra distribui?*[2]

The council of Auxerre (578) directed women to receive Holy Communion with their hands covered by a cloth, which was known by the name of *dominicale*.[3]

The offering of bread and wine by the faithful at the offertory was prescribed by the second council of Mâcon (585); 'On every Sunday an offering, as well of bread as of wine, be made at the altar (*aris*) by all, men and women, that by these oblations (*immolationes*) they may obtain remission of their sins and may deserve to be sharers with Abel and the rest of just offerers.' The canon ends with threats of anathema against all those who should fail to comply.[4]

A censing of the *oblata* after the offertory in commemoration of the death of our Lord was prescribed by the council of Rouen (650).[5] A canon also directed that the Host should be placed in the mouth of the communicant with the formula: *Corpus Domini, et Sanguis prosit tibi ad remissionem peccatorum et ad vitam aeternam.*[6] The priest's own Host was not to be given to layfolk.

---

[1] Counc. II Tours, 567, can. 3. Labbe, *op. cit.*, t. V, col. 853.

[2] Mabillon, *De Lit. Gall.*, pp. 92 seq.; Duchesne, *op. cit.*, chap. VII, pp. 219–20, n. 1.

[3] Counc. Auxerre, 578, can. 36: forbids a woman to receive the Host in her bare hands; whereas can. 42 prescribes the use of a *dominicale*. Some writers have seen no connection between the two canons, and consider the *dominicale* to have been a head-covering. Labbe, *op. cit.*, t. V, cols. 960, 961. Cf. Hefele–Leclercq, *Conciles*, t. III, part III, liv. XV chap. I, p. 220.

[4] Counc. II Mâcon, 585, can. 4. Labbe, *op. cit.*, t. V, col. 981.

[5] Counc. Rouen, 650, can. I; Hef.–Lecq., *op. cit.*, t. III, part I, chap. II, p. 288.

[6] *Ibid.*, can. 2; *ibid.*

The council of Nantes (658) prescribed *eulogiae* to be given on Sundays and feasts to those who did not receive Holy Communion.[1] They were to be blessed with the following prayer: *Domine sancte, Pater omnipotens, aeterne Deus, benedicere digneris hunc panem tua sancta et spirituali benedictione, ut sit omnibus salus mentis et corporis, atque contra omnes morbos et universas inimicorum insidias tutamentum.*

SUPPRESSION OF THE GALLICAN RITE

It is difficult to say when the Roman liturgy first began to infiltrate into Gaul, but there would not appear to have been any opposition to accepting Roman *libelli* and codices.

Pope John III (561–74), when sending the pallium to Edaldus, bishop of Vienne, commented on the diversity of liturgies, and at the same time pointed out that it was his duty to follow Roman usages: *De officiis missarum de quibus in litteris vestris requisistis, sciat caritas vestra quia varie apud diversas ecclesias fiant: aliter enim Alexandrina ecclesia, aliter Hierosolymitana, aliter Ephesina, aliter Romana facit, cujus morem et instituta debet servare ecclesia tua, quae fundamentum sancti habitus ab illa sumpsit.*[2]

The Popes do not seem to have made any concerted efforts to suppress the Gallican rite, but the liturgical *dubia* submitted from time to time by the bishops provided opportunities for the Apostolic See to make known its wishes.

'Romanising' was probably accelerated after the time of St. Virgilius (*c.* 610), when the metropolitans of Arles no longer occupied an important position in determining the destiny of the Church in southern Gaul, and there was no other prelate of sufficient influence to take their place.

Gaul submitted to an indiscriminate introduction of Roman texts and formulas, incorporating selections from Gelasian and Gregorian *libelli missarum*, according to the codices that the several churches might chance to have. Elsewhere, we find a continuation of the traditional liturgy, but often in a very corrupt

---

[1] Counc. Nantes, 658, can. 9; Hef.–Lecq., *op. cit.,* p. 297.
[2] Labbe, *op. cit.,* t. V, col. 827.

state. The result of this state of affairs was little better than 'liturgical anarchy'.

A very widespread adoption of Roman codices would seem to have been noticeable from about the year 750. An introduction of the integral Roman rite would have been effected by the foundation of Benedictine monasteries, and a religious house that accepted the Holy Rule would in all probability adopt the Roman liturgy.[1]

The great work of St. Boniface (*ob.* 752) in propagating Roman usages was mainly as against pagan customs. Thus the *Concilium Germanicum* (742) condemned the 'offerings of animals, which foolish folk perform in the churches, according to pagan custom, in the name of holy martyrs or confessors, thereby calling down the wrath of God and his saints'.[2] The same council ordered that 'every priest living within a diocese shall be subject to the bishop of that diocese. Annually during Lent he shall render to the bishop an account of his ministry, in regard to baptism in the Catholic faith, to prayers, and the order of the Mass.'[3]

A similar injunction is found later in the century. The work of St. Boniface had been ordered by Pope Zachary (741–52): *Omnibus praedica, omnesque doce sicut a sancta Romana, cui Deo auctore deservimus, accepisti Ecclesia.*[4] Boniface himself in a letter to the Roman pontiff speaks of the decadence of religion: *Et promisit (Carlomannus) se de ecclesiastica religione quam jam longo, id est non minus quam per sexaginta vel septuaginta annos calcata et dissipata fuit aliquid corrigere vel emendare velle.*[5]

Zachary was appealed to also by Pepin, who was mayor from 741 to 751 and king from 751 to 768. Papal guidance was sought in a questionnaire numbering twenty-seven points.[6]

With Pepin and his more illustrious son, Charlemagne, we come into direct contact with the Gallican rite or such of it as still remained in Gaul.

---

[1] e.g. St. Virgilius gave the church of St. Honorat les Alyscamps at Arles to the Black monks in 601, and Aygulf, about the year 660, introduced the Holy Rule at Lérins.

[2] *Mon. Germ. Hist., Leges* III, conc. II, i, pp. 3–4.

[3] *Ibid.*, p. 3.   [4] *Pat. Lat.*, t. LXXXIX, col. 952.

[5] Bonifac., *Epist.* XLII; *Mon. Mogunt.*, edit. Jaffe.

[6] Wilhelm Levison, *England and the Continent in the Eighth Century* (Oxford, 1946), p. 89.

The initiative for the official suppression of the Gallican rite came from the State rather than from the Church. Pope Stephen II (III; 752–57) sought refuge in Gaul when fleeing from Astulf, king of the Lombards, in 753. He was accompanied by Chrodegang of Metz, the uncle of Pepin and a zealous promoter of the Roman liturgy. In the following year, Stephen crowned Pepin as king of the Franks in the abbey church of St. Denis near Paris. The presence of the Pope would certainly have encouraged a general adoption of the Roman rite, but it is clear that the demand for the universal suppression of the Gallican liturgy came in the first instance from the king, and not from the Pope. 'At Pepin's request', says Walafrid Strabo (*ob.* 849), 'the papal clerics introduced the chant (Roman), and thence its use spread far and wide.'[1] Charlemagne, in his *Admonitio Generalis* (789), says that his 'royal father, King Pepin, . . . suppressed the Frankish chant, out of unanimity with the Holy See and peaceful concord in the Church of God'.[2]

The successor of Stephen on the Chair of Peter, Paul I (757–67), sent Pepin 'as many books as we could find, that is, an antiphonal and a book of responses, and also texts for secular education'.[3] The service-books were made to fit Pepin's sacramentary, which would seem to have been the 8th-century Gelasian compilation. Edmund Bishop says that he has no hesitation in calling this book 'The Roman Sacramentary of King Pepin'.[4] 'The number and rapid spread of known copies prove its instant popularity. It stands as the first notable monument of the decision of Pepin's to abolish the Gallican rite, which is connected with the sojourn of Pope Stephen II (III) and his brother and future Pope Paul as Pepin's guests in 754.'[5]

It was, however, an exaggeration on the part of the synod of Frankfurt (794) to say that all the churches had adopted Roman usages in the time of King Pepin. The constant concern of

---

[1] Wal. Str., *Lib. de exord. et increm.* . . ., cap. XXV; Hittorp, *De div. Cath. Eccl. offic.* (Paris, 1610), col. 690; *Pat. Lat.*, t. CXIV, col. 957.

[2] *Mon. Germ. Hist.*, *Leges*, capit. I, p. 61.

[3] *Mon. Germ. Hist.*, *Epist.* III, p. 529.

[4] Bishop, *Lit. Hist.*, p. 152, n.

[5] *Ellard, Master Alcuin, Liturgist* (Chicago, 1956), chap. I, p. 28.

Charlemagne as to whether churches had introduced the Roman chant and rite seems to indicate that in some places at least the clergy were unwilling to abandon their traditional usages. Pope Hadrian during Easter Week of 774 asked Charlemagne to continue what his father Pepin had begun in spreading the liturgical uses of Rome in his wide kingdoms, although this would seem to refer more especially to those Lombard regions just then being absorbed in the Carolingian orbit.

Metz under St. Chrodegang became early a foyer of Roman liturgical life. Paul the Deacon (Warnifrid) tells us that he imposed 'the manner and use of Rome, something that had never before been done at Metz'.[1] Stational churches were introduced in imitation of the eternal City, but it was the chant for which Metz became so justly famous: 'To Rome for rubrics, to Metz for chant' says Alcuin's biographer.[2] Rouen also excelled in its chant, and in 760 the Pope, at the request of St. Remedius (*ob.* 772), later bishop, sent Symeon, the *secundercius* in his *schola cantorum*, as instructor.[3] Later (787), we find a school of chant established in the abbey of Fontanelle (St. Wandrille).

The extinction of the Gallican rite was greatly furthered by the great Benedictine houses, and 'no single ecclesiastical centre is oftener mentioned in this whole programme (Roman chant and rite) than St. Peter's Abbey, Corbie, in the diocese of Amiens'.[4]

'If the father (Pepin) was satisfied with a half measure, the son (Charlemagne) will demand of the Pope an "unadulterated" Roman book, which his subjects can reject only at their peril'.[5] The counsel of the 'young men' to Roboam might well have been called to mind by those who wished for a continuance of the Gallican rite: 'And now my father put a heavy yoke upon you: but I will add to your yoke. My father beat you with whips: but I will beat you with scorpions.' [6]

---

[1] Paul D., *Gesta episc. Mettensium: Mon. Germ. Hist., Script. rer. Germanic.*, II, p. 268.

[2] *Romamque ecclesiasticum ordinem discendum . . . fuerat, necnon Mettis civitatem causa cantus directus. Ibid.*, XV, i, p. 189.

[3] Ellard, *op. cit.*, chap. I, p. 21.

[4] *Ibid.*, chap. III, p. 50.

[5] *Ibid.*, chap. I, pp. 29–30.

[6] III *Kings*, XII, ii.

The campaign for liturgical uniformity undertaken by Charlemagne was 'stepped up' by the arrival at court of the Anglo-Saxon Alcuin in 782.

An appeal was made to the Pope for an 'unadulterated' Roman sacramentary, and Hadrian (772–95) sent a Gregorian book, which by reason of its donor received the name of 'Hadrianum'. It seems certain that this sacramentary reached Charlemagne by the end of 785, or not much later.[1] It was not, however, presented to the clergy of the Frankish dominions as it left Rome, and a very substantial supplement was added by Alcuin. The vast bulk of the materials gathered for this purpose seems to have been taken from the 'Sacramentary of Pepin', the 8th-century Gelasian codex.[2] There does not seem to be any evidence that formulas were borrowed from the now illegal Gallican liturgy. New Mozarabic material was provided in the Masses for the dead, but a clean sweep was made of nearly the whole of the twenty or twenty-one prayers found in these services in Gaul.[3]

The difference between the 'Imperial' liturgy and that of the city of Rome was observed by Walafrid Strabo (*ob.* 849), who says: 'The Churches of Gaul had their own prayers, which are still used by many'.[4]

The year 789 has been described as 'the year one of complete liturgical uniformity',[5] when the *Hadrianum*, together with the Supplement, was published. In the same year, Charlemagne issued his famous *Admonitio Generalis*, in which it was said: 'that bishops, throughout their jurisdictions, diligently examine the priests, as to their orthodoxy, their (way) of baptizing and celebrating Mass; that they may hold to the true faith and following the Catholic form of baptism; to find out if they understand the Mass prayers well . . .'[6]

The emperor, as Charlemagne had now become, was nothing if not thorough, and in 806 he ordered 'inspectors' to be sent into

---

[1] Ellard, *op. cit.*, chap. VI, p. 107.

[2] The votive-Mass section came down fairly intact since embodied in the Supplement.

[3] Bishop, *op. cit.*, p. 168.

[4] Wal. Str., *De rebus eccles.*, cap. XXV; Hittorp, *op. cit.*, col. 690; *Pat. Lat.*, t. CXIV, col. 957.

[5] Ellard, *op. cit.*, chap. IV, p. 72.

[6] *Mon. Germ. Hist.*, *Leges*, II, capit. I, p. 59.

Abbey Church, St. Victor, Marseilles
(founded by St. Cassian)

Chapel of the Holy Trinity,
Lérins (? seventh century)

Chapel of St. Saviour, Lérins

St. Honoratus, Founder of Lérins
(ob. 429). Fifteenth-century statue

Cloisters, Lérins (seventh century)

Chapel of St. Cyprian and
St. Justina, Lérins

Cell of Leobard, Marmoutier
(seventh century)

the towns and villages in order that they might see whether his decrees respecting the Roman rite and chant were observed.

His concern in matters affecting the liturgy would seem to have gone to extreme lengths, as, for example, whether priests wore sandals at Mass, and whether the sacred ministers at a solemn Mass gave each other the *pax*.[1]

About the year 800, the bishops of the Frankish kingdom, at the instance of the emperor, drew up a questionnaire for priests: *Interrogo vos, presbiteri, . . . Missam vestram secundum ordinem Romanum quomodo nostis vel intellegitis*,[2]

It can hardly be supposed that the Gallican rite ceased everywhere and at once, although it would seem to have become little more than a memory in a very short time.

Hildwin, abbot of St. Denis, in a letter to King Louis the Pious, written in 835, refers to the Gallican Mass as 'very ancient', but says that the missals are in such a bad condition that they are impossible to use: *Cui adstipulari videntur antiquissimi et nimia pene vestustate consumpti missales libri continentes missae ordinem more gallico, qui ab initio receptae fidei usu . . . usque quo tenorem, qui nunc utitur, romanum susceperit*.[3]

About forty years later, the Gallican liturgy would appear to have been extinct, and when Charles the Bald (*ob.* 877) expressed a desire to witness the traditional rite of his kingdom, it was found necessary to obtain priests from Toledo, as the Mozarabic liturgy was somewhat similar in its structure and arrangement. The king, it would seem, was desirous of attending the various rites with a view to deciding which one he preferred. Charles finally chose the Roman rite, and, in a letter to the clergy of Ravenna, he said: 'For us, we judge that it is the Roman Church that it is necessary to follow in the celebration of Mass'.[4]

The *Hadrianum*, as we have seen, was imposed by Charlemagne on all the churches of his kingdom: the Supplement would seem

---

[1] *Ut confectis sacris mysteriis in missarum solemniis omnes generaliter pacem ad invicem praebeat. Ibid.*, sect. II, t. I, p. 61.

[2] *Mon. Germ. Hist., Leges* II, capit. I, p. 234.

[3] Bona, *Rer. Lit.*, lib. I, cap. VIII, 5, p. 76; *Pat. Lat.*, t. CVI, col. 13.

[4] *Sed nos sequendum ducimus Romanam Ecclesiam in missarum celebratione.* Bona, *ibid.*; Baluze, *Capitularia Regum Francorum*, t. II, p. 730.

H

to have been at first optional. It came, however, to be integrated in the Gregorian book, and it was this Franco-Roman liturgy which largely modelled the Roman rite of the future. 'The Church of Gaul', says Dom Fernand Cabrol, 'had her revenge, for, from the 9th century, whilst losing her own liturgy, she took the lead in the liturgical movement, remodelled the Roman sacramentary, and added numerous formulas which, securely incorporated in the text of the Roman missal, are now recited everywhere.'

The same thing happened to the pontifical, ritual, martyrology, breviary and ceremonial of bishops, all of which retain traces of the various influences to which they were subjected through the centuries.[1] It is interesting to note that the expression *Salvator mundi*, which we find at prime in the prayer *Dirigere et sanctificare*, was a distinctive characteristic of the Gallican and North Italian liturgies.[2] It is found also in the Mozarabic rite in the *Ad pacem* prayer for the Second Sunday in Lent,[3] and in the *Missa* of the fifteenth Sunday '*de Quotidiano*'.[4]

CHURCH ARCHITECTURE

The first 'cathedral' of St. Gatian, the apostle of Touraine (*ob.* probably *c.* 337), would seem to have been a cave at Marmoutier near Tours, beneath which an important Benedictine abbey was erected in later centuries. The baptismal font for the immersion of the Saint's converts is still visible. Two other caves, inhabited by saints, are also shown: St. Patrick and St. Libert (Léobard). The latter is said to have lived in the cave for twenty-two years, and to have left instructions that he was to be buried standing upright, in order that he might be ready for the Last Judgment! St. Libert was the last of the hermits, and monks living in community took their place. St. Lidorius, successor of St. Gatian, appears to have officiated in the house of a senator on the site of the present cathedral. St. Martin, when bishop of Tours (*ob.* 397), preferred to live a solitary life in a cave at Marmoutier,

---

[1] Cabrol, *Books of the Latin Liturgy*, chap. VII, 4, p. 99.
[2] Baumstark, *Liturgie Comparée* (1953), chap. IV, p. 77.
[3] Férotin, *Lib. Moz. Sacram.*, col. 167.
[4] *Ibid.*, col. 639.

rather than to reside in his episcopal city. The cemetery to the
west of the town became the burial place of the Saint, where a
modest *cella* of straw and rushes was erected by St. Britius (Brice),
which under St. Perpetuus developed into a basilica consecrated
on 4 July 482. St. Martin had lived for ten years at Ligugé near
Poitiers before being raised to the episcopate, and to his honour
a votive hypogeum was built, the remains of which were discovered under the tower of the 15th-century abbey church in
1953.

On the evangelisation of the country, it had been the Christian
instinct to destroy all vestiges of paganism,[1] but, with the disappearance of the old religion, such pagan works of art as still
remained were sometimes employed in Catholic worship. Thus,
for example, in the Romanesque church of Belloc-Saint-Clamans,
Gers, we find a pagan sarcophagus, with 'little loves' symbolising
the seasons, transformed into a Christian altar. Saints also were
at times laid to rest in coffins prepared for heathens: St. Aphro-
disius at Béziers, St. Ludre at Déols (Indre) and St. Andéol at
Bourg-Saint-Andéol.

The profound decadence in the architecture and art of the
churches of Gaul from the middle of the 7th century until the
Carolingian renaissance has been explained by the fact that the
rapid conquest of Syria, Palestine, Egypt and North Africa by
Islam had dried up the source from whence Gaul derived her
inspiration. On the other hand, a recent scholar, while admitting
the presence in the country of a large number of Jews and Syrians,
has doubted the 'free communication between the East and West
of the Mediterranean' in Merovingian times by reason of the pirate
fleet of Vandal Carthage.[2] 'Gaul of the Merovingians, so far as
vital contacts with the Empire were concerned, was from the
first marooned'.[3] Nevertheless, Gallican contacts with the East
in the matter of church building are important, and serve to support the hypothesis of Oriental borrowings in the liturgy.

---

[1] In the Limousin, the cross at the cross-roads was sometimes accompanied by a little
oratory known as *Ouradour* (*Oradour*), which in all probability had been substituted for
the pagan *lararia*.

[2] Norman H. Baynes, *M. Pirenne and the Unity of the Mediterranean World*, *Byzantine
Studies*, XXII, p. 316. London, 1955. [3] *Ibid.*, p. 315.

In the 6th century, when the Gallican rite received its more or less final form, we find colonies of Greeks or Syrians in most of the cities of southern Gaul.

Cassian, bishop of Autun, who was a native of Alexandria, had been previously a bishop in Palestine; while the Syrian merchant Eusebius, who had secured the bishopric of Paris by bribes, was said by St. Gregory of Tours (*ob.* 594) to have replaced all the dignitaries of his Church by compatriots. The Gaulish bishops, moreover, seem to have been attracted to the East, and to have gathered Orientals around them.

St. Amator, bishop of Auxerre, is known to have visited Antioch; Licinius, bishop of Tours, resided for some considerable time in the East; while St. Just, bishop of Lyons, left his diocese in order to live with the monks of the deserts of Egypt. Pilgrimages to the Holy Places must have influenced the Gallican Church, and it was from returned pilgrims that Gregory of Tours learned of the names and virtues of the saints of Syria and Asia Minor. Gregory speaks also of a Syrian merchant at Bordeaux, who cherished a relic (finger) of St. Sergius.[1] It would seem to have been a pilgrim who informed Bishop Perpetuus as to the plan of the church of the Cenacle at Jerusalem, as a mosaic in the nave of the basilica of St. Martin at Tours, which was in process of building at the time, represented the interior of the church with exactitude. Further than this, the architect of the Tours basilica may well have seen Carthage, Egypt and Anatolia.[2] It was in this basilica that Clovis received the consular purple tunic and chlamys, and placed on his head the royal crown of the Franks.

Many of the Merovingian bishops were great church-builders: Leontius of Bordeaux expended much of his fortune in this way; Felix of Nantes (597) completed the cathedral which has been described by Fortunatus;[3] St. Venantius of Viviers (517–37) erected several churches and a baptistery adorned with marbles; and St. Gregory of Tours (*ob.* 594) rebuilt his cathedral, which had been destroyed by fire in 561. Fortunatus has left us a

---

[1] *Greg. Turon., Hist. Franc.*, lib. VII, cap. XXXI. *Pat. Lat.*, t. LXXI, col. 435.

[2] Emile Mâle, *La Fin du Paganisme en Gaule et les plus anciennes basiliques chrétiennes* (Paris, 1950), chap. V, 3, p. 153.

[3] Fortun., *Miscell.*, lib. III, cap. IV. *Pat. Lat.*, t. LXXXVIII, cols. 120–4.

description of the Martinian themes which adorned the new building.[1]

The many churches and monasteries of the period show that, despite the anarchy prevailing in the country, the 6th century was one of the finest in the history of Christian art in Gaul.

The ecclesiastical remains of Merovingian Gaul are not very numerous, but those that survive often point to Oriental influence.

The foundations of a church at Arles, discovered in 1835, have been said to be those of an oratory built by St. Trophimus in commemoration of a martyred relation of the name of Stephen, but, apart from the doubtfulness of the apostolate of St. Trophimus, the remains could not be of an earlier date than the 4th century. They may well be those of a basilica dedicated to the protomartyr Stephen, cited in the life of the bishop St. Hilary (429–49) and again in that of St. Caesarius (502–43).[2]

The excavations undertaken at Lyons, at the time of the restoration of the site of the ancient high altar in 1936, revealed an apse of ancient type with benches for the clergy, which recalls the 6th-century church of Annona in Algeria. We find in the mosaic pavement of black, white and red cubes the representation of the façade of a church with an embattled tower to the right, reminiscent of a mosaic of the 4th–5th century, discovered at Tabarka in Tunisia.[3] Sidonius Apollinaris, towards the end of the 5th century, tells us in three letters that the bishop Patiens erected and embellished a church between a road and the port of the Saône, which, orientated to the east, was adorned with marbles and mosaics. The writer does not supply the name, and many have thought that the reference was to St. Nizier, but, as M. Coville says, it was the church of St. John that was normally termed *ecclesia*, the 'church of the bishop', whereas St. Nizier was always known as the 'basilica'. It would seem, therefore, that the remains are more likely to be those of the church erected by St. Patiens

---

[1] The immense Romanesque basilica, erected over the tomb of St. Martin in the first half of the 11th century, was destroyed at the Revolution. Two towers are all that remain. A modern church was built in the 19th century.

[2] L. H. Labande, *L'Eglise Saint-Trophime d'Arles* (Paris, 1930), I, pp. 6–10.

[3] Leclercq, *Eglises, Dict. d'Archéol. Chrét. et de Lit.*, t. IV, part 2, col. 2232.

(451–91).[1] A crypt of the 6th century still exists under the choir of St. Nizier, and a further work of St. Patiens is to be found in the crypt of St. Irenaeus, which was constructed to serve as a resting place for the relics of the second bishop and those of the early martyrs.

The 5th-century vaulted oratory, erected by St. Cassian at Marseilles and now forming a part of the crypt of the abbey church of St. Victor, and the foundations of the early monastery at Glenfeuil show a plan similar to one of the churches of Ben Bir Kilisse near Iconium.[2]

The adoption of a vault may have been derived from Asia Minor, a country bordering on Persia, the home of the vaulted palaces of the Sassanides. The apsidal part of the cathedral church of Vaison, which probably dates from the end of the 5th century, shows three apses with architectural features common to the churches of Syria.[3]

Two of the seven chapels constructed on the island of Lérins call for special mention: St. Saviour and Holy Trinity. The chapel of St. Saviour, surmounted by a cupola, is reminiscent of the monastic churches of Upper Egypt. It is impossible to assign a date with any certainty, but the hypothesis offered by Mâle may supply the answer. He considers that it was built in the 7th century by Eastern monks, who had fled to Lérins from the all-conquering Arabs. The island suffered from a raid in 725, which annihilated the monastic community, and it must therefore have been built before that date.[4] The neighbouring chapel of the Holy Trinity shows the normal plan of Gallican baptisteries, but without an interior colonnade. Here again the plan suggests an Eastern origin, with the sanctuary of St. Gregory at Ani in Armenia as the model. The chapel may well be of the same date as that of St. Saviour.[5]

The tribunes in the Merovingian basilica of St. Martin at Tours, which were somewhat similar to those in the *martyrium* at Jerusalem and the Egyptian basilica of St. Menas, were common fea-

---

[1] Armand Macé, *Restauration du Choeur de la Cathédral Saint-Jean à Lyon* (Lyons, 1936), pp. 55–61.

[2] Mâle, *op. cit.*, chap. V, 4, pp. 155–6.   [3] *Ibid.*, p. 157.

[4] *Ibid.*, chap. V, 7, pp. 185–7.   [5] *Ibid.*, p. 187.

tures in Asia Minor, and only appeared later, under Oriental influence, at Rome.

Contact with the East was almost certainly responsible for the semicircular atrium encircling the apse at Tours, and a prototype is found at Carthage.[1]

Eastern peculiarities are met with in the basilica of St. Peter at Vienne, now a museum, which in its original state dates from at least the 5th century. The square chamber to the left of the apse probably corresponded to the Byzantine *prothesis*, and a similar structure, serving as the *diakonikon*, would have existed at one time on the other side. The foundations of the church of St. Romain d'Albon (Epaone), a building which appears to be contemporary with that of Vienne, show two quadrangular chambers, one on either side of the apse.[2] The basilica at Vienne has Eastern features also in the windows and wall arcading, which are reminiscent of the Baptistery of the Orthodox at Ravenna and the Palace of Diocletian at Split (Spalato). Wall arcading originated with the Sassanides in Persia, showing the source from whence the churches of Armenia and the monastic churches of Egypt borrowed this form of decoration.[3]

Merovingian baptisteries show similar signs of Oriental origin. The 7th-century baptistery of Poitiers, which is the only monument of the period which in its external appearance remains unchanged, recalls the Mausoleum of Galla Placidia at Ravenna. Fragments of a similar type are found in the baptistery of St. Rémi in Provence, which, as at Djemila in North Africa, was provided with a bathroom for the catechumens.[4]

The 6th-century baptistery of Riez, with its interior colonnade, was long thought to have been a pagan temple, but its true prototype was rather the *martyrium* of St. George at Ezra in Syria.[5] Marseilles had a baptistery of a similar plan (4th century), which was one of the largest known and greater than that of St. John Lateran; while another of the beginning of the 5th century existed at Aix en Provence.

---

[1] Mâle, *op. cit.*, pp. 152-3.
[2] Cf. Basilica of S. Maria delle Grazie, Grado (6th century).
[3] Mâle, *op. cit.*, chap. V, 4, p. 159.
[4] *Ibid.*, chap. VII, 2, p. 221.   [5] *Ibid.*, chap. VII, 3, pp. 222-3.

The baptistery of Fréjus (beginning 5th century) seems to have been one of the smallest in southern Gaul, but it remains substantially intact. The disappearance of monumental baptisteries was hastened by an enactment of Charlemagne (789), which prescribed the baptism of infants in their first year.

The porphyry and jasper columns of the 7th-century Merovingian crypt at Jouarre (634) remain intact, much as the original builders left them.[1]

Fortunatus (*ob.* beginning 7th century), describing the basilicas of Gaul, says that they 'shine and sparkle' (*fulgor, nitet, rutilat*): doubtless as the sun catches the mosaics that cover the walls. Mosaics originated in the Persian palaces, and found a place also in the Palace of Diocletian at Spalato.

St. Gregory of Tours (*ob.* 594) speaks of hangings between the columns, suspended before the sanctuary and round the ciborium.

The *Gesta Dagoberti* records the work of St. Eloi at St. Denis: a *tugurium* (ciborium) with marble columns was erected over the tomb of the Saint, which was encrusted with gold and precious stones. The balustrade of the choir was covered with gold, and the ambo with silver; while a great cross of gold set with gems was erected behind the altar. King Dagobert himself provided the sumptuous hangings for the walls and arcades.[2]

A *chorus psallentium* or closed choir with ambones is mentioned in a text of the second council of Tours, which met in the basilica of St. Martin. Choirs of this kind were a common feature in many of the churches of Syria, but, as they were normally constructed in wood, they have long since disappeared.[3] The carved wooden desk from the abbey of the Holy Cross at Poitiers, now in the Benedictine convent of Sainte Croix, is said to have been used by St. Radegunde herself. However that may be, it is certainly of Merovingian workmanship, from an Eastern model.

Representations of the crucifixion appeared in the East in the 6th century, and it was not until later that they became usual in the West. St. Gregory of Tours (*ob.* 594) tells us that when a

---

[1] The crypt was extended in the 10th century.
[2] *Gest. Dag.*, cap. XX; Mâle, *op. cit.*, chap. V, 6, pp. 182–3.
[3] Mâle, *op. cit.*, chap. V, 3, p. 152.

picture depicting our Lord on the cross was exhibited in a church at Narbonne, the faithful were so shocked that it had to be covered with a veil.[1]

Merovingian shrines would seem to have been modelled on Jewish ossuaries, which in their turn were derived from Syrian originals, as, for example, the shrine in the museum at Poitiers and the 7th-century shrine of St. Benedict at Fleury.

The manuscripts of the period reveal Eastern contacts, and the illuminators appear to have derived their inspiration from the Thebaid or Sinai.[2] The ivory book-covers preserved at Saulieu in Burgundy and in the *Bibliothèque Nationale* at Paris (from the monastery of Lupicinus in the Jura) are almost identical in workmanship with two ivories from Etchmiadzin in Armenia and the chair of Maximian at Ravenna. It has been suggested that all five objects came originally from the same workshop, which was at Alexandria.[3]

Eastern influence is discernible also on the tombs of the period, as may be seen from those of Angilbert, bishop of Paris, at Jouarre, and of the abbot Mellebaude in the Gallo-Roman necropolis outside Poitiers. The representation of the archangel Raguel on the latter indicates that it was executed before 745, the year in which figures of Raguel and Uriel were forbidden on the ground that they were apocryphal.

The finely sculptured 5th- and 6th-century tombs of south-west France from the workshops of Narbonne, Toulouse and Bordeaux have led some writers to ascribe the skill and ingenuity of the carvings to the Visigoths, in whose kingdom they were designed, but in point of fact the Visigoths invented nothing, and they were merely reproducing Eastern art. Oriental influence is seen in the subjects depicted on the tombs, which have been largely inspired by the Antiochene *Commendatio animae*, a prayer of the 2nd or 3rd century, and attributed to St. Cyprian of Antioch.

In other matters also, Merovingian Gaul looked to the East,

---

[1] *Greg. Turon., De Gloria Martyrum*, cap. XXIII; *Pat. Lat.*, t. LXXI, cols. 724-5.
[2] Mâle, *op. cit.*, cap. X, i, p. 263.
[3] *Ibid.*, chap. XI, i, pp. 285-6.

and St. Radegunde turned to Constantinople when she needed
relics for her religious house at Poitiers. The emperor Justin II
(565–78) acceded to her request, and the royal foundress was
given a relic of the true Cross, which Venantius Fortunatus wel-
comed with the composition of the hymn *Vexilla Regis.*

The churches of Gaul until the 5th century would seem to have
followed the ancient custom of adopting the names of their
founders, and we find the basilica at Clermont known as the
Basilica Joviniana.

In country districts, churches were built and supported by the
great landowners, and these 'proprietary chapels' became parish
churches later.[1] Thus we find Sulpicius Severus erecting a basilica
on his estate at Primuliacum in 402.[2]

The adoption of celestial patrons for churches was popularised
by the finding of the body of St. Stephen (415) and the promulgation of the title 'Mother of God' (*Theotokos*) for the Blessed Virgin
at the council of Ephesus in 431.

There does not appear to be any justification for the statement
that churches in Gaul had been dedicated to the Virgin as early as
the 4th century. The cultus of Mary, however, was earlier here
than in Rome, and seems to have been received directly from the
East. A marble plaque, dating from the end of the 5th century,
with the inscription: *Maria virgo minister de tempulo gerosale,* is
found in the crypt of the church of St. Maximin.

ALTARS

Merovingian altars often took the form of a cube of stone,
sometimes with a pilaster at each corner. An example of this
kind, with a *chi rho*, alpha (missing) and omega sculptured on the
front, may be seen in the *Musée de Cluny* at Paris.[3]

Elsewhere, we find a slab of stone lying on one or four sup-

---

[1] Cf. *Ursland* chapel system in early mediaeval Norway, Iceland and Orkney.

[2] A portrait of St. Martin was placed in the church, and, as a recent writer says, 'Sulpicius
had devoted himself exclusively to the furtherance of the cult of St. Martin as the pioneer of
asceticism and the monastic life in Gaul' (N. K. Chadwick, *Poetry and Letters in Early
Christian Gaul* (London, 1955), chap. IV, p. 98). Primuliacum has never been satisfactorily identified.

[3] *Musée de Cluny*, Paris, n. 22392.

ports, as at Tarascon. The altars are usually incredibly small, and
they would have been devoid of ornaments, save, possibly, a
single candle at the time of Mass.

HOLY OIL IN THE CHURCH OF GAUL

It is uncertain when the ceremony of the blessing of the oils
was fixed for Holy Thursday.

We know that St. Caesarius, bishop of Arles (*ob.* 543), blessed
them on Holy Saturday, but this may have been a peculiarity of
the Arlesian Church.[1]

St. Eloi, bishop of Noyon (*ob. c.* 656), refers to the consecration of the chrism in the Mass *in Cena Domini* on Holy Thursday
as a universal practice.[2]

The austere Roman form for the consecration of a church was
elaborated in the Gallican rite by two new elements: Unction
with holy oil and repeated aspersions with lustral water. The use
of oil was borrowed from the East, where it was already attested
in the second half of the 4th century.[3] It would seem to have been
adopted in Gaul by the end of the 5th century, and its use was
confirmed by the council of Agde in 506: *Altaria placuit, non
solum unctione christmatis, sed etiam sacerdotali (episcopali) benedictione consecrari.*[4]

The *Statuta Ecclesiae antiqua* (6th century) make no reference
to the use of oil at an ordination, but a formula at the anointing
of the priest's hands is found in the *Missale Francorum* of the first
half of the 8th century. Such an anointing was probably adopted
in imitation of its use at the coronation of a king.

There is no evidence in support of the testimony of Warren
and Duchesne that priests in the Celtic Church were anointed at
their ordination at the end of the 6th century.

The Gallican custom of deferring the use of oil at the Baptismal

---

[1] G. Morin, *Une particularité arlésienne de la liturgie du samedi saint. Ephem. Liturg.*,
XLIX (1935), pp. 146–9.

[2] *S. Elig. Noviom., Homil.* X *in Cena Domini: Pat. Lat.*, t. LXXXVII, col. 629.

[3] e.g. St. Ephrem (*ob.* 373), *Hymn. de oleo chrismatis:* Dion. Areop., *De Hierarchia
ecclesiae*, IV; *Testamentum Domini* (edit. Rahmani), p. 156.

[4] Counc. Agde, 506, can. 43. Cf. Counc. Epaone, 517, can. 26.

rite until the subsequent Confirmation has been thought to indicate a close Roman relationship.[1]

BAPTISMAL LITURGY

Before the end of the 7th century we have no more than scattered references in ecclesiastical writers, but the Baptismal ritual
of the Frankish Churches is given in the *Gallicanum Vetus, Gothicum* and Missal of Bobbio. The liturgical books do not present
perfect harmony in all details, but there is nevertheless a general
agreement.

It will suffice here to indicate the points of difference between
the Gallican and Gelasian rites:

> 1. An absence of the distribution of the ceremonies pre-
> paratory to Baptism in a fixed series of scrutinies.
> 2. A joining in the same liturgical function of the re-
> nunciation of the devil, the profession of faith and the actual
> Baptism. At Rome the renunciation is united to the giving of
> the Symbol and the *Effeta*: two things which were unknown
> in Gaul.
> 3. The deferring of unction until the Confirmation, which
> followed the Baptism.
> 4. A washing of feet.

With the exception of the ceremony of the washing of feet,
Gallican peculiarities were very similar to those of the primitive
Latin rites. Gaul showed little or no agreement with Eastern
usages, and there were noteworthy divergences.[2]

The Carolingian liturgical reform saw to it that the manuals
gave the baptismal form clearly and without the extraneous additions, such as had been common in the Gallican rite. One of the
commonest of these additions was the clause '*ut habeas vitam
aeternam*'.

In spite of these injunctions, however, a fresh copy of the now
'outlawed' Sacramentary of Pepin appeared about the end of

---

[1] P. de Puniet, *La Liturgie Baptismale en Gaule avant Charlemagne*, ap. *Revue des
questions historiques*, October, 1902, pp. 28–9.

[2] De Puniet, *op. cit.*, pp. 40–1.

Alcuin's life (*ob.* 804). The production comes down to us in MS.-*Bibliothèque Nationale*, Paris, lat. 816, in the ritual for a sick-room baptism after the direction for trine immersion. The following form is given: *Baptizato ill(um) in nomine Patris et Filii et Spiritus Sancti ut habeas vitam aeternam.*[1] So, after half a century of effort, this battle was not yet won.[2]

LAUS PERENNIS

Laus perennis signifies 'perpetual psalmody', which was a continuous recitation of the canonical hours at every moment of the night and day in the same religious house.[3] The practice seems to have been borrowed from Constantinople for the church at Agaunum (St. Maurice en Valais), on the occasion of the restoration of the basilica, erected over the relics of the Martyrs of the Theban Legion by Sigismund, king of Burgundy. The exact date is said to have been 22 September 522, on the feast of St. Maurice. There is no doubt that such an institution was a novelty in the Gallican Church, and the bishops to whom the king submitted his plan spoke of it as *inusitatum opus.*[4] Some fifty years later, King Gontram of Burgundy instituted an observance *ad instar monasterii Agaunensis* at St. Marcel near Chalon sur Saône and also at St. Benignus, Dijon. In 625, the practice was introduced at St. Denis, and it had been already adopted at St. Martin, Tours. Other sources, though without any explicit reference to Agaunum, tell us that the *Laus perennis* was carried out at St. Germain des Prés (Paris), Soissons (St. Medard), Luxeuil, Remiremont and Laon. The latest recorded instance comes from St. Riquier in the time of Charlemagne, when the Gallican rite had already given place to the Roman.[5] Such a late introduction was, however, unusual, and one would have supposed that the practice would have been abandoned after the suppression of the traditional liturgy.

---

[1] Paul Cagin, *Le Sacramentaire Gélasien d'Angoulême*, fo. 138. *Société Historique et Archéologique de la Charente*, 1918.

[2] Ellard, *op. cit.*, chap. IV, p. 84.

[3] Stanley Luff, *British Monasteries and the Laus Perennis*, *Pax*, Spring, 1953.

[4] *Acta SS.*, 1 May. *Vita Alia S. Sigismundi*, para. 6.

[5] Luff, *op. cit.*, p. 149.

RELICS

Great importance was attached to relics in the Merovingian period, and 'relic hunting' was a favourite pastime with those who aspired to sanctity.

St. Gregory of Tours (*ob.* 594), as we have seen, speaks of a certain Euphronius, a Syrian merchant of Bordeaux, who collected relics of St. Sergius: *hujus sancti reliquias collocavit.*[1] From the same source also we read of a deacon of Tours who was sent to Rome in order to acquire relics of saints: *diaconus noster ab urbe Roma cum sanctorum pignoribus veniens.*[2] Gregory himself, in describing the dedication of an oratory, says that relics of St. Saturninus, martyr; St. Martin, bishop; and St. Illidius, confessor, have been placed in it.[3]

St. Radegunde (*ob.* 587), the wife of King Clothair, who left her husband in order to become a nun, seems to have been an inveterate collector of relics. Even before her marriage, when she was living in the royal villa at Athies, Radegunde resorted to this hobby, although, in the hurry of her departure to the court, she inadvertently left them behind. Years later, after her separation from the king, when the Queen in her solitude at Saix was making another collection, the missing relics are said to have been miraculously restored to her.[4] The convent of the Holy Cross, founded by St. Radegunde at Poitiers, owed its name to a relic of the true Cross which had been sent by the emperor. Political connections between the Frankish courts and that of Constantinople were frequent, and the royal abbess asked the Eastern emperor Justin II to send her a portion of the true Cross. In 568 or 569 envoys brought to Poitiers many relics of apostles and martyrs, a gospel-book and no less than five pieces of the Holy Cross. The occasion of the solemn entry into the city led Venantius Fortunatus to compose the two famous hymns: *Vexilla Regis prodeunt*[5] and *Pange Lingua.*[6] The celebrated strophe, *O*

---

[1] *Greg. Turon., Hist. Franc.*, lib. VII, cap. XXXI; *Pat. Lat.*, t. LXXI, col. 435.
[2] *Ibid.*, lib. X, cap. I; *ibid.*, col. 527.
[3] *Greg. Turon., Glor. Confess.*, cap. XX; *Pat. Lat.*, t. LXXI, col. 842.
[4] René Aigrain, *Ste. Radegonde*, chap. III, p. 71. Poitiers, 1952.
[5] *Vexilla Regis*, Fortun. *Miscell.*, lib. II, cap. VII; *Pat. Lat.*, t. LXXXVIII, col. 95.
[6] *Pange Lingua*, Fortun. *Ibid.*, lib. II, cap. II; *Pat. Lat.*, t. LXXXVIII, cols. 88–9.

crux, ave, spes unica, and the doxology, found today in the *Vexilla Regis,* were not in the original hymn. The liturgical edition in use since Urban VIII (1623–44) has omitted three of the strophes of Fortunatus. A modern convent of Benedictine nuns, near the Baptistery of St. John, claims to have some of the relics of the Holy Cross preserved since the days of St. Radegunde.

Relics of the Cross were received also by Sulpicius Severus from St. Paulinus of Nola and by St. Avitus of Vienne from the patriarch of Jerusalem.

A magnificent reliquary in gold adorned with precious stones was fashioned in 630 by St. Eloi for the relics of St. Martin, at the request of King Dagobert.

Sources for the Rite

1. Letter of Pope Innocent I (416) to Decentius, bishop of Gubbio.[1]

2. Three Homilies of Faustus, bishop of Riez (*ob. c.* 485), on the Creed.[2]

3. St. Caesarius of Arles (*ob.* 543); Sermons on the Creed [3] and *Regula ad Monachos.*[4]

4. Aurelian of Arles (*ob.* 553): *Regula ad Monachos et ad Virgines.*[5]

5. Pseudo-Germanus: *Expositio brevis antiquae liturgiae gallicanae.*[6] In all probability an anonymous treatise of the end of the 7th century. Righetti considers the document to be of but relative value, and not portraying the official Gallican Mass. He believes it to be a production of the Church of Burgundy, perhaps Autun.[7]

6. Gregory of Tours: *De cursibus ecclesiasticis.*[8] A liturgical

---

[1] *Pat Lat.,* t. XX, col. 463.

[2] Engelbrecht, *Studien über die Schriften des Bishofes von Reii Faustus* (1889), pp. 47–101.

[3] In Sermons of St. Augustine. *Pat. Lat.,* t. XXXVIII–XXXIX, cols. 2194–6 and 2233–40.

[4] *Pat. Lat.,* t. LXVII, col. 1099.

[5] *Pat. Lat.,* t. LXVIII, cols. 385 and 397.

[6] *Pat. Lat.,* t. LXXII, col. 77; Duchesne, *op. cit.,* chap. VII, pp. 189 seq.

[7] Righetti, *op. cit.,* t. I, part 2, cap. III, p. 115.

[8] Krusch, *Gregorii Turon. opera, Monum. Germ. histor. Script. rer. Meroving.,* t. I, 2, pp. 854–72.

manual, containing an instruction to determine the order of
Offices or ecclesiastical lessons (*Cursus ecclesiastici*).

7. Venantius Fortunatus: *Expositio symboli* and many of his
poetical works.[1]

LITURGICAL BOOKS

The Gallican books are not so well documented as those of
other rites, and those that have survived, mutilated or mixed with
Roman elements, date from the later Merovingian period.

Gennadius writes of his contemporary, a priest of the name of
Musaeus (*ob. c.* 460), who compiled a lectionary at the request of
Venerius, bishop of Marseilles (*c.* 431–51). This was followed up
in the episcopate of Eustachius by a sacramentary—*egregium et
non parvum volumen*—containing lessons, psalms, chants, prayers
(*supplicationes*) and prefaces (*contestationes*). A book of homilies
completed his liturgical output.[2]

It must not be supposed, however, that the composition of a
sacramentary implied a change of liturgy. The term would probably mean no more than a compilation of collects and prayers for
various feast days. On the other hand, the substitution of variable for fixed formulas was certainly a new departure.

About the same time, Claudian, brother of St. Claudian Mamertus, bishop of Vienne (*ob. c.* 475), edited a lectionary: the lessons
of which harmonised with the text of the sacramentary.[3]

Sidonius Apollinaris, bishop of Clermont (470–80), in a letter
to his colleague Megethius, admitted the composition of a number
of Masses: *Sidonius domino papae Megethio. Diu multumque
deliberavi, quamquam mihi animus affectu studioque parendi sollici-
taretur, an destinarem, sicut injungis, contestatiunculas quas ipse
dictavi. Vicit ad ultimum sententia, quae tibi obsequendum definie-*

---

[1] *Pat. Lat.*, t. LXXXVIII.

[2] *Musaeus Massiliensis ecclesiae presbyter vir in divinis scripturis doctus. . . . Sed et ad
personam sancti Eusebii episcopi successoris supradicti hominis dei composuit sacramentorum
egregium et non parvum volumen per membra quidem opportunitate officiorum et temporum
pro lectionum textu . . .* Gennadius, *Liber de Viris Illustribus*, cap. LXXIX (al. LXXX),
edit. Carl Albrecht Bernoulli. Leipzig, 1895.

[3] Sid. Apollin., *Epist.*, lib. IV, ii; *Pat. Lat.*, t. LVIII, col. 516. Mamertus is said to
have 'marked the lessons that should be read on the several feasts of the year'. An epitaph
to his memory was composed by Sidonius: *Hic sollemnibus annuis paravit—quae quo
tempore convenirent.*

76401

人;七

Ste. Marie aux Alyscamps, Arles

Ancient Sarcophagi and Chapel
of the fifth century. SS. Honoratus
and Geniès, Les Alyscamps, Arles

SS. Honoratus and Geniès,
Les Alyscamps, Arles. Founded
by St. Virgilius (588–606)

St. Jean de Moustier,
Arles. Convent dependent on
St. Caesarius

House of St. Columba, Kells,
Co. Meath

Round Tower, Glendalough,
Co. Wicklow

St. McDard's Island, Co. Galway

bat.[1] The *contestatiunculae*, referred to in the letter, were probably either prefaces or prayers of the Mass. The liturgical work of Sidonius, however, would seem to have been more extensive than incidental Masses or a *libellus missarum*, and it may well be that Gregory of Tours (*ob.* 594) compiled his sacramentary from this collection. Gregory relates how on one occasion Sidonius was invited to celebrate Mass *ad festivitatem basilicae monasterii* and, on arrival at the church, found that his *libellus missarum* had been stolen (*ablatoque sibi nequiter libello per quem sacrosancta solemnia agere consueverat*). Nothing daunted, however, Sidonius proceeded to offer the holy Sacrifice without a book, with the result that the faithful declared that they had witnessed a Mass celebrated by an angel.[2]

St. Hilary of Poitiers (*ob.* 366) has been accredited with the composition of a sacramentary, but the short existing fragment is rather a book of homilies or a work of spirituality.[3]

John the Precentor (*archicantor*), whom St. Benedict Biscop (*ob.* 690) had brought from Rome to teach chant and liturgy at Wearmouth and Jarrow, was astonished to find liturgical books attributed to Hilary, Martin, Germanus and Ambrose, although allowance must be made for exaggeration, as the English were anxious to maintain the excellence and antiquity of the Gallican liturgy.[4]

Roman formulas penetrated early into the Gallican rite, and, in addition to the Gelasian codices, there were a number of other texts, which can only be explained by the widespread diffusion of *libelli missarum*.

By the beginning of the 8th century, says Bourque, the Gelasian sacramentary was without a rival in Gaul, having succeeded in almost exterminating the traditional liturgy. The Gallican liturgy no longer existed in 700: some fragments of mixed texts survive, but it is impossible to reconstitute the original form.[5] It

---

[1] Sid. Apollin., *op. cit.*

[2] *Greg. Turon., Hist. Franc.*, lib. II, cap. XXII; *Pat. Lat.*, t. LXXI, cols. 217–8.

[3] Hil. Poit., *Pat. Lat.*, t. CXLII, cols. 1086–7.

[4] C. Silva-Tarouca, *Giovanni Archicantor; Atti della pontificia Accademia Romana di Archeologia, Memorie* I (1923), pp. 215–16.

[5] Bourque, *Etude sur les Sacramentaires Romains; Les Textes Primitifs* (Rome, 1948), chap. III, art. I, 2, p. 197.

I

is necessary to envisage more than a century of slow Roman infiltration, and to fix the 6th century as the date of the first arrival
of the Gelasian sacramentary in Gaul.[1] It would seem, however,
to be somewhat of an exaggeration to speak of the 'extermination'
of the Gallican liturgy at this early period. It is clear that, when
Pepin and Charlemagne demanded the universal adoption of the
Roman rite, liturgical usage in Gaul, although intermingled with
Gelasian formulas, was by no means identical with contemporary
Roman usage.

There is a single existing MS. which appears to be of a date
earlier than the latter part of the 7th century. The letters of
pseudo-Germanus are of an unknown date and authorship.

(1) *Lectionary of Wolfenbüttel.* A palimpsest of the 5th–6th
century, containing MS. 4160 Wissenburg 76 under a text of *De
Vita Contemplativa* of Julian Pomerius (master of St. Caesarius)
in uncials of the 7th century.[2] The document, as we find also in
the later Lectionary of Luxeuil, gives normally three lessons, with
pieces of chant corresponding to our gradual: originally known
as the 'psalm', as they were taken from the psalter. The texts, as
in most Gallican books, derive almost entirely from Scripture, but
arranged in the form of a mosaic, and a passage in the *ipsissima
verba* of the Bible is rare. The Vulgate has been mainly used,
although we find examples of more ancient versions.

The MS. has been thought to come from the Arles–Marseilles
district, largely colonised by Greeks, where Eastern usages lin-
gered long. A recent study, however, inclines to the view that
the lectionary came from the Church of Clermont Ferrand, rather
than from that of Arles.[3]

The text begins with Easter, and we read in the life of St.
Caesarius that still in the 6th century the Church of Arles followed the same order for the Paschal baptism and confirmation
as prescribed in the Apostolic Tradition of Hippolytus, which
had been abandoned almost everywhere else.

The lessons edited by Musaeus served as a model and proto-

---

[1] Bourque, *op. cit.*, p. 199.

[2] G. Morin, *Ephem. Liturg.*, January–March 1937, fasc. I, p. ii.

[3] Giovanni Berti, *Il più antico Lezionario della Chiesa*, *Ephem. Liturg.*, vol. LXVIII
(1954), fasc. II, pp. 147–54.

type for the codex, which gives chants both between and after the pericopes. Gennadius says expressly that Musaeus provided *responsoria Psalmorum capitula*, an ancient technical expression for what we call the gradual.

(2) *Reichenau Fragments or Masses of Mone.*[1] The second of these titles is due to the discovery of the 'fragments' in a palimpsest MS. by Francis Joseph Mone in 1850. The Masses, which appear to be of the late 7th century, were at one time in the possession of John II, bishop of Constance (760–81). Mone recovered the primitive text with observations and notes, as the text of the Masses had been erased in the 8th century, in order to make way for the Commentary of St. Jerome on St. Matthew. Fr. Lucas, who considers the fragments to be 'within the limits of the 5th century', says that they reveal a stage of liturgical development intermediate between the fixed formulas, beyond which the Eastern Churches never advanced, and the collects varying from day to day or from season to season of the ecclesiastical year, which are the common characteristics of the later Western sacramentaries, both Roman and Gallican. The Reichenau Masses, he considers, to be of a time when a departure from the fixed prayers of the primitive liturgy was customary, although only one or at the most two seem to be for use on any particular feast. The others are of that indeterminate character which marks the *Missae Cottidianae* of later liturgical books. We have, then, Fr. Lucas concludes, a witness to the relatively late development in Gaul of a liturgical system in harmony with the ecclesiastical calendar.[2] Wilmart believes that the original MS. once formed part of a small Gallican missal: one of those *libelli missarum* which were the earliest form of liturgical book. The text is purely Gallican in type, without any Roman interpolations. There are, however, but seven Masses, not eleven, as was originally supposed. Six of these are of the Sunday, while the seventh is for the feast of St. Germanus of Auxerre. The MS., which was probably written in Burgundy, shows considerable theological precision, especially in the *contestationes* or prefaces, and a strongly marked

[1] Carlsruhe 253. *Pat. Lat.*, t. CXXXVIII, cols. 863–82.
[2] H. Lucas, *Early Gallican Liturgy, Dublin Review*, July 1893, pp. 570–1.

local character is apparent. Two of these prefaces are provided for each Mass, and the celebrant may make his choice. One of the Masses, with the exception of the *Post pridie*, has been composed in hexameter verse: a feature which Baumstark considers to indicate Syrian influence.[1]

(3) *Peyron, Mai and Bunsen Fragments*.[2] These fragments consist of disjointed palimpsest leaves. Those of Mai and Peyron are preserved in the Ambrosian Library at Milan; while the Bunsen codex is found at St. Gall.

Peyron has what appears to be a Lenten *contestatio*, with other prayers of a Gallican type. Mai begins with a part of a bidding-prayer, and contains a fragment of a *contestatio* (under that title) and portions of other prayers: two of which have the title *Post Nomina*, while two others appear to be prayers *Ad pacem*. The Bunsen fragment has a part of a Mass for the dead (*Post Sanctus; Post pridie*), and several pairs of bidding-prayers and collects, the former bearing the title *Exhortatio* or *Exhortatio matutina*.

(4) *Missale Gothicum*.[3] The title of the codex dates from the 15th century, and Tommasi (1680) and Mabillon (1685) have attributed the MS. to the Narbonne district, which was at one time included in the Visigothic kingdom.[4] Duchesne [5] and Baumstark,[6] on the other hand, consider its provenance to be Autun, as Masses are found for St. Symphorian and St. Leger (Leodegarius), but, if it emanated from there, it is strange that there is no mention of St. Nazarius, the patron of the cathedral church, which was consecrated in 542. The editor of the missal produced by the Henry Bradshaw Society says: 'We seem to be driven to assign the compilation and the writing of the MS. to some place outside Autun which had received from that city the two *libelli missarum* for the feasts of St. Leger and St. Symphorian'.[7] He does not,

---

[1] Baumstark, *Liturgie Comparée* (Chevtogne, 1953), chap. IV, 2, p. 79.

[2] *Pat. Lat.*, t. LXXXVIII, cols. 883–4.

[3] *Missale Gothicum*, MS. *Vat. Regin.*, lat. 317. *Pat. Lat.* LXXII, cols. 325–58; *Henry Bradshaw Society*, vols. LII (1917), LIV (1919).

[4] *Nempe apud Septimanos vel Novempopulanos.* Mabillon, *De Lit. Gallic.*, p. 175—in which it is styled *seu Gothico-Gallicanum.*

[5] Duchesne, *op. cit.*, chap. V, II, 7, p. 151.

[6] Baumstark, *Lit. Rom. e Lit. dell'Esarcato*, cap. I, p. 34.

[7] H. M. Bannister, *Missale Gothicum*, vol. I (*H.B.S.*, vol. LII, 1917), p. lxii.

however, leave it at that, and Bannister suggests that the MS. came from the scriptorium of a house founded from Luxeuil, such as Besançon, Corbie or Murbach. Palaeological considerations have strengthened this view.[1] Dom Germain Morin has proposed an altogether novel provenance, and thinks that the codex came from some monastery dedicated to St. Gregory the Great near Münster in Alsace, in fact Gregorienmünster (Gregoriental).[2]

As to the date of the MS., 'if one were pressed to name any one quarter of a century it would be between 690 and 715, with a preference to the earlier rather than to the later part of that period'.[3]

The 'missal' appears to be a collection of *libelli* or *missae*, taken from different codices and from different districts, and then passed on from church to church. It has all the characteristics of the Merovingian epoch, and seems similar in many respects to the Lectionary of Luxeuil.[4] The Masses are numbered, and the MS. begins with Christmas Eve (III). There were two Advent Masses at one time, as we find in *Gallicanum Vetus*. A Mass for the neophytes is provided for each of the days in the octave of Easter. All the Masses are Gallican in respect to their order, but many of the prayers are Roman, and Mabillon over-emphasised the Gallican element (*'purus ordo gallicanus'*).[5] The formulas proper to the particular Mass, except on rare occasions, are not continued after the preface, although a proper preface is provided for each of the sixty-eight Masses. No more than thirteen feasts and the six Sunday Masses have complete formularies as far as the postcommunion.[6]

The last of the eighty-one numbered sections is the first prayer of the *Missa Cotidiana Romin(sis)*, with which the MS. breaks off.

(5) *Missale Gallicanum Vetus.*[7] *Missa Romana* was added to

---

[1] H. M. Bannister, *op. cit.*, p. lxv.
[2] Morin, *Rev. d'Hist. Ecclés.*, vol. XXXVII (1941), pp. 24–30.
[3] Bannister, *op. cit.*, p. l.
[4] *Lect. Lux.*, Paris, *Bibl. Nat.*, MS. lat. 9427.
[5] Mabillon, *De Lit. Gallic.* lib. III, *Pat. Lat.*, t. LXXII, cols. 217–18.
[6] Cf. *Communicantes* and *Quam oblationem* in the Roman rite. Bernard Capelle, *La Messe Gallicane de l'Assomption, Miscellanea Mohlberg*, vol. II (Rome, 1949), p. 47.
[7] *Missale Gallicanum Vetus*, MS. *Vat. Palat.* 493. *Pat. Lat.*, t. LXXII, cols. 339–82.

the title in the 17th or 18th century, possibly to distinguish it from the *Missale Gothicum*. It looks as if the two MSS. were copied immediately or remotely from a single exemplar, and many of the formulas are identical: both are mutilated, but one completes the other.[1] The 'missal', which is approximately of the same date as the *Missale Gothicum*, begins with a Mass for St. Germanus of Auxerre (9 October), from which Baumstark and others have considered the place of origin to be Auxerre.[2] This Mass is followed by prayers for the blessing of virgins and widows, and Masses for Advent (two), Christmas Eve and Christmas (midnight). Then come the *Expositio* and *Traditio Symboli*, presentation of the Gospel (*In aurium apertione*) and other ceremonies preparatory to Baptism; finally, the Masses for the Sundays after Easter until the Rogation Mass, after which the MS. breaks off. A prayer for Good Friday well exemplifies the rhetoric of antiquity, of which Gaul was one of the last homes in the West: *O salutaris hora passionis! O magna maximarum gratiarum! Nona hodierna maxima horarum hora. Hanc nunc tu, noster dilecte sponse, osculare de cruce, licet post crucis trophaeum. Osculare precamur; salutare tuum impertire nobis; triumphator mirabilis, auriga supreme, Deus pie, gloriosissime propugnator.*[3] Baumstark suggests that the prayer reveals something Germanic in its profundity and Celtic in its spontaneity; while there is possibly also an affinity to that strong Syrian element which existed among the population of Merovingian Gaul.[4]

(6) The *Missale Francorum*,[5] which most writers collate with the *Gothicum* and the *Gallicanum Vetus*, although dating from about the same period, has considerably more extensive Roman elements. Duchesne, in fact, classed it among the Roman documents akin to the Gelasian sacramentary.[6]

Little more than a fragment remains, comprising the ordinary of the Mass, blessing of virgins and widows, consecration of an

---

[1] *Unde colligere licet, has orationes fuisse communes, non loci alicujus peculiaris, ad quem haec missalia pertinuerint.* Mabillon, *De Lit. Gallic.*, p. 376, n. a.

[2] Baumstark, *Lit. Rom. e Lit. dell'Esarcato*, cap. I, p. 34.

[3] *Pat. Lat.*, t. LXXII, col. 361.

[4] Baumstark, *Lit. Comp.*, chap. I, pp. 4–5.

[5] *Missal. Franc., Vat. Regin. Chris.*, MS. lat. 257; *Pat. Lat.*, t. LXXII, cols. 317–40.

[6] Duchesne, *op. cit.*, chap. V, 3, p. 134.

altar [1] and eleven Masses with the *canon actionis* as far as the *Nobis quoque*.

The provenance of the MS. has been much disputed: Liège, Paris and Burgundy have all been suggested by liturgists; while Dom Cabrol and Luigi Barin consider Poitiers to have been its place of origin.[2]

Vestiges of Gallican terminology appear in the rubrics, but all the Masses are of the Roman type. The first Mass is *pro regibus*, the second of St. Hilary; while the remainder comprise the common of saints and 'other intentions'. Allusions to the Roman Empire have been changed to *Regnum Francorum*.

(7) The Missal of Bobbio [3] was discovered in the monastery of that name by Mabillon, who subsequently edited it.[4]

The MS. was at first considered to date from the 7th century, but, on palaeographic grounds, it is now assigned to the first half of the following century.[5]

The question of provenance has been hotly debated, and by no means satisfactorily determined. Edmund Bishop is persuaded that the MS. was written in Upper Italy in the neighbourhood of Bobbio in the 7th century, and that it was principally the work of the Irish: 'I am disposed to say that in the Bobbio missal we have an example of the kind of book in vogue in the second age of the Irish saints', that is in the time of St. Columba (*ob.* 597).[6] The canon (*missa romensis cottidiana*) [7] is practically identical with that of the Missal of Stowe, and, 'allowing therefore for variations arising from local causes, it is evident that the compilers of the Bobbio and Stowe missals copied from

---

[1] There is no reference to relics. 'It can hardly be denied that some churches in Gaul, spoken of by St. Gregory (Tours), were consecrated without the inclusion of relics'. Wickham Legg, *Three Chapters in Recent Liturgical Research* (London, 1903), III, p. 61.

[2] Barin, *Storia del Messale Romano* (Rovigo, 1920), tit. II, cap. III, p. 113.

[3] *Missal of Bobbio*, Paris, *Bibl. Nat.*, MS. lat. 13246; *Pat. Lat.*, t. LXXII, cols. 447–580; *Henry Bradshaw Society*, vols. LIII (1917), LXI (1924).

[4] Mabillon, *Musaeum Italicum*, t. I.

[5] E. A. Lowe, 'The Paleography of the Bobbio Missal, The Bobbio Missal, Notes and Studies' (*H.B.S.*, vol. LXI, 1924), p. 98.

[6] Bishop, *Liturg. Hist.* (Oxford, 1918), III, p. 58, n. 3; *Book of Cerne*, p. 239, n.

[7] A similar title is found before the collect (*Deus qui culpa offenderis*) at the very end of the *Missale Gothicum*, and it occurs also in the Missal of Stowe and the Gregorian sacramentary.

the same source, which was current in the early years of the 7th century'.[1]

On the other hand, the character of the handwriting is by no means Irish, and there is a complete absence throughout of any Irish saints. Bishop, however, continues: 'Spanish forms lay behind the most interesting and characteristic features of the Bobbio missal',[2] which again points to Irish origin.[3] 'Spanish symptoms' for Dom Morin suggest south-west France in the district of Narbonne by way of provenance. A region which, from the 5th to the 8th century, was under Visigothic rule.[4]

Dom André Wilmart describes the missal as *une capricieuse compilation faite aux environs de Bobbio pour les besoins d'une colonie de Scots émigrés*.[5]

Earlier liturgists, like Neale and Forbes, think that the missal originated from Besançon, as a Mass of St. Sigismund (1 May) has been provided. They have therefore styled the book *Missale Vesontionense*.[6]

The missal, which contains sixty-two Masses, is divided into three parts: Masses of the temporal from Advent to Pentecost, Masses of saints and votives (four), and Sunday Masses (seven) and requiems. Roman and Gallican elements have been strangely intermingled.

The codex is a missal rather than a sacramentary, and includes the epistles and gospels. It is probably the most ancient example of its kind extant.

The MS. begins with a 'Mass to be said daily', which has lessons and prayers for use on days when no other Mass is prescribed.

The prayers are for the most part Gallican in plan until the preface, with Roman formulas for the canon, communion and thanksgiving, which have been taken from the *Missa romanensis cottidiana*.[7] Seventy-six prefaces are provided for the sixty-two

---

[1] 'Belonging to the Irish family'. Bishop, *Book of Cerne*, p. 229. Cf. *Liturg. Hist.*, pp. 90–1.

[2] Bishop., *Liturg. Hist.*, VII, p. 163, note b.

[3] *Ibid.*, VIII, 4, p. 179.

[4] Morin, *Rev. bénéd.*, vol. XXXI (1914), p. 332.

[5] Wilmart, *St Ambroise et la Légende Dorée, Ephem. Liturg.* (1936), p. 202.

[6] Sigismund, king of the Burgundians, was defeated and murdered by Chlodomir in 523.   [7] *Missa romanensis cottidiana* is Gallican until the preface.

Masses. Some of these *contestationes* are paraphrases of the sermons of St. Augustine, St. Maximus and St. Ambrose.

Gallican terms appear frequently in the missal, as, for example, *collectio post nomina, collectio ad pacem, contestatio, benedictio turris*. The terms *contestatio* and *praefatio* jostle each other in a curious manner, and here and there we find a Gallican rubric [1] with Roman prayers, and vice versa. The ordinary and canon of the Mass have been taken from the Roman liturgy. The phrase *quam tibi offerimus in honorem nominis tui Deus* has been inserted after the words *cunctae familiae tuae*, and the *Communicantes* includes the names of Hilary, Martin, Ambrose, Augustine, Gregory, Jerome and Benedict.[2]

The Mass *In Symboli traditione* gives the *Expositio* and *Traditio Symboli*; Mass for Holy Thursday is followed by the Good Friday *Lectio Passionis*; while that of Holy Saturday is preceded by the *preces* and intercessory *orationes*, similar to those we find on Good Friday.

The candle is blessed during the *Exsultet*. Rogation days are marked by *legenda* and a *missa in letaniis*. Pentecost is styled: *in Quinquaginsimo*. Proper Masses have been provided for St. Michael, St. Stephen, St. James, St. John, St. John Baptist, SS. Peter and Paul and St. Martin.

(8) *So-called Letters of St. Germanus of Paris*.[3] This is a most important document, as it is the only one from which we are able to reconstruct the *Ordo Gallicanus*.[4] The first of the two letters bears the title: 'Germane, bishop of Paris, has written about the Mass', but, as Dom Wilmart says, it could not have been written before the end of the 7th century, whereas Germanus was bishop of Paris from 555 to 576.[5] Mgr. Batifol, on the other hand, believes the writer to have been at least someone of the same period, who came from a milieu in which just such a liturgy was in use.[6]

---

[1] e.g. *Post prophetiam.*
[2] Mabillon, *Mus. Ital.*, I, p. 207.
[3] Pseudo-Germ., Autun, *Bibl. municip.*, MS. 184; *Pat. Lat.*, t. LXXII, cols. 83–98.
[4] Duchesne, *op. cit.*, chap. VII, pp. 189–227.
[5] A. Wilmart, *Germain de Paris (Lettres attribuées à Saint), Dict. d'Archéol. Chrét. et de Lit.*, t. VI, part I, col. 1102.
[6] Batifol, *Etudes de Liturgie et d'Archéologie Chrétienne* (Paris, 1919), chap. VIII, p. 251.

He thinks it possible that the appeal to tradition in the short prologue refers to a time when the Roman rite was threatening to supplant the Gallican, but when the authority of the old liturgy was still able to carry some weight.[1]

The conclusion of Edmund Bishop would seem, however, to be the most probable: the document is a production of the 7th century or even, it may be, of the early 8th century.[2]

This *Expositio antiquae liturgiae gallicanae*, as it is called, is an anonymous treatise in the form of two letters, containing certain mystical interpretations of the Mass and other services, which throws considerable light on the Gallican liturgy, as it was performed at this period at Autun or some other Burgundian church.

The MS. was discovered at Autun by Mabillon, and edited by Martène and Durand in the fifth volume of the *Thesaurus novus anecdotorum* (1717).[3]

(9) *Benedictional of Autun-Freising.* This codex of the 8th–9th century is a curious type of Gallican book, containing formulas for the blessing given by the priest before Communion. The first part of the MS., which may date from the 7th century, shows traces of having come from Autun, and is related to the *Missale Gothicum*. Then the MS. appears to have been taken to Freising, no one knows how, where it received considerable additions, and an attempt was made to coalesce the Gallican usages with the Roman rite.

Some of the blessings in the codex are uncommon, particularly those for the consecration of a king and the anointing of hands.

The document is completed by a benedictional now in the Fitzwilliam Museum, Cambridge, in which we find similar blessings.[4]

(10) *Lectionary of Luxeuil.*[5] This *antiquissimum lectionarium Gallicanum* was discovered by Mabillon at Luxeuil in 1683. Its origin has been disputed. Duchesne and Morin consider that the

---

[1] Batifol, *op. cit.*, chap. VIII, p. 251.

[2] Bishop, *Liturg. Hist.*, chap. VI, p. 131, n. 1.

[3] Cf. Martène, *De antiq. Eccles. rit.*: *Pat. Lat.*, t. LXXII, cols. 83–98.

[4] Morin, *Rev. bénéd.* (1912), t. XXXIX, pp. 168 seq.; Leclercq, *Gallicane (liturgie)*, *D.A.C.L.*, t. VI, part I, cols. 497–504.

[5] *Lect. Lux.*, Paris, *Bibl. Nat.*, MS. lat. 9427. *Pat. Lat.*, t. LXXII, cols. 171 seq.

names of Geneviève (3 January) and Julian (6 January) in the very
limited calendar are a sufficient guarantee of its Parisian origin,
and the codex is in general agreement with the pericopes of a 7th-
century MS. from St. Denis.[1] Masai goes one step further, and
fixes the house of its origin at Morigny near Etampes, where in
the early Middle Ages there was a house of nuns under the patron-
age of St. Julian: *L'exclusivité jalouse du culte de Geneviève ne peut
convenir qu'au Pagus Parisiensis.*[2] The existence of a convent at
Morigny in Merovingian times is, however, very doubtful, and
the claim of St. Julian to be its patron rests on a discovery of his
alleged relics in 1648.[3] A similarity between the Luxeuil codex
and MSS. 600 and 403 of Lyons have led Dom Célestin Charlier
to consider the provenance to have been south-east France, and
more especially the region of Autun.[4]

Abbé Philippeau agrees that the MS. originated from Luxeuil,
but says that it was written for the parish church, although transcribed in the monastic scriptorium.[5] It is, however, unlikely that
there was a church for externs at Luxeuil before the end of the 8th
century, and, as we shall see, there can be little doubt that the
lectionary was written either for a bishop or for some cathedral
church.

Other contemporary Gallican books have no pontifical, and
the codex under consideration is the only one to have as complete a series. The inclusion of Masses which require the participa-
tion of a bishop show that the MS. was intended for his use: *in
natale episcopi, in natale episcoporum, in depositione episcopi, in
dedicatione, in natale ecclesiae, in velatione virginum, quando episcopi
praedicare debent ut plebs decimos reddat, quando diaconus ordinatur,
quando presbyteri benedicentur.*

Dom Pierre Salmon, with every appearance of accuracy, has
attributed the MS. to the Church or bishop of Langres, not only
on account of its proximity to Luxeuil, but also because a series

---

[1] Duchesne, *op. cit.*, chap. V, p. 155. Morin, *Rev. bénéd.* (1893), p. 438.
[2] Masai, *Scriptorium*, II, p. 37.
[3] Cottineau says that Morigny was an abbey of Benedictine monks, dedicated to the
Holy Trinity. *Répertoire . . . des Abbayes et Prieurés*, vol. II, col. 1984.
[4] Charlier, *Note sur les Origines de l'écriture dite de Luxeuil*, *Rev. bénéd.* (1948), p. 149.
[5] Philippeau, *Rev. du Moyen Age Latin* (1946), p. 183.

of comparisons makes such a hypothesis possible. He considers further that it was written in one of the many abbeys which admitted Columbanian usages, although there is no evidence of any Irish influence respecting the date of Easter, and the Paschal computation is that of the Gallican churches at the end of the 7th century.[1] If, as is supposed, the lectionary remained in use until the 10th century, the Church for which it was written would have retained its peculiarities and ancient texts longer than other churches.[2]

The lectionary is wholly Gallican, without any apparent Roman influence, but Fr. Radó suggests that internal evidence points to connections with an Eastern lectionary.[3]

The book contains one hundred and eighty-eight lessons, from Christmas Eve onwards, including eight which have been borrowed from a passional and homily-book. The lessons of certain proper Masses are found at the end. Each of the days is provided with three lessons.

In conclusion, we may say that the lectionary throws light on a liturgy celebrated in a country which was still largely barbarian.

(11) *Lectionaries of Schlettstadt and Würzburg.* The MSS. were discovered by Dom Morin.

The lectionary of Schlettstadt is Merovingian in origin, but the MS. comprises no more than the prophetical lessons. The Lectionary of Würzburg has been ascribed recently to Claudian Mamertus (*c.* 470), but there seems little doubt that it is fundamentally Roman, as may be seen from the six lessons for the *Natale Papae*.[4]

A letter from St. Lupus, bishop of Troyes (*ob.* 478), and St. Euphronius, bishop of Autun, to Talasius, bishop of Angers, says that the lessons of the Vigil of the Nativity should be observed in a different way from those of the Vigil of Easter. Talasius would seem to have sent a memorandum on the subject to the bishops.[5]

A letter of Hildwin, abbot of St. Denis, to King Louis the

---

[1] Salmon, *Le Lectionnaire de Luxeuil et ses Attaches Columbaniennes, Mélanges Colombaniens* (Paris, 1951), p. 254.

[2] *Ibid.,* pp. 248–9. [3] Radó, *Ephem. Liturg.* (1931), pp. 8, 100.

[4] Righetti, *op. cit.,* vol. III (1949), sect. 2, cap. II, p. 194.

[5] *Pat. Lat.,* t. LXVI, cols. 66–8.

Pious, written in 835, is extant, in which he speaks of the deplorable condition of the codices of the now superseded Gallican Mass: *In quibus voluminibus habentur duae missae quae sic inter celebrandum ad provocandam divinae miserationis clementiam, et corda populi ad devotionis studium excitanda tormenta martyris sociorumque ejus succincte commemorant, sicut et reliquiae missae, ibidem scriptae aliorumque apostolorum, vel martyrum, quorum passiones habentur notissimae, decantant.*[1]

LITURGICAL YEAR

The Gallican calendar has varied at different times and in different places. The Hieronymian martyrology shows a considerable assimilation to Roman usage.

St. Gregory of Tours (*ob.* 594), in a chapter of his *History of the Franks* entitled *De vigiliis*, gives a list of the feasts observed in Tours, together with the stational churches: Christmas, Epiphany, Easter, Ascension, Quinquagesima [2] or Pentecost, SS. Peter and Paul, St. Symphorian, St. Lidorius, St. Martin, St. Britius and St. Hilary.[3] Of the last four, only St. Martin was observed as a feast everywhere in Gaul.

The calendar appears to have been edited by the bishop Perpetuus (461–91).

De vigiliis is followed by *De jejuniis*: a register of the days of fasting.[3]

Advent

The key-day for Advent Sunday was fixed by the first council of Mâcon (581) for the feast of St. Martin (11 November), so that, as in the Ambrosian and Mozarabic liturgies, we find six Sundays in Advent. The *Gallicanum Vetus* provides two Sunday Masses. An alleged work of St. Hilary of Poitiers (*ob. c.* 368), quoted by Migne and ascribed to Berno of Reichenau (*ob.* 1048), gives Advent no more than three Sundays: *tres tantum hebdomadae in adventu Domini.*[4] It is, however, impossible to attribute a three

[1] *Mon. Germ., Epist. Carol. aevi*, t. III, p. 330; *Pat. Lat.*, t. CVI, col. 13.
[2] Pentecost is termed 'Quinquagesima' in the council of Orleans.
[3] *Greg. Turon., Hist. Franc.*, lib. X, cap. XXXI; *Pat. Lat.*, t. LXXI, cols. 566–7
[4] *Pat. Lat.*, t. CXLII, col. 1053.

weeks' Advent either to St. Hilary or to the 4th century. The book must be either spurious or a *libellus officiorum* of some church dedicated to St. Hilary.

Christmas to Lent

For some unaccountable reason, it was a general belief of the time that our Lord was born on a Wednesday, and St. Gregory of Tours tells us that St. Radegunde was accustomed to carry out important undertakings on this day.[1] It was indeed on Wednesday, 13 August 587 that she died.

Christmas Eve is given as the beginning of the year in the Lectionary of Luxeuil and the *Missale Gothicum*, whereas the more primitive Lectionary of Wolfenbüttel (5th–6th century) has Easter Eve, as in the Eastern liturgy.

St. James and St. John are commemorated together on 27 December, as we find in the Celtic Felire of Oengus (*Leabhar Breac*).

A passage in the *Post secreta* for the Mass of the Circumcision in the *Gothicum* is reminiscent of the Roman canon: *Per quem omnia creas.*[2]

A Sunday after the Circumcision and two Sundays after Epiphany are given in the Lectionary of Luxeuil.

The Baptism of Christ as the chief commemoration of the Epiphany is suggestive of Eastern origin.[3]

Cassian (*ob. c.* 435) attests the custom on the feast of the Epiphany of announcing the date of Easter, and reminds us that 'ancient tradition' (Nicea, 325) has appointed the patriarch of Alexandria to make the necessary annual computation: *Intra Aegypti regionem, mos iste antiqua traditione servatur, ut peracta Epiphaniorum die . . . epistolae pontificis Alexandrini per universas Aegypti ecclesias dirigantur, quibus initium quadragesimae et dies Paschae non solum per civitates, sed etiam per universa monasteria designantur.*[4] Cathedral churches were reminded of their obligation to make this announcement in at least two 6th-century coun-

---

[1] *Greg. Turon., Hist. Franc.*, lib. IX, cap. II.
[2] *Missal. Goth., Henry Bradshaw Society*, vol. LII (1919), p. 19.
[3] Morin, *Ephem. Liturg.*, January–March 1937, p. 8, n. ii.
[4] Cassian, *Collat.*, X, 2.

cils: IV Orleans (can. 1, 541) and Auxerre (can. 2, 578). Spain in the 5th century made it at Christmas rather than the Epiphany.[1]

Lent and Holy Week

It is interesting to note that the lessons appointed for the beginning of Lent and Good Friday in the Luxeuil codex are identical with those read at the same season in the East Syrian rite. The Lenten text, moreover, is similar to the Talmud (Treatise *Maghillâ* 31a) at the Jewish feast of the Atonement.[2]

The *Missale Gothicum* provides five Lenten Masses and a Mass *In Symboli Traditione* which is not found in any Roman sacramentary.[3] The *Expositio* and *Traditio Symboli* are in the *Gothicum* and, at length, in the *Gallicanum Vetus*. The *Expositio* or *Explanatio* appears in all three Gallican MSS.

Gaul in the 7th and 8th centuries had retained this feature, which had long since been abandoned by Rome.[4] The four gospels and the Lord's prayer were given to the *competentes*, with a short commentary on each, as we learn from the *Gallicanum Vetus*.[5] The duty of directing the catechumens to repeat the sacred formulas devolved upon the *primicerius*: a dignitary still existing in Gaul in the 9th century.[6] The office is found in Pannonia in the 3rd century, as we learn from the Acts of St. Pollio (*ob.* 304).[7] It appears also at Rheims in the time of St. Remigius [8] (*ob. c.* 533), and in an inscription at Lyons dated 555.[9] Is it possible that Rome had suppressed the office? Gaul, as we know, had in the first place received her faith and hierarchy from the Apostolic See. The title of *primicerius* was instituted for a capitular dignity at Milan by the archbishop, Francesco Piccolpasso, in 1440.

The ancient Gallican books make no mention of scrutinies: the *Gallicanum Vetus* alone, under the title of *Praemissiones ad scruta-*

[1] *Lib. Ord.*, edit. Férotin (1904), pp. 527–8.
[2] *Isa.* LVIII; LII, 13–LIII, 12. Baumstark, *Lit. Comp.*, chap. VII, 2, p. 142.
[3] *Missal. Goth. Henry Bradshaw Society*, vol. LII (1919), pp. 50–62.
[4] De Puniet, *Lit. Bapt. en Gaule avant Charlemagne*, pp. 9–10.
[5] *Gallic. Vet.*, *Pat. Lat.*, t. LXXII, cols. 348–54.
[6] Amalar., *De eccles. Offic.*
[7] *AA. SS.*, April, t. III (3rd edit.), col. 572d.
[8] Remig., *Epist.* IV; *Pat. Lat.*, t. LXV, col. 969.
[9] Edmund Le Blant, *Inscrip. Chrét. de la Gaule*, t. I, p. 142.

men, contains two prayers, which are to be said at the delivery of the Gospel and the Lord's Prayer. The scrutinies make their appearance where the Gelasian sacramentary is in use, but they were a recent Roman importation. Primitive Gallican usage is in agreement with the pre-Gelasian Church, that is with the usage that preceded the organisation of the scrutinies.[1]

The ceremony of the *Traditio Symboli* originally took place on Palm Sunday in both Gaul and Milan, but it was later transferred to the preceding Saturday. The Baptism of Clovis (496) seems to have taken place on an extra liturgical day, and without any of the ceremonies of the catechumenate, with the exception of the *Traditio Symboli*. The scene has been described by Gregory of Tours (*ob.* 594). The Creed presented to the Frankish king contained the clause: *Deum verum factorem coeli et terrae crederet*. De Puniet suggests that this slight variation may have been customary in the Church of Rheims, and adopted under the influence of Irenaeus, who several times in his works uses the word *factorem*.[3] In any case, it was not a corruption of *creatorem*.[4] The Baptism itself admitted almost all the customary rites. Gregory, in describing the ceremony, says: 'The basilica was adorned with coloured hangings and dazzlingly white veils. The baptistery had been prepared for the function: the chrism lavishly applied, the lighted candles emitting a pleasant smell; while the interior of the basilica was filled with a perfume reminiscent of heaven.'[5]

The ceremony of the *Traditio Symboli*, as we learn from pseudo-Germanus[6] and Venantius Fortunatus,[7] was originally combined with the consecration of the chrism. The day for the chrism, however, seems to have been changed to the generally accepted day—Holy Thursday—about the end of the 7th century. The consecration of the chrism in the *Missa in traditione Symboli* is not found in any of the Gallican sacramentaries, and St. Eloi,

---

[1] De Puniet, *op. cit.*, p. 14.
[2] *Greg. Turon., Hist. Franc.*, lib. II, cap. XXXI. *Pat. Lat.*, t. LXXI, cols. 226–7.
[3] Iren., *Adv. Haereses*, I, cap. XVI; III, cap. III. *Pat. Graec.*, t. VII, cols. 635, 850.
[4] De Puniet, *op. cit.*, pp. 8–9.
[5] *Greg. Turon., Hist. Franc.*, lib. II, cap. XXXI. *Pat. Lat.*, t. LXXI, col. 226.
[6] Pseudo-Germ., *Epist.* II; *Pat. Lat.*, t. LXXII, cols. 96–7.
[7] Ven. Fortun., *Miscell.*, lib. I, cap. IX (*In laudem chrismatis*), 4 seq. *Pat. Lat.*, t. LXXXVIII, col. 97 and n.

bishop of Noyon (*ob.* 660), says in his homily *in Coena Domini* (IX) that, throughout the whole world, the ceremony takes place on Holy Thursday.[1]

Palm Sunday is already found in the Lectionary of Luxeuil.

The first three days of Holy Week were styled *Authentica Hebdomada*, as is still the practice in the Ambrosian rite.

Holy Thursday was known as *Natale Calicis* in South Gaul in the 6th and 7th century.[2]

The *Gothicum* and the *Gallicanum Vetus* both devote a large space to the liturgies of Good Friday and Holy Saturday. The days were termed *Biduana*: a relic of the time when the Lenten fast was restricted to these two days.[3]

Opus ad Baptizando (*sic*) in *Gallicanum Vetus* is preceded by the offices for the *Triduum Sacrum*. The ceremonies, however, which in the two codices are intermingled with the baptismal service, are not very characteristic.

The couplets of invitatory and prayer, such as we find in the Roman liturgy on Good Friday, are found, with verbal variations, in the *Gallicanum*, and both MSS. have prayers similar to those in the hours for the day.

The Blessing of the Fire on Holy Saturday is absent from both *Gothicum* and *Gallicanum*. There is, however, the Blessing of the Candle, which begins with the *praefatio antequam excorcidietur* and a collect.[4] The exorcism and blessing of the font follow: with the infusion of the chrism in tracing three crosses. The *Exsultet* is similar to that of the Roman rite,[5] with a general prayer for the clergy and faithful, and one for the bishop: *Praecamur ergo, Domine, ut nos famulos et famulas tuas omnem clerum et devotissimum populum una cum patre nostro beatissimo illo.*[6] A *collectio post benedictionem cerei* and a *collectio hymnum cerei* follow.

---

[1] Eloi, *Homil.* IX *in Coena Domini: Homil.* VIII. *Pat. Lat.*, t. LXXXVII, cols. 623, 629.

[2] Avitus of Vienne (*ob.* 518), *Pat. Lat.*, t. LIX, cols. 302, 308, 321; Eloi of Noyon (*ob.* 656?), *Hom.* X, *Pat. Lat.*, LXXXVII, col. 628.

[3] *Incipiunt orationes in biduana. Missal. Goth.*, fo. 148b. *Henry Bradshaw Society*, vol. LII, p. 64. Cf. Baumstark, *Lit. Comp.*, chap. X, 2, pp. 215–16.

[4] *Gallicanum Vetus, Pat Lat.*, t. LXXII, col. 363.

[5] Our actual formula is found in a 7th-century Gallican sacramentary.

[6] *Missal. Goth., Henry Bradshaw Society*, vol. LII, p. 69.

K

Easter

The Gallican Church, unlike that of the Celts, had adopted the
Paschal computation of Victorius of Aquitaine (457), but, when
Rome received the cycle of Dionysius Exiguus in 525, Gaul
continued to follow Victorius.

It is interesting to note that the lessons appointed to be read on
Easter Sunday were very similar to those in the lectionary of the
Jacobite patriarch Anastasius V.[1]

Low Sunday is termed *Quasimodo* in the Lectionary of Wolfenbüttel, and *Clausum Paschae* in that of Luxeuil and the *Missale
Gothicum*.

There were five Sundays after Easter.

Rogation Days

Sidonius Apollinaris says that his friend Mamertus, bishop of
Vienne (*ob.* 474), 'invented, introduced and established' the
'solemnity of the Rogations' at a time of public adversity, but he
adds that rogations for the weather had been observed in the
diocese before his time. These, however, were only attended in
an off-hand sort of way—*vagae, tepentes, infrequentes . . . oscita-
bundae supplicationes*. Sidonius introduces a humorous touch in
describing the original celebration, which, he says, had 'often been
interrupted for refreshment'. The prayers were for the most part
intercessions for either 'rain or fine weather, so the potter and the
gardener could never decorously attend together'. Mamertus
fixed and regularised them in an observance of prayer and fasting,
singing of psalms and shedding tears of compunction.[2]

We learn from Avitus, the successor of Mamertus (*c.* 494–517),
that the observance of the Rogations spread from Vienne to
other churches, although celebrated on other days. St. Caesarius
of Arles (*ob.* 543), in two homilies for the Rogations, says much
the same as Sidonius Apollinaris and Avitus.[3] There is, however,
no indication that litanies, as we know them, were at first sung on

---

[1] Baumstark, *Lit. Comp.*, chap. VII, 2, p. 142.
[2] Sidon. Apollin., *Epist.* V, 14. Cf. *Epist.* VII, i.
[3] Caesar. Arel., *Pat. Lat.*, t. XXXIX, cols. 2076–9.

these three days at all.[1] The substance of the devotion was rather the chanting of psalms, with, perhaps, prayers or collects. The whole question of the Rogations has been examined by Edmund Bishop in an article on the *Kyrie eleison*.[2]

Holy Cross

The cult of the Holy Cross received a great impetus in Frankish Gaul after the reception of the relics at Poitiers in 568 or 569.

Six Sunday Masses are provided in the *Missale Gothicum*.

Assumption of the Blessed Virgin

The Gallican Church observed the feast of the Assumption two days after the Petrine commemoration in January, that is on 18 January: *Adsumptio S. Mariae*.[3] It would seem to have been originally celebrated as a festival of the Divine Maternity (*Maria Theotokos*),[4] probably borrowed from Syria, where, at the beginning of the 6th century, we find it attested by two homilies of Severus of Antioch (Μνήμη τῆς ἁγιάς θεοτόκου καὶ ἀειπαρθένου Μαρίας). A similar commemoration is found in the Syrian Jacobite calendars on 15 January.

The Bobbio missal gives two Masses of 'Our Lady in January'. The formulas of one Mass—*In S. Mariae solemnitate*—treat exclusively of the Divine Maternity.

The second Mass—*In adsumptione S. Mariae*—has the Byzantine gospel of Martha and Mary.

The Assumption is styled *Festum Sanctae Mariae* in the Lectionary of Luxeuil, and supplied with lessons.[5]

A relic of the old Gallican commemoration is found in a 9th-century antiphoner of Senlis on 19 January: *Natale Sanctae Mariae*. The title *Adsumptio S. Mariae* is given in a gospel-book of St. Denis (7th century) and also in the Calendar of St. Willibrord, which is approximately of the same date as the *Missale*

---

[1] The term 'litanies' that we find in a canon of the council of Orleans (511) may well imply no more than penitential supplications.

[2] Bishop, *Liturg. Histor.*, *Kyrie eleison*, VI, pp. 128–9.

[3] *Mediante mense undecimo celebratur.* Greg. Turon., *Glor. Mart.*, lib. I, cap. IX; *Pat. Lat.*, t. LXXI, col. 713.

[4] *Lect. Lux.; Pat. Lat.*, t. LXXII, col. 180.

[5] Morin, *Ephem. Liturg.*, January–March 1937, p. 7, n. 9.

Gothicum. Traces of the *Gothicum* Mass are contained in a responsorial of Compiègne (probably 860–80).

The Mass of the Assumption in the *Missale Gothicum* is one of the most important Western Mariological documents.[1]

The *contestatio* seems to have been inspired by a sermon (IX) that was at one time ascribed to St. Ildefonsus of Toledo (*ob.* 667).[2] Abbot Capelle, however, who has made a special study of this Mass, discounts any such borrowing, and maintains that they are mutually independent.[3] The formularies in the *Gothicum* proper to the Assumption originally went as far as the preface, but, with the increasing importance of the feast, the texts of the rest of the Mass were completed by the end of the 7th century. Curiously enough, however, the compiler of these formularies never took the trouble to compose new texts, but borrowed from existing ones which had little or no reference to the Assumption. The *Benedictio populi*, for example, although Marial in character, treats exclusively of the Divine Maternity, which seems to suggest that the additions were taken from an earlier Mass: *Festivitas sanctae Mariae.*[4] The most ancient attestation of the corporal Assumption of the Blessed Virgin, apart from apocryphal and legendary literature, is found in the *collectio post nomina* of this Mass: *Illuc defuncti liberentur a Tartaro quo Beatae Virginis translatum est corpus de sepulchro.*[5] There is little doubt that the *Gothicum* was influenced by the *Transitus Mariae* in the version known as Pseudo-Melito. Gaul showed a confidence towards the apocryphal writings which Rome never had.

The most ancient representation of the Assumption known in the West, dating from the end of the 6th or the beginning of the 7th century, is found in the cathedral church of Sens: a piece of linen in which relics were at one time wrapped, which bears a representation of the Blessed Virgin being taken up to heaven, accompanied by two angels and in the presence of the Apostles.

---

[1] *Missal. Goth.*, fols. 73b–85a. *Henry Bradshaw Society*, vol. LII (1917), pp. 30–4.

[2] *Pat. Lat.*, t. XCVI, col. 272. Cf. Bishop. *Liturg. Histor.*, chap. VIII, 3, pp. 177–8.

[3] Capelle, *La Messe Gallicane de l'Assomption, Miscellanea Mohlberg*, vol. II (Rome, 1949), pp. 51–5.

[4] *Ibid.*, pp. 48–51.

[5] *Missal. Goth.*, fols. 76a–76b. *H.B.S.*, vol. LII (1917), p. 31.

An inscription in debased Latin says: *Con transisset Maria Mater Domino de Apostolis.*[1]

The *contestatio* of the *Gothicum* Mass, which is perhaps its most interesting feature, appears also, in a shorter form, in the Bobbio missal.[2] Dom Germain Morin has drawn attention to the almost unique reference in this prayer to the Nativity of the Virgin: *Cujus sicut gratulati sumus ortu, tripudiavimus partu, ita glorificamur in transitu. Parum fortasse fuerat, si te Christus solo sanctificasset introitu, nisi etiam talem matrem adornasset egressu.*[3] It would seem, says Dom Morin, to have been borrowed from a Church which observed the feast of the Nativity: a commemoration unknown at that time in Gaul. The Gallican milieu which received the feast in about the end of the 7th century was under strong Roman influence.

The feast is found on 9 September in the Calendar of St. Willibrord, who was consecrated bishop by Pope Sergius in 695, but he would seem to have been one of the first to have adopted it. Apart from this Ecternach document, there is no trace of the observance of the feast in Gaul until the appearance of the Gelasian sacramentary in the 8th century.

The refusal on the part of the Gallican Church to celebrate the feast of the Nativity seems to have been intentional, unless it had been admitted and then speedily dropped. The Bobbio missal, which is closely related to the *Gothicum*, has the same *contestatio* for the Mass of the Assumption in January, although only in part, and the editor has suppressed the reference to the Nativity.

The scribe of the *Gallicanum Vetus* ignores both the Assumption and the Nativity. The omissions may have been either an instinctive dislike of innovations of the kind or an antipathy to apocryphal origins. The *Transitus Mariae* certainly had a marked influence on the observance of the feast of the Assumption.

A festival of the *Nativity of the Virgin* would seem to have been condemned in a sermon attributed to St. Augustine, which until quite recently was recited in monastic choirs on 24 June. The

---

[1] Mâle, *op. cit.*, chap. VI, 5, pp. 210–11.

[2] Mabillon, *Liturg. Gall.*, p. 212; *Pat. Lat.*, t. LXXII, col. 245.

[3] *Missal. Goth.*, fols. 80a–80b. *H.B.S.*, vol. LII, p. 32; *Rev. bénéd.*, t. LVI (1945–46), pp. 9–11.

introduction of the feast appears to have met with opposition similar to what we find in respect to that of the Conception in the 12th century.[1]

While on the subject of the cult of the Blessed Virgin in the Gallican liturgy, it might be of interest to make some reference to those Gallo-Roman figurines in terracotta which have been repeatedly mistaken for statuettes of our Lady. The pagan Gauls reverenced a goddess who symbolised the fruitfulness of nature, and in the time of the Romans received the name of *Mater*. These feminine divinities were seated, holding a child in their arms—sometimes at the breast. Sanctuaries of the Virgin, as Notre Dame de l'Epine in Champagne and Notre Dame de la Déliverande in Normandy owe their origin to a chance discovery of such a statuette, and indeed many of the cherished black virgins came into existence as Gallo-Roman *Matres*.[2]

Chair of St. Peter

A feast of the Chair of St. Peter was observed on 16 January,[3] and the Lectionary of Luxeuil gives three 'Sundays after St. Peter's Chair'. The commemoration in the Lectionary of Wolfenbüttel is on 22 February. Mgr. Duchesne says that the Gallican Church, unwilling to admit the feasts of saints in Lent, did not observe the February feast before its acceptance of the Roman books.[4]

Later Poitevin calendars commemorated St. Radegunde [5] on 13 August and St. Venantius Fortunatus on 14 December. Ancient English calendars observed St. Radegunde on 11 February, probably because two names were confused. A Berne MS. of the Hieronymian martyrology gives a clue as to the confusion. 11 February in that MS. cites an abbess of the name

---

[1] Morin, *Rev. bénéd.*, t. LVI (1945–46), pp. 9–11.

[2] Mâle, *op. cit.*, chap. XIII, 4, pp. 319–20.

[3] *Missal. Goth.* (*H.B.S.*, vol. LII, 1917), pp. 48–50. Cf. Felire of Oengus, *Leabhar Breac.*

[4] Duchesne, *op. cit.*, chap. VIII, 7, p. 279.

[5] The antiphon for second vespers refers to Radegunde as 'mother of the fatherland': in remembrance of the many moving letters, written to the Merovingian princes in the interests of peace. On the testimony of a nun of the name of Baudonive, a contemporary of Radegunde, *Alleluia* was sung at the funeral ceremonies of the royal foundress. Aigrain, *op. cit.*, chap. IX, p. 199, n. 17.

of Baldegonde, from a convent of the Holy Cross in the 7th century.

The Mass for the feast of St. Ferreolus and St. Ferrucio on 16 June in the *Missale Gothicum* seems unique in Gallican *liturgica*. The cult of these saints was practically restricted to Burgundy and to monasteries founded from Burgundy.[1]

A Mass *de novo fructus* (*sic*) is found in the Lectionary of Luxeuil, and a Mass of St. Sixtus (6 August) in the *Gothicum*, although the latter makes no mention of any blessing of fruit.

St. Germanus of Auxerre is provided with a Mass before the two Advent Masses in the *Gallicanum Vetus*.

A not very intelligible passage in a canon of the second council of Tours (567) speaks of *festivitates et missae sanctorum* as taking place all through the month of August, but no existing sacramentary or lectionary makes any mention of them.[2]

An office of St. Stephen on 9 September, which is probably a vestige of some Gallican commemoration, is found in a 9th-century antiphoner of Senlis. Traces of a similar feast exist also in liturgical books of Châlons sur Marne, in which the Office is styled *De costa Sancti Stephani*, probably to distinguish the September feast. *Adventus reliquiarum Stephani* was observed at Châlons on 20 June.[3]

VESTMENTS

The vesture for the celebration of Mass would appear to have been the customary civilian dress of a Roman until at least the 6th century, even if clothes of a somewhat richer material were reserved for liturgical occasions. When, however, secular fashions changed, the Church, in its conservatism, retained the old dress, which thus became ecclesiastical vestments.

Pope Celestine I, in the letter *Cuperemus quidem*, written to the bishops of Narbonne and Vienne on 26 July 428, condemns the practice of wearing a pallium and girdle in church. The usage

---

[1] The two saints are said to have been brothers, disciples of St. Irenaeus, and to have been martyred half a league to the north of Besançon.

[2] *Toto Augusto manicationes fiant, quia festivitates sunt et missae.* Counc. II Tours, 567, can. 18. Labbe, *op. cit.*, t. V, col. 857.

[3] Morin, *Ephem. Liturg.*, January–March 1937, p. 7, n. 9.

would seem to have originated in the ascetic movement, which at
that time was gaining ground in the Western Church. The Pope,
like many of the Gaulish bishops, would seem to have viewed the
growth of monasticism with deep distrust. 'It is not surprising',
says Celestine, 'that they who have not grown up in this Church
act contrary to the Church's usages, and that, coming from other
customs, they have brought their traditional ways with them into
our Church. They consider that they will be fulfilling the letter
rather than the spirit of the Scriptures, if they wear a pallium, with
a girdle round the loins. . . . Such a course may perhaps be followed as a matter of custom rather than of reason by those who
live in remote districts and pass their lives far from their fellow-
men. But why should they dress in this way in the churches of
Gaul, changing the age-long usage of distinguished prelates for a
different attire?' [1]

The old civilian mode of dress was still customary in church in
the time of St. Caesarius of Arles (*ob.* 543).

It has been suggested by some liturgists that the surplice,
which probably originated in either France or Germany, was connected in some way with the old Gallican form of alb, which took
the form of an ungirdled tunic. [2]

Pseudo-Germanus tells us that the deacon in his day was accustomed to wear a stole over the alb, for which a fanciful symbolism
was invented: *Stola autem, quam super alba diaconus induit, significat subtilitatis intelligentiam in divina mysteria.* [3] The use of the
term 'stole', in place of 'orarium', is unusual at such an early date.

The chasuble was sometimes called an 'amphibolus', and Sulpicius Severus tells us that St. Martin (*ob.* 397) offered the holy
Sacrifice vested in tunic and amphibolus. [4] Pseudo-Germanus
(? 7th–8th century) refers to it as a specifically sacred vestment:
Casula amphibolus vocant, quod (sic) sacerdos induitur (for Mass)
unita intrinsecus, non scissa, non aperta tota unita sine manicis. [5]

---

[1] Labbe, *op. cit.*, t. II, col. 1618; *Pat. Lat.*, t. L, col. 430.
[2] Joseph Braun, *Cath. Encyclop.*, vol. XIV, art. 'Surplice', p. 344.
[3] Pseudo-Germ, *Exposit. Brev. Antiq. Lit. Gall.*, Epist. II; *Pat. Lat.*, t. LXXII, col.
98.
[4] Sulpic. Sev., *Dial.* II, cap. I.
[5] Pseudo-Germ., *Epist.* II; *Pat. Lat.*, t. LXXII, col. 97.

The testament of St. Caesarius (*ob.* 543) bequeaths to his successor in the see of Arles (Auxanus): *Indumenta Paschalia, quae mihi data sunt, omnia illi serviant, simul cum casula villosa, et tunica, vel galnape,*[1] *quod melius dimisero.*[2] Again, in the Life of St. Caesarius, we read: *Ambulans* (Caesarius) *per plateam civitatis, vidit contra in foro hominem, qui a daemonio agebatur, in quem cum attendisset, habens manum sub casula, ut a suis non videretur, crucem eum fecit.*[3] Fortunatus, in his Life of St. Medard, bishop of Noyon and Tournai (*ob. c.* 558), speaks of the Saint giving a 'chasuble' to a poor man by way of alms.[4]

Dalmatics were conceded by Pope Symmachus (498–514) to the bishops and deacons of Arles: *diaconos quoque ipsius, ac Romanae instar ecclesiae, dalmaticarum fecit habitu praeeminere.*[5] A similar privilege was accorded by St. Gregory I (590–604) to the bishop and archdeacon of Gap.[6]

Tunicles were certainly worn in Spain in the 6th century, and probably also in Gaul.

The pallium was mentioned in the first council of Mâcon (581),[7] and also by pseudo-Germanus.[8]

Pseudo-Germanus speaks of priests who wore metal bracelets or cuffs of silk or some other handsome material: *Manualia vero, id est manicas induere sacerdotibus mos est instar armillarum, quas regum vel sacerdotum brachia constringebantur. Ideo ex quolibet pretioso vellere, non metalli duritia extant, vel ut omnes communiter sacerdotes, etiam minoris dignitatis in saeculo facilius inveniant.*[9]

From the same source also we learn that girdles were not worn by the minor clergy: *Alba non constringitur, sed suspensa tegit levitae corpusculum.*

---

[1] *Galnape*, mantle or cloak.

[2] Du Cange, *op. cit.*, t. II, p. 273.

[3] Bona, *op. cit.*, lib. I, cap. XXIV, p. 212.

[4] *Casulam igitur, quae per eum a matre dirigebatur artifici egeno illi misericordia modus tribuit.* Fortun. *Vita S. Medardi*, cap. V; Du Cange, *op. cit.*, art. *Casula*, t. II, p. 273.

[5] *Pat. Lat.*, t. LXVII, col. 1016.

[6] Greg., *Epist.*, lib. IX, cap. CVII. *Pat. Lat.*, t. LXVII, cols. 1034-5.

[7] *Ut archiepiscopus sine pallio missas dicere non praesumat.* Counc. I Mâcon, 581, can. 6. Labbe, *op. cit.*, t. V, col. 968.

[8] *Pallium vero quod circa collo usque ad pectus venit, rationale vocabatur in Vetere Testamento.* Pseudo-Germ., *Epist.* II; *Pat. Lat.*, t. LXXII, col. 97.

[9] *Ibid., Epist.* II. Cf. ἐπιμανίκια in the Byzantine rite.

A life of St. Caesarius of Arles (*ob.* 543) refers to a staff, but it is not clear whether in the 5th and 6th centuries such a staff pertained to a pastoral staff properly so called: *Cum vir Dei ad aliquam ecclesiam pergeret, clericus cui cura erat baculum illius portare (quod notariorum officium erat) oblitus erat.* An ebony staff, preserved in the church of Notre Dame la Major in Arles, is said to have belonged to the Saint.[1] The reference in the letter of Celestine I to the bishops of Gaul has probably no more than an allegorical meaning.[2] Finally, it may be noted that Romanus, bishop of Rouen, was given a staff by the king in 623: *rex . . . baculum illi contulit pastoralem.*

OFFICE OF DEACONESS

The office of deaconess, although persisting for a long time elsewhere, was an object of disfavour in the Gallican Church. After the councils of Orange (can. 26; 441) and Epaone (can. 21; 517), an unsuccessful attempt was made to retain the institution, but in 535 the second council of Orleans (can. 17) categorically stated: 'Henceforward, on account of the frailty of the sex, no woman is to be for the future consecrated a deaconess.' The prohibition was reiterated in the second council of Tours (can. 21; 567). Such legislation was peculiar to Gaul, and received the confirmation of the majority of the bishops. It was therefore all the more strange that we find St. Medard in 544/5 'ordaining' St. Radegunde as a deaconess at Noyon, after the separation from her husband, Clothair. Her precious embroideries and 'bands of purple' were given to the basilica to be made into trappings for the altar.[3]

LIGHTS AND INCENSE

The great basilicas were illuminated by thousands of lights on solemnities, and we read that St. Radegunde (*ob.* 587) was accustomed to make candles with her own hands. Fortunatus, her great friend, says in the life of the Saint: *Illud qua pietate peragebat sollicita, ut quae per oratoria vel loca venerabilia tota nocte per-*

---

[1] Joyeux, *op. cit.*, III, p. 24.   [2] Labbe, *op. cit.*, II, col. 1618.
[3] Aigrain, *op. cit.*, chap. III, pp. 59–66.

lucerent, candelas suis manibus factas jugiter ministrabat?[1] Lights were carried in the gospel procession, but pseudo-Germanus makes no allusion to the use of incense.[2]

There is, however, no doubt that the Gallican Church had incense, despite the fact that neither 'Germanus' nor the rubrics of the existing MSS. make any mention of it.

In fact, the earliest reference in the Western Church to the use of incense at funerals is found in a sermon of St. Hilary of Arles (*ob.* 449) on his predecessor St. Honoratus (*ob.* 429).[3] St. Gregory of Tours (*ob.* 594) speaks of incense at the translation of the relics of St. Lupicinus (*c.* 488): *dispositis in itinere psallentium turmis cum crucibus cereisque atque odore fragrantis thymiamatis.*[4] Portable lights and incense both appeared at the triumphal entry of the relic of the true Cross into Poitiers at the instigation of St. Radegunde in 568 or 569. A more ceremonial use of incense seems to be envisaged in the *Missale Francorum* (8th century) at the consecration of a church, where we find directions for the censing of the altar. The strictly 'ceremonial' use of incense appears to have been Gallican in origin, and received later in the Roman rite through the adoption of Carolingian usages. The censing of the *oblata* at the offertory was prescribed by the first canon of the council of Rouen in *c.* 650, when it was regarded as symbolical of the death of Christ.[5] The ceremony was adopted in the Carolingian liturgy, and Amalarius, on his visit to Rome in 831, refers to it as one of the differences between his own Church and that of Rome: *Post evangelium non offerunt (Romani) incensum super altare.*[6] The Gallican custom had been probably derived from the Byzantine liturgy, in which incense was carried at the Great Entrance, and the gifts censed as soon as they had been placed on the altar.

---

[1] *Fortun., Sanct. Rad. Reg. Vita,* lib. I, 7; *Pat. Lat.,* t. LXXII, col. 654.

[2] *Pat. Lat.,* t. LXXII, col. 91.

[3] *Praelata tunc ad feretrum ipsius aromata et incensum vidimus. Hil. Arelat., Sermo de Vita S. Honorat.,* cap. VIII; *Pat. Lat.,* t. L, col. 1269.

[4] *Greg. Turon., Vitae Patrum,* cap. XIII; *Pat. Lat.,* t. LXXI, col. 1067. Cf. *Pat. Lat.,* t. XCVI, col. 371.

[5] Mansi, *Concil.,* t. X, col. 1199.

[6] Amal., *pref. alt.*; Hittorp, *De div. Cath. Eccles. Offic.,* col. 737; *Pat. Lat.,* t. CV, col. 992.

EUCHARISTIC BREAD

St. Radegunde (*ob.* 587), in her retirement at Saix and again later in the convent at Poitiers, made a practice of making altar breads for the neighbouring churches.[1] There is, however, no indication as to whether the bread was unleavened or fermented. Today, the Benedictine nuns of Sainte Croix carry on the same work.

RESERVATION OF THE BLESSED SACRAMENT

Mabillon, in his dissertation on the Gallican Liturgy (*De Liturgia Gallicana*), makes it clear that the reserved Sacrament was for the exclusive use of the sick, and that the reception of Holy Communion out of Mass was a very rare occurrence: *Ceterum ex asservata Eucharistia soli communicabant infirmi non sani, quibus vix unquam extra missam communio a sacerdote porrigebatur.*[2] There was, he says, a contrary custom in the Church of Jerusalem.[2]

The earliest method of reservation would seem to have been in a *canistrum* (*vimineum*) or (wicker) basket, which belonged to both Jewish and pagan sacrificial cults.[3] These baskets are represented on two 2nd-century frescoes in the Catacombs of St. Calixtus, Rome, and in mosaics of a 4th-century pavement in the basilica of Aquileia. Their use in Gaul is attested in a letter of St. Jerome to Rusticus, a monk from southern Gaul, in which he praises St. Exuperius, bishop of Toulouse (*ob.* after 410), for his Christian poverty and endurance, but adds that no one has greater riches than he who carries the Lord's Body in a wicker basket and his Blood in a glass vessel.[4]

Later, we find the Eucharist reserved in a pyx which was kept in the *secretarium* in a circular vessel surmounted by a small conical tower, known as a *turris* or *turriculum*. The origin of the name has been supplied by pseudo-Germanus: 'The Body of the

---

[1] Aigrain, *op. cit.*, chap. III, p. 70.

[2] Mabillon, *De Lit. Gallic.*, lib. I, cap. IX; *Pat. Lat.*, t. LXXII, col. 166.

[3] S. J. P. van Dijk and J. Hazelden Walker, *The Myth of the Aumbry*, I, p. 27. London, 1957.

[4] *Nihil illo divitius, qui corpus Domini in canistro vimineo portat.* Jer., *Epist.* CXXV *ad Rusticum. Pat. Lat.*, t. XXII, col. 1085.

Lord is carried in towers, because the tomb of the Lord was cut out of the rock in the shape of a tower.'[1]

It was in a 'tower' also that the deacon brought the bread at the offertory of the Mass. St. Gregory of Tours (*ob.* 594) says: *Acceptaque turre diaconus, in qua mysterium dominici Corporis habebatur.*[2]

From the earliest days, one of the offices of the deacon was the administration of the Sacrament to the sick, and the tower therefore became one of his especial attributes. A miracle related by St. Gregory of Tours tells of a tower which moved by itself to the altar from the hands of an unworthy deacon.[3]

Leo, the thirteenth successor of St. Martin in the see of Tours (526), is said to have been a skilful carpenter who constructed wooden Eucharistic towers overlaid with gold.[4]

St. Venantius Fortunatus (*ob.* between 530 and 540) composed an epigram on the golden *turris* of Felix, bishop of Bourges.[5]

A 'tower' is referred to also in the testaments of Remigius, bishop of Rheims [6] (*ob.* 533); Aredius, abbot of Atane [7] (6th century), and Landunus, bishop of Rheims (*ob.* 648), although their Eucharistic association is not expressly mentioned.[8]

Lebrun says that the 18th-century method of reservation in France—*suspension*—was a Gallican usage which originated in the East.[9]

The testament of Perpetuus, bishop of Tours (*ob.* 491), mentions as a bequest to the presbyter Amalarius: *capsulam communem unam de serico, item peristerium et columbam ad repositorium dat.*[10]

---

[1] Pseudo-Germ. *Pat. Lat.*, t. LXXII, col. 93.

[2] Greg. Turon., *De Glor. Mart.*, cap. LXXXVI. *Pat. Lat.*, t. LXXI, col. 781; Righetti, *op. cit.*, vol. I, part III, cap. VII, 3, pp. 452–3.

[3] *Ibid. Pat. Lat.*, t. LXXI, col. 781.

[4] *Fuit autem faber lignarius, faciens etiam turres holochryso tectas, ex quibus quaedam apud nos retinentur: in aliis etiam operibus elegans fuit.* Greg. Turon., *Hist. Franc.*, lib. X, cap. XXXI; *Pat. Lat.*, t. LXXI, col. 569.

[5] Venant. Fortun., *Miscell.*, lib. III, cap. XXV; *Pat. Lat.*, t. LXXXVIII, cols. 114–15.

[6] *Pat. Lat.*, t. LXV, col. 971.

[7] *Ibid.*, t. LXXI, col. 1147. Atane, known as St. Yrieix-la-Perche: a dependence of St. Martin, Tours.

[8] Laurent Köster, *De Custodia SS. Eucharistiae* (Rome, 1940), cap. III, art. 3, p. 39.

[9] Lebrun, *op. cit.*, t. II, pp. 270–1.

[10] Mabillon, *De Lit. Gall.*, lib. I; *Pat. Lat.*, t. LXXII, col. 162.

MASS OF THE GALLICAN RITE

The obligation of assisting at Mass on Sunday was enforced by the council of Agde (506), and the faithful were bidden to remain until after the blessing before Communion.[1] The regulation was renewed in the first (511) and third (538) councils of Orleans.[2]

The features of the Gallican Mass introduced at the beginning of the 6th century are considered by Thibaut to have been an imitation of the Byzantine liturgy; while the Mass of the faithful is said to have been largely borrowed from the early liturgy of Jerusalem.[3] Such a categorical and sweeping statement, however, must be treated with a certain amount of reserve, although the Mass is in many ways indebted to Oriental influence.

Claudian Mamertus (*ob.* 473/4) would seem to have acted as a kind of 'auxiliary' to his brother, the bishop of Vienne (St. Mamertus). We read that he acted as 'precentor and leader of the Psalms' and that he 'taught the trained group of singers (*schola cantorum*) to chant before the altar'. Sidonius Apollinaris has in fact left us a most instructive inventory of the scope and activities of a bishop's presbyter. 'The 5th century', says Miss Chadwick, 'has no finer example of classical learning and Christian integrity.'[4]

The characteristics of the Gallican liturgy in the Merovingian period may be classified under seven headings:

(1) Use of psalms, each followed by a collect. St. Cassian refers to the practice as a feature of the monastic liturgy.[5]

(2) Three lessons at Mass. The lesson from the Old Testament, attested in the second book of the Apostolic Constitutions, was suppressed at an early date in Rome and Africa, while a psalm-chant held first place.[6] Sulpicius Severus (*ob. c.* 420/5) mentions a prophetical lesson in his Life of St. Martin.[7]

---

[1] Counc. Agde, 506, can. 47. Labbe, *op. cit.*, t. IV, col. 1391.
[2] Counc. I. Orleans, 511, can. 26; Counc. III Orleans, 538, can. 29.
[3] Thibaut, *op. cit.*, III, p. 79.   [4] N. Chadwick, *op. cit.*, chap. VII, p. 209.
[5] Cassian, *De Instit. Coenob.*, lib. III, cap. XI.
[6] The Ambrosian rite has three lessons on Sundays, *Solemnitates Domini* and *Solemnia*: the Mozarabic rite has suppressed the three lessons on Sundays, but on fast days and in Lent there are four.
[7] *Lectione prophetica tunc notatum* . . . Sulpic. Sev., *Vita S. Martini*, cap. VII.

(3) Prayers for the people before the offertory. The prayers at the dismissal of the penitents and catechumens had disappeared by the time of pseudo-Germanus, whoever he may have been, but the prayer for the faithful was retained. The author of the letters tells us that the original form of such prayer had been in accordance with the nineteenth canon of the council of Laodicea (*c.* 370), and followed the arrangement found in book VIII of the Apostolic Constitutions: *postea deprecarent pro illis levitae, diceret sacerdos collectam post precem.* The prayers were probably introduced into the liturgy of the Provençal monasteries through St. Cassian.

(4) The recital of names immediately after the offertory: a practice which still obtains in the Mozarabic rite. A similar place in the liturgy is attested by pseudo-Denis the Areopagite and the East Syrian rite.

(5) The position of the kiss of peace: after the offertory. At an early date, Rome, Milan and North Africa deferred the *pax* until after the canon, as a preparation for Holy Communion.

(6) The *Pater noster* at the conclusion of the Eucharistic prayer. St. Augustine (*ob.* 430) says that the Lord's prayer after the canon was a well-nigh universal usage.[1] It may have been introduced into the Gallican rite under the influence of North Africa.[2]

(7) Solemn Blessing before Communion. This would seem to have been a feature of the Church of Jerusalem in the 4th century.[3] It may have reached Gaul by way of Africa, which had extended its influence to Spain, Narbonnaise Gaul and Provence. The blessing, however, cannot be considered a distinctive Gallican trait, although it was adopted early in the liturgy.[4]

No exemplar of a Gallican antiphoner has survived, with the resulting loss of antiphons, graduals, etc. But Mgr. Duchesne has endeavoured to repair the lacuna by borrowing the appropriate chants from the Mozarabic liturgy.[5] Charles the Bald (*ob.* 877),

---

[1] *Petitionem fere omnis Ecclesia dominica oratione concludit.* Aug., *Epist.*, CXLIX.
[2] Thibaut, *op. cit.*, III, p. 86.
[3] Ethérie, *Journal de Voyage*, XXV (edit. Hélène Pétré, Paris, 1948), pp. 198–201.
[4] Thibaut, *op. cit.*, III, p. 87.
[5] Duchesne, *op. cit.*, chap. VII, pp. 189–227.

as we have seen, obtained the services of a Mozarabic priest when he wished to witness the Gallican liturgy which had ceased to exist for well nigh a century. The similarity between the two rites was remarked on by Cardinal Bona (*ob.* 1674): *Caeterum non absurdam neque incredibilem esse hanc sententiam de utriusque Missae Gallicanae et Hispanicae similitudine, praeter ea quae dicta sunt, alia etiam pertinentes.*[1]

THE LITURGY

Preparatory Prayers

The purely Gallican Rheinau MS. (Masses of Mone) has no *apologiae* or *praeparatio sacerdotis*, either before or at the beginning of Mass. We find one, however, in the Missal of Stowe, and the Bobbio missal provides a prayer which can pass for an *apologia*. The *Missa prima die sanctum Paschae* in the *Gothicum* contains the prayer *Ante tuae immensitatis conspectum*,[2] which closely resembles one of a similar character in the so-called Mass of Illyricus.[3] A later hand has written the word *Sanctus* at the foot of the folio in the *Gothicum*, indicating that the prayer was to be said by the priest during the singing of the *sanctus*.[4] *Apologiae* would not seem to have formed any part of the original Gallican liturgy, but rather to have been an importation from Roman or Carolingian codices.

Introit

The liturgy began with an antiphon specially intended to enhance the entry of the ministers, after the manner of the Μονογενής in the Byzantine rite. Pseudo-Germanus says: *Antiphona ad praelegendum canitur ... Psallentibus clericis procedit sacerdos in specie Christi de sacrario.*[5] The title *antiphona ad praelegendum* seems to imply words of exhortation under the form of a reading, which the beginning and end of his explanation appears to justify: *Antiphona ad praelegendum canitur* and *ut tam*

---

[1] Bona, *op. cit.*, lib. I, cap. XII, 6, p. 77.
[2] *Missal. Goth.*, H.B.S., vol. LII (1917), no. 275, p. 81.
[3] Bona, *op. cit.*, append., p. 484.
[4] *Missal. Goth.*, H.B.S., vol. LII, p. 81.
[5] Pseudo-Germ., *Epist.* I; *Pat. Lat.*, t. LXXII, col. 89; Duchesne, *op. cit.*, p. 190.

monendum quam exhortandum nutriat in plebe bona opera et ex-tinguat. The antiphon is referred to in a canon of the council of Agde (506): *Et quia convenit ordinem Ecclesiae ab omnibus aequaliter custodiri, studendum est, ut sicut ubique fit, et post anti-phonas collectiones per ordinem ab episcopis vel presbyteris dicantur.*[1] St. Gregory of Tours (*ob.* 594) adds the further information that the chant was concluded with *Gloria Patri: Et ecce chorus psal-lentium qui ingressus basilicam, postquam dicta Gloria Trinitati, Psalentii modulatio conquievit.*[2] *Sicut erat,* as a protest against Arianism, was probably added after the second council of Vaison (529).

Monition for Silence

It is clear, however, that the original liturgy in Gaul, as every-where else, began with the lessons. This is attested by Gennadius in *De viris illustribus,* when he speaks of Museus of Marseilles, who compiled a 'remarkable sacramentary' for Eustace his bishop.[3]

The lessons were introduced by a diaconal monition for silence. Pseudo-Germanus says: *Silentium diaconus annuntiat . . . sacerdos ideo datur populo ut dum ille benedicit plebem, dicens: Dominus sit semper vobiscum, ab omnibus benedicatur dicentibus: Et cum spiritu tuo.*[4] *Silentium facite* is also the Mozarabic formula, where it occurs before the reading of the epistle. The diaconal monition is mentioned by St. Gregory of Tours (*ob.* 594): *Quadam die dominica, postquam diaconus silentium ut missae auscultarentur populis indixit.*[5]

Dominus sit semper vobiscum is the form of salutation in the Mozarabic liturgy.

Chants

Three introductory canticles, however, precede the lessons in the description of the liturgy given by pseudo-Germanus: *Ajus*

---

[1] Counc. Agde, 506, can. 30. Labbe, *op. cit.,* t. IV, col. 1388.
[2] *Greg. Turon. Glor. Mart.* Cf. *Hist. Franc.*
[3] Gennad., *De Script. Eccles.,* LXXIX. *Pat. Lat.,* t. LVIII, col. 1103.
[4] Pseudo-Germ., *Epist.* I; *Pat. Lat.,* t. LXXII, col. 89; Duchesne, *op. cit.,* p. 190.
[5] *Greg. Turon., Hist. Franc.,* lib. VII, cap. VIII; *Pat. Lat.,* t. LXXI, col. 421. Cf. Isid., *De eccles. offic.* I, 10.

L

vero ante prophetiam pro hac canitur in graeca lingua quia . . .
Incipiente praesule ecclesia Ajus psallit, dicens latinum cum
graeco . . . Dictum Amen ex hebraeo . . . Tres autem parvuli qui ore
uno sequentes Kyrie eleison . . . Canticum autem Zachariae ponti-
ficis in honorem sancti Johannis Baptistae cantatur . . .; ideo pro-
phetiam quam pater ejus ipso nascente cecinit alternis vocibus ecclesia
psallit.[1]

The *aius* (ἅγιος) would seem to have been the trisagion,
although Dom Cabrol maintains that it was neither the trisagion
nor the *sanctus*, although he fails to tell us what he thinks it was.[2]
The chant, as we learn from pseudo-Germanus, was bilingual—
Greek and Latin—with the Hebrew Amen at its conclusion.[3]
The Bobbio missal (7th–8th century) gives two prayers *post aios*,
which suggests that the chant may have been still in use. The
separation of the two forms in the MS. could be accounted for
by the twofold use of the chant—at the beginning of the liturgy
and before the gospel.[4]

A reference to the trisagion in the Gallican Church is found in
the almost contemporary life of St. Gery (Gaugericus), bishop
of Cambrai (*c.* 600), but the occasion of its use was not the
Eucharist: *Ajus, ajus, ajus, per trinum numerum imposuit in nomine*
Trinitatis.[5] Netzer and Thibaut, following Duchesne, consider
the use of the trisagion at all Masses throughout the year to have
been prescribed by the third canon of the second council of
Vaison (529). Gregory Dix, on the other hand, says, with some
show of probability, that the canon refers to what we call the
sanctus, and not to the chant of which pseudo-Germanus speaks.[6]
The Syrian Monophysite interpolation in the trisagion—'Who
was crucified for us'—was condemned by St. Avitus, bishop of
Vienne (*ob. c.* 519), in a letter to Gondebaud, king of the Burgundians, but it is clear that the chant had not at that time found

---

[1] Pseudo-Germ. *Pat. Lat.*, t. LXXII, cols. 89–90; Duchesne, *op. cit.*, p. 191.
[2] Cabrol, *Western Rites*, chap. VII, p. 139.
[3] Cf. Roman rite on Good Friday. Also the trilingual title on the cross.
[4] Nos. 25 and 32, *The Bobbio Missal, Notes and Studies, Henry Bradshaw Society*, vol.
LXI (1924), pp. 113–4; *Pat. Lat.*, t. LXII, cols. 455, 457.
[5] *Anal. Bolland.*, VII (1888), p. 393.
[6] Dix, *Shape of the Liturgy*, chap. XIII, p. 467, n. 1.

Gallican Rite

its way into the Gallican liturgy.[1] The Bobbio missal, however, seems to infer that the trisagion with the interpolation was sung in the liturgy.

The threefold *Kyrie eleison*, which followed the *aius*, is found in a similar position in the Syriac liturgy of St. James. 'Taking this in conjunction with the Antiochene greeting immediately before the trisagion in "Germanus" ', says Dix, 'it seems fairly easy to see whence the model for all this part of the "Germanus" rite in its present form was derived—from Syria.' [2] The *Kyrie* was sung by three boys in unison. The expression *qui ore uno*, found in pseudo-Germanus, is borrowed from *Daniel* III, 51: *Tunc hi tres quasi ex uno ore laudabant, et glorificabant, et benedicebant Deum in fornace.*

The use of the *Kyrie* was probably not very general in Gaul before the second council of Vaison (529), when, after the example of Rome, Italy and the East, its frequent recitation was prescribed.[3] The singing of the *Kyrie* by children was a feature of the *lucenarium* in the 4th century at Jerusalem: *Et diacono dicente singulorum nomina semper pisinni plurimi stant respondentes semper: kyrie eleison, quod dicimus nos: miserere Domine, quorum voces infinitae sunt.*[4]

The third canticle, *Benedictus* or *Prophetia*, according to St. Gregory of Tours, was intoned by the bishop: *quo (Palladio episcopo Santonensis) incipiente prophetiam.*[5] Two choirs then continued the verses alternately (*alternis vocibus*). Mabillon and others after him have confused the prophecy (*Benedictus*) with the prophetic lesson, but it is evident that St. Gregory had the canticle in mind. The *Benedictus*, says Dix, 'evidently held the place in the 6th-century French rites that *Gloria in excelsis* held in the 6th-century Italian rite, as the "hymn" before the collect. Its use in place of the *Gloria* is probably due to the fact that in the 6th century the *Gloria* in France was used at lauds in the place

---

[1] Avit., *Epist.* III; *Pat. Lat.*, t. LIX, col. 211.
[2] Dix, *op. cit.*, chap. XIII, p. 466.
[3] Counc. II Vaison, 529, can. 3. Labbe, *op. cit.*, t. IV, col. 1680.
[4] Ethérie, *op. cit.*, p. 192. Cf. St John Chrysostom, *In Matth. Hom.* LXXI (al. LXXII); *Pat. Graec.*, t. LVIII, col. 666.
[5] Greg., *Hist. Franc.*, lib. VIII, cap. VII. *Pat. Lat.*, t. LXXI, col. 453.

where the Italian office-books used the Benedictus'.[1] The Missal of Bobbio gives the *Gloria in excelsis*, but the two *post prophetiam* prayers show the Gallican substratum of the MS.[2] The *Gloria* appears as a thanksgiving after the *post aius*.[3]

Pseudo-Germanus, in his second letter, tells us that *Alleluia*, *Trisagion* (*Sanctus*), *Benedictus* and *Benedicite* were omitted in Lent. A special canticle, unknown elsewhere, was sung in their place: *Sanctus Deus Archangelorum in quadragesima concinetur et non canticum Zachariae . . . nec* (MS. *vel*) *alleluia in nostra ecclesia, sanctus vel prophetia, hymnus trium puerorum vel canticum Rubri maris, illis diebus decantantur.*[4] The avowal of 'Germanus' is in itself a proof of the late production of the letters, and both St. Caesarius (*ob.* 543) and St. Aurelian (*ob.* 551) attest the retention of Alleluia in Lent in 6th-century Arles.

Collect

The *collectio post prophetiam*, which followed the *Benedictus*, was usually either a paraphrase of the most significant verses of the preceding chant or an allusion to the feast. Its position was similar to Eastern usage, and was alluded to by Cassian: *psalterium cum orationibus interjectis.*[5] St. Caesarius refers to it in one of his homilies: *Non ergo foris fabulis, sed intus psalmodiae et orationibus studete.*[6]

An allocution to the faithful seems to have preceded the collect.[7] There is no mention of the collect in pseudo-Germanus, although we have abundant evidence for its existence in the Gallican rite. Two such prayers are found in the 'Masses of Mone', six in the *Gallicanum Vetus*,[8] seven in the Bobbio missal, and a number in the *Gothicum*.[9] A *collectio* for Christmas in the *Gothicum* is said to show a reference to the Frankish king, Clovis.[10]

---

[1] Dix, *op. cit.*, chap. XIII, p. 467.
[2] *Pat. Lat.*, t. LXXII, cols. 455–57.
[3] Mabillon, *Mus. Ital.*, t. I, pp. 281–2; *Pat Lat.*, t. LXXII, col. 456.
[4] 'Germ'. *Pat. Lat.*, t. LXXII, col. 98; Duchesne, *op. cit.*, p. 193, n. 3.
[5] Cassian, *De Instit. Coenob.*, lib. II, cap. XI; lib. III, cap. XI.
[6] Caesar., *Hom.* CCLXXX, 4 (append. Aug.).
[7] Righetti, *op. cit.*, vol. I, part II, cap. III, p. 118.
[8] e.g. Advent, St. John Baptist (2), Sunday (3).
[9] *Pat. Lat.*, t. LXXII, cols. 227, 277, 337, 462, etc.
[10] Fols. 6a–6b. *Missal. Goth.*, *H.B.S.*, vol. LII, pp. 3–4.

Lessons

St. Caesarius speaks of the three lessons—prophetic, apostolic, evangelical—as *expositio: Nam lectiones sive propheticas, sive apostolicas, sive evangelicas etiam in domibus vestris aut ipse legere, aut alios legentes audire potestis.*[1]

They are attested also by St. Gregory of Tours in his *Historia Francorum: Positis clerici tribus libris super altarium, id est Prophetiae, Apostoli, atque Evangeliorum, oraverunt ad Dominum . . . simulque unam habentes conniventiam, ut unusquisque in libro quod primum aperiebat hoc ad missas etiam legeret.*[2] Again later in the same work, he says: *Adveniente die Dominico Rex ecclesiam ad spectanda Missarum sollemnia petit, fratres vero consacerdotesque qui aderant, locum Palladio Episcopo ad agenda festa praebuerunt. Quo incipiente Prophetiam, Rex interrogat quis esset.*[3] The Lectionary of Luxeuil [4] and the Bobbio missal both provide the three lessons.

Lebrun speaks of them as a 'truly Gallican usage': *on ne peut pas douter que cet usage ne soit véritablement Gallican.*[5] There is, however, little doubt that the three lessons were at one time in the Roman liturgy.

In Eastertide, the first pericope was from the Acts of the Apostles, and the second from the Apocalypse; while the historical books of the Old Testament were read in Lent and the *acta* of the saints on their feast days: *Actus autem Apostolorum vel Apocalypsis Johannis pro novitate gaudii paschalis leguntur, servantes ordinem temporum, sicut historia testamenti veteris in Quiquagesimo vel gesta sanctorum, confessorum ac martyrum in solemnitatibus.*[6] The Eastertide pericopes are attested in the Lectionary of Luxeuil and the Bobbio missal. The recital of the *acta* of the saints is well attested in the Gallican liturgy. St. Avitus, before beginning a sermon in the basilica of St. Maurice—*in novatione monasterii ipsius*—on 22 September 515 speaks of the custom of reading the

---

[1] Caesar., *Hom.* CCLXXXI, i (append. Aug.)
[2] *Greg. Turon., Hist. Franc.*, lib. IV, cap. XVI. *Pat. Lat.*, t. LXXI, col. 282.
[3] *Ibid.*, lib. VIII, cap. VII. *Pat. Lat.*, t. LXXI, col. 453.
[4] *Lect. Lux. Pat. Lat.*, t. LXXII, cols. 171–216.
[5] Lebrun, *op. cit.*, t. II, p. 269.
[6] Pseudo-Germ. *Pat. Lat.*, t. LXXII, col. 90; Duchesne, *op. cit.*, chap. VII, 3, p. 194.

Gesta martyrum before the homily: *ex consuetudine sollemni series lectae passionis explicuit.*[1] We hear also of a special concession which St. Caesarius (*ob.* 543) made for those who were weak and feeble in body: they were permitted to sit down for long lessons: *Passiones prolixae aut certe aliquae lectiones longiores leguntur.*[2] Biographical lessons are mentioned also by St. Aurelian in his Rule[3] (*ob.* 551), St. Ferreolus, bishop of Uzès[4] (*ob.* 581), and St. Gregory of Tours[5] (*ob.* 594). A letter of a cleric of the name of Warnacharius to Ceraunus, bishop of Paris, refers to a passional which the bishop was compiling.[6]

A noticeable feature of deacons in the early centuries would seem to have been their extreme youth. Sidonius Apollinaris (*ob.* 482) writes of a bishop: *Lector hic primum sic minister altaris, idque ab infantia.*[7] The Coptic and Ethiopic dissident churches have retained this primitive trait, and the 'little deacon', who was assisting his grandfather at the liturgy on 21 May 1924 in the church of Abu Sergeh in Cairo, was no more than six years of age. Deacons in the Ethiopic Church are often young boys, barely able to read.

'Alcuin thought his revision of the Bible a suitable present for Charlemagne on the occasion of his coronation as emperor on Christmas Day, 800', writes Beryl Smalley in a history of Bible study recently revised.[8]

The emperor in the months that followed issued a proclamation to 'all those serving as lectors in the churches of our realms': 'Among other things', he says, 'we have carefully corrected all the books of the Old and New Testament, corrupted by the ignorance of scribes . . . Lessons for the night office . . . set out without the words of the authors, and bristling with countless mistakes.'[9]

---

[1] *Mon. Germ. Auct. antiq.*, t. VI, 2, p. 145.   [2] Caesar., *Hom.* CCC.
[3] *Reg. Aurel.*, *Pat. Lat.*, t. LXVIII, cols. 396, 406.
[4] Ferreol., *Reg. ad Monachos*, cap. XVIII. *Pat. Lat.*, t. LXVI, col. 965.
[5] *Greg. Turon. De Glor. Mart.*, lib. I, cap. LXXXVI (*P.L.*, t. LXXI, col. 781); *De Mirac. Mart.*, lib. II, cap. XXIX (*P.L.*, t. LXXI, col. 954); lib. II, cap. XLIX (*P.L.*, t. LXXI, col. 963).
[6] *Mon. Germ.*, *Epist.*, t. III, p. 457.
[7] Sid. Apollin., *Epist.*, IV, 25.
[8] Smalley, *The Study of the Bible in the Middle Ages*, p. 37. Oxford, 1952.
[9] *Mon. Germ. Hist.*, *Leges* II, cap. I, pp. 80–1.

It is clear from this proclamation that a corrupt text of the Bible would have greatly added to the 'liturgical anarchy' of later Merovingian Gaul. A lectionary seems to have been the earliest contribution of Alcuin after his arrival at the royal court.

Chants

On Sundays and feasts, the Canticle of the Three Children (*Benedicite Omnia Opera*) was sung between the epistle and gospel: *Hymnum autem trium puerorum, quod post lectiones canitur.*[1] The Lectionary of Luxeuil prescribed the singing of the *Benedicite* before the apostolic lesson on Christmas Day, but the normal Gallican usage was followed at other times. A rubric for the Sunday after Easter says: *Clausum paschae: Danihel cum benedictione sicut primo die sanctae paschae.*[2] The *Benedicite* and *Benedictus* are said to have been prescribed in commemoration of the Baptism of Clovis (496).[3]

The canticle should, in principle, be followed by a prayer, although it is not generally specifically mentioned.

A *collectio post benedictionem* is, however, found in the Bobbio missal.[4] A prayer of the kind occurs in the Gelasian and Gregorian sacramentaries, and also in our Roman missal, after *Benedictus es* on Ember Saturdays: *Deus qui tribus pueris.*

The canticle was followed by a responsary, which was sung by boys in remembrance of the Hebrew youths who chanted 'Blessed is he who cometh in the name of the Lord'. The chant served as an appropriate prelude to the gospel: . . . *Ecclesia servat ordinem, ut inter Benedictionem et Evangelium non intercedat, nisi tantummodo responsorium quod a parvulis canitur.*[5] It took the place of the Alleluiatic verse or the *antiphona ante Evangelium* of the Ambrosian liturgy. *Lauda alleluia* in the Mozarabic rite was similar in purpose, but the fourth council of Toledo (633) directed it to be sung *after* the gospel: *propter gloriam Christi, quae per idem evangelium praedicatur.*[6] St. Gregory of Tours

---

[1] Pseudo-Germ. *Pat. Lat.*, t. LXXI, col. 91; Duchesne, *op. cit.*, p. 194.
[2] *Lect. Lux. Pat. Lat.*, t. LXXII, col. 201.
[3] Thibaut, *op. cit.*, II, p. 37.
[4] Missal Bobbio. *Pat. Lat.*, t. LXXII, col. 458.
[5] Pseudo-Germ. *Pat. Lat.*, t. LXXII, col. 91; Duchesne, *op. cit.*, p. 194.
[6] Counc. IV Toledo, 633, can. 12. Labbe, *op. cit.*, t. V, col. 1709.

(*ob.* 594) says that the responsary was sung by the deacon, but this may have been a local custom proper to Tours, or to Orleans, where the service to which the bishop alludes took place.[1]

Gospel

A certain solemnity attended the singing of the gospel from the *tribunal analogii* or ambo.[2] The trisagion (*aius*) was sung in the procession, and the gospel-book, preceded by a seven-branched candlestick was covered with a veil.[3] A description of the ceremony has been left us by pseudo-Germanus: *Tunc in adventu sancti Evangelii claro modulamini denuo psallit clerus Ajus . . . Egreditur processio sancti Evangelii velut potentia Christi triumphantis de morte, cum praedictis harmoniis et cum septem candelabris luminis, quae sunt septem dona spiritus sancti vel v(eteris) legis lumina mysterio crucis confixa ascendens in tribunal analogii, velut Christus sedem regni paternae, ut inde intonet dona vitae clamantibus clericis: Gloria tibi Domine . . . Sanctus autem quod redeunte sancto Evangelio clerus cantat . . .*[4] The response of *Gloria tibi Domine* to the announcement of the gospel was, as we see, similar to Roman custom. The *sanctus*, which 'Germanus' says was sung in the procession back to the altar, was probably a farced or paraphrased trisagion, as we find in the Mozarabic rite. The passage in the Apocalypse (IV, 10–11) to which 'Germanus' alludes was precisely one which occurs in one of the forms of the paraphrased trisagion in the traditional Spanish liturgy.[5]

Sermon

The priest was directed after the gospel either to deliver a homily from one of the Fathers or to comment on the lessons. St. Caesarius (*ob.* 543) seems to have been accustomed to lend his sermons for others to preach in their churches, and Cyprianus, in his life of the Saint, refers to the frequency with which this was done.[6] St. Hilary of Arles (429–49) is said to have preached on

---

[1] *Greg. Turon., Hist. Franc.*, lib. VIII, cap. III. *Pat. Lat.*, t. LXXI, col. 451.

[2] The desk for the gospel-book in the Byzantine rite is the ἀναλόγιον.

[3] Pseudo-Germ., *Epist.* II; *Pat. Lat.*, t. LXXII, col. 96.

[4] *Ibid., Epist.* I; *Pat. Lat.*, t. LXXII, col. 91; Duchesne, *op. cit.*, pp. 196–7.

[5] Louis Brou, *Etudes sur la Liturgie Moẓarabe. Le Trisagion de la Messe d'après les sources manuscrites. Ephem. Liturg.*, vol. LXI (1947), fasc. IV, append., p. 333.

[6] Cyprianus, *Vita S. Caesarii*, I, v. 42; *Pat. Lat.*, t. LXVII, col. 1021.

occasions for the space of four hours, so that his provision for seats in churches was not to be wondered at![1] Pope Celestine I (422–32), in a letter to the bishops of Provence, had forbidden priests to preach, but the prohibition would seem to have gone unheeded, and the second council of Vaison (529) not only confirmed the practice, but extended it to rural parishes. Deacons, however, might read one of the homilies of the Fathers to the faithful, but they were not allowed to preach.[2] This distinction was not given by pseudo-Germanus, who merely said: *Homiliae autem sanctorum quae leguntur pro sola praedicatione ponuntur, ut quicquid Propheta, Apostolus vel Evangelium mandavit, hoc doctor vel pastor Ecclesiae apertiori sermone populo praedicet, ita arte temperans ut nec rusticitas sapientes offendat, nec honesta loquacitas obscura rusticis fiat.*[3]

Litany

The sermon or homily was followed by a litanic prayer for 'all sorts and conditions of men': *Preces vero psallere levitas pro populo ab origine libri Moysacis ducit exordium, ut audita Apostoli praedicatione levitae pro populo deprecentur et sacerdotes prostrati ante Dominum pro peccata populi intercedant . . .*[4] In an earlier century, Caesarius of Arles (*ob.* 543) had spoken in one of his homilies of the prayer of the deacon to which the priest added a collect. The faithful, even when infirmity prevented their kneeling, could at least bow their heads.[5] Yet, continued the bishop in the following homily, 'When the deacon bids *Flectamus genua*, I see many men remain standing, immoveable as pillars.' [6]

---

[1] Gibert, *Arles Gréco-Romaine* (Arles, 1949), pp. 189–90.

[2] 'If deacons were worthy to read the gospel, how could they be unworthy to recite publicly the expositions of the Fathers?' Counc. II Vaison, 529, can. 2. Labbe, *op. cit.*, t. IV, col. 1680.

[3] Pseudo-Germ., *Epist.* I. Duchesne, *op. cit.*, p. 197.

[4] *Ibid.*, p. 198.

[5] Caesar., *Hom.* CCLXXXV. *Pat. Lat.*, t. XXXIX, col. 2284. It will be noticed that these Homilies of St. Caesarius have been inserted in an appendix to the works of St. Augustine (*Pat. Lat.*, t. XXXIX, the 5th tome devoted to the writings of the Latin Doctor).

[6] *Oratio diacono clamante indicitur, non solum corda, sed etiam corpora fideliter inclinetis. Nam dum frequenter, sicut oportet, et diligenter attendo, diacono clamante, Flectamus genua, maximam partem, velut columnas erectas, stare conspicio . . .* Caesar., *Hom.* CCLXXXVI. *Pat. Lat.*, t. XXXIX, col. 2285.

The extant Merovingian books do not provide any text of the litany, but give only the prayer of the priest.

The *preces* in the Mozarabic liturgy, which we find in the *Missale Mixtum* before the epistle (apostle) on Passion Sunday, are considered to be litanic in form: *Insidiati sunt mihi adversarii mei gratia*.[1]

Prayers for 'all sorts and conditions of men', prefaced by monitions, are given in the *Gallicanum Vetus* for Holy Saturday.[2]

The title *collectio post precem*, which we find in the *Gothicum* for Christmas and Easter, may possibly refer to a preceding litany, although Mabillon thinks otherwise.[3] It is interesting to note that the Christmas prayer, as well as the *collectio post prophetia* (*sic*) for that day, have the words *Salvator mundi*, so characteristic of Gallican texts.[4]

Litanies of a similar type are found in the Missal of Stowe (*Deprecatio Sancti Martini*) between the epistle and gospel; the Ambrosian missal, in place of the *Gloria in excelsis* on the Sundays in Lent; and the Mozarabic missal, also on Sundays, but between the lesson and the epistle. The Spanish litany is said by the priest as he prostrates at the foot of the altar (*prosternat se ad pedem altaris*).

The position of the Gallican litany may possibly be indicated by pseudo-Germanus, when he says: *audita Apostoli praedicatione*, that is after the epistle. In the Roman rite, the solemn prayers on Good Friday follow the gospel, as we find also for the great *synapte* of the Apostolic Constitutions and in the Byzantine liturgy, which have petitions of the same type. The Gallican *prex* may have sprung from an Oriental source.

It may be said perhaps that the prayers for 'all sorts and conditions' (*prône*) that we find before the sermon in many of the churches of France take the place of the litanic prayer and collect in the Gallican liturgy.

---

[1] *Missal. Mixt. Pat. Lat.*, t. LXXXV, cols. 372–3.
[2] Mabillon, *De Liturg. Gall.*, lib. III; *Pat. Lat.*, t. LXXII, cols. 365–7. Cf. Solemn prayers in the Roman rite on Good Friday.
[3] *Missal. Goth.*, H.B.S., vol. LII, pp. 4, 80; *Pat. Lat.*, t. LXXII, cols. 227, 277.
[4] *Missal. Goth., Ibid.*, p. 4.

Dismissal of Catechumens

This litany and prayer may well have been vestiges of the prayers and blessings at the dismissal of the catechumens and penitents, which were suppressed when the catechumenate ceased to serve any useful purpose. An invocation in the litany in the Stowe missal seems to point to this conclusion: *pro . . . paenitentibus et catachomenis*.[1]

If, however, the prayer was the *oratio fidelium*, Thibaut says that we have here the only example known of the dismissal taking place *after* a prayer of the kind.[2] Yet such phrases as: *postea deprecarent pro illis levitae diceret sacerdos collectam* and *post precem exirent postea foris . . .*, would seem to suggest prayers before the dismissal, rather than the prayer of the faithful.

The collect corresponds with the prayer κύριε παντοκράτορ in the Apostolic Constitutions and with the shorter formulary in the liturgy of Constantinople κύριε ὁ θεὸς ἡμῶν, τὴν ἐκτενῆ ταύτην.[3]

By the time of pseudo-Germanus, the discipline of the catechumenate had become little more than a memory, which the author of the *Expositio* found it necessary to explain, without, however, supplying a formula: *Catechuminum ergo diaconus ideo clamat juxta anticum Ecclesiae ritum, ut tam Judaei quam haeretici vel pagani instructi, qui grandes ad baptismum veniebant et ante baptismum probantur, starent in ecclesia et audirent consilium Veteris et Novi Testamenti; postea deprecarent pro illis levitae, diceret sacerdos collectam, post precem exirent postea foris, qui digni non erant stare dum inferebatur oblatio, et foras ante ostium auscultarent prostrati ad terram magnalia: Quae cura ad diaconum vel ad ostiarium pertinebat ut illis admoneret exire, iste provideret ne quis indignus retardaretur in templo, dicendo: Nolite dare Sanctum canibus, neque mittatis margaritas ante porcos*.[4]

Pseudo-Germanus, in almost the same words as James of Edessa (640–708) in respect to his own rite [5] (Syrian), says that

---

[1] Stowe Missal, *H.B.S.*, vol. XXXII (1915), p. 6.

[2] Thibaut, *op. cit.*, p. 43.

[3] Brightman, *Liturgies Eastern and Western*, p. 373.

[4] Pseudo-Germ. *Pat. Lat.*, t. LXXII, col. 92; Duchesne, *op. cit.*, col. 202.

[5] Ignace Ephrem II Rahmani, *Les Liturgies Orientales et Occidentales*, part I, chap. IV, p. 109. Beirut, 1929.

the deacon dismisses the unworthy *juxta antiquum Ecclesia ritum.* In the 6th century, the catechumenate was still a reality, and the first council of Lyons (517) directed that the penitents should be dismissed after the prayer (*post precem*): *Domini quoque gloriosissimi regis sententiam secuti, id temperamenti praestitimus ut Stephano praedicto vel Palladiae, usque ad orationem plebis, quae post evangelia legeretur, orandi in locis sanctis spatium praestaremus.*[1] A council held at Epaone in the same year (517) speaks of the discipline as 'customary': *cum catechumeni procedere commonentur.*[2]

Cassian, a century earlier, refers incidentally to the catechumenate: . . . *mutatio rursum officio celebrare velut diaconum catechumenis missam.*[3]

Offertory

The procession of the oblations at the beginning of the Mass of the faithful was the nearest approach to the Byzantine 'great entrance' known in the West.

The ceremony called for a demand for silence and an injunction to keep a watch over the doors: *Spiritualiter jubemur silentium facere observantes ad ostium, id est ut tacentes a tumultu verborum . . . hoc solum cor intendat ut in se Christum suscipiat.*[4] The doors of the church are interpreted by 'Germanus' as the 'gates of the soul' or, in other words, the senses, since the shutting of doors to exclude the unworthy was no longer a reality.[5]

A chant of antiphon or psalm, known as the *sonus* and similar in purpose to the Byzantine *cherubikon*, was sung during the procession. It concluded, like the Eastern hymn, with *Alleluia: De sono. Sonum autem quod canitur quando procedit oblatio, hinc traxit exordium. Praecepit Dominus Moysi . . . Nunc autem procedentem ad altarium corpus Christi non jam tubis irreprehensibilibus, sed spiritalibus vocibus praeclara Christi magnalia dulci modilia psallit*

---

[1] Counc. I Lyons, 517, can. 6. Labbe, *op. cit.*, t. IV, col. 1585.

[2] Counc. Epaone, 517, can. 29. *Ibid.*, t. IV, col. 1579.

[3] Cassian, *Instit.*, lib. XI, cap. XVI.

[4] Pseudo-Germ. Duchesne, *op. cit.*, p. 203; *Pat. Lat.*, t. LXXII, col. 92.

[5] The injunction in respect to the doors is still heard in the Byzantine liturgy, but after the great entrance with the holy gifts: in a pontifical function after the kiss of peace.

Ecclesia.[1] The reference to Moses recalls the silver trumpets of the levites at the offering of a victim, although there is no reason to suppose that like instruments were in use in the Gallican liturgy.[2]

The Mozarabic rite used the term *lauda*[3] for the responsary sung at this time, and *sonus* was the name given to similar responsaries at lauds and vespers.

The *oblata*, which were brought to the altar, had been almost certainly prepared before the liturgy, as in the Byzantine rite. It would therefore be a mistake to cite the second council of Mâcon (585), which directed the faithful to offer bread and wine on Sundays, as a proof that the actual preparation of the elements took place at this time.[4] Moreover, these offerings of the people were made in imitation of Roman practice. St. Caesarius (*ob.* 543) attests the custom of offering *before* the Mass: *Ille bonus christianus est, qui quando ad ecclesiam venit, et oblationes quae in altario mittantur exhibet.*[5]

The bread for the liturgy was brought to the altar by the deacon in a vessel shaped like a 'tower', while the wine was carried in a chalice: *Corpus vero Domini ideo defertur in turribus quia monumentum Domini in similitudinem turris fuit scissum in petra, et intus lectum ubi pausavit corpus dominicum unde surrexit Rex gloriae in triumphum. Sanguis vero Christi ideo specialiter offertur in calice quia . . . Aqua autem ideo miscetur vel quia . . .*[6] The bread and wine, it will be noticed, are already referred to as the 'Body and Blood of Christ'.[7] The *prolepsis* is found also in St. Gregory of Tours (*ob.* 594). The Saint, describing a miracle at a Mass on the feast of St. Polycarp at Riom, infers that the offertory procession started from the *secretarium: Lecta igitur passione (S. Polycarpi) cum reliquis lectionibus quas canon sacerdotalis invexit, tempus ad sacrificium offerendum advenit. Accepta*

---

[1] Pseudo-Germ. Duchesne, *op. cit.*, p. 203; *Pat. Lat.*, t. LXXII, cols. 92–3.

[2] *Canetis tubis super holocaustis. Num.* X, 10.

[3] Isid., *De eccles. offic.*, I, 13; Counc. IV Toledo, 633, can. 12. Labbe, *op. cit.*, t. V, col. 1709.

[4] Counc. II Mâcon, 585, can. 4. Labbe, *op. cit.*, t. V, col. 981.

[5] Caesar., *Hom.* CCLXVI, 2. Cf. . . . *oblationes quae in altario consecrantur offerte. Erubescere debet homo idoneus, si de aliena oblatione communicaverit. Qui possunt, aut cereolos aut oleum quod in cicindilibus mittatur exhibeant.* Caesar., *Hom.,* CCLXV, 2.

[6] Pseudo-Germ., Duchesne, *op. cit.*, p. 203; *Pat. Lat.*, t. LXXII, col. 93.

[7] Cf. *Cherubikon* in the Byzantine liturgy.

quoque turre diaconus, in qua mysterium dominici corporis habebatur, ferre cepit ad ostium ingressus templum ut eam altari superponeret, elapsa de manu ejus ferebatur in aera, et sic ad ipsam aram accedens, nunquam eam manus diaconi potuit adsequi; quod non alia credimus actum de causa, nisi quia pollutus erat in conscientia.[1]

Water was probably added to the wine after the oblations had been brought to the altar. The sacred vessels were then covered with a rich veil of silk.

The three cloths or veils employed in the Gallican liturgy have been enumerated by pseudo-Germanus, who, after the fashion of the times, has added a fanciful symbolism: *Palla vera linostima in illius indumenti tenet figuram, quia in gyro contexta a militibus non fuit divisa, tunica scilicet Christi. Corporalis vero palla ideo pura linea est super quam oblatio ponitur, quia corpus Domini puris linteaminibus cum aromatibus fuit obvolutum in tumulo.*

Coopertum vero sacramentorum ideo exornatur quia omnia ornamenta praecellit resurrectio Christi, vel camara celi quae nunc Dominum teget ab oculis nostris. Siricum autem ornatur aut auro, vel gemmis, quia Dominus Moysae in tabernaculo fieri velamina jussit ex auro, jacinto et purpura, coccoque bis tincto et bysso retorta: quia omnia illa mysteria in Christi praecesserunt stigmata.[2]

The first of these, the *Palla linostima*, is a table-cloth covering the *mensa* of the altar and falling all round it. St. Isidore speaks of it as a material woven of flax and wool.[3] It is mentioned also in the prayer at the ordination of subdeacons in the *Missale Francorum: Pallae vero quae sunt in substraturio in alio vase debent lavi, in alio corporales pallae. Ubi pallae corporales lavatae fuerint, nullum linteamen ibidem aliud debet lavi; ipsa aqua in baptisterio debet vergi.*[4] The *palla linostima* was said to symbolise the seamless coat of Christ.

(2) *Corporalis palla* was a corporal of pure linen on which the Host was laid. It symbolised the winding sheet of Christ.

---

[1] *Greg. Turon., De Glor. Mart.*, cap. LXXXVI. *Pat. Lat.*, t. LXXI, cols. 781–2. Cf. *Cum sacrificii offerendi tempus advenisset diaconus turrim, in qua corporis Dominici mysterium continebatur, attulit.* Mabillon, *De Lit. Gall.*, lib. I, cap. V, 9. *Pat. Lat.*, t. LXXII, col. 133.

[2] Pseudo-Germ., *Epist.* I; *Pat. Lat.*, t. LXXII, col. 93; Duchesne, *op. cit.*, p. 203.

[3] Isid., *Orig.*, XIX, 22.

[4] *Missal. Franc., Allocutio ad subdiaconum ordinandum. Pat. Lat.*, t. LXXII, col. 319.

(3) *Coopertorium* (*coopertum*) *sacramentorum*, or 'veil of the holy mysteries', was stretched over the oblations on the altar. It was made of silk, adorned with gold or precious stones. The veil recalled those with which the Mosaic tabernacle was enveloped. Pseudo-Germanus compares it to 'the heavens which encircle Christ', since the veil serves to cover his Eucharistic body: *amictus lumine sicut vestimento.*[1]

It is termed indifferently by St. Gregory of Tours: *pallium siricum, pallium altaris* [2] and *coopertorium.*

The council of Rouen (*c.* 650), in imitation of Byzantine usage, prescribed the censing of the *oblata*, after they had been placed on the altar and veiled,[3] but it is uncertain whether the practice existed in churches outside the province.

The *laudes* were sung at the conclusion of the *sonus*, taking the form of a threefold *Alleluia: Laudes autem, hoc est Alleluia, Johannes in Apocalypsi post resurrectionem audivit psallere. Ideo hora illa Domini pallio quasi Christus tegitur caelo* (corrupt passage), *ecclesia solet angelicum canticum* (*cantare*). *Quod autem habet ipsa Alleluia prima et secunda et tertia, signa tria tempora ante legem, sub lege, sub gratia.*[4]

The ceremonies connected with the offertory would seem to have varied in the different churches. St. Caesarius (*ob.* 543) is said to have introduced the solemn procession of the oblations, with the *sonus* and *laudes*, at Arles in imitation of a practice recently started in neighbouring churches.[5] The fifth council of Arles (554), some eleven years after the death of Caesarius, directed the suffragans of the province to transfer the *oblata* ceremonially to the altar, according to the use of the mother-church, and to the exclusion of any other custom: *Ut oblatae quae in sancto offeruntur altario, a comprovincialibus episcopis non aliter nisi ad formam Arelatensis offerantur ecclesiae.*[6]

---

[1] *Psl.* CIII, 2.
[2] *Greg. Turon., Hist. Franc.*, lib. VII, cap. XXII. *Pat. Lat.*, t. LXXI, col. 429.
[3] Counc. Rouen, *c.* 650, can. I. Mansi, *Concil.*, t. X, col. 1199.
[4] Pseudo-Germ. Duchesne, *op. cit.*, p. 203; *Pat. Lat.*, t. LXXII, col. 93.
[5] Thibaut, *op. cit.*, pp. 48–9.
[6] Counc. V. Arles, 554, can. I. Labbe, *op. cit.*, t. V, col. 782.

Prayers after the Offertory

The prayer after the offertory, which Duchesne calls the 'prayer of the veil',[1] is not mentioned by pseudo-Germanus. It was preceded by a bidding prayer which took the form of a preface exhorting the faithful to pray that they might receive grace from the 'mystery of the day'. The bidding prayer was termed *prefatio missae*; while the collect, which was addressed to God, was preceded by the rubric: *collectio sequitur*. The two prayers varied with the day, and are found in the *Gothicum*,[2] *Gallicanum Vetus*, Bobbio missal and Masses of Mone.[3] The *collectio* seems to have been a counterpart of the *super oblata* or *secreta* in the Roman missal. A somewhat similar combination appears in the *post communio* and the *collectio sequitur* at the end of the Gallican Mass.[4]

The structure and arrangement of these formularies correspond with those in the Roman and African Churches, rather than with the form of collective prayers that we find in the Eastern liturgies. The Mozarabic rite has similar prayers in the *missa* and *alia* (*alia missa*), which St. Isidore describes as the first prayers of the Mass.[5] Normally, *missa* is a bidding prayer addressed to the faithful, while *alia* is a prayer addressed to God, although sometimes we find the two prayers both addressed either to God or to the people.

The forms of exhortation or invocation are clearly derived from the ancient solemn prayers of the Roman Church.[6]

Recital of Names

The position of the recital of the names—after the *collectio*—is exceptional, although we find it in the liturgies of 'Denis the Areopagite',[7] East Syria and Spain.

It was probably of this place in the Mass that Pope Innocent I

---

[1] Duchesne, *op. cit.*, pp. 206–8.

[2] *Gothicum. Pat. Lat.*, t. LXXII, cols. 227, 230, etc.

[3] Mone. *Pat. Lat.*, t. CXXXVIII, cols. 869, 870.

[4] Fols. 15a–15b, *Missal. Gothicum. H.B.S.*, vol. LII, p. 7.

[5] Isid., *De eccles. offic.*, lib. I, cap. XV. Hittorp, *op. cit.*, col. 188.

[6] Thibaut, *op. cit.*, II, p. 54.

[7] Pseudo Denis Areop., *De Hier. Eccles.*, lib. III, cap. IX.

(401–17) complained in his celebrated letter to the bishop of Gubbio (416).[1]

Pseudo-Germanus speaks of a recitation of the names of the dead, without, however, mentioning those of the living: *Nomina defunctorum ideo hora illa recitantur qua pallium tollitur, quia tunc erit resurrectio mortuorum quando adveniente Christo caelum sicut liber plicabitur*.[2] There can nevertheless be little doubt that the living were also named, and we find the second council of Vaison (529) ordering the inclusion of the name of the Pope: *Et hoc nobis justum visum est ut nomen domini papae, quicumque sedi apostolicae praefuerit, in nostris recitetur*.[3]

The names were often inscribed on tablets of ivory (diptychs), and Martène tells us that he saw a tablet of the kind at Bourges.[4]

A specimen of the Gallican diptychs is met with in the commemoration at the end of the Rule of Aurelian, bishop of Arles (546–51), which includes a list of the dead. One of the most recent names is that of King Childebert, who died in 562; while eternal rest for the departed through the intercession of the Blessed Virgin and certain *beati*, the last of whom is Caesarius (*ob.* 543), is a further guide as to the date.[5]

Pseudo-Germanus tells us that the priest removed the veil over the *oblata* at the moment of the recital of the names:[6] a symbolical gesture inspired by the Apocalypse.[7]

The *collectio post nomina* sometimes refers to the 'Book of Life': a feature borrowed from the East.[8] Thus in the *post nomina* prayer for Christmas in the *Gothicum: Nomina quorum sunt recitatione conplexa scribi jubeas in aeternitate*.[9]

In the same codex also, for the second and third of the Lenten Masses: *caelesti cyrographo in libro vitae jubeas adscribi*.[10] The

---

[1] Innoc. I, *Epist.* XXV; *Pat. Lat.*, t. XX, col. 553.
[2] Pseudo-Germ. Duchesne, *op. cit.*, p. 208; *Pat. Lat.*, t. LXXII, col.
[3] Counc. II Vaison, 529, can. 4. Labbe, *op. cit.*, t. IV, col. 1680.
[4] Mabillon, *Admonitio* to works of 'St. Germ.' *Pat. Lat.*, t. LXXII, col. 87.
[5] Mabillon, *De Lit. Gall.*, lib. I, cap. V, 12. *Pat. Lat.*, t. LXXII, cols. 135–6.
[6] Pseudo-Germ. *Pat. Lat.*, t. LXXII, col. 93.
[7] *Et qui non inventus est in Libro vitae scriptus, missus est in stagnum ignis. Apoc.* XX, 14.
[8] The Syrian Moses bar Kepha refers in the 9th century to the *Liber Vitae*. Rahmani, *op. cit.*, part III, chap. III, p. 674.
[9] *Missal. Goth.*, fo. 9. *H.B.S.*, vol. LII, p. 5.
[10] *Ibid.*, fols. 133b, 135a. *Ibid.*, pp. 55, 56.

M

third Mass for Lent in the *Gallicanum Vetus* gives a similar text,[1] but in the second we find: *In coelesti pagina conscribi praecipias.*[2] References to the 'Book of Life' are found also in the Mozarabic liturgy for the Sunday before the Epiphany,[3] Sunday *ante Carnes Tollendas* [4] and Easter.[5] It occurs again in the Ambrosian 11th-century Missal of Aribert.[6]

The third set of prayers for the living and dead in the Roman missal, which, before the 'simplification of the rubrics' in 1955, were directed to be said on the Lenten ferias, are Gallican survivals, introduced by way of the Carolingian liturgy. The secret, in which reference is made to the 'Book of Life', is clearly a *collectio post nomina: Deus cui soli cognitus est numerus electorum in superna felicitate locandus: tribue, quaesumus; ut, intercedentibus omnibus sanctis tuis, universorum, quos in oratione commendatos suscepimus, et omnium fidelium nomina, beatae praedestinationis liber adscripta retineat.*

A text is found in the Leonine sacramentary in which the names are restricted to those of the living.[7]

A public recital of the names of the 'offerers' at Mass was a very general Gallican custom. The *Missale Gothicum* refers to it in the Mass of St. Andrew: *Et offerentum et pausantum quae recitata sunt nomina.*[8] Again, in the Mass of St. Symphorian: *Recitatis nominibus offerentum, fratres carissimi.*[9] Some of the *post nomina* prayers take the form of bidding prayers, as we find in the Reichenau fragment (Masses of Mone) for prayers *ante nomina*.

A regulation in the *Admonitio Generalis* of Charlemagne (789) directed that the names should not be read out earlier in the Mass as formerly, but only in the canon.[10]

Kiss of Peace

The position of the *pax*, separated from the offertory by the recital of names, is a Gallican characteristic, and was a cause of

---

[1] *Gallic. Vetus. Pat. Lat.*, t. LXXII, col. 261.   [2] *Ibid. Ibid.*, col. 260.

[3] *Missal. Mixt. Pat. Lat.*, t. LXXXV, col. 225.   [4] *Ibid. Ibid.*, col. 286.

[5] *Ibid. Ibid.*, col. 483.   [6] King, *Liturgies of the Primatial Sees*, p. 439.

[7] *Sacram. Leon.*, edit. Muratori, p. 318.

[8] *Missal. Goth.*, fo. 107b. *H.B.S.*, vol. LII (1917), p. 42.

[9] *Ibid.*, fo. 225b. *Ibid.*, p. 116.   [10] Sect. 54.

complaint to Innocent I as expressed in his letter to the bishop of
Gubbio (416). The kiss of peace for Innocent, as it had been for
Tertullian,[1] was the seal of the Eucharistic prayer, the seal of the
sacrament of Christian unity, which is the oblation of the holy
Sacrifice, but, says the Pope, it was not to be given *ante confecta
mysteria*.[2] Innocent refers to the position of the *pax* before
Communion as of 'Apostolic tradition', apparently unmindful of
the testimony of St. Justin Martyr.[3] The idea of christian charity
is reiterated by pseudo-Germanus: *Pacem autem idea Christiani
mutuo proferunt ut per mutuum osculum teneant in se caritatis
affectum.*[4]

The kiss would seem to have been given to all the faithful on
the lips. The collect *ad pacem* for the Epiphany in the *Missale
Gothicum* says: *ut osculum quod in labiis datur in cordibus non
negetur.*[5] A somewhat similar idea is found in the *Gallicanum
Vetus: Pacem qua in labiis proferimus in intimis teneamus visceribus.*[6] The Romanised Missal of Bobbio has retained the prayer
ad pacem, but it is unlikely to have been used after the adoption
of the Gelasian canon. It is interesting to note that this old
Gallican collect is found in the Missal of Robert of Jumièges,
which was written in England sometime between 1016 and 1051.
It appears here as the postcommunion for the Mass of St. Leger
(2 October).[7]

Creed

The creed was not recited in the liturgy of Gaul before the
Carolingian reform. The reference to 'Gaul' in a canon of the
fourth council of Toledo (633) was exclusively to 'Narbonnaise
Gaul', where the Mozarabic and not the Gallican rite prevailed.[8]

---

[1] *Alia jam consuetudo invaluit, jejunantes habita oratione cum fratribus subtrahunt osculum
pacis, quod est signaculum orationis. Quae oratio cum divortio sancti osculi integra? Quale
sacrificium est, a quo sine pace receditur?* Tertull., *De Orat.* XIV (alias XVIII). *Pat. Lat.*,
t. I, cols. 1176–7.

[2] *Innoc.*, epist. XXV, cap. I; *Pat. Lat.*, t. XX, col. 553.   [3] Justin, *Apol.* I, 65.

[4] Pseudo-Germ., Duchesne, *op. cit.*, p. 211; *Pat. Lat.*, t. LXXII, col. 93.

[5] *Missal. Goth.*, fo. 66b. *H.B.S.*, vol. LII (1917), p. 27.

[6] *Gallic. Vet.* Lebrun, *op. cit.*, t. II, p. 592.

[7] The prayer is found in this place in missals of Verdun (1481) and Liège (1540), and
also in a sacramentary of Reichenau. Oxford, Bodl. MS. *Liturg. Misc.* 319.

[8] Counc. IV Toledo, 633, can. 2. Labbe, *op. cit.*, t. V, col. 1704.

The creed in the Spanish liturgy was recited immediately before
the *Pater noster*. Alcuin (*ob.* 804), who has been described as
'liturgist extraordinary to Charlemagne',[1] introduced the profession of faith, with the *filioque*, into the Mass of the Frankish
dominions. He had heard it chanted in Northumbria by the Irish
monks, who had picked up the custom from Visigothic sources.

Dialogue

Pseudo-Germanus gives little more than a passing reference
to the great sacerdotal prayer of the holy Mysteries, and one must
therefore look to some other source.

The *Sursum corda* is certainly mentioned, but not a word as to
what followed it: *Sursum corda ideo sacerdos habere admonet, ut
nulla cogitatio terrena maneat in pectoribus nostris in hora sacrae
oblationis . . .*[2] A curious variant of the dialogue before the *illatio*
(preface) is found in the Mozarabic liturgy, but the form used in
Gaul is uncertain.

Preface

The preface in the Merovingian books and the Bobbio missal
is termed *contestatio*, while the *Gothicum* and the *Gallicanum Vetus*
employ a variety of names: *contestatio, immolatio, praefatio missae*.

Contestatio is used in the classical sense of attestation, pro-
testation, confession or profession of faith. Its use would probably have originated from the 'attestation' of the pontiff and faithful which marks the beginning of the Eucharistic canon: *Habemus
ad Dominum*.[3] Gennadius, in the 5th century, speaks of it at the
conclusion of a reference to Musaeus of Marseilles (458): *Composuit sacramentorum egregium . . . sed supplicandi Deo et con-
testandi beneficiorum ejus sodalitate sui consentaneum*.[4] In the
following century, St. Gregory of Tours (*ob.* 594), in his
'Miracles of St. Martin', employs *contestatio* as the current word:
At ubi, expedita contestatione, omnis populus Sanctus in laudem

---

[1] Ellard, *op. cit.*, chap. XII, p. 225.

[2] Pseudo-Germ., *Epist.* I. Duchesne, *op. cit.*, p. 213; *Pat. Lat.*, t. LXXII, col. 94.

[3] Cf. *Respondetis; Habemus ad Dominum. Laborate ut verum respondeatis. Quia apud
acta Dei respondetis.* Aug., *Serm.* II, i. Also, Cyril. Jer., *Catech. Mystagog.*, V.

[4] Gennad., *De Script. eccles.*, LXXIX. *Pat. Lat.*, t. LVIII, col. 1103.

Domini proclamavit.[1] *Contestatio* is a distinctive Gallican term, but we find it also in the Carolingian sacramentary of St. Alban's, Mainz, dating from the second half of the 9th century. The Masses for the thirty-seven Sundays are all provided with a proper preface (*contestatio*).[2]

Immolatio is a difficult word to translate in any other way than 'Sacrifice of the Mass', although it connotes no more than the preface of the canon. It would seem, however, that the term is a modification of *illatio* (*inlatio*): the name given to the preface in the Mozarabic rite. *Illatio* is the simple translation of the Greek Ἀνάφορα, a word characterising the form of speech by which the thanksgiving of the Pontiff ascends to heaven during the offering of the Holy Sacrifice.[3]

St. Caesarius of Arles (*ob.* 543), in admonishing those who leave the church after the lessons, pointedly asks who in that case will be found to respond to the *Sursum corda* of the priest: *Cum enim maxima pars populi, imo, quod pejus est, pene omnes, recitatis lectionibus exeunt de ecclesia, cui dicturus est sacerdos, Sursum corda? Aut quomodo sursum se habere corda respondere possunt, qui deorsum in plateis et corpore simul et corde discedunt?* [4]

A proper 'preface' is provided for every Mass in the Gallican and Mozarabic liturgies: the *Missale Gothicum* has sixty-eight prefaces for as many Masses, and the Bobbio missal seventy-six for sixty-two formularies. The texts are considerably more diffuse in expression than is customary in the Roman liturgy, although their general form is similar. The conclusion of a *contestatio* is indicated by *per quem*.

Sanctus

No extant Gallican book provides the text of the *sanctus*, but the formula, together with that of the *benedictus*, are quoted by St. Caesarius.[5] It is possible, says Henry Jenner, that the phrase

---

[1] *Greg. Turon., De Mirac. S. Mart.*, lib. II, cap. XIV. *Pat. Lat.*, t. LXXI, cols. 946–7. Cf. Du Cange, *Gloss. Man.*, t. II (Halle, 1773), p. 687.

[2] Robert Amiet, *Trois Manuscrits Carolingiens de St.-Alban de Mayence. Ephem. Liturg.*, vol. LXXI (1957), fasc. II, p. 103. The sacramentary is now in the Seminary at Mainz, cod. I. [3] Thibaut, *op. cit.*, II, p. 59.

[4] St. Caesar., *Hom.* CCLXXI, 2. *Pat. Lat.*, t. XXXIX, col. 2277.

[5] *Ibid., Hom.* CCLXXXI, 2 (append. Aug.). *Ibid.*, t. XXXIX, col. 2277.

gloria majestatis tuae, which is found in the *sanctus* of the Mozarabic rite, may have occurred also in the Gallican liturgy.[1] St.
Gregory of Tours (*ob*. 594) tells us that it was customary for the
people to join in the *sanctus: Ubi expedita contestatione omnis
populus sanctus in laudem Domini proclamavit*.[2]

The *collectio post sanctus*, in which the celebrant attests the
holiness of Christ, takes up the theme of the preceding chant and
amplifies it, thus leading to the recital of the Institution, which
began with the Roman formula *Qui pridie*. The prayer, variable
at every Mass, generally commenced with the words *vere sanctus,
vere benedictus*, after the example of the Eastern liturgies. They
were, however, replaced in the Mass of Christmas in the *Missale
Gothicum* by the opening phrase of the song of the angels: *Gloria
in excelsis Deo*.[3] The *post sanctus* ends normally with *per Christum
Dominum nostrum*, which serves as an antecedent to *qui pridie*.
Some form of *post sanctus* is found in all liturgies, with the
exception of the Roman and the Romanised Missal of Bobbio.
Fr. Lucas, however, on the strength of the *post sanctus* on Holy
Saturday in the Ambrosian rite, says: 'What possible difficulty
can there be in supposing that the Roman Mass also originally had
this same form, even though it has not retained it in even a single
Mass?'[4] The hypothesis is, of course, possible, but, with a total
absence of evidence, extremely improbable.

A definite epiclesis is met with in the so-called *post sanctus* for
Holy Saturday in the *Gothicum: Te oramus uti hoc sacrificium tua
benediccione benedicas et Spiritus sancti tui rore perfundas ut sit
omnibus legitima eucharistia per Christum Dominum nostrum*.[5] On
the other hand, the prayer may possibly be a *post pridie*, as that
which follows is termed *colleccio ad panis fraccionum*.

Consecration

'In the ancient Gallican books', says Duchesne, 'the account of
the institution of the Eucharist is always omitted, or is merely

[1] Jenner, art. *Gallican Rite, Cath. Encyclop.*, vol. VI, p. 363.
[2] *Greg. Turon., De Mirac. S. Mart.*, lib. II, cap. XIV; *Pat. Lat.*, t. LXXI, cols. 946–7.
[3] *Missal. Goth.*, fo. 12a, *Henry Bradshaw Society*, vol. LII (1917), p. 6.
[4] Lucas, *Early Gallican Liturgy, Dublin Review* (January 1894), p. 122.
[5] *Missal. Goth.*, fols. 168b–169a. *H.B.S.*, vol. LII, p. 80.

indicated by the first words of it. The celebrant must have known it by heart'. [1] The original cause of the omission may have been due to the *disciplina arcani*, as was probably the reason for the lacuna in the East Syrian liturgy of Addai and Mari. The consecration was referred to incidentally by pseudo-Germanus, but by his time there was no longer any need for reticence.

The expression *mysterium fidei* would seem to have been a distinctive trait of the Gallican liturgy.

At the moment of consecration, says St. Gregory, the priest signs the *oblata: Cum ventum est ut sanctum munus, juxta morem catholicum, signo crucis superposito, benediceretur . . .*[2] This, however, must surely have taken place at the words: *gratias agens benedixit.* Pseudo-Germanus, in his second letter, which is largely concerned with the baptismal Mass of Holy Saturday, adds: *Angelus enim Dei ad secreta super altare tamquam super monumentum descendit, et ipsam hostiam benedicit, instar illius angeli qui Christi resurrectionem evangelisavit.*[3]

Oriental influence never seems to have introduced *in qua nocte tradebatur* as the opening phrase of the recital of the institution, as we find in the Mozarabic liturgy.

Post secreta, as the title of the prayer following the consecration, is evidence of a silent canon; while the alternative, *post mysterium*, indicates that the words of institution were held to effect the consecration.

There seems little doubt that the Host was consecrated on the paten, not the corporal: *Patena autem vocatur ubi consecratur oblatio, quia mysterium Eucharistiae in commemoratione offertur passionis Domini.*[4]

Faustus, bishop of Riez (*ob.* between 490 and 495), in a sermon entitled *Magnitudo*, which appears to owe something to the *De Mysteriis* and *De Sacramentis* of St. Ambrose, speaks of the change in the Eucharist as effected by the words of our Lord: *Quando benedicendae verbis caelestibus creaturae sacris altaribus*

---

[1] Duchesne, *op. cit.*, p. 215.
[2] *Greg. Turon., De Vit. Patr.*, XVI, *De sancto Venantio Abbate. Pat. Lat.*, t. LXXI, col. 1075.
[3] Pseudo-Germ., *Epist.* II; *Pat. Lat.*, t. LXXII, col. 96.
[4] Pseudo-Germ., *Epist.* I; *Pat. Lat.*, t. LXXII, col. 93.

*imponuntur, antequam invocatione sancti nominis consecretur, sub-
stantia illic est panis et vini: post verba autem Christi corpus et
sanguis Christi.*[1] A true epiclesis through the invocation of the
Father is expressed by the words 'invocation of the holy name'.

Post Secreta

The prayer which follows the consecration is known as *post
secreta*, *post pridie* or *post mysterium*.

It was a formula of oblation, taking the place of the com-
plementary prayers of the anamnesis and epiclesis of the Holy
Spirit, and ending with the great doxology of the Eucharistic
canon.

This was a variable prayer which took various forms: sometimes it was addressed to the Father and sometimes to the Son;
while in the Mozarabic liturgy we find it as a bidding prayer. The
petitions often include a kind of oblation, after the manner of the
Unde et memores: others have a more or less definite epiclesis.
Just such an invocation is found in four of the so-called Masses
of Mone; one has a *post pridie* without an epiclesis; while another
is unfinished, although without anything of the kind so far as it
goes.

The prayers in the *Gothicum* are for the most part without any
form of epiclesis, although in nine of the Masses we find one of a
sort, in some cases very vague. Thus the *post secreta* for the
Circumcision says: *ut fiat nobis eucharistia legitima in tuo filique
tui nomine et Spiritus sancti, in transformationem corporis ac
sanguinis Domini Dei nostri Jesu Christi, unigeniti tui.*[2] The
prayer in the Mass of St. Germanus in the *Gallicanum Vetus* asks
that the Word may descend upon the *oblata: Descendat, precamur,
omnipotens Deus, super haec, quae tibi offerimus, Verbum tuum
sanctum: descendat inaestimabilis gloriae tuae spiritus: descendat
antiquae indulgentiae tuae donum ut fiat oblatio nostra hostia spiritalis in odorem suavitatis accepta; etiam nos famulos tuos per
sanguinem Christi tua manus dextera invicta custodiat.*[3]

---

[1] *Pat. Lat.*, t. XXX, col. 272. The sermon has been variously ascribed to Eusebius of Emesa, St. Jerome and St. Caesarius, but it is more probably the work of Faustus.
[2] *Missal. Goth.*, fols. 44a–44b. *H.B.S.*, vol. LII, pp. 18–19.
[3] *Gallic. Vet.* Mabillon *De Lit. Gallic.*, lib. III; *Pat. Lat.*, t. LXXII, col. 342.

The Cistercian liturgist, Cardinal Bona, assures his readers that the position of the invocation in no way contravenes the faith: *nam haec oratio nihil habet alienum a fide!* [1]

An addition to the text of the *Hanc igitur* is found in the *Missale Francorum: in honore domini martyris tui illius*.[2] Pope Vigilius in his letter to Profuturus, bishop of Braga (538), may possibly have had some such variable clause in mind. Yet another variant, not in the ordinary Roman text, occurs in the Bobbio missal: *in honorem nominis tui*.[3] This is found also in a prayer in the *Gothicum*, which seems to have been based on the *Hanc igitur*. Frankish, Spanish and Irish compilers have made use of and combined what were originally Roman formulas. Attempts to reconstitute the Gallican canon have produced a difference in detail, but all liturgists have agreed on its brevity.[4]

Fraction

The complicated ceremonial connected with the fraction, as we find in some of the Eastern liturgies, occupied an important place in the Gallican rite. Pseudo-Germanus resumes here his description of the liturgy, which he had discontinued at the *Sursum Corda: Confractio vero et commixtio corporis Domini tantis mysteriis declarata . . . In hac confractione sacerdos vult augere; ibidem debet addere, quia tunc caelestia terrenis miscentur et ad orationem sacerdotis caeli aperiuntur. Sacerdote autem frangente, supplex clerus psallit antiphonam, quia (Christo) patiente dolore mortis, omnia trementis testata sunt elementa. Oratio vero dominica pro hoc ibidem ponitur ut omnis oratio nostra in dominica oratione claudatur*.[5]

The fraction has retained its original position, as in the liturgy of 'Denis the Areopagite', whereas Rome and Byzantium have deferred it until after the *Pater noster*. The ceremony is attested by St. Gregory of Tours (*ob.* 594).

---

[1] Bona, *op. cit.*, lib. I, cap. XIII, 7, p. 88.
[2] *Missal. Franc.* Mabillon, *Lit. Gallic.*, lib. III; *Pat. Lat.*, t. LXXII, col. 339.
[3] *Missal. Bobbio*, fo. 13. *H.B.S.*, vol. LVIII (1920), p. ii.
[4] Netzer, *Introduction de la Messe Romaine en France sous les Carolingiens* (Paris, 1910), chap. I, p. ii.
[5] Pseudo-Germ. Duchesne, *op. cit.*, p. 218; *Pat. Lat.*, t. LXXII, col. 94.

It is possible that there may have been an elevation before the fraction, if we may judge from the life of Euvertus, a 4th-century bishop of Orleans. The author, a certain subdeacon of the name of Lucifer, tells us that, at the time of the fraction, the bishop, following priestly precedent, raised his hands and offered the Host which was to be blessed by the Holy Trinity. Thereupon a beautiful cloud appeared above the head of the celebrant, and out of the cloud a hand with extended fingers was seen blessing the oblations.[1]

The fraction, according to Eutychius, patriarch of Constantinople (552–82), symbolised the supreme moment of the death of our Lord.[2] St. Caesarius (*ob.* 543) referred to the rite, without, however, describing it: *Credimus secundum sermonem divinum id esse corpus dominicum quod in divina mensa sancte consecrantur, ut universo coetui sacro absque sectione dividitur, et absque defectu participatur.*[3]

The complicated ritual of the fraction in the Mozarabic and Celtic liturgies is well known, but we have not the same detail respecting Gallican usage. We know, however, that it was a similarly complicated affair. The second council of Tours (567) legislated for the arrangement of the particles on the corporal: *non in imaginario ordine sed sub crucis titulo.*[4] It seems clear from this that a certain amount of superstition was connected with the ceremony. Superstition would seem to have been encouraged by the 'miracles' described in the *Verba seniorum*, a Greek work which had been translated by the Roman deacon, Pelagius, who has been identified with the Pope of that name (556–61).[5] On the other hand, the Pope, in a letter to Sapaudus, bishop of Arles (558), condemned the superstitious practice of arranging the particles in the form of a human figure.[6]

Pseudo-Germanus says that an antiphonal chant was sung during the fraction by a cleric in a 'suppliant tone', as befitted a

---

[1] *Acta SS.*, Sept., t. III, p. 45; *Dictionnaire d'Archéologie Chrétienne et de Liturgie*, t. IV, col. 2666.

[2] Eutych., *De Paschate et SS. Euch.*; *Pat. Graec.*, t. LXXXVI, col. 2396A.

[3] Caesar., *Dialog. interrog.*, lib. III, 169.

[4] Counc. II Tours, 567, can. 3. Labbe, *op. cit.*, t. V, col. 853.

[5] We have here a further example of Gaul influenced by the East.

[6] Righetti, *op. cit.*, t. I, part 2, cap. III, p. 122.

commemoration of the death of Christ.[1] The name of the chant is not given, but it served a purpose similar to the *confractorium* in the Ambrosian rite.

Lord's Prayer

The Lord's Prayer, as in most liturgies, was framed in a prologue and epilogue, which in Gaul varied with the Mass.[2] The prologue took the form of a prayer *ante orationem dominicam*, and the epilogue, a prayer *post orationem dominicam*. The text of the prologue in the Bobbio missal has been altered: 'Instructed by divine teaching, and (following) divine institution we are bold to say' has been changed, in conformity with Roman usage, to 'Admonished by saving precepts', etc.

The Lord's Prayer was recited by the people in the Gallican rite, after the manner of the Eastern liturgy. St. Cassian (*ob. c.* 435) refers to the custom in his ninth Conference, addressed to Leontius, bishop of Fréjus (*c.* 426), and the monk Helladius, when speaking of the abbot Isaac in the Egyptian desert of Scetis.[3] In the following century, the custom was attested by St. Caesarius of Arles [4] (*ob.* 543) and St. Gregory of Tours (*ob.* 594). St. Gregory refers to it in narrating the miracle of the deaf mute. He tells how on a certain Sunday the invalid was able to recite the Lord's prayer at Mass with the rest of the faithful.[5]

Commixture

The commixture followed the *Pater noster*, but we have no information as to how it was carried out. It would be interesting to know whether it was in any way similar to the elaborate ceremony found in the Syrian rite.

---

[1] Pseudo-Germ. *Epist.* I. *Pat. Lat.*, t. LXXII, col. 94; Duchesne, *op. cit.*, p. 218.

[2] In the Mozarabic rite, the introduction is variable: the embolism constant.

[3] *Quod formidantes nonnulli, cum in ecclesia haec oratio ab universa plebe concinitur* . . . Cassian, *Collat.* IX, cap. XXII. *Pat. Lat.*, t. XLIX, cols. 797–8.

[4] *Aut quando oratio dominica dicitur, quis est qui humiliter et veraciter clamet; Dimitte nobis debita nostra* . . . ? Caesar. *Hom.* CCLXXXI, 2. *Pat. Lat.*, t. XXXIX, col. 2277.

[5] *Aperto ore cepit sanctam orationem cum reliquis decantare.* Greg. Turon., *Mirac. S. Martini*, lib. II, cap. XXX. *Pat. Lat.*, t. LXXI, col. 955.

Blessing before Communion

St. Caesarius suggests that the solemn blessing of the bishop before Communion served as a kind of general absolution, which followed naturally from the closing petitions of the Lord's Prayer: 'forgive us our sins' and 'deliver us from evil'.[1] The blessing is often claimed to be a distinctive Gallican usage, but it would probably have been borrowed from the Church of North Africa. A diaconal monition preceded the blessing: *Humiliate vos benedictioni*, which St. Caesarius referred to in a homily: *Et hoc admoneo simul et rogo, fratres, quoties clamatum fuerit, ut vos benedictioni humiliare debeatis, non vobis sit laboriosum capita inclinare; quia non vos homini, sed Deo humiliatis.*[2] The solemn pontifical blessing, as in Africa,[3] consisted of a number of phrases, varying according to the days of the liturgical year.[4] The Gallican blessings abound in Scriptural allusions and patristic rhetoric, and the Old Testament references are often explained with the help of St. Paul. Later Carolingian texts are shorter, less poetic, more abstract and more theological. The African practice of reserving the blessing to the bishop was prescribed in the council of Agde (506), and the usage was forbidden to simple priests: *Benedictionem super plebem in ecclesia fundere aut poenitentem in ecclesia benedicere presbytero penitus non licebit.*[5] Later, as we learn from pseudo-Germanus, a short and fixed formula of blessing was permitted to priests: *Benedictionem vero populi sacerdotibus fundere Dominus per Moysen mandavit ... Propter servandum honorem pontificis sacri constituerunt canones ut longiorem benedictionem episcopus proferret, breviorem presbyter funderet, dicens: Pax, fides et caritas et communicatio corporis et sanguinis Domini sit semper vobiscum.*[6] On the other hand, a

---

[1] Caesar., *Hom.* CCLXXXVI, 7. *Pat. Lat.*, t. XXXIX, col. 2285.

[2] *Ibid.*, *Hom.* CCLXXXV, 2. *Ibid.*, col. 2284.

[3] *S. Aurelii Augustini sermonum quorumdam fragmenta: Pat. Lat.*, t. XXXIX, col. 1721.

[4] e.g. *Missal. Goth.*, Christmas, fo. 13b; *Henry Bradshaw Society*, vol. LII (1917), pp. 6–7.

[5] Counc. Agde, 506, can. 14; Labbe, *op. cit.*, t. IV, col. 1390. Cf. Counc. Orleans, 511, can. 21.

[6] 'Germ.' Duchesne, *op. cit.*, p. 222; *Pat. Lat.*, t. LXXII, col. 94. Cf. Stowe and Ambrosian liturgies.

number of lengthy formulas of blessing in the *Missale Gothicum*
would not seem to have been reserved to the bishop.[1] Clergy
were ordered by the fourth council of Toledo (633) to follow
the prescribed order of ceremonies, as some of the priests delayed
to give the blessing until after the Communion.[2]

Holy Communion

A fixed order regulated the administration of Holy Communion, and the second council of Tours (567) legislated for it:
*Ad orandum et communicandum laicis et feminis, sicut mos est,
pateant sancta sanctorum.*[3] St. Caesarius tells us that the men
received the Host in their bare hands, while the women covered
their hands with a veil appointed for the purpose: *Omnes viri,
quando ad altare accessuri sunt, lavant manus suas; et omnes
mulieres nitida exhibent linteamina ubi corpus Christi accipiant.*[4] A
similar injunction in respect to women was issued by the council
of Auxerre [5] (578), and the *dominicale* that we find mentioned in
another canon was probably the name of the cloth for covering
the hands.[6] Women who failed to bring this cloth were forbidden
to use the linen cloth on the altar (*palla dominica*).[7]

It is difficult to say how frequently the faithful in Merovingian
Gaul received Holy Communion. A monastic rule of a 'certain
father to his monks', which borrows extensively from the Celtic
usages of St. Columban and dates from the 7th century, directs
the community to receive Holy Communion every Sunday.[8]

Pseudo-Germanus gives us no details for Communion, but he
tells us that a chant (*trecanum*) was sung at this time, expressive

---

[1] *Missal. Goth. Pat. Lat.*, t. LXXII, cols. 226, 229, 232, 234, 235, 238, etc.

[2] Counc. IV Toledo, 633, can. 18; Labbe, *op. cit.*, t. V, col. 1711.

[3] Counc. II Tours, 567, can. 4; *Ibid.*, t. V, col. 854. Cf. *Greg. Turon., Hist. Franc.*, lib. IX, cap. iii; *Ibid.*, lib. X, cap. VIII: *ad altarium.*

[4] Caesar., *Hom.* CCLII: *de tempore; Pat. Lat.*, t. XXXIX, col. 2168.

[5] Counc. Auxerre, 578, can. 36: *Non licet mulieri nuda manu eucharistiam accipere.* Labbe, *op. cit.*, t. V, col. 960.

[6] *Ibid.*, can. 42: *Ut unaquaeque mulier quando communicat dominicalem suum habeat: quod si qua non habuerit, usque in alium diem dominicum non communicet. Ibid.*, t. V, col. 961.

[7] *Ibid.*, can. 37: *Non licet mulieri manum suam ad pallam dominicam mittere. Ibid.*, t. V, col. 960.

[8] *Regula cujusdam Patris ad Monachos. Pat. Lat..* t. LXVI, col. 987. Gaudemet, *Les Aspects canoniques de la Règle de Saint Colomban, Mélanges Colombaniens* (Paris, 1951), p. 174.

of faith in the Holy Trinity: *Trecanum vero quod psallitur signum est catholicae fidei de Trinitatis credulitate procedere. Sic enim prima in secunda, secunda in tertia et rursum tertia in secunda et secunda rotatur in prima. Ita Pater in Filio mysterium Trinitatis complectit: Pater in Filio, Filius in Spiritu sancto, Spiritus sanctus in Filio et Filius rursum in Patre.*[1] The chant has not been identified with any certainty, but Lebrun is probably correct in collating the Gallican *trecanum* with the *ad accedentes*.[2] The Mozarabic liturgy, for example, has *Gustate et videte*, which consists of three verses borrowed for the most part from *Psalm* XXXIII: each verse accompanied by a threefold *Alleluia*.[3] This more or less corresponds with the *trecanum* described by pseudo-Germanus, who has in fact alluded elsewhere to the psalm by way of a pious aside: *Jam vero quam dulcis sit animae et corpori sacra communio.* St. Cyril of Jerusalem (*ob.* 386) speaks of this psalm as a communion chant,[4] and it is found in this connection in the Apostolic Constitutions [5] and the Liturgy of St. James.[6] An incidental allusion to it was made by St. Caesarius (*ob.* 543): *Gustabis et panem, illum scilicet qui dixit: Ego sum panis vivus qui de coelo descendi; gustabis et videbis quam suavis est Dominus.*[7] His successor in the see of Arles, St. Aurelian, referred in 546 to a chant at the time of Communion, which seems to call for a rubric: *Psallendo omnes communicent.* The correct name of the chant would appear to be *tricanum* rather than *trecanum*, as the word is derived from τρίκανῶν, that is 'three rules', 'three principles' or 'three bars'.

Thanksgiving

The thanksgiving, which was known as *post communionem* or *post eucharistiam*, was in the form of a variable *praefatio* or bidding prayer, followed by a collect under the rubric *collectio sequitur*.

---

[1] Pseudo-Germ. Duchesne, *op. cit.*, p. 224; *Pat. Lat.*, t. LXXII, col. 94.
[2] Lebrun, *op. cit.*, t. II, pp. 350–1.
[3] *Missal. Mixt. Pat. Lat.*, t. LXXXV, col. 119.
[4] Cyril Jer., *Catech. Mystagog.*, V.
[5] Apost. Constit., lib. VIII, cap. XIII (al. cap. XX).
[6] Lit. St James, Brightman, *op. cit.*, p. 64.
[7] Caesar., *Hom.* CVI, 10. *Pat. Lat.*, t. XXXIX, col. 1955.

Dismissal

There is no formula of dismissal in the existing Merovingian books, but it was probably analogous, if not identical, with the simple form in the Celtic missal of Stowe: *Missa acta est—in pace.* St. Avitus, bishop of Vienne (*ob. c.* 519), says that the dismissal formula was used equally at the conclusion of assemblies in church, palace or praetorium: *In ecclesiis, palatiisque sive praetoriis, missa fieri pronunciatur, cum populus ab observatione dimittitur.*[1]

Blessed Bread

Blessed bread (*benedictio, eulogia*) was given by the inferior ministers at the end of the Mass to those who had not received Holy Communion. The custom, which was probably borrowed from the East, is several times mentioned by St. Gregory of Tours (*ob.* 594).[2]

It is noteworthy that the Gallican liturgy was largely composed of variables, with a very small number of fixed formulas.

The scheme of rites and ceremonies was more or less the same throughout the country, but there would have been considerable variations in the different provinces.

BIBLIOGRAPHY

1. L'*Abbaye de Lérins*: Histoire et Monuments. Henri *Moris*. Paris, 1909.
2. Notice sur l'Antique *Abbaye de Saint-Victor de Marseille*. L. *Laurin*. Marseilles (5th edit.), 1948.
2a. Master *Alcuin, Liturgist*. Gerald *Ellard*. Chicago, 1956.
3. L'*Ancienne Liturgie Gallicane*, son Origine et sa Formation en Provence au Ve et Ve siècles sous l'influence de Cassien et Saint Césaire d'Arles. J. B. *Thibaut*. Paris, 1929.
4. *Ancient Liturgies of the Gallican Church*. J. M. *Neale* and G. H. *Forbes*. Burntisland, 1855.
5. *Arles Gréco-Romaine*, Seuil des Gaules Chrétiennes. J. *Gibert*. Arles, 1949.
6. *Bobbio Missal*: Text (Paris, *Bibl. Nat.*, MS. lat. 13246). Edit. E. A. *Lowe*. *Henry Bradshaw Society*, vol. LVIII. London, 1920.

---

[1] Avit., *Epist.* I; *Pat. Lat.*, t. LIX, col. 199.
[2] *Greg. Turon., Hist. Franc.*, lib. VI. *Pat. Lat.*, t. LXXI, cols. 371–414.

7. *Bobbio Missal*: Notes and Studies. Edit. André *Wilmart*, E. A. *Lowe* and H. A. *Wilson*. *H.B.S.*, vol. LXI. London, 1924.
8. Le *Canon du Concile d'Agde sur l'Assistance à la Messe*. Germain *Morin*. *Ephemerides Liturgicae*. July–October, 1935.
9. *Christian Worship*. Louis *Duchesne* (2nd Eng. edit.). London, 1904.
10. *Chronologia Sanctorum et aliorum virorum illustrium, ac Abbatum Sacrae Insulae Lerinensis*. Vincent *Barrali Salerno*. Lyons, 1613.
11. The *Early Gallican Liturgy. Dublin Review. Herbert Lucas*. July 1893 and January 1894.
12. *L'Eglise Saint-Trophime d'Arles*. L. H. *Labande*. Paris, 1930.
13. *Etudes de Liturgie et d'Archéologie Chrétienne*. Pierre *Batifol*. Paris, 1919.
14. *Explication . . . de la Messe*. Pierre *Lebrun*. t. II. Paris, 1726.
15. *Expositio brevis antiquae liturgiae gallicanae (Pseudo-Germanus)*. *Migne*, *Pat. Lat.*, t. LXXII, cols. 83–98.
16. *La Fin du Paganisme en Gaule et les plus anciennes Basiliques Chrétiennes*. Emile *Mâle*. Paris, 1950.
17. *Gallican Rite*. Henry *Jenner*. *Catholic Encyclopedia*, vol. VI.
18. *Gallicane (Liturgie)*. H. *Leclercq*. *Dictionnaire d'Archéologie Chrétienne et de Liturgie*. Vol. VI, part I.
19. *Gregorius Turonensis, Opera*. *Migne, Pat. Lat.*, t. LXXI.
20. L'*Ile et l'Abbaye de Lérins*: Récits et Description. *Moine de Lérins*. Lérins, 1929.
21. L'*Introduction de la Messe Romaine en France sous les Carolingiens*. H. *Netzer*. Paris, 1910.
22. *Jean Cassien*: La Spiritualité du Desert. Vols. I, II. Léon *Cristiani*. Figures Monastiques. Editions de Fontanelle. Abbaye de St. Wandrille, 1946.
23. *John Cassian*: A Study in Primitive Monasticism. Owen *Chadwick*. Cambridge, 1950.
24. *Lectiones Hagiographicae in Liturgia Occidentali*. V. *Raffa*. *Ephemerides Liturgicae*, vol. LXIX (1955), fasc. I.
25. *Lérins et ses Fondateurs*. Léon *Cristiani*. Editions de Fontanelle. Abbaye de Saint Wandrille. 1946.
26. *Littérature latine au moyen âge*. Vol. I. J. *de Ghillinck*. Brussels, 1939.
27. De *Liturgia Gallicana*, lib. 3. John *Mabillon*. Paris, 1685. Migne, *Pat. Lat.*, t. LXXII, cols. 99–382.
28. De *Liturgia Gallicana*: Dissertatio. Rudolph *Buchwald*. Breslau, 1890.
29. La *Liturgie Baptismale en Gaule avant Charlemagne*. P. *de Puniet*. *Revue des Questions Historiques*, October, 1902. Paris, 1902.
30. *Liturgie Comparée*. Anton *Baumstark* (edit. Bernard Botte). Chevtogne, 1953.
31. *Liturgie Gallicane dans les huit premiers siècles de l'Eglise*. Louis *Marchesi* (trans. Gustave Gallot). Lyons, 1869.
32. Les *Liturgies Orientales et Occidentales*. Ignace Ephrem II *Rahmani*. Beirut, 1929.
33. *Manuale di Storia Liturgica*. Mario *Righetti*. Vols. I (1945), IV (1953). Milan.

34. *Mélanges Colombaniens.* Actes du Congrès International de Luxeuil: 20–23 July, 1950.
35. *Missale Gothicum* (Vat. Regin., MS. lat. 317). Edit. H. M. *Bannister.* Vol. I (*Henry Bradshaw Society*, vol. LII, 1917), II (*H.B.S.*, vol. LIV, 1919).
36. *Poetry and Letters in Early Christian Gaul.* N. K. *Chadwick.* London, 1955.
37. La marveilleuse vie de *Saint Césaire d'Arles.* J. A. *Joyeux.* Aix en Provence, 1942.
38. *Sainte Radegonde.* René *Aigrain.* Poitiers, 1952.
39. *Storia del Messale Romano.* Luigi *Barin.* Rovigo, 1920.
40. *Stowe Missal*, edit. G. F. *Warner. Henry Bradshaw Society*, vol. XXXII. London, 1915.

Chapter Four

CELTIC RITE

HISTORICAL BACKGROUND

'THERE is strong circumstantial evidence', says F. E. Warren, 'in favour of the immediately Gallican origin of the British Church, and for fixing the date of its foundation between A.D. 176 and 208.'[1] The statement, however, is misleading, as it seems to suggest that the Gallican rite was introduced into Britain in the 3rd century, whereas the Christians of the period could have had no more than the liturgical minimum, which was common to Christendom, East and West, amplified by improvisation on the part of the celebrant. Warren, moreover, appears to have been influenced by the 'Ephesine' myth, and on the very next page he says: 'Any features of Oriental ritual in the British Church may be accounted for and traced, as has been already suggested, through this immediate channel' (Lyons).[2]

It is unnecessary to dwell on such unsubstantiated legends as those of Joseph of Arimathea and Bran the Blessed (father of the great Caractacus), but a story gained credence at Rome, as early as the 7th century, to the effect that Pope Eleutherius (175–89), at the request of a British chieftain of the name of Lucius, sent two bishops to Britain about the year 180.[3] The story appears first in Bede, who got it from the *Liber Pontificalis*, but it would not seem to have been known to Gildas, Augustine or Aldhelm.

There can, however, be little doubt that Christianity first came to this country with the Roman legionaries. St. Irenaeus in his enumeration of the Christian Churches in 176 makes no allusion to a British Church,[4] but Tertullian, writing about the year 208,

---

[1] Warren, *Liturgy and Ritual of the Celtic Church* (Oxford, 1881, chap. I, p. 57.
[2] *Ibid.*, p. 58.   [3] Bede, *Hist. Eccles.*, lib. I, cap. IV; lib. V, cap. XXIV.
[4] Iren. *Haer.*, lib. I, cap. X.

says: . . . *Galliarum diversae nationes, et Britannorum inaccessa Romanis loca Christo vero subdita . . . in quibus omnibus locis Christi nomen qui jam venit regnant . . . utpote in quibus omnibus locis populus nominis Christi inhabitet . . .*[1] The places 'inaccessible to the Romans' are believed to be districts in Scotland. The persecution of Diocletian (*c.* 304) brought its British martyrs in Alban at Verulamium and Julius and Aaron at Caerleon on Usk.

The first certain evidence for an organised Church in Britain is found in the presence of three British bishops (London, York and, perhaps, Lincoln) at the council of Arles in 314; while others again assisted at the council of Rimini in 359. At Silchester, on the site of the little town of Calleva, the foundations of a 4th-century basilica were uncovered in 1892.

Professor Lloyd considers that at the time of the severance of the country from the Empire (410) the whole province, so far as it was really Roman, may be regarded as Christian.[2]

'It is difficult, however, to believe that there were Christian Churches in Wales before the beginning of the 5th century.'[3] In Ireland, Christianity may well have been preached throughout the country by Irish-speaking Britons in the 4th century.[4]

Towards the close of the 4th century, St. Ninian (*?ob.* 432), a Briton, who is said to have been consecrated by Pope Siricius (384–99) at Rome, carried out an apostolate among the Southern Picts of Galloway, and in 397 dedicated a stone church in honour of St. Martin at Whithorn (Candida Casa) in Wigtownshire. An Ogham inscription on a stone, found in the Shetlands on St. Ninian's Isle in the parish of Dunrossness, has been deciphered: 'The community of Ninian the baptizer.'[5] Recent excavations at the east end of the priory church at Whithorn have disclosed remains which are thought to be those of a fifth century church.[6]

---

[1] Tertull., *Adv. Jud.*, VII; *Pat. Lat.*, t. II, cols. 610–11.
[2] J. E. Lloyd, *A History of Wales*, vol. I, chap. IV, 3, p. 104.
[3] Hugh Williams, *Cymr. Transact.* (1893–94), p. 68.
[4] Zimmer, *Celtic Church*, p. 26.
[5] The stone is now at Edinburgh. The name of Ninian follows that of Martin in a litany of the Culdees of Dunkeld. Haddan & Stubbs, *Documents relating to Gt. Brit. & Ireland*, vol. II, append. C.
[6] V. G. Childe & D. Simpson, *Ancient Monuments of Scotland* (Ministry of Works, 1952), p. 119.

It would seem, however, that many of St. Ninian's converts relapsed into Paganism, and St. Patrick, in a letter to Coroticus, speaks of the Picts as 'apostates'. Gildas (*ob. c.* 570), who was himself a native of the district round the Clyde, writes of the 'fierce hordes of the Picts and Scots, shaggy-haired and of indecent nakedness'.[1] A reconversion of the country appears to have been effected by St. Columba and his Irish missionaries.[2]

In 396, St. Victricius, bishop of Rouen, came to Britain to establish peace in a discordant Church, and in the following century we find two further missions from Gaul, which were to have considerable influence in the country. The immediate cause of the first of these missions would seem to have been the prevalence of Pelagianism in Britain: 'the national heresy', as Dom Louis Gougaud calls it.[3] Christianity by this time had clearly won, in some form or other, the allegiance of the whole country, for heathenism makes no appearance in the story: the conflict lies solely between heresy and the Orthodox faith. The so-called Alleluia victory over the barbarians is a narrative suggestive of a Christian atmosphere.[4] The first visit was undertaken by St. Germanus, bishop of Auxerre, and St. Lupus, bishop of Troyes, in 429–31: the second, supposedly by St. Germanus and St. Severus, bishop of Trier, probably some time between 441 and 448.[5] Some writers, however, have thought that the second mission looks suspiciously like a duplication of the first, possibly incorporating a variant tradition, and Prosper of Aquitaine makes no mention of it.

The missioners may well have concerned themselves with liturgical matters, and the introduction of the method of psalmody, which came later to be known as the *Cursus Scottorum*, could have been effected by them.[6] This *Cursus*, which is said to have

---

[1] Gild., *De Excid. Brit.*, part I, cap. XV; *Pat. Lat.*, t. LXIX, col. 341.

[2] St. Columba came to Iona (Hy) in 565.

[3] Gougaud, *Christianity in Celtic Lands* (London, 1932), chap. II, p. 25. *Pelagianism* rejected original sin, claiming death to be no more than a law of human nature. Baptism therefore was merely a title of admission to the kingdom of heaven, and grace was not necessary for salvation.   [4] Lloyd, *op. cit.*, chap. IV, 3, pp. 106–07.

[5] Severus might also be identified with Severus of Vence, who attended the synods of Riez (439) and Vaison (442).

[6] Patrice Cousin, *La Psalmodie Chorale dans la Règle de Saint Colomban, Mélanges Colombaniens* (Paris, 1951), p. 183.

originated in the monastic settlements of Egypt, will be discussed later in the chapter.

One result of the Gallic visitations would seem to have been the impetus given to monasticism in Cornwall and Wales, and 'the most ancient and celebrated monasteries of Cambria owed their origin, if not to the bishop of Auxerre, at least to a movement of reform instituted by him'.[1] The tradition that St. Illtyd was associated with St. Germanus is corroborated in the life of St. Samson of Dol, written by a Breton monk of Rhuys.[2]

The dedication of churches in Britain to St. Germanus was by no means uncommon, and his cult was admitted by the monk Heiric in the second half of the 9th century: *Haec beato Germano peculiari devotione submissa.*[3] The town of St. German in Cornwall has been named after him. St. Lupus, under the name of Bleiddian, is honoured by two churches in Glamorganshire.

British bishops assisted at the Gallican councils of Tours (461), Vannes (465), Orleans (511) and Paris (555). At Tours, the British representative was a certain Mansuetus: *Mansuetus episcopus Brittanorum interfui et subscripsi.*[4] The delegate was in all probability an *episcopus vagans*, who had been forced to leave his country as a result of the Teutonic invasion.

In central Britain, the Celtic Church was well-nigh extinct by the end of the 5th century, surviving for another two centuries in Cornwall (West Wales) and Wales.

The liturgy, at least in respect to its framework, was undoubtedly Gallican, although Celtic individuality would have shown itself in additions and embellishments. 'Such therefore', says William Maskell, 'was the use (Gallican) which the English Church most probably observed in celebrating the Holy Eucharist until the end of the 6th century.' [5]

The period, however, would be in total darkness if it had not been for Gildas (*ob. c.* 570), the author of *De Excidio Britanniae*,

---

[1] Leclercq, *Cénobitisme, Dict. d'Archéol. Chrét. et de Lit.*, t. II, part 2, col. 3205.

[2] *Acta SS.*, 28 June, *Vita Samsoni*, cap. IV, para. 42.

[3] Heiric, *Miracula Germani*, lib. II; *Pat. Lat.*, t. CXXIV, cols. 1244–5.

[4] Counc. I. Tours, 461. Labbe, *Concil.*, t. IV, col. 1053.

[5] Maskell, *Ancient Liturgy of the Church of England* (London 1846), pref., chap. III, p. lii.

who drew his inspiration from the waning civilisation of Rome and painted the blackest picture of the contemporary Celtic Christians. The British Church was considered to be rushing headlong into ruin, and nothing except monasticism could save it. He would appear to have been himself a monk, looking upon religious as the true 'saints' of God. Gildas gives us but little information concerning the liturgy: he was of the order of prophets. The monastery at Rhuys in Brittany claimed him as the founder and patron: his name occurs in an early Breton litany, and two of the old MSS. of *De Excidio* were transcribed at Rhuys.

Monasticism in Wales made remarkable progress in the second half of the 6th century: due in part to the influence and vigour of St. Illtyd, abbot of the important monastery at Llanwit Major in Glamorgan, where St. Samson, the future bishop of Dol, was trained. No church in Wales would seem to have been dedicated to St. Samson, but we find them in Cornwall (Southill), Guernsey and the Scilly Isles.[1] Samson assisted at the council of Paris in 555 (557), at which he signed as *Samson peccator episcopus*.

Dubricius (Dyfrig), a bishop and great supporter of the monastic movement in the 6th century, seems to have had Archenfield in Herefordshire as the special scene of his activity, if one may judge from the dedication of churches in the district.[2] St. David (*ob. c.* 588), who founded the monastery of Mynyw (Menevia), later to be known as St. David's, became the patron saint of Wales, and has somewhere in the region of fifty-three churches dedicated to his memory.

The important abbey of Bangor-is-Coed on the Dee was founded by Deiniol or Daniel in the middle of the 6th century. It seems clear that by the 9th century monasticism had entered upon a period of decadence from which it never fully recovered until the Cistercian renaissance of the 12th century. Clerical marriage and family property in church offices were pretty firmly established.[3]

Cornwall, where paganism seems to have been still strong, was

---

[1] Middleton in Dorset is dedicated to SS. Mary and Samson.

[2] e.g. Llanfrother (now extinct), with its chapels of Henland and Ballingham; Whitchurch by Monmouth.

[3] Lloyd, *op. cit.*, chap. VII, 2, p. 215.

evangelised by the post-Patrician missions of Ia, Piran, Senan and Petrock in the late 5th and early 6th centuries.

The first known apostle of Ireland, if we may trust Prosper of Aquitaine, was a certain Palladius, who was sent by Pope Celestine I (422–32) 'to the Scots who believed in Christ' in 431.[1]

The fact that Rome should send a bishop to Ireland suggests the existence of Christian communities of some importance, although we know from the apostolate of St. Patrick that paganism was everywhere in the ascendant. The Stowe missal, dating probably from the first decade of the 9th century, has a prayer for the conversion of the heathen, although this may well have been a survival from an earlier mass-book: *adque omnem populum ab idularum cultum eripias et ad te deum verum patrem omnipotentem convertas.*[2]

The work of Palladius in the country was of short duration, and it was overshadowed by the more fruitful apostolate of St. Patrick (*ob. c.* 461). The 'Confession' and the 'Letter to Coroticus' are two genuine works of the Saint, which may be safely used as guides in threading the mazes of his history, but unfortunately they tell us nothing about the liturgy. It would appear from them, however, that Patrick came of a clerical family: his father was a deacon and his grandfather (? great-grandfather) a priest. The names suggest also that he represented the Roman rather than the Celtic element in the province.

The oldest text to record the *Natale* of St. Patrick on 17 March seems to have been the *Life of St. Gertrude of Nivelles* (*ob.* 659), which was written about the year 670. The commemoration is found also in the Calendar of St. Willibrord (beginning of the 8th century), the fragmentary Calendar of Luxeuil (8th century), and the early Irish martyrologies of Tallaght and Felire of Oengus, both of which were compiled at Tallaght, the latter some time between the years 797 and 808, and the former a little earlier. The name of St. Patrick occurs no less than four times in the

---

[1] *Ad Scottos in Christum credentes ordinatus a papa Caelestino Palladius primus episcopus mittitur.* Prosper, *Epitoma Chronicon*, part I; *Pat. Lat.*, t. LI, col. 595. *Scotti* was the general name for the Irish until about the 12th century.

[2] Fo. 27v., *Stowe Missal*, vol. II, *Henry Bradshaw Society*, vol. XXXII (1915), p. 12.

Ordinary of the Mass in the Stowe missal,[1] and it is found in the embolism in a liturgical fragment in the library of St. Gall (?9th century).[2]

The Celtic Church knew little of any diocesan hierarchy, and the bishop (*epscop*), even when he is not the abbot, normally resided in a monastery.

The asceticism and mortification practised in many of the religious houses, as, for example, Mynyw (St. David's), was of the most rigorous kind, equalled only by the Fathers of the Egyptian desert.[3] The 'desert places' or 'retreats of the martyrs' have left their imprint on our maps in such names as Diserth, Dysart (Latin, *Desertum*) and Merthyr (Latin, *Martyrium*).[4]

The oldest of the Irish monastic centres is believed to have been at Killeany (Cell Enda) in Aranmore, the largest of the Aran Islands in Galway Bay, and founded by St. Enda (*ob. c.* 530). Bangor on the southern shore of Belfast Lough in Ulster, which was established by St. Comgall (*ob.* 602), is one of the best known of the Irish monasteries, and it was here that St. Columban and St. Gall received their training before setting out for their missionary work on the Continent of Europe. It is from Bangor also that we have a 7th-century antiphoner: a purely Celtic book without Roman additions or interpolations.

The Celtic lands produced also an 'Order' of religious whose manner of life is but little known: Culdees or *Céli Dé*.[5] The title would seem to have been given in Middle Irish MSS. to foreign monks and to religious Irishmen practising poverty.[6] These Culdees had a centre of considerable importance at Tallaght near Dublin in the 8th and 9th centuries, from whence came the martyrologies of Tallaght and Oengus, and the so-called Stowe

---

[1] e.g. Litany (*H.B.S.*, ibid., p. 14); after *Memento Domine* (ibid., p. 15); *Nobis quoque peccatoribus* (*Ibid.*, p. 16); Embolism (*Ibid.*, p. 17).

[2] St. Gall, *Stiftsbibl.*, 1394, 4, 97.

[3] Three fasts were observed annually: before Christmas, before Easter and after Pentecost. There was also a weekly fast on Wednesday and Friday.

[4] N. Chadwick, *Poetry and Letters in Early Christian Gaul* (London, 1955), chap. VIII, pp. 217–18.

[5] The plural *Céli Dé* came ultimately to denote a kind of secular canons, who occupied an intermediate position between monks and secular clergy.

[6] *Martyrol. of Oengus the Culdee. Henry Bradshaw Society*, vol. XXIX (1905), pref., pp. XXVII–XXVIII.

missal. They were numerous also in Scotland, and we find them at Bardsey (Ynys Enili), an island off the coast of Carnarvon. The Welsh settlement appears to have been founded some time before 516, and to have survived until the later Middle Ages, when it seems to have become Augustinian.

Missionary enterprise was from the first characteristic of Celtic monasticism. In 563, St. Columba crossed the Irish Sea to Iona, an island off the West coast of Scotland, where a monastery was founded which was to play an important part in subsequent ecclesiastical history.

The Celts had a predilection for islands. Here they could pray and study undisturbed; while the settlements afforded a convenient point of departure for missionary journeys.

By the time of the death of St. Columba in 597, Christianity had reached Caledonia and all the islands of the West coast. It was from Iona also that St. Aidan and his companions went South to evangelise Northumbria, Mercia and Essex. Lindisfarne, for the thirty years preceding the synod of Whitby (664), was, as St. Bede tells us, the most important Christian centre in England.[1]

The southern districts seem to have been but little affected by the Irish missions. Malmesbury in Wiltshire had a monastic establishment under Maelduth (Maelduin), from whom St. Aldhelm (*ob.* 709) received his early education.[2] Two small Celtic monasteries existed in Sussex before the arrival of St. Wilfrid in 681: Bosham, mentioned by St. Bede, where Dicuil lived with five or six brethren,[3] and Lewes, the home of St. Lewinna. Tradition speaks of two local villages as being founded by Celtic monks from the Bosham monastery: Ditchling [4] and Steyning.[5] Two villages are said to have been named after St. Chad: Chiddingly ('Land of the children of Chad') and Catsfield ('Chad's field' or 'district').

---

[1] Bede, *Hist. Eccles. Gent. Angl.*, lib. III, cap. V.

[2] *Ibid.*, lib. V, cap. XVIII.

[3] *Ibid.*, lib. IV, cap. XIII.

[4] Ditchling is referred to in King Alfred's will as *Diccelingum*: 'the place of the people of Diccel' (Dicuil).

[5] Steyning is occasionally spoken of before the Norman Conquest as 'St. Cuthman's parish' after St. Cuthman, who, as the old story goes, conveyed his old mother thither in a wheelbarrow from Chidham near Bosham, and built the first church there.

Continental Europe also owed much to Celtic missionaries: especially in Brittany, Galicia (North Spain) and the far-flung districts in which 'Columbanian' monasteries were founded. Missionaries and refugees put new life into the somewhat decadent Merovingian Church, but their activities were not always appreciated by the Gaulish hierarchy.

It would hardly seem necessary to point out that there were no doctrinal differences between the Celtic and Roman churches. The Celts, in common with the faithful throughout Christendom, acknowledged the supreme jurisdiction of the successor of St. Peter, even though distance and the exigencies of the time often made direct influence well-nigh impossible.

It is true that St. Columban (*ob.* 615) on two occasions wrote somewhat strongly worded letters to the Pope in respect to the correct computation of Easter: the first to St. Gregory I (*c.* 600); the second to either Sabinian (604–6) or Boniface IV (608–15). In the first of these, he calls the Pontiff: 'the brightest ornament in the Church, the most noble flower in all disordered Europe, the lofty guardian, and the master of the divine science of chastity'.[1] In the second letter, St. Columban says: 'By reason of Christ's twin apostles (Peter and Paul), you hold an all but celestial position, and Rome is the head of the world's Churches, if exception be made of the singular privilege enjoyed by the place of Our Lord's resurrection (Jerusalem).'[2] And again, the Saint speaks of 'that spiritual source (Papacy), the waters of life'.[3] St. Kilian (*ob. c.* 689) refers to Rome as 'the head of the world, apex of the Catholic faith';[4] while the 7th-century Antiphonary of Bangor gives a hymn of St. Sechnall, written in the 5th century in praise of St. Patrick, in which the Church is said to have been founded on St. Peter.[5] If indeed the Celtic Church had not been orthodox, how comes it that its bishops assisted at the proceedings at Arles in 314, St. Augustine's Oak in 603 and

---

[1] Eugène Martin, *Vita di S. Colombano* (Bobbio, 1923), lib. I, cap. III, pp. 87–89.
[2] Letter to Bonif. IV; *Mon. Germ. Hist.* (new series), *Epist.*, t. III, pp. 174–75.
[3] Martin, *op. cit.*, p. 90.
[4] *Ibid.*, prelim. chap., p. 10.
[5] *Antiph. Bangor*, part 2, edit. F. E. Warren, *Henry Bradshaw Society*, vol. X (London, 1895), p. 14.

Whitby in 664? In spite, however, of these clear proofs that the Celtic Church was at all times a part of the Universal Church of Christ in communion with Rome, we find non-Catholic writers persistently asserting that the faith of the Celts was derived direct from the East, thereby by-passing Rome and its Sovereign Pontiff. So recently as 1956, Sir Winston Churchill, in his *History of the English-Speaking Peoples*, says that the 'form of Christianity which reached England through the mission of St. Columba . . . was monastic in form, and travelled from the East through Northern Ireland to its new home without touching at any moment the Roman centre. . . . It was not in these early decisive periods associated with the universal organisation of the Papacy.'[1] There is, however, as we have seen, not the slightest evidence for such an assertion. There were certainly differences with the English, and also between the Celtic and Gallo-Roman Churches, largely owing to a lack of diocesan ties in the bishops, who were either resident in monasteries or, as it were, *episcopi vagantes* with 'roving commissions'.[2] The main cause of complaint on the part of the clergy trained on the Continent was the Celtic computation of Easter, which will be considered later, and to a lesser degree the style of tonsure. A strongly worded letter was sent to the 'itinerant' priests in Brittany by the metropolitan Licinius of Tours and the bishops of Angers (Eutochius) and Rennes (Melanius) in 515 and again in 520, in which portable altars were forbidden, and strict injunctions were issued to the effect that all churches must be consecrated.

The monastery of Landevennec, founded by St. Winwaloe (*ob.* 529), seems to have retained Celtic usages until the 9th century.[3] The most important Celtic infiltrations on the Continent were those introduced by the Columbanian missionaries.

---

[1] Winston S. Churchill, *Hist. of the English-Speaking Peoples*, Vol. I, *The Birth of Britain*, chap. V, p. 57. London, 1956.

[2] In Brittany, diocesan sees were established at St. Brieuc by the saint of that name (*ob. c.* 502), Tréguier by St. Tugdual (6th century), Dol by St. Samson (*ob. c.* 565), and St. Pol de Léon by St. Paul Aurelian (*ob. c.* 573).

[3] The ruins of the abbey are being restored today as a religious house. *A domus* of St. Winwaloe existed at Wereham in Norfolk, which was granted to the Premonstratensian abbey of West Dereham in 1336. A farm, known by the name of 'Winnals', incorporates a part of the old buildings.

St. Columban, an alumnus of St. Comgall at Bangor, left Ireland with twelve companions in 590, and founded monasteries at Annegray, Luxeuil and Fontaines. In 610, at the instigation of Queen Brunehild and, possibly, not without the connivance of the Frankish episcopate, he was expelled from the kingdom, and, after a series of wanderings, retired to Bobbio in Italy. St. Columban died on 23 November 615. It would indeed be difficult to over-estimate the work and influence of this great monk and missionary. An anonymous life, edited by Adso, abbot of Montier en Der in *c.* 990, says: 'And now what place, what city does not rejoice in having for its ruler a bishop or an abbot trained in the discipline of that cloister (Luxeuil)? For it is certain that by the virtue of its authority almost the whole land of the Franks has been for the first time properly furnished with regular institutions.'[1] Merovingian Gaul in the first half of the 7th century may well claim St. Colomban as the 'father of monasticism'. In all, about fifty houses would seem to have owed their foundation to the sons of Colomban.

St. Colomban was the author of *Regula monachorum, Regula coenobialis* and a Penitential.[2] The first of these, comprising ten chapters, consists of maxims for the direction of individual conduct. It distinguishes between the obligatory collective prayers (canonical) and the simple private devotions left to individual discretion (*in cubiculo suo*). It is noteworthy that whereas the Rule of St. Benedict is itself the focus of obedience, the Rule of St. Colomban directs obedience to the person of the abbot rather than to the written rule. The *Regula coenobialis* contains fifteen chapters of penal sanctions. It is important as prescribing frequent private auricular confession, rather than the public confession and episcopal absolution which seem to have been general elsewhere. His Penitential is the earliest example that we know to have been in use on the Continent: with a list of appropriate penances for specific sins. The disciples of St. Colomban, as we have seen, founded a number of houses, especially in north-east France and

---

[1] Adso, *Vita Bercharii*, I, 8; *Acta SS.*, October, t. VII, p. 1012.
[2] Colomb., *Reg. mon.* and *Reg. coenob.*, *Pat. Lat.*, t. LXXX, col. 209. Penitent., *ibid.*, t. LXXX, col. 324.

Flanders, but in addition to these we find monasteries which followed a double rule: St. Colomban and St. Benedict, and the two observances persisted until the introduction of lay abbots by Charles Martel (730–40). Thus a charter of Faro, bishop of Meaux, for the monastery of Rebais (1 March 637) says: *Regula Benedicti ad modum Luxoviensis monasterii*.[1] Luxueil itself would seem to have introduced the Holy Rule alongside the existing Columbanian usages about the year 629. Celtic monks were found in considerable numbers throughout the territory of the Franks from the 6th to the 9th century, and we hear of them at Waulsort, St. Gall, Mainz, Würzburg, Cologne and Ratisbon. It is evident that they were faithful to their own customs and usages. A passage in the life of St. Gerard, bishop of Toul (936–94), says: 'It was their (Scotti) custom to assemble daily at the different altars in the chapel, where they offered the services of supplication and praise to God after the manner of their own countries' (*more patrio*).[2] There does not seem to have been any concerted opposition to Celtic usages other than a general disapproval of an antiquated computation of Easter, although we hear of Agrestius, himself a monk of a Columbanian monastery, complaining of the multiplicity of collects *et multa alia superflua* at a council of Mâcon (?620).[3]

Irishmen (*Scotti*), as we have seen, went to the Continent as missionaries in considerable numbers, but, at least in the early years of the 12th century, there seems to have been a 'two-way traffic'. Abbot Dionysius (Domnus) about the year 1111 is known to have sent four of his community (two of good family and two of lesser degree) to Ireland, in order to beg funds for the building of the monastic church of St. James at Ratisbon. Later in the century, an abbot of this house (Christian MacCarthy,

---

[1] Pardessus, *Diplomata*, n. 275, t. II, p. 39. A blending of the two rules was found also at Bèze (620), Solignac (632), St. Jean de Laon (640), Sithiu (640), Fontenelle (649), Fleury (651), Jumièges (654), Corbie (656), Hautevilliers (680) and Noirmoutier (680).

[2] Widric, *Vita Gerardi*, III, 25; *Acta SS.*, April, t. III, p. 213.

[3] Agrestius, a former notary of Thierry II, would seem to have been a thoroughly disturbing element, and, among other things, he attempted to involve the two successors of St. Columban at Luxeuil in the schism of the 'Three Chapters'. Martin, *op. cit.*, epil. pp. 186–7; Counc. Mâcon, ?620, Labbe, *op. cit.*, t. V ,cols. 1686–7.

succ. 1133) came to Ireland twice, definitely on collecting tours, and on the second occasion he died and was buried there.[1]

CELTIC SINGULARITY

Celtic singularity may be classified under three heads: Tonsure, Date of Easter and Baptism.

Tonsure. A tonsure does not appear to have been customary for clerics before the second half of the 4th century, and for monks before the end of the 5th century or the beginning of the 6th.[2] An injunction not to wear the hair long sufficed. The primitive tonsure, which bore the name of 'St. Paul', was a total shaving of the head.[3] It was maintained in the East until the 7th century. The tonsure of 'St. Peter' left a circle of hair around a shaven head. St. Gregory of Tours (*ob.* 594) seems to have been the first to mention this form, which was employed by his great namesake of Rome,[4] and probably introduced into Britain by St. Augustine.[5] The exact appearance of the tonsure, which was so dear to our Celtic forefathers, and known as the tonsure of 'St. John' is uncertain.[6] Two suggestions have been made as to its form: (1) The forepart of the head, in front of a line drawn from one ear to the other, was completely shaved, while behind this line the hair was left to grow. (2) The hair was long behind, although the forepart of the head was not wholly shaven, since a semicircle of hair was permitted to grow from ear to ear above the forehead. Dom Louis Gougaud considers the second of these to have been the more probable,[7] and he thinks that this Celtic form may well have been an insular invention derived from some national tradition, as the Druids were also accustomed to have a

---

[1] Leask, *Irish Churches and Monastic Buildings*, vol. I (Dundalk, 1955), cap. VIII, p. 114. Ireland appears to have been the 'happy hunting ground' for ecclesiastical 'beggars', much as we find the United States today.

[2] Bock, *Tonsure Monastique et Tonsure Cléricale, Revue de Droit Canonique*, t. II, n. 4, December 1952, p. 376.

[3] Cf. *Qui sibi totonderat in Cenchris caput; habebat enim votum. Act. Apost.* XVIII, 18.

[4] Pope St Gregory the Great, 590–604.

[5] The question of the tonsure does not seem to have been debated in the conferences between St. Augustine and the British bishops, but it was frequently discussed in later times.

[6] The Saxons called it the 'tonsure of Simon Magus'.

[7] Gougaud, *op. cit.*, chap. VI, p. 202.

tonsure.[1] St. Patrick seems to have been unsuccessful in opposing the national fashion. The Roman tonsure would seem to have been accepted by the various Churches at the same time as the Roman Easter. The fourth council of Toledo (633) included the abolition of the 'insular' tonsure among the decrees for promoting a unity of rite.[2]

Computation of Easter. The Celts seem to have regarded the celebration of Easter on their traditional date as a matter of supreme importance, and we find St. Colomban (*ob.* 615) writing to St. Gregory the Great (590–604): 'I must confess that I am amazed that this Gallican error (date of Easter), which is little less than schismatic, has not been corrected by you.' The question of computation looms large in the history of the early Church. Pope St. Victor I (189–99) had condemned certain Churches of Asia for celebrating Easter on the same day as the Jewish Passover,[3] and the council of Arles (314), at which three British bishops were present, insisted that the feast should be observed *uno die et uno tempore per omnem orbem*.[4] Unfortunately, however, Rome herself effected changes in the computation. The council of Nicea (325) had directed that Easter was to be observed on the same Sunday throughout the world, and never on the same day as the Jewish Passover, but in order to make the paschal moon (that is the moon whose fourteenth day falls at the earliest on the equinox) agree for a series of years as closely as possible with the course of the sun, the Churches were forced to change their computus several times.[5]

So important, however, was it that the Churches of Christendom should all observe the feast of Easter on the same day that it became customary, generally on the Epiphany, to announce publicly, in a formula recited after the gospel, the day on which it was to be kept that year. The treasury of the cathedral church

---

[1] Gougaud, *op. cit.*, pp. 204–5.

[2] Counc. IV Toledo, 633, can. 41. Labbe, *op. cit.*, t. VI, col. 1716.

[3] The supporters of the Asiatic computation were known as Quarto-decimans.

[4] Counc. Arles, 314, can. I. Labbe, *op. cit.*, t. I, col. 1427.

[5] The patriarch of Alexandria, as the Egyptians were considered to be the best astronomers, was to communicate the correct day in an annual pastoral letter to the Pope. Edward Landon, *A Manual of Councils of the Holy Catholic Church*, vol. I (Edinburgh, 1909), p. 407.

of Ravenna has a slab of marble on which a calendar has been carved for the express purpose of enabling one to find the date of Easter in any year from 532 to 626: the slab dates from the 6th century. Serious complications sometimes arose from the fact that whereas Rome was forced from time to time to make adjustments in the computation, other Churches did not always follow her lead. Thus it came about that towards the end of the 6th century no less than three different systems were found in the Western Church. Rome, since 525, had followed the reckoning of Denis Exiguus; Gaul had retained the computation of Victorius of Aquitaine, which Rome had herself adopted in 457 and St. Augustine had introduced into England; while the Celtic Churches followed the system, erroneously ascribed to Anatolius of Laodicea, which had been brought to the British Isles in the 4th century. The Celts clung to their usage with unbelievable tenacity, and would seem to have considered any change on their part as an act of schism, if not of downright heresy. Such obstinacy inevitably caused confusion and ill-will. In the year 603, for example, we find the Gallican Church keeping Easter on 7 April, whereas the Irish missionaries in that country were observing it on 31 March.[1] The decision in favour of Rome reached at the council of Whitby (668) was in fact precipitated by the anomaly of the Northumbrian king celebrating Easter, while his queen and her retinue were observing Palm Sunday.[2] The fact that the Celtic date sometimes coincided with the Jewish Passover was looked upon by the Roman party as particularly reprehensible. The bitterness of the conflict may seem strange to us, but we may remember that somewhat similar passions were aroused in the 19th century over the respective merits and demerits of the Julian and Gregorian calendars in the Eastern churches.

---

[1] It was an exception for the Roman and Celtic dates to coincide. Among the Celts, Easter was on a day between 25 March and 21 April: among the Romans, between 22 March and 25 April.

[2] According to Lingard: 'Even at the close of the 8th century, the Scottish liturgy was in daily, though not exclusive, use in the Church of York'. *Anglo-Saxon Church*, vol. I, p. 299. It is, however, unlikely that this is correct. Alcuin certainly wrote to the archbishop (Eanbald) concerning divergencies in the liturgy, but there is no reason to suppose that his reference was to other than non-Gregorian books.

Several centuries were to elapse before the Celtic Easter came to be abandoned everywhere.

Brittany, under pressure from King Louis le Débonnaire, gave up its Celtic usages in 817, and monasteries adopted the Benedictine rule. In England, Somerset and Devon had conformed to Roman practice at the beginning of the 8th century through the efforts of St. Aldhelm, abbot of Malmesbury (671) and bishop of Sherborne (705). The diocese of Crediton in Devon was founded in 909, and the Saxon Eadwulf was appointed bishop, with the task of undertaking an annual visitation in Cornwall, in order to root out the 'errors' of the people, 'for', as a text in St. Leofric's missal says, 'they had hitherto resisted with all their might the truth and the apostolic decrees, refusing to obey them'.[1] The bishop in Cornwall did not become subject to the see of Canterbury until the time of King Athelstan (925–40), and the submission of Bishop Kenstec to the archbishop Ceolnoth (833–70) had been an exceptional case. In 936, however, Athelstan nominated the British bishop Conan to the see of Bodmin, and Cornish separatism came to an end, although this is not to say that Celtic usages did not persist here and there.

The Church in Northumbria established by King Oswald (634–35), which had flourished under Aidan, Finan and Colman, conformed to Roman usage at the synod of Whitby (664). Colman, the protagonist of the Celts, rather than submit, retired to Ireland under the mistaken notion that his computation of Easter was of Ephesine origin!

Strathclyde adopted the Roman Easter in 688, on the occasion of the visit of Adamnan, abbot of Iona, who had conformed himself about the same time. It was not, however, until 721 that Sedulius, British bishop of Strathclyde, submitted: at a council held at Rome under Pope Gregory II (715–31).

In 768, 'Easter was altered among the Britons, the reform being the work of that man of God, Elbodugus'.[2] The reference is to North Wales, while Elbodug (Elfodd), who died in 809, is described as 'chief bishop in the land of Gwynedd'. South Wales

---

[1] *Missale vetus Leofrici* (edit. F. E. Warren, Oxford, 1883), pp. 1–2.
[2] Harl. MS. 3859; *Cymr.* IX, 162.

o

is said to have adopted the Roman Easter in 767, after a certain amount of conflict, but the supposed 'conflict' may have been invented to show the unwillingness of the south to follow the north. Despite, however, the acceptance of the Roman Easter, the supremacy of the see of Canterbury was not fully established in Wales until the 12th century.

An unsuccessful endeavour to bring the Scottish Church into line with Rome on the Paschal question was attempted by Adamnan on his return from a second mission to Aldfrith, king of Northumbria, in 688. This was effected by a decree of Nectan, king of the Picts, in 710, although Iona (Hy) refused to submit for another six years. The abbot Duchan (710–17) had indeed conformed to Roman usage in 716, but it was not before 729 that the monastery agreed to celebrate Easter on the Roman date, and even then we find a rival abbot continuing 'schismatic' practices until 772.[1]

In Ireland, the adoption of the Roman Easter took place in the 7th century. Bede tells us that the southern 'Scots', thanks to the exhortations of the Apostolic See (Honorius I, 625–38), submitted in 634.[2] The 'Scots' of the north refused to follow their example, and gave their reasons in a letter to Rome in 640. Later in the century, however, Adamnan, at the synod of Tara (692), was successful in getting the north to follow Roman usage, with the exception of the 'family of Columba'. St. Columban, as we have seen, was fanatically attached to the Celtic Easter, thereby antagonising many of the Gaulish bishops, although Eustace, his successor at Luxeuil, 'in the interests of peace and unity', adopted the date followed by the 'Church of the country'.

Baptism. We learn from Bede that St. Augustine directed the Celtic Church to 'complete' the ordinance of Baptism according to the Roman rite.[3] The exact meaning of this requirement is uncertain, and we do not hear of it again. It may refer to the absence of Confirmation or to a defect in the manner in which the Sacrament was administered. On the other hand, Gilbert, bishop

---

[1] A 'schism' between the two parties had existed at Iona since 704.

[2] *Ad admonitionem apostolicae sedis antistitis Pascha canonico ritu observare didicerunt.* Bede, *op. cit.*, lib. III, cap. III; Cf. *ibid.*, lib. II, cap. XIX.

[3] *Ibid.*, lib. II, cap. II.

of Limerick, in his treatise *De Statu Ecclesiae* (*c.* 1100), which was composed to help eradicate the last vestiges of the Celtic rite, laid it down that priests were to administer Baptism by triple immersion, and, except in a case of necessity, in church. Holy Communion was to be given immediately after Baptism.

A further difference would seem to have been in that the Celts failed to conform to the canonical regulation requiring the assistance of three bishops at an episcopal consecration. It appears that the British bishops met annually in synod to raise three priests to the episcopate.

RACE HATRED

The request of St. Augustine to the British bishops at the conference, that the Celtic Church might assist in the work of evangelising the heathen English, met with a flat refusal. The hatred, however, was by no means confined to the unbaptised, and 'It is to this day', writes Bede in 731, 'the fashion among the Britons to reckon the faith and religion of Englishmen as naught, and to hold no more converse with them than with the heathen'.[1] Laurence, the successor of Augustine in the see of Canterbury, complains that Dagan, an Irish bishop, had not only refused to eat at his table, but also would not take his food anywhere under the roof which sheltered him.[2] The irreconcilable attitude of the Celts was not solely due to the authoritarian demeanour of Augustine at the conferences!

CESSATION OF CELTIC USAGES

Celtic usages, as we have seen, were in certain districts an unconscionably long time dying.

In 906, in a council on the Hill of Credulity near the royal city of Scone in Perthshire, an engagement was entered into to observe, 'in conformity with the customs of the Scots (*pariter cum Scottis*), the laws and discipline of the faith and the rights of churches and the Gospels', whatever all that may mean precisely.[2] Lingering Celtic practices were suppressed in 1069 by St. Margaret,

---

[1] Bede, *op. cit.*, lib. II, cap. XX.
[2] Gougaud, *op. cit.*, chap. XI, p. 410.

wife of Malcolm III (1054–93), who is said to have banished 'certain barbarous rites' from the Mass, but here again we have no means of knowing what they were. Fifty years later, in the time of King David, the chronicler records that the Culdees 'in a corner of their church, which was very small, used to celebrate their own office after their own fashion'.[1] One would like to know what this meant!

Ireland was equally conservative, and the work of reform in the 12th century included the suppression of Celtic usages. Canterbury would seem to have been the prime mover in the reform, with the help of the bishops in the Scandinavian pale— Dublin, Wexford, Waterford, Limerick—who presented a model of church government very different from that to which the Celts had been accustomed. The leading spirit was the papal legate, Gilbert, bishop of Limerick (1106–39), who in the prologue to *De Statu Ecclesiae* (*c.* 1109), a summary of Christian doctrine and ecclesiastical law, dedicated to the bishops and priests of Ireland, refers to liturgical disorders and irregularities as 'those diverse and schismatical orders, with which nearly all Ireland has been deluded'. The remedy advocated is uniformity with the rest of the Christian Church by the adoption of 'one Catholic and Roman Office'.[2] A national synod was held at Rathbreasail (?Westmeath) in 1110, and 'it is passing strange', as Fr. Ailbe Luddy says, 'in view of Gilbert's ardent desire to see the Roman liturgy universally adopted, that we find no legislation on the point'.[3] The reform was continued in the northern part of the country by St. Malachy, both as vicar general of Celsus, archbishop of Armagh (1105–30), and as bishop of Connor (1124). St. Bernard (*ob.* 1153) says of him that he introduced Roman laws and ecclesiastical customs into his native country.[4] And again, that 'he established in all churches the apostolic constitutions, and the decrees of the holy fathers, and especially the

---

[1] *Chron. Picts and Scots* (edit. W. F. Skene, Edinburgh, 1867), p. 190.

[2] *Ut diversi et schismatici illi ordines, quibus Hibernia poene tota delusa est, uni Catholico et Romano cedant officio.* Gilbert, *S.E.*, col. 995.

[3] Luddy, *Life of St. Malachy* (Dublin, 1930), chap. II, p. 14.

[4] *Fiunt de medio barbaricae leges, Romanae introducuntur. Recipiuntur ubique ecclesiasticae consuetudines, contrariae rejiciuntur. Vit. et Reb. Gest. S. Malachiae,* cap. VIII, 17; Mabillon, *Omnia Opera S. Bern* (Paris, 1719), t. II, opusc. XII, col. 672.

customs of the holy Roman Church'.[1] Later in the century, we
find two synods returning to the question of the enforcement of
the Roman rite and usages: Kells under the legate John Paparo
in 1152, and Cashel with Christian, bishop of Lismore and papal
legate, in 1172. 'From this time forward', says the synod of
Cashel, 'let all the divine offices of the holy Church be performed
in all parts of the (Irish) Church according to the use of the
Church of England', that is of the Universal Church.[2] The 12th
century would seem to have seen the last of the Celtic practices
in Ireland. The introduction of Romanesque architecture, more
or less embellished with carved ornament, and the erection of
larger churches may well have been the occasion for the adoption
of the Roman rite pure and simple; while the foundation of
Augustinian and Cistercian houses would help also in the extermination of the last traces of Celtic customs.

DISAPPEARANCE OF 'SAINTS AND SCHOLARS'

The incursions of the Danes and Norsemen destroyed well-
nigh all the Celtic monasteries, and with their destruction civilisation, art and learning suffered an eclipse from which they never
fully recovered.[3] Some idea of the sufferings of the Irish Church
may be gauged from the vicissitudes through which the cathedral
church of St. Brendan at Clonfert in Galway passed: from the
middle of the 7th century till the late 12th century the church was
either plundered or burnt no less than nine times.

Lindisfarne was plundered in 793 and Iona in 802. In Wales,
the Danish raids became serious in the second half of the 9th
century. The whole of the sea-coast of Brittany was laid waste by
Norsemen in 919, and from 921 to 936 they remained absolute
masters of the country. The Breton monks either crossed the
Channel to England or sought refuge in France. It is to these
refugees that we must assign the origin of two litanies in which

---

[1] *Apostolicas sanctiones, ac decreta sanctorum Patrum, praecipueque consuetudines sanctae Romanae Ecclesiae in cunctis ecclesiis statuebat. Op. cit.,* cap. III, 7; *ibid.,* col. 668.

[2] *Omnia divina ad instar sacrosanctae ecclesiae, juxta quod Anglicana observat ecclesia, in omnibus partibus ecclesiae (Hibernicae) amodo tractentur.* Mansi, *Concil.,* t. XXII, cols. 133-6.

[3] The monastic schools of Ireland had gained a deservedly international reputation, and students had resorted to them from many parts of Europe.

the names of Anglo-Saxon saints are found, together with those
of Celts, many of whom were Bretons.

Celtic learning decayed for want of teachers, although intellectual life continued in a diminished form throughout the 10th
and 11th centuries, as may be seen from Irish literature, as well
as from the persistent cultivation of the plastic arts. The work of
Marianus Scotus (*ob.* 1082/3 at Mainz) is regarded as one of the
last literary activities of the itinerant *Scotti*.[1]

CHURCH ARCHITECTURE

The Irish names for 'church' were borrowed from the corresponding Latin terms. Celtic churches, at a very early date, were
sometimes constructed of earth, although wood was more
general. The wind-swept western coast lands, however, could
not support forest or even usable woods, and St. Patrick was
forced to use moist earth for the building of a church somewhere
in Tyrawley.[2] The use of wood in the construction of churches
was known as the 'Scottish style'; while the Gauls called it *opus
Gallicum*.[3] The building might be of wattle-work (*ex virgis*),
rough-hewn timber (*de robore secto*) or smooth planks (*de lignis
levigatis; tabulis dedolatis*). St. Bede (*ob.* 735) says that when St.
Finan of Iona, who had been ordained and sent by the 'Scots',
became bishop of Lindisfarne in the middle of the 7th century, he
built a church of sawn wood covered with reeds, 'after the Scotic
manner'.[4] A later bishop, Eadbert (*ob.* 698), removed the thatch,
covering both roof and walls with plates of lead.[4]

The perishable character of much Irish building, at least as late
as the 10th century, with the frequent records in the various
annals of the total burnings of monastic settlements, indicate the
general use of inflammable materials: easily destroyed and easily
replaced.[5] The Annals of Ulster (849) record that two hundred
and sixty persons were burned in a wooden church at Trevet in

---

[1] De Ghillinck, *Littérature latine au moyen âge* (Brussels, 1939), chap. II, p. 61.
[2] Tirechan, *Life of St. Patrick*, *Book of Armagh*, VII, fo. 14, b. 2.
[3] A work of stone went by the name of *opus Romanense*.
[4] Bede, *Hist. Eccles.* (London, 1847), lib. III, cap. XXV.
[5] Leask, *Irish Churches and Monastic Buildings*, vol. I (Dundalk, 1955), chap. II, pp.
5–6.

Meath; while the description of the great church of St. Brigid at
Kildare, given by the 8th-century monk Cogitosus, suggests that
the building was in all probability of timber construction.[1] Small
cells, known as *dairtheach* or *deartheach* ('oak houses'), have been
mentioned since the 8th century, but they were probably much
older. The latest reference to them in the Annals is found in the
12th century. A vigorous impetus to stone building was afforded
by the raids and burnings of the Vikings in the 9th and 10th centuries, but in the West, where timber was scarce, stone must have
been used much earlier than in other districts. Tradition ascribes
the first stone building to St. Ciannan's Duleek (co. Meath):
hence the name Duleek, that is *Diamliac* or 'house of stone'.

Stone churches were regarded as 'Roman' or 'Gaulish', and so
late as the 12th century, when St. Malachy (*ob.* 1152) decided to
build a large stone oratory at Bangor, the inhabitants protested:
'Why have you thought good to introduce this novelty into our
regions? We are Scots, not Gauls. What is this frivolity? What
need was there for a work so superfluous, so proud?'[2] St.
Malachy, however, by no means despised the more homely construction of wood, as may be seen in St. Bernard's life of the Saint.[3]
Stone nevertheless was an early medium for churches, and at the
end of the 4th or the beginning of the 5th century we find a stone
church erected by St. Ninian at Whithorn in Galloway. The
occurrence must have been somewhat exceptional, as the place
was renamed in consequence 'Candida Casa': *qui locus . . . vulgo
vocatur ad Candidam Casam, eo quod ibi ecclesiam de lapide, insolito Brettonibus more fecerit.*[4] In Scotland, it was not before the
early 8th century that we hear of Nectan, king of the Picts, sending to England for stonemasons, where they had been lately
introduced into the country by St. Benedict Biscop (*ob.* 690).
The saintly founders of monasteries in Ireland would unquestionably often have erected small and humble oratories of

---

[1] Leask, *op. cit.*, p. 7.

[2] *Quod in terra illa necdum ejusmodi aedificia inveniuntur, Scotti sumus non Galli . . . .
Quid opus erat opere tam superfluo, tam superbo.* Bern. *Vit. Mal.*, cap. XXVIII, 61; *Pat.
Lat.*, t. CLXXXII, col. 1109.

[3] *Porro oratorium intra paucas dies consummatum est de lignis quidem levigatis, sed apte
firmiterque contextum opus Scoticum pulchrum satis. Ibid.*, cap. VI, 14.

[4] Bede, *op. cit.*, lib. III, cap. IV.

stone in the 5th, 6th and 7th centuries. It is, however, impossible to give the precise dating of any work of primitive building. A very rude-looking structure is not necessarily an early one. Many buildings, which can be shown from their details to be of quite late date, are more rudely constructed than others no less certainly early.[1]

The native building tradition had its roots in the megaliths and in the technique of simple timber construction.[2] The use of mortar and knowledge of the round arch must have come to Ireland from the Continent, most probably in the 7th century, and certainly in the succeeding hundred years.[3]

The type of Irish churches, from the earliest times until the coming of the great monastic orders, is the rectangular building, gabled at both ends and small in size.[4] There was perhaps no chancel before the 10th century.[5] One of the peculiar features of the early Irish churches is their diminutive size. Many of them would not have held a congregation of more than three or four in addition to the priest and his server. It is possible, however, that the faithful were accustomed to gather in the open space before the church, and the climate of the 6th and 7th centuries, though deteriorating slowly during the latter, was much finer and warmer than it is today.[6] An increase in the numbers of a religious community or a desire for extension did not, as generally elsewhere, take the form of an enlargement of the church, but rather the erection of yet more small oratories. The whole group of churches, together with the various domestic buildings, were normally surrounded by a low enclosure wall or *cashel*. The oratories were often seven in number, probably on account of the very general belief that seven was a sacred number. Such was the case at Lérins, Glendalough and Cashel. These monastic centres of the early Celtic Church seem to have been formed on

---

[1] Leask, *op. cit.*, chap. VII, p. 53.

[2] *Ibid.*, chap. I, p. 1.

[3] *Ibid.*, pp. 1, 2.

[4] *Ibid.*, chap. II, p. 8. Cf. St. Mary's Glendalough.

[5] *Ibid.*, chap. V, p. 31.

[6] *Ibid.*, chap. VII, p. 60. Something similar may be witnessed today at the annual pilgrimage to Croaghpatrick, when thousands of the faithful gather outside the tiny oratory in order to 'hear' Mass.

the model of those of Syria and Egypt: the whole grouping was known as a *laura*.

A primitive architecture of stone, contemporary with wood elsewhere, arose in the exposed and treeless coast lands and islands remote from the woodlands of the interior. Vestiges of this period are to be found in the beehive huts of stone or *clocháns* and the diminutive oratories.[1] These early monastic settlements were normally encircled with ramparts of earth or stone (*cashels*). Some complete specimens of *clocháns* survive in the coastal areas: from Inishmurray to Dingle Peninsula, and the Skelligs. The rude oratories of uncemented stone may be in the form of the keel of an upturned boat, a truncated pyramid or a circular bee-hive, but, whether rounded or oval in external shape, they were always quadrangular in the interior. Similar communities existed also for women in the time of St. Columba, and his biographer, Adamnan, refers to *monasteria puellarum*.[2]

The nine buildings—two oratories, six dwelling huts and the church of St. Michael—at Skellig Michael, seven miles out from the rocky coast of Kerry, have been described as 'the most western of Christ's fortresses in the ancient world'. With the single exception of Inishmurray, no Irish settlement gives so per-fect a picture of the eremitical monastic plan, resembling the *laura* of the eastern Mediterranean.[3] The buildings, other than the tiny church of St. Michael, are *clocháns* of dry stone. A cross, formed by white stones set in the stonework, is found over the doorway of the second oratory.

The primitive oratory of Gallarus, near Kilmalkedar in county Kerry, is believed to be the earliest surviving building in the country devoted to Christian use as a place of worship. The Stone House on the south island of Aran (Inisheer) may have provided the model.[4] It is completely rectangular in plan, and has stood perhaps for more than twelve hundred years. From outside it is not unlike a well-built peat-rick or an inverted

---

[1] Leask, *op. cit.*, chap. IV, p. 17.
[2] Adamnan, *Vita Columb.*, lib. III, cap. XLI.
[3] Leask, *op. cit.*, chap. IV, p. 19.
[4] W. Gamble, *Irish Antiquities and Archeology*, p. 41.

boat; while internally its shape is that of a roughly pointed vault.[1]

The group of buildings on Inishmurray, an island off the coast of Sligo, enclosed within a monastic *cashel*, presents an Irish monastery much as it appeared in the 7th or 8th century. All that are wanting are a few extra huts and several community buildings.[2]

While on the subject of Celtic *clocháns* and other primitive buildings, it might be of interest to make some reference to houses of a somewhat similar type elsewhere, although they have little or no connection with the Celtic rite.

Unique houses, known as *trulli*, formed of a rough cylinder of limestone blocks, topped by a semi-spherical or conical roof of the same material, laid one upon the other in concentric courses narrowing as they reach the apex, are to be found in a small area, inland and south of Monopoli in Apulia. It has been thought that these *trulli* were the local equivalent of the original African homes of early immigrants. The name, however, is Greek, and therefore comparatively late.[3] The style of dwelling may be compared with the Eskimo *igloo*, where ice takes the place of limestone. A still further comparison is found in the *nuraghi* of Sardinia: towers in the shape of a truncated cone, constructed sometimes of hewn and sometimes of unhewn stone without mortar.[4]

One is on surer ground in respect to the dating of the larger and more developed buildings. The earliest of these is perhaps St. Columba's House at Kells, which was in all probability completed in 814. The first church of the monks had been destroyed in 807. We read also that in 819 the *domliac* (stone church) of *Cennanus* (Kells) was broken by the 'Gentiles', that is the Norsemen. St. Kevin's church at Glendalough, known popularly as the 'Kitchen', is probably of the same century, although somewhat later. In both churches we find an upper chamber, a circumstance by no means uncommon in early churches in Ireland.[5] Larger

---

[1] Leask, *op. cit.*, chap. IV, pp. 21–3.   [2] *Ibid.*, chap. III, p. 14.
[3] Harry Hodgkinson, *The Adriatic Sea* (London, 1955), part I, pp. 17–19.
[4] Cf. Beehive tombs of Mycenae.   [5] Leask, *op. cit.*, chap. V, p. 35.

than either of the two foregoing is the similarly constructed
oratory of St. Flannan at Killaloe, but its construction suggests a
relatively late date, with a chancel from the first.

Windows in the early churches, and even so late as the 12th
century, were few in number and small in size. Often there
appears to have been only an east window above the altar. Glass
seems to have been unknown, but sometimes there were external
shutters, and in the small church once on Friar's Island, Killaloe,
we find rusted iron in the outer joints, revealing their one-time
existence. The introduction of glass into England is attributed by
Bede to Benedict Biscop, who is said to have imported glaziers
from Gaul in 676.

The date of the first appearance of a structural chancel in Irish
churches has been disputed. A recent writer is of the opinion
that two of the churches at Glendalough—Holy Trinity and
Reefert—both of which have coeval nave and chancel, may be
amongst the earliest in the country, and date from the 10th
century.[1]

A unique feature among Irish churches existed at Rahan in
County Offaly, where there were two small chambers flanking the
chancel to the north and south, and entered from it by means of
two small doorways. The chambers answered to the *diaconicon* [2]
and *prothesis* [3] found in churches of the Byzantine rite. Similar
features existed in Syria and North Africa in the 5th and 6th
centuries, and in some English churches in the 7th century.[4]

The Celtic church or oratory had but a single altar, which was
of wood or stone indifferently. It is of interest to note that the
altar in the monastery at Luxeuil was in all probability consecrated by the Celtic bishop Aidus, and not by the ordinary,
notwithstanding a canon of the third council of Orleans (538),
restricting the consecration of altars to the bishop of the diocese.[5]

One of the most distinctive features of Irish architecture is the

---

[1] Leask, *op. cit.* chap. VII, p. 76.
[2] The *diaconicon* served as a sacristy for the vesting of the celebrant and his assistants.
Possibly also for the reserved Sacrament.
[3] In the Eastern church, the *prothesis* was used for the preparation of the elements.
[4] Leask, *op. cit.*, chap. VIII, pp. 90, 92.
[5] Counc. III Orleans, 538, can. 15. Labbe, *op. cit.*, t. V, col. 299.

round tower, of which there seem to have been at one time about a hundred. The earliest record of such a tower is 965, but they probably originated in the preceding century, serving as watch towers, refuges and treasure houses at a time when Danish invasions were all too frequent. The towers were normally un-attached to any building, but we find them connected with the church at Clonmacnoise and Glendalough.

Sculpture and carving were rare in Celtic churches, but on a small number of doorway lintels a cross is carved or engraved, as, for example, at St. Molaise's House, Inishmurray; Gallen; St. Mary's Glendalough; Fore and Clooneamery. The cross—decorated lintel—at St. Fechin's church at Fore is considered to have a marked similarity to certain of the 6th-century doorways in Syria: 'One is almost compelled to assume that someone present at its erection had seen Levantine examples.' [1] The door-way probably dates from the 9th century, between the years 875 and 916, when Ireland was sufficiently at peace to receive refugees or visitors from the East. It was in this very period that Irish annalists record the arrival and departure of Analeon the Pil-grim 'with the epistle which had been given from Heaven at Jerusalem'.[2]

An archway at Rahan (Co. Offaly) has been assigned by some writers to the 7th or 8th century on account of some of its decoration, which is similar to what we find in the chapel of the palace at Ani in Armenia, and it is known that Armenian clerics lived not far from here about this time. It is now considered, however, to be rather of the end of the 11th or the beginning of the 12th century.[3] Celtic art is chiefly associated with the monu-mental crosses which are to be found in cemeteries, near round towers and by the roadside.

Memorial stones would seem to have been inherited from pre-Christian times. The most ancient Christian variety are those in Galloway, which in some instances may date from the end of the 5th century: lechs or rude pillars of stone.

The crosses in Cornwall are considered to date from the 8th

---

[1] Leask, *op. cit.*, chap. VII, p. 69.   [2] *Ibid.*, pp. 69–70.
[3] *Ibid.*, chap. VIII, p. 90.

and 9th centuries; while the 'high-crosses' of Ireland range from the 7th or 8th century until the 12th. The two or three surviving wayside crosses of the 9th or 10th century to be met with in Brittany are of a period subsequent to the abandonment of the Celtic liturgy.

The Irish examples exhibit to perfection the two principal Celtic motifs of decoration: spirals and interlacings. Giraldus Cambrensis (*ob.* 1216/20) has described them as the 'work of angels'. These Irish interlacings were borrowed by the Carolingians, who in their manuscripts employed great capital letters composed of small cords in which monsters sported. The representation of human figures on the crosses was a dismal failure: barbarous and without either proportion or life. It is thought that they may have been deformed models offered by the manuscripts of Syria and Egypt.[1]

An incomplete slab of local Manx slate, which was found in the ruins of a *keeill* or Celtic chapel on the Calf of Man in 1773, displays a remarkable 'Celtic' interpretation of the 'Syrian' type of Crucifixion.[2] The type, in which Christ was represented as if alive and fully robed, between flanking soldiers (the spear- and the sponge-bearer respectively), with cherubim above.[3] It was indeed just such a type which directly inspired the Crucifixion page in the Durham Gospels: produced in one of the Irish monasteries in Northumbria towards the close of the 7th century, forming a fascinating link between the Late Antique art of the eastern Mediterranean and the profoundly different Irish style. The long-robed 'living Christ' reappeared in late Saxon art. The Calf of Man Crucifixion is of the 8th century: the plain lower half of the slab was evidently intended to be set in the ground, or in a

---

[1] e.g. the cross at Cardonagh shows the figure of the Crucified clothed in a long robe, as we find represented in Syria; while the several episodes taken from the lives of the Egyptian desert Fathers can only have been taken from Alexandrian miniatures. Emile Mâle. *La Fin du Paganisme en Gaule et les plus anciennes Basiliques Chrétiennes* (Paris, 1950), chap. XIII, 3, pp. 314-15.

[2] The Calf of Man is a small island off the south-west coast of the Isle of Man. The slab has no known parallel, either as regards subject or form. The figure of the Crucified is 'barbarous' in the extreme.

[3] The slab from the Calf of Man is incomplete, and the sponge-bearer is missing. It is one of the earliest representations of the subject in stone in the British Isles.

masonry base, and the carving may have formed the central panel of a masonry altar. It may be seen today in the Manx Museum at Douglas in the Isle of Man.

The carvings on some of the Irish crosses would seem to have been inspired by Oriental MSS. of the *Commendatio animae*: the prayer for the dead. Thus one finds Daniel in the lions' den, Three Children in the furnace of fire, Jonas and the whale, Miracle of Cana, and the Multiplication of loaves and fishes. The illuminated MSS. from which these themes were taken would very probably have come from Antioch, where this Jewish prayer had received its Christian form.[1]

The finest of the Irish crosses is considered to be that of Muiredach, abbot of Monasterboice (890–923), which is of the 10th century. Good examples of such crosses are to be met with at Ahenny (Co. Tipperary), Kells (Co. Meath), Monasterboice (Co. Louth), Clonmacnoise (Co. Offaly), Durrow (Co. Offaly), Moone (Co. Kildare), and Drumcliff (Co. Sligo).

We have seen that many of the motifs on these crosses have been in all probability inspired by Eastern models, but the sculptors themselves may well have been Gallo-Roman artists.[2] We know from Bede that Anglo-Saxon England employed workmen from Gaul.[3]

Two fine crosses, probably dating from the 7th or 8th century, have survived in Northumberland: Bewcastle and Ruthwell. It is interesting to note that these Northumbrian crosses have certain characteristics similar to what we find on the 7th-century tomb of Angilbert at Jouarre.[4]

Nearly one hundred stones with Celtic ornament upon them have come to light in Wales.

Welsh crosses are inferior in design and workmanship to the Irish ones; spirals are almost wholly absent, there is little figure sculpture, and there is less grace of form. The artists and gravers had not the Irish cunning.[5] Among the more notable Welsh crosses are those of Nevern and Carew. An important group of

---

[1] Mâle, *op. cit.*, p. 315. [2] *Ibid.*, p. 177.
[3] Bede, *Hist. Eccles.* V, 21. [4] Mâle, *op. cit.*, pp. 176–77.
[5] J. E. Lloyd, *op. cit.*, chap. VII, 3, p. 221.

these carved tombstones belongs to Glamorgan, where we find over thirty stones showing Celtic ornament: twelve belong to Margam and Llanwit Major, and may be seen in their respective churches.

The inscriptions on the Welsh stones, with one exception (Towyn), are in Latin, not, as in Ireland, in the vernacular. Culture in the Welsh Church was on traditional Roman lines, rather than a native growth, drawing its inspiration from popular sources.[1]

The churches of Celtic Wales would seem to have been constructed exclusively of wood, and nothing prior to the Norman Conquest has survived.[2]

The remains of primitive Celtic oratories can be seen at Perranzabulo (St. Perrans) and Gwithian in Cornwall.

Brittany has little that dates with any certainty from the Celtic period, with the exception of the crypt of St. Melar at Lanmeur (Morlaix).

OGHAM SCRIPT

Ogham, the ancient alphabet used by the Goidelic Celts of Great Britain and Ireland, consisted of perpendicular strokes placed above or below a horizontal line, and of strokes crossing the line either at right-angles or obliquely. The key to its composition was found in the Book of Ballymote, a MS. of the 14th century. Ogham inscriptions on stones are found in Wales and southern Ireland, providing decisive evidence of Goidelic occupation, as a standing stone with a sepulchral epitaph had little or no currency among the Brythonic tribes.[3] In the 5th and 6th century a process was going on which gradually drove Goidelic speech altogether out of Wales.

Ogham stones probably had a pagan origin, but more than half of those in Wales were found in close connection with churches or ancient chapels.[4]

---

[1] J. E. Lloyd., *op. cit.*, pp. 221–22.
[2] *Ecclesiam de lapide, insolito Brettonibus more.* Bede, *op. cit.* lib. III, cap. IV.
[3] Lloyd, *op. cit.*, chap. IV, p. 115.
[4] *Ibid.*, p. 116.

LITURGICAL BOOKS

Prior to the 6th century, the Celtic Churches used a version of the Scriptures anterior to the Vulgate of St. Jerome.[1] Biblical glosses, of which there are a comparatively large number, provide the earliest surviving examples of the old Irish language, but they are not earlier than the 8th century.[2] A specimen of the kind of psalter used at Iona in the 6th century is found in the MS. known as the *Cathach* of St. Columba.[3]

Apochryphal writings were very generally received by the Celts, and popular superstition encouraged fantastic names of angels, as may be seen in prayer books of the early Middle Ages.[4]

The oldest Irish ecclesiastical law inflicted the same punishment on anyone who dared to offer violence to a bishop, anchorite, scribe or *excelsus princeps*.

The most famous of the Irish MSS. is probably the 'Book of Kells', containing the four gospels, a fragment of Hebrew names and the Eusebian canons. It is known also as the 'Book of Columba', probably because it was written in the monastery of Iona in honour of the Saint. The book, on palaeographic grounds and judging by the character of the ornamentation, can hardly be placed earlier than the end of the 7th or the beginning of the 8th century. It would seem to have been at Kells for a long time during the Middle Ages, hence its usual name, but it was presented to Trinity College, Dublin, in the 17th century. The miniature of the Blessed Virgin and Child on fo. 7v derives from a Hellenistic current still alive in the Greek East in the 7th and 8th centuries.[5]

The rich ornamentation of the Irish MSS. was frequently adopted on the Continent, though nowhere, save perhaps in

---

[1] Gougaud, *op. cit.*, chap. VIII, p. 260.

[2] *Ibid.*, p. 265.

[3] The MS. is described by H. C. Lawlor in *Proceedings of the Royal Irish Academy*, vol. XXXIII, sect. C, no. ii, pp. 241–6.

[4] e.g. Book of Cerne.

[5] E. Kitzinger, *Coffin-Reliquary*, d, *The Iconography, Relics of St. Cuthbert* (London, 1956), chap. II, p. 260. The illuminations, says Blouet: *représent une synthèse originale, au confluent des courants celtique, anglo-saxon et copte*. L. Blouet. *Le Chrismale de Mortain*, chap. IV, p. 40. Coutances, n.d.

Northumbria,[1] did the imitators approach the skill and delicacy of the scribes and artists of Ireland.

Wales furnishes no evidence of any skill in illuminating, and the Book of Chad (*Efengyl Teilo*) at Llandaff was there by purchase, and may well be a further example of Irish art.

Two sacramentaries of the end of the 8th and the beginning of the 9th century, written for the Church of Cambrai in the time of Bishop Hildoard [2] (790–816), suggest 'at once the usual character of the more ordinary Irish codices'.[3]

Existing Codices

(1) *Turin Fragment.* A MS. now in the Library of Turin (F. IV, 1), probably originally from Bobbio, and consisting of six leaves. It includes the canticles *Cantemus Domino, Benedicite* and *Te Deum*, with their ensuing collects; the *Laudate* Psalms (CXLVIII–CL); and the *Benedictus* (text not given).

(2) *Carlsruhe Fragment A.* A MS. in the Library of Carlsruhe, comprising four pages in an Irish hand of the late 8th or early 9th century. There are parts of three Masses: one of which is *pro captivis*. The arrangement resembles the Missal of Bobbio, as the epistle and gospel seem to have preceded the other variables under the title: *lectiones ad misam.*

(3) *Carlsruhe Fragment B.* Here again we have four pages in an Irish hand, probably of the 9th century. The MS. has fragments of Masses, with a variant of the intercessions found in the Stowe missal and in Witzel's extracts from the Fulda MS. Some Irish also appears in the document.

(4) *Piacenza Fragment.* Four pages in an Irish hand, possibly of the 10th century, but the two outer pages are illegible. The inner pages contain parts of three Masses: one of which is headed *Ordo missae sanctae Mariae.* In the other Masses, we have the prefaces of two of the Sunday Masses in the Missal of Bobbio, one of which is found on the 8th Sunday after Epiphany in the Mozarabic rite.

---

[1] e.g. Book of Lindisfarne.
[2] Cambrai, MS. 162–3 (158) and 164 (159).
[3] Edmund Bishop, *Journal of Theological Studies*, IV (1903), pp. 414–15.

(5) *St. Gall Fragments.* The fragments, which are of the 8th and 9th centuries, are preserved in the Library of St. Gall (MSS. 1394, 1395). One of the MSS. contains part of the Ordinary of the Mass which, so far as it goes, resembles the Stowe missal. Another has a confession and litany which are also found in Stowe, a fragment of a Mass for the dead, a prayer for the visitation of the sick and three forms for the blessing of salt and water.

(6) *Basle Fragment.* The MS., which is in the Library of Basle (A VII, 3), is a Greek psalter with a Latin interlinear translation. The fly-leaf gives two hymns in honour of the Blessed Virgin and St. Bridget; a prayer to the Virgin, angels and saints; and a long prayer: *De conscientiae reatu ante altare.* The psalter contains an outline of the so-called Letter of our Lord to Abgar, which found a place in the Irish *Liber Hymnorum*, and was read in the Office.

(7) *Book of Dimma.* This Irish fragment is ascribed to a certain Dimma who lived in the 7th century, but it was probably written in the 8th century. It is a copy of the four gospels, together with the order for Unction and Communion of the sick, bound up between the third and fourth gospels (fols. 52–4). It is now in Trinity College, Dublin.

(8) *Book of Mulling.* Another Irish fragment is preserved in Trinity College, which is of the 8th and 9th centuries and ascribed to Mulling, bishop of Ferns (*ob.* 697). It contains an office of Unction and Communion of the Sick, with a part of a directory or plan of service.

(9) *Book of Deer.* A Scottish gospel-book of the 10th century, now in Cambridge University Library. A portion of an office for the Communion of the sick has a certain resemblance to Mozarabic and Gallican texts. There is a Gaelic rubric in a hand which is thought to be of the 11th century.

(10) *Book of Cerne.* The actual MS. is of the first half of the 9th century, but it is thought to have been the composition of Aeduald, bishop of Lindisfarne (721–40). The 'Hispano-Hibernian character of the document makes it extremely unlikely to have been compiled by his namesake, the 9th-century bishop

of Lichfield (818–30).[1] Some of the prayers, and more particularly those relating to the Blessed Virgin, may have come
from Spain almost as they stand.[2] Association or influence
between England and Spain existed in the first half of the 8th
century, whereas by the end of that century or the beginning of
the 9th, 'Hispanism' and 'Irishry' in religion and devotion had
fallen into disrepute. The book contains excerpts from Scripture
and *carmina* showing acquaintance, not only with the Mozarabic,
but also with the Gelasian, Gregorian and Gallican liturgies.
Many of the prayers are derived, either wholly or in part, from the
Acta Johannis, *Passio Petri et Pauli* and *Passio Andreae*. The
document seems to have been 'made up from different booklets'.[3]
Léon Blouet considers the schematic design of the long and un-
articulated fingers in the illuminations to be a trait which has
passed from Coptic art into that of the Irish.[4]

(11) *Book of Armagh.* A MS. now in Trinity College, Dublin,
and written by Ferdomnach the Scribe at the beginning of the
9th century. It contains the only complete exemplar extant of
the New Testament as read in the early Irish Church, together
with certain liturgical prayers which afford evidence that the
Gregorian canon was known in Ireland in 807. The codex has
also the apocryphal Epistle to the Laodiceans, with the cautionary
note that its Pauline authorship had been rejected by St. Jerome:
Incipit aepistola ad laudicenses sed hirunimus eam negat esse pauli.[5]

(12) *Antiphonary of Bangor.* A monastic book strictly Celtic
in character, which was discovered at Bobbio, and is now in the
Ambrosian Library at Milan. It would seem to have been written
between the years 680 and 691, as fifteen abbots of Bangor are
named in the hymn copied on the last page: (*In*) *memoriam
abbatum nostrorum.* The last abbot but one, Caman (*ob.* 680), is
said to be 'singing hymns with Christ', whereas Cronan (*ob.* 691),
who concludes the list, was still alive, as the scribe piously says:
'may the Lord preserve him'. The book contains canticles,
hymns, collects, versicles and antiphons, in addition to Eucharistic

---

[1] Bishop, *Liturg. Histor.*, VIII, pp. 192–7. [2] *Ibid.*, pp. 169, 174.
[3] Kuyper, *Book of Cerne* (Cambridge, 1902), introduct., p. XVIII.
[4] L. Blouet, *op. cit.*, chap. IV, p. 39. [5] *Book of Armagh*, fo. 139r.

and other texts. It was probably compiled for the abbot when presiding in choir. There are twelve hymns: eight are not found elsewhere, and ten are certainly intended for liturgical use. The collects are for the most part addressed to our Lord, as we find in the Gallican and Mozarabic liturgies, and the frequent use of the expression *Salvator mundi* is a further indication of Hispano-Gallican influence.[1] In many of its details, the antiphonary inclines to Eastern rather than to Western usage. The ranking of Saturday (Sabbath) with the feasts of martyrs shows that the day was observed at Bangor as a feast and not as a fast, in which the 7th-century Irish practice was Oriental, and not Roman.[2]

(13) *Leabhar Breac* or 'Speckled Book'. An Irish MS. of the 14th or early 15th century, and now in the Royal Irish Academy. It contains a variant of the tract on the Mass which is found in the Stowe missal.

(14) *Martyrology of Tallaght*.[3] This was probably a copy of an older martyrology that was associated with St. Willibrord (*ob.* 739), who may have brought the MS. with him from Ireland: to which Irish commemorations were added for each day. The Tallaght martyrology seems to have been compiled in the monastery of that name some time between the years 797 and 808, although the latest name recorded is Coirpre of Clonmacnoise (*ob.* 899).

(15) *Martyrology of Oengus the Culdee*. The Martyrology was composed about the same time as that of Tallaght. Oengus was a monk of Clonenagh (Co. Offaly), then of Tallaght, and later abbot and bishop. He died about the first quarter of the 9th century.

(16) *Martyrology of Gorman*. A MS. written probably between the years 1166 and 1174 by Marian Gorman, abbot of the Hill of the Apostles, a house of Augustinian canons at Knock (Co. Louth).

---

[1] Cf. *Collectio post Praecem* for the Mass of Christmas in the *Missale Gothicum* (*H.B.S.*, vol. LII (1917), p. 4) and the *Ad Pacem* in the Mozarabic liturgy, First Sunday in Lent, *De Samaritana* (*Missal. Mixt.; Pat. Lat.*, t. LXXXV, col. 302).

[2] Cf. Gallican and Milanese rites.

[3] Book of Leinster (12th century) and MS. 5100–4 in the Royal Library, Brussels (abstract of the 17th century).

(17) *Missal of Stowe*. This most important document for a study of the Celtic rite was discovered on the Continent in the 18th century. It may be seen today in the Royal Irish Academy in Dublin,[1] after having belonged to the libraries of Stowe House (Bucks), whence its name, and Asburnham Place (Sussex). The book may have been taken from Ireland as one of the offer-ings of Tordelbach O'Brian, king of Munster, to the monastery of Ratisbon in 1130.[2] Interpolations have been made in the missal by a certain Moelcaich, and, in a few rubrics and two inserted collects, also by a later hand, but both scribes were probably contemporary members of the community at Tallaght. The primary object of the book seems to have been to provide the monastery with an authoritative ritual. Maelruain (*ob.* 792), the founder of Tallaght, appears in the diptychs after the names of the bishops. There is no mention of his successor Eochaid (*ob.* 812), under whom the MS. with its interpolations was probably written. The latest saint to be invoked is Samdine (Samthann, Samdann), a virgin of Clonbroney (Co. Longford), who died in 739. Opinions have differed as to the date of the missal, but 'on palaeo-graphical grounds, no less than for other reasons, there seems to be sufficient warrant for dating the original text in the early part, or even written within the first decade, of the 9th century'.[3] In addition to the prayers of the Mass, the MS. contains extracts from the Gospel of St. John, the order for Baptism, order for the visitation of the sick, litanies and other prayers or blessings. A treatise on the Mass in Irish appears at the end, and seems to be of no later date than the other insertions,[4] although Dom Louis Gougaud has considered it to be of the 10th or 11th century. The Mass shows an acquaintance with the Gelasian, Gregorian, Gallican and Mozarabic books. The Missal of Stowe was pre-served in a *cumdach* or oak box ornamented with silver, which was made some time between 1023 and 1052, possibly in the

---

[1] Lib. Royal Irish Academy, Dublin, MS. D. ii, 3.

[2] Abbey of St. James the Great, Ratisbon, founded for Irish Benedictines in 1075.

[3] *Stowe Missal*, vol. II, *Henry Bradshaw Society*, vol. XXXII (1915), introduct., p. XXXVI. None of the inserted matter would seem to be later than the first half of the 9th century, and it is quite conceivable that the missal was subjected to revision almost immediately after it was written. *Ibid.*, pp. XXXVI–XXXVII.

[4] *Ibid.*, p. XXXVI. Cf. *Leabhar Breac*.

monastery of Lothra (Co. Tipperary), which had been founded
by St. Ruadhan (*ob.* 584).[1]

The mediaeval missals, known by the names of Drummond
(11th century), Corpus (12th century) and Rosslyn (13th or 14th
century), contain the names of certain of the Irish saints. Those
in the *Missale Drummondiense* [2] seem to have been taken from the
Martyrology of Oengus: the canon includes the name of St.
Bridget. The Rosslyn missal is probably a 13th-century Irish
book, written for Downpatrick cathedral, and possibly brought
to Scotland by the expedition of Edward Bruce in 1316. It was
in the library of the St. Clairs of Rosslyn at the end of the 16th
century.[3]

No early British liturgical book has survived, and the most
ancient Breton missal—St. Vougay—dates from the end of the
11th or the beginning of the 12th century, some considerable
time after Celtic usages had been abandoned, although the litany
of Holy Saturday has preserved a considerable number of Celtic
saints, especially those connected with Brittany.

LITURGICAL YEAR

It is impossible to reconstruct the entire liturgical year of the
Celtic Churches, and each of the several groups would have had its
own calendar. The *Communicantes* in the Stowe missal gives the
chief feasts of the *temporale* as observed at Tallaght in the 9th
century: *In natale Domini* (Christmas), *Kalendis* (Circumcision),
Stellae [4] (Epiphany), *Natalis Calicis* (Holy Thursday), *Pasca*
(Easter), *In clausula Pasca* (Low Sunday), *Ascensio, Pentecosten.*

The mutilated fragments of an Irish sacramentary of the 10th
or 11th century give a Mass of the Circumcision in which the
gospel is taken, not from the canonical gospels, but from an
apocryphal work, hitherto unknown, of James the son of

---

[1] One side of the *cumdach* was renewed about 1375.

[2] The missal takes its name from Drummond Castle, where it is preserved. *Missal.
Drummond.*, edit. G. H. Forbes, Burntisland, 1882.

[3] *Rosslyn Missal*, edit. H. J. Lawlor, *Henry Bradshaw Society*, vol. XV, London, 1899.

[4] Epiphany, Welsh: *Dydd Gwyl Ystwyll*; Cornish, *Degl Stul*; St. Cuthbert's Gospels:
In stilla Domini.

Alphaeus.[1] The Return from Egypt, Presentation of our Lord in the Temple and his Victory over the Devil were liturgical memorials in 9th-century Ireland. The Martyrology of Oengus says: 'Out of Egypt—splendid gladness! came Mary's great Son'[2] (11 January), and 'The reception of Mary's Son in the Temple, sure inestimable'[3] (2 February). The 'Defeat of the Devil' was also commemorated. On these days the office of Sunday is to be said: 'We never saw dinner in the daytime on these feasts'. 'The first taking of Christ into the Temple with Mary—a gracious man's course' is the entry for 2 February in the Martyrology of Gorman,[4] and, for the same feast, the Drummond missal (11th century) says: *Purificatio sancte Marie semper virginis*. At Iona and elsewhere, a forty days' fast was kept in preparation for Easter, with two other 'Lents' in the course of the year. Lent began on the first Monday, and the introduction of Ash Wednesday was one of the reforms instituted in Scotland by St. Margaret in the 11th century.

25 March has a composite entry in the Martyrology of Tallaght: *Dominus noster Jesus Christus crucifixus est, et conceptus, et mundus factus est. Passio Jacobi fratris Domini. Et conceptio Mariae. Et immolatio Isaac a patre suo Abraham in Monte Morae.*[5] The Martyrology of Gorman has for the same day: 'Jesus' Conception on the same day as his crucifixion without respect'.[6] 27 March in Tallaght is *Resurrectio Domini*[7] and in Gorman: 'Mindful Christ's Resurrection'.[8]

The Stowe missal refers to Holy Thursday as *Dies sacratissima natalis calicis domini nostri Jesu Christi*.[9] The expression *Natalis calicis* is found in the calendar of Polemius Silvius[10] (403) for 24 March, and it occurs also in the tenth homily of St. Eloi, bishop of Noyon (*ob.* 660). The day was especially devoted to

---

[1] H. M. Bannister, *Liturgical Fragments, Journal of Theological Studies*, IX (1908), pp. 417–18. [2] *Martyr. Oengus, H.B.S.*, vol. XXIX (1905), p. 35.
[3] *Ibid.*, p. 58. [4] *Martyr. Gorman, H.B.S.*, vol. IX (1895), p. 29.
[5] *Tallaght, H.B.S.*, vol. LXVIII (1931), p. 27.
[6] *Gorman, H.B.S.*, vol. IX (1895), p. 63.
[7] *Tallaght, H.B.S.*, vol. LXVIII, p. 27.
[8] *Gorman, H.B.S.*, vol. IX, p. 63.
[9] Holy Thursday, Irish, *Cennlá* or 'Supper day'; *Dia dardáin cennlá lá senaid an Tigerna* or 'The day of the Lord's synod (*Coena Domini*); *Caplait* (Low Latin, *capillatio*; Welsh, *Dydd iau cablyd*). [10] *Pat. Lat.*, t. XIII, col. 678.

the care of the person, and monks washed their heads, had their hair cut, etc., probably as a reminder of St. John XIII, 9: *Domine, non tantum pedes meos, sed et manus et caput.* The *Mandatum* is prescribed in a 9th-century regulation of the Culdees: 'At the washing of the feet the *Beati* are recited as long as the washing lasts. After that comes the sermon on the washing.' In some places, a regular bath is ordered, possibly a survival of the custom observed by the catechumens in the early Church, of which St. Augustine gives an explanation.[1] A canon, which has been attributed to St. Patrick, refers to three baptismal festivals: *Octavo die chatechumeni sunt; postea solemnitatibus Domini baptiʒantur, id est, Pascha et Pentecoste et Epiphania.*

The blessing of the new fire on Holy Saturday, unknown to the liturgical books of Rome and Gaul, seems to have originated in Ireland, and, if we may trust the evidence of Muirchu (*ob.* 690), to have existed in the time of St. Patrick: *Sanctus ergo Patricius sanctum pasca celebrans incendit divinum ignem valde lucidum et benedictum, qui in nocte refulgens a cunctis pene per planitiem campi habitantibus visus est.*[2] 'The Scotti scattered throughout England and the continental countries', says Dom Gougaud, 'first made it known to the Anglo-Saxon missionaries with whom they had such close relations, and that the latter, practising it themselves on their own behalf, helped to diffuse it abroad.' [3] The ceremony may well have been a 'baptised' pagan usage of the ancient Irish. Many writers, however, consider it to have originated in the 'lighting of the lamp' at the beginning of the night vigil: the *Lucenarium.*[4] If such was the case, it seems strange that the ceremony should have developed in Ireland. The blessing of the candle is found in the purely Celtic antiphonary of Bangor, in which there is a hymn, *quando cereus benedicitur*, which occurs nowhere else,[5] followed by a short formula: *ad cereu(m) bene-dice(ndum).*[6]

---

[1] St. August., *Epist.*, LIV, 9–10.

[2] Edit. Whitley Stokes (London, 1887), p. 279.

[3] Gougaud, *op. cit.*, chap. IX, p. 338.

[4] Righetti, *Manuale di Storia Liturgica*, vol. II, cap. V, p. 168.

[5] *Creator igneus* (9 verses) fols. iit, iiv; *Henry Bradshaw Society*, vol. X (1895), p. ii.

[6] *In nocte tu fuisti columna ignis, Domine, . . .* , fo. 36r; *ibid.*, p. 33.

The controversy in respect to the date of Easter ('Feast of Gladness') has been previously mentioned. The rubric *In Pascha annotina*, which follows the title *Dominica octavum Paschae* in the gospel-book of Landevennec, refers to a public renewal of Baptismal vows by those who had been baptised in the previous year.

The Transfiguration is commemorated in the Martyrology of Oengus on 26 July: 'The Transfiguration, at daybreak, of Jesus on Mount Tabor'.[1] It is found also in the Martyrology of Gorman: 'Christ's Transfiguration—a beautiful tale'.[2]

Notices of this kind, however, are no indication of a definite liturgical observance.

Saturday, as we have seen, had something of a festive character. Several texts prescribed a due observance of Sunday, and that known as *Cain Domnaig* had a great influence in the country.

Blessed Virgin. The three existing Irish martyrologies give the January and August commemorations of the death and assumption of our Lady, as we find in the Coptic Church of Egypt, but with the addition of the Chair of Peter in the January feast:

Tallaght, 18 January: *Sanctae Mariae matris Domini, hac die ejus dormitatio in Roma audita est; Cathetra Petri in Roma.*[3] 14 August (*sic*): *Assumptio Mariae Virginis.*[4] 16 August: *Nativitas sanctae Mariae et concordiae Mariae Elizabeth coronae.*[4]

Oengus, 18 January: 'The magnifying in Rome of the Apostle Peter—a saying that is higher—at the festival that is nobler, the great death of Jesu's Mother'.[5] 15 August (vigil): 'On the great feast of her commemoration, very Mother of our Father, with a host of kings, right splendid assembly!'[6] 16 August (feast): 'The Nativity of Mary, a virginal strong diadem, the holy Mother of my Prince.'[6]

Gorman, 18 January: 'The sharp report (of the death) of Mary, a goodly vigil. The enthronement of pre-eminent Peter in royal

---

[1] *Oengus, H.B.S.,* vol. XXIX, p. 165.   [2] *Gorman, ibid.,* vol. IX, p. 145.

[3] *Tallaght, H.B.S.,* vol. LXVIII, p. 9. A commemoration of the Chair of St. Peter is found in the Philocalian calendar, and was introduced into Gaul at an early date. It is mentioned at Tours in 567. The Stowe missal, under the rubric: *In sollemnitatibus petri et christi,* gives the Roman collect for the feast before the *Gloria in excelsis. H.B.S.,* vol. XXXII, p. 4.   [4] *Tallaght, ibid.,* vol. LXVIII, p. 63.

[5] *Oengus, ibid.,* vol. XXIX, p. 36.   [6] *Ibid.,* p. 176.

vast Rome.'[1] 14 August: 'The great vigil of Mary.'[2] 15 August: 'The death of great Mary, Jesu's Mother, the true Virgin, whom surely I shall meet.'[2] 22 August: 'The great octave of Mary.'[3]

The three martyrologies commemorate also the Conception and Nativity of the Blessed Virgin:

Tallaght, 1 April: *Sanctae Mariae nativitas.*[4] 3 May: *Crucis Christi inventio. Mariae virginis conceptio.*[5] 7 May: *Agnitio sanctae crucis. Conceptio Mariae i. utero* (borrowed from 3 May).[6] 8 September: *Nativitas Mariae matris Jesu.*[7]

Oengus, 1 April: Glosses connect the feast of St. Mary with her visit to Elizabeth, not, as in Tallaght, with her nativity.[8] 3 May: 'The first finding of Christ's cross with (its) many virtues: . . . the great feast of the Virgin Mary' (Conception).[9] 8 September: 'Thou shalt commemorate Mary: thou art not deadened on a scanty meal' (Nativity).[10]

The obscure entries in these martyrologies do not suggest that a feast of the Conception was observed in early days in Ireland, and Fr. Paul Grosjean has shown that the name of Mary in the Félire of Oengus was a compiler's error. The corresponding name in the martyrology attributed to St. Jerome is that of St. Marianus, martyred in Numidia.[11] Even so, the entry became Mary's Conception in Tallaght. The Irish commentators showed their acquaintance with the 2nd-century *Protevangelium Jacobi,* which recorded a miraculous conception announced to Joachim and Anne by an angel. They also knew a much later document, *Liber de Ortu Mariae,* attributed to St. Matthew. This placed the birth of Mary four months after conception, according to some texts, and well fitted the accidental record of the conception at the beginning of May.

Gorman, 8 September: 'Great Mary's holy nativity.'[12] 15 September: 'The great octave of Mary.'[13] 8 December: 'The conception of great Mary.'[14]

---

[1] *Gorman, H.B.S.,* vol. IX, p. 19. The Drummond calendar gives: *Annuntiatio quoque assumptionis beatissimae Dei genitricis Mariae semper virginis fidelibus Romanis.*
[2] *Ibid.,* p. 157. [3] *Ibid.,* p. 163. [4] *Tallaght, ibid.,* vol. LXVIII, p. 29.
[5] *Ibid.,* p. 39. [6] *Ibid.,* p. 40. [7] *Ibid.,* p. 69.
[8] *Oengus, ibid.,* vol. XXIX, p. 104. [9] *Ibid.,* p. 122. [10] *Ibid.,* p. 193.
[11] Paul Grosjean, *Analecta Bollandiana* LXI (1943), pp. 91-5.
[12] *Gorman, H.B.S.,* vol. IX, p. 173. [13] *Ibid.,* p. 177. [14] *Ibid.,* p. 235,

The martyrologies of Tallaght and Oengus commemorate the 'Dedication of the basilica of Mary'.[1] There is no indication as to the name of the basilica, but it may possibly refer to the 'Dedication of the Sovereign Lady at Atrib', which we find in the Coptic rite on 16 June.

The Visitation of the Blessed Virgin is found in Tallaght, 18 December: *Salutatio Mariae ab Elizabeth matre Johannis.*[2]

St. Joseph. The inclusion of the name of Joseph in the three Irish martyrologies may be a further borrowing from Egypt, where a calendar of the 8th century, under 20 July (26 *Abib*), gives the entry: 'the Carpenter Joseph'.

The Martyrology of *Tallaght* records his name on 19, 20 and 21 March: *Joseph sponsi Mariae.*[3]

Oengus, 19 March: 'Joseph, name that is nobler—Jesu's pleasant fosterer.'[4]

Gorman, 19 March: 'Joseph, a tower against burnings,[5] the dear fosterer of appointed Christ.'[6]

Sanctorale. From an early period, the sanctorale has included the great saints of the Universal Church. The *Division of the Apostles* was commemorated on 15 July. *Oengus*: 'The twelve apostles, who surpass every number, before a countless host Jesus distributed them throughout the race of Adam.'[7] *Gorman*: 'The distribution of Jesu's apostles.'[8] Oengus commemorates the consecration of the Roman basilicas, 18 November: 'Sing the consecration of the churches of Peter and of excellent Paul.' 19 November: 'Tell of the consecration of the basilica of John, a son without reproach.'[9] The Roman list of martyrs in Tallaght has no less than fifty-seven doublets.

The commemoration of Mamertus (*ob. c.* 480), with the reference to the introduction of the Rogation litanies, that we find in Tallaght, suggests a Gallican origin, 9 May: *Memmertius episcopus*

---

[1] *Tallaght, ibid.*, vol. LXVIII, p. 71; *Oengus, ibid.*, vol. XXIX, p. 194.
[2] *Ibid.*, vol. LXVIII, p. 86.
[3] *Ibid.*, p. 25.   [4] *Oengus, ibid.*, vol. XXIX, p. 83.
[5] Possibly an allusion to one of the purposes of the round towers.
[6] *Gorman, ibid.*, vol. IX, p. 59.
[7] *Oengus, ibid.*, vol. XIX, p. 162.
[8] *Gorman, H.B.S.*, vol. IX, p. 137.
[9] *Oengus, H.B.S.*, vol. XXIX, p. 235.

et confessor qui ob imminentem cladem sollenes ante ascensionem Domini letanias instituit cantari.[1]

'The solemn observance of the day of a holy man's death was a custom inherited from primitive times, and there is every reason to think', says Professor Lloyd, 'that the dates connected with the names of the patron saints of Welsh churches are, for the most part, genuine anniversaries.' [2]

The lives of the Welsh and Irish saints contain in most cases a nucleus of truth, but the panegyrics subordinate everything to the enhancement of the hero's glory, admitting elements of exaggeration and most unlikely miracles. Dispositions of this kind grow more and more pronounced as the story is told and retold in successive ages.[3]

Gildas (*ob. c.* 570), the author of *De Excidio Britanniae*, styles the martyrs of Britain as 'lamps of exceeding brightness set alight for us, lest Britain should be involved in the thick darkness of pitchy night'.[4] St. Alban (22 June) and SS. Julius and Aaron (3 July) are singled out for especial mention.

CELTIC IRELAND AND COPTIC EGYPT

The Copts, before the Moslem conquest of Egypt, were great travellers, and we find traces of their presence in Celtic Ireland. The kind of asceticism associated with the Desert Fathers was especially congenial to the Irish, and Dom Henri Leclercq mentions the unsubstantiated hypothesis that Celtic monasticism was directly derived from Egypt.[5] Certainly the grouping together of several small churches within a *cashel* or fortified enclosure seems to support this view. One of the commonest names for townlands or parishes is *Disert* or 'Desert': a solitary place in which anchorites were established. Monasteries, particularly those in Connor and Down, frequently had some such solitude connected with them. Warren tells us of seven Coptic monks who were buried at

---

[1] *Tallaght, H.B.S.*, vol. LXVIII, p. 41.

[2] Lloyd, *op. cit.*, chap. V, 3, p. 149.

[3] It is often quite impossible to distinguish fact from fiction, history from legend in the lives of the Welsh and Irish saints.

[4] Gild., *De Excid. Brit.*, part I, cap. VIII; *Pat. Lat.*, t. LXIX, col. 337.

[5] Leclercq, art. *Irlande, Dict. d'Archéol. Chrét. et de Lit.*, t. VII, part 2, col. 1479.

Disert Ulidh in Ulster,[1] and we find their names invoked in a litany in the Martyrology of Oengus: *Morfesseor do manchaib Egipr(e) in Disiurt Uilaig*.[2] An Ogham inscription on a stone near St. Olan's Well in the parish of Aghabulloge (Co. Cork) has been interpreted by scholars to read: 'Pray for Olan the Egyptian.' Irish monks are known also to have visited Egypt, and we hear of Dicuil, the author of *Liber de Mensura orbis terrae*, who probably came from Clonmacnoise, travelling to the Pyramids on his way to Palestine.[3]

A number of similarities in the Coptic and Irish Churches have been recorded: (1) glass chalices, such as the monks used in Egypt, have been found in Co. Waterford; (2) both Copts and Irish employed a metal case for the book of the Gospels; [4] (3) the 5th-century bell of St. Patrick is a direct imitation of those in use in Egypt; [5] (4) a similarity in the two Churches in respect to feasts of our Lady. The *Saltair Na Rann*, which is no more than an Irish 11th- or 12th-century edition of the *Book of Adam and Eve*, which was composed in Egypt in the 5th or 6th century, is known in no other European country except Ireland.[6]

HISTORY OF THE RITE

It would seem, says Dom Cabrol, that there has never been a Celtic liturgy in the ordinary sense of the word.

The Celts were great travellers and ardent lovers of the liturgy: indefatigable in collecting every book on the subject, copying, retouching and sometimes adding a formula here and a rite there.[7] It is only in the domain of private prayer, outside the scope of the official liturgy, that Celtic originality appears. Here Celtic piety has a free course, with interminable litanies, *loricae* or 'shields' for

---

[1] Warren, *Liturgy and Ritual of the Celtic Church* (Oxford, 1881), p. 56.

[2] 'Seven monks of Egypt in Disert Uilaig'. *Oengus; H.B.S.*, vol. LXII, pp. 64-5.

[3] George T. Stokes, *Ireland and the Celtic Church* (London, 1928), lect. XI, pp. 24-16.

[4] Warren, *op. cit.*, p. 21; Alfred J. Butler, *Ancient Coptic Churches of Egypt*, vol. II (Oxford, 1884), p. 61.

[5] W. Gamble, *Irish Antiquities and Archeology*, p. 62; Butler, *op. cit.*, vol. II, p. 81.

[6] Published in *Anecdota Oxoniensia*, Whitley Stokes, Oxford, 1882. English translation, S. C. Malan, London, 1882.

[7] Cabrol, *Les livres de la liturgie latine* (Paris, 1930), chap. VII, 6, p. 104.

protection against the evil one, *apologiae* or confessions of sin, and invocations to national saints.[1]

The liturgy of the Celtic Churches certainly differed from that of Rome, and Dr. Lingard was guilty of an understatement when he said: 'Whether the sacrificial service of the Scottish missionaries varied from that of the Roman we have no means of knowing.' [2] It is probable also that considerable diversity existed among the various Churches, with no attempt at a uniform liturgy. As regards Britain, there is no evidence before the 6th century, and very little then. A passage attributed to Gildas (*ob.* 590) says that the Britons are at variance with the whole world, and are opposed to Roman customs, not only in the Mass, but also in their tonsure.[3] The reference, however, is more likely to date from the 7th century. The only reliable information that we have concerning the rites of the British Church, apart from the three controversial points already mentioned, is a single statement of Gildas, who says that certain lessons, differing from those of any known rite, were recited at Ordinations; and he makes a possible allusion to the anointing of the hands at Ordination. The reply of St. Gregory to the inquiry of St. Augustine shows clearly that the British liturgy was not identical with the Roman.[4] The British bishops at the conference at Bangor were directed to observe the Roman computation of Easter, the Roman usages in Baptism, and to assist in the conversion of the English people (*Anglorum genti*), but it was significantly added: 'We will tolerate all your other customs, though contrary to our own.' [5]

The supposition of a difference in rite is strengthened by the fact that Luidhard, bishop of Senlis and chaplain to Queen Bertha, was officiating in the church of St. Martin at Canterbury, and would consequently have used the liturgy to which he had been accustomed.

The Gallican rite was undoubtedly the nucleus of the early

---

[1] Cabrol, *op. cit.*, p. 105.

[2] Lingard, *Anglo-Saxon Church* (edit. 1858), vol. I, p. 271.

[3] *Britones toti mundo contrarii, moribus Romanis inimici, non solum in missa sed in tonsura etiam. Epist.* II, Haddan and Stubbs, *Councils* etc, t. I (Oxford, 1869), p. 112.

[4] Bede, *op. cit.*, lib. I, cap. XXVII.

[5] *Ibid.*, lib. II, cap. II.

Celtic liturgy,[1] although in an earlier form than we find in pseudo-Germanus, which represents a later usage probably augmented and embellished by the Church of Arles. We know, for example, that the list of the orders of the hierarchy in the *Statuta Ecclesiae Antiqua* [2] corresponds to Roman usage, whereas the list in a letter of Faustus, bishop of Riez (*ob. c.* 493), to Rusticus, bishop of Narbonne, is dissimilar: *fossarii* and *ostiarii* are included, but acolytes and exorcists are omitted. The list given by Faustus, moreover, corresponds in general to a list found in the *Chronicon antiquissimum*, a document composed in Great Britain, which ends with the emperor Justin in 578. Faustus himself would seem to have been a Celt, either British or Breton. The term *fossor* is used also in the *Life of St. Cadoc* (6th century), which, although a text of the 11th century, is believed on other grounds to contain early material.[3]

The success of the Saxons in effecting a settlement in southeast Britain and their ultimate conquest of well-nigh the whole country interposed a heathen barrier between the British Churches and those of the nearest part of the Continent. There was indeed communication at the western end of the English Channel through the British settlement on the Armorican peninsula, but the Celtic colonists would seem to have had almost as little to do with their Frankish neighbours as had the insular Britons with their English foes.

St. Patrick expressed the wish that he could leave the great work that he is doing in Ireland, in order to visit the brethren in Gaul and meet the saints of that country face to face, but there is no evidence that he found time to do so.[4] Relations between British and Continental Christianity became casual and unauthoritative. The Celtic Churches could no longer keep abreast with any changes which the Gauls might think fit to make in their liturgy. Thus, for example, St. Augustine found the Britons following rules for the computation of Easter which

---

[1] *Lit. Hibern.* Mabillon, *De lit. Gallic.*, I, 2, 3c; *Pat. Lat.*, t. LXXII, pp. 114, 119.

[2] A document probably of the late 5th or early 6th century.

[3] N. Chadwick, *Poetry and Letters in Early Christian Gaul* (London, 1955), chap. VII, pp. 205–6.

[4] Haddan and Stubbs, *op. cit.*, vol. II, pp. 308–9.

had been abandoned by Gaul about the time of the conquest of Kent.

Celtic Christianity ceased to share in the general movement of the West, yet in the hundred and fifty years between the first settlement of the English in Britain and the coming of St. Augustine we find that the Welsh tribes had cast off all traces of heathenism, and, in common with the more civilised Britons, had become well organised Christian communities: it was the age of Gildas and David.[1]

It is unfortunate that we know so little about the Celtic rite: if only Gildas had given us a detailed account of the liturgy as performed in his day instead of depicting the vices of his contemporaries!

Two interesting examples of the practice of *Laus Perennis* in the Welsh Church have come to light.[2] The *Laus Perennis* was a service of uninterrupted psalmody, performed by choirs of religious in relays. The first example is found in St. Illtyd's monastery of Llanwit Major in Glamorgan. The Iolo MS. tells us that the community numbered 2,400, and that batches of a hundred relieved each other at all the offices of the day and night.[3] The monastery had seven churches, as was so often the case in Celtic communities, and it would seem likely therefore that the monks were divided into companies apportioned to the several churches.[4]

The other reference to 'perpetual psalmody' comes from North Wales in the second half of the 6th century. St. Kentigern (*ob.* 603), in exile from his diocese of Glasgow, founded a monastery at what was known to later ages as St. Asaph. Here, says Jocelin of Furness, the 12th-century biographer of Kentigern, 365 of the community out of a total of 965 were wholly engaged in performing the Divine Office: *nec facile quemquam illorum egredi . . . instituit*. The monks were divided into groups or choirs which succeeded one another at the hours, apparently all in one church.[5]

---

[1] Lloyd, *op. cit.*, chap. V, p. 124.
[2] S. Luff, *British Monasteries and the Laus Perennis*, Pax, Spring, 1953.
[3] *Acta SS.*, 6 November, *Comm. Praev., Vita S. Illtudi*, para. 3.
[4] Luff, *op. cit.*, p. 150.
[5] Jocel., *Vita S. Kentigerni* (*Nova Legenda Angliae*, ed. Horstman, vol. II, pp. 120–1).

St. Gobnact's Church, Inishere, Aran

Muiredach Cross, Monasterboice,
Co. Louth

Stone of Lugneadon,
Inchasgath, Co. Galway

Ruined Celtic Church of Rigfert,
Glendalough (sixth century)

Basilica of St. Columban, Bobbio

St. Columban, Luxeuil

Abbey Church and Abbot's House,
Abbey of St. Peter, Luxeuil

Ceaseless psalmody was practised at Constantinople in the opening years of the 5th century by a community of monks, who received the name of *Acoemetae* or 'the Sleepless Ones'. In the following century we find the *Laus Perennis* introduced into the West at Agaunum (St. Maurice en Valais), where it was started on 22 September 522, and from whence it was extended to churches in Gaul.

It would be from the Gallican Church, rather than from the East, that the Celts adopted the practice.

A somewhat confusing document,[1] drawn up by some Irish monk on the Continent, probably in the 8th century, assumes that the Scottish (Irish) and the British (after 429) *cursus* were one and the same (*Cursus Scottorum*), tracing it through Germanus and Lupus to St. Mark. The writer distinguishes it from the Gallican, thus making it Alexandrine in origin.[2] This *cursus* was the disposition of the Psalms in the Divine Office: a matter of considerable importance to monastic founders. Colman at the Synod of Whitby (664) claimed an Alexandrine origin for his Office, but his arguments were hotly contested by St. Wilfrid.

More exact information respecting the Canonical Hours and the Eucharistic liturgy was forthcoming from the *Catalogus sanctorum Hiberniae secundum diversa tempora*, a document dating from about the year 750. The MS. is believed to have been the work of Tirechan, the author of the Annotations on the Life of St. Patrick in the Book of Armagh. The Irish saints are arranged in three sections. The first order or *Ordo sanctissimus* (*c.* 440–544) comprises St. Patrick's auxiliaries and his first successors down to 544: 'The first order of Catholic saints was in the time of St. Patrick; and then they were all bishops, famous and holy, and full of the Holy Ghost; three hundred and fifty in number, founders of churches. They had one head, Christ; and one chief, Patrick; they observed one mass, one celebration, one tonsure from ear to ear. They celebrated Easter on the

---

[1] Brit. Mus., London, Cotton MS., Nero A ii.
[2] Patrice Cousin, *La Psalmodie Chorale dans la Règle de Saint Colomban*, pp. 183–4. Cf. Haddan & Stubbs, *op. cit.*, vol. I, pp. 139–40; Leclercq, *Office Divin*, Dict. *d'Archéol. Chrét. et de Lit.*, t. XII, col. 1978; Gougaud, *Celtiques (Liturgies)*, *ibid.*, t. II, col. 299.

Q

fourteenth moon after the vernal equinox, and what was excommunicated by one Church, all excommunicate.

'The second order or *Ordo sanctior* (544–98) was of Catholic presbyters. For in this order there were few bishops, and many presbyters, in number three hundred. They had one head, our Lord. They celebrated different masses, and had different rules; one Easter on the fourteenth moon after the equinox; one tonsure from ear to ear. They received a mass from Bishop David and Gillas (Gildas) and Docus (?Cadoc), the Britons.'

'The third order or *Ordo sanctus* (598–665) was of this sort. They were holy presbyters and a few bishops; a hundred in number . . .; they had different rules and masses; and different tonsures, for some had the coronal, and others the hair (behind), and a different Paschal festival. For some celebrated the Resurrection on the fourteenth moon or on the sixteenth, with hard intentions.' [1] The Divine Office is implied by the 'uniform *celebratio*' of the first period, and no doubt also by the *diversas regulas* of the second and third. We find the term *celebratio* used several times in the Stowe missal.[2] *Unam missam* of the first age is evidently the Mass introduced into Ireland by the undisputed leader (*dux*) of the time, St. Patrick. Tirechán mentions a *Missa Patricii* as adopted by the community of Achad Fobuir in the time of St. Patrick, but without giving any information as to its nature. The second period seems to indicate a new Mass introduced into Ireland by David, Gildas and Docus at about the time of the mission of St. Augustine (597). The close relations between Britain and Ireland would make such a contribution by no means unlikely. Later, we find the reverse process, with the Anglo-Saxons borrowing a goodly proportion of their formulas of prayer from the Irish.[3] In France, also, we find a similar borrowing in Alcuin's collections of prayers, and in the *Libellus precum* of Fleury.[4]

The Irish contributions, however, were in the nature of private prayers and devotions rather than of the Celtic rite properly so-called, and the Anglo-Saxon council of Clovesho (747) made it

---

[1] Haddan and Stubbs, *op. cit.*, vol. II, p. 292.
[2] Irish, *celebrad*.
[3] e.g. MS. *Reg.* 2AXX, Brit. Mus.; Book of Nunnaminster; Book of Cerne.
[4] Gougaud, *Celtiques (Liturgies)*, *D.A.C.L.*, t. II, part II, col. 3028.

quite clear that no liturgy other than the Roman was to be tolerated: *In baptismi officio, in Missarum celebratione, in cantilenae modo celebrantur, juxta exemplar videlicet quod scriptum de Romana habemus Ecclesia* . . .[1] In 816, a synod of the bishops of the South of England held at Celchyth went so far as to exclude 'Scottic' clergymen from all sacred ministrations, warning the faithful to have nothing to do with them.[2]

The Irish, as Walafrid Strabo (*ob.* 849) observed in the 8th century, had a quite extraordinary capacity for devotion: *Quamvis autem geniculationis morem tota servet ecclesia, tamen praecipue huic operi Scotorum insistit natio; quorum multi pluribus, multi paucioribus, sed tamen certis vicibus, et dinumeratis per diem vel noctem genuflectentes, non solum pro peccatis deplorandis, sed etiam pro quotidianae devotionis expletione, studium istud frequentare videntur.*[3] Celtic liturgical compositions are replete with prolixity, repetition of the same formulas and verbosity, but it is nevertheless difficult to say what is specifically Celtic. Edmund Bishop speaks of the 'tinkering methods' of the Irish, and, in the Celtic liturgical texts extant, there is a mixture of Roman and Gallican elements, and from another provenance still.[4] The 'Spanish symptoms' had been already influenced by the sort of piety and devotion dominant in East Syria in the 5th and 6th centuries. This further provenance is shown in passages which are common to both the Mozarabic and Celtic liturgies.[5] Syriac religious influence came from Spain, and the Spanish Church inoculated the Irish. Dom Louis Gougaud thinks that Gaul was the intermediary by which Hispanism, liturgical and devotional, found its way into early Irish and English documents,[6] but Edmund Bishop is probably more correct when he says that 'the facts that can at present be ascertained . . . point rather to a direct draft by the early Irish on the Spanish Church'.[7] Then, by way of an afterthought, Bishop continues: 'Of course it is quite

---

[1] Counc. Clovesho, 747. Labbe, *op. cit.*, t. VI, col. 1577.
[2] Can. 5. Haddan and Stubbs, *op. cit.*, vol. III, p. 581.
[3] Wal. Str., *De Rebus Eccl.*, cap. XXV; Hittorp, *De Div. Offic.*, col. 686.
[4] Bishop, *Liturg. Hist.*, VII, p. 166.
[5] Cf. Borrowing in the Celtic texts extant.
[6] Gougaud, *Celtiques (Liturgies)*, *D.A.C.L.*, t. II, part II, col. 2992.
[7] Bishop, *op. cit.*, VIII, 4, p. 181.

probable that such a feature as the order of Apostles or the order "John, Mary" in the Stowe diptychs was derived by some Irishman—and the Irish were in those days a people enamoured of the strange, the odd, the rare—directly from some Syrian, and taken directly to Ireland. Traces of this Syrian piety in forms of prayer, in prayer books or devotional literature on the Continent north of the Alps and Pyrenees in the 9th and 10th centuries are to be ascribed to the influence of Irish or English missionaries or to wandering scholars in the 8th or 9th century.' [1]

Roman interpolations probably made their appearance in the Celtic liturgy at a time when Ireland adopted the Roman Easter, and the Antiphonary of Bangor (7th century) is still wholly Gallican.

It has been said, notably by the historian Lingard, that the Celtic liturgy, which had been introduced by 'Scottish' missionaries into the North of England, survived at York until the end of the 8th century.[2] The assertion was made on the strength of the letter of Alcuin to Eanbald II, archbishop of York, but there is nothing in it to suggest any Celtic reference.[3] It would seem only that Eanbald was wanting to do something about his use, and that Alcuin told him not to bother.

There are no historical documents extant respecting the character of the Scottish liturgy, but its existence is proved by the solitary fragment of the Book of Deer, the many allusions in the works of Adamnan and other writers on the Celtic Church in Scotland, and by the action taken by Queen Margaret in the 11th century in suppressing its last vestiges. The Aberdeen breviary says that St. Serf (? date) lived *sub forma et ritu primitivae ecclesiae*,[4] and when Palladius arrived in Scotland he is said to have found individuals: *habentes fidei doctores et sacramentorum ministros presbiteros et monachos, primitivae ecclesiae solum modo sequentes ritum et consuetudinem*.[5] The breviary says also that Palladius found St. Serf at Culross: *virum devotum, mansuetum, et pium*

---

[1] Bishop, *op. cit.*, VII, p. 163, note b.
[2] Lingard, *Anglo-Saxon Church*, vol. I, p. 299.
[3] Alcuin, *Epist.* LVI *ad Simeonem* (Eanbald); Epist. LXV.
[4] *Brev. Aber.*, fo. XV, 1 July.
[5] *Ibid.*, fo. XXIV, 6 July.

quem, ejus exigentibus meritis, catholicum juxta Romanae Ecclesiae morem rite ordinavit episcopum, et in eadem fide divinitus informavit . . .[1] Then, passing on through Scotland: *ecclesias consecravit, vestimentis sacerdotalibus modum imposuit, et ab eisdem horas canonicas dicendas, prout ecclesia instituebat Romana, sollenniter jussit.*[2] A certain amount of doubt surrounds the visit of Palladius to Scotland,[3] but documents such as the Aberdeen breviary, even where they are historically valueless, often preserve authentic allusions or indications of otherwise unknown or forgotten circumstances.

It was not until the time of St. Margaret (*ob.* 1093), wife of King Malcolm III, that Celtic practices came to be finally suppressed. The reforms included the abolition of the following 'abuses': (1) the beginning of Lent on the Monday after the first Sunday, instead of on Ash Wednesday; (2) failure to receive the Eucharist on Easter Day; (3) working on the Lord's Day; and (4) 'Strange customs in the Mass'. It is difficult to know exactly what is implied by the second of these 'abuses', and, as we shall see, the Irish Church refused to recognise one who neglected Communion on this day as 'faithful'. The only possible explanation seems to be that the laity never communicated at all! As to the 'strange customs' in Mass, Theodoric, St. Margaret's chaplain and biographer, says that in some places Mass was celebrated in an irregular manner, 'contrary to the custom of the Church' and 'by some barbarous rite, which the Queen, kindled with God's zeal, so laboured to destroy and bring to nothing, that henceforth there appeared no one who dared to do such a thing'.[4] However, as we learn from the Register of St. Andrews (1144–53), the Culdees continued to recite the Office according to their own use for at least another fifty years. There is no indication in either Theodoric or the Register as to what the 'barbarous rite' might have been. It was, in all probability, no more than a Romanised form of the Celtic (Gallican) liturgy, and we know

---

[1] *Brev. Aber.*, fo. XXV, lect. V.   [2] *Ibid.*, lect. VI.

[3] W. F. Skerne *Celtic Scotland*, vol. II, p. 27.

[4] *Contra totius Ecclesiae consuetudinem, nescio quo ritu barbaro, missas celebrare consueverat.* Theodoric, *Vita S. Marg.*, cap. VIII seq; Haddan and Stubbs, *op. cit.*, t. II, part II, p. 158.

how would-be 'purists' are apt to magnify and exaggerate the simplest variation from what is considered to be liturgically *à la mode*. The suggestion that Mass in remote and mountainous districts was sometimes said in the vernacular has no evidence to support it.

On the Continent, the Celtic usages of St. Columban and his monks do not appear to have roused much opposition from the Gaulish clergy, with the exception of the computation of Easter. We find, however, a certain Agrestius, who was himself a Columbanian monk, complaining to a council at Mâcon (*c.* 620) of deviations in the celebration of Mass. One of his chief grievances seems to have been the multiplicity of collects *et multa alia superflua*.[1] More than one interpretation has been given as to the exact meaning of this 'multiplicity of collects'. Pope Benedict XIV (1740–58) thinks that it refers to the use of several collects before the epistle, instead of the single prayer which was at that time customary in the Roman Mass, but others consider that the expression implies a 'multiplicity' of variables throughout the Mass, as we find in the Gallican and Mozarabic rites. In addition to this, Agrestius, who seems to have been a difficult and unstable character, complained that the Rule of St. Colomban differed from the monastic usages current in Gaul. Eustace, abbot of Luxeuil, replied to his charges, and it is possible that, for the sake of unity, he introduced the Rule of St. Benedict, as we know that his successor St. Walbert (630–35) followed the Holy Rule from the beginning of his abbacy.

A certain amount of feeling seems to have been aroused also by the Irish *episcopi vagantes*, who had no fixed see and apparently exercised their ministry wherever they might happen to be. The Orders given by these roving prelates were declared by a Gaulish council to be null and void. In the 7th century, many of the Columbanian monasteries in Gaul adopted the *Laus perennis*, a service of uninterrupted psalmody, performed by choirs of religious in relays. The practice, as we have seen, was observed

---

[1] *In summa quod a caeterorum ritu ac norma desciscerent et sacra missarum sollemnia orationum et collectarum multiplici varietate celebrarent.* Mabillon, *Annal. Ord. S. Ben.*, t. I, p. 320; Labbe, *op. cit.*, t. V, cols. 1686–7.

at St. Asaph and Llanwit Major in Wales in the previous century, when the only Western monastery outside Britain to follow a similar custom was Agaunum or St. Maurice in Switzerland.

Latin terms entered largely into the ecclesiastical vocabulary of Celtic Ireland and Scotland: *easpuig* (*episcopus*), *sagart* (*sacerdos*), *aifreann* (*offerendum*), *caisg* (*pascha*), *nollaig* (*Natale Christi*), *altaire* (*altare*), *bachull* (*baculum*), etc.

We do not know whether the liturgical chant was accompanied by any instrument. The organ was known to St. Aldhelm of Malmesbury (*ob.* 709), but perhaps not as an instrument of accompaniment. The earliest allusion to the organ in Brittany is found in the 9th-century life of St. Paul Aurelian, written by Wrmonoc.

VESTMENTS AND PONTIFICALIA

A prophetic utterance, purporting to be of Druidic origin, is believed to be the oldest allusion to the chasuble and pastoral staff. It is to be found in the Book of Armagh, quoted by Muirchu (*ob.* 670) in his 'Life of St. Patrick': 'Adze-head (Irish form of tonsure) will come with a crook-head staff; in his house head-holed (*in sua domu capiti perforata*, i.e. chasuble) he will chant impiety from his table (altar) from the front (i.e. east) part of his house, all his household (assistant ministers) will respond. So be it, So be it.'

The life of St. Bridget (*ob.* 525) tells us that she gave away to the poor the transmarine and foreign vestments of Bishop Condlaedh, of glorious light, which he was accustomed to use when offering the holy mysteries at the altars, on the festivals of our Lord and the vigils of the Apostles.[1] The Book of Deer, a Scottish gospel-book of the 10th century, depicts two priests in chasubles.

A curious little 9th-century Irish treatise on the vestments of

---

[1] *Vestimenta transmarina et peregrina Episcopi Conlaith, decorati luminis, quibus in solemnitatibus et vigiliis Apostolorum, sacra in altaribus offerens mysteria utebatur, pauperibus largita est.* Cogitosus (8th century monk, Kildare), *Vita S. Brigid.*, cap. XXIX.

the Mass gives eight colours for the chasuble—gold (yellow), blue, white, green, brown, red, black and purple.[1] Similar colours are prescribed in the 'Speckled Book' (*Leabhar Breac*), a document of the 14th or early 15th century. Adamnan speaks of the monks of Iona (Hy) as wearing white garments on festivals. Their habit consisted of the *tunica candida* or *pallium*, with an outer cloak known as the *amphibalus* or *cuculla*.[2]

Sandals are styled indifferently by Adamnan as *calceus, calceamentum* or *fico*: words frequently to be met with in the lives of the Celtic saints.

The ordinary outer dress of a British priest seems to have been a long hair cloak, known as a *caracalla*. It was in such a garment, St. Bede tells us, that St. Alban attempted to disguise himself, having changed clothes with a priest who had sheltered him during the persecution of Diocletian (c. 304).[3]

Crowns are said to have been worn by Celtic bishops, and it is related of St. Samson of Dol (c. 557) that he had a dream in which he saw 'three eminent bishops adorned with golden crowns standing before him'.[4] There is a representation of a bishop with a crown on a sculptured bas-relief in a ruined chapel in the valley of Glendalough, Co. Wicklow.

The figure depicted in the Golden Psalter of St. Gall has been thought to be wearing a rationale, but the alleged vestment is probably no more than a book held on the chest.

The pastoral staff or *cambutta*[5] was in shape like a primitive walking-stick, which, when damaged or worn, was sometimes covered with silver or gold. The shrine of St. Madoc of Ferns (6th century) depicts a short staff of wood, which was rounded at

---

[1] Moran, *Essays on the Early Irish Church*, Dublin, 1864; Mario Righetti, *Storia Liturgica*, vol. I (Milan, 1945), part III, cap. VIII, p. 496.

[2] The mistranslation by Geoffrey of Monmouth of the word *amphibalus* produced the 'life' of a purely fictitious martyr. This non-existent Saint is said to have been put to death at Redbourn, four miles from St. Alban's, in the Diocletian persecution. He was identified as the priest whom St. Alban had sheltered: 'St. Amphibalus'! *Amphibalus* was also a name given to the chasuble: *Casula, quam amphibolum vocant.* Pseudo-Germanus *Explic. antiq. lit. gallic.: Pat. Lat.*, t. XLIII, col. 97.

[3] *Mox se sanctus Albanus pro hospite ac magistro suo ipsius habitu, id est, caracalla, quae vestiebatur, inductus, militibus exhibuit.* Bede, *Hist. Eccles.*, lib. I, cap. VII.

[4] Mabillon, *Acta SS.*, t. I, p. 176, sect. 43.

[5] *Cambota*, more rarely *cambo*. Walafrid Strabo, *Vita S. Galli*, I, 26.

the top and truncated at the bottom.[1] The more modern form of pastoral staff appeared in the 9th or 10th century. The manufacture of staffs was a regular monastic industry in Ireland. Reference has been made already to the 7th-century prophecy respecting the *Bachall Isa* of St. Patrick,[2] but the earliest mention of the staff (*cambutta*) was probably to that of St. Columban (*ob.* 615), which, after his death, was sent to the monastery of St. Gall. It is stated in the 'Rites of Durham' [3] that when the coffin reliquary of St. Cuthbert (*ob.* 687) was opened the saint was found with his 'met-wand (?crozier) lying beside him'. Was this the *baculus* used by St. Cuthbert in accordance with the custom common to all Celtic saints? St. Cuthbert followed the Roman rite, but as a monk at Melrose and Lindisfarne he must have come across many old Celtic usages. The adoption of the Roman liturgy and reckoning of Easter did not mean that all previous customs vanished over-night! When, however, the feretory grave of the Saint was opened in 1827 there was no trace of any met-wand, which, if not a mere figment of the imagination, must have been taken by the Commissioners of Henry VIII at the spoliation of the shrine, probably in 1540.[4]

The comb of St. Kentigern (*ob.* 603), which was preserved as a relic in Glasgow was probably for liturgical use,[5] as was also that of St. Cuthbert (*ob.* 687), which was buried with him [6] and was extracted when the feretory grave of the saint was opened in 1827.

LIGHTS

A reference to lights (*lucernae ministerium*) is found in the life of St. Comgall, abbot of Bangor in Ulster (*ob. c.* 601), where we read of the monk Lugidius, who fell asleep as he was holding a

---

[1] The shrine is at least a century later than the time of St. Madoc.
[2] Preserved by the Scholiast on Fiacc's hymn. J. H. Todd, *St. Patrick*, p. 411.
[3] *Rites of Durham*, edit. Fowler, *Surtees Society*, 1903.
[4] *The Relics of St. Cuthbert*, Chr. Hohler and Others, introduct., XIII, p. 85. Oxford, 1956
[5] *Regist. Glasg.* (Edinburgh, 1843), vol. II, p. 330.
[6] *Reginald de Adm. S. Cuthberti Virtut.*, p. 89.

light by the side of his abbot during the Paschal vigil, letting the candle fall into the consecrated Easter water.[1]

It has been suggested that the small projecting stones high up in the east wall of the primitive oratory at Gallarus near Kilmalkedar originally supported the altar lights, but they may equally have served as pegs from which book-satchels depended.[2]

CHURCH ORNAMENTS, ETC.

It is possible that incense was used in the Celtic Church, although there is no reference to it in any of the surviving liturgical books.[3]

The *flabellum* or liturgical fan [4] seems to have been employed at Mass. It is found in an Irish gloss of the Soliloquies of Angus [5] (9th century), as well as in designs in the Book of Kells (8th century), in which angels holding *flabella* are depicted. An allusion to the *culebath* of St. Columba occurs in the *Annals*, and, in a somewhat late reference, in the *Voyage of Snedgus and Mac-Riagla*. The fan of St. Emin is mentioned in a quatrain published by E. O'Curry.[6]

The paten was known as the *discus*, *patena* or *patinus*: the chalice as *calix Domini*, *vas*, *laguncula*, *'coilech* or *'cailech*.

The sacred vessels in early times were probably made of glass, but at a little later period we find bronze chalices in Irish monasteries on the Continent.[7] The two-handled chalice of Ardagh in the National Museum, Dublin, may be possibly of the 8th century. It is thoroughly Celtic in decoration, and fashioned of gold, silver, bronze, lead, enamel, glass, amber and mica. Tradi-

---

[1] *In nocte Paschae, cum sanctus Congallus sacrificium offeret, Lugidius coram illo in manu sua lucernam tenebat. Cum autem Lugidius paulisper dormitasset, lucerna de manu ejus juxta altare cecidit in aquam Paschae consecratam, et Congallus increpavit eum. Acta SS.,* August., t. I, die IV, p. 345.

[2] Leask, *op. cit.*, chap. IV, p. 23.　　[3] Warren, *op. cit.*, chap. II, p. 127.

[4] Irish, *culebad*; Old Irish, *culebath*.　　[5] Carlsruhe Library.

[6] Gougaud, *Celtiques (Liturgies), Dict. d'Archéol. Chrét. et de Lit.*, t. II, part II, col. 3,000.

[7] The *Liber Pontificalis* says that in the time of Pope Zephyrinus (199–217) it was customary for ministers to hold glass patens before the celebrating bishop, while assistant presbyters took the consecrated *coronae* to the people. *Lib. Pontif.*, I, 139. The most ancient glass paten extant (3rd or 4th century), which is now in the British Museum, was found at Cologne.

tion recalls Assicus (Tassach), a disciple of St. Patrick, who was a skilful worker in bronze (*faber aereus*), and one who designed liturgical ornaments.

Little bells have been found in most of the districts known to have been visited by Celtic saints. It would seem to have been customary for a bishop to receive a staff and a bell at his consecration. The Book of Armagh refers to bells as *clocos*, and Adamnan, in his life of St. Columba, writes of *clocca*.[1] The almost contemporary life of St. Columban (*ob.* 615) uses the word *signum*.[2]

St. Patrick's bell, now in Dublin, is said to be one of the oldest iron relics of the Christian period. Small bronze bells, preserving the quadrangular shape of the earlier iron ones, were cast from, at least, the 9th century.[3] Legend ascribes to St. Dega the making of three hundred bells, the chiselling of three hundred crosses and the transcribing of three hundred gospels.[4]

Bells of the old Celtic form have been found in two or three places in Wales, but only in a single case with any ornamentation.

Celtic reliquaries were rectangular in form with a roof-shaped top, generally made of yew and covered with metal: decorated with designs familiar to Celtic craftsmen. The most ancient example of the kind is believed to be the one discovered at Melhus in Norway in 1906, where it might have been taken as plunder by the Vikings in the 7th century.

Oaths were sworn on the relics of saints, and special penalties were reserved for the men who thus perjured themselves. 'Gospels', says a Welsh historian, 'were of less account in this respect than such precious objects as the torque of St. Cynog or the bell of St. David kept at Glascwm, for the Saints of Wales, like those of Ireland, were held to be pitiless in vengeance when their ire was kindled by an indignity'.[5]

Leather book-wallets or satchels (*tiag lebair*), furnished with a strap, were provided to carry reliquaries or liturgical books. The

---

[1] Irish, *clog*.   [2] Krusch, *Script. Merov.*, IV, 85.
[3] e.g. Bells of St. Fillan (Edinburgh Museum), Clogher and Armagh (Dublin), St. Pol de Léon (Finistère).
[4] Léon Blouet, *Le Chrismale de Mortain*, chap. II, p. 22, n. 10. Coutances: Editions Notre-Dame, n.d.   [5] Lloyd, *op. cit.*, chap. IX, 3, p. 307.

Irish name, *tiag lebair*, is an early derivative from the Latin *theca* (θήκη), and used in Middle Irish literature of a bag or wallet of various descriptions. The Latin word *theca* occurs alone in the same sense, also *cetha* and *scetha*. *Capsella* and *capella* are found also in early Latin hagiographical literature for a wallet or case for carrying books and relics. The Irish term may have been suggested by the Latin *bibliotheca*, which in the Book of Armagh is used of a receptacle or case for books.

It would seem to have been the custom among the Celtic clergy to carry a copy of the Gospels in just such a wallet, slung round the neck or from the shoulders.

The Gospels in a *tiag lebair*, with the *bachall* (staff) and bell, seem to have been always carried by the Celtic saints, forming part of the armour in which these early missionaries battled against the heathenism of their time.

The most treasured books were kept in rectangular ornamented caskets, called *cumdachs*, and those in which were preserved the Gospel-book of St. Molaise (1001–25), Missal of Stowe (1023–52 in its oldest parts), Psalter (*cathach*) of St. Columba (1084) and Book of Deer (1150) may be seen today.

It was customary for Celtic monks, when working in the fields or going on a voyage, to carry the Blessed Sacrament with them, either in a small receptacle (*chrismals* [1]), worn bandolier-fashion, or in a little bag (*perula*), hung round the neck under the clothes. Frequent mention of the practice is found in Irish and British texts.[2] The carrying of the Eucharist was believed to ensure safety in battle and to serve as a talisman against the attacks of brigands. The life of St. Comgall (*ob. c.* 601) tells how on one occasion the Saint was attacked by heathen Picts while working in a field, but, on seeing the chrismal on his cloak, the pagans did not dare to touch it, under the belief that it was Comgall's God. The Saint was much moved, and said: 'Lord thou art my strength, my refuge and my redeemer.' So late as the 12th century

---

[1] *Chrismale* or *Kiismeel* has derivative forms: *Chrismarium* or *Chrismatorium*. The term is used also for the ampulla for chrism and the white garment at Baptism. The Rheims codex of the Gregorian sacramentary says: *Ubi chrismalis, seu chrismal, sive chrismale sumitur pro vase in quo Christi corpus servatur'.* Pat. Lat., t. LXXVIII, col. 421.

[2] e.g. *Poenitentiale Cummeani*, XI, 3.

(1150), we hear of four priests who were attacked by brigands while carrying the Eucharist. The Sacrament was profaned, but misfortune overtook the assailants, who ended by hanging themselves.[1] In the time of St. Laurence O'Toole, archbishop of Dublin (*ob.* 1180), when brigandage was rife, priests, with the protection of the sacred species, escorted parties of travellers along the roads.[1]

Serious penances were prescribed in the *Regula Coenobialis* of St. Colomban for dropping the Eucharist accidentally or leaving it behind through negligence: anything up to a year on bread and water.[2] Elsewhere we find a penance of forty days inflicted on anyone who should fall into the water while carrying the Eucharist. The traveller, in such a case, is ordered to drink any water that has seeped into the chrismal, and reverently to consume the particle. In yet another place, the Rule prescribes *quinis quinquies percussionibus* for forgetting to wear a chrismal, and *duodecim percussionibus* for dropping it.

St. Brigid of Kildare (*ob. c.* 525) was herself referred to by the Book of Lismore as a Eucharistic coffer: 'She was a consecrated casket for the keeping of Christ's Body and Blood';[3] while St. Aldhelm, bishop of Sherborne (*ob.* 709), addressed a poem to the chrismal.[4]

A leather 'tabernacle pyx' overlaid with gold, dating from the 7th–8th century, is found in the treasury of the cathedral church of Chur (Coire) in Switzerland.

The most perfect example of a Celtic chrismal is probably that of Mortain in Normandy: a beechwood coffer with the figures of Christ Pantocrator, St. Michael and St. Gabriel on the outside; a seraphim with outstretched wings surrounded by birds on the lid. The back of the lid has a Runic inscription: 'May God help Eado who made this chrismal.'[5] The iconography is partly reminiscent

---

[1] L. Blouet, *op. cit.*, chap. II, p. 21.

[2] St. Col., *Reg. Coenob.*, cap. XV. Jean Gaudemart, *Les Aspects Canoniques de la Règle de Saint Colomban, Mélanges Colambaniens*, p. 171.

[3] P. M. Harney, *Life in an Ancient Irish Monastery*, p. 10. Dublin, 1950.

[4] Blouet, *op. cit.*, chap. V, p. 47.

[5] The origin of the Runic alphabet seems uncertain, but it may be Romanised-German: used first on the Continent and later in England. It would appear to have been in use in this country for about five centuries (until about the year 900).

of Coptic art and partly of Celtic.[1] The coffer in all probability
originated in Northumbria 'between 660 and 700, perhaps rather
725'.[2] It would have been given by Robert, Count of Mortain
and brother of William the Conqueror, who in 1082 had founded
the collegiate church (St. Evroult) of Mortain.[3] In addition to the
coffer, the Norman foundation received an illuminated 10th-
century gospel-book of the Winchester School, which was unfortunately destroyed in June 1944. An *ordo* of 1741, now in the
archives of the town of Mortain, notes a curious liturgical custom
on the feast of St. Mark (April 25): The subdeacon, in the procession to the church of Notre-Dame du Rocher, vested in alb,
carries the book of the gospels (*codicem Evangeliorum*) and a 'little
golden coffer' (*parvam capsam aureatam*): the latter suspended
round his neck.[4]

Before leaving the subject of the Celtic chrismal, we may
conclude with a summary of the various types of art employed in
the Northumbrian chrismal of Mortain: '*Les runes des anglo-
saxons, réservées la plupart du temps aux formules païennes et
magiques, apparaissent ici radicalemant exorciseés; les images des
archanges sont gravés dans la langue de Rome; les images saintes
nous viennent de l'orient byzantin; et les oiseaux du toit se sont envolés
des miniatures syriennes et irlandaises.*'[5]

Holy Communion

Circular azyme bread, stamped with a cross, was in use in Ireland in the 7th century, as may be seen in the design at the foot of
the monogram in the Book of Kells. Holy Communion was normally given under both kinds, but the Rule of St. Colomban
directed that 'novices shall not be permitted to receive the
chalice'.[6] The Rule speaks of the act of Communion as 'going to
the chalice' (*accedere ad calicem*), an expression that was used also
by the Irish Culdees.[7]

Communion was given in the Mass, and a prescription of Cum-

---

[1] Blouet, *op. cit.*, chap. IV, p. 33.   [2] *Ibid.*, chap. II, pp. 16, 19.
[3] René Herval, *En Normandie, de la Dives au Mont-Saint-Michel*, pp. 119–20. Gre-
noble, 1951.
[4] Blouet, *op. cit.*, chap. III, p. 30.   [5] *Ibid.*, chap. V, p. 61.
[6] *Pat. Lat.*, t. LXXX, col. 220.   [7] *Ibid.*, cols. 217c, 220d.

mian says: *Sacrificium non est accipiendum de manu sacerdotis qui orationes et lectiones secundum ritum implere non potest.*[1] Gildas (570) tells us that in the Welsh Church of the 6th century the punishment for certain offences was exclusion from the kiss of peace and Holy Communion.[2] An ordinance ascribed to St. Patrick says that he who neglects to receive Holy Communion on Easter night is not one of the 'faithful'. The 12th-century reform in Ireland extended the days for a general Communion to Christmas, Easter and Pentecost.

The Eucharist was administered to children after Baptism, and a formula of Communion[3] and several thanksgiving prayers are found in the Stowe missal. The sick and dying received the reserved Sacrament by intinction, and formulas are given in Dimma,[4] Mulling,[5] Stowe[6] and Deer.[7]

The 8th-century rule of the Irish Culdees prescribed a seven years' probation for admission into the community: during the first year the novice was not allowed to receive Holy Communion, only to 'hear Mass'; then in the second year his Communions began, gradually increasing in number until they attained in his seventh year to Communion every Sunday.

EULOGIAE

Adamnan speaks of the table in the refectory at St. Kenneth's monastery at Aghaboe in Ireland, on which the *eulogiae* were cut up for distribution. *Eulogiae* were received at the afternoon meal in 6th-century Ireland,[8] and a similar custom existed at Iona.[9] At

---

[1] *De Mensura poenitentiarum*, cap. XIV; Gougaud, *Celtiques (Liturgies)*, *D.A.C.L.*, t. II, part II, col. 3021.

[2] Gildas, *Prefatio de Penitentia*, I.

[3] *Corpus et sanguinis (sic) domini nostri Jesu Christi sit tibi in vitam aeternam. Amen.* Fo. 59, *Henry Bradshaw Society*, vol. XXXII, p. 32.

[4] *Corpus et sanguis domini nostri Jhesu Christi filii dei vivi conservat animam tuam in vitam perpetuam.* Warren, *op. cit.*, p. 170.

[5] *Tum reficitur corpore et sanguine; Corpus cum sanguine domini nostri Jhesu Christi sanitas sit tibi in vitam aeternam.*

[6] *Corpus et sanguis domini nostri Jesu Christi dei vivi altissimi—reliqua.* Fo. 63v. *H.B.S.*, vol. XXXII, p. 35.

[7] *Hisund dubar sacofaicc dau* ('Here give the sacrifice to him'): *Corpus cum sanguine domini nostri Jhesu Christi sanitas sit tibi in vitam perpetua (sic) et salutem.*

[8] Adamnan, *Vita S. Columbae*, II, 12.   [9] *Ibid.*, II, 4.

Lindisfarne in the time of St. Cuthbert (*ob.* 687), the distribution
took place at the third hour after Mass, and in the Continental
houses of St. Colomban on Sundays and holy days after Mass.
These *Eulogiae* are mentioned in the *Vita prima* of St. Samson of
Dol (*ob. c.* 565).

RITES AND CEREMONIES OF MASS

The Mass was known by many names in the Celtic Churches:
*Communio, Communio altaris, Comna, Conviaticum, Eucharistia,
Hostia, Oblatio, Oiffrenn, Sacorfaicc, Sacrificium, Sacrificiale mys-
terium, Viaticum.*

In all European languages, with the exception of the Celtic,
the word for the Mass was derived from *Missa,* but *Oiffrenn* was
taken from *Offerendum.*[1] The name was already in use in the time
of St. Patrick.[2]

Gildas reproaches the British priests with not celebrating often
enough,[3] but he unfortunately gives no indication as to what this
may mean.[4] At Iona in the time of St. Columba (*ob.* 597), Mass
was said on Sundays and feasts, but by the 7th century we hear of
priests celebrating twice on the same day. Celtic priests were certainly unaccustomed to daily Mass as a norm, although we read of
two Breton priests, Riwenno and Condeluc, disciples of St.
Conwoïon of Redon (*ob.* 868), who said Mass every day.[5]

The Holy Sacrifice was usually offered in the morning, but
Adamnan speaks also of the afternoon, when the Mass was preceded by a washing of hands and feet. It is not certain, however,
whether these ablutions were ceremonial in character, but they
have been reminiscent of the prescription in the book *Exodus.*[6]

The only 'Celtic' missal that has survived is the so-called

---

[1] Old Irish, *oifrend*; Welsh, *offeren.*

[2] Cf. *Offerenda,* a chant sung in the Ambrosian rite at the offertory: that is at the
beginning of the Mass of the faithful.

[3] Gildas, *De Excidio Britanniae,* cap. LXVI.

[4] Cf. *De quibus dicitur quod rarissime celebrant et abstinent ab altari.* A reprimand from
the General Chapter of the Cistercians (1202) to the Welsh abbots of Aberconway,
Carleon (Llantarnam) and Valle Crucis. *Cap. Gen.,* 1202, XXV; Canivez, *Stat.,* t. I,
p. 281. Here again it is impossible to say how infrequently the defaulting abbots said
Mass.

[5] Mabillon, *Acta SS., O.S.B.,* t. IV, 2, p. 205.

[6] *Lavabunt in ea Aaron et filii ejus manus suas ac pedes. Exod.* XX, 19.

Cathedral Church, Salisbury: Exterior and Interior

York Minster: The Nave

Hereford Cathedral

Missal of Stowe, which contains the Irish ordinary for the daily Mass in a late Romanised form.[1] Certain of the prayers and phrases are found also in the 'Mass of Illyricus', but there is nothing more than an accidental resemblance between the two.[2] Stowe, which is said to be the smallest known volume which ever passed under the title of a missal, seems to be a *missale itinerantium*, with an ordinary that might serve for almost any occasion, a general common of saints and two Masses for special intentions—for penitents and for the dead.

Baptism is given as part of the liturgy for Holy Saturday, but as a separate office, as we find in the *Gothicum*, *Gallicanum Vetus* and Bobbio.

The text for those parts of the Mass in which the people join are, in several cases, indicated by incipits and endings.

The title *Missa Romensis cottidiana* occurs also in the Bobbio missal, and it is found at the very end of the *Missale Gothicum* before the collect *Deus qui culpa offenderis*.

The text of the Stowe missal has three somewhat differing elements, all more or less contemporary: the original text (9th century), correction of Moelcaich and interpolations of a later hand. Then, at the end of the book, the Mass, as far as it goes, is described in an Irish tract.

The Mass begins with a confession of sins (*Peccavimus, Domine. Peccavimus, parce peccatis nostris . . .*) and a litany of the saints, as in the St. Gall fragment.[3] It is not found in the Bobbio missal. The original compiler of the litany inserted no more than thirteen invocations (Blessed Virgin, ten Apostles, St. Mark and St. Luke), to which Moelcaich added a further thirty-two names, twenty-four of which are Irish.[4] These additions, on fols. 30-30v, were bound up in a wrong place in the MS., where at first sight they would appear to be connected with the diptychs in the canon. The list of Apostles, though imperfect, agrees with the order in St.

---

[1] *Stowe Missal*, printed text, vol. II, edit. *H.B.S.*, vol. XXXII, 1915.

[2] The so-called Mass of Illyricus is a collection of Franco-Roman prayers, dating from the 9th–10th century (*c.* 1030, Jungmann, *Missarum Sollemnia*, t. I, p. iii).

[3] St. Gall, MSS. 1395.

[4] In the Fulda MS. numerous invocations are followed by the patriarch Secundinus and 23 more names of men and women, doubtless all Irish. Witzel says in reference to these names: *nostris temporibus ignotissima.*

R

Matthew (X, 2–4), and the compiler, in all probability, took them from the diptychs. St. Madianus (Mathias) occupies the same position in the Stowe missal and St. Gall litanies as in the list of saints in the canon.

The litany or *praeparatio sacerdotis*, as we should now call it, was rudimentary in the early Western books, and represented by no more than a single prayer: *apologia sacerdotis*. Before the interpolations of Moelcaich, Stowe had a short prayer with penitential supplications, a litany of the saints and a prayer followed by a short ejaculation (in the form of a prayer). The conception breathed the spirit of the Eastern liturgies, and Stowe appears to represent the stage immediately following the simple *apologia* of the 7th century.[1] The framework of the *praeparatio* in Stowe, Fulda and MS. 2 A XX is identical.[2] The *Ordo* of St. Amand and the Irish interpolator in Stowe both used a late and corrupt text of the litany taken from Gaul, in which the order of the concluding suffrages had been inverted.[3] The litany in Stowe is followed by still more *apologiae*, and, 'with the peculiar character of Irish piety and devotion, a development of this kind is likely to be marked and accentuated earlier and more readily in Ireland than perhaps in any other Western country'.[4] The 'Mass of Illyricus', to which we have already referred, has some fifteen or twenty *apologiae*, besides a fully developed scheme of vesting prayers.[5] Bishop speaks of the Mass as an '*Ordo Missae* farced with apologies'.[6]

Oratio Augustini: Rogo te Deus Zabaoth, which follows in Stowe, is found also in 'Illyricus', pontifical of Troyes (9th century), Tours missal (9th century), Rheims pontifical, sacramentary of Corbie (10th century) and elsewhere. A faulty binding of the Stowe MS. places the greater part of the *Oratio Ambrosii: Ante conspectum divinae majestatis* in the canon,[7] and

---

[1] Bishop, *Liturg. Hist.*, VII, p. 138.

[2] The Fulda MS. was published by G. Witzel in 1855. 'I think', says Bishop, 'that the English and the Irish were the propagators of such litanies of the saints in the 8th century in Gaul and Germany'. Bishop, *op. cit.*, VII, p. 150.

[3] *Ibid.*, p. 160.   [4] *Ibid.*, pp. 138–9.

[5] The litany in 'Illyricus' is preceded by a rubric: *flexis genibus coram altare*. Bona, *Rer. Lit.*, append., p. 471.

[6] Bishop, *op. cit.*, p. 138, n. 2.

[7] Stowe missal, fols. 31–31v.

only the last part, beginning: *profeta omnes justitiae* appears in its proper place, but after the heading *Oratio Augustini*. The so-called prayer of St. Ambrose, inserted by Moelcaich, occurs in the *Libellus precum* of Fleury and several other French books. It seems clear enough from the Irish tracts that the chalice was prepared before the introit. In the first place, water was poured into the chalice,[1] as the priest said: *Peto*[2] *te, Pater, deprecor te, Fili, obsecro te, Spiritus sancte*: a drop at the name of each of the Divine Persons. Bread was then placed on the altar, after which the wine was added to the chalice with the formula: *Remittit Pater, indulget Filius, miseretur Spiritus Sanctus*:[3] again in three assignments. The later text of Stowe regarding the 'partial uncovering of the chalice' seems to indicate that the *oblata* were set on the altar before the beginning of Mass. The Irish tracts refer to the introit, but it is not mentioned anywhere in the missal, and was probably sung from the psalter.

After the prayers of 'St. Augustine' and 'St. Ambrose', the Stowe missal gives a short prayer: *Ascendat oratio nostra*, prefaced by a rubric: *Haec oratio in omni misa cantatur*. It is found after the creed and Lord's prayer in the *Liber Hymnorum*. 'On solemnities of Peter and Christ' (*sic*), says a corrector other than Moelcaich, the prayer is followed by the collect for St. Peter (*III Kal. Julias*): *Deus qui beato Petro apostolo*.[4] A similar collect appears in the Gelasian sacramentary and the Bobbio missal.

The *Imnus angelicus* or *Gloria in excelsis* in Stowe is begun in the original hand, but continued by Moelcaich on an inserted slip. It may be noted that the canticle is found here in its Roman position, whereas in the purely Celtic antiphonary of Bangor it occurs *ad vesperum et matutinam*, after the manner of the Greeks, who employed it at compline ('Αποδειπνον) and lauds ('όρθρος), where it formed a part of the Δοξολογία μεγάλη.[5] The text of the

---

[1] The pouring of water first into the chalice is unknown elsewhere.

[2] *Quaeso*, Leabhar Breac.

[3] Stowe, fo. 65v; *H.B.S.*, vol. XXXII, pp. 37-40. *Mittet Pater, Leabhar Breac.*

[4] The corrector interpolated the days on which it was to be said, not the collect itself.

[5] The Celtic monks were great reciters of psalms, and St. Colomban prescribed in two offices the recitation of the entire psalter. The version used would appear to have been the second revision of St. Jerome (387-91): the so-called 'Gallican' psalter.

Gloria in Stowe differs from that in Bobbio, and Edmund Bishop considers the Irish version to be the more ancient.[1]

Moelcaich has inserted the collect *Deus qui diligentibus te* over erasures which probably represented the original continuation of the canticle. Another hand has prefixed a direction to the effect that the prayer shall be said *in cotidianis diebus* in place of the prayer which follows.

Deus qui diligentibus te, which is found in the Gelasian sacramentary, is the collect for the Fifth Sunday after Pentecost in our Roman missal.

The original hand had inserted the prayer: *Deus qui culpa offenderis*, with the heading: *Orationes et preces misae aeclesiae romane haec oratio prima petri* . . . We find it in the Bobbio missal after the collect for St. Peter.

As we have seen, the multiplicity of prayers in Mass was one of the grievances of Agrestius at the council of Mâcon (*c.* 620).

The words *Hic augmentum* ('Here is extension') were added by Moelcaich before the title of the epistle. They refer, either to 'some unwritten addition', as, for example, an extra proper collect, or, less probably, to the unwritten conclusion of the collect: *Jesum Christum*, etc. The Irish tract speaks of *augmentum* as *tormach*, 'increase' or 'expansion', whereas St. Colomban uses the word in the sense of 'addition', with reference to the petitions added to the psalms at the day hours: *cum versiculorum augmento intervenientium*.[2] One finds, later, at the offertory in Stowe: *secunda pars augmenti hic super oblata*. The word, which is used by Arnobius,[3] has been defined by Varro: *quod ex immolata hostia dejectum in jecore in porriciendo augendi causa*.[4] The single fixed epistle for the daily Mass is an indication of antiquity,[5] but, unlike Bobbio, there is no mention of a prophetic lesson. The Irish tract refers to the gradual as *salm digrad*: a term which possibly applies to all the prayers and chants between the epistle and gospel.

The prayer *Deus qui nos regendo* was added by a hand other

---

[1] Bishop, *Journal of Theological Studies*, XII, p. 411, n.
[2] *Reg. S. Columb.*, cap. VII.
[3] Arnobius, *Adv. Gentes*, lib. VII, cap. XXIV.
[4] Varro, *De Lingua Lat.*, lib. V (edit. 1833), 112, p. 44.
[5] I *Cor.* XI, 26–52.

than Moelcaich. It is found in Gerbert's *Monumenta Veteris Liturgiae Alemannicae*[1] and in the later Gelasian MSS. Another prayer follows, which is an Easter collect in Bobbio, and referred to by Gerbert as Ambrosian:[2] *Omnipotens sempiterne Deus qui populum tuum.*

The psalm is taken from *Psalm* CIV, verses 4, 1–3, 4.

The prayer: *Grata sint tibi, Domine,* is the secret of an Advent Mass in the Gelasian sacramentary. It is followed by *Alleluia,* with *Psalm* CXVII, 14 and the prayer: *Sacrificis (sic) presentibus, Domine.* The prayer is found as the secret in another Gelasian Mass for Advent, and in our Roman missal it occurs on the Fourth Sunday in Advent.

A bidding-prayer or *prex,* to which Moelcaich has added a title: *Deprecatio sancti Martini pro populo,* does not appear between the epistle and gospel elsewhere. In the mediaeval English Church, bidding-prayers or *preces dominicales* were recited during the procession before the solemn Mass in cathedrals and collegiate churches: after the gospel and offertory in parish churches.

A near approach to the whole passage of the Stowe *deprecatio,* both in form and substance, is found in the missal litany transcribed by Witzel from an ancient MS. in the library at Fulda.[3] It seems clear that the *deprecatio* came to Ireland by a Gallican channel, and the character of these intercessions corresponds to those enumerated, in a somewhat different order, in a passage of the Rule of St. Columban. The original source of the *deprecatio* must be looked for in the Byzantine rite,[4] and Dom Capelle speaks of the Irish diaconal litanies as almost direct translations of the litany in use in the Church of Jerusalem: *la source est unique et hierosolymitaine.*[5] *Dicamus omnes,* which occurs twice in the Stowe *deprecatio,* recalls the Lenten litanies in the Ambrosian rite. There is no mention either of the Pope or of minor orders.

---

[1] *Mon. Vet. Lit. Alemann.,* t. I (1771), p. 191.

[2] *Ibid.,* t. I, p. 95.

[3] Bona, *op. cit.,* lib. II, cap. IV, 3.

[4] Cf. διακονίκα, εἰρηνικὰ, δέησεις, μεγαλὴ συναπτή in the liturgy of St. John Chrysostom.

[5] Capelle, *Le Kyrie eleison et le pape Gelase, Revue bénéd.,* vol XLVI (1934), p. 134. Duchesne, commenting on the Stowe litany, says: 'The examples given are nothing more than translations of a Greek text'. Duchesne, *op. cit.,* chap. VII, 6, p. 200.

The petition *pro pissimis* (*sic*) *imperatoribus et omni romano exercitu* is a strange one to find in an Irish book, but it was imported verbatim from the Continent without consideration as to its relevancy. In the Fulda MS. we have the singular *piissimo imperatore*, while in the much later Corpus Irish missal *rex* and *exercitus Hibernensium* have been substituted for the Roman emperor and his army. *Piissimi imperatores* is a direct translation of εὐσέβεστατοι βασιλεῖς in the liturgy of St. John Chrysostom.

The bidding-prayer in Stowe is followed by two collects: (1) *Sacrificium tibi, Domine*, which is an Advent secret in the Gelasian sacramentary, and, possibly, in Stowe an *oratio post precem* of the Gallican type; (2) *Ante oculos tuos*, which occupies the same place in the so-called Mass of Illyricus.[1]

At the conclusion of these prayers, there is a rubric in Irish: *Lethdirech sund*, 'Half-covering here', and followed after the creed by another rubric: *Landirech sund*, 'Full covering here': both rubrics were apparently inserted by Moelcaich. The Irish rubric prescribing the 'half-covering' is continued in Latin: *Dirigatur Domine usque vespertinum . . . ter canitur . . . hic elivatur lintiamen de calice.* This seems to mean that the chalice was partially uncovered, in removing a first veil, at the beginning of Mass: the complete uncovering not taking place till the offertory. In the Gallican liturgy, this was the place for the preparation of the *oblata*, but there are no traces of such a rite in Stowe. The Penitential of Cummian supposes a double veil: *Perfundens aliquid de calice super altare quando auferuntur linteamina, septem dies poeniteat.*[2] The verses indicated of the psalm *Dirigatur*[3] were sung thrice, and then, after the partial uncovering, a formula, almost identical with our Roman offertory prayer, was recited three times: *Veni, Domine, sanctificator omnipotens et benedic hoc sacrificium preparatum tibi. Amen.* The rite is described in the Irish treatise on the symbolism of the ceremonies of the Mass appended to the Stowe missal: 'The uncovering, so far as half, of the Host and Chalice, and what is chanted thereat, both Gospel

---

[1] Bona, *op. cit.*, append., p. 482.
[2] Gougaud, *Celtiques* (*Liturgies*), *D.A.C.L.*, t. II, part II, col. 3008.
[3] *Psl.* CXL, 2.

and Alleluia as far as the *oblata*, it is a commemoration of the law of the Prophets, wherein Christ was manifestly foretold, save that it was not seen until he was born.' [1] The 'partial uncovering' is associated in the rubric with the gospel and *allóir*, but in the text of the missal it follows the gradual. The ceremony is described also in the *Leabhar Breac*: 'The two uncoverings, including the half of the chalice of the offertory and of the oblation, and what is chanted with them, both in the gospel and *alleoir*, figure the written law in which Christ was manifestly foretold, but was not seen until his birth. The elevation of the chalice of the offertory and the paten, after the full uncovering, at which is sung the verse *Immola Deo sacrificium laudis.*' [2] The prayers and ceremonies possibly continued while the psalms and alleluia were being sung.

The fixed gospel [3] in the Stowe missal begins on an inserted sheet in the handwriting of Moelcaich, and concludes, after the 'prayer of Gregory', in the original hand. According to the tracts, the gospel was followed by *allóir*,[4] which Stokes describes as *alleluia* and Macgregor as 'blessing'.[5]

The *oratio Gregorii super evangelium* was inserted by the scribe who succeeded Moelcaich. It is found in the Gregorian sacramentary for the second Saturday and third Sunday in Lent, but not in connection with the gospel: [6] *Quessumus, Domine, omnipotens Deus ut vota nostra tibi immulata clementer respicias atque ad defentionem nostram dextram tuae majestatis extendas . . . per Dominum nostrum . . .*

The Antiphonary of Bangor gives a *collectio post evangelium* (*Exultantes gaudio*) and four other formulas *post evangelium*. There is no collect thus entitled or found in any liturgy other than the Irish.

The creed, written in the original hand with the *filioque* inserted between the lines,[7] was certainly in the Stowe missal before

---

[1] *Stowe*, fo. 65b; *H.B.S.*, vol. XXXII, pp. 37 (Irish), 40 (English).

[2] Fo. 251, col. 1.   [3] *Johan.* VI, 51–7.

[4] Cf. Ambrosian *antiphona post evangelium*. The *laudes* of the Mozarabic and Gallican liturgies had a threefold *alleluia*.

[5] Cf. *Per evangelica dicta* in the Roman rite.

[6] Cf. Collect for 3rd Sunday in Lent in the actual Roman missal.

[7] The *filioque* was possibly inserted by Moelcaich.

the Adoptionist controversy, and the conformity of its text with the creed of Alcuin suggests the possibility of its adoption from Carolingian usage.[1] This, however, is not to say that the creed in the Stowe missal is a Carolingian product, and, if Alcuin cites it, this is because it was a familiar formula which was in use in the district where he had lived. It is unlikely to have been introduced into Ireland after 798, and appears to be contemporary with the insertion of the *Gloria in excelsis* in the Mass.[2] On the other hand, the creed may have come to Ireland directly from Spain, where it was prescribed by the third council of Toledo in 589, or by way of Gaul or England. The conformity with Alcuin's text permits the three hypotheses. Ireland then, either directly or indirectly, adopted the creed from Spain, but, faithful to its original way of treating everything, it was placed after the gospel, not, as in Spain and the East, after the *Pater noster*, and we may be sure also that the Irish text was different from that of Spain. The omission of the words *Deum de Deo* was a Gelasian peculiarity. The creed (*symmulus*)in the Antiphonary of Bangor differs in its wording from all other forms which are known to exist, although it has marked traces of affinity to the creed in the *Gallicanum Vetus*. Its liturgical position, immediately before the *Pater noster*, is that of the Mozarabic rite.[3]

In the Stowe missal, an Irish rubric, indicating the position of the offertory, follows the creed: *Landirech sund*, 'full covering here'.

Then, versicles are sung three times: *Ostende nobis Domine misericordiam et salutare tuum dabis (da nobis)*, followed by a prayer: *Oblata, Domine, munera sanctifica nosque a peccatorum*

---

[1] Capelle, *Recherches de Théologie ancienne et médiévale*, VI (1934), p. 255.

[2] *Ibid.*, p. 258.

[3] *Credo in deum patrem omnipotentem invisib(i)lem, omnium creaturarum visibilium et invisibilium conditorem. Credo et in ihesum Christum, filium ejus unicum dominum nostrum, deum omnipotentem, conceptum de spiritu sancto, natum de maria virgine, Passum sub pontio Pylato, qui crucifixus et sepultus descendit ad inferos, tertia die resurrexit a mortuis, ascendit in caelis, seditque ad dexteram dei patris omnipotentis, exinde venturus judicare vivos ac mortuos. Credo et in spiritum sanctum, deum omnipotentem, unam habentem substantiam cum patre et filio, sanctam esse aecclesiam catholicam, ab remisa peccatorum, sanctorum commonionem carnis resurrectionem. Credo vitam post mortem, et vitam aeternam in gloria Christi. Haec omnia credo in Deum. Amen.* Antiphonary of Bangor, Henry Bradshaw Society, vol. X (1895), introd., p. XXVII.

nostro (rum) maculis emunda: per Dominum. The prayer is found in the Bobbio missal, where it is called *collectio post nomina*, and it occurs also in the Gelasian and Gregorian sacramentaries. It is the secret of the third Christmas Mass in our Roman missal. The Irish tract says that during its recitation the chalice was elevated after the 'full covering': 'The elevation of the chalice, after the full uncovering thereof, *quando canitur oblata*, that is a commemoration of Christ's birth and of his glory through signs and miracles'.[1]

The *Leabhar Breac* prescribes the elevation of both chalice and paten *quando canitur Imola Deo sacrificium laudis*, and the wording of the prayers seems to suggest this.

The Stowe missal is a book for the priest, a sacramentary in fact, and it is consequently silent as to the antiphon. The following prayer, which was inserted in Stowe by Moelcaich over an erasure which began with *G*, is found in one set of the *orationes et preces divinae* in the Leonine sacramentary: *Hostias quesumus, Domine, nostrae devotionis benignus adsume et per sacrificia gloriosa subditorum tibi corda purifica: per Dominum.*[2] The prayer with *G* as the first letter was in all probability *Grata sit tibi*, which follows *Oblata, Domine* in the Bobbio missal, and occurs later in Stowe in an amplified form.

Hostias . . . is followed by a prayer in Moelcaich's hand, which is evidently a relic of the time when the 'names' were recited here, as in the Hispano-Gallican liturgies: *Has oblationes et sincera libamina immolamus tibi Domine Jesu Christi qui passus es pro nobis et resurrexisti tertia die a mortuis pro animamus (animabus) carorum nostrorum n. et cararum nostrarum quorum nomina recitamus et quorumcumque non recitamus sed a te recitantur in libro vitae aeternae propter misericordiam tuam eripe qui regnas in secula seculorum. Amen.* The names of the living would seem to have been recited here, but the memento of the living occurs after the *Te igitur* in the canon.

The author of the life of St. Samson says: 'Many times have I

[1] *Stowe*, fo. 65v; *H.B.S.*, vol. XXXII, pp. 37 (Irish), 40 (English).
[2] Muratori, t. I, col. 352; Feltoe, *Sacramentarium Leonianum* (Cambridge, 1896), p. 56.

heard read at St. Samson's altar, when Mass was sung, the names of both his parents.' [1]

A similar position for the remembrance of the dead is found in the Penitential of Cummian, in which the deacon is directed to place the *oblata* on the altar at the offertory: *Diaconus obliviscens oblationem afferre, donec auferatur linteamen quando recitantur nomina pausantium similiter poeniteat.*[2] This prayer and the one that follows closely resemble the *collectio post nomina* of the Gallican and the *oratio post nomina* of the Mozarabic rites.

The reference to the 'Book of Life' is of frequent occurrence in the Eastern and Gallican service-books.

A rubric, which is found here, probably refers to additional proper prayers analogous to the Roman secrets: *Has oblationes Secunda pars augmenti hic super oblata.*

Grata sit tibi would seem to have been an expanded form of the prayer which, in the original text, followed *Oblata, Domine.*[3] It was transferred here, when a long passage relating to the 'names' was inserted: *Grata sit tibi haec oblatio plebis tuae quam tibi offerimus in honorem Domini nostri Jesu Christi et in commemorationem beatorum apostolorum tuorum ac martirum tuorum et confessorum quorum hic reliquias spicialiter recolimus n. et eorum quorum festivitas hodie celebratur et pro animamus (animabus) omnium episcoporum nostrorum et sacerdotum nostrorum et diaconorum nostrorum et carorum nostrorum et cararum nostrarum et puerorum nostrorum et puellarum nostrarum et penitentium nostrorum cunctis proficiant ad salutem: per Dominum.* The recitation of names may have been followed at one time by an anthem known as the *deprecatio*, containing the names of the departed for whom prayers were asked and of those saints whose intercessions were sought. The *deprecatio* at Iona concluded with the name of St. Martin, and we read that St. Columba, offering the holy Sacrifice on the day after the news of the death of Bishop Columban had reached him, directed the cantors to add the name of the lately deceased bishop.

---

[1] Lloyd, *op. cit.*, chap. V, 3, p. 149.

[2] Cummian, *De Mens. Penitent.*, cap. XIII.

[3] The prayers *Oblata* and *Grata* are both found in the Bobbio missal, with the titles *Post nomina* and *Ad Pacem* respectively.

It is possible that the kiss of peace was given here in the 7th century, as was customary in the Gallican and Mozarabic liturgies.

The *Sursum corda* was not preceded by *Dominus vobiscum*, as was also the case in the Gelasian sacramentary.

The dialogue was identical with that in our Roman missal, but the preface in the Stowe MS. is not found elsewhere, although the words *sanctus, fortis, immortalis* occur in the trisagion on Good Friday, and *non unius singulariter personae sed unius trinitatis substantiae* are in the Roman preface of Trinity.[1] The preface for the *misa pro mortuis pluribus* [2] is a Mozarabic prayer for the dead, taken from a missal of the second half of the 8th century, and cited by Elipandus, bishop of Toledo, in his Adoptionist controversy with Alcuin in 793/4.[3] It is found also in a preface of a Mass for the dead in the Irish fragment of Reichenau-Carlsruhe, where it is nearer to the text quoted by Elipandus.[4] It does not appear in the actual *Missale Mixtum*.[5] A rubric in Irish at the end of the common preface in Stowe says that here the *dignum* of the addition (*dignum intormaig*), that is the proper preface, is inserted, if it ends with *Per quem*: after the *Per quem* clause there is a similar direction, if the addition ends with *Sanctus*. A proper preface for the feast of St. Patrick—*sollemnitas dormitationis ejus*—is alluded to by Tirechán in his *Annotationes*, but the text has not survived.[6] The direction in the Book of Armagh: *offertorium ejus* (St. Patrick) *proprium immolari* probably refers to a proper preface, for which the Gallican name was *immolatio*.[7] The 9th-century fragment in the library of St. Gall contains part of a preface for the Circumcision.[8]

The variable *Post Sanctus* after the *Benedictus* in the Stowe missal is similar to that in the Mozarabic liturgy for Christmas

---

[1] A profession of the Holy Trinity is of frequent occurrence in Celtic liturgical books.

[2] *Vere dignum cujus promisionis plenas aeternorum bonorum.* Fols. 45, 45v; *Stowe Missal, H.B.S.*, vol. XXXII, p. 23.

[3] *Pat. Lat.*, t. XCVI, col. 875.

[4] *Journal of Theological Studies*, V, pp. 57, 59, 69. Cf. Liturgical note by Edmund Bishop in *Book of Cerne* (edit. Kuypers), p. 270.

[5] Férotin, *Liber Ordinum* (Paris, 1904), col. 422.

[6] J. H. Todd, *Life of St. Patrick* (Dublin, 1864), p. 430.

[7] The expression *immolabat altissimo* occurs in the Hymn of St. Comgall in the *Antiphonary of Bangor*, fo. 17r, stanza 22. *H.B.S.*, vol. X, p. 19.

[8] *Bibl. St. Gall*, MS. 1394.

Day [1] and the *Missale Gothicum* for the Vigil: *Benedictus qui venit de celis ut conversaretur in terris homo factus est ut per passionem suam vitam aeternam credentibus daret: per Dominum.* Another *Post Sanctus* is given in the *Misa apostolorum* . . . in Stowe: *Vere sanctus vere benedictus vere mirabilis in sanctis suis Deus noster Jesus Christus ipse dabit virtutem et fortitudine(m) plebis suae benedictus Deus quem benedicimus in apostolis et in om(n)ibus sanctis suis qui placuerunt ei ab initio sae(culi) per eundem Dominum nostrum Jesum Christum qui pridie.* [2] A *Post Sanctus* is found also in the Reichenau-Carlsruhe and Piacenza fragments.

It may be seen that the *Post Sanctus* was originally followed immediately by *Qui pridie*, and here it is in all probability a vestige of the Irish Mass before the introduction of the Roman canon.

The Book of Armagh attests the use of the Roman canon in the Celtic Church at the beginning of the 9th century. *Te igitur* is prefaced in Stowe by the title: *Canon dominicus pape gilasi*, although it is in fact the Gregorian canon with a long list of Irish saints. The beginning of the Stowe canon, till *memoriam venerantes*, was the work of Moelcaich, but an examination of the palimpsest folio indicates that this part was included by the original hand, but without the development of *Memento etiam Domine*. The words *Episcopo sedis apostolicae* [3] are added after *papa nostro*, and *abbato nostro n. episcopo* after *fidei cultoribus*. The reference to the name of the abbot shows that the missal was written for the use of religious.

The rubric: *Hic recitantur nomina vivorum* prefaces the memento of the living in Stowe, but it is not found in the later Irish missals. The memento has a long list of intercessions for various classes of persons, which occurs also in Carlsruhe fragment B and the Fulda MS., but not in the Bobbio missal. The 10th-century additional clause: *pro quibus tibi offerimus vel* is wanting in Stowe,[4] which has the curious intercession: *pro imperio romano.*

---

[1] *Vere sanctus; vere benedictus Dominus noster Jesus Christus filius tuus qui venit e celis: ut conversaretur in terris: caro factus est ut habitaret in nobis Christus Dominus ac Redemptor eternus. Missal. Mixt.*; Pat. Lat., t. LXXXV, col. 189.

[2] *Stowe*, fo. 41v; *H.B.S.*, vol. XXXII, pp. 20–1.

[3] The words *sedis apostolicae* are found also in the Bobbio missal.

[4] Cf. Corpus missal (p. 3), where the omission still survives in a 12th-century text.

Pro fratribus in via directis [1] may be compared with a *contestatio paschalis* in the *Gallicanum vetus*: *dum justos per viam rectam gradientes caelestem ducit ad patriam*,[2] and also with the Holy Rule, in which St. Benedict says: *De fratribus in viam directis*.[3]

Stowe gives variants for the *Communicantes* of Christmas, Circumcision, Epiphany, Holy Thursday, Easter, Low Sunday, Ascension and Pentecost. The original hand in the missal begins with *Et memoriam venerantes*, continuing, as in the actual Roman canon, without variation until the next clause.

Hanc igitur, with the Gregorian *Diesque quoque nostros*, provides two interesting variants: (1) *in hac aeclesia quam famulus tuus ad honorem nominis gloriae tuae aedificavit*. (2) *Quessumus Domine ut placatus suscipias eumque adque omnem populum ab idulorum cultura eripias et ad te Deum verum patrem omnipotentem convertas*. The first of these seems to suggest the possibility of the canon being part of a Mass of dedication. The allusion to a particular church occurs in a diaconal litany in the Byzantine liturgy and also in a York MS. of the 10th century.[4] In the second variant, the prayer for the founder or builder, who was still living, seems to imply that he was a pagan. In any case, it is clear that at the time the original missal [5] was written paganism was not extinct in Ireland.[6] The phrase *et in commemoratione beatorum martirum* in the *Hanc igitur* occurs also in the Reichenau fragment, but it is not found in texts that are certainly Roman, although it is possible that the Irish compilers may have made use of and combined what were originally Roman formulas. Edmund Bishop suggests that this may be 'an interesting example of the gradual and progressive way in which the Irish corrupted the ancient liturgical texts to suit their own type of piety'.[7] The Book of Armagh (807) contains the *Hanc igitur* in the *ipsissima verba* of our Roman missal, with a cross rubricated between *accipias* and *diesque nostros*.[8] The variations in the *Quam oblationem* and *Qui*

---

[1] Stowe, fo. 25.　　　　　[2] *Gallicanum Vetus*, Mabillon, *Mus. Ital.*, I, p. 332.
[3] *Reg. S. Ben.*, cap. LXVII.
[4] *Early English Text Society*, vol. LXXI, p. 62.
[5] Stowe, possibly, may have copied prayers from an earlier MS.
[6] Cf. Counc. Merida, 666, can. 19. Labbe, *Concil.*, t. VI, col. 507.
[7] Bishop, *op. cit.*, p. 82, n. 6.　　[8] *Lib. Armacan.* (Book of Armagh), fo. 19a.

pridie sections are small: *egit* for *agens*; *accepit* (*calicem*) for *acci-piens*;[1] and *calix sancti sanguinis mei* until the end, where Moel-caich has added the Ambrosian phrase: *passionem meam praedica-bitis resurrectionem meam adnuntiabitis adventum meum sperabitis donec iterum veniam ad vos de caelis.* Similar endings are found in the liturgies of St. Mark and St. James, Coptic St. Mark and St. Basil, and in the Ambrosian and Mozarabic rites.

The St. Gall MS. directs the sign of the cross to be made once over the chalice, while Stowe prescribes its use five times in the canon, none of which are at the words of institution. In one of the fragments of the Irish sacramentaries published by Bannister, we find *Amen* said after the consecration: *Qui pridie quam. . . . Amen dicitur!* 'These last words have been added by another hand, but they witness none the less in favour of a liturgical usage'.[2] Adamnan seems to suggest in his life of St. Columba that the words of consecration were said audibly at Iona: *Quendam audiens presbyterum sacrae eucharistiae mysteria conficientem.*[3] The importance of the formula of consecration is emphasised in the Irish treatises on the Mass. The treatise appended to the Stowe missal says: '*Quando canitur: Accepit Jesus panem,* the priest bows himself thrice to repent of his sins. He offers it (chalice) to God (and chants *Miserere mei Deus*), and the people kneel, and here no voice cometh lest it disturb the priest, for that is the right of it, that his mind separate not from God while he chants this lesson. Hence its *nomen* is *periculosa oratio.*'[4] The Penitential of Cummian (*c.* 650) inflicts a penance of fifty stripes for a priest who has been found guilty of having once stumbled in pronounc-ing the 'prayer of the Lord, which is called *periculosa*'.[5] It is clear from the Irish treatises of Stowe and *Leabhar Breac* that the *oratio periculosa* was not the Lord's prayer, as Warren maintains.[6] The penance prescribed in the Penitential of Bobbio for a like offence was one day's fast on bread and water. A monition in the Roman

---

[1] This is found also in the Bobbio missal.

[2] Bannister, *Journal of Theological Studies*, t. V (October 1903), p. 69.

[3] Adamnan, *Vit. S. Columbae*, I, 40.

[4] *Stowe*, fols. 65v, 66; *H.B.S.*, vol. XXXII, pp. 37 (Irish), 40 (English).

[5] *Si titubaverit sacerdos super orationem dominicam, quae dicitur periculosa, si una vice quinquaginta plagas . . . .*

[6] Warren, *op. cit.*, p. 98.

pontifical, for the instruction of newly ordained priests, says: *Res quam tractaturi estis satis periculosa est.* The penitential attributed to Gildas seems to suggest that the word *periculum* was sometimes inscribed in the margin of the missal, in order to put the celebrant on his guard as he pronounced the words of consecration.[1] The Stowe treatise then continues: 'The three steps which the ordained man steppeth backwards and which he again steps forward, this is the triad in which everyone sins, to wit, in word, in thought, in deed; and this is the triad of things by which he is renovated iterum and by which he is moved to Christ's body.' [2]

The *Leabhar Breac* directs the priests to recite the *Miserere* at the moment of consecration.

Unde et memores has few evident mistakes, and it follows the Gelasian text in adding *sumus* after *memores*.

Supplices te rogamus adds *et petimus* and omits *caelesti*.

The memento of the dead in the Celtic liturgy is of especial interest. The opening words: *Memento etiam, Domine, et eorum nomina* are reminiscent of a passage in the Mozarabic Mass: *Commemoratio pro vivis: Offerunt Deo Domino ... in honorem sanctorum pro se et suis.*[3] They recall also the *collectio post nomina* for Holy Saturday in the *Missale Gothicum*: *Oremus pro his qui offerunt ... clementer exaudire dignetur. Per resurgentem.*[4] The clause *Memento etiam, Domine, ... in somno pacis* is wanting in the Gelasian sacramentary, but it agrees with the Bobbio text.[5] The expression *sacrificium spirituale (Cum omnibus in toto mundo offerentibus sacrificium spirituale)* is uncommon in Western liturgical phraseology, but it is found in the postcommunion for St. Patrick in the Drummond, Corpus and Rosslyn missals. *Spiritalis*, however, as an epithet of *cibus* or *poculum* is frequently met with.[6] The title *senior (ac venerabilibus sacerdotibus offert senior*

---

[1] *Si quis errans commotaverit aliquid de verbis sacris ubi periculum adnotatur, triduanum aut tres superpositiones faciat.* 'Gildas', *De Poenitentia*, XX; Haddan and Stubbs, *op. cit.*, t. I, p. 115.   [2] *Stowe*, fo. 66; *H.B.S.*, vol. XXXII, pp. 37–8 (Irish), 41 (English).

[3] *Missal Mixt.*; *Pat. Lat.*, t. LXXXV, col. 414.

[4] *Missal. Goth.*; *H.B.S.*, vol. LII, p. 78.

[5] The words *commemoratio defunctorum* follow in Bobbio.

[6] Cf. Mozarabic preface for the second Sunday after the octave of the Epiphany. *Miss. Mixt.*; *Pat. Lat.*, t. LXXXV, col. 249.

noster N. praespiter) occurs in the Rule of St. Colomban and the *Gallicanum Vetus.* The Irish rule of St. Columba calls the head of a community *senora.* The offertory prayer in 'Illyricus' contains the word *senior: Suscipe Sancta Trinitas hanc oblationem quam (offero tibi) pro seniore nostro et cuncta congregatione sancti Petri . . .*[1] The memento in Stowe contains a reference to the *anathletico gradu venerabilium patriarcharum,*[2] and the *Liber Hymnorum* has *Electus Dei anthleta.*

The missal, as we have seen, wrongly inserts the preparatory litany and 'prayer of St. Ambrose' before the intercessory interpolation with its long list of names. The intercession includes more than a hundred righteous, of the Old Law as well as of the New, together with saints who are not found in Holy Scripture and a number of Irish bishops and abbots—from Abel to Coemgen (Kevin). The local entries are not of a date later than the 6th and 7th centuries, and it is clear that the 9th-century scribe had a missal before him of the middle of the 7th century at latest.

The position of the Blessed Virgin in the order of names is of especial interest, and, coming after that of St. John Baptist, it may well be a further example of 'the indubitable influence of Syriac devotion and piety on Ireland'.[3] The only instance in the West of the same 'historical order' is found in the litany of MS. *Reg.* 2 A. XX, and documents relating to this. In the East, we find the order 'John Baptist, Stephen, Mary' is given in the priest's intercession in the Syriac liturgy of St. James.[4] The list of apostles in Stowe is that of the Roman canon, whereas the order in the Gallican and Mozarabic liturgies is taken from the Acts of the Apostles, although the Irish diptychs would seem to have drawn on the Mozarabic.[5] The majority of the Irish litanies follows, with a few minor variations, the list of Apostles' names in Matthew X, as we find inscribed also on the Ardagh chalice.

It is interesting to note, in view of the prolonged and somewhat

---

[1] Bona, *op. cit.*, append., p. 495.

[2] Stowe, fo. 29v.

[3] Bishop, *op. cit.*, VII, p. 161, note b.

[4] Archdale A. King, *Rites of Eastern Christendom*, vol. I, chap. II, pp. 174-5. Cf. Jacobite liturgy of Cyriacus of Nisibis (793-817).

[5] *Act. Apost.* I, 13. The order of the names of the Apostles in the Book of Cerne and in MS. *Reg.* 2 A. XX follows the Roman canon.

acrimonious controversy respecting the computation of Easter,
that the names of the second, third and fourth archbishops of
Canterbury figure in the canon.[1] There is, however, no Augustine, although he is commemorated in the Felire of Oengus on
24 May.[2] The feeling of resentment against the 'Apostle of the
English' on the part of the Celtic clergy may have persisted, but
we know that Laurence wrote, at least on one occasion, to the
Irish bishops inviting them to unite with the Anglo-Saxon
Church.[3]

The list of names concludes with a commemoration of the
dead: *Et omnium pausantium qui nos in dominica pace precesserunt
ab Adam usque in hodiernum diem quorum Deus nomina nominavit
et novit Ipsis et omnibus in Christo quiescentibus locum refrigerii
lucis et pacis ut indulgeas deprecamur.*

The term *pausantes* is applied to the dead in the *Missale
Gothicum, Gallicanum Vetus*, Penitential of Cummian and the
Commemoratio pro defunctis in the Mozarabic liturgy. Adamnan
refers to the grave of St. Columba as: *locus in quo ipsius sancta
pausant ossa.*[4] The use of the word *pausantes* instead of *mortui*
and *pausatorium* for *sepulchrum* is uncommon in late Latin. The
Annals of Ulster (14th–15th century) generally have *pausare* in
recording the deaths of bishops and abbots, whereas for kings
and other lay persons we find *quievit, mortuus est*, etc. *Pausare*
occurs in a similar sense for early mortuary inscriptions in the
Roman Catacombs, as well as for Christian inscriptions in Gaul.
The Byzantine liturgies frequently make use of such words as
Ἀνάπαυσις and ἀναπαύσασθαι. A canon of St. Theodore of Canterbury (*ob.* 690) says: *Quando recitantur Pausantium nomina.*[5]

Pausatorium in the sense of cemetery was used by Papias,
bishop of Hierapolis and Colossae, in the first half of the second
century.[6] We find it again in the life of St. Deicola (Dicuil,
Desle), a disciple of St. Columban, who, after the exile of his

---

[1] Stowe, fo. 32v. Laurence (604–19), Mellitus (619–24), Justus (624–27).
[2] *Mart. Oengus the Culdee. H.B.S.*, vol. XXIX, p. 126.
[3] Bede, *op. cit.*, lib. II, cap. IV.
[4] Adamnan, *Vita S. Columb.*, lib. III, cap. XXIII.
[5] Canons of St. Theodore, can. 55.
[6] *Kimeterium, Pausatorium, vel dormitorium*, Papias. Du Cange, *Gloss. Man.*, t. V
(Halle, 1778), p. 206.

S

master, founded the monastery of Lure in the diocese of Besançon.[1]

The earliest life of St. Samson (7th century) speaks of the reading of the diptychs in which were the names of the dead entitled
to a share in the Eucharistic sacrifice. The passage is thought to
refer to the monastery of Llanwit Major in Glamorgan rather
than to Dol.

The *Nobis quoque peccatoribus* differs from the Gelasian sacramentary in the order of the names of the female saints, but, apart
from the omission of the name of Eugenia, it agrees with the
Bobbio missal. Eugenia, however, appears in the canon of the
Drummond missal (also Bridget), and also in the *Gallicanum
Vetus*, where we find it in the *commemoratio pro defunctis* in the
canon,[2] as well as in the *collectio ad pacem* for the Vigil of Christmas.[3] It appears also in the *Liber Sanctae Trinitatis*, a 14th-
century Irish martyrology, on 25 December, and, together with
Anastasia, in the Leonine sacramentary.[4] After *Per quem haec
omnia*, etc., Moelcaich has added *ter canitur*, with a direction in
Irish to elevate the principal Host over the chalice, and to dip half
of it therein: 'Here the oblation is lifted over the chalice, and half
of the bread is dipped in the chalice.' [5] Then follows in the original hand: *Fiat, Domine, misericordia tua super nos quemadmodum
sperabimus (speravimus) in te*,[6] to which the *ter canitur* probably
refers. A second Irish rubric says: 'Here the bread (literally cake
or wafer) is broken.' The fraction, it may be noted, precedes the
Pater noster, as in the Roman rite before St. Gregory.

The original hand of the scribe had written: *Cogno(v)erunt
Dominum . . . in remissionem peccatorum nostrorum*, which was
interspersed with six *alleluias*. Then Moelcaich inserted over an
erasure: *Fiat, Domine*, etc.; *Cognoverunt Dominum, alleluia*, and a
prayer or confession of faith: *Credimus, Domine, credimus in hac
confractione corporis et effussione sanguinis nos esse redemptos et
confidimus sacramenti hujus adsumptione munitos ut quod spe in-*

---

[1] *Concremare tanti patris Pausatorium studentes, Vita S. Deicoli Abbatis Lutrensis,*
num. 3; Du Cange, *op. cit.*, t. V, p. 206.

[2] Mabillon, *Mus. Ital.*, t. I, p. 281.　　　　[3] *Ibid.*, p. 289.

[4] *Sacram. Leon.*, ed. Feltoe, p. 159.

[5] Cf. Syrian rite.　　　　[6] *Psl.* XXXII, 2.

*terim hic tenemus mansuri in celestibus veris fructibus perfruamur:
per Dominum.*

The responsary *Cognoverunt*, which was not apparently variable, answers to the Ambrosian *confractorium* and the Mozarabic
antiphona ad confractionem panis. Fiat misericordia tua, Domine
is the actual Mozarabic antiphon for Lent.[1] The prayer *Credimus*
has a slight resemblance to the creed, which is recited at this point
in the Mozarabic rite.[2] The expression *confractione corporis* in the
prayer has led Warren to infer that it was also used in the Celtic
prayer of consecration, especially as the word *confringo* occurs in
the Gallican words of institution.[3] However this may be, Warren
is certainly mistaken in supposing that concelebration was the
general practice of the Celtic Church.[4] The theory has been maintained from a passage in Adamnan's *Life of St. Columba*,[5] but the
reference is to cofraction not to concelebration, and there is not
the smallest evidence for supposing that consecration and fraction
were equivalents. In the time of St. Columba, the expression
fractio panis no longer denoted the liturgy as a whole, and the
Antiphonary of Bangor makes it quite clear that one priest said
Mass, while the others who were present received Holy Communion: *Ymnum quando commonicarent sacerdotes.*[6] The rite of cofraction at Iona in 563 has been thus described by Adamnan: If
the celebrant was a simple priest, another priest joined him in
order to break the Body of the Lord with him, but if the celebrant
was a bishop he broke the Host alone. The idea was obviously
familiar to the author of the first life of St. Samson, edited probably in the second half of the 7th century: *Quando* (Samson)
*missam cantabat, angeli semper Dei sancti ministri altaris ac sacri-
ficii apud ipsum videbantur oblationemque cum suis manibus illo solo
vidente frequenter frangebant.*[7] Ireland in the 10th century appears

---

[1] *Missal. Mixt.; Pat. Lat.*, t. LXXXV, col. 309.

[2] Similar confessions of faith are found in Syriac St. James and the Ethiopic liturgy.

[3] Warren, *op. cit.*, p. 265, n. 149. Cf. *Post secreta* for Christmas in the *Missale Gothicum, H.B.S.*, vol. LII, p. 6.

[4] Warren, *op. cit.*, chap. II, pp. 128–9.

[5] Adamnan, *Vita S. Columb.*, lib. I, cap. XLIV. Adamnan, abbot of Iona, was the
eighth successor of St. Columba (679–704).

[6] *Antiph. Bangor, H.B.S.*, vol. X, pp. 10, 11.

[7] *Acta SS.*, July, t. VI, col. 584. The passage is thought to refer to Llanwit in South
Wales rather than to Dol. F. C. Burkitt, *Journal of Theological Studies*, XXVII, p. 49.

to have had a double fraction between the Consecration and Communion: first for the commixture and then for Holy Communion.

The commixture took place after the *Pater noster* and embolism.

The Host was broken over the paten, not, as is customary to-day, over the chalice. The rite of intinction, which is not the same as that of the commixture, is said by the Irish treatises to represent the flowing of the blood of Christ on his body on the cross. The two halves of the Host are dipped in the chalice.[1]

The rare and laconic rubrics in the Stowe missal make no mention of the second fraction for Holy Communion, but the appended treatise on the Mass describes the eight different ways in which, following the feasts, the priest accomplishes the rite. It is possible that the first fraction was made with the Host of the celebrant, and the second with that of the communicants, but the texts are not clear on the point. The *Leabhar Breac* omits what concerns the second fraction and Holy Communion. The Stowe treatise says: 'The particle that is cut off from the bottom of the half which is on the (priest's) left hand is the figure of the wounding with the lance in the armpit of the right side; for westwards was Christ's face on the cross; to wit, *contra civitatem*, and east-wards was the face of Longinus; what to him was the left, to Christ was the right.'[2]

The complicated modes of fraction are described in the Stowe treatise, which says also how the particles are to be arranged on the altar at Easter and Christmas.[3] On ordinary days, the Host was divided into five parts; for feasts of saints (confessors) and virgins, seven; for martyrs, eight; on Sundays, 'for the oblation of Sunday as a figure of the nine households of heaven and the nine grades of the Church', nine; for the apostles, eleven; on the Circumcision and Holy Thursday, twelve; on Low Sunday (*Minchasc*) and Ascension, thirteen; and for the great feasts of Easter, Christmas and Pentecost, sixty-five, the sum of all pre-

---

[1] *Stowe, Missal*; H.B.S., vol. XXXII, pp. 38 (Irish), 41 (English). Cf. Syrian rite, Renaudot, *Liturg. Orient. Collect.*, t. II, p. 111; Archdale A. King, *Rites of Eastern Christendom*, vol. I, p. 184.

[2] Stowe, *H.B.S., ibid.*

[3] Cf. Mozarabic and Byzantine (*prothesis*) usages.

ceding. Each of the numbers was given a mystical significance. At Christmas and Easter, there was a complicated arrangement of the particles on the paten, figuring a kind of wheel-cross, such as we see in ancient Celtic art. The particles were apportioned to different classes of people.[1]

As in the case of the Gallican liturgy, it would seem that a certain amount of superstition attended the rite of the fraction. The peculiar custom of cofraction existed at Iona, but liturgical usages in the Celtic Church were many and diverse (*diversas missas celebrabant*), and there is nothing, for example, to show that the rites of the fraction described in the Stowe treatise were ever observed in the Scottish monastery. The Missal of Bobbio makes no reference either to a fraction or a commixture, but, like the Gelasian sacramentary, passes immediately from the *Per quem haec omnia* clause of the canon to the introduction of the *Pater noster*.

All that are given between the preface and the *Pater noster* in the St. Gall fragment are three collects (found in the three Roman sacramentaries) and a *collectio ante orationem Dominicam*, which concludes with an introduction to the Lord's Prayer, similar to that which we find in Stowe and Bobbio.

The Stowe text, until the end of the Communion, is in the handwriting of Moelcaich. The introduction to the *Pater noster* is the same as in the Book of Dimma, Bobbio missal and St. Gall fragment: [2] *Divino magisterio edocti*, but otherwise identical with the Roman form. There is nothing to suggest that either the introduction or the embolism were ever variable, as in the Gallican and Mozarabic rites, but a variant appears in the office for the visitation of the sick in the Stowe missal: *Concede, Domine, nobis famulis tuis ut orantibus cum fiducia dicere meriamur* (sic) *Pater noster*.[3] The following introduction is found in the *Missa de infirmis* in the Scottish Book of Deer and the Irish Book of Mulling: *Creator naturarum omnium Deus et Parens universarum in celo et in terra originum, has trementis populi tui religiosas preces ex illo*

---

[1] *Stowe missal*; *H.B.S.*, vol. XXXII, pp. 38–9 (Irish), 41–2 (English).
[2] Cf. Ambrosian rite for Easter Sunday.
[3] *Stowe*, fo. 63; *H.B.S.*, vol. XXXII, p. 35.

inaccessibiles lucis trono tuo suscipe, et inter hiruphin et saraphin indefessas circumstantium laudes exaudi spei non ambigue precationes.[1] The embolism in the Stowe missal and the St. Gall fragment is almost exactly the same as in the Gelasian sacramentary, except that it omits the name of the Blessed Virgin and inserts St. Patrick in place of St. Andrew. The Bobbio missal includes our Lady, but gives neither Patrick nor Andrew. Variants for the embolism are found in the Books of Deer and Mulling: (1) *Libera nos, Domine, a malo, Domine Christe Jesu, custodi nos semper in omni opere bona, fons et auctor omnium bonorum Deus evacua nos vitiis, et repre nos virtutibus bonis per te Christe Jesu.*[2] (2) *Libera nos a malo, Domine Christe Jhesu, et custodies nos in omni opere bono, auctor omnium bonorum, manens et regnans in saecula saeculorum. Amen.*

It is possible that the position of the *pax* was originally in connection with the offertory, but in all the extant MSS. we find it in the Roman place before Holy Communion. The word for an ordinary kiss in all the Celtic languages is derived from *pacem*, the liturgical kiss.[3] The following formula is found in the Antiphonary of Bangor, *ad pacem celebrandum: Pax tua, Domine Rex caelestis, permaneat semper in visceribus nostris, ut non timeamus a timore nocturno.* It was not, however, recited at Mass, but at the beginning of the night office, and such a usage is still extant in the night office of the East Syrians.[4]

The Stowe missal and the St. Gall fragment give the formula for the *pax* after the embolism: *Pax et caritas Domini nostri Jesu Christi et commonicatio sanctorum omnium sit semper nobiscum et cum spiritu tuo.* In the St. Gall MS., it is preceded by a rubric: *(Sacerdos) tenens sancta in manibus signat calicem cruce et hie pax datur et dicit sacerdos.* The Book of Dimma has a similar form in the *Missa de infirmis: Pax et commonicatio sanctorum tuorum, Christe Jhesu, sit semper nobiscum.* The description of the Mass celebrated by Bishop Cronan at Iona, which Adamnan gives in his *Life of St. Columba*, suggests a blessing after the fraction and

---

[1] Cf. Mass for the Nativity of St. John Baptist in the Mozarabic rite.
[2] Cf. Gallican liturgies. The last passage is found in the Reichenau fragment.
[3] e.g. Breton, *pok*.
[4] Gougaud, *Celtiques (Liturgies)*, *D.A.C.L.*, t. II, part II, cols. 3012–13.

before the commixture.[1] If we may judge from a representation of
our Lord in glory in the 9th-century Irish MS. of the gospels,
preserved at St. Gall, it may have been the Celtic practice to give
the blessing after the Eastern manner.[2]

The collect which follows *Pax et caritas* in Stowe is a formula
for the giving of the *pax*: *Pacem mandasti, pacem dedisti, pacem
dirilinquisti, pacem tuam, Domine, da nobis de Coelo et pacificum
hunc diem et ceteros dies vitae nostrae in tua pace disponas . . . per
Dominum . . .* The formula for the commixture is given in Stowe,
but it is not found in either the Bobbio missal or the St. Gall fragment: *Commixtio corporis et sanguinis Domini nostri Jesu Christi
sit nobis salus in vitam perpetuam. Amen.* St. Gall gives a rubric:
mittit sacerdos sancta in calicem, and directs the *pax* to be given.[3]
A formula, similar to that which is given for the *pax* in Stowe, is
found in the Gallican liturgy of pseudo-Germanus, but it was not
associated with the kiss of peace, which, as still in the Mozarabic
rite, was given before the *Sursum corda.*

A single *Agnus Dei* follows the commixture in the Stowe missal,
but it is not found in either Bobbio or St. Gall. A rubric in the
latter MS. prescribes the Communion of the people after the *pax.*
The *Agnus Dei,* which was introduced at Rome by Pope Sergius
(687–701), does not appear in other Celtic books, although its
use in Brittany is attested in the lives of St. Malo (Machutus) and
St. Samson in the first quarter of the 9th century.[4] The *Agnus
Dei* is followed in Stowe by *Pacem meam do vobis, Pacem relinquo
vobis.*[5] *Pax multa . . . Dominus regit me,*[6] with an *Alleluia* after
each verse. The St. Gall MS. gives only the quotation from St.
John before *Psalm XXII: Venite comedite* comes later.

A hymn *quando commonicant sacerdotes,* which has been called
'the oldest Eucharistic hymn in existence', is found in the Antiphonary of Bangor. The preface to the *Leabhar Breac* says that it
was sung by angels at Dunshauglin in Co. Meath on the occasion

---

[1] Adamnan, *op. cit.*, lib. I, cap. XLIV.

[2] i.e. first, second and fourth fingers extended, with the third closed down upon the
extremity of the thumb over the palm of the hand.

[3] *Et dat sibi populus p(a)cem, (atque commo)nicant, et juxta commonionem canitur . . . .
Pacem do vobis . . . .*

[4] *Vita secunda Samsonis.*

[5] *Joann.* XIV, 27.   [6] *Psl.* XXII, 1.

of a visit of St. Patrick to his disciple, St. Sechnall (*ob.* 447). The hymn has eleven four-lined stanzas: [1]

> *Sancti venite*
> *Christi corpus sumite,*
> *Sanctum bibentes*
> *Quo redempti sanguinem.*

It is found also, in slightly varying forms, in the Stowe missal and the St. Gall fragment.[2] Dom Cagin thinks that the hymn, taken from a Byzantine tropary, may have been introduced in the West to serve as a chant at the fraction before the appointment of the *Agnus Dei* by Pope Sergius (*ob.* 701).[3] *Venite populi* is sung today between the first and second *Agnus* in the rite of Lyons at the Pontifical Mass on Holy Thursday and Easter Day, and it is found in the Ambrosian rite as the *confractorium* for Easter.

Communion antiphons are given in Stowe, St. Gall, and the *Missa de infirmis* of Stowe, Deer, Dimma and Mulling. Seven of these antiphons appear in the Antiphonary of Bangor, the first of which occurs as a Mozarabic *ad accedentes* and an Ambrosian *transitorium*: *Corpus Domini accepimus et Sanguine(m) ejus potati sumus; ab omni malo non timebimus quia Dominus nobiscum est.*[4] Baumstark considers the first part of the text to be an almost verbatim translation of a Greek original of the 6th century, and of Palestinian origin.[5]

No two sets of communion antiphons in the Celtic books are alike, although some of them are common to nearly all.

The antiphons in Stowe are followed by the colophon: *Moel-caich scripsit*, which indicates the end of his corrections and additions in the text. It may be noted that Moelcaich was a mere eclectic, devoid of any liturgical bias, and introducing Roman and Gallican interpolations indifferently.

The two postcommunion prayers in the Stowe missal and St. Gall fragment are substantially identical, and have been borrowed

---

[1] *Antiph. Bangor*, fols. 10r–11r; *H.B.S.*, vol. X, pp. 10–11.
[2] *St. Gall*, MS. 1394. Cf. *Trecanum* in the Gallican rite.
[3] Cagin, *Paléographie Musicale*, t. V, p. 186.
[4] *Antiph. Bangor*; *H.B.S.*, vol. X, p. 31; *Pat. Lat.*, t. LXXII, col. 106.
[5] Baumstark, *Liturgie Comparée*, p. 108, Editions de Chevetogne, 1953.

from Roman books. (1) *Quos coelesti, Domine, dono satiasti* appears as a Sunday postcommunion in the Gelasian sacramentary; for the Sixth Sunday after Pentecost in the Gregorian sacramentary; and for the Sixth Sunday after Trinity and the Mass *contra paganos* in the Sarum missal. The actual Roman missal gives it as the postcommunion for the Fifth Sunday after Pentecost. The same prayer occurs also in the daily Mass of the Bobbio missal, with the title *post communionem*. (2) *Gratias tibi agimus ... qui nos corporis et sanguinis Christi filii tui communione satiasti ...* is given as the *consummatio missae* in the Bobbio missal and also in the 9th-century St. Gall fragment. The first part of it (*Gratias ... veniam*) seems to have been taken, with verbal variations, from the Leonine sacramentary, *mense Julio XXIV*:[1] the remainder from the same source, but *mense Septembri*.[2] It is found as a variable prayer in the Gallican books, and in part also as the postcommunion *pro vivis et defunctis* in our Roman missal. The 9th-century *Vita secunda* of St. Samson speaks of the final collect at the end of the Mass as *ultimam collectam complere*. A postcommunion is given in the three proper Masses in Stowe. The first two (*Sumpsimus, Domine, Sanctorum tuorum* and *Deus qui confitentium tibi*) are Gelasian; the third, in the *Missa pro mortuis*, is in the form of a Gallican *praefatio* or bidding-prayer: *Oremus, fratres carissimi, per caris nostris N*. A thanksgiving formula occurs in the *Missa de infirmis* in Deer, Dimma and Mulling.

In the Book of Deer, the collect *Deus, tibi gratias agimus* is preceded by *Reffecti Christi corpore et sanguine*, etc. Both forms are met with in the *Missale Gothicum*.[3] The collect, with variations, is found in Dimma, Mulling and Stowe. Before the thanksgiving in the Mulling fragment, there is an *oratio post euchari(s)tiam*: *Custodi intra nos, Domine*, which recalls a prayer in the *Gothicum*.[4] The prayer in the Book of Dimma is preceded by a

---

[1] *Sacram. Leon.*, edit. Feltoe (Cambridge, 1896), p. 71.

[2] *Ibid.*, p. 126.

[3] *Refecti corporis et sanguinis, Missal. Goth., Consummacio Missae* in *Missa Dominicalis* I. *H.B.S.*, vol. LII, p. 131. *Deus tibi gracias agimus, Missal. Goth., Consummacio Missae* in *Missa Dominicalis* VI. *H.B.S.*, vol. LII, p. 141.

[4] *Custodi intra nos, Domine, Missal. Goth., Consummacio Missae* in *Missa Dominicalis* III. *H.B.S.*, vol. LII, p. 135.

blessing: *Benedicat tibi Dominus et custodiat te*, and followed by a signing of the cross and the words: *Pax tibi in vitam aeternam*.

A formula of dismissal is found in the Stowe missal: *Missa acta est in pace*.

The long formula for the blessing of the font and the baptismal water in Stowe are a combination of the Gelasian and Gregorian forms. A rubric prescribes a litany: *circa fontem canitur*, but the text is not given. The first part of the blessing of the font consists of exorcisms, which, though they are found in various parts of the Gelasian books, are always connected with the blessing of either the font or the water. The final section, with some few verbal differences, is the prayer: *Omnipotens sempiterne Deus, adesto magnae pietatis tuae mysteriis*, which with the preface and prayers that follow are in the Gelasian, Gregorian and modern Roman Holy Saturday ceremonies, down to the pouring of the chrism into the font.

The chrism is directed to be poured *in modum crucis*, after which the rubric continues: *et quique voluerit implet vasculum aqua benedictionis ad domos consecrandas et populus praesens aspergitur aqua benedicta*.

BIBLIOGRAPHY

1. *Antiphonary of Bangor*. Henry *Bradshaw Society*, vol. IV (part 1), 1893; vol. X (part 2), 1895. London.
2. *Celtic Rite*. Henry *Jenner*. *Catholic Encyclopedia*, vol. III.
3. *Celtic Scotland*. W. F. *Skene*. Edinburgh, 1876.
4. *Celtiques (Liturgies)*. Louis *Gougaud*. *Dict. d'Archéol. Chrét. et de Lit.*, t. II, part II, cols. 2970–3032.
4a. Le *Chrismale de Mortain*. Léon *Blouet*. Coutances, n.d.
5. *Christianity in Celtic Lands*. Louis *Gougaud*. London, 1932.
6. *Councils and Ecclesiastical Documents relating to Great Britain and Ireland*. A. W. *Haddan* & W. *Stubbs*. Oxford, 1869.
7. The *Early Scottish Church*: Its Doctrine and Discipline. Columba *Edmonds*. Edinburgh–London, 1906.
8. *Gaelic Pioneers of Christianity*. The Work and Influence of Irish monks and saints in Continental Europe (6th–12th century). Louis *Gougaud*. Dublin, 1923.
9. A *History of Wales* (vol. 1). J. E. *Lloyd*. London, 1954.
10. *Ireland and the Celtic Church*. George T. *Stokes*, revised by H. J. *Lawlor*. London, 1928.
11. *Irish Antiquities and Archeology*. W. *Gamble*. Redhill, Co. Cavan. N.D.

12. *Irish Churches and Monastic Buildings* (vol. 1). Harold G. *Leask*. Dundalk, 1955.
13. *Life of St. Malachy*. Ailbe J. *Luddy*. Dublin, 1930.
14. *Litany of the Saints in the Stowe Missal*. Edmund *Bishop*. *Liturgica Historica*. Oxford, 1918.
15. Les *Liturgies Celtiques*. Louis *Gougaud*. *Liturgia*, XXII, part IV. Paris, 1930.
16. *Liturgy and Ritual of the Celtic Church*. F. E. *Warren*. Oxford, 1881.
17. *Martyrology of Gorman*. Henry Bradshaw Society, vol. IX. London, 1895.
18. *Martyrology of Oengus the Culdee*. Henry Bradshaw Society, vol. XXIX. London, 1905.
19. *Martyrology of Tallaght*. Henry Bradshaw Society, vol. LXVIII. London, 1929.
20. *Mélanges Colombaniens*. *Actes du Congrès International de Luxeuil*, 20–3 July, 1950. Paris, 1951.
21. La *Messe Celtique*. Fernand *Cabrol*. *La Messe en Occident*. Paris, 1932.
22. *Missale Gothicum*. Henry Bradshaw Society, vol. LII, London, 1917.
23. The *Prayer Book of Aedulf the bishop, commonly called 'The Book of Cerne'*. Edit. A. B. Kuypers. Cambridge, 1902.
24. *Recherches de Théologie ancienne et mediévale*, VI. Abbot *Capelle*. Mont César, Louvain, 1934.
25. *Relics of St. Cuthbert*. Chr. *Hohler* & Others. Oxford, 1956.
26. Les *Rites de la Consecration et de la Fraction dans la Liturgie Celtique de la Messe*. Louis *Gougaud*. *Report of the Nineteenth Eucharistic Congress*, Westminster, 1908.
27. *Scottish Mediaeval Liturgical Books and Fragments*. David *McRoberts*. Glasgow, 1953.
28. *Spanish Symptoms*. Edmund *Bishop*. *Liturgica Historica*, VIII. Oxford, 1918.
29. The *Stowe Missal*, edit. G. F. *Warner*. Henry Bradshaw Society, vol. XXXII. London, 1915.
30. *Tonsure Monastique et Tonsure Cléricale*. Colomban *Bock*. Revue de Droit Canonique, t. II, no. 4. December, 1952.
31. *Vita di S. Colombano*. Eugène *Martin* (Ital. trans., Giuseppe Monteverde). Bobbio, 1923.

Chapter Five

ENGLISH MEDIAEVAL RITES

AN enumeration of the rites or uses existing in England at the time of the Reformation is given in a preface to the Book of Common Prayer entitled 'Concerning the Service of the Church': 'And whereas heretofore there hath been great diversity in saying and singing in churches within this realm; some following Salisbury use, some Hereford use, and some the use of Bangor, some of York, some of Lincoln; now from henceforth all the whole realm shall have but one use.' One of the reasons for this liturgical uniformity was alleged to be the complicated system by which it was 'many times more business to find out what should be read, than to read it when it was found out'.[1] The rules governing the 'manifold changings of the Service' were known as the 'Pie', a name which came to be given to the *Ordinale* itself: *Quod usitato vocabulo dicitur Pica, sive directorium sacerdotum.*[2] The term 'Pie' is a French form of the Latin *Pica*, a magpie, so-called from the confused appearance of the rules, which were printed in old black-letter type on white paper, thus resembling the colours of the magpie.

It is no object of this book to enter into controversy, but it may be pointed out in passing that the nature and character of the books that resulted from this desire for uniformity were altogether changed by the very deliberate suppression of well-nigh every thing that pertained to sacrifice.

In the 16th century, however, the desire for liturgical uni-

---

[1] Pope Pius XII would seem to have come to a somewhat similar conclusion in respect to the Roman books, if we may judge from the general decree of the Congregation of Rites on the 'Simplification of the Rubrics' (23 March 1955).

[2] *Incipit ordo Breviarii seu portiforii secundum morem et consuetudinem ecclesiae Sarum (seu Sarisburiensis) Anglicanae una cum ordinali, seu quod usitato vocabulo dicitur Pica, sive directorium sacerdotum; Pica de dominica prima Adventus. Breviarium edit. Londini* an 1555, fo. 1.

formity was by no means a Protestant trait. It might in fact be regarded rather as 'Tridentine', 'papal' and 'Counter-Reformation', marking the end of the Middle Ages with its liberally interpreted episcopal *jus liturgicum*. The fathers of the twenty-fifth and final session of the council of Trent, who met on 4 December 1563, requested the Pope, in the interest of the whole Church, to accomplish the reform of the missal and breviary. The result of the petition was forthcoming in the breviary of 1568 and the missal of 1570. St. Pius V (1566–72) in the bull *Quo primum tempore* (14 July 1570) enforced the exclusive use of these books on all the churches and monasteries of Western Christendom, unless they could show a liturgy that had been in continuous use for at least two hundred years. Such was the final decision of the Apostolic See on the question of liturgical uniformity, but a similar movement on a national or diocesan basis had been apparent in Europe throughout the century. In Scandinavia, the Trondheim (Nidaros) missal, printed in 1519, was declared to be the norm for the kingdom of Norway. In 1549, the provincial synod of Trier prescribed a single missal for each of the dioceses in the province, and, if such was impossible, the diocese in question must adopt that of the metropolitan church. Italy demanded a reformed missal in 1546, and a similar line was taken in Spain and Portugal, where it was suggested that the Masses of saints proper to each diocese should be relegated to supplements. As regards England, we shall see how the Sarum rite, by reason of the excellence of its liturgical books, gradually prevailed throughout the country, and also in Scotland and Ireland, so that York, Hereford and Bangor scarcely obtained outside their own dioceses. A final move towards uniformity, before the spate of Protestant prayer books set in, was undertaken by the Convocation of Canterbury in 1542, which, although schismatic in that the jurisdiction of the Pope had been repudiated in 1534, was nevertheless still Catholic in outlook. The Convocation of that year enjoined that the Sarum rite was to be the sole rite throughout the province. The decision, if it had been carried out, would have suppressed the uses of Hereford and Bangor, leaving the rite of York as the only rival. It is, however, doubtful whether any such unification was ever attempted, as seven years later (1549) the old Catholic liturgies were swept away in favour of a Protestant prayer book.

It may perhaps, with a certain amount of justice, be objected that the term 'rite' as applied to the English mediaeval liturgies is incorrect, since they are all, without exception, no more than local variants of the Roman rite. It is, however, customary in common parlance to speak of the Sarum rite, York rite, etc., no less than of the Sarum use and York use, and the two terms have been retained indifferently.

The liturgy of the Mother-Church of Christendom was introduced by St. Augustine (597) into a country, which, except for Cornwall and Wales, was predominantly pagan. The Roman rite therefore had a comparatively free field, and ultimately superseded the Celtic liturgy in the West country, Scotland and Ireland. The Anglo-Saxon synod, held at Cloveshoo in 747, made it clear that the only liturgy to be tolerated was the Roman: 'that in one and the same manner we all celebrate the sacred festivals pertaining to our Lord's coming in the flesh; and so in everything in the way we confer Baptism, in our celebration of Mass, and in our manner of singing. All has to be done according to the pattern which we have received in writing from the Roman Church.' [1] A similar enactment was made respecting the Divine Office: 'That the seven Canonical Hours be everywhere gone through with the fitting Psalmody and with the proper chant; and that no one presume to sing or to read aught save what custom admits, what comes down to us with the authority of Holy Scripture, and what the usage of the Roman Church allows to be sung or read.' [2]

The Norman Conquest (1066) brought in its wake a rebuilding of churches on a very different scale from what had been customary in Anglo-Saxon times. Cathedrals were provided with chapters on the continental model, and the liturgical services came to assume a wealth of ceremonial. For the due ordering of Divine worship, cathedral and monastic churches, with a somewhat broad interpretation of the *jus liturgicum*, compiled their own

---

[1] Counc. Cloveshoo, 747, can. 13; Labbe, *op. cit.*, t. VI, col. 1577.
[2] *Ibid.*, can. 15; Labbe, *ibid.*

service-books. The books were never other than of the Roman rite, but within this framework considerable latitude existed, although the books so compiled would seem to have been largely the result of borrowing from those composed by others. The compilation of diocesan and monastic uses was more or less complete by the 13th century, but that is not to say that minor alterations and additions were not frequently made.

The religious orders, with the exception of the Gilbertines, were international in character, and would therefore in many cases follow the rite of their brethren on the Continent.

The Benedictines, however, were not an 'Order' in this sense, and their service-books varied from house to house.

Augustinian practice also, contrary to what is sometimes said, differed in much the same way, although a greater uniformity is found among the centralised congregations.[1] It would seem also that groups of churches of Austin Canons banded themselves together to follow similar rites and ceremonies.

Prayers, customs and practices existing in churches of the Duchy of Normandy were certainly drawn upon in the compilation of English uses, but, with the possible exception of Hereford, it has been found impossible to detect an unquestioned adoption of a Norman liturgy by an English diocese. Liturgical peculiarities would probably have existed in well-nigh every diocese, but the Sarum use became early a model for other churches, with the result that by the time of the change of religion in the 16th century there were no more than four or five distinctive secular uses in operation.

The adoption by churches of the Sarum use did not, however, necessarily entail a rejection of all their existing usages in favour of those at Salisbury, but rather the fitting of them into the framework outlined in the Sarum books. We will in fact find several examples of Churches which, while adopting the Sarum use, still retained at least something of their own peculiar usages.

---

[1] e.g. The Congregation of Windesheim, founded in 1387, followed the use of Utrecht.

SARUM RITE

The diocese of Salisbury (Sarum) was created out of the united sees of Ramsbury and Sherborne, and Herman, bishop of Ramsbury (*ob.* 1078), became the first occupant of the new diocese, the seat of which was transferred in 1075 to what came to be known as Old Sarum. The town consisted of little more than a fortress built over a hill, which Peter of Blois (*ob. c.* 1202) was to speak of as the 'ark of God shut up in the temple of Baal'.[1] St. Osmund, the second bishop (1077–99), was a Norman nobleman of some distinction, who had come to this country with William the Conqueror. He it was who consecrated the cathedral church in 1092, and was buried within its walls until 1457, the year of his canonisation by Pope Calixtus III, when his body was translated to the lady chapel in the 'new' cathedral in Salisbury.[2] A slab from the destroyed tomb of this great bishop may be seen today in one of the bays of the nave.

It has been said times without number that the Sarum use had St. Osmund for its author, but, before accepting the statement, it would be well to look into the matter a little closer. We read in the *Catholic Encyclopedia*: St. Osmund 'compiled the books corresponding to our missal, breviary and ritual, which revised and fixed the Anglo-Saxon readings of the Roman rite. With these he appears very naturally to have incorporated certain liturgical traditions of his Norman fellow-countrymen.'[3] And again: 'It must not be forgotten that the Sarum use represents in the main the Roman rite as carried out in the eleventh century.'[4] Much the same was said by Dr. Rock,[5] and also by Fr. Thurston in his edition of *Alban Butler's Lives of the Saints*.[6] It seems probable that the above writers found their source in Dugdale's *Monasticon Anglicanum*, which quotes an excerpt from the

---

[1] Peter of Blois became chancellor to the archbishop of Canterbury and archdeacon of Bath in 1176.

[2] The bishop, Richard Poore, had unsuccessfully petitioned for his canonisation in 1228.

[3] F. Thomas Berg, *Sarum Rite, Catholic Encyclopedia*, vol. XIII, p. 479.

[4] *Ibid.*, p. 480.

[5] Rock, *Church of our Fathers*, vol. III (London, 1853), part II, p. 121.

[6] Thurston, *Alban Butler's Lives of the Saints*, vol. XII (London, 1938), p. 62.

Chronicle of John Brompton (col. 976, num. 60): *Hic (Osmundus) composuit librum ordinalem Ecclesiastici Officii, quem Consuetudinarium vocant; quo, fere tota nunc Anglia, Wallia et Hibernia utitur.*[1] This is the tradition, but is it worthy of credence? It is possible for a tradition to be a valuable and trustworthy witness to the truth, but, on the other hand, it may well be no more than an 'old wives' fable', which has come to be established through unremitting repetition. We know that St. Osmund introduced the Norman conception of a cathedral chapter,[2] and, as we have seen, consecrated a cathedral church. Such innovations would undoubtedly entail a certain overhauling and revision of the liturgical books, but there is no evidence whatsoever to suggest that St. Osmund left behind him any liturgical regulations. 'It is quite conceiveable', as Dr. Frere says, 'that some book such as an ordinal or *consuetudines* of St. Osmund has perished . . ., but it would be risky to assert or even to conjecture that this was the case.'[3] St. Osmund definitely took a hand on the constitutional side, notwithstanding that the consuetudinary used at Salisbury in the 13th century, while containing some undoubted work of the Saint, was a later 'explanation' of the *Institucio* of St. Osmund. The numerous references to St. Osmund in documents of the 13th century always allude to constitutional questions, never to liturgical.[4] An ascription to him of definitely liturgical statutes does not seem to have arisen till the beginning of the 14th century, when the tractate was already a century old. The Sarum statutes of 1319 appear to have been prepared to ascribe anything old to St. Osmund, and from that time the compiler of the Sarum use has been regarded as the first Norman bishop of the see. Internal evidence of the rite points also to a development later than the closing years of the 11th century: the ceremonial is too

---

[1] Dugdale, *Monasticon Anglicanum* (London, 1673), vol. III, t. V, p. 375.

[2] Cathedral chapters after the Norman model were established in 1090 by Thomas of Bayeux at York, Remigius of Fécamp at Lincoln, and, within a few months, St. Osmund at Old Sarum. It is interesting to recall that the abbot of St. Wandrille de Fontanelle in Normandy was made an ex officio canon of Salisbury. No act has repealed this privilege. Cf. Anglican bishop of Norwich, who is still abbot of the non-existent abbey of St. Benet of Hulme.

[3] Frere, *The Use of Sarum*, vol. I, *The Sarum Offices as set forth in the Consuetudinary and Customary*, p. XVIII.

[4] e.g. *Lincoln Cathedral Statutes*, vol. II, pp. 873–4, 884.

T

elaborate and intricate to date from the time of the first Norman king.

It would seem probable therefore that the Sarum ordinal [1] and consuetudinary [2] are twin products of the early 13th century, while the revised consuetudinary, which Frere has called the customary, dates from the first half of the 14th century. The first mention of the ordinal as a recognised service-book in England comes from Lichfield in the statutes of Bishop Nonant (1188–98), and about twenty years later we hear of a Sarum ordinal. Before the middle of the 13th century the ordinal has become one of the books which every parish church must possess.[3] There were in all, five recensions of the Sarum ordinal current in the 14th century: (I) The original ordinal of *c.* 1215, which is the rubric of the Arsenal missal; (2) the revised use of Sarum, probably due to St. Edmund Rich, which is the rubric of the Crawford missal; (3) the Ordinal of precentor Wellwick, of which the chapel of St. George's Windsor had a copy; (4) the Ordinal of St. Stephen's Westminster, which in all probability is embodied in the Bologna MS.; (5) the New Ordinal, which is in fact a revision of numbers (2) and (3).[4]

The earliest Sarum ordinal extant dates from about 1270. The first definite reference to the 'new use of Sarum' is found in a will of 1389–90: 'To John Penne my clerk, a missal of the new use of Sarum.' [5] This 'new ordinal' in its turn became superannuated, largely, it would seem, owing to the increasing prominence given to the feast of Corpus Christi. Like its predecessors, the book had no Pie. Clement Maydestone, however, a Brigittine of Syon Convent at Isleworth (*ob.* 1456), compiled a *Directorium Sacerdotum* with a Pie, which by the end of the 15th century had superseded all such books, and, until about 1501, was itself called the 'Sarum Ordinal'. Later, the shorter ordinal, under the name of

---

[1] Service-book for choir use.

[2] Book for use in the chapter house.

[3] In 1250, Walter Gray, archbishop of York, directed that an ordinal should be provided for every church, and a similar injunction was made at Merton by Robert Winchelsey, archbishop of Canterbury, in 1305.

[4] For this resumé of editions of the ordinal the writer is indebted, as for so much else in this chapter, to Mr. Christopher Hohler.

[5] Gibbon, *Early Lincoln Wills*, p. 87; ap. *Lincoln Cathedral Statutes*, vol. III, p. 841.

Pica Sarum, 'the rules called the Pie', was cut up and redistributed according to the seasons of the year, and then incorporated in the text of all future editions of the Sarum breviary.

The ordinal was an object of hate to John Wycliff (*ob.* 1384) and his followers, as it was just in his time that great efforts were being made to see that all priests conformed exactly to the rubric of the New Ordinal. The commonest type of Old Use missal had been the Bologna type, but it was the Crawford type which was used for the standard printed texts, and which for this and other reasons must have been the true Salisbury version. Wykeham (and Wykehamists like Maydestone) clearly objected to this diversity. In their view, the only authentic Sarum use is that of Salisbury cathedral: consequently they pressed the new ordinal on the clergy, which meant that everybody had either to buy new books or else do a lot of revising. It was all the fuss and bother about what to people like Wycliffe seemed such a very secondary matter that caused his explosion. 'Song and Salisbury use', said the heresiarch in his tract, were two of the four 'sathenas disceitis' which militated against those saving instruments, the 'foure Evangelistis'.[1]

The earliest existing MS. of the consuetudinary seems to have been compiled sometime between the years 1173 and 1220, in all probability in the closing years of Richard Poore as dean of the cathedral church of Salisbury (1197–1215). This Richard Poore, who became subsequently the seventh bishop of the see (1217–28), was instrumental in the translation to New Sarum or Salisbury, as we call it today, and also in the building of the present cathedral church, the foundation stone of which was laid on 28 April 1220. The bishop lived long enough to see the consecration of the lady chapel on 28 September 1225, when among those present was the treasurer, Edmund Rich, who was later archbishop of Canterbury and a saint.[2]

---

[1] *Tracts of Clement Maydeston*, edit. Chr. Wordsworth, *Henry Bradshaw Society*, vol. VII (London, 1894), introd., p. XVI. To appreciate the point, one should try conforming exactly with the rubric of a Sarum breviary without a Pie!

[2] The building was completed, apart from the spire which was no part of the original design, in 1266, having taken nearly half a century to accomplish. It stands alone among English cathedrals in having been built all of a piece, and thus possesses an architectural unity which is exceptional.

In 1319, Bishop Roger de Mortival spoke of Richard Poore as having 'amplified and systematised the liturgical provisions of St. Osmund'. Is it not possible that he did a great deal more than this? As we have seen, there is no evidence that St. Osmund issued any liturgical directions, and it is therefore impossible to get behind the consuetudinary of Richard Poore, in which liturgical customs were set out in the second and third divisions of the book, as a sequel to the first section containing the ancient constitutional legislation of St. Osmund.

The elaboration of the rites and ceremonies in the 'Illustrious Church of Sarum' was almost certainly coeval with the foundation of the new cathedral, but it is obvious that a 'rite' must have existed before the 13th century. We do not know, however, how much in the ordinal of *c.* 1215 was novel at the time; how early the peculiarities of the sacramentary had come into being; and whether there was an earlier edition of the ordinal.

An interesting digression concerns the conjecture that the Sarum use was followed in the diocese of Lisbon from shortly after the capture of the city from the Moslems in 1147 until 1536. This, if true, would suggest that the rite was considerably earlier than the time of Bishop Poore. Gilbert, first bishop of Lisbon, is said to have been an English priest from Hastings, who was consecrated by the archbishop of Braga, introducing the breviary and missal of Salisbury into his Portuguese diocese. The story of the Sarum rite at Lisbon was repeated by Rodrigo da Cunha, who was primate of Braga (1627–36) and later of Lisbon (1635–43), and it has been resuscitated by Mr. Livermore in his *History of Portugal*.[1] A distinctive use was certainly followed in the diocese until the 16th century, but we are by no means clear as to its character. A French writer has accounted for the story by suggesting that the Sarum rite was introduced in the private chapel of Queen Philippa, daughter of John of Gaunt, on her marriage with John I of Portugal in 1387, as this use had been adopted since the time of Edward III (1327–77) in the chapel of the kings of England.[2] The date and circumstances make this

---

[1] H. V. Livermore, *A History of Portugal* (Cambridge, 1947), chap. V, p. 80.

[2] David, *Etudes Historiques sur la Galice et le Portugal due VIe au XIIe siècle* (Lisbon–Paris, 1947), p. 560, note I.

supposition considerably more tenable. In addition to this, the library at Evora possesses a book, written by the dean of the chapel royal of Henry VI for a Portuguese nobleman who was interested, detailing the usages to which the dean was accustomed, and saying: 'In all things we follow the use of the Church of Sarum, certain details excepted.' [1] On the other hand, the royal confessors from Henry III to Richard II were almost all Dominicans, although we know that in Edward III's reign a Thomas Brinton, bishop of Rochester (1373–89), who was a Benedictine, was a royal confessor.[2] A letter of Pope Boniface IX (1384–1404), dated 8 September 1398 and addressed to King Richard II, states plainly that the king and clergy of the court (including seculars) recited the Divine Office according to the rite of the Friars Preachers.[3]

The House of Lancaster, however, beginning with John of Gaunt, the father of Queen Philippa, favoured the Carmelites as confessors and chaplains.[4] Yet even in the 15th century, an exception to the White friars is found in a certain Blakman, a Carthusian, who was confessor to Henry VI.

Was it therefore possible that the rite at which Queen Philippa assisted at her chapel in Lisbon was that of the Carmelites? Alternatively, was it that of the Dominicans? The Queen took a keen interest in the building of the Dominican church and convent of Batalha, the memorial to the great national victory of Aljubarrota (1385), where she and her husband lie buried.

Sarum, Carmelite or Dominican: any of the three uses could have been followed in the royal chapel in Lisbon in the second half of the 15th century.

To return to England and the fortunes of the Sarum rite. The use of Salisbury became early a model for other churches, and in the 13th and following centuries the members of the cathedral chapter seem to have assumed a role of 'Congregation of Rites', to whom queries and doubts might be deferred. At first it

---

[1] The royal chapel referred to was probably that of St. Stephen's, Westminster.
[2] Steele, *Richard II*, p. 30; *Dict. of Nat. Biog.*, Art. *Brinton*, vol. VI, London, 1886.
[3] *Bullarium Ordinis Praedicatorum*, II, 352.
[4] David Knowles, *The Religious Orders in England* (Cambridge, 1948), chap. XIV, p. 167.

would seem to have been the constitutional influence rather than the liturgical, but in course of time the roles were reversed, and the Sarum rite was substituted for many of the local uses.

In 1223, the bishop and chapter of St. Davids enjoined that the services of the Blessed Virgin and the dead should be celebrated *secundum Ordinale Ecclesiae Sarum.*[1] Three years later (1226), we find the statutes of Peter de la Roche, bishop of Winchester, directing the use of Sarum to be followed in the church of Wherwell (Merewell) in Hampshire.[2] Pope Gregory IX in 1228 affirmed that the institutions of St. Osmund were followed by the greater part of England,[3] and an explicit approval of these customs was given by Gregory X in 1274, although it must be admitted that the papal references were to the constitutional rather than to the liturgical side of things.

The fame of the use of Salisbury grew with the years, and in 1256 Bishop Giles de Bridport was able to boast that 'among the churches of the whole world, the church of Sarum hath shone resplendent, like the sun in his full orb, in respect of its divine service, and its ministers'.[4] The collegiate church of Lanchester in the diocese of Durham was permitted to choose its mode of chant (*modus psallendi*) in 1283: use of York or use of Sarum.[5]

It has been said repeatedly that the clerks of the Oxford colleges, even though the city was in the diocese of Lincoln, were bound by oath to follow the Sarum use. A tract of Clement Maydestone was quoted to support this view.[6] Happily Mr. Christopher Hohler was good enough to look through the typescript before it was too late, and was able to give me the true reading of the passage in Maydeston. Two colleges only were in the writer's mind: one in each place. Now Clement Maydestone was a Wykehamist, and his reference was therefore to Win-

---

[1] MS. Harl. 1249, fo. 2; Haddan and Stubbs, *op. cit.*, vol. I, p. 459.

[2] *Divina vero officia secundum Saresberiam celebrentur.* Dugdale, *Monast. Ang.*, vol. III et ult., t. V (London, 1673), aaa, p. 56.

[3] Wilkins, *Concilia*, vol. I, p. 562. London, 1737.

[4] *Stat. Eccles. Cath. Sarum* (edit. 1883), p. 54; Wilkins, *op. cit.*, vol. I.

[5] *Et modum psallendi teneant secundum morem Ecclesiae Eborum vel Sarum.* Dugdale, *op. cit.*, vol. III, t. V, aaa, p. 39.

[6] *Nam clerici Collegiorum Winton et Oxonie (qui prestant juramentum ad servandum usum Sarum).* Tracts of Clement Maydestone, *Defensorium Directorii Sacerdotum*, Henry Bradshaw Society, vol. VII (1894), p. 6.

chester College and New College, Oxford. There is absolutely
nothing in the University statutes to support the wider interpretation, which is indeed clearly incorrect, since no member of
several of the religious orders could ever have taken a degree if
it had been so. As regards the oath, says Mr. Hohler, this concerns the statutes as a whole, without any specific oath concerning
the use. The Oxford clerks, other than at New College, certainly
followed Sarum, probably of the type associated with the Bologna
MS. In any case, the calendar of the Queen's College obit book is
Sarum. The founder of the College sealed the Statues on 10
February 1340/1 and, when he came to the provisions for the
chapel service, the chaplains at the peril of their souls are ordered
to say on the proper days the services for the dead (benefactors)
according to the use of Sarum in the chapel of the college, or in
the parish church, if such a one should be annexed or appropriated thereto.

It would seem, however, that until the appearance of the New
Ordinal people did not bother very much about 'use'.[1]

Scotland would appear to have been one of the first to adopt
Sarum usages, and it may well be that the newly founded religious
houses in the country assisted in popularising it. Moray had
turned first for statutes to Lincoln,[2] but in 1242 the cathedral
chapter of Elgin decided to follow the Sarum use 'not only in
reading and in singing, but in other things pertaining to divine
services': *Ut in divinis officiis in psallendo, legendo et cantando ac
aliis ad divina spectantibus servetur ordo qui in ecclesia Salis-
byryensi esse noscitur institutus.*[3] We find the statute, inserted by
the respective editors, in the Arbuthnott missal [4] of 1491 and the
Aberdeen breviary of 1510.[5] In 1259, the bishop of Glasgow
made inquiries as 'What the use of Sarum might be', although his

---

[1] e.g. Sarum missals appear in the inventories of Canterbury cathedral. The Lincoln
use would have been confined to the cathedral church of Lincoln and, perhaps, its prebendal churches.

[2] F. C. Eeles, *King's College Chapel, Aberdeen* (Edinburgh, 1956), append. 2, pp. 123-4.

[3] *Registrum Episcopatus Moraviensis*, edit. Bannatyne Club (Edinburgh, 1837), vol.
XCIII, p. 107. Elgin moved from Moray in 1222.

[4] The *Arbuthnott Missal* was written by James Sibbald: now in the Museum and Art
Galleries at Paisley.

[5] The *Aberdeen Breviary* was an example of Bishop Elphinstone's work towards systematising a Scottish adaptation of the Sarum use.

cathedral church had already adopted the Salisbury constitutions.
The bishop would seem to have been satisfied with the result of
his investigation. Two leaves from a noted Sarum breviary of
the 13th century, probably forming part of a Glasgow cathedral
choir book, are used today to bind an early book of the Incor-
poration of Skinners in the city.[1]

There is little doubt that the Sarum use was followed throughout Scotland in the later Middle Ages, unless some of the churches
in Galloway had the use of York, for which there is no evidence.
All the surviving mediaeval Scottish liturgical books and fragments, except the monastic, are of the Sarum use. The introduction of Celtic saints was unsystematic, and made little impression
on the *sanctorale* apart from disorganising it and multiplying the
occasions for using the 'common of saints'. Names were freely
added to calendars and litanies, but with few proper services to
correspond with them.[2]

The early years of the 16th century were a time for the furtherance of nationalism in which liturgical unification played a part.
The so-called Aberdeen use was mooted, which was to be identified with the Scottish use in much the same way as the Sarum use
was identified with the English use. A first instalment for the reformation of the liturgical books was foreshadowed by King
James IV (1488–1513) and his Privy Council in the privilege to
the printers, which provides that 'mess bukis efter our awin
Scottis use, and with legendis of Scottis sanctis, as is now gaderit
and ekit be ane Reverend fader in God, and out traist consalour,
Williame, bishope of abirdene and utheris, be usit generaly within
al our Realme alssone as the sammyn may be imprentit and pro-
vidit, and that na maner of sic bukis of Salusbery use be brocht
to be sauld within our Realme in tyn cuming'.[3] The reference is
to the attempt made by William Elphinstone, bishop of Aberdeen, to provide a Scottish liturgical use by a conservative reform
of the Sarum books. Aberdeen would seem to have been the first
Church in Scotland to adopt Sarum rules, and in the Middle Ages

---

[1] *Official Historical Catalogue, Scottish Exhibition, Glasgow,* 1911, p. 1051, no. 3.
[2] *Epistolare . . . . Aberdonensis,* 1527, edit. F. C. Eeles, pp. XI–XII.
[3] R. Dickson, *Introduction of the Art of Printing into Scotland,* p. 94. Aberdeen, 1885.

it was the most easily accessible cathedral city in Scotland with a secular chapter.[1] The Aberdeen breviary (1509–10) was more or less the Sarum breviary with a full and well-regulated provision for Scottish saints' days, coupled with a few other changes and some necessary simplification. Of the existing provision for these days he says: *sparsim in incerto antea vagabantur*. The title of the breviary makes it clear that the bishop identified the Aberdeen use with the use of the whole of Scotland: *Breviarii Aberdonensis ad percelebris ecclesie Scotorum potissimum usum et consuetudinem*, and in the colophon: *non solum ad ecclesie sue Aberdonensis verumciam ad tocius ecclesie Scoticane usum percelebrem*. There is no evidence that the Elphinstone reform effected more than the breviary, but some tradition of the Aberdeen use persisted. An epistolary (1527), issued on the authority of Gavin Dunbar (1518–31), claims to be *ad cathedralis ecclesie Aberdonensis usum et consuetudinem*, but the scheme of reform never reached the missal.[2] The series of epistles accurately corresponds with the Sarum missal, although there are certain omissions, and the title *De non virginibus* has been altered to *De una matrona*, as in the Aberdeen breviary, Arbuthnott missal and York missal. The work of Bishop Elphinstone was continued by Bishop William Stewart, who in 1540 ordered the cathedral *ordinale* to be reformed and rewritten.[3] A MS. martyrology, written for Elgin cathedral so late as 1552–60, says: *secundum usum ecclesie Aberdonensis*.[4]

Bishop Elphinstone, says Dr. Eeles, 'visualised a Scottish use, though with a moderation that paid the greatest respect to the use of Sarum which had so long been established in Scotland'.[5]

In some quarters, also, about this time we find traces of an introduction of the Roman rite. Thus the papal rescript of 1501, transforming the Chapel Royal in Stirling Castle into a collegiate church, grants to the king the right to follow either the local

---

[1] *Epist.* (1527), edit. Eeles, p. XII.
[2] *Ibid.*, p. XIII.
[3] *Registrum Episc. Aberdon.*, edit. Edinburgh, 1845, vol. II, p. 116.
[4] C. R. Borland. *A Descript. Catal. of Western mediaeval MSS. in Edin. Univ. Lib.* (Edin. 1916), p. 93.
[5] Eeles, *King's College, Aberdeen*, append. 2, p. 132.

liturgical use or the Roman rite in the offices of the new collegiate church.[1] In Edinburgh University Library there is a copy of the first recension of the breviary compiled by Cardinal Quignon: *Breviarium Romanum nuper reformatum*, Paris, 1536. The inscription on the title-page and at the end of the text shows that the book was in use in Scotland.[2] Among the faculties granted in the bull of Pope Paul III, appointing Cardinal Beaton legate *a latere* in 1543,[3] and again in the bull of Julius III, appointing Archbishop Hamilton to the same office in 1552,[4] we find the permission for secular priests to recite the Divine Office *secundum usum et morem Romanae ecclesiae, etiam juxta ritum Breviarii noviter impressi, extra tamen chorum*. Eight breviaries and two missals of this Quignonian revision of the Roman rite are still extant, suggesting that a significant proportion of the clergy were fully alive to the need for a revision of the mediaeval liturgical books, but sought a revision along lines different from that of Bishop Elphinstone of Aberdeen.[5] It is interesting to note that in 1509, at the time when the Aberdeen breviary was being printed, Archbishop Alexander Stewart of St. Andrews petitioned and obtained from Pope Julius II a dispensation to recite the Divine Office according to the Roman rite, in place of the rite followed by the Augustinians of his cathedral chapter.[5] This may indeed have been a normal proceeding, since Bishop James Kennedy had a Roman breviary among his liturgical books, which he may have recited with his chaplain, Master John Balfour.[5] A *Missale ad sacrosancte Romane ecclesie usum*, printed in Paris in 1546, contains the proper for a Mass of St. Ninian inserted in a 16th-century hand, thereby showing that the missal had been in use in Scotland.[6]

A Protestant Communion service (Second Prayer Book of Edward VI) was celebrated by John Willock, an apostate Franciscan, in the Collegiate Church of St. Giles, Edinburgh, in

[1] *History of the Chapel Royal of Scotland*, C. Rogers, Grampian Club, 1882.
[2] Edin. Univ. Lib., Df. 8, 41. D. McRoberts, *Catalogue of Scottish Mediaeval Liturgical Books and Fragments* (Glasgow, 1953), p. 18.
[3] Burnet's *History of the Reformation*, vol. IV, p. 345.
[4] *The Warrender Papers*, vol. I, p. 26.
[5] McRoberts, *op. cit.*, p. 18.
[6] Eeles, *Scottish Historical Review*, vol. X, pp. 35–8.

August 1559, but in November of that year we hear of the Bishop of Amiens, Nicholas de Pelleve, in his capacity of papal legate 'purgins the High Church of Edinburgh from heretical pollutions with great show of piety and devotion'.[1] This was on 9 November 1559, but Catholic worship finally ceased on 1 April of the following year, so that the last Mass was probably said on 31 March, 1560.

In *Ireland*, we find a canon of the synod of Cashel (1172) directing the 'use of the English Church' to be followed throughout the Church of Ireland in all religious observances. There was no reference to any specific 'use', and the enactment probably implied no more than a strict adherence to Roman usages.[2] The synod was in fact the death knell of lingering Celtic customs. In 1163, the archbishop of Dublin, St. Lorcan O'Tuathail, introduced Arroasian canons into his cathedral church of Christ Church. A successor, Henry of London (1212–28), who united Glendalough to his archdiocese, adopted the Sarum model for his chapter, and he may well have followed the rites and ceremonies of that Church. We know that in the following century (c. 1300–10), the Consuetudinary of Sarum was transcribed in its entirety for use in the diocese of Dublin.

The Reformation in Ireland followed much the same course as in England, but with less success. The 'Order of Communion' existed side by side with the Catholic liturgy in Dublin for three years (1548–51).[3] This temporary adjunct was translated into Latin for the benefit of those clergy who knew no English.

Then, on Easter Sunday (29 March) 1551, the First Prayer Book of Edward VI was used in the cathedral church of Christ Church in place of the Sarum liturgy. Two years later (2 February 1553), two Protestant bishops were consecrated with the ordinal in the Second Prayer Book of Edward VI.[4]

---

[1] J. Cameron Lees, *St. Giles' Edinburgh: Church, College and Cathedral* (Edinburgh, 1889), pp. 116–17. Nicholas de Pelleve became subsequently archbishop of Sens and cardinal.

[2] *Item quod omnia divina ad instar sacrosanctae ecclesiae, juxta quod Anglicana observat ecclesia, in omnibus partibus ecclesiae amodo tractentur.* Syn. Cashel, 1172, can. 7. Wilkins, *op. cit.*, vol. I, p. 473.

[3] M. V. Ronan, *Reformation in Dublin*, part III, p. 346.

[4] *Ibid.*, pp. 385–7.

Protestant service-books, however, were not accepted by the mass of the people: 'Even where the bishop had adopted the Book of Common Prayer, priests said their Mass as of old, and the people continued to hear it, and those priests who used the Common Prayer introduced into it some of the Roman Mass.' [1]

When the Catholic religion was officially restored by Queen Mary, the archbishop of Dublin, George Browne, remained in his see, and continued in his ministrations, as if the Mass had never been abolished! [2] Later, however, he was ejected, as he had contracted matrimony. In 1555, Hugh Comen, archbishop of Dublin, held a provincial synod for the reformation of religion and the restoration of the Catholic liturgy. Former religious customs were also revived.[3] With the accession of Elizabeth, the old faith was once again proscribed, and the ancient liturgy vanished from the churches of the Island.

The use of Sarum, which its liturgical books describe as *insignis ac preclara* and *insignis ac inter occiduous nominatissima*, was the most important factor in the liturgy of the English Church from the 13th century until the change of religion in the 16th.

William Lynwood, bishop of St. Davids and the greatest of English canonists (*ob.* 1446), tells us that when the archbishop of Canterbury officiates at a provincial synod or on some similar occasion, the bishop of Salisbury, according to ancient custom, rules the choir as precentor.[4] The liturgical fame of Salisbury extended also to Rome, and the *English Martyrology*, which appeared in 1608, says that 'in ancient tymes the Catholicke bishops of Salisbury obtayned the titles of the Pope's maister of cermonyes, and had their places always assigned them in the Pope's chappell and other solemnityes at Rome, according to the dignity'.[5]

Passing to the influence of Sarum in the English dioceses, it may be noted that *Wells* had taken practically the whole Sarum consuetudinary by 1298. *Lincoln* under Bishop Remigius of

---

[1] M. V. Ronan, *op. cit.*, pp. 389–90.

[2] *Ibid.*, part IV, pp. 410–11. Edward Staples, bishop of Meath, was equally accomodating!

[3] *Ibid.*, p. 434.   [4] Lynwood, *Provinciale*, lib. II, tit. III.

[5] Wilson (Watson), *English Martyrology*, 1608, p. 194.

Fécamp (1067–94) had to some extent introduced Rouen customs, as we learn from the Register of William of Alnwick (1436–50), who, in treating of the translation of the see from Dorchester to Lincoln, said that its divine service was derived from the rites of the Church of Rouen, although nothing specifically was mentioned about the Mass.[1] Lincoln came early on the constitutional side under the spell of Salisbury. A *consuetudinarium de divinis officiis*, the ceremonial portion of the *Liber Niger*, was compiled in the time of Richard de Gravesend (1258–79). The book contains a somewhat detailed description of the preparation of the chalice before the gospel.[2]

Lincoln in the 14th century was still considered to have a 'use' of its own, but, although a reference to such a 'use' is found in the preface of the Book of Common Prayer, Edmund Bishop considers that it was 'little more than a half-forgotten tradition' by the 16th century.[3] The Sarum use would probably have prevailed by that time throughout the diocese, apart from a few local peculiarities, possibly in respect to the chant. In any case, Mr. Christopher Hohler thinks that the Lincoln use was 'effectively confined to Lincoln cathedral, and, perhaps, its prebendal churches'. A recent book on *English Art, 1216–1307*, says that both the Huth Psalter [4] and the Salvin Hours [5] have connections with Lincoln, but without giving any further explanations.[6] A MS. in the British Museum has been ascribed to Lincoln, as the calendar gives the Translation of St. Hugh, in addition to the Deposition, and a sequence in his honour has been added at the end.[7] Wickham Legg says of this MS.: 'a correcting hand has passed over the rest of the book, so that by additions in the margins or erasures, the greater part of the missal has been

---

[1] *Remigius . . . . canonicos ibidem saeculares ordinavit et posuit ad deserviendum ibidem in officio divino juxta ritum Ecclesiae Rothomagensis quae est totius Normandiae metropolis. Novum Registrum Ecclesiae Lincolniensis, Stat. Eccles. Cathedr. Lincoln.*, edit. Chr. Wordsworth (London, 1873), p. 3.

[2] Wickham Legg, *Eccles. Essays* (London, 1905), V, pp. 154–5.

[3] Bishop, *op. cit.*, XII, p. 277.

[4] Brit. Mus., London, MS. Add. 38116. The MS. dates from the 1280's.

[5] Formerly Yates Thompson Coll., no. LXXX; then Chester, Beatty MS. 60. A Book of Hours of Sarum use.

[6] Peter Brieger, *English Art, 1216–1307*, chap. XII, pp. 220–2.

[7] Brit. Mus., London., MS. Add. 11414.

brought into conformity with Sarum, though here and there the Gregorian collects remain'.[1] A more exact picture of what was done has been given by Mr. Christopher Hohler, who points out that the 'correcting hand' was in fact no more than bringing a missal of the 'Arsenal type' into conformity with the 'New Use', probably very late in the 14th or even well on in the 15th century.[2] The book as a whole is 14th century. The supplement, comprising the prayers of the 'New Use' not found in the Arsenal MS. and the sequences, being quite separate and simply a supplement. Wickham Legg, on the other hand, had said that the calendar is written in a late-14th-century hand, while the rest of the book is made up of quires written at various times: the earliest hand being of the middle of the 14th century, if not later, the others being of the 15th century.[3]

Unfortunately no complete indubitable service-book of Lincoln is known. The Bodleian Library, Oxford, has three leaves of a 14th-century missal, whose identity is attested by the rubric in the second column: *Et sciendum . . . secundum usum lincoln cantari debet sequentia.*[4]

The absence of Lincoln books is not surprising. In the first place, an order of Edward VI (25 December 1549) called in 'all pies . . . and ordinalles after the use of Sarum, Lincoln, York, or any other private use.' Then, in the reign of Elizabeth, we find an organised holocaust carried on by the churchwardens of Lincolnshire in the years 1559–66: of 'Mass-bookes, and other latin bookes of popish peltrie . . . belonging to the popishe sinfull service . . . whose names we know not'.

In the huge Mercian diocese of *Lichfield and Coventry*, we find the statutes of Hugh Pateshull (1239–41) drawn largely from the second part of the Sarum consuetudinary, with occasional excerpts from the third part; while two centuries later, in the episcopate of William Heyworth (1420–47), the Sarum ordinal would seem to have been officially prescribed in the cathedral church: *formam ordi-*

---

[1] Wickham Legg, Liturg. introduct., *Missale ad usum Ecclesie Westmonasteriensis*, fasc. III, *Henry Bradshaw Society*, vol. XII (1897), pp. 1408–9.
[2] The rubric of the Arsenal MS. 135 seems to give the original ordinal of *c.* 1215: the New Ordinal was a late 14th century recension.
[3] Wickham Legg, *ibid.*   [4] Bodl. Lib., Oxford, MS. Tanner 4 (9824).

nalis Sarum. In fact, all the evidence we have points to the use of
Sarum liturgical books in that diocese. The collegiate churches of
St. Bartholomew, Tong (1410), and St. Mary Magdalene, Battle-
field (1444), both in the county of Shropshire, were directed by
their foundation statutes to follow the use and ordinal of Salisbury. The diocese retained certain local peculiarities for the
feasts of St. Cedde (Chad), St. Catherine and St. Nicholas, as well
as for the first three days of the Octave of Pentecost, as we learn
from the later statute of Galafrid Blyth (1503–24).[1]

Some printed Sarum breviaries refer to a 'Lichfield use' for the
feast of the patron of the Mercian diocese on 2 March (St. Chad):
secundum vero usum Lichfeldensem.[2]

The Sarum rite was followed also in the area which now forms
the Anglican diocese of Liverpool, as may be seen from a will
quoted by Henderson: *Lego ecclesiae meae de Prestecott unum
Portiphorium magnum notatum Sarum.*[3]

There is some reason to believe that Sarum was followed in the
diocese of *Durham*, but we find cases in which churches were permitted to follow either York or Sarum.[4]

Exeter. In the 12th century, we hear of a clerk of the bishop
of Exeter visiting Lisieux, *ut divinis informaretur officiis*, as if there
was some suggestion of borrowing from the usages of the Norman Church.[5] Whether this was done or not, Exeter was in
possession of a Sarum missal at a very early date. A memorial to
Henry of Chichester, canon of Exeter, appears on the fly-leaf of a
missal in a later-13th-century hand, now in the John Rylands
Library, Manchester.[6] The initial to the canon has the Crucified

---

[1] *Item, quia comperimus pleraque circa divina officia, in cantuum modulatione, et aliis, ab
Ordinale Sarum longe discrepasse: idcirco, de consensu et assensu supramentionatis, statuimus
et ordinamus: quod forma Ordinalis Sarum, tempore divinorum, in omnibus praeterquam in
festis divi Ceddae patroni nostri, Catherinae, et Nicholai: ac etiam diebus Lunae, Martis et
Mercurii in festo Pentecostes, in quanto convenientius fieri poterit, inviolabiliter observetur.*
Dugdale, *op. cit.*, vol. III, *Eccles. Cathedr. Canonic. Secular.*, p. 255.

[2] *Brev. Sar.*, edit. Proctor and Wordsworth, Cambridge, 1886, fasc. III, col. 193.

[3] F. C. Eeles, *On a 15th-century Missal formerly used at Broughton-in-Amounderness*,
pp. 1–2. Manchester: Printed for Chetham Society, 1935.

[4] *Ibid.*, p. 1, n. 1. Vide York rite.

[5] Launoy, *De Scolis celebrioribus*; ap. T. F. Simmons, *Lay Folks Mass Book* (London,
1879), introduct., p. XXXV, n. 2.

[6] Manchester, John Rylands Lib., MS. 24. The MS. is known today as the 'Crawford
missal.'

between the Church and the Synagogue, as in the Amesbury Psalter.[1] In the following century, John de Grandisson (1327–70), at the beginning of his episcopate, sent to Salisbury for a pontifical to serve as an examplar, and the ordinal prescribed by him in 1337 was largely taken from the use of Sarum. This ordinal refers to the feast of Corpus Christi as a 'novelty',[2] which was gaining ground and likewise causing difficulties.[3] Here, as elsewhere, the 'Sarumising' of the service-books seems to have been carried out in successive stages, but so late as 1502 it was necessary for Bishop Hugh Oldham to direct his chapter to conform exactly to the ordinal and customary of Sarum. Statutes for the new foundation of a collegiate church at Ottery St. Mary, which were drawn up by Bishop Grandisson in 1339, show that Sarum was the then received use of the diocese, although they 'no less show a sort of jealousy still existing, and an earnest desire upon the part of the bishop to establish an 'Exeter use'.[4] Thus in the seventh statute he speaks of the Divine Office as being performed, on certain occasions, *secundum ordinale et consuetudinarium quae fecimus et extraximus ex Exoniae et Sarum usibus*.[5] The two uses appear to be identified in statute thirty-six: *Item volumus quod in majoribus festis—sicut Sarum et sicut Exon*. Once more in the seventy-seventh chapter, the bishop says very plainly: *Item statuimus quod ubicumque ordinale vel consuetudinarium vel statuta nostra non sufficiant forte in multis faciendis per totum annum, quod tunc recurratur ad ordinale et consuetudinarium Sarum. Ita tamen quod semper omnia per nos disposita firmiter observentur. Nolumus tamen quod allegent vel dicant unquam se usum tenere Sarum, sed magis Exoniae, vel, ut verius dicant, usum per nos eis traditum proprium et specialem*.[6] We do not know how far the bishop's wishes in the matter were carried out. The blessing of the oils on Holy Thursday in the pontifical of Bishop Edmund Lacy (1420) was taken almost verbatim from Sarum. In 1436, the founder of

---

[1] Oxford, All Souls, MS. 6.

[2] *Tamen quia id festum est mobile et novum. Ordin. Exon.*, 1337, p. LIII.

[3] The synod of Exeter, held in 1287, makes no mention of Corpus Christi.

[4] Maskell, *Ancient Liturgy of the Church of England . . . .* (London, 1846), pref., chap. IV, p. LXII.

[5] Maskell, *Monumenta Ritualia*, vol. I, p. XLIII.

[6] Oliver, *Monasticon Exon*, pp. 268 seq.

'Godeshous', a charitable institution for the poor of Exeter, stipulated that the chaplain should say his office *secundum usum Sarum*.[1]

St. Paul's Cathedral Church, London, had its own distinctive use until 1414, when an order was made by the bishop, Richard Clifford (1407–22), 'with the assent of the chapter, that from the first of December following, Divine Service should be performed in his cathedral, *secundum usum Sarum*: and that the old form and rubric called St. Paul's should be laid aside'.[2] It would appear from entries in the report of the visitation of the treasury of the cathedral church, made in 1295, that some time before that date the chant had been changed, as we read: *In capella Carnarie* in the cemetery: *Missale vetus cum veteri nota*; altar of St. Hippolytus: *Unum missale de antiqua nota, non regulata*; altar of St. John the Evangelist: *Unum missale plenarium cum nota antiqua*. The inventory of the church of St. Faith in the crypt enumerates *Unum missale de usus S. Pauli*.[3] A later inventory, which was made in 1486, after the change of use, lists a number of the old books as stored in the lower room (*in inferiori domo*) of the treasury: *Vetus missale secundum usum S. Pauli; aliud vetus missale secundum usum S. Pauli; unum manuale antiquum; unus textus antiquus; unum psalterium antiquum; unum ordinale secundum primariam ordinationem et antiquam Ecclesiae S. Pauli Londiniensis*.[4] The use of the cathedral church would have been followed, at least in theory, by the parish churches, and a MS., written about 1395, informs us that it was employed for Mass in the Benedictine abbey of Barking, where there seems to have been a certain amount of controversy as to the usages proper to the convent: *Nota quod diversis temporibus intra conventum nonnullae emanarunt altercationes— igitur nos cupientes dictas altercationes et discordias radicitus extirpari praesenti extirpamus edicto secundum antiquas consuetudines istius domus approbatus, quod conventus predictus tres modos diversos habeat sui servitii dicendi: primo horas suas dicat secundum regulam Sancti Benedicti: Psalterium suum secundum cursum Curiae Romanae; Missam vero secundum usum ecclesiae Sancti*

---

[1] Oliver, *op. cit.*, p. 404.
[2] Collier, *Ecclesiastical History*, vol. I, p. 649.
[3] Dugdale, *op. cit.*, vol. III, t. V, pp. 327, 328, 330, 332.
[4] *Ibid.*, pp. 364, 365.

U

Pauli Londiniarum.[1] The church of St. Giles without Cripplegate petitioned Rome for the Sarum use, because in 1376 their old books were worn out.[2] In 1414, as we have seen, the distinctive use of St. Paul's was replaced by the rite of Sarum, but the *Defensorium Directorii Sacerdotis*, which in all probability was written by the Brigittine Clement Maydestone (*ob.* 1456) in defence of his own work, makes it clear that some of the old rites and ceremonies were retained and incorporated in the Salisbury service-books: *Probatur ista assertio esse vera per venerabiles viros et patres canonicos ecclesie sci Pauli London, qui totum divinum officium in cantando et legendo observent secundum usum ecclesie Sarum. Sed de ceremoniis vel observationibus ejusdem nil curantes, sed custodiunt antiquas observantias in ecclesia sancti Pauli a primordio illic usitatas.*[3]

The catalogue in the British Museum cites a MS. missal as *Missale in usum D. Pauli,* but it is later than 1414. The rubrics throughout speak of, and are according to, the use of Sarum, but there is nothing very remarkable in that, as the rubric of all these books, irrespective of what sort of church they were to be used in, is the Ordinal of Salisbury cathedral. A tradition that the book had once belonged to the cathedral church seems to have earned for it the title of 'of St. Paul's'. Some of the rubrics, however, could refer only to a large establishment of priests and ministers, and the book must at least have been the property of some great London church. This is clear from the rubric on the feast of St. Mark, directing the procession on that day to go to some church in the city or the suburbs, and return after the celebration of Mass to their own church.[4] The missal provides one interesting and important exception to the Sarum use: the communion prayer *Agimus tibi Deo Patri gratias.* We find it also in the Hereford [5] and Gilbertine [6] liturgies, but the prayers which precede it in the

---

[1] MS. Wood F XXX; Dugdale, *op. cit.*, vol. I (edit. 1817), p. 437, note K. Barking followed the Benedictine breviary for the Divine Office, the Roman Curia for the psalter, and the use of St Paul's for Mass.

[2] 1376, *Cal. Papal Regist.* IV. VI Greg. XI.

[3] *Defensorium Directorii Sacerdotum*, cap. XLI, *Tracts of Clement Maydestone*, edit. Chr. Wordsworth, *Henry Bradshaw Society*, vol. VII (London, 1894), pp. 15-16.

[4] Maskell, *op. cit.*, pref., chap. IV, p. LXI.   [5] *Ibid.*, pp. 121, 123.

[6] *Gilbertine Rite*, vol. II, edit. R. M. Woolley, *H.B.S.*, vol. LX (London, 1922), p. 90.

London missal are not according to Hereford, but to Sarum, and it is thought to have been a survival of the old use of St. Paul's. There would seem to have been some intention of extending the use of the Sarum rite beyond the Humber in the latter part of the 15th century, if we may judge from the MS. York missal in the library of Sidney Sussex College, Cambridge. We have here what was apparently an attempt to assimilate the York use to that of Sarum, but that it was abortive is evident from the fact that the proposed changes are not admitted in any of the printed editions of the York missal. An entry in the 15th-century York missal, formerly used at Broughton-in-Amounderness in Lancashire, records that one Nicholas Walmysleye gave two vestments to the parish, together with 'a masse boke of Saroume use'.[1] This would in all probability have been in the early years of the 16th century. There is, moreover, little doubt that at the time of the change of religion a certain number of churches in the diocese of York followed the Sarum use.

Towards the end of the 13th century we find Anthony Beck, bishop of Durham and former canon of Lincoln, giving churches a choice of use: York or Sarum. It was thus for the collegiate church of Lanchester in 1283 and for the colleges of Chester le Street in 1286 and St. Andrew at Bishop Auckland in 1292: *modum psalterii secundum usum Eborum vel Salesberie.*

As we have seen, the great Benedictine houses enjoyed a certain amount of liturgical freedom, so that while Westminster, St. Albans, Abingdon and Tewkesbury were strongly influenced by Sarum, others, as Worcester and Peterborough, do not seem to have been in the least affected.[2]

As regards the Austin Canons, we find some churches which followed the Sarum use, as, for example, the oratory of the Holy Trinity at Barton in the Isle of Wight, which was served by the Order.[3] Others again, like the congregation of Arrouaise canons at Notley in Buckinghamshire, obtained a papal indult to enable the community to 'go over' to Sarum. Their old use, by reason of the rigour of the Order, had become 'too burdensome' (*nimis*

---

[1] Eeles, *op. cit.*, p. 1.   [2] Eeles, *Holyrood Ordinale*, introduct., p. xxxii.
[3] *Archeologia*, LII, pp. 297, 301.

grave).[1] A Sarum antiphoner exists at Cambridge, probably from the house at Barnwell, in which the prominence of St. Augustine alone distinguishes it from a Sarum book. Parts of the customary of this house are identical with the corresponding Sarum book, and we know that Salisbury influenced the liturgy of this house.[2] There is, says Dr. Eeles, 'abundant proof that the original of Holyrood Ordinal was known and used by English Augustinian canons soon after the middle of the 13th century, and by those whose rite was influenced by Sarum.' [3] On the other hand, we know that Sarum books were not used at Guisborough, Oseney, Westacre, Kirkham or Cottingham. Local variation continued down to the eve of the Reformation, as is proved by the Statutes for Canons Regular issued by Cardinal Wolsey: 22 March 1519. After ordering the Victorines, Arroasians and all other Austin Canons throughout England to unite in one general chapter, the Cardinal says: *Item statuimus quod omnes et singuli canonici regulares juxta morem singulorum locorum psalmorum et alia ad divinum cultum pertinencia . . . cantent.*[4]

St. Albans, already by the middle of the 12th century, used service-books of the 'Sarum family': Ely, and, probably, Peterborough in the 13th century, and Abingdon in the 15th century. Mr. Hohler things it possible that Salisbury abandoned its older books in favour of a rehash of Westminster in 1180 or thereabouts.

The Sarum rite was adopted in churches, formerly monastic, which survived the dissolution of the religious houses (1536, 1539), as well as by those dispossessed monks and friars who continued to exercise their clerical calling in parishes. The number of those who accepted benefices would seem to have been considerable,[5] but ex-religious who lived on into the reign of Elizabeth were subject to strange theological and liturgical tergiversations. An extreme example is found in Peter Hutchison, who, until the suppression of his abbey in 1536, had been a Cistercian monk at Sibton in Suffolk. He was appointed vicar of Westleton

---

[1] 1391 *Cal. Papal Regist.* IV.
[2] Eeles, *op. cit.*, introduct., p. xxxiv.   [3] *Ibid.*, p. xxxvii.
[4] Wilkins, *Concilia Mag. Brit. et Hib.*, III, pp. 683 seq.
[5] G. Baskerville, *English Monks and the Suppression of the Monasteries.* London, 1937.

in 1545, a position he retained until his death on 8 September 1584. Thus Mr. Hutchison, on receiving the benefice, gave up the Cistercian use in favour of Sarum. Then, in 1548, a vernacular formula for the distribution of Holy Communion was appended. In the following year (1549) the Mass itself gave place to the First Prayer Book of Edward VI, which in its turn was succeeded by a more markedly Protestant service-book in 1552. Then came the Marian interlude, when Mass according to the use of Sarum was restored, but on the accession of Elizabeth (1558) the Catholic religion was again proscribed, and a reformed prayer book reintroduced. The parishioners of Westleton must have been somewhat bewildered at the 'quick-change artist' that was their vicar! 'Is it from these generations', says Philip Hughes, 'that we must date the beginnings of what has troubled so many good men, of all kinds of belief . . ., namely the unruffled "religionlessness" of so very many—indeed of whole sections, and of the very mass of the nation?'.[1] 'After sixty years of upheaval (1529–89), religious conviction had well nigh disappeared, outside the minorities called Papist and Puritan.'[2]

The Sarum Mass was restored in St. Paul's Cathedral by order of Queen Mary on 27 August 1553, and throughout her short and troubled reign would have been the principal use throughout the country. Priests accustomed to the service-books of York and Hereford continued their distinctive usages, although it was seriously considered by Convocation, which met under Cardinal Pole in 1557, whether it would not be advisable to enforce the Sarum books throughout the whole realm: *uniusmodi per totum regnum.*

A Sarum missal appeared in 1557, and in the following year a Sarum manual, which proved to be the last of the books of the mediaeval *Ecclesia Anglicana.*

The Royal Injunctions issued in 1559 made it quite clear that the old service-books would be no longer tolerated, and Elizabeth more or less reiterated a former Act of Edward VI in which it was stated that Catholic liturgical books should be 'clearly and

---

[1] Philip Hughes, *Reformation in England*, vol. III ('*True Religion now established*'), chap. V, p. 235. [2] *Ibid.*, chap. V, p. 146.

utterly abolished, extinguished and forbidden for ever to be used or kept'. In spite of this, however, the hunt persisted throughout the reign, and, as late as 1590, we find the archbishop of York still asking: 'Whether all and every antiphoner, mass-book, grail, portess, processional, manual, legendary, with all other books belonging heretofore to your church or chapel, and which served for the superstitious popish service be defaced, abolished and utterly gone; and if not, then where and with whom are they?' [1] Eleven years later, a somewhat similar inquiry was made by Bancroft, bishop of London: 'Whether there be in your parish who are noted, known, or suspected to conceal or keep hidden in their houses any mass-books, portesses, breviaries or other books of popery or superstition . . . uncancelled or defaced, which it is to be conjectured they do keep for a day, as they call it.' [2]

The rite was maintained secretly by some few Marian priests in the early years of the reign of Elizabeth, but the 'missioners' who came to this country from the Continent brought with them the reformed missal of St. Pius V (1570). The English College at Douai abandoned the use of Sarum in 1577, and all that has survived of the use which for three hundred years 'shone resplendent, like the sun in his full orb' are some distinctive customs in the English Catholic marriage service which derive from the ritual of the 'Illustrious Church of Sarum'. It has been said that there was some talk of a revival of the Sarum use after the re-establishment of the diocesan hierarchy in 1850, but other views prevailed.[3]

Origins of the Sarum Rite

'The main characteristic of the Sarum sacramentary and its allies', says Mr. Christopher Hohler, 'is the rejection of an extremely large number of prayers found in the *Hadrianum* in favour of others which are sometimes the Gelasian alternatives, but more often are not.' [4] 'Gregorian' English books are not

---

[1] Philip Hughes, *op. cit.*, chap. IV, p. 120.   [2] *Ibid.*, p. 121.

[3] *Butler's Lives of the Saints*, edit. Thurston, vol. XI (London, 1935), p. 62. The writer has been unable to obtain any confirmation of this.

[4] Chr. Hohler, *Sonderdruck aus St. Bonifatius Gedenkgabe zum zwölfhundertjährigen Todestag, The Type of Sacramentary used by St. Boniface*, p. 90. Fulda, 1954.

essentially different from any other European missals: in some
cases certainly, and in all fairly certainly, they are in fact French
books taken over and adapted at some date between 800 and 1200.
Sarum books differ from all others in Europe, their only comparable group being the St. Amand family with which they are in
some way connected. The *Hadrianum* uses the same prayers for
a number of different occasions quite often, whereas the St.
Amand and Sarum books reject these doublets. They are, however, based on some form of Gregorian, very possibly the
Hadrianum, but in principle they never use the same prayer twice.
The prayers which are found in several places in the *Hadrianum*
are, broadly speaking, found only once in the Sarum and St.
Amand books. When they would have been used again, the compilers of these works turned to some different source for a fresh
prayer to replace them. The problem in all this is, first, why was
this done only in these two families of books; secondly, what
were the 'different sources' used by the Sarum compiler; and
thirdly, when and where did he work?

Some of the prayers in these Sarum books have been so far
untraced, while others are found in the 'Leonine' or Ambrosian
sacramentary. The real peculiarity of Sarum is in fact the number
of Leonine prayers, which are not found in any MS. (of which the
text has been published) intermediate in date between the Leonine
sacramentary itself (*c.* 600) and the St. Alban's sacramentary of
the middle of the 12th century. Seemingly they are not in the
MS. mass-books of Fécamp or Newminster at Winchester.

The archetype of the Sarum books must have been introduced
at one of three periods: the Conversion of the country in the 6th
and 7th centuries; the Monastic Revival in the 10th century; or
the Reorganisation of the English Church after 1066. The 11th
century is apparently excluded, as we find no trace of Sarum
peculiarities in the Norman mass-books, and the two English
Benedictine missals (St. Augustine's Canterbury; Durham),
which certainly depend on the book approved at Canterbury by
Lanfranc, do not show them either.

The 10th century is also excluded, as the five sacramentaries
earlier than *c.* 1050 and connected with the reformed monasteries

show no Sarum peculiarities. We are forced therefore, says Mr.
Hohler, to look to the 'dark ages' for the arrival of the archetype
to this country. The remains, however, of English sacramentaries
earlier than the middle of the 10th century are so insignificant that
any generalisation is impossible, although we find some characteristic Sarum formulas for the proper Masses of various English
saints in 10th- and early-11th-century monastic books. On the
Continent, a comparable sacramentary is found only in the so-
called family of St. Amand, which is usually easiest to detect in
formularies for the Sundays after Pentecost, when most of its
peculiarities are shared by the entire Sarum group.[1] Missals of
this group include Sens,[2] St. Amand,[3] Soissons?,[4] Utrecht,[5] St.
Thierry,[6] Niederalteich, Regensburg, Breslau, Esztergom, and
Fulda (10th century).

Dr. Wickham Legg, taking the secrets and postcommunions
as the criterion, has divided the English missals into two groups:
Sarum group and Gregorian group. In the former he has included Salisbury, St. Albans, Tewkesbury, Abingdon, Westminster, and the Drummond, Rosslyn and Corpus missals;
while the latter comprises York, Durham, St. Augustine's Canterbury, Whitby, Sherborne, Leofric, Winchcombe, Robert of
Jumièges [7] and *Vitellius*,[8] as well as the continental missals of
Rouen, Bayeux, Coutances, Evreux, Paris, Dominicans, Cistercians and Carthusians.[9]

The earliest MS. of the Sarum group is that of St. Albans,
dating from *c.* 1150.[10] The abbey was reformed in 1077, and, if
St. Osmund was really the author of the Sarum use, it is indeed
strange that a great religious house, undoubtedly proud of its
traditions, should have so changed its liturgy to follow that of a

---

[1] The St. Amand group is so-called from the home of its oldest known representative.
[2] Sens, Brit. Mus., MS. Ad. 30058.
[2] St. Amand, Paris, *Bibl. Nat.*, MS. lat. 2291.
[4] Soissons?, Paris, *Bibl. Nat.*, MS. lat 12051.
[5] Utrecht, Brit. Mus., MS. Ad. 18955.
[6] St. Thierry, Rheims, MS. 213, supplement.
[7] The missal was written in England sometime between 1016 and 1051.
[8] *Vitellius*, Cotton MS. *Vital.* A 18.
[9] Wickham Legg, liturg. introduct., *Westminster Missal*, fasc. III, *Henry Bradshaw Society*, vol. XII (1896), p. 1418.
[10] St. Alban's MS., Bodl. Lib., Oxford, MS. Rawl. liturg., c. 1.

Wiltshire diocese. The sacramentaries that have come down to us from Anglo-Saxon times are, without exception, Gregorian, whereas the missals of the Sarum group are post-Conquest. There is little doubt that there was a liturgical reorganisation in England during the first half-century of Norman rule, and the various uses would in all probability have borrowed something from the continental missals. There seems, however, no reason to suppose that any one Norman use was accepted whole and entire, and it is difficult to determine the Church, if any, from which prayers were borrowed. 'When the precise relation of any one of the chief Norman rites to our English uses has been fixed', says Edmund Bishop, 'a considerable step will have been taken towards clearing up the obscurity in which the whole subject of the origins of these latter is involved.'[1] The task is the more perplexing in that the liturgy of each particular Church was not stereotyped in the Middle Ages; each use was from time to time borrowing from its neighbours, adding, retrenching, changing.[1]

It is thus impossible to determine the origin of the book on which the so-called Sarum group of missals depends. No member of this family exists in a manuscript earlier than the middle of the 12th century, although books of the kind were extremely widespread. 'When the Sarum use became standard throughout the British Isles, many churches, instead of buying a complete set of new books, appear to have contented themselves with buying the Ordinal which gives no cues for secrets and postcommunions: for there are a whole series of highly aberrant Sarum missals which must be the result of combining the rubric of the Ordinal with the sacramentary of churches other than Salisbury. All, however, belong to the same general group.'[2]

The resemblances in Sarum and Rouen, as shown, for example, in John of Avranches (*De Officiis Ecclesiasticis*), are no more than items whch formed a part of the substructure of all the late mediaeval uses. The tract of John of Avranches is a recension or adaptation for Rouen of the *Ordines Romani*, which as a book

---

[1] Bishop, *op. cit.*, XII, p. 300.
[2] Hohler, *Type of Sacramentary used by St. Boniface*, p. 90.

passed away as Germanism and Romanesque gave place in the 12th century to Frenchified fashions and Gothic architecture.[1]

Bayeux, whose *ordinarium* has been printed, shows equally that its Church was not the source from which Salisbury derived its use. There are, however, some similar features in Bayeux and Sarum, as for instance the ceremony of the removal of the Blessed Sacrament from the sepulchre before matins on Easter Day.[2] A more vital similarity between Sarum and a Norman book is found in the secret for the Second Sunday after Epiphany, which begins *Ut tibi grata*. The prayer, which is one of the distinctive features of the St. Amand family, has been described by Dr. Wickham Legg as 'one of the most constant peculiarities of the Sarum use that I have yet found'.[3] It appears in England only in missals *secundum usum Sarum*, but not in all of them, and the related books of Westminster, Tewkesbury, etc., all have *Placare*. Neither is it to be found in any of the books collated by Wickham Legg for his Westminster missal: printed missals of Rouen, Bayeux and Coutances. It is absent also from those of Jumièges, St. Wandrille, Mont St. Michel, St. Martin de Troarn and St. Evroult; while on the evidence of the missals of St. Augustine's Canterbury and Durham, it is pretty certain that *Ut tibi grata* was not found at Bec.

There is, however, one Norman missal in which it appears: Fécamp, where we find it in both the 12th-century sacramentary [4] and the 14th-century missal.[5] Fécamp has also *Sacris muneribus* as the secret (*alia*) for the Third Sunday after Pentecost, which occurs in the Westminster, St. Albans and Abingdon books, as well as in the Newminster missal at Le Havre. This is interesting, but

---

[1] Bishop, *op. cit.*, XII, p. 277.

[2] *Ordinaire et Coutumier de l'Eglise Cathédrale de Bayeux* (*Bibl. Lit.*, t. VIII), edit. Ulysse Chevalier, p. 139 (end of the 13th century). Cf. *Breviarium ad usum insignis Ecclesiae Sarum*, fasc. I, edit. Proctor and Wordsworth (Cambridge, 1882), col. dcccvii. A later ordinal of Bayeux (early 14th century) directs the clergy and people to be blessed with the Sacrament in the form of a cross: *et cum ea clero et populo in modum crucis benedicit more consueto.*

[3] Wickham Legg, *The Sarum Missal edited from three early manuscripts* (Oxford, 1916), pref., p. XIV.

[4] Fécamp Sacramentary (12th century), fo. 17v, Rouen, *Bibl. Municip.*, MS. 290 (A 313).

[5] Fécamp Missal, fo. 22v, Rouen, *Bibl. Municip.*, MS. 292 (Y 181).

it is impossible to say whether there was any direct relationship between Sarum and Fécamp. It is, for instance, perfectly possible that Sarum had *Placare* as the secret for the Second Sunday after Epiphany (like St. Albans, etc.) during the 12th century.[1] Several of the Sarum postcommunions are not found in any other English use, although they are met with in the Roman sacramentaries.

The prayers for vesting, given in the Sarum MS. missals, are very similar to those in the French *ordines missae*, from which it may be perhaps inferred that the Norman borrowings were reduced later, and interpolations from other sources added.

However, when all is said and done, and in spite of what has been discovered in the way of similarities with other uses, it must be confessed that with our present knowledge it is quite impossible to identify any specific 'ancestor' for the Sarum use. Its essential framework is indeed in the same line of development as Lanfranc's statutes for Canterbury, the Ecclesiastical Offices of John of Avranches and ultimately, perhaps, the *Ordines Romani*. In this skeleton, St. Osmund may possibly have had a hand, but he was far from producing the liturgy that we know today as Sarum. Edmund Bishop is probably correct when he says: 'Is not "Sarum", the missal, simply, and no more than, a good sort of thirteenth-century compilation, and had not St. Edmund of Canterbury (of Abingdon, that is) a hand in it?[2] Whenever I read the book this comes to me as patent enough on the surface; and it is long indeed that it has been a wonder to me that our experts can imagine it to be an eleventh-century book and a production of St. Osmund's episcopate.'[3]

The 13th-century Dominican rite has many points in common with Sarum.

It has been pointed out also that 'Haymo's style is typically English and fundamentally identical with that of the Sarum Ordinal of the early 13th century'.[4] The Haymo in question was

---

[1] Mr. Christopher Hohler in a letter to the author (17 December 1955).

[2] St. Edmund in *c.* 1222 accepted a canonry at Salisbury, with the office of treasurer. He received the prebend of Calne, and donated a quarter of his income to the building fund.

[3] Bishop, *op. cit.*, p. 300, n. 1.

[4] Van Dijk, *Sacris Erudiri* (1954), p. 136.

the great English Franciscan Haymo of Faversham (*ob. c.* 1243), whom Pope Gregory IX employed to revise the breviary of the Roman Curia.

MISSALS OF THE SARUM USE

English mediaeval service-books are scarce, for, as we have seen, the votaries of the new religion ordered them to be 'defaced, abolished and utterly gone'.

Until the latter part of the 13th century, missals and other liturgical books were for the most part written in monastic scriptoria, but by the time of Edward I (1272–1307) we find the monks hiring scribes instead of doing the writing themselves. They were unable to deal with the products of the new learning in the Universities and the closely written books which are so typical of the century.[1]

There are, however, signs, at least in the first half of the 13th century, that some of the monastic scriptoria, like that of Winchester or St. Albans, continued to be active, but very little is known about the scriptoria of the secular cathedrals, and the catalogues of their libraries do not furnish proof whether these books were produced there or acquired elsewhere.[2]

The Ordinary of the Mass in the three earliest existing MSS. is not identical with that in the printed missals, and the rubrics are considerably fewer in number.

The earliest form of Sarum rubric known is Wickham-Legg's MS. A (not C, the basis of his text, which is a mid-century revision probably), since this reappears in the Gradual edited by Frere for the Plainsong Society, and the Gradual is liturgically earlier than the adoption at Salisbury of the feast of St. Wulstsan (*c.* 1220).[3]

The Crawford Missal, which owes its name to a former owner, the Earl of Crawford and Balcarres, has a note: *Memoriale Henrici de Cicestria Canonici Exon. precis LXs.*[4] The end of the

---

[1] N. R. Ker, *Mediaeval MSS. from Norwich Cathedral Priory, Camb. Biograph. Soc. Trans.* I (1949), 8.

[2] Peter Brieger, *English Art, 1216–1317.* Oxford, 1957.

[3] St. Wulfstan, not St. Malo, as Dr. Frere absent-mindedly writes.

[4] Henry of Chichester was precentor of Crediton, and resigned in 1264.

Ordo Missae is concluded with the words: *Sicque completur officium misse secundum usum Sarum.* Some intimation as to the date of the MS. is given in the calendar on September 15: *Festivitas reliquiarum.* The Feast of Relics was assigned to this date by Bishop Jocelin in *c.* 1150,[1] and, by reason of its clashing with the Octave of the Nativity of the Blessed Virgin, moved to the Sunday after the Translation of St. Thomas of Canterbury (7 July) in 1319.[2] The MS. was written therefore between these two dates. There is no mention of the feast of Corpus Christi, and the Conception of the Blessed Virgin is given as a feast of nine lessons.

The missal in the Arsenal Library, Paris, dates from about the end of the 13th century, and the exemplar in the Library of the University of Bologna is probably of the first quarter of the 14th century. *Octava S. Mariae* takes the place of the Feast of Relics on 15 September in the Bologna missal.

These early missals bear witness to the original practice of breaking the Host at the word *fregit* in the canon: *Hic faciat (facit) signum fractionis dicendo: fregit.*[3] The practice of elevating the Host, *ut videatur ab omnibus*, is well developed, but not so the chalice, which is only raised *contra pectus*.[4] The printed editions of the missal give the rubric in respect to the chalice: *usque ad pectus vel ultra caput.*

The *Veni Creator* is said at the beginning of Mass in the Crawford and Arsenal MSS., and while vesting according to the printed books. Prayers for each vestment are given in the Bologna and Morris missals; the *Veni Creator* is postponed until the offertory. In the Crawford missal, the vesting prayers have been added in a very late hand (?15th century) in a vacant space at the bottom of the page.

The Morris missal, which is of the early 14th century, is somewhat similar, especially in its first part, to the French *Ordines Missae*, and the several prayers to be said at the washing of the

---

[1] W. H. Rich Jones, *Vetus Registrum Sarisberiense, Rolls Series* (1883), vol. I, p. 227.

[2] E. A. Dayman and W. H. Rich Jones, *Statuta et Consuetudines Ecclesiae Cathedralis Sarisberiensis* (Bath, 1883), p. 68.

[3] *Sarum Ordin.*, 13th century (Crawford missal), edit. Wickham Legg, *Tracts on the Mass.* H.B.S., vol. XXVII (1904), p. 223.

[4] *Ibid.*, p. 224.

hands and vesting resemble those in the French missals.[1] The
secret for St. Thomas of Canterbury is *Munera tibi*, as we find in
the 14th-century Westminster missal, not *Salutaris* as in the
printed Sarum text. Variations from the usual Sarum collects
occur also in the secrets for Whitsun Tuesday and Wednesday,
and in the postcommunion for the following Friday. The MS. has
illuminations of the East Anglian School, and it is of interest to
note that many of the best existing Sarum MSS. emanated from
the diocese of Norwich.

The *editio princeps* of Sarum missals was printed at Paris in
1487. The Bodleian Library, Oxford, has a rubricated missal,
printed at Basle by Michael Wenssler, *c.* 1489: from MS. additions
to this copy it appears that it was used in the parish church of
South Littleton near Evesham in Worcestershire.[2] A fragment of
a missal printed at Rouen in 1492 (*Missale secundum usum
ecclesie sarisburien*) is found in the same library: the missing folios
may be gauged by collating the MS. with one similarly printed at
Rouen in 1510. Sarum missals appeared from the printing press
in London in 1498 (Winkin de Worde) and 1501 (Richard
Pynson). The last edition, as we have seen, was produced in
1557.

A number of Sarum books for use in Scottish dioceses have
been preserved. The Lesmahagow Missal of the early 13th century, with a special Mass for St. Machutus (15 November), shows
a curious mixture of English and Scottish local feasts, pointing to
an early period in the adaptation of the Sarum use in Scotland.
A similar feature is noticeable in the Blantyre Psalter (13th century), now in the Chapter Library at Durham. A text similar to
the Sarum use is found also in the eight leaves of a 13th-century
missal from Jedburgh Abbey (Austin Canons), now in the
National Library of Scotland. Three Sarum missal-fragments
and one of a Sarum breviary, all of the 15th century, are the sole
survivors of the mediaeval service-books of the cathedral church
of Glasgow. What became of the 'XVI buikis or thareby of musik

---

[1] The Feast of Relics is on 15 September. The Morris missal is now in New York:
Pierpont Morgan MS. 9.
[2] Bodl. Lib., Oxford, Gough missal 33.

of sangis and messis', which had found their way to the library of the University by 1582?[1]

The Sarum missal, written by James Sibbald in 1491 for use at Arbuthnott, has been previously mentioned. Two interesting books from Aberdeen date from the time of Bishop Elphinstone's reform. The one, a missal for the church of St. Nicholas, was printed at Rouen in 1506, and shows the calendar used in the diocese prior to the reform: [2] the other, a breviary which appeared in 1510, gives Bishop Elphinstone's attempt at systematising the Scottish adaptation of the Sarum use.[3] The Rothiemay Sarum missal was printed at Paris in 1523.[4]

COLOUR SEQUENCE

The Sarum colour sequence was ill-defined, but, as in the Dominican rite, the most precious vestments were worn on solemnities, irrespective of colour. Otherwise we find white, red, green and yellow, with black for the dead. In the later centuries, purple (violet) and blue were very generally added. Yellow was prescribed for confessors, and white for the Blessed Virgin. Blue, which had been introduced from the Continent, was no more than a substitute for purple. The colour for Passiontide, including Good Friday, was red, as we find today in the Ambrosian rite and for the blessing and procession of palms in the new order of the Roman rite. A striking peculiarity of Sarum usage was the use of white vestments in Lent, but a red cope was worn at the blessing of the ashes. Pictures and statues were veiled in white, not purple, and from the beginning of Lent until Easter Sunday morning.

Neither in the Sarum ordinal nor apparently in either version of the customary is there any clear indication as to the Advent colour.[5]

The colour sequences of Sarum, Lichfield and Wells are obviously closely connected: the two latter being derived from the

---

[1] McRoberts, *op. cit.*, p. 8.
[2] The missal of St. Nicholas Aberdeen is preserved in Blairs College.
[3] The Aberdeen Breviary is in the National Library of Scotland.
[4] Rothiemay Sarum Missal, St. Andrews University Library.
[5] W. St. John Hope and C. F. Atchley, *English Liturgical Colours* (London, 1918), p. 38.

former, with a few additions and an omission. The same phrases
are used, as will be seen by a study of the Latin texts, and in
the same order. Nevertheless, though all have the same framework, the details are local, showing that already small variations
in the colour use had begun.[1]

Yet 'there is abundant evidence that, widespread as was the
Sarum missal, the average parish church made no attempt to
follow the few rules for colours that are given in it.' [2]

ORNAMENTS OF THE MINISTERS

A rubric in the Sarum ordinal says: 'Throughout Advent and
from Septuagesima to Maundy Thursday let the deacon and subdeacon be vested in chasubles at Mass, except on Saints' days, for
then they ought to wear dalmatics and tunicles; and except on
ember-fasts and vigils on which they ought only to be in albes,
save Whitsun embertide, for then they use dalmatics and tunicles.
For the rest of the year let them use dalmatics and tunicles'.[3] The
same custom prevailed at Wells and Exeter; and a similar one at
York and Hereford.

The destruction of vestments at the Reformation was thorough
and systematic, and comparatively little has survived. A chasuble
in the Victoria and Albert Museum, London, must date from the
late 1260s or early 1270s, since a shield with arms on its back connects it with Edmund of Cornwall and his wife Margaret de
Clare.[4]

English embroidery, known as *Opus Anglicanum*, was in high
repute, not only in England, but also on the Continent. It is indeed thanks to the work sent abroad that we know of the quality
and richness of the work. Examples before 1250 are very rare.
Matthew Paris tells us that Pope Innocent IV (1243–54) wrote to
all the Cistercian abbots in England that they might send him
embroideries in gold.[5] The papal interest was maintained by his
successors, since in a Vatican inventory of 1293 the *Opus Angli-*

---

[1] W. St. John and C. F. Atchley, *op. cit.*, p. 131.
[2] F. C. Eeles, *Holyrood Ordinale*, introduct., p. xc. Edinburgh, 1914.
[3] W. H. Frere, *The Use of Sarum*, vol. II, *Ordinal and Tonal* (Cambridge, 1901), p. 149.
[4] Brieger, *op. cit.*, chap. XII, p. 210.
[5] Matthew Paris, *Chronica Majora*, 1246, IV; *Rolls Series*, LVII (1877), p. 546.

canum is mentioned no less than 113 times. The highest excellence of this 13th-century work may be admired today in the Syon cope in the Victoria and Albert Museum, London, and the cope sent by Pope Nicholas IV (1288–99) to the cathedral of Ascoli Piceno.

LITURGICAL YEAR

Sarum customs, at least in the centuries preceding the Reformation, included elaborate ceremonial observances on the three days after Christmas: feast of deacons on St. Stephen (26 December), feast of priests on St. John (27 December) and feast of children on Holy Innocents (28 December). Much also was made of the traditional rehearsing of the twofold Genealogy of our Lord: on Christmas Day the Genealogy according to St. Matthew, and on the Epiphany that according to St. Luke.

The suppression of the Alleluia from Septuagesima until Easter was dramatised by a chorister, who, representing the Alleluia, was whipped out of the cathedral church.

During the season of Lent, a great veil was hung before the sanctuary, concealing the altar from the rest of the church.[1] It was divided and drawn aside at the words in the Passion: 'And the veil of the temple was rent in the midst.'

An imposing Palm Sunday procession moved to a chapel or tent some distance from the church, whither the Blessed Sacrament was conveyed more or less privately. Then, in the return procession, the Eucharist was borne in a feretory on the shoulders of two priests. This *Corps Saint* procession, as it was called at Rouen until the end of the 18th century, formed no part of the original rite, but, by the close of the 13th century, some of the churches that had adopted the Sarum use borrowed this ceremony. The exact date of its acceptance at Salisbury is unknown, but from whatever quarter it was taken, it was clearly not from Hereford, which had received it from Rouen. Its introduction was a symptom of the increasing prominence given in England, and

---

[1] The lenten veil is still prescribed in the Premonstratensian Order, as well as in the rite of Braga. The General Chapter of 1958 abolished its use in Cistercian churches.

elsewhere, to the cultus of the Blessed Sacrament. This may be seen in the ceremony of adoration at the first station, which was substantially the same as at Rouen and Hereford. Then again, when the procession went into the cathedral, it passed underneath the Blessed Sacrament held aloft in the doorway, as the responsary *Ingrediente Domino* was sung. The early Sarum MS. in the University Library at Bologna has a rubric which shows that originally relics, and not the Blessed Sacrament, were carried in the procession: *Tunc intrent in ecclesiam sub capsula reliquiarum ex transverso ostii elevata, cantando* . . . Later usage prescribed that the Blessed Sacrament should be taken to the temporary chapel, after the procession had left the church, by two clerks with cross, lantern and two banners, and that it should come into sight as the words *Benedictus qui venit*, etc., were being recited in the gospel. The fourth and last station before the great cross, with *Ave Rex noster*, was similar in character to the usages at Hereford and Rouen.

The office of tenebrae was almost identical with the actual use of the Dominicans and Carmelites. The herse had twenty-four candles, not fifteen, as in the Roman rite.

Three hosts were consecrated on Holy Thursday:[1] the third was placed in a sepulchre, and on Good Friday an unveiled crucifix was added. The 'Easter sepulchre' was often a permanent stone structure, recalling in shape and decoration the altar tombs of the period. The return of the Eucharist and cross to the high altar on Easter Sunday morning was a solemn occasion. The Blessed Sacrament was restored to the customary place of reservation: a pyx, frequently in the form of a dove, hanging over the altar, or an aumbry, generally in the north wall of the sanctuary.

The liturgy on Holy Saturday was very similar to what we find in our missal, but two litanies were sung before the blessing of the font, while a third preceded the Mass. This third litany was *Rex sanctorum angelorum* in the Sarum use: a form common in Germany and known even in Italy, but not found in any other English missal.

A visit to the font was made during the second vespers of

---

[1] Cf. Rite of Braga.

Easter, as is customary today in Carmelite, Premonstratensian and some other churches.

Salisbury followed the Roman calendar, but with a multiplicity of local feasts. Among the variants, we find the Apparition of St. Michael at Mont St. Michel in Normandy (16 October), in place of the Apparition at Monte Gargano in Apulia (8 May); SS. Crispin and Crispinian instead of SS. Chrysanthus and Daria (25 October); and the Most Sweet Name of Jesus on 7 August.

The feast of the Holy Name was a *novum festum* in the 15th century, but it appeared as a votive Mass long before it was in the *sanctorale*.

The cult of St. Anne was popular in the 14th century, and the feast was prescribed for the Universal Church in the bull *Splendor paternae gloriae* of Urban VI, dated 21 June 1381. It was, however, no more than the recognition of an existing devotion, and the feast is found in fourteen English calendars of the 14th century, more than half of which date from before 1340. A chapel of St. Anne existed at Evesham before 1229.

The Feast of Relics was first observed at Sarum on a date which is unknown, but it was transferred by Bishop Jocelin (1142–84) to 15 September.[1] In 1243/4 Pope Innocent IV gave an octave to the Nativity of the Blessed Virgin, which was prescribed in England in 1252. The octave day thus clashed with the feast of relics, so that the latter solemnity was once again transferred, and in 1319 it was fixed for the Sunday following the Translation of St. Thomas of Canterbury (7 July).[2]

The classification of feasts in the Sarum use was more complicated than in the modern Roman rite. 'Pica' or 'Pie', as we have seen, was the name given to the book of rules for finding out the Office or Mass that was to be said on any given day.

Feasts were either double or simple. Double feasts were subdivided into principal, major, minor and inferior. Christmas, Epiphany and the Assumption were the only principal double feasts that were immovable: Easter, Pentecost, Ascension, Patronal and Dedication, movable.

---

[1] Frere, *Use of Sarum*, II, XX, n. 2.
[2] The cathedral church of Christ Church in Dublin observed the feast of relics on 31 July.

Major double feasts comprised the Purification, Nativity of our Lady, All Saints and St. George (after 1413).

Minor doubles were the Annunciation, Nativity of St. John Baptist and the Conception of the Blessed Virgin.

Inferior doubles: SS. James, Bartholomew, Matthew, Simon and Jude, Andrew and Thomas.

The Commemoration of All Souls: *quasi duplex festum secundum Sarum*. Some of the saints were accorded no more than a memorial. Days within octaves ranked as simples.

The order of the collects, epistles and gospels was not identical with that of the Pian missal.

Sarum had Sundays after Trinity, not Pentecost, and we find some slight inversion of order. The Second Sunday in Lent had its own proper gospel (*Matt.* XV, 21), not that of the Transfiguration, now repeated from the preceding Sunday; while the gospel for the Sunday next before Advent was not the Last Judgment, but the entry of our Lord into Jerusalem on Palm Sunday.

The Sarum gospels for the Second, Third and Fourth Sundays in Advent are in the Roman missal those for the First, Second and Third Sundays.

Ceremonial

The elaborate splendour of Sarum ceremonial, as carried out in the cathedral church in the centuries immediately preceding the Reformation, contrasted vividly with the comparative simplicity of the practice of the Roman Church.

Three, five or even seven deacons and subdeacons, two or more thurifers, and three crucifers figured on solemnities; while two or four priests in copes (*rectores chori*) acted as cantors. There was the censing of many altars, and even during the lessons at matins vested priests offered incense at the high altar. Processions were frequent, and those before High Mass on Sundays were especially magnificent.

On the altar itself there were rarely more than two lights, but on feasts there were many others, either standing on the ground or suspended from the roof.

A *flabellum* or liturgical fan, made of rich materials, was often waved over the *oblata* by the deacon during the canon.

Mass According to the Sarum Use

The text of the Mass, except where noted, is taken from the late printed missals.

The missal of 1492 directed the prayer *Deus qui de indignis dignos* to be recited in the sacristy before Mass.

The customary prayers, which were said while vesting, included *Veni Creator*, with versicle and response, and the prayer *Deus cui omne cor patet*. *Judica me Deus* and its antiphon (*Introibo*) were sometimes said going to the altar, followed by *Kyrie eleison*, *Pater noster* and *Ave Maria*.

At a solemn Mass, the celebrant and his ministers went to the step of the altar during the *Gloria Patri* of the *officium* (introit), where the verse of the Psalm *Confitemini*[1] and a short *Confiteor* were recited:

Confiteor Deo, beatae Mariae, omnibus sanctis et vobis: quia peccavi nimis cogitatione, locutione, et opere mea culpa: precor sanctam Mariam, omnes sanctos Dei, et vos orare pro me.

Misereatur,[2] *Absolutionem*[3] and two versicles and responses followed.[4] Then, if it was a solemn Mass, the celebrant gave the *pax* to the assistant ministers, with the formula: *Habete osculum pacis et dilectionis: ut apti sitis sacrosancto altari ad perficiendum officia divina.* A rubric says: *Et hoc semper observetur per totum annum: nisi tantum in missis peo defunctis et in tribus proximis feriis ante Pascha. His itaque peractis: ceroferarii candelabra cum cereis ad gradum altaris dimittunt.* A variant of the formula is given in missals of the 13th (Crawford)[5] and 14th (Morris)[6]

---

[1] *Confitemini Domino quoniam bonus. Quoniam in saeculum misericordia ejus.* Cf. Dominican rite.

[2] *Misereatur vestri omnipotens Deus, et dimittat vobis omnia peccata vestra, liberet vos ab omni malo, conservet et confirmet in bono, et ad vitam perducat aeternam.*

[3] *Absolutionem et remissionem omnium peccatorum vestrorum, spatium verae penitentiae et emendationem vitae, gratiam et consolationem sancti Spiritus, tribuat vobis omnipotens et misericors Dominus.*

[4] *Adjutorium nostrum (Qui fecit); Sit nomen (Ex hoc nunc).*

[5] *Sarum Ordinary of the Thirteenth Century, Tracts on the Mass,* edit. J. Wickham Legg, Henry Bradshaw Society, vol. XXVII, p. 220. London, 1904.

[6] *Sarum Ordinary of the Fourteenth Century, ibid.,* p. 4.

centuries, which more or less corresponds with that which Maskell ascribed to the use of Bangor: *Habete pacis osculum ut apti sitis sacrosancti altaris domini ministerio*.[1] 'This ceremony', says Maskell, 'is peculiar in this place to the Sarum and Bangor Churches: nor is it easy to say from whence it was introduced.'[2] This assertion, however, has been shown by Dr. Wickham Legg to have no foundation in fact, since it is found in many of the *Ordines Romani*, Innocent III, the Churches of Siena, Stavelot, Vienne, Bayeux, and elsewhere.[3]

The prayer *Aufer a nobis* was said before the middle of the altar, after which, if the Mass was solemn, the priest signed himself at the words *In nomine Patris*, etc., and blessed the incense.

The altar was censed in the middle and at each corner, and the priest himself was censed.

Then, kissing the gospel-book (*textus*), he recited, if it was a private Mass, the *officium*, *Kyrie* and *Gloria in excelsis*. If, however, these chants were sung by a choir, the celebrant filled in the time by saying silently the so-called *Oratio sancti Augustini*[4] or some other *apologia*. The following rubric is found in the missal which was given by the prior of Worcester to the church of Bromsgrove in 1511: *Oratio sancti Augustini dicenda a sacerdote in missa dum canitur Officium et Kyrie et Gloria in excelsis et Credo in unum: vel tota dicitur ante Missam quod melius est*.[5] It would seem that the custom of the recitation by the celebrant of the parts sung by the choir had already made its appearance.

The *officium* was repeated, not only after the *Gloria Patri*, but also after the psalm-verse which precedes it.

On certain occasions, especially in Masses of the Blessed Virgin, the *Gloria in excelsis* was farced.

After the *officium* at High Mass, one of the taperers was directed

---

[1] Maskell, *op. cit.*, p. 14.

[2] *Ibid.*, p. 14, n. 15. The rite ascribed by Maskell as the 'rite of Bangor' is in point of fact Sarum.

[3] *Tracts on the Mass*, edit. J. Wickham Legg, p. 233, n.

[4] *Summe sacerdos et vere pontifex, Jesu Christe.* The prayer is found also in the 1512 missal.

[5] T. F. Simmons, *Lay Folks Mass Book* (London, 1879), introduct., pp. XXXV–XXXVI.

to bring up the matter for the Sacrifice: the other carried a dish and towel for the *lavabo*.

The deacon, as well as the priest, turned to the people at the salutation.

On Sundays and certain other days, the epistle was read from the screen: at other times from the choir step.

Sometimes during this lesson the chalice was taken into the sanctuary, and the corporals unfolded on the altar by an acolyte.

The gradual was sung from the step of the screen by two boys in surplices; while two cantors in silk copes, taken from a higher tier of seats, chanted the *alleluia*.[1] The subdeacon, in the meanwhile, washed his hands and prepared the *oblata*. The water was blessed by the priest sitting in the sedilia. A sequence followed, if it was prescribed for the day.

The deacon, before reading the gospel, censed the middle of the altar, but the book was not censed (*numquam thurificetur.*) A blessing was given with the formula: *Dominus sit in corde tuo et ore tuo ad pronuntiandum sanctum evangelium Dei. In nomine patris, etc.* The deacon in the gospel procession was directed to carry the book *super sinistram manum*.[2] If the epistle had been read from the screen, it was also for the gospel.

The creed, when ordered, followed.

The deacon, after the *offertorium*, brought the vessels to the priest, and the bread and wine were offered together with a single prayer: *Suscipe sancta Trinitas, hanc oblationem quam ego indignus peccator offero in honore tuo et beatae Mariae, et omnium sanctorum tuorum, pro peccatis et offensionibus meis: pro salute vivorum et requie omnium fidelium defunctorum. In nomine Patris, et Filii, et Spiritus Sancti acceptum sit omnipotenti Deo hoc sacrificium novum.*[3]

An alternative and longer prayer is given in the missal, which has a marked resemblance to the prayer before the *Orate fratres* in the Roman rite: *Suscipe sancta Trinitas, hanc oblationem.* Then,

---

[1] The occupants of the various seats and stalls in the choir at Salisbury are detailed in the consuetudinary.

[2] Cf. Dominican rite.

[3] Maskell omits the words *acceptum . . . novum. Op. cit.*, p. 56.

placing the host before the chalice on the corporal, the celebrant kissed the paten, putting it partially under the corporal.

At a solemn Mass, the censing followed: *Thurificet sacrificium: videlicet ultra ter signum crucis faciens, et in circuitu et utraque parte calicis et sacrificii: deinde locum inter se et altare. Et dum thurificat dicat: Dirigatur Domine ad te oratio mea, sicut incensum in conspectu tuo.* The deacon censed the priest, and the sub-deacon gave him the gospel-book to kiss, while the deacon continued the censing, as he made a circuit of the altar. If there was a creed, an acolyte censed the choir.

While washing his hands, the priest said: *Munda me, Domine, ab inquinamento mentis et corporis: ut possim mundatus implere opus sanctum Domini.* Then, returning to the middle of the altar: *In spiritu humilitatis et in animo contrito suscipiamur, Domine, a te: et sic fiat sacrificium nostrum in conspectu tuo, ut a te suscipiatur hodie, et placeat tibi Domine Deus.*[1]

Bidding-prayers were said on Sundays in parish churches after the gospel and offertory, either before some altar or in a pulpit for the purpose (*ad hoc constituto*):[2] in cathedrals and collegiate churches they were said in the procession before High Mass. The Sarum manual variously describes them as 'the bedes on the Sunday', '*preces dominicales*', '*preces pro*' or '*in diebus dominicis*'.

The priest then kissed the altar, and signed himself, as he said: *In nomine Patris,* etc. Turning to the people, he asked for their prayers: *Orate fratres et sorores pro me: ut meum pariterque vestrum acceptum sit Domino Deo sacrificium.* The response was directed to be said *privatim* (*tacita voce*), although this can hardly have been originally the case: *Spiritus sancti gratia illuminet cor tuum et labia tua, et accipiat Dominus digne hoc sacrificium laudis de manibus tuis, pro peccatis et offensionibus nostris.*

Special formulas were provided for Masses for the dead: *Orate fratres pro fidelibus defunctis,* with the response: *Requiem eternam dona eis Domine, et lux perpetua luceat eis. Quam olim Abrahae promisisti et semini ejus.*[3]

---

[1] Cf. Prayer before the *lavabo* in the Roman Presanctified rite.
[2] *Processionale ad usum insignis Ecclesiae Sarisburiensis,* London, 1554, fo. 56.
[3] *Sarum Missal from three early MSS.,* edit. Wickham Legg (Oxford, 1916), p. 219.

The subdeacon held the paten in a veil (*offertorium, sudarium*) from the *Sursum corda* until the *Pater noster*.

The canon was the same as in our missal, apart from a memento of the King, and some few ceremonial variations.[1]

The Ordinary rubric, as Fr. van Dijk points out, is obviously related to that used by Haymo of Faversham (*ob.* 1243) in the standard Franciscan book. Which way the influence went is, however, not absolutely clear, as there is a shortage of documents illustrating the Sarum rubric of the canon before *c.* 1260.

A short rubric followed the word *fregit* in the recital of the Institution in the New Ordinal: *Hic tangat hostiam dicens*. It was probably borrowed from abroad, and the explanation, taken from the *Oculus sacerdotis*, or some such work, belongs to a rubric of the canon as incorporated in the manual. The 13th-century Crawford missal says: *Hic faciat signum fractionis dicendo: fregit.* There seems very little doubt that we have here a reminder of the time, before the Elevation of the Host, when the sacramental bread was broken at the word *fregit*. Some of the French missals go a step farther than those in England, and the Paris missal of 1489 says: *frangat modicum*. It would surely be very simple to change *frangat* into *tangat*. The memory of the fraction at the Consecration, however, passed into oblivion, and the Sarum missal of 1554 speaks of some 'silly fellows' (*fatui*) who understand it of breaking the bread, whereas the Church consecrates before breaking, and so does otherwise than Christ did—*sic aliter facit Ecclesia, quam Christus fecit.*

At the beginning of the *Pater noster*, the deacon received the paten from the subdeacon and held it aloft, uncovered, until the words *Da propitius pacem in diebus* in the embolism. The neo-Gallican missal of Paris (1738) refers to this practice as a *signum communionis*: that the people might know that the time of communicating was close at hand. We find a somewhat similar elevation of the paten prescribed in the early-14th-century ordinary of Bayeux, and in the actual use of the Premonstratensians the deacon is directed to raise the paten (uncovered) from the words *Sursum*

---

[1] e.g. profound inclination of the head and shoulders in place of a genuflection; raising of the arms in the form of a cross (*in modum crucis*) at *Unde et memores*.

corda till *Domino Deo nostro*, and again in the same manner at *Panem nostrum quotidianum* in the *Pater noster*.[1]

On receiving the paten, the priest kissed it, placed it to his left and right eyes, and made the sign of the cross with it *ultra caput*. The fraction was made in the ordinary way, after which, if the Mass was pontifical, the bishop gave an elaborate form of blessing, which varied with the day, consisting of a number of phrases.

It was here also that the suffrages, ordered for some special purpose, were said: *ut psalmos et orationes pro pace, antequam dicatur 'Pax Domini', intra missas*.[2]

Pax Domini and *Agnus Dei* followed, after which the commixture took place, not before the *Agnus*, as in our Roman rite.[3] *Haec sacro + sancta commixtio corporis et sanguinis Domini nostri Jesu Christi, fiat mihi omnibusque sumentibus salus mentis et corporis, et ad vitam aeternam promerendam et capescendam praeparatio salutaris. Per.*

Then, before the kiss of peace, the following prayer was said: *Domine, sancte Pater, omnipotens aeterne Deus, da mihi hoc sacrosanctum corpus et sanguinem Filii tui Domini nostri Jesu Christi ita digne sumere ut merear per hoc remissionem omnium peccatorum meorum accipere et tuo Sancto Spiritu repleri; et pacem tuam habere; quia tu es Deus solus et praeter te non est alius, cujus regnum et imperium gloriosum sine fine permanet in saecula saeculorum. Amen.* The celebrant kissed the right side of the corporal, the bowl of the chalice, and, finally, the deacon, saying: *Pax tibi et Ecclesiae Dei*, to which the response *Et cum spiritu tuo* was given.

Holding the Host in his two hands, the priest said the following communion prayers:

Deus Pater, fons et origo totius bonitatis, qui ductus misericordia Unigenitum tuum pro nobis ad infima mundi descendere et carnem sumere voluisti, quam ego indignus hic in manibus meis teneo.

Te adoro, te glorifico, te tota mentis ac cordis intentione laudo et precor; ut nos famulos tuos non deseras, sed peccata nostra dimittas,

---

[1] *Ordin. Prem.*, 1739, p. 177; *Ordin. Prem.*, 1949, part I, cap. IX, art. VI, no. 381, p. 107; *ibid.*, no. 385, p. 109.

[2] Wilkins, *Concil.*, t. II, p. 222, for year 1296.

[3] Cf. Dominican rite.

quatenus tibi soli vivo ac vero Deo, puro corde et casto corpore, servire valeamus. Per.

The next prayer is found almost verbatim in our Roman Mass: *Domine Jesu Christi, Fili Dei vivi.* The expression *Salvator mundi,* which is in the Sarum liturgy before the doxology, has a Gallican flavour.

Corporis et sanguinis túi, Domine Jesu Christe, sacramentum, quod licet indignus accipio, non sit mihi judicio et condemnationi; sed tua prosit pietate corporis mei et animae saluti.

There is no *Domine non sum dignus*, and the words said by the celebrant at the moment of his Communion seem peculiar to Sarum: *Ave in aeternum, sanctissima caro Christi, mihi ante omnia et super omnia summa dulcedo. Corpus Domini nostri Jesu Christi sit mihi peccatori via et vita. In nom + ine Patris, et Filii, et Spiritus Sancti. Amen.*

Before receiving the precious Blood: *Ave in aeternum, coelestis potus, mihi ante omnia et super omnia summa dulcedo. Corpus et sanguis Domini nostri Jesu Christi prosint mihi peccatori ad remedium sempiternum in vitam aeternam. Amen. In nom + ine Patris,* etc.

Then, before taking the ablutions: *Gratias tibi ago, Domine, sancte Pater, omnipotens aeterne Deus, qui me refecisti de sacratissimo corpore et sanguine Filii tui Domini nostri Jesu Christi; et precor, ut hoc sacramentum salutis nostrae quod sumpsi indignus peccator, non veniat mihi ad judicium neque ad condemnationem pro meritis meis; sed ad profectum corporis mei et animae saluti in vitam aeternam.* A somewhat similar prayer is found in the old rite of the Benedictines of the Congregation of Tibães in Portugal, directed to be said after the ablutions.[1]

The Sarum method of ablutions is somewhat different from our own. For the first ablution, the subdeacon [2] ministers wine and water, and the celebrant may rinse his fingers. Then a prayer is said: *Quod ore sumpsimus, Domine, pura mente capiamius; et de munere temporali fiat nobis remedium sempiternum.* After this, the priest washes his fingers in the chalice with wine, and there is a

---

[1] *Ceremonial Monastico reformado da Congregacão de S. Bento de* Portugal, 1820.
[2] Deacon, missal of 1554.

second prayer: *Haec nos communio, Domine, purget a crimine et coelestis remedii faciat esse consortes*.[1] Then, having taken the ablutions, and laid the chalice on the paten to drain, he inclines before the altar, and says: *Adoremus crucis signaculum: per quod salutis sumpsimus sacramentum*. He washes his hands, while the deacon folds the corporals, after which the minister raises the chalice to the lips of the priest, in case any drop of liquid should remain. The sacred ministers say the *communio* together. The missal of 1554 prescribes a third ablution of water, as we find in the use of Hereford, and also in the Arbuthnott missal (1491).[2] There is also in the same book a somewhat different and more extensive rubric: When the priest has said the prayer: *Haec nos, Domine, communio*, the deacon pours water into the chalice, which the priest consumes. Then, going to the middle of the altar, he places the chalice on the paten to drain, and says: *Gratias . . . corpore et sanguine Domini nostri Jesu Christi. Te precor . . . corporis mei et animae meae salutem in vitam aeternam*. Again at the corner of the altar he washes his hands, assisted by the subdeacon, while the deacon folds the corporals. The book is moved by the subdeacon, who receives from the deacon the chalice lying on the paten. Then, when the chalice has been placed to the lips of the celebrant by the deacon, an acolyte, during the *communio*, removes the corporals, *offertorium* (veil) and chalice.

This would seem to have been the later Sarum practice, as represented by the printed missals, but we find considerable variation in the MSS., in which the ceremony of the ablutions is simpler. If the celebrant was required to say a second Mass, the ablutions were omitted, and the sacred vessels were placed *in sacrario*.

Postcommunions, dismissal and *Placeat* followed, but there was no blessing. Many of the missals described the *Placeat* as *post missam*, and *Micrologus* (c. 1100) says: *Finita Missa, dicit, Placeat tibi, Sancta Trinitas*.[3]

---

[1] *Participes*, missal of 1554.

[2] The missal was written by James Sibbald, vicar of Arbuthnot in the diocese of St. Andrews (*ob.* 1507).

[3] *Microl.*, cap. XXIII; Hittorp, *De Divinis Catholicae Ecclesiae Officiis* (Paris, 1610), col. 746.

The priest, having said the *Placeat*, signed himself (*In nomine Patris*, etc.), and returned to the sacristy, in reciting the gospel *In principio*.

VARIABLES IN MASS ACCORDING TO THE SARUM USE

No more than seven collects were permitted. The Norman churches usually had the Gregorian distribution of collects without any of the Sarum characteristics.[1]

The lesson from Isaias for the Octave of the Epiphany is a relic of the Old-Latin translation, and has been taken from the Septuagint, not the Hebrew: *Domine Deus meus honorificabo te*. The Sarum sequences in Advent are very similar to those in other English and Norman uses, and those for Christmas and Epiphany are found in almost every English missal. In Easter week, however, there is a great variation, and for the Thursday nearly every use has a different sequence from its fellows.

An ancient feature has been retained in the last three weeks of Lent and at certain other times: versicles are appended to the *offertorium* to be sung, it would seem, as the time was prolonged during which the faithful made their offerings.

Some of the Sarum secrets and postcommunions are found in the Gregorian sacramentary, but on a different day; while others again are in the Gelasian and Leonine sacramentaries. There is, however, a somewhat large residuum, almost a third, which cannot be found in any Roman sacramentary. From the First Sunday in Advent until Easter there are more than fifty of these varying secrets and postcommunions: from Easter to Advent more than twenty.[2] Whence do these secrets and postcommunions come? They are not in any of the Roman sacramentaries, but neither are they to be found in any one Norman missal. One or two of the Sarum texts are in the 12th-century Rouen book, as, for example, the secret for Ember Saturday in Advent: *Super has fidelium hostias*, whereas the printed Rouen missal of 1499 gives *Ecclesiae*

---

[1] Liturg. introduct., Wickham Legg, *Westminster Missal*, fasc. III, *Henry Bradshaw Society*, vol. XII (1897), p. 1420.

[2] e.g. the secret on Ember Friday in Advent in the Sarum book and the other missals of the same group is *Sacrificiis quaesumus*; whereas the late 13th century Arsenal (Sarum) missal follows the Gregorian sacramentary: *Muneribus nostris*.

tuae, Domine, in common with Hereford, Durham, St. Augustine's Canterbury, Whitby, Bayeux, Coutances and Nidaros (1519). York follows the Gregorian sacramentary with *Sacrificiis praesentibus.* The Sarum secret for the Holy Innocents is found in both Rouen missals: *Adesto Domine muneribus.*

The Sarum peculiarity of *Ut tibi grata* as the secret for the Second Sunday after Epiphany, which is found at Fécamp in a 12th-century sacramentary and a 14th-century missal, as well as in the books of the St. Amand family, has been already considered.

The Coutances missal affords no resemblance to Sarum, and we find none of the characteristic Salisbury prayers in either Bayeux or Evreux.

The course of the Sarum group of missals, as we have seen, is exceedingly obscure.

The pontifical benedictions, which varied according to the occasion, were preceded by the diaconal monition: *Humiliate vos ad benedictionem,* to which the choir responded *Deo gratias.*

The following rubric is found in the Sarum missal of 1554: *Deinde si episcopus celebraverit, diaconus ad populum conversus baculum episcopi in dextera tenens, curvatura baculi ad se conversa, dicat hoc modo . . . Postea, eucharistia super patenam reposita, episcopus super populum faciat benedictionem. Post benedictionem sequatur Et cum spiritu tuo, tribus vicibus, cum hac additione, sempiternam tertia vice.*

The benedictional of John Peckham, archbishop of Canterbury (1279–92), was probably adopted, after it had been compiled (1280–90), by Salisbury, as it was by Anian, bishop of Bangor (1267–1305). A similar collection is found in the Exeter pontifical of Edmund Lacy (1420–58).

Origins of the York Rite

Christianity came to York at an early date, and a bishop assisted at the council of Arles in 314: *Eborius episcopus de Civitate Eboracensis, provincia Britannia.*[1] There was, however, no continuity

---

[1] Labbe, *op. cit.,* t. I, col. 1430.

with the later archbishops, and, after the withdrawal of the Romans, the country relapsed into paganism. St. Paulinus, who had been one of the monks sent to join St. Augustine in Kent (601), became archbishop of York in 625, and, two years later, baptised the king, Edwin. A church dedicated to St. Peter, on the site of the present minster, was established in the same year. The pallium was given to Paulinus in 631, but on the appearance of the pagan Mercians in 633, the archbishop fled to Kent, leaving the deacon James to minister to the Christians, and there was no primate until St. Wilfrid in 664.[1] The Roman mission ended somewhat ingloriously, but Northumbria was not to be left desolate, and the work was supplemented by a band of Celtic monks from Iona under the leadership of St. Aidan.[2] We learn that the brethren of the Church of York came to be known as *Colidaei* or Culdees, a name that they retained until the time of Henry I (1100–1135), when canons on the Norman model replaced the old arrangement.[3]

It was not until after the Norman Conquest that York attained complete independence of Canterbury. In 1188, the Scottish dioceses, with the exception of Whithorn (*Candida Casa*), were released from jurisdiction to York and made directly subject to the Holy See: in the 14th century the last of the Scottish sees severed its ecclesiastical ties with England. Man, together with Orkney, had been transferred to the province of Nidaros (Trondheim) in Norway in 1154.

We are not concerned with Orkney, which never had any connection with York, but Man was admitted to the province of York in 1458. Innocent IV in 1244 had approved the consecration of the bishops of Man by the archbishops of York, but with the consent of Nidaros.[4] The change of consecrator was doubtless on account of the dangerous sea passage to Norway.

The use of York lays no claim to a saint for its compiler, and

---

[1] The pallium was not granted again until it was given to Egbert in 732.
[2] Bede, *Hist. Eccles.*, III, 3.
[3] Raine, *Fasti Eboracenses*, t. I, p. 21; Simmons, *Lay Folks Mass Book* (London, 1879), p. 324.
[4] Munch, *Chronicle of Man and the Sudreys*, vol. II, append. XIX, pp. 309–10. *Manx Society*. Douglas, 1874.

there is no one individual to whom its origin may be ascribed. It belongs, as we have seen, to the Gregorian rather than to the Sarum group: a fact which may possibly afford some clue as to its first beginnings.

St. Paulinus (627) would have brought with him the Roman rite introduced into England by St. Augustine, but, as we know, his time in York was short-lived and the mission came to an untimely end. With the advent of the 'Scottish' missionaries from Iona, we can hardly doubt that the Celtic rite would have been introduced, even if it was augmented by Roman formulas.

The letter of Alcuin (*ob.* 804) to Eanbald II, archbishop of York (796– after 808), has been variously interpreted: *Presbyteri non despiciant Romanos discere ordines.*[1] And again: *Nunc quid non habes Romano more ordinatos libellos sacratorios abundanter? Habes quoque et veteris consuetudinis sufficienter sacramentaria majora . . . Aliquid voluissem tuam auctoritatem incepisse Romani ordinis in clero tuo, ut exempla a te sumantur, et ecclesiastica officia venerabiliter et laudabiliter vobiscum agantur.*[2]

Lingard, for example, says: 'Even at the close of the 8th century, the Scottish liturgy was in daily, though not exclusive, use in the Church of York.'[3] There is, however, no possible reason for thinking that Celtic usages had survived in this Northern city. Mr. Christopher Hohler considers that the letter in question implies no more than that Eanbald wished to do something about altering his use, and that Alcuin told him not to bother to do so.

On the other hand, there are those who think it possible that a Carolingian liturgy was introduced at this time. Alcuin, although an important figure at the Frankish court of Charlemagne, had not altogether relinquished his personal interest in the English cathedral church. He was indeed non-residentiary, but, in writing to excuse his absence from the election of an archbishop, he refers to the minster clergy as *familia nostra*. The editor of the *Lay Folks Mass Book* considers that the MS. of the York Mass, written *c.* 1425 and now in the library of York Minster,[4] not-

---

[1] Alcuin, *Epist. LVI ad Simeonem* (Eanbald).
[2] *Ibid., Epist.* LXV.
[3] Lingard, *Anglo-Saxon Church*, vol. I, p. 299.
[4] York Minster Lib., MS. XVI, A. 9.

withstanding some later and easily recognisable interpolations, was in the main the Gregorian Mass of the 8th century—*secundum ritum sacri palatii* which Charlemagne enforced in the churches of his Empire.[1] The expression *secundum ritum palatii* had been used by Leidrad, archbishop of Lyons, in his letter to the emperor.[2] If, however, such a hypothesis is correct, it refers to the essential framework of the liturgy, and it is evident that the Mass, as it has come down to us in the York books, has been considerably altered and enriched. It was inevitable that the Norman Conquest should have left its mark on the rite, and Rouen is considered to have been the source from which York borrowed, as agreement with that Church is found in points where its use differed from any English use.[3] The *Lay Folks Mass Book*, which was a translation from the French for the Church of York, contemplates a ritual founded on the usages of the cathedral church of Rouen.[3] Among the similarities existing between Rouen and York, it is pointed out that the rubric as to the vesting of the celebrant is translated almost word for word, and there is an identity of form of confession in the treatise with the earlier Rouen form, possibly in a point where the Rouen use appears to have been peculiar.[3]

Finally, the York use would have submitted to an enrichment of ceremonial in the 13th century, much as we find took place in other English churches.

The Augustinian breviary [4] and missal [5] of Guisborough show a considerable amount of Durham influence, and the former has also texts in common with York.[6]

It is possible, although far from certain, that the use of York was followed in some places in the diocese of Galloway, which until the year 1472 was a suffragan see of York. A page from a 14th-century antiphoner of the York use, discovered in the binding of a manuscript which was at Sweetheart Abbey

---

[1] Simmons, *op. cit.*, append. I, pp. 352–4.
[2] Coville, *Recherches sur l'hist. de Lyon, du Ve siècle au IXe siècle* (Paris, 1928), p. 284.
[3] Simmons, *op. cit.*, introduct., p. xxxv.
[4] Woolhampton, Douai College, Brev., 14th cent.
[5] Brit. Mus., MS. Add. 35286, Missal, 13th–15th cent.
[6] *Holyrood Ordinale*, edit. F. C. Eeles, introduct., pp. xxxiii–xxxiv.

(Cistercian) in the 15th century, is now in the University Library of Edinburgh.[1]

In addition to this, several pages of a 14th-century York breviary, found at Carnwath in Lanarkshire, were on view at the Scottish Exhibition at Glasgow in 1911.[2]

The attempt to extend the Sarum use to the province of York, traces of which are visible in a MS. missal (*c.* 1425) now in the library of Sidney Sussex College, Cambridge, failed in its purpose, and the absence of the proposed changes in the printed York missals is a witness to the sturdy independence of the Northern Church. Such agreement as exists between York and Sarum would seem to point to a borrowing from some common source rather than from the Church of Salisbury. The York rite appears to have 'kept itself to itself', and there is no direct evidence of its use outside the province. On the other hand, the collegiate churches of Chester-le-Street (1286) and Bishop Auckland (1292) were given the choice by their founder of following either the York or the Sarum use, and the option was confirmed by Thomas Langley, bishop of Durham, in 1428. The Augustinian canons of Hexham, also in the diocese of Durham, were recommended by the archbishop of York, William Merton, in 1323 to adopt *usum ecclesie nostre Ebor.*[3]

LITURGICAL BOOKS

York missals are exceedingly rare, and no more than some five or six complete copies are known to exist. A rubricated missal of the second half of the 14th century, formerly belonging to the church of St. Mary at Norton-Cuckney in Nottinghamshire, may be seen in the Bodleian Library, Oxford: the decoration and script are those of a cheap liturgical book, intended for a small and poor church. The 15th-century missal from Broughton-in-Amounderness, which until 1541 was in the archdeaconry of Richmond and diocese of York, although a part of Lancashire, is owned by Colonel Butler-Bowden of Pleasington Hall.

---

[1] C. R. Borland, *A Descriptive Catalogue of the Western Mediaeval Manuscripts in Edinburgh University Library* (Edinburgh, 1916), p. 159.

[2] *Official Historical Catalogue, Scottish Exhibition, Glasgow*, 1911, p. 1051, no. 4.

[3] *Priory of Hexham*, Surtees Society, I, append., p. lxix, no. xlix.

A comparison with the York missal edited by Henderson shows that the text is almost identical with that of the late mediaeval printed missal, except that the rubrics in the MS. are somewhat shorter. We may therefore consider that the text of the printed missals represents what had become uniform and stabilised for a considerable time.[1] The ordinary and canon are identical with the printed text, but the canon in the Broughton book has few rubrics. There is, however, a rubric prescribing the elevation of the Chalice, which seems to suggest that the ceremony had been recently introduced, especially as there is no corresponding rubric for the Host.[1] St. Sytha (27 April) is the sole addition to the calendar, although Masses for the Conversion of St. Paul, Feast of Relics and St. Andrew have been inserted in a late cursive hand: probably omitted by mistake. The name of St. Thomas of Canterbury has not been erased in the MS., but this has been done in the case of the collects *pro Papa*, while in the canon the original *Rege* has been crossed out and inserted in the place of the Pope.[2] The sequences at the end of the book are incomplete, and some folios are wanting. At the end of the *sanctorale*, the collect, secret and postcommunion from the Mass *pro speciali amico* have been added from the Sarum missal:[3] possibly after the gift of the Salisbury book already mentioned.

The earliest printed missal seems to have been that of 1509, a *missale pressum* produced at Rouen. Evidence for its existence is found in an inventory of 1520, in which it is catalogued as belonging to the chapel of St. Stephen in York Minster.[4] Editions of the York missal appeared at Rouen in 1516, 1517 and 1530, and at Paris in 1533. The British Museum has a fragment of the 1516 missal and a complete copy of that of 1533. The sixteen leaves of the former comprise the calendar, *sequentiae communes*, four additional Masses and the *Cautelae*. The 1517 edition has been followed in the Ordinary of the Mass given by Maskell.[5]

---

[1] Eeles, *On a 15th-century York Missal formerly used at Broughton-in-Amounderness, Lancashire* (Manchester: Printed for Chetham Society, 1953), p. 3.
[2] A witness to the claim of Henry VIII to be the Head of the Church.
[3] *Missale . . . Sarum*, Burntisland (London, 1861), cols. 813, 814.
[4] York Fabric Rolls, 301.
[5] Maskell, *op. cit.*, pp. 2–142.

The York liturgical books were printed for the Surtees Society of Durham: missal (1874), manual and processional (1875), pontifical (1873). All these were edited by Henderson; while the breviary was undertaken by Lawley in 1880–82. An article on the 'Newly found York gradual' appeared from the pen of Dr. Frere in the *Journal of Theological Studies* in 1901.[1]

MSS. are easily defaced, and the text is liable to be corrupted by careless copyists. It was therefore determined by a council, held in York in 1195, that the archdeacons in their visitations should make a point of seeing that the missals were corrected from an exemplar type, particularly in respect to the text of the canon (*secretum*).[2]

LITURGICAL COLOURS AND VESTMENTS

The missal provided no general rubric on liturgical colours, but scattered rubrics, wills and inventories made it possible to determine some sort of sequence in the York use.

White was used for Christmas, Easter, Palm Sunday and, probably, Pentecost, as well as for feasts of the Blessed Virgin. If an altar had no blue vestments, white was substituted for all Sundays and feasts of nine lessons, not being doubles. The officiant wore a white cope for the blessing of the fire on Candlemas and Holy Saturday.

Red was the colour for all doubles, except feasts of our Lady, but in chapels and chantries with only two sets of vestments it was used on all feasts and Sundays.

Blue served for Sundays and feasts of nine lessons, not being doubles, but if an altar was provided with only blue and green sets, then blue was the festal colour and green the ferial. We read in an inventory of the time of Edward VI: 'a vestement of blew with tunicles for funeral days'. It would seem from this that the church had no purple vestments, and that blue and purple were reckoned as the same colours.

Green was the ferial colour in summer, that is from Trinity to Advent, and also for the feast of relics.

---

[1] Frere, *Journal of Theological Studies*, II, pp. 575–86.
[2] Counc. York, 1195, can. 2. Labbe, *op. cit.*, t. X, col. 1792; Wilkins, *Concil.*, vol. I, p. 501,

Purple was used for the more solemn offices of the dead, as was customary also at Lincoln and Sarum.

Black was the normal colour for the dead, and the missal directed that the sequence on the Fourth Sunday in Advent should be sung in the cathedral church by four vicars in black copes.

Yellow is found also in some inventories, and it was probably used indifferently with green, as was violet with black or purple.

Blue and White seem to have been the colours for Lent.[1]

The following colour rubrics are found in the York liturgical books:

Sabbato quattuor temporum Adventus: Haec lectio sequens legatur in medio chori ab aliquo Vicario seniori in superpelliceo et capa rubea serica: V. Lectio Danielis Propheta. (All MSS.)

Sequatur in medio chori a duobus Vicariis in capis sericis rubeis secundum dispositionem Succentoris tractus: Benedictus es. (MS. 14th century.)

Ad missam in auroram in Nativitate Domini: Sacerdos cum suis ministris ad altare et Rectores chori omnes sint in vestimentis albis. (MSS. 14th century.)

Sexta die a Nativitate Domini: Chorus regatur a duobus in capis sericis albis. (MS. 14th century.)

Dominica in Ramis Palmarum, ad palmas benedicendas: Praelatus, si praesens fuerit, exeat in vestiarium, et induat se stola et capa serica alba ad palmas benedicendas.

In Sabbato sanctae Paschae: benedictio novi ignis: Praelatus (executor officii) vero, post Nonam decantatam sacris vestibus et capa serica alba indutus, etc. (All MSS.)

The Alleluia after the epistle in the liturgy of Holy Saturday was sung by two of the vicars in white copes.

In Purificatione B.M.V.: benedictio ignis: Impendatur benedictio a sacerdote faciente officium in alba capa induto cum aliis indumentis sacerdotalibus. (MS. 14th century. York missal, Surtees Society, 59, I, XIX, XX.)

The fabric rolls sometimes throw a light on the colour of the

---

[1] Henderson, *Manuale et Processionale . . . .*, *Surtees Society* (1875), p. xxiv.

vestments. One from York Minster, *c.* 1500, says: *Una secta blodia del bawdekyn pro adventu et septuagesima.*[1]

The 'amendynge' of the dalmatykes for the Advent and Septuagesym' is referred to in 1519.[2]

Unlike Sarum, the use of chasubles for the assistant ministers was restricted to Sundays in the 'rites' of York and Hereford: albs only were worn on the ferias of Advent and Lent.

Ornaments of the Church

Vesting for Mass, especially in small churches, took place at the altar, and chests were provided *pro vestimentis conservandis.* Thus a will of Richard de Dalton, barber of York (1392), says that he leaves to the high altar of Holy Trinity in Miklegate York: *unam cistam ferro ligatam pro custodiendis ornamentis dicti altaris.*[3] Another, of 'Richard Shirburn squyer' of Mitton (1436): 'betwitting' (bequeathing) to the altar of St. Nicholas in the 'parysh kirke of Mitton', service-books, vestments, altar cloths, chalice, paxbrede, other ornaments, 'and a kiste to keep all this gere in, with the appurtenance that langes to the same auter'.[4] The vestments were sometimes kept in 'aumbries' below the altars, and we read of Richard Russel, citizen and merchant of York, who in 1435 left to the now demolished church of St. John in Hungate, York, a wooden altar with an aumbry below. He directs: *quod unum altare fiat bene et effectualiter de tabulis, in parte boreali dictae ecclesiae, coram ymagininbus Beatae Mariae et Sanctae Annae et subtus idem altare unum almariolum pro libris et vestimentis iidem altari pertinentibus fideliter conservandis.*[5]

The council of York, held in 1195, directed that the Blessed Sacrament was to be renewed in the pyx every Sunday, and that the priest, when taking the Eucharist to the sick, was to be preceded by a light. The same council laid it down also that the minister of the altar should see that the bread and the wine were

---

[1] York fabric rolls 233.
[2] *Ibid.,* 268.
[3] *Surtees Society, Test. Ebor.,* vol. I, p. 183, edit. Raine.
[4] *Ibid.,* vol. II, p. 75.
[5] *Ibid.,* vol. II, p. 53.

ready for the Sacrifice. No priest was permitted to say Mass *sine ministro literato*.[1]

The regulations concerning altar lights would have been similar to those elsewhere, but in the 14th century we find a chandelier with seven lights in the minster, lighted on Sundays and feasts 'in honour of God Almighty the maker of that prayer, of St. Peter the glorious confessor, of St. William and all Saints'. The chandelier had been an offering on the part of the local Guild of the Lord's Prayer, the ordinances of which were returned in obedience to the king's writ in the year 1388–89. The York missal, formerly belonging to the church of Broughton-in-Amounderness in Lancashire, has an entry to the effect that a parish priest of the name of Edward Ball (from 1481) presented the church with an iron bar (*pertica ferrea*) to hold lights, which was to hang before the altar in the choir in honour of the Saints: *perticam ferream pendentem in alto choro coram altare in honore omnium sanctorum*.[2] Something of the kind existed in the chapel of Farnworth in the parish of Prescot near Liverpool, where we read that in the time of Queen Mary a warden of the chapel, a certain John Woodfall, was charged with detention and embezzlement of a 'ranche of iron used for lights before the Holy Sacrament in Farneworth Chapel'.[3]

LITURGICAL YEAR

The differences between the 12th-century calendar and those from about 1400 onwards are very considerable.

The old calendar had no distinction of double feasts: principal and minor. The twenty-five doubles found in it became the principal doubles of the later calendars, to which were added in later centuries: Translation of St. William (January, I Epiphany), Visitation of the Blessed Virgin (2 April) and Holy Name of Jesus (7 August).

---

[1] Counc. York, 1195, can. I. Labbe, *op. cit.*, t. X, col. 1792; Wilkins, *op. cit.*, vol. I, p. 501.

[2] The Latin word *pertica* in the Broughton missal suggests something long and strait, but a more common form was circular, as the trendall or rowell so often listed in inventories.

[3] Eeles, *op. cit.*, p. 5.

The blessing of candles on the feast of the Purification (2 February) was preceded by a blessing of the fire, for which the officiant wore a white cope.[1] There was a single prayer: *Domine sancte Pater, omnipotens aeterne Deus; bene + dicere, et sancti + ficare digneris ignem istum . . .*[2]

On Ash Wednesday, the ashes were blessed before the absolution of the penitents, which was thrust into the office between the blessing and the distribution. A similar arrangement is found in the Bayeux, Evreux and Rouen books, and York in all probability borrowed the disposition from Rouen.

The *Corps-Saint* procession on Palm Sunday was introduced at York, but it was no more a part of the genuine rite that it was at Salisbury. So far as it is possible to judge from the printed missals and MSS., used by Dr. Henderson for the reprint, the procession looks like a mere addition, a loan from the use of other churches, awkwardly and ungraciously foisted into the original rite.[3] The 14th-century MS. ordinal (1390) of St. Mary's abbey, York, shows that the practice did not then obtain there.

A Carolingian origin for the York rite seems to be supported by a passage in the solemn prayer for the Emperor on Good Friday: *et faciat sapere ea quae recta sunt, atque contra inimicos Catholicae et Apostolicae Ecclesiae triumphum largiatur victoriae ad nostram perpetuam pacem.*[4] This has been thought to be suggestive of the Frankish wars with the Saxons and other heathen tribes.[5] The text is not found in the corresponding prayer in the Roman and Sarum liturgies. A further reference to these 'Carolingian' wars 'of the Cross' seems to be indicated in the *Missa contra paganos* in the York MS. missals,[6] which is not in the printed missals, nor yet in the Roman and Sarum books.

The liturgy of Holy Saturday provided five lessons, as we find in the 14th-century missal of Westminster.

Sundays were reckoned 'after the Octave of Pentecost', not

---

[1] A white cope was worn also for the blessing of the fire on Holy Saturday.
[2] *Miss. . . . Ebor.*, vol. II, edit. *Surtees Society*, vol. LX, p. 17.
[3] Bishop, *op. cit.*, XII, pp. 279, 293.
[4] *York missal*, edit. Henderson, vol. I, pp. 103–4.
[5] Simmons, *op. cit.*, p. 353, n. 3.
[6] *York missal*, edit. Henderson, vol. II, p. 178.

'after Trinity': another Gregorian feature, which it shared also with Westminster.

St. William Fitzherbert, archbishop of York (*ob.* 8 June 1154), was one of the principal feasts. His career was singular for a saint, as having been successively canon, treasurer and archbishop of the cathedral church, St. William, at the instigation of St. Bernard and his fellow Cistercians, was solemnly deposed at the council of Rheims in 1147, on the supposition that he owed his election to the see to bribery and royal influence. St. Bernard, like so many other good people, always ready to believe the worst, had employed his choicest invectives: 'rotten from the soles of his feet to the crown of his head'; [1] 'a vile and infamous person'; [2] 'a man to be shunned and repelled for he is a thief and a robber'. [3] Some years later, however, when his enemies were dead, William was reinstated, but he had no more than a month in which to enjoy the restored primacy. He was canonised by Pope Honorius III about the year 1226, in consequence of the many wonders reported at his tomb. The feast of the Translation of St. William was observed on the First Sunday after Epiphany (*duplex festum principale*), and the principal feast (*festum principale, cum octavo*), with a commemoration of SS. Medard and Gildard, on 8 June.

There were two feasts also of St. Wilfrid: 24 April (*Translatio*) 12 October (*Depositio*); and two of St. John of Beverley: 7 May (*Depositio*) and 25 October (*Translatio*).

25 March was not only the Annunciation of our Lady, but also *Hac die Christus passus est.*

The York calendar was distinctive in its choice of date for the Visitation of the Blessed Virgin: 2 April. A date which seems to harmonise with the gospel narrative better than the more usual 2 July. [4]

---

[1] Letter 187, *To Pope Innocent II, Letters of St. Bernard of Clairvaux*, edit. Bruno Scott James, p. 261. London, 1953.

[2] Letter 202, *To Pope Celestine II*, ibid., p. 272.

[3] Letter 205, *To Pope Eugenius III; ibid.*, p. 279.

[4] The Visitation was extended to the Universal Church in 1389, and the feast was confirmed by the council of Basle in 1441. It has been celebrated on various dates: York, 2 April; Prague and Ratisbon, 28 April; Paris, 27 June; Rheims and Geneva, 8 July. It is now observed throughout the Western Church on 2 July. An Office is said to have been drawn up by Adam Cardinal Easton (*ob.* 1397), a Benedictine of Norwich, who in 1381/2 was nominated dean of York. Later, he held a prebend in Salisbury cathedral.

The Conception (8 December) was a *duplex principale*, whereas Hereford kept it as a simple *duplex*.

The Feast of Relics was observed on 19 October.

The calendar prefixed to the York missal, as edited by Dr. Henderson, has for certain feasts the words: *ab operibus feminarum* (*ferianda* to be supplied); while the Hereford missal, written *c.* 1350 and formerly in the possession of Mr. Dewick (treasurer of Henry Bradshaw Society), gives a list of saints preceded by the words *Ista festa ferianda sunt ab operibus mul* (*ierum*). In several Sarum calendars also we find: *Omnino tenenda.* A long list of *festa ferianda ex toto in episcopatu Wigorniae* occurs at the end of the Constitutions of Walter de Cantelupe, bishop of Worcester, promulgated on the feast of St. James the Apostle, 1240.[1] A similar, but not identical, list is found for Hereford in Dewick's missal.

The meaning of the injunction is clear: a holiday is to be kept on these days, with abstention from servile work. The reference to women in particular was in all probability an allusion to a capitulary of the emperor Charlemagne, issued at Aachen in 789, in which he specified the kinds of work forbidden to women on Sundays: 'Moreover let women not do works of weaving, nor cut out dresses, nor sew, nor do embroidery, nor let them think it lawful to pluck wool, nor to beat flax, nor in public to wash clothes, nor to shear sheep'.

Mass According to the Use of York

The missal is distinguished for the paucity and brevity of the rubrics, but a very long one is given respecting the symbolism of the number of the collects, and their correct endings. A shorter regulation of a similar character is found in the Sarum *Cautelae Missae*.

The introductory rubric, directing the priest to wash his hands before Mass, is not found in either Sarum or Hereford, but the omission is not by any means a proof that the rite was neglected. York provided a prayer: *Largire sensibus nostris omnipotens Pater: ut sicut hic abluuntur inquinamenta manuum, ita a te mun-*

---

[1] MS. *Cotton Claudius* A VIII, fol. 209b; Wilkins, *Concilia*, vol. I, p. 677.

dentur pollutiones mentium, et crescat in nobis augmentum sanctarum virtutum. Per.

This was followed by the antiphon *Introibo ad altare Dei*, psalm *Judica me, Kyrie, Pater*, and versicles.[1]

Then came two prayers, which are not in the 15th-century MS.:[2]

Actiones nostras quaesumus Domine aspirando praeveni, et adjuvando prosequere: ut cuncta nostra operatio et a te semper incipiat et per te coepta finiatur. Per Dominum.

Aures tuae pietatis, mitissime Deus, inclina precibus meis et gratia sancti Spiritus illumina cor meum: ut tuis mysteriis digne ministrare, teque eterna caritate diligere, et sempiterna gaudia percipere merear. Per Christum.

It would seem from the rubric that the priest said *Confitemini Domino* on his way to the altar: *Sacerdos introiens ad altare et procedentibus in ordine ministris dicat: Confitemini Domini quoniam bonus. Quoniam in saeculum misericordia ejus.*

Confiteor, Misereatur and *Absolutionem* were said at the foot of the altar:

Confiteor Deo, et beatae Mariae, et omnibus sanctis, et vobis fratres: quia ego peccator peccavi nimis, corde, ore, opere, omissione, mea culpa. Ideo precor gloriosam Dei genetricem Mariam, et omnes Sanctos Dei, et vos orare pro me.

Misereatur vestri omnipotens Deus: et dimittat vobis omnia peccata vestra: liberet vos ab omni malo, servet et confirmet in omni opere bono et perducat vos ad vitam aeternam.

Absolutionem et remissionem omnium peccatorum vestrorum, spatium verae penitentiae, emendationem vitae, gratiam et consolationem sancti Spiritus, tribuat vobis omnipotens et misericors Dominus.

Versicles and responses were recited as the priest ascended the steps of the altar: *Deus tu conversus vivificabis nos (Et plebs tua laetabitur in te); Ostende nobis Domine (Et salutare tuum); Sacerdotes tui (Domine Deus virtutum); Domine exaudi orationem meam (Et clamor meus); Dominus vobiscum (Et cum spiritu tuo).*

---

[1] *Ostende nobis Domine: Sacerdotes tui induantur: Domine exaudi: Et clamor: Dominus vobiscum. Domine Deus virtutum converte nos* is found also in the 1425 MS.

[2] *C.* 1425, York Minster Library, MS. XVI, A. 9.

Then, inclined before the altar: *Aufer a nobis, Domine, omnes iniquitates nostras, ut ad sancta sanctorum mereamur puris mentibus introire. Per Christum.*

The *officium* (introit) was said at the south side, after which the censing would seem to have taken place. A rubric says: *Et in dextro cornu altaris, dicat officium. Et postea incenset altare.* There was no triple repetition of the *officium*, as we find at Salisbury and Hereford.

The 1425 MS. omits a clause in the *Gloria in excelsis: Qui tollis peccata mundi, miserere nobis*, but it is more likely to have been a copyist's error than an intentional variant.

A rubric, as we have seen, supplies a fanciful symbolism for the number of the collects—one, three, five or seven, beyond which it was not permitted to go.

The celebrant and his ministers sat in the sedilia from the epistle until it was time to read the gospel.

On the First Sunday in Lent and Passion Sunday, the gradual consisted of a whole psalm, as at Sarum and Hereford. York had a greater number of sequences than Sarum, but they were for the most part of an indifferent quality.

The missal fails to tell us whether the chalice was prepared during the chants between the epistle and gospel or at the offertory. Dr. Wickham Legg, who has made an exhaustive study of the preparation of the chalice in the liturgies of Christendon, can say no more respecting the use of York than that: 'It would seem not unlikely, however, that the elements were ready on the altar when the priest said the anthem of the offertory.' [1]

The blessing of the deacon before the gospel, and the response are peculiar to the York rite. *Vicarius* (vicar choral), in place of *diaconus*, is found in the 1425 MS., showing that the missal was intended for use in the minster.

Dominus aperiat tibi os ad legendum et nobis aures ad intelligendum sanctum evangelium Dei pacis. In nomine Patris, etc.

The deacon responds: *Da mihi Domine sermonem rectum et bene*

---

[1] Wickham Legg, *A Comparative Study of the Time in the Christian Liturgy at which the Elements are prepared and set on the Holy Table. Ecclesiological Essays*, V (London, 1905), p. 153.

sonantem in os meum, ut placeant tibi verba mea et omnibus audient-
ibus propter nomen tuum in vitam aeternam. Amen. The response
has an affinity with the prayer in the Mozarabic rite, which the
priest at a private Mass says before the gospel: *Conforta me, Rex*
sanctorum, summum tenens principatum; da sermonem rectum et bene
sonantem in os meum: ut placeam tibi et omnibus circumstantibus.[1]

Dominus vobiscum before the gospel is not found in the York
missal, and there is no further rubric until: *Post lectum evangelium*
dicat sacerdos secrete: Benedictus qui venit in nomine Domini, and
he kisses the book. The injunction *secrete* is not given in the 1425
MS. A long rubric provides an instruction as to the days on
which the Creed was to be recited: On the feast of St. William
(8 June) in the mother-church only. While it was being sung at
a solemn Mass, the choir kissed the gospel-book, presented to
them by the subdeacon, and were censed by the thurifer.[2]

A rubric directs the celebrant and ministers, after the customary
salutation and *Oremus,* to sing the *offertorium: Et cantat cum suis*
ministris offertorium. It is possible, however, that they merely
said it, and then carried on with the offertory. Metrical compositions, bearing a strong resemblance to the Carmelite *O Flos*
Carmeli, figured among the *offertoria.*[3]

In Masses for the dead, it would seem that the priest himself
began *Hostias et preces,* as in the Scandinavian rites of Lund and
Roskilde.[4] The offertory rubrics are remarkably few in number,
but the general outline of the ceremonies would probably have
been somewhat similar to those at Salisbury. York directed the
celebrant to wash his hands twice: before touching the Host, and,
apparently, after the censing of the *oblata* and altar. No prayer is
prescribed at the first *lavabo.* The rubric says merely: *Postea*
(offertorium) lavet manus et componat hostiam super corporales
pannos et dicat. The prayer which follows is similar to Sarum:
Suscipe, sancta Trinitas, hanc oblationem quam ego miser et indignus
peccator offero in honore tuo et beatae Mariae, et omnium sanctorum

---

[1] *Missale Mixtum, Pat. Lat.,* t. LXXXV, col. 535, n. a; *Devocionario Muzárabe*
(Toledo, 1903), p. 65.   [2] Cf. *Present use of Bayeux.*
[3] Frere, *Journal of Theological Studies* II (1901), p. 585.
[4] Segelberg, *De Ordine Missæ secundum Ritum Scandinavicum Medii Aevi, Ephem.*
Liturg., vol. LXV (1951), fasc. IV, p. 255. Cf. Missals of Hereford and Westminster.

tuorum, pro peccatis et offensionibus meis: pro salute vivorum et requie fidelium defunctorum. In nomine Patris, et Filii, et Spiritus sancti. Amen.

A second rubric and prayer follow: *Item calicem cum vino et aqua et dicat: Acceptum sit omnipotenti Deo, sacrificium istud: in nomine Patris, et Filii, et Spiritus sancti. Amen.*

Separate prayers for the host and the chalice seem to suggest that the elements were offered separately.

An interesting note respecting the washing of the corporals at York, taken from the Churchwarden's Accounts of the Parish of St. Michael, York, in the year 1521, is given by Maskell: 'P^d for a pair of mosfits for to wase the Corporase.' These 'mosfits' are thought to be 'mosticks', which dictionaries refer to as 'steadying rods used by painters'; and that such sticks or rods were used in the old fashion of washing by what was called 'bucking', and in the 'bucking tub'.[1]

The York missal makes no reference to incense at the offertory, and a similar omission is found in the Hereford book. The rubric as to the second *lavabo*, however, seems to infer the use of incense: *Interim lavet manus et dicat.* There is no indication whether the priest went to the piscina or was served at the corner of the altar. The prayers prescribed comprise: *Lavabo inter innocentes manus meas: et circumdabo altare tuum, Domine,* and the hymn *Veni creator spiritus, mentes tuorum.*[2] Then, inclined before the middle of the altar, the priest continued: *In spiritu humilitatis et in animo contrito suscipiamur, Domine, a te: et sic fiat sacrificium nostrum ut a te suscipiatur hodie, et placeat tibi Domine Deus meus.* The offertory concluded with the kissing of the altar and the signing of the sacrifice, with the formula: *Sit signatum + ordinatum + et sanctificatum + hoc sacrificium nostrum.*

On Sundays in parish churches the bidding-prayers were then said in the vernacular. Five exemplars of these prayers have survived, the earliest of which is said to date from the 10th or 11th century. Of the others, three are of the 15th century, and one as late as 1509.

---

[1] Maskell, *op. cit.*, p. 37, n. 43.

[2] Cf. Swedish rite of Straengness and Missals of Hereford and Westminster.

The *Orate fratres* is similar to Sarum, but the response is distinctive. *Orate fratres et sorores pro me peccatore: ut meum pariterque vestrum Domino Deo acceptum sit sacrificium.* The printed missal (1517) directs the choir to respond *secrete*, but the tone of voice is not indicated in the 1425 MS. The response takes the form of the first three verses of Psalm XIX: *Exaudiat te Dominus in die tribulationis: protegat te nomen Dei Jacob. Mittat tibi auxilium de sancto: et de Sion tueatur te. Memor sit omnis sacrificii tui: et holocaustum tuum pingue fiat.* Evidence of Sarum influence at York is seen in the York printed *horae*, for the use of those who were simply hearing Mass, in which the Sarum response, with verbal variations, is given: 'Whan the preest turneth after the lavatory. *Spiritus sancti gratia illustret et illuminet cor tuum et labia tua et accipiat dominus hoc sacrificium de manibus tuis dignum pro peccatis et offensionibus nostris.*' [1]

The York secrets are Gregorian in character, and, as a rule, we find them similar to those in the Whitby missal, but, for some parts of the Mass, Whitby, although in the diocese of York, seems more inclined to follow Durham, which was monastic in character.[2]

A long rubric is found before the preface in the 15th-century MS.: *Subnotatur. Pelagius (papa) constituit cantari has IX praefationes: I de Nativitate; II de Apparitione; III de Quadragesima; IIII de Passione et de Cruce; V de Pascha; VI (de) Ascensione; VII de Pentecoste; VIII de Trinitate; IX de Apostolis Petro et Paulo, et etiam de pluribus apostolis dicitur. Gregorius (papa) decimam adjecit de sancto Andrea apostolo, et etiam Urbanus (papa) undecimam de Sancta Maria addidit.* The substance of this rubric is to be found in a letter from Pelagius II (579–90) to the bishops of Germany and Gaul, which Baronius ascribes to the year 590. Its authenticity, however, has been questioned by Bona,[3] and Muratori in *De Rebus Liturgicis* considers it to be a forgery of pseudo-Isidore in the time of Charlemagne.[4] This limitation of

---

[1] York *Horae*, fo. 13b.
[2] Whitby was refounded as a Benedictine house in the reign of William the Conqueror. Reinfrid, a monk of Evesham, was the first prior.
[3] Bona, *Rer. Lit.* (Rome, 1671), t. II, cap. X, 3, p. 378.
[4] Muratori, *Liturgia Romana Vetus* (Venice, 1748), t. I, pp. 66–7.

the number of prefaces was the fruit of a campaign in the 11th and 12th centuries to expel the non-Gregorian prefaces.[1] The campaign was over by 1200, and the rubric in a 15th-century MS. is simply a survival.

The preface for Trinity Sunday was said also on the Sundays after Pentecost.

The York missal gives a special form of *Benedictus* for Masses of our Lady: *Benedictus Mariae filius qui venit in nomine Domine, osanna in excelsis.*

The text of the canon, apart from one small addition, is identical with that of the Pian missal. The name of the king was added after those of the Pope and bishop. A variant is found in the insertion of the words *atque omnium fidelium Christianorum* after *omnium circumstantium*, an addition of which Bona disapproved: *sed omnino rejicienda haec additio tamquam superflua; nam in fine praecedentis orationis praemissa est pro omnibus fidelibus deprecatio illis verbis, et omnibus orthodoxis.*[2] The reason for this addition seems to have been the absence of the words *et omnibus orthodoxis* in some MSS., but here we have both clauses.

The 1425 MS. and the printed missal of 1517 provide a variation of rubric. The latter says: *Hic respiciat hostiam cum veneratione dicens;* and the former: *Eugenius VII instituit. Et cum dicat, parum tangat calicem, dicens.* To what does the allusion to Pope Eugenius I (654–57) refer? The number seven is unlikely to relate to seven signs of the cross, but it may well refer to the seven words in the preceding *Communicantes: genetricis Dei et Domini nostri Jesu Christi,* which may have been interpolated before the time of St. Gregory (590–604). A rubric in the 15th-century Sidney Sussex York MS. directs the priest to incline as he says these words: *Hic parum inclinatus dicat ad istam septem verba sequentia.*[3]

Yet another reference to a Pope is found in the 1425 MS., before the recital of the words of institution: *Alexander papa instituit. Inclinato capite, super linthiamina, hostiam accipiendo.*

---

[1] i.e. the (usually) 'Gelasian' prefaces.
[2] Bona, *op. cit.*, lib. II, cap. XI, 5, p. 388.
[3] Sidney Sussex Coll., Cambridge, MS. D; Henderson, *Missale. . . . Eboracensis*, vol. I, p. 182.

This legend respecting Alexander I (105–15) is at least as old as the time of Durandus (*ob.* 1296), who, in commenting on this part of the canon, says: *Haec verba dicitur Alexander Papa primus addidisse, ut praemissum est.*[1] The rubric had been changed in the printed missal: *Hic erigat sacerdos manus et conjungat: postea tergat digitos, et elevet hostiam dicens.*

As in the Sarum use, York directed the priest to touch the Host at the word *fregit* (*hic tangat hostiam*). The above reference to an 'elevation' implies raising the Host in order to consecrate it, and there is no rubric prescribing an elevation after consecration. There is, however, no doubt but that the ceremony was observed at York, as elsewhere, and the York *horae* give *Ave verum corpus natum* as the prayer to be said 'At the elevation of our Lord'. The missal of 1517 says respecting the chalice: *Hic elevet calicem usque ad caput*, whereas the 1425 MS. gives: *Hic superponit corporalia.*

All the known York MS. missals direct the priest to extend his arms in the form of a cross at *Unde et memores* (*Hic extendit brachia in modum crucis*), but the printed missals omit the rubric. A somewhat far-fetched and improbable explanation of this omission has been given by Simmons: 'possibly from a desire to conform to the Roman use in that spirit of deference to Rome, which was a marked characteristic of the northern province, and traceable, at all events in some degree, to a jealousy of the preponderance of the see of Canterbury'.[2]

The Sarum rubric before *Supplices te rogamus*, which was wanting in the 1425 MS., is found in the 1517 edition: *Hic corpore inclinato et cancellatis manibus.*

York appears to be the only English use which does not enjoin a striking of the breast at *Nobis quoque peccatoribus.*

The following rubric is found in the 15th-century MS. after *Da propitius pacem* in the embolism: *Hic accipiat patenam et osculetur istam: signat eadem in facie + pectore + a capite vertite usque ad pectus + ad dextram usque ad sinistram, dicendo: Da propitius.* The same MS., after *Per eundem Dominum nostrum* of the doxology, says: *Et frangat corpus in tres partes.* The formula for

---

[1] Durandus, *Rat.*, IV, LXI, i. These rubrics, however, are no part of the York rubric as such.   [2] Simmons, *op. cit.*, p. 289, n. 4.

z

the commixture has two slight variants from the Sarum use: *fiat nobis* in place of *fiat mihi*, and the omission of the word *promerendam*. The doxology, also, has been extended: *Per eundem Dominum nostrum Jesum Christum Filium tuum. Qui tecum vivit et regnat.*[1]

The 1425 MS. has a rubric before the formula for the *pax*: *Det osculari calicem et corporalia et (? ut) postea erectus dare(t) ministris, dicens.* The formula is almost identical in the York and Hereford missals: *Habete vinculum pacis et caritatis, ut apti sitis sacrosanctis mysteriis Dei.* The *osculatorium* or pax brede is mentioned in a constitution (1250) of Walter Gray, archbishop of York (1216–55), as one of the ornaments of the parish church to be provided by the parishoners.[2]

The communion prayers are said by the priest, as he holds the Host in his two hands.[3] Three prayers were said before Communion:

(1) *Domine, sancte Pater, omnipotens aeterne Deus, da nobis hoc corpus et sanguinem Filii tui Domini Dei nostri Jesu Christi ita sumere, ut mereamur per hoc remissionem peccatorum nostrorum accipere et tuo sancto Spiritu repleri: quia tu es Deus, et praeter te non est alius nisi tu solus. Qui vivis et regnas Deus.* The prayer is similar to the first communion prayer in the Hereford missal. *Oremus* is found in the printed edition of the York missal before the second and third prayers, but it is not given in the MS.

(2) *Perceptio corporis et sanguinis tui, Domine Jesu Christe, quam indignus sumere praesumo: non mihi veniat ad judicium nec ad condemnationem, sed pro tua pietate prosit mihi ad tutamentum animae et corporis. Qui cum Deo Patre et Spiritu sancto vivis et regnas Deus.* A variant of this prayer is found in our Roman missal.

(3) The third prayer: *Domine Jesu Christe, Fili Dei vivi*, is perhaps the most general of all the communion prayers, and, varying in no more than a few words, is in nearly all the mediaeval missals.

---

[1] *Qui tecum* etc is wanting in the 1425 MS.

[2] Wilkins, *Concil.*, t. I, p. 698. A similar direction was given in the province of Canterbury at the Council of Merton in 1305 (*ibid.*, t. II, p. 280).

[3] The rubric enjoining this is not found in the 15th-century MS.

The formulas for Communion were similar to those in the Hereford use, but York had a further prayer, distinctive of that Church: *Corpus Domini nostri Jesu Christi sit mihi remedium sempiternum in vitam aeternam.*[1]

Sanguis Domini nostri Jesu Christi conservet me in vitam aeternam.

Corpus et sanguis Domini nostri Jesu Christi: custodiat corpus meum et animam meam in vitam aeternam.

The MSS. missals make no mention of ablutions, and the printed editions say nothing as to the rinsing of the chalice and the washing of the hands. Two rubrics are found in the 1517 missal: *Post primam ablutionem dicetur haec oratio* and *sumat hic calicem et ponat super patenam, et postea inclinando se dicat.* It may, however, be inferred from these directions that the two ablutions were taken in the customary manner, and that the chalice was afterwards placed sideways on the paten to drain.

The ablution prayers were similar to those in the Sarum rite, except that at York *Quod ore sumpsimus* concluded with the words *in vitam aeternam*, in place of *sempiternum*, and in the second prayer we find *Domine* before, instead of after, the word *communio*, and *Per Christum Dominum nostrum* at the end.

The postcommunions, like the secrets, were Gregorian in character.

The York missal gives no further rubric, except one before the *Placeat*, directing the priest to say the prayer *tacita voce* in the middle of the altar, inclined and with hands joined.

There is no mention of either blessing or last gospel.

The thanksgiving after Mass included the *Benedicite*,[2] versicles and responses, and the collect *Deus qui tribus pueris*. In one missal, also, we find the long prayer: *Gratias ago tibi, dulcissime Domine Jesu Christe, lux vera.*[3]

---

[1] Cf. missal of Straengness.

[2] The *Benedicite* is found as a thanksgiving after Mass in the Rouen and Sarum books, but not at Hereford.

[3] The so-called Prayer of St. Augustine: *Summe sacerdos*, is given in this missal as a prayer to be said before Mass.

HEREFORD RITE

The diocese of Hereford probably originated with Putta, the exiled bishop of Rochester (676), but the limits of the see were still undetermined at the end of the 8th century.

Prosperity came to Fernley, as Hereford was at first called, with the arrival of the relics of the martyred king of the East Angles, Ethelbert, who had been treacherously put to death at the Mercian court in 793.[1]

The cathedral church was dedicated to the Blessed Virgin and St. Ethelbert.

The diocese comprised nearly all Herefordshire, part of Shropshire and parishes in the counties of Worcester, Monmouth, Montgomery and Radnor.

The Danes severely damaged the cathedral in 1055, when the shrine of St. Ethelbert was destroyed.

Hereford again suffered severely in the civil war early in the reign of Stephen (1135–54): the cathedral was sacked, divine service suspended and the bishop (Robert de Bethune) forced to retire and seek refuge elsewhere for two or three years. It will be seen how important this period was when we come to consider the origins of the rite.

The reign of Henry III saw a host of aliens, for the most part Savoyards, intruded into the highest offices of the Church. In 1240, Peter of Aigueblanche (*ob.* 1268), one of the principal counsellors of the king, was recompensed with the see of Hereford; while his nephew, Peter de Morestel, became dean, and another nephew, Pontius de Salins, canon. In addition to this, we find yet more members of the bishop's family holding important posts in the cathedral church. The bishop greatly concerned himself with affairs of state, and was constantly absent from the country. In 1263 the king sent Peter a letter in which he ordered him to return from Savoy immediately. Henry had lately visited Hereford, but found no bishop, 'official' or dean to exercise spiritual functions; while even the canons were living at a dis-

---

[1] Relics accounted for the growth and prosperity of many churches and towns.

tance.[1] Matthew Paris has never a good word to say for the bishop, whose memory reminds one of a 'detestable odour of sulphur'. The annalist rejoices in the misfortune of the man, who had a polypus in his nose, which, like a kind of leprosy, ate his face.[2] Peter of Aigueblanche, nevertheless, is, as we shall see later, important for the use of Hereford. The bishop died in 1268, after a period of imprisonment by the barons in Eardisley Castle.

A saint occupied the see of Hereford later in the century: Thomas de Cantelupe (1272–82), who died at Orvieto in 1282 on a journey to the Pope, which had been made necessary by a serious dispute with Archbishop Peckham on a question of jurisdiction.

Few of the bishops in the Middle Ages were saints, and Thomas Polton (1420–21) distinguished himself by never once setting foot in his diocese. Ordinations, etc., were taken by the bishop of Annadown, county Clare! [3]

The last Catholic bishop of Hereford, Thomas Reynolds (1557), died a prisoner for the faith before consecration.

ORIGINS OF THE RITE

As we have seen, a source for the distinctive features of the Sarum use must be sought for elsewhere than at Rouen, despite the many assertions to the contrary for which no evidence has been produced.[4] Hereford, on the contrary, at least in the printed missal, shows very marked affinities with that Church, which would seem to have been textually related to Westminster. The borrowing is especially noticeable in the ceremonies of Palm Sunday and Holy Week.[5]

When and how were the Rouen usages admitted at Hereford? Who brought them thither? The probable answer to these questions has been supplied by Edmund Bishop.[6]

---

[1] François Mugnier. *Les Savoyards en Angleterre au XIIIᵉ siècle et Pierre d'Aigue-blanche, Evêque d'Héreford*, chap. IX, pp. 222–3. Chambéry, 1890.

[2] Matth. Paris, *Chronica Majora*. Vol. V (edit. H. R. Luard), p. 647. London, 1880.

[3] *Extracts from the Cathedral Registers* (1275–1535), edit. E. N. Dew, p. 102. Hereford, 1932.

[4] Bishop, *op. cit.*, XII, *Holy Week Rites of Sarum, Hereford and Rouen compared*, p. 278.

[5] *Ibid.*, pp. 276–300.

[6] *Ibid.*, pp. 299–300.

The borrowing must have taken place before the loss of Normandy in the time of King John (1199–1216), and all the evidence points to the episcopate of Robert de Bethune (Betun), who was bishop of Hereford from 1131 to 1148. Robert, as Wharton has shown in his *Anglia Sacra*, was a man who devoted time, care and thought to all that concerned the celebration of divine service.[1] He restored and reformed the cathedral church, which had been turned into a fortress, and renewed the celebration of Mass and Office.[2] The work had been rendered necessary by the civil war, and was undertaken by the bishop on the recovery of the city by the forces of King Stephen in 1141.

There is no direct evidence that the ritual observances of the diocese were changed on this occasion, but Robert de Bethune had a golden opportunity, and it could have been effected without much difficulty. Edmund Bishop in fact has shown how Robert de Bethune had the occasion to become acquainted with Rouen customs, but whether he took advantage of this to introduce them into his diocese must remain uncertain. There is indeed proof that the tractate of John of Avranches, which was the Rouen ceremonial of the 11th century, was known in the Augustinian house of Llanthony in Monmouthshire, from the priorship of which Robert was called to be bishop of Hereford. A MS. in the British Museum, comprising a miscellaneous collection and entitled *Exceptiones variae ex patribus*, is known from its calendar at fols. 11–13 to have been written at Old Llanthony.[3] The calendar does not give the name of St. Thomas of Canterbury, who was canonised in 1173, and the handwriting of the MS. may be fairly assigned to the middle of the 12th century. Folios 132–33 contain an extract *Ex consuetudinario Rotomagensi*, which is nothing else but a fragment of John of Avranches. It appears

---

[1] *Porro quam sedulus, quam devotus fuerat in divinis officiis.* Wharton, *Anglia Sacra*, p. 309.

[2] *Episcopus igitur cum, pace restituta, in sua redisset, ecclesiam suam reformavit, hostica de fortis munimenta diruit et complanavit, spurcitias de intus eliminavit clerum dispersum revocavit, divinum officium innovavit. Ibid.*, p. 314.

[3] London, Brit. Mus. Royal MS. 8 D VIII. Ker gives the title of the MS. as *Excepciones Rob. de. Braci*, and says that it came from Llanthony Secunda near Gloucester (*Mediaeval Libraries of Great Britain* (London, 1941), p. 60. This was a daughter of the Monmouth house, and there was nothing to prevent the MS. being taken there.

therefore that a copy of what is practically the most ancient Rouen *ordinarium* now extant was known under the title of the 'Rouen Consuetudinary' in the house of Llanthony, where it must have come under the notice of Robert de Bethune.[1] The calendar of Hereford included the names of two archbishops of Rouen: St. Ouen (*ob.* 684) on 24 August and St. Romanus (*ob.* 639) on 23 October.

The liturgical books of the Austin Canons, says Dr. Eeles, have affinities with Rouen and Hereford, especially in the Alleluia verses of the Sundays after Pentecost.[2] The so-called Hanley Castle missal, now in the Cambridge University Library, although it is doubtful how far it depicts Augustinian usage, probably represents early Hereford practice, before the use of that diocese became fixed and most assimilated to Sarum. The MS. is largely 12th century, but the calendar, canon and sequences are much later than the rest: 14th century. The sequences are in fact simply Sarum.[3]

Hereford owed nothing to Sarum before the 14th century, but the episcopate of John Trilleck (1344–61) would seem to have been a time of liturgical modification and expansion. The MS. ordinal and the printed missal and breviary have all borrowed from the new Sarum ordinal. It was from Salisbury also that Hereford in the course of the 15th century adopted the custom of placing the Blessed Sacrament in the 'sepulchre' on Good Friday, together with the cross.

We have spoken of the Gregorian and Sarum group of prayers. All the MS. missals are purely 'Gregorian' in their prayers. The 'Sarum' prayers in the printed missal replace a few Gregorian doublets: they are peculiar to this printed text, and collation shows that they were taken from some monastic member of the Sarum group, not from any book of Salisbury itself, and later than 1200 in any case. Wickham Legg says that the inclination of Hereford to Sarum is evident in the postcommunion for the Vigil of the Epiphany, the secret for the Second Sunday in

---

[1] Bishop., *op. cit.*, pp. 299–300.
[2] F. C. Eeles, *Holyrood Ordinale* (Edinburgh, 1914), introduct., p. xxxii.
[3] *Ibid.* Camb. Univ. Lib., MS. Kk. 2. 6.

Lent and the *super populum* prayers for the Monday after Passion Sunday, but the collects for these days are definitely Gregorian in character. If the MS. assigned by Dr. Henderson to the 14th century represents the earlier use of Hereford, the changes would point to an increase of Sarum influence there, just as the substitution of Gregorian collects for Sarum in the later MS. of St. Albans points to a diminution of Sarum influence at St. Albans from what it was in the 12th century.[1]

It seems strange to learn that the liturgical books of Hereford were in use in a collegiate church in the diocese of St. Jean de Maurienne in Savoy. The use of Hereford was indeed specifically prescribed in the foundation statutes of the collegiate church of St. Catherine, Aiguebelle (Aquabelle) in 1267. The founder was Peter de Aigueblanche, who we have already seen as bishop of Hereford in the reign of Henry III. The statute of foundation, which was dated 21 April 1267, enjoined two daily Masses: a matutinal Mass for the dead at a side altar, and a Mass *de tertia* of the feast or feria at the high altar, with deacon and subdeacon. The use of Hereford was prescribed in the following terms: *Omnia vero officia ecclesiae in matutinis missis et in omnibus aliis horis fiant secundum consuetudinem herefordensis ecclesiae ut in libris ordinatum invenietur; et si libri in ordinatione discordent cantor ordinet et concordet libros prout viderit expedire.*[2] Until 1305 the dean of Hereford was the patron of the collegiate church, but in that year the privilege devolved upon the Counts of Savoy.[3] The use of Hereford, however, persisted in the church until June 1580, in spite of the attempts of the bishops of Maurienne to get the canons to conform to the use of the diocese.[4] The archives of Hereford cathedral have preserved a piteous appeal from the prior and canons of the collegiate church to the bishop, Charles Boothe, in 1533. The letter, which shows the tenacity with which the use of Hereford was maintained in this far off Savoyard valley, is im-

---

[1] Wickham Legg, liturg. introduct., *Westminster Missal*, fasc. III, *Henry Bradshaw Society*, vol. XII (1897), pp. 1418–19.

[2] F. Mugnier, *Les Savoyards en Angleterre au XIIIᵉ siècle et Pierre d'Aigueblanche, Evêque d'Héreford*, part III, Document IX, p. 303.

[3] *Ibid.*, chap. IX, pp. 250–1.

[4] The bishop of Maurienne, Peter de Lambert, edited nineteen articles for the reform of the collegiate church in 1567.

portant, and no apology is needed for quoting it more or less in full: 'We rejoiced in the Lord to hear that your lordship presides over the see of Hereford, for until now we have been as members without a head. . . .[1] It remains for us to approach our father and Hereford our mother, and signify some matters concerning the state of the servants and suppliants of *your* church. Bishop Peter de Aquablanca in founding the church . . . ordered and willed the office according to the use of Hereford to be said or sung by the said prior and canons. Until now we, your servants and suppliants, as also our predecessors have done this (*decantavimus*) daily. But while our founder was alive he provided all the books for the church and for our use, but they are now worn out and tattered by age after being used for 369 years.[2] We understand, too, that since that time your office has been enlarged and amended, and we your servants are attached to the said use. . . . So we beg your lordship to make provision for us and *your* church. We have had hard times (*plurimis et repetitis vicibus incitati*) and have been worried (*interpellati*) by the bishops of Maurienne to adopt their use. Had we been willing to comply with their demands by singing the office according to their use, they would have provided the necessary books, but this we decline to do out of respect for the memory of our pious founder and your church of Hereford. The aforesaid bishops were annoyed on this account and have usurped our liberties and pre-eminence, for according to our foundation our prior instituted canons and priests without the superior's consent being required, and we could not meet such forfeitures on account of failure of rights of the pious foundation. . . . Moreover, we, your petitioners, would have your lordship know that the vestments and ornaments of our church are worn out. . . . Our founder provided these when the church was built. . . . We are poor and helpless (*debiles*) and have lost much that he gave. . . . Thus we your servants and petitioners are unable to provide vestments and ornaments for the church. . . . We, therefore, appeal to your lordship, our father, for books,

---

[1] Why 'members without a head'? A succession of bishops of Hereford was maintained throughout the Middle Ages.

[2] There seems to have been no previous attempt to obtain fresh copies of the Hereford books, or inquiry as to whether there had been any alteration in the liturgy.

vestments and ornaments for the more honourable serving of God and the church.' [1]

The bishop's reply is not recorded, but, as England was severed from Catholic unity in the following year (1534), it may well be that no answer was received.

The Hereford use, as we have seen, continued at Aiguebelle until June 1580, but by that time it existed no more than in that one church in Savoy. England had abandoned the old religion, and the Catholic service-books fed bonfires and served to wrap up provisions and other commodities.

In the early years of the 15th century we hear of a personal permission for the use of the Hereford rite outside the limits of the diocese. Pope John XXIII (1410–15) on 1 May 1413 gave an indult to Richard Kyngeston, dean of St. George's Chapel, Windsor, permitting him to follow the Hereford use for the rest of his life, although he was no longer resident in that diocese. The dean had been archdeacon of Hereford from 1379 until 1404, and prebendary of Charminster and Bere in the diocese of Salisbury in 1406. The papal privilege, however, was not to last for long, as Richard Kyngeston seems to have died, or at least resigned in the year following the issue of the indult (1414).

LITURGICAL BOOKS

Books of the Hereford use are scarce. A rubricated missal of the early 15th century, formerly belonging to the church of St. Dubritius (Dyfrig) at Whitchurch in Monmouthshire, is in the Bodleian Library, Oxford,[2] and a fragment of a missal is found in St. John's College, Cambridge. The British Museum has a missal,[3] and also an ordinal of the 14th century, as well as a draft for a revised breviary ordinal on the back of a roll of accounts.[4] A missal of the Hereford use is in the library of Worcester cathedral,[5] but no exemplar survives at Hereford, although we find here a breviary with music, dating from 1265 to 1270.

---

[1] *Extracts from the Cathedral Registers, 1275–1535.* Edit. E. N. Dew, pp. 154–5. Hereford, 1932.

[2] Bodl. Lib., Oxford, MS. Univ. Coll. 78a.   [3] Brit. Mus., MS. Add. 39675.

[4] *Ibid.*, MS. Harl. 2253, fly leaves.   [5] Lib., Worcester Cath., MS. F. 161.

Dr. Henderson's edition of the missal (1874) purports to have been taken from the printed missal of 1505, but it has been described by Mr. Christopher Hohler as an 'incompetent partial collation with York'.

The Hereford breviary was edited by Frere and Brown for the 'Henry Bradshaw Society': vol. I, no. XXVI (1904); vol. II, no. XL (1911). A calendar in the library of St. John's College, Oxford, would seem to have been written for or under the influence of the Victorine Augustinian canons, who had settled at Wigmore in the diocese of Hereford. There appears to be little doubt that the original scribe wrote under Hereford influences in the latter part of the 13th century: St. Ethelbert is given on 20 May and St. Milburga on 23 February. The mention of St. Hugh (17 November) and St. Edmund (16 November) precludes an earlier date. The introduction of a number of French abbots, St. Victor (21 July), St. Aurea (3 October) and St. George with Companions (27 August), which refers to the translation of George and Aurelia to Paris, renders it likely that the calendar may have been written for or under the mother house of St. Victor in Paris.

LITURGICAL YEAR

Ash Wednesday. The blessing of the ashes has a single prayer: *Deus qui non mortem.*

Palm Sunday. The procession of the Blessed Sacrament on Palm Sunday is of paramount importance, for, as we have seen, it was of a character so similar to the *Corps-Saint* procession at Rouen that it affords certain evidence of a borrowing of Rouen customs by Hereford. A comparison of the Hereford ceremony with a Rouen *ordinarium* of c. 1450 [1] and the processional of 1645, which was the last book to represent the traditional rite, shows us that the two ceremonies are almost identical. [2] The Blessed Sacrament was taken privately outside the city wall before the palm ceremony in the church. The palms were blessed and distributed

---

[1] In the appendix to Le Prevost's edition of John of Avranches; *Pat. Lat.*, t. CXLVII, cols. 117–19.

[2] Process. 1645, published by the archbishop, François II de Harlay, in which Le Prevost had a considerable hand.

at a side altar, after which a procession was made to the place
where the Sacrament had been taken. Then, after a gospel (*Turba
multa*) and a sermon, the procession returned to the cathedral
with the Eucharist. A station was made at the city gate, from the
top of which five or seven boys sang *Gloria laus*. On entering the
city *Ingrediente Domino* was sung, with *Collegerunt pontifices* at the
door of the cloisters and *Unus autem* at the door of the cathedral.[1]
The procession then entered the church, passing underneath the
Blessed Sacrament, which was held aloft transversely in the doorway. This was done in silence at Rouen, whereas Hereford prescribed the antiphon *Occurrunt turbae*. A fourth and last station
was made before the great crucifix at the entrance to the choir,
which was saluted by *Ave Rex noster*. Then two priests [2] in black
copes sang antiphons in the rood loft, during which the procession entered the choir, and Mass began.

Holy Thursday. The *mandatum* at Hereford had many of the
features of the Rouen use, notwithstanding a difference in the
psalms and antiphons.

Good Friday. The cross for adoration was uncovered *cum
baculo*, that is by the bishop, in the Rouen and Hereford uses: by
the priests who hold it, in Sarum. The same two churches place
the cross in the sepulchre some time between the veneration and
the procession of the Blessed Sacrament for the Mass of the Presanctified: Sarum after vespers. The 'genuine' Hereford rite, as
exemplified in the 14th-century *ordinale*, followed the Rouen
custom of putting the cross, but not the Eucharist, in the sepulchre; whereas the printed missal (1502) directed the inclusion of
both cross and Sacrament, in a rubric which was a mere copy of the
Sarum rubric. It would appear that Hereford adopted the Sarum
practice in the course of the 15th century. The cross was washed
with wine and water before putting it in the sepulchre at both
Rouen and Hereford, but not so at Sarum.

Holy Saturday. Further resemblances between Rouen and
Hereford, and dissidence as between them and Sarum, are found
in the liturgy of Holy Saturday. A single prayer for the blessing
of the incense is provided in the Rouen and Hereford books:

---

[1] Bishop, *op. cit.*, p. 292.   [2] Rouen, four deacons.

Sarum gives three prayers and not this one—*Veniat omnipotens Deus.* In the *Exsultet* of Hereford, after naming Pope and Ordinary, the text continues: *Necnon et pro Anglorum rege N. et principe nostro N.* Who is the *princeps?* Edmund Bishop has supplied the answer. The Hereford form is found also in missals of Rouen, of course with the necessary variant: 'King of the French' for 'King of the English', and must have been used some six centuries after it had lost its meaning. The 12th-century sacramentary of Rouen [1] unfortunately does not contain the *Exsultet*, but a 13th-century missal says: *cum antistite nostro N., necnon Francorum rege N. et principe nostro N.,*[2] which is also the form in the missal of 1499, and retained in the neo-Gallican missal of 1728, published under the aegis of Archbishop de Lavergne de Tressan, which was in use at Rouen until the 19th century.[3] The municipal library at Rouen has also a 13th century missal from the Benedictine abbey of St. Ouen (Rouen), in which we find: *antistite nostro et abbate nostro et principe nostro.*[4] The *princeps* for whom prayer is offered is clearly the Duke of Normandy: 'The words in question, occurring in unbroken tradition in the Rouen *Exsultet,* date from a time when there were Dukes of Normandy who owned the King of France as their suzerain; and it may perhaps be considered safe, in view of all that has been said hitherto, to conclude further that the Hereford form was simply borrowed from Rouen at some time during that period.' [5]

The third litany, sung during the return from the font, is replaced at Sarum by what Edmund Bishop has called 'a doggerel which hardly deserves the name of litany or hymn—*Rex sanctorum angelorum*'.[6] The Hereford rubric, at the end of the litany, directed the cantors to say in a loud voice (on a high note) *Accendite:* [7] 'Light up', and all the candles, throughout the church, were

---

[1] London, British Museum, Addit. MS. 10028.
[2] Rouen, *Bibl. Municip.,* MS. Y 50. [3] Bishop, *op. cit.,* p. 298.
[4] Rouen, *Bibl. Municip.,* MS. H 459. [5] Bishop, *op. cit.,* p. 298.
[6] *Ibid.,* p. 296.
[7] The monition *Accendite* is still to be heard on this day in the rites of Lyons and Braga. It would seem to have originated in the 8th-century stational Mass at Rome, when the subdeacon, standing at the door of the *secretarium,* directed the lights of the basilica to be lit, before the procession of the Pope proceeded to the altar. *Ord. Rom.,* I, 7; *Pat. Lat.,* t. LXXVIII, col. 940. Lyons, in the 'restored' order of Holy Week, has abandoned its traditional use.

lighted, while the ruler of the choir sang the *Kyrie eleison*, which was the beginning of the Mass. The monition *Accendite* is not found in the Sarum books. Rouen, however, which, as we have seen, influenced Hereford, has a rubric in the missal of 1499: *Statim accensis cereis incipiatur celebratio misse; et incipiant cantores solemniter Accendite. Sequitur Kyrie el. iii.* A revised rubric appeared in the missal of 1645: *Accenduntur luminaria in altari et cantores incipiunt Kyrie.*[1]

The classification of feasts at Hereford included *festum principale*, *duplex*, *semiduplex* and *simplex*.

Sundays, as in the Sarum use, were reckoned 'after Trinity'.

In addition to the solemnities of our Lord and his blessed Mother, the Dedication of the Cathedral Church on 11 May [2] and the Feast of Relics on the first Sunday after the Translation of St. Thomas of Canterbury (7 July) were observed as *festa principalia*.[3]

St. Ethelbert, king and martyr, co-patron of the cathedral church, was honoured with a feast (*festum principale* with octave) on 20 May. He was a king of the East Angles who was murdered at the Mercian court at the instigation of the queen in 793. First buried at Mardon, the remains of the king were translated later to a 'fair church' at Fernley, which in course of time received the name of Hereford. St. Ethelbert obtained a considerable cultus as a martyr, although the cause of his death was a desire on the part of the queen to annex his kingdom rather than *pro odio fidei*. In 1121, a three days' fair at his feast was granted by King Henry I to Richard de Capella.[4]

St. Thomas de Cantelupe, bishop of Hereford (1272–82), had no less than three feasts: 25 August, the day of his death (*Depositio; Semiduplex*); 2 October, the principal feast (*Festum Principale* with octave; commemoration of St. Leodegard); 25 October,

---

[1] Bishop, *op. cit.*, p. 297.

[2] The missal, formerly belonging to Whitchurch and now in the Bodleian Library, Oxford, kept its local dedication on 11 March, and the feast of its patron saint, St. Dubritius (Dyfrig), on 14 November. Dubritius would seem to have worked in these parts, and his name has been given also to the churches at Hentland, Ballingham and St. Devereux.

[3] Sarum adopted the same day in 1319, as the original date (15 September) clashed with the Octave of the Nativity of the Blessed Virgin, the importance of which increased towards the middle of the 13th century.

[4] A three days' fair at the feast of St. Denis (9 October) was granted by King Henry III in 1227.

the translation of his relics (*Festum Principale*). A certain amount of confusion seems to exist today as to when the feast of St. Thomas should be observed: the Canons Regular of the Lateran and the dioceses of Birmingham, Salford and Shrewsbury keep it on 3 October; Cardiff on 5 October; Westminster on 22 October.

The litany in the Hereford use inserted the name of St. Thomas as the first among confessors, as St. Ethelbert was the first among martyrs.[1] St. Thomas died at Orvieto in 1282, while on a visit to Pope Martin IV. The bishop was engaged in an acrimonious dispute with the Franciscan archbishop of Canterbury, John Peckham, on a matter concerning jurisdiction. The primate had excommunicated Thomas, and when the bones of the bishop were brought back to Hereford he refused to permit a burial until he had been satisfied that the papal pentitentiary had granted a certificate of absolution!

Thomas de Cantelupe, notwithstanding the quarrel with Canterbury, was canonised by Pope John XXII in 1320, and in the *acta* of canonisation no less than four hundred and twenty miracles were ascribed to him.[2] So late as 1610, we find the relics of the Saint carried in procession by the people of Hereford during a plague.[3]

The feast of St. Andrew (30 November) was observed with an octave. Eight French saints were admitted in the Hereford calendar: Leufroi (21 June), Grimbald (8 July), Ouen (24 August), Bertin (5 September), Fermin (25 September), Leodegar or Leger (2 October), Romanus (23 October), Anian or Aignan (17 November). St. Anian was originally observed in the Sarum use on 17 November, and also invoked in a litany which was said on the Saturdays in Lent. Later, however, the feast of St. Hugh (canonised in 1220) came to be substituted for that of St. Anian on 17 November.

SS. David, Cedd, George and Winifred were added to the Hereford calendar, at the request of the archbishop of Canterbury, in 1415.

---

[1] The French bishops, Romanus and Ouen, find a place in the litany.

[2] St. Thomas of Hereford was the last Englishman to be canonised before St. Thomas More and St. John Fisher in 1935.

[3] Edwin Burton, *Hereford*, *Catholic Encyclopedia*, vol. VII, p. 255.

The only instance in which the actual authorship and appointment of any Hereford service has been recorded was for the institution of the feast of St. Raphael in 1445. It had been previously adopted in the diocese of Exeter by Edmund Lacy, who
had held the see of Hereford from 1417 to 1420.[1] A letter of the
bishop of Hereford, Thomas Spofford (1422–48), to his dean and
chapter prescribed the observance of the feast in the cathedral
church: 'We order and decree the commemoration or feast of St.
Raphael to be included (*connumerari*) in the other feasts of nine
lessons of our cathedral, with nine proper lessons, hymns, responses, antiphons, versicles, chapters, collects and invitatory,
with Mass from the proper and the collect, *Rege, quaesumus,
Domine, famulum tuum Edmundum pontificem*, for the good estate
of the said Edmund, bishop of Exeter . . . on the 5th day of
October.'[2]

The 14th-century Hereford missal, as we have seen, provides
a list of *festa ferianda*: saints' days to be observed as holy days,
with abstinence from servile work.

LITURGICAL COLOURS

The Hereford sequence of colours is uncertain, and but few
indications are found in the service-books that have survived.

The missal and 14th-century ordinal give rubrics in respect to
the vestments to be worn on Good Friday and All Souls.

On Good Friday, we learn that the bishop (celebrant) had
'Lenten' vestments; two priests in red chasubles brought in the
veiled cross and sang *Popule meus* after the solemn prayers; while
two other clerics chanted the response *Agios o Theos* vested in
black silken copes.[3]

---

[1] Spofford's successor, Richard Beauchamp, on his translation from Hereford to
Sarum, licensed its use in his new diocese on 20 August 1456. William Boothe, archbishop of York, adopted it also for use in his cathedral church on 10 October 1454.

[2] *Extracts from the Cathedral Registers* (1275–1535), edit. E. N. Dew, pp. 114–15. The
Roman missal observes the feast on 24 October.

[3] *Hora sexta episcopus cum ministris suis vestibus quadragesimalibus indutis. Post
Orationes (Sollemnes) duo presbyteri, albis et casulis rubeis revestiti, crucem velatam, assu-
mant, cantantes hos versus juxta altare; Popule meus. Alii duo in capis nigris de serico
stantes in medio chori, respondeant scilicet; Agios o Theos. Missale ad usum percelebris
ecclesiae Herfordensis* (Leeds, 1874), pp. 90, 93, 94; *Hereford Breviary (Henry Bradshaw
Society,* vol. XLVI, 1915), vol. III, p. 72.

The Commendations on the Commemoration of All Souls were said by the officiant in a black samite cope.[1]

The registers of the cathedral give a number of references to vestments, but only in one case do we find mention of the days on which they were to be worn.

Adam de Orleton (1317–27), who was appointed bishop in 1317, supplied a receipt for vestments which were the property of the see, and which he pledged himself to return to the dean and chapter, either in person or by his executors: 'A mitre of pearls with arches (*voltis*) worked in gold and enamels (*amalatis*) of precious stones . . . a chasuble of red stuff lined with yellow, worth 40s.; also a chasuble with tunicle and dalmatic of white samite on the one side and crimson stuff (*sindone*) on the other, worth £10; also a third chasuble of azure [2] silk lined in green with lined tunicle and dalmatic of red stuff on the one side and azure on the other, worth 40s.; also a chasuble, tunicle and dalmatic with cope of white samite, and of crimson cloth new and recently cut from the same.' [3]

The will of John de Aquablanca, dean of Hereford (1320), mentions 'a double (duplicem, ? stout) chasuble of red and white silk with its belongings—alb, amice, stole and maniple of crimson, embroidered with gold griffins and pearl lozenges (*losongis*) for the high altar (cathedral) and no other use. . . . To the altar of Blessed Ethelbert one of my green cloths with large eagles, and to the Lady chapel one of my green cloths with smaller eagles for the service of the altar on Sundays and holy days.' [4]

Another reference in the registers would suggest that the vestments described were for use on the newly instituted feast of St. Raphael (1445). They were a gift of Edmund Lacy, bishop of Exeter, who had been formerly bishop of Hereford (1417–20). The bishop greatly favoured the observance of the feast, and we read: 'And lest the performance of the obligation should . . . in

---

[1] *Executor officii in alba revestitus et desuper capa de nigra samita indutus, cum suis ministris coram altari dicat sollemniter commendationem.* Missal, *op. cit.*, p. 353.

[2] Lit. indigo, but explained as skyblue at Exeter in 1337.

[3] *Extracts from the Cathedral Registers* (1275–1535), edit. E. N. Dew, pp. 43–4. Hereford, 1932.

[4] *Ibid.*, p. 46.

A A

time to come fall into desuetude, or the commemoration (*obsequium*) of the great angelic spirit cease (*incidat in occasum*) . . . the bishop of Exeter has given and assigned to you the Dean and Chapter . . . one priest's chasuble (*planetam*) with three tunicles for deacon and subdeacon, and three copes of red velvet with orphreys of gold (*de panno aurato rubeo*) with three apparelled albs (*cum eorum plenis apparatibus*), stoles, girdles (*limbis*), maniples (*sive fanellis*), and three apparelled amices with velvet embroidery; also one superfrontal and a frontal with one frontal of deep red cloth worked with gold and falcons for the high altar, and two of the same material for the two side altars in the choir, worth 200 marks and more, acquired at considerable expense and labour, and in consideration of the notorious poverty of our cathedral. . . . These he has sent for the use and beauty of the said church and to remain in perpetuity.' [1] The only colour mentioned is red for the copes, but it is uncertain whether this indicates that this was the colour for the feast. White is now prescribed in the Roman rite.

If we may judge from a record of the institution of William Brown to the living of Kington in 1365, it would seem to have been customary at such a time to hand the vestments for the high altar and a missal to the newly appointed parish priest.[2]

MASS ACCORDING TO THE USE OF HEREFORD

The celebration of a Mass for the dead was unusual on a Sunday, but in 1353 we hear of a foundation solemn Mass for the soul of Sir Lawrence of Ludlow in the church of St. Laurence (Ludlow) on the Sunday next after the Epiphany.[3]

The foundation of the chantry at the altar of St. John Baptist and St. Nicholas in the church of All Saints, Newland, in 1446 enjoined a votive Mass for each of the days of the week.[4]

A record in the registers for the year 1488 prescribes that the vicar of Aymestrey should say Mass in the chapel of Leinthall every Tuesday. On the Lord's day he is instructed to say one

---

[1] *Op. cit.*, pp. 114–15.   [2] *Ibid.*, p. 73.   [3] *Ibid.*, p. 68.
[4] Sunday, Holy Trinity; Monday, Angels; Tuesday, *Salus Populi*; Wednesday, Holy Spirit and Requiem (if no principal feast); Thursday, Peace; Friday, Holy Cross; Saturday, St. Mary. *Ibid.*, p. 117.

gospel (?dry Mass) and to bless water and bread for the infirm and aged.[1]

In 1385 we find the bishop of Hereford issuing an order to the chantry priests of Ledbury, forbidding them to begin Mass until the parish high Mass had begun and the gospel had been sung. It would seem that the faithful had been fulfilling their Sunday obligation by only hearing a low Mass in a chantry chapel, instead of assisting at matins and high Mass.[2]

Prayers for the benefactors of the cathedral church were ordered by the bishop, Charles Boothe, in 1523 to be said kneeling immediately after the asperges on Sundays. A *Pater* and *Ave* were to be followed by the antiphon *Mater ora filium*, and then the verse, *Ora pro nobis sancta Dei genetrix*, with the prayer *Meritis et precibus*.[3]

The first rubric in the missal, directing the psalm *Judica me* with its antiphon (*Introibo ad altare Dei, ad Deum qui laetificat juventutem meam*) and certain other prayers to be said by the priest 'standing before the altar', would seem to suggest a practice such as we find in our Roman missal. It is, however, expressly said: 'When he has put on amice and alb', as if the other vestments were to be taken later.

A second rubric orders *Confitemini* and the *Confiteor* to be recited 'standing before the step of the altar'. When did the priest put on the chasuble? Was it before or after this second series of preparatory prayers? There is no mention of a washing of the hands in the sacristy before Mass, although the absence of a rubric does not preclude the practice.

Judica me and its antiphon were followed by a threefold *Kyrie*, *Pater noster*, versicles and the prayer *Actiones nostras*, which the York priest was instructed to say before going to the altar. The versicles at Hereford omitted *Sacerdotes tui induantur* and its response, and included: *Domine Deus virtutum converte nos (Et ostende faciam tuam et salvi erimus)*.

The second series of prayers admitted: *Confitemini Domino quoniam bonus. Quoniam in saeculum misericordia ejus; Confiteor, Misereatur;* and *Absolutionem*. The versicles recited as the priest

[1] *Op. cit.*, p. 132.   [2] *Ibid.*, p. 82.   [3] *Ibid.*, p. 150.

ascended the steps of the altar were similar to those in the Roman rite, with an additional four: *Sacerdotes tui induantur justitia* (*Et sancti tui exsultent*); *Ab occultis meis munda me Domine* (*Et ab alienis parce servo tuo*); *Sancta Dei genitrix virgo semper Maria* (*Intercede pro nobis*); *Domine Deus virtutum converte nos* (*Et ostende faciem tuam.*) Then, before the altar, the prayer: *Aufer a nobis Domine cunctas iniquitates* was said: a prayer, which, with small and unimportant variations, is found also at Sarum, York and in the Pian missal.

Hereford made no mention of incense either at the beginning of Mass or at the offertory, but its use is unlikely to have been omitted.

After the prayer *Aufer a nobis*, the priest kissed the altar, and, going to the right side, said: *Adjutorium nostrum in nomine Domine. Qui fecit coelum et terram. Sit nomen Domini benedictum. Ex hoc nunc et usque in saeculum.* The *officium* (introit) was repeated three times, followed, as usual, by the *Kyrie* and *Gloria in excelsis.* The number of collects was not permitted to exceed seven. When the priest turned to the people, as, for example, at the salutation (*Dominus vobiscum*), a rubric prescribed that the deacon should turn also, while the subdeacon was to kneel and adjust the chasuble (*de casula aptanda subministret*).

The epistle was read from a lectern (*super lectrinum*) at the choir step. At its conclusion, the gradual (*gradale*), with its verse, and *Alleluia* or tract followed, according as time allowed. There is no direction as to where or by whom the chants were to be sung, as we find in the rubrics of the Sarum missal, nor is there any reference to a sequence.

Before the announcement of the gospel, the deacon, as in the Sarum rite, censed the middle of the altar, with instructions that the lectern was not to be censed. The deacon was blessed with the formula: *Dominus sit in corde tuo et in labiis tuis ad pronuntiandum evangelium pacis. In nomine Patris, + et Filii, et Spiritus sancti.* Then, announcing the gospel from a pulpit or lectern, the deacon signed himself on the forehead (only).[1] At the conclusion

---

[1] The announcement, as in the Roman missal, was either *Sequentia sancti evangelii* or *Initium sancti evangelii.*

of the gospel, the deacon kissed the book, and the priest intoned the creed.

Hereford would seem to have been the only English use to prescribe a genuflection at the *Incarnatus* in the creed: *Et fiet genuflexio dum dicitur.*

In Masses for the dead, the celebrant himself began the *offertorium, Hostes et preces*, as at York and Westminster.[1]

The mingling of water with the wine appears to have taken place at the offertory.[2] In fact, the Hereford rubrics suggest that the setting of the bread and wine on the altar did not take place until after the anthem of the offertory.[3]

The water was blessed in response to the petition *Benedicite: Dominus. Ab ipso sis benedicta, de cujus latere exivit sanguis et aqua. In nomine + Patris, etc. Amen.*

Then, placing the paten on the chalice, the bread and wine were offered together with a single prayer, which is also the offertory prayer in the Dominican rite: *Suscipe, sancta Trinitas, hanc oblationem quam tibi offero in memoriam passionis Domini nostri Jesu Christi, et praesta, ut in conspectu tuo tibi placens ascendat, et meam et omnium fidelium salutem operetur aeternam, per Christum.* The chalice was returned to the altar and covered with the corporal, while the Host was placed before it: the paten kissed and partially hidden under the corporal.

The missal made no reference to incense at the offertory, but provided a rubric in respect to the washing of hands. This would seem to have taken place at the piscina, as the rubric says: *in eundo.* The following formulas are given for the *lavabo: Veni Creator* (omitting the verse *Dudum sacrata*); *Emitte spiritum tuum, et creabuntur. Et renovabis faciem terrae* and the prayer *Ure igne sancti Spiritus.*[4]

Ure igne sancti Spiritus renes nostros et cor nostrum, Domine, ut tibi casto corpore serviamus et mundo corde placeamus. Per Christum Dominum nostrum.

---

[1] Cf. Scandinavian liturgies of Lund and Roskilde.

[2] Hereford Missal (1502), edit. Henderson, p. 17.

[3] Wickham Legg, *A Comparative Study of the Time in the Christian Liturgy at which the Elements are prepared and set on the Holy Table. Ecclesiological Essays*, V (London, 1905), p. 153.   [4] Cf. Swedish rite of Straengness and Missal of Westminster.

Then, returning to the middle of the altar, the priest said: *In spiritu humilitatis et animo contrito suscipiamur a te, Domine: et sic fiat sacrificium nostrum ut a te suscipiatur hodie, et placeat tibi Domine Deus.* The prayer is found in both the Sarum and York missals.

The offertory concluded with the celebrant kissing the altar and, with hands joined over the chalice, as he said: *Veni Sanctificator, omnipotens aeternae Deus* (signing the chalice) *bene + dic et sanctifica hoc sacrificium, quod tibi est praeparatum.* Then signing himself, he continued: *In nomine Patris*, etc.

The priest turned to the people for the *Orate fratres*, which, unlike Sarum and York, made no reference to *sorores*: *Orate fratres ad Dominum, ut meum pariter et vestrum in conspectu Domini acceptum sit sacrificium.* There was no response.

Secrets and preface followed in the usual way.

Hereford interpolated a prayer after the *Sanctus* and *Benedictus*, which the priest said while venerating a representation of the Crucified (*adorans crucifixum*): *Adoramus te, Christe, et benedicimus tibi quia per sanctam crucem tuam redemisti mundum. Miserere nobis, qui passus es pro nobis.* This 'representation' was the picture of the Crucified which was usually to be found in the missal on the page preceding the canon. It was customary to kiss it.

The Hereford prayer is cited by Cardinal Bona, quoting from Petrus ab Opmeer *in assertione Missae*. A second prayer is also given: *Domine Jesu Christe Fili Dei vivi adjuva infirmitatem meam, et conforta me nunc in hac hora.*[1] Interpolations of the kind were disapproved of by the author of the *Micrologus: Nimis temerarium videtur.*[2]

The name of the King, as in other English missals, was inserted in the canon. Certain rubrics in the canon call for mention. Thus, for example, a reverent inclination at *Hanc igitur*, in place of the more recent stretching of the hands over the oblations. The rubric directing the Host to be elevated after consecration 'that it might be seen by all', at the same time forbids any kissing of the

---

[1] Bona, *op. cit.*, lib. II, cap. XI, p. 382.
[2] *Microl.*, cap. XII, Hittorp, *op. cit.*, col. 738.

Host,[1] and directs the fingers to be kept joined until after the ablutions. A similar injunction for the people to be 'able to see' is made in respect to the elevation of the chalice: *elevet calicem in altum ut videatur ab omnibus*. This must surely have been a comparatively recent interpolation. Durandus (*ob.* 1296) admits that the elevation of the chalice is not a superfluous act, although the precious Blood cannot be seen,[2] but the practice did not become common until the middle of the 14th century, and in many churches it was adopted considerably later. Its introduction may be not unreasonably associated with the time of Bishop Trilleck (1344–61). At *Unde et memores*, the priest extended his arms *in modum crucifixi*, and for *Supplices te rogamus* joined his hands together in the form of a cross.

Before the words *Da propitius pacem* in the embolism, a rubric directed the priest to touch each of his eyes with the paten before kissing it. The paten was kissed again at the word *adjuti*. Two particles of the Host were held in the left hand, and a third particle in the right, as the celebrant said: *Per omnia saecula saeculorum.*[3]

Preces in prostratione or suffrages for special intentions were recited before *Pax Domini*, as in the Sarum and York uses. *Pax Domini* and *Agnus Dei* followed, and a particle was placed in the chalice with a formula identical to that found in the Sarum rite: *Haec sacrosancta commixtio corporis et sanguinis. . . .* The prayer: *Domine Jesu Christe, qui dixisti Apostolis tuis* was said as in our Roman missal, but omitting the words *pacem do vobis*.

The priest kissed the chalice and the altar before giving the formula for the *pax*, which was similar to the use of York: *Habete vinculum caritatis et pacis, ut apti sitis sacris mysteriis Dei.* The minister responded: *Pax Christi et sanctae ecclesiae tibi et cunctis ecclesiae filiis.* There were four Communion prayers:

(1) *Domine, sancte Pater, omnipotens aeterne Deus, da mihi hoc sacrosanctum corpus et sanguinem Filii tui ita digne sumere ut*

---

[1] The kissing of the Host is prescribed in the missal of Evreux-Jumièges of the 14th–15th century.

[2] Durandus, *Rat. div. off.*, IV, 41, 50.

[3] One particle was put into the chalice; a second, consumed by the priest; and a third given in Holy Communion to the deacon and subdeacon.

merear per hoc remissionem omnium peccatorum meorum accipere: et tuo sancto Spiritu repleri: quia tu es Deus solus, et praeter te non est alius: cujus regnum et imperium sine fine permanet in saecula saeçulorum. Amen. The prayer is found also among the Communion prayers in the York use.

(2) The second prayer is inscribed in the missal as *Alia oratio*, which seems to suggest that it was an alternative: *Domine Jesu, Christe, Fili Dei vivi,* etc. It was almost identical with a prayer in our Roman missal,[1] and one which occurs in most of the mediaeval missals.

(3) This prayer was very nearly the same as the first Communion prayer in the Sarum rite: *Deus Pater, et origo totius bonitatis, qui misericordia ductus Unigenitum tuum pro nobis ad infima mundi descendere, et carnem sumere voluisti, quem ego indignus et miserrimus peccator hic manibus teneo, te adoro, te glorifico, te tota cordis intentione laudo, et precor ut nos famulos tuos non deseras sed peccata nostra deleas: quatenus tibi soli Deo vivi et vero, puro corde et casto corpore semper servire valeamus. Per eundem.*

(4) *Agimus tibi Deo Patri gratias pro jam beatificatis, postulantes eorum interventu apud te adjuvari: pro his autem qui adhuc sunt in purgatoriis locis, offerimus tibi Patri Filium: supplicantes ut per hanc sacrosanctam hostiam eorum poena levior sit et brevior: pro nobis autem quos adhuc gravant peccata carnis et sanguinis immolamus tibi Patri Filium: obsecrantes ut peccata quae ex carne et sanguine contraximus caro mundet, sanguis lavet Unigeniti Filii tui Domini nostri Jesu Christi. Qui tecum vivit.* This uncommon prayer, as we have seen, is found in a MS. missal which is said to have belonged to the cathedral church of St. Paul's, London, and we meet with it again in the missals of the Gilbertines [2] and the Benedictines of Westminster.[3] The 14th-century missal of Westminster gives three Communion prayers, one of which was to be said, according to the preference of the celebrant: *Deus Pater fons*

---

[1] The Hereford prayer had *obedire* (*mandatis*) instead of *inhaerere*, and a different doxology: *Qui vivis et regnas cum Deo Patre in unitate ejusdem,* etc.

[2] The *Gilbertine Rite*, vol. II, edit. R. M. Woolley, *Henry Bradshaw Society*, vol. LX (London, 1922), p. 90.

[3] *Miss. ad usum Eccles. Westmonast.*, fasc. II, edit. Wickham Legg, *H.B.S.*, vol. V (London, 1893), col. 519.

et origo, as at Hereford and Sarum; *Domine Jesu Christe, Fili Dei vivi*, as in most of the mediaeval missals and the Pian liturgy; *Agimus tibi Deo Patri*, as at Hereford.[1]

Before receiving the Host, the priest said: *Corpus Domini nostri Jesu Christi sit animae meae remedium in vitam aeternam. Amen.*[2] Before receiving the Chalice: *Sanguis Domini nostri Jesu Christi conservet animam meam in vitam aeternam. Amen.*

The first ablution with wine was taken at the corner of the altar. The prayer prescribed is found in the Sarum, York and Pian missals: *Quod ore sumpsimus, Domine, pura mente capiamus: et de munere temporali fiat nobis remedium in vitam aeternam. Amen.*

In the second ablution, the priest washed his hands with wine and water over the chalice, and said a prayer which occurs in the uses of Sarum and York: *Haec nos communio, Domine, purget a crimine: et coelestis remedii faciat esse consortes. Per Christum Dominum nostrum. Amen.*

A third ablution was taken at Hereford, with water only, for which the priest returned to the middle of the altar, reciting a variant of the prayer in the Pian missal: *Corpus tuum, Domine, quod sumpsi, et calix, quem potavi, adhaereant semper visceribus meis: et praesta, ut in me non remaneat macula peccati, in quem pura et sancta introierunt sacramenta corporis et sanguinis tui. Qui vivis et regnas.* Then, placing the chalice horizontally on the paten, the priest washed his hands at the piscina (*sacrarium*), as he said: *Lavabo inter innocentes manus meas: et circumdabo altare tuum, Domine.*

The Mass concluded in the ordinary way with communion, postcommunion, dismissal and *Placeat*, after which the celebrant kissed the altar, and returned to the sacristy.[3] He was directed to say the antiphon *Trium Puerorum, Benedictite* etc., as he took off his vestments, or as he went to the sacristy (*vestibulum*).

BANGOR RITE

The diocese of Bangor seems to have been founded at the end of the 6th century, but the exact date is uncertain. The history of

---

[1] *Op. cit.*, cols. 518–19. [2] Cf. missal of Straengness (Sweden).
[3] The priest signed himself before turning to the people for the salutations.

the see before the Norman Conquest is in fact so obscure that Godwin does not allow any bishops before that time.[1] The first Welsh bishop to be present at an English council was Hervey, bishop of Bangor, who attended the council held at Westminster under St. Anselm in 1092. A Norman by birth, he was ignorant of the language and customs of his people, and unpopularity forced him to take refuge in England, receiving by way of compensation the see of Ely (1108). The cathedral church of Bangor had been destroyed by the Normans in 1071, and it is probable that it was rebuilt by Hervey.

There is no record as to the liturgy in these early centuries, but we may reasonably suppose that the original Celtic rite would have given place to the Roman, as it was observed in Anglo-Saxon England, at about the same time as North Wales adopted the Roman computation of Easter (768). This is not to say, however, that Celtic usages did not survive here and there, but we may be sure that if any such remained they would have been suppressed by the Norman Hervey. The 'Bangor use' has been ascribed to Anian (1267–1305), the bishop who rebuilt the cathedral after it had suffered severely in the wars between the English and Welsh in the time of Henry III (1227–72), and who baptised the future King Edward II. In 1402 the church and palace were burned down by Owen Glendower, remaining in ruins for nearly a century. The choir was rebuilt in 1496 by Henry Deane, who was bishop of Bangor and Augustinian prior of Llanthony near Gloucester. On his translation to Salisbury in 1500, the bishop is said to have left his mitre and crozier to his successor, on condition that he continued with the restoration of the cathedral church. Nothing, however, was done until the appointment of the Cistercian abbot of Beaulieu, Thomas Skevington or Pace (1509–33), who, in spite of the fact that he never resided in his diocese, completed the cathedral church, rebuilding the nave and tower.[2] As Geoffrey Baskerville says: 'It was not usual for Bishops of Welsh sees in the Middle Ages to set foot inside their

---

[1] Godwin, *De praesulibus Angliae*, 1743.
[2] The four bells given by the bishop to his cathedral church were sold by the first Protestant bishop.

dioceses', and at the dissolution of the monasteries (1539) we find all the bishoprics in Wales given to dispossessed religious: Bangor to the abbot of Hyde, Llandaff to the abbot of Eynsham, St. Asaph to the abbot of Bermondsey, and St. David's to the prior of Bisham.[1] The last Catholic bishop of Bangor was William Glynn (1553-58).

To return to the liturgy: What was the rite of Bangor? No printed missal *in usum Ecclesiae Banchorensis* is known to exist, and the MS. missal, formerly in the posesssion of William Maskell, although believed by him to be a Bangor book, is almost certainly one of the many variants of Sarum. There is, however, a pontifical, which is said to have belonged to Bishop Anian (1267-1306), and to have been given to the cathedral by Richard Ednam, the then bishop, in 1485. It was for some time lost to the cathedral, but found its way back through Bishop Humphreys in 1701. The forms of giving troth and at the putting on of the ring, which are to be met with in the service-books of other English uses, are absent from this pontifical, and yet in its non-pontifical sections the book is Sarum. Maskell, in support of his claim to possess a Bangor missal, written in *c*. 1400, says that while it is an undoubted English book, it nevertheless follows neither Sarum, York nor Hereford. The differences in the ordinary and canon, he maintains, are confirmed by the many variations in the collects and offices.[2] In addition to this, there are several remarkable points of agreement with the pontifical,[3] and the *Ordo sponsalium* is similar in the two MSS.[4] A note at the end of the calendar tells us that the missal was given to Oswestry in the time of Queen Mary: 'This Booke was geuen to the hye Alter of the Paryshe Churche of Oswestry by S[r] Morys Griffith Prist, To pray for all Christen Soules, the yere of oure Lorde god a thowsande fyve hundred fyfty and foure.' Maskell intimates that the book had been alienated from the church in the days of Edward VI, and restored to it on the return of the Catholic religion. There is,

---

[1] Baskerville, *English Monks and the Suppression of the Monasteries* (London, 1937), chap. X, p. 248.

[2] Maskell, *op. cit.*, pref., chap. VIII, p. cliv.

[3] *Ibid.*, p. clvi, n. 42.

[4] *Ibid.*, p. cliv.

however, nothing in this note to suggest that the missal had previously belonged to Oswestry. It may have been so, but it is rash to affirm it. If it was an Oswestry book, all the more reason for it not representing the use of Bangor. Oswestry was in the county of Shropshire, diocese of Lichfield and archdeaconry of Shrewsbury. Lichfield, as we have seen, followed the Sarum use with some few diocesan peculiarities. The church at Oswestry, which had been monastic in Anglo-Saxon days, had been appropriated to the Benedictine abbey of Shrewsbury before 1085, and it is equally certain that the rite of Bangor was not followed there. Leland, who toured England in 1536-42, says that the Church of St. Oswald at Oswestry was sometime a monastery 'caullid the White Minster. After turned to a Paroche Chirch, and the Personage impropriate to the Abbey of Shreusbyri'.[1]

A comparison between the Ordinary of the Mass ascribed by Maskell to Bangor and the Ordinary in the Sarum use will show but little dissimilarity. Variations in missals occur most frequently in the preparatory, offertory and communion prayers, and in these the two books are practically identical. Here and there we find words transposed or some small and unimportant variant, but no more than could be accounted for by a defective scribe. One single variation is perhaps worth mentioning: the addition of the words *Salvator mundi* in the Communion prayer *Domine Jesu Christe Filii Dei vivi*, which, says Maskell, are found also in the Bangor pontifical.[2]

The actual wording of the rubrics in the missal is in some cases dissimilar from the printed Sarum text, but no change in the ceremonial is involved. The direction for the deacon to continue the insensation while the priest washed his hands, which is given by Maskell as a distinctive rubric of the use of Bangor, is found verbatim in the Burntisland edition of the Sarum missal.[3]

Finally, it may be noted that the calendar of the MS. contains the dedication of a church in Essex.

If therefore the rite of Bangor was a distinctive 'rite', like those

---

[1] John Leland, *Itinerary*, vol. V, p. 37, edit. 1737.

[2] Maskell, *op. cit.*, pp. 118, 119, n. 66. Cf. Gallican, Celtic and Mozarabic rites.

[3] *Miss. ad usum insig. et praeclarae Eccles. Sarum*, edit. Burntisland (London, 1861), part I, col. 595.

of York and Hereford, it seems clear that the MS. cited as 'Bangor' is in fact a missal of the 'Illustrious Church of Sarum'.

While admitting the possibility of a mediaeval rite of Bangor, we must at the same time confess that we know nothing whatever about it.

BIBLIOGRAPHY

1. Ancient *English Holy Week Ceremonial*, H. J. *Feasey*, London, 1897.
2. The *Ancient Liturgy of the Church of England according to the Uses of Sarum, Bangor, York and Hereford and the Modern Roman Liturgy*. 2nd edit. William *Maskell*. London, 1846.
3. *Catholic Encyclopedia: Bangor*, Edwin *Burton*, vol. II; *Hereford*, Edwin *Burton*, vol. VII; *Salisbury*, Edwin *Burton*, vol. XIII; *Sarum Rite*, F. Thomas *Bergh*, vol. XIII; *York*, Edwin *Burton*, vol. XV; *York, Use of*, Herbert *Thurston*, vol. XV.
4. *Ceremonies and Processions of the Cathedral Church of Salisbury*, Chr. *Wordsworth*. Cambridge, 1901.
5. *Church of Our Fathers*, as seen in St. Osmund's Rite for the Cathedral of Salisbury, with Dissertations on the Belief and Ritual in England before and after the coming of the Normans. Daniel *Rock*. 4 vols. London, 1905.
6. A *Comparative Study of the Time in the Christian Liturgy at which the Elements are prepared and set on the Holy Table*. J. *Wickham Legg*. *Ecclesiological Essays*, V. London, 1905.
7. *English Liturgical Colours*. W. *St. John Hope* and Cuthbert F. *Atchley*. London, 1918.
8. *Epistolare* in usum Ecclesiae Cathedralis *Aberdonensis*, 1527. Introduct. F. C. *Eeles*. Edit. Edinburgh, 1924.
9. *Hereford. Extracts from the Cathedral Registers*, 1275–1535. Edit. E. N. *Dew*. Hereford, 1932.
10. *Hereford Breviary*, edit. W. H. *Frere* and L. E. G. *Brown*. Henry Bradshaw Society, vols. XXVI (1904), XL (1911), XLVI (1915).
11. *Holyrood Ordinale*. Edit. F. C. *Eeles*. Edinburgh, 1914.
12. *King's College Chapel, Aberdeen*. F. C. *Eeles*. Edinburgh, 1956.
13. *Lay Folks Mass Book* or the Manner of Hearing Mass . . . and Offices in English *according to the Use of York*. Edit. T. H. *Simmons*. London, 1879.
14. *Liturgica Historica*, XII. *Holy Week Rites of Sarum, Hereford and Rouen compared*. Edmund *Bishop*. Oxford, 1918.
15. *Missale* ad usum insignis et praeclarae *Ecclesiae Sarum*. Parts I (1861), II (1867). Burntisland, London.
16. *Missale* ad usum insignis *Ecclesiae Eboracensis*. Surtees Society, vols. LIX, LX. 1872.
17. *Missale* ad usum Ecclesiae *Westmonasteriensis*, fasc. III. Edit. J. *Wickham Legg*. Henry Bradshaw Society, vol. XII. London, 1897.

18. *Missale* ad usum percelebris *Ecclesiae Herfordensis.* Reprint of Missal of 1502, collated with MS. of 14th century (Univ. Coll. Lib., Oxon). Leeds, 1874.

19. *Obituary Book of Queen's College, Oxford.* An ancient Sarum Calendar. Edit. J. R. *Magrath.* Oxford, 1910.

20. *Ordinale Sarum* sive *Directorium Sacerdotum.* Edit. Chr. *Wordsworth. Henry Bradshaw Society,* vols. XX (1901), XXII (1902).

21. The *Reformation in Dublin, 1536–1558.* Myles V. *Ronan.* London, 1926.

22. *Sarum Missal,* edited from three early MSS. J. *Wickham Legg.* Oxford, 1916.

23. Les *Savoyards en Angleterre au XIIIᵉ siècle et Pierre d'Aigueblanche, Evêque d'Héreford.* François *Mugnier.* Chambéry, 1890.

24. *Scottish Mediaeval Liturgical Books and Fragments.* David *McRoberts.* Glasgow, 1953.

25. *Tracts of Clement Maydeston,* with the remains of *Caxton's Ordinale.* Edit. Chr. *Wordsworth. Henry Bradshaw Society,* vol. VII. London, 1894.

26. *Use of Sarum.* Vol. I. The Sarum Offices as set forth in the *Consuetudinary* and *Customary.* W. H. *Frere.* Cambridge, 1898.

27. *Use of Sarum.* Vol. II. *Ordinal* and *Tonal.* W. H. *Frere.* Cambridge, 1901.

28. *York Missal,* formerly used at *Broughton-in-Amounderness,* Lancashire. F. C. *Eeles.* Manchester, 1935.

Chapter Six

RITE OF NIDAROS (TRONDHEIM)

THE province of Nidaros in Norway would seem to have been one of the most extensive in Christendom, embracing Orkney, Isle of Man, Iceland, Greenland and the Faröe Islands.

HISTORICAL BACKGROUND

The Church in Norway was a daughter of the Anglo-Saxon Church, and to England may be ascribed the honour of bringing the faith of Christ to the country. Many of the early kings of Norway were educated in England, and, on claiming their kingdom, brought with them a number of priests. It is understandable therefore that the ecclesiastical terminology and institutions of the Anglo-Saxons should have been introduced.

It seems strange that there was practically no attempt on the part of either Sweden or Denmark to evangelise Norway, although they had already received the Faith.

The kingdom of Norway was founded by Harold the Fair-haired (*Haarfagre*) in the second half of the 9th century. He was succeeded in 935 by his illegitimate son Hákon (*ob.* 981), who had been brought up as a Christian at the court of King Athelstan. Priests were summoned from England, but the attempt to force Christianity on the Norwegian people failed, and a heathen reaction ensued. A like failure attended the missionaries from Bremen, who had come to that part of the country known as Viken. Bremen, which had become a metropolitan see in 849, was indeed the first mother-church of Norway. The province included the three Scandinavian kingdoms: an arrangement confirmed by Popes Nicholas I in 858 and Victor II in 1055.

The establishment of Christianity in the country was due to Olaf Tryggvason (*ob.* 1002), who had returned from England to

claim the kingdom in 994, bringing with him the bishop Sigurd
and several priests. The success of the apostolate was such that
in the space of four years Norway became virtually Christian.[1]
The king established a royal residence at Nidaros, where he
erected a timber church dedicated to St. Clement: the ancestor of
the future cathedral church of the Norwegian province.

Under Olaf's direction, Christianity spread also to Orkney,
Iceland, Greenland and the Faröe Islands. In Iceland, we find the
local 'parliament' (*Althing*) accepting it as the religion of the
country in 1000.

The work of consolidating the Faith in Norway was undertaken by another Olaf, Olaf Haraldsson (1015–30), better known
as St. Olaf. 'He had with him', says Adam of Bremen (1070),
'many bishops and priests from England, by whose admonition
and doctrine he himself prepared his heart for God, and to whose
guidance he committed the people subject to him; among those
famous for teaching and virtues were Sigafrid, Grimkil, Rudolf
and Bernard.'[2] Rudolf and Bernard worked later in Iceland. St.
Olaf was killed in battle with the Danes at Stiklestad in 1030, and,
regarded as a martyr, he came to be honoured as the foremost of
Norway's three patron saints.[3] His body, after being buried in a
sandy bank alongside the river, was placed in a shrine over the
altar of the church of St. Clement on 3 August 1031. Then, on
the erection of Christ Church (1077), it was transferred there, as
being a more worthy resting place. Adam of Bremen (*c.* 1070)
has described the stream of pilgrims that visited the shrine of the
Saint: 'The body of the most blessed king and martyr Olaf re-
poses there, at whose grave God until this day performs great
miracles of healing, so that thereto come great numbers from distant lands in the hope that they can be helped by the holy martyr's

---

[1] The stone cross which may be seen today at Gulen in West Norway is believed to be
a memorial to the missionary zeal of Olaf Tryggvason. F. N. Stagg. *West Norway and
its Fjords* (London, 1954), chap. I, p. 28.

[2] Adam of Bremen, *Gesta Hammaburgensis Ecclesiae Pontificum*, t. II, p. 55. Hamburg,
1876.

[3] In addition to St. Olaf: *St. Sunniva* (8 July), reputed daughter of an Irish king, who
died on the Island of Selje in the 10th century; St. Halvard of Huseby (14 May), cousin of
St. Olaf, who in *c.* 1043 was murdered while going to the rescue of a woman who had
been attacked.

intercession.' In 1537, when the Danes had introduced Protestantism into the country, the shrine was removed to Copenhagen,
where it was robbed of its jewels and melted down. The relics,
however, retained their place on the high altar until the capture of
Trondheim by the Swedes in 1564.[1] The body was then buried
in a little church at Skatval in the fjord until the Swedes, in the
same year, were driven out, and the holy relics were ceremoni-
ously shipped back to Trondheim. They were placed in an open
grave in the cathedral church, but four years later (1569), on the
order of the Danish king, the grave was filled in with earth, and
now nobody knows where the Saint lies buried.[2]

The helmet and spurs of St. Olaf were taken to Stockholm by
the Swedes.[3] The only known relic of the Saint is today happily
in Catholic hands, and may be seen under the altar of the cathedral in Oslo. The story of its recovery from the National Museum
in Copenhagen is interesting. When in 1861 Josephine, the
Catholic queen of King Oscar I of Sweden, assisted at Mass in
Oslo for the feast of the Saint, Mgr. Studach, the Vicar Apostolic,
requested the Queen to ask for the return of the relic. In the
following year (1862) King Frederick VII of Denmark acceded
to the request, and sent it to the queen in a reliquary, the exact
facsimile of an ancient one, which the Danish museum had retained. The relic was brought in solemn procession to the
Catholic cathedral at Oslo on the feast of the Translation of St.
Olaf, 3 August 1862. The relic, which would appear to be that
of the tibia of the saint, is enclosed in a reliquary of gilded bronze
and enamel surmounted by a silver hand. In the middle of one
side is a great crystal through which the relic may be seen: four
half circles surround the crystal, in each of which are enamels depicting an angel; while on the other side is a medallion showing

---

[1] The retention of the relics on the altar would seem to have been due to a desire on the
part of the Lutherans to hide from the simple people the fact that there had been a change
of religion.

[2] The foregoing account of the vicissitudes of the relics of St. Olaf is taken from *A
Guide to the Cathedral of Nidaros* (pp. 19–20), written by Aug. Albertsen, the architect
of the cathedral church, and published at Trondheim in 1946. The *Passio et Miracula
Beati Olavi*, edited by F. Metcalfe (Oxford, 1881), introduct., p. 30, gives a somewhat
different version.

[3] The cathedral church of Upsala had been dedicated to SS. Eric, Olaf and Laurence.

our Lord in an attitude of benediction holding the book of the gospels. Alpha and Omega appear over his shoulder. Under and round the base are four saints: an apostle, a bishop, an abbot and an abbess, beneath which is the inscription: *Dextera Domini fecit virtutem.* The original in the museum at Copenhagen is believed to be Cologne work, dating from about 1200.[1] The reliquary and its sacred contents were probably a part of the loot taken from Norway by the Danes at the Reformation. On the other hand, we know that King Christian II had asked for a relic of the Saint from Trondheim on 6 August 1514. Some few years earlier, in 1493 to be exact, Magnus, bishop of Åbo in Finland, had made a similar request, but specifying that the relic should be *ex ossibus.* In return, the bishop promised to send the Norwegian cathedral a relic of St. Henry, Finland's patron saint.[2] Unfortunately, however, there is no record as to whether either of these requests were acceded to.

The successors of St. Olaf on the throne of Norway were said, by a pious fiction, to have received the kingdom from his hands, and, on the death of the king, the crown was placed on the altar. When, later, this was found to be impracticable, the relics of St. Olaf were carried in solemn procession to where the new king was acclaimed. The custom seems to have originated in 1204.[3]

The principal feast of St. Olaf was observed on 29 July, with a secondary commemoration (Translation) on 3 August. Adam of Bremen in his *Lives of the Archbishops of Hamburg* tells us that 29 July was a day of reunion for 'all the nations of the Northern Seas, Norwegians, Swedes, Goths, Cimorians, Danes and Slavs'.[4] The cultus of the 'Perpetual King of Norway' spread to Sweden, Denmark, the British Isles and beyond. The name 'Tooley', given to a London street, is a corruption of 'St. Olaf's', and marks the site of a former Scandinavian colony in London; while the London churches of St. Olave in Hart Street and St. Olave Up-

---

[1] J. J. Duin, *Helligdomsarmen, St. Olavs Kirke 100 År*, p. 39. Oslo, 1956.
[2] *Ibid.*, p. 38.
[3] Faehn, *Gudstjenestelivet I Nidaros Domkirke I Middelalderen*, ap. *Nidaros Erkebispestol og Bispesete*, p. 602. Oslo, 1953.
[4] Adam of Bremen, *op. cit.*, t. II, p. 82.

well in Old Jewry were also named after him.[1] The oldest representation of St. Olaf comes from Vernes in Stjordalen: very
different in appearance from the later 12th-century literary
tradition.[2]

A third Olaf, Olaf III Kyrre (1066–93), seems to have been a
deeply religious king, and the annals of the monk Simeon tell of
how he was accustomed to assist the priest at Mass.[3] He brought
from England a priest of the name of Turgot (Torgaut), to whom
the Norwegian Church 'owes much of its early organization'.[4] It
was probably due to Olaf Kyrre that the system of guilds, for the
promotion of social security and sickness benefits, was introduced
into Norway, and the king himself became a member of the
Miklegild (Guild of the Holy Cross) at Nidaros.[5] Gildeskaal in
Haalogaland is believed to owe its name to the erection of a
church in the time of Olaf Kyrre. There would seem to have
been no regular diocesan organisation in Norway before his
reign, although the system of parishes was considerably older,
and may have been an adaptation of the pagan community (*fylke*),
each with its own temple and priest. The first bishops, who had
been consecrated in England, were accustomed to reside at the
royal court and to follow the king on his journeys, much as we
find *abuna* in Ethiopia, of whom it was said that his 'episcopal see
was the back of his mule'.[6] The introduction of tithes, as a means
of financing the Church, is believed to have originated with King
Sigurd I Jorsalfar (1103–30).

The dependence of Norway on the English Church, which
lasted until at least the middle of the 12th century, was strongly
resented by the archbishops of Bremen, who were the metropolitans of the country until 1103, but their remonstrances were
unheeded. England seems to have been, before about 1290, the
normal route to Rome, and every archbishop had to go to Rome

---

[1] Churches dedicated to St. Olaf are found at Chester, Exeter, Chichester, York,
Fritwell (Oxon), Gatcombe (Hants), Poughill (Cornwall) and Ruckland (Lincs).
[2] Stagg, *Heart of Norway*, part 2, p. 25.
[3] Rolls, *Symeon. Mon. Hist. Reg.*, II, p. 203 (*an.* 1074).
[4] Stagg, *Heart of Norway*, part 2, p. 23.
[5] *Ibid.*, part 2, p. 22.
[6] These *hird-bishops*, as they were called in Norway, were personal to the royal establishment.

to receive the pallium.[1] The days of English affiliations, however, were over by the 14th century, and in 1338 we find Bishop Hákon in a letter to John, bishop of Skalholt in Iceland, bewailing the fact that wine no longer came from Flanders and England, but from Germany only.[2] 'The time of greatest intimacy between the clergy of Norway and England, as may be seen from the English Rolls, was the reign of Hákon Hákonarsson (1217–63), and especially the decade ending in 1230.'[3] After 1290 all is changed. The records of Norwegian clerics in England become meagre, and those for France plentiful.[4]

A century earlier, however, we read of Archbishop Eric Ivarsson (1188–1205) having studied at the abbey of St. Victor in Paris. Shortly before 1295, a certain John the Fleming is found as the right-hand man to the archbishop of Nidaros: 'so great a jurist that no one in Norway was his like'.[5]

Contact with France was further extended in the 14th century by the employment of Bruges as the normal route for Norwegians on their way to the papal court at Avignon.

King Olaf Kyrre established three dioceses, formed from districts attached to the principal *Things* ('Parliaments'), and hallowed by associations connected with the three patron saints of Norway: Nidaros (St. Olaf), Oslo (St. Halvard) and Bergen (St. Sunniva).[6] Stavanger and Hamar were later foundations.

The first monastery in the country appears to have been founded by Canute the Great, shortly before the death of St. Olaf (1030), on the island of Nidarholm (Munkholm) in the fjord near Nidaros. The earliest monks, who were Benedictines, were undoubtedly Englishmen, as were the first secular priests.[7] A second religious house, dedicated to St. Alban, was established on the island of Selje. Later, we find Augustinians at Elgesaeter near Nidaros, Bergen and Halsno: Cistercians at Lysekloster (1146), Høvedø (1147) and Tutterø (1207). Lysekloster had been

---

[1] The metropolitan see of Nidaros was established in 1154.

[2] *Dipl. Nor.* VII, no. 155; Leach, *Relations between England and Scandinavia from 1066 until 1399 in History and Literature, Proceedings of American Academy of Arts and Sciences* (1909), p. 546.   [3] *Ibid.*, p. 560.   [4] *Ibid.*, p. 556.

[5] *Ibid.*, p. 557; *Laurentius Saga*, cap. IX.

[6] The relics of the Saint were brought to Bergen by Bishop Paul in 1170.

[7] Willson, *History of Church and State in Norway*, chap. X, p. 130.

founded from Fountains and Høvedø from Kirkstead, and it would seem probable that English monks would have been in the majority for a number of years. In the 13th century, the abbots and priors of Lysekloster were frequently employed as ambassadors to England.

Bremen, as we have seen, was the first metropolitan see for the Scandinavian countries, but it was inconveniently situated, and the Norwegian kings resented its jurisdiction. A change of province was effected in 1103, as a result of the visit of a legate of Pope Paschal II (1099–1118) to Denmark. The bishop of Lund was nominated metropolitan, and given the pallium. So matters stood until 1152, when Eugenius III (1145–53) took the necessary steps for providing Norway with an archbishop of its own. Nicholas Breakspear, Cardinal bishop of Albano, was sent to effect this and other matters connected with the Norwegian Church, such as the introduction of a cathedral chapter with their appointment of bishops.[1] Cardinal Nicholas, who later ascended the Throne of Peter as Adrian IV (1154–59), won golden opinions: 'There never came a foreigner to Norway', says Snorre Sturlason, 'whom all men respected so highly, or who could govern the people so well as he did. After some time he returned to the South with many friendly presents, and declared ever afterwards that he was the greatest friend of the people of Norway.' [2] The province of Nidaros, which had been established by Pope Anastasius IV (1153–54) on 28 November 1154, comprised eleven sees, but the great distances between those which were outside Norway made effective control well nigh impossible: [3]

Norway: Nidaros, Bergen, Stavanger, Oslo, Hamar.
Iceland: Skalholt, Holar.
Greenland: Gardar.
Faröe Islands: Kirkebo in Straumo.
Orkney: Kirkwall.
Sodor and Man: St. Germans.

---

[1] There were at first 12 canons, later increasing to 18, and perhaps 24: each with his own stall and altar. The *Ave Maria* was probably introduced into Norway by Nicholas Breakspear. Willson, *op. cit.*, chap. XI, p. 143.
[2] Heimskringla, *Saga of Sigurd, Inge and Eystein*, cap. XXIII, Laing translation.
[3] Bishops of the Norwegian Church in Ireland were subject to Irish metropolitans.

'Perhaps the most remarkable man in the long list of the archbishops of Nidaros'[1] is to be found in Eystein (Augustine)
Erlendsson (1157–88), who has been described as 'learned, pious,
eloquent . . . filled with the loftiest ideas as to the power and
authority of the Church'.[2] There is indeed a marked resemblance
between the Norwegian archbishop and his more famous contemporary, St. Thomas of Canterbury, whom he met in England.
They had both served as a secretary to a king before their respective consecrations, and, in defence of the liberty of the
Church, they had each undergone a period of exile.[3] One of the
earliest representations of the martyrdom of St. Thomas is to be
met with in Norway: a little brass reliquary at Hedal in Valders,
dating from about the year 1220. Archbishop Eystein was appointed papal legate in *c.* 1171, an honour which was to be denied
to his successors until the 15th century. The most lasting
memorial to the primate is to be found in the existing cathedral
church of Trondheim, despite the very considerable restoration
due to successive fires and Protestant neglect. It is interesting to
note that Eystein, prior to his exile in England, was constructing
his cathedral in the Romanesque style, as may be seen today in
the transepts and chapter house, but that after his return to Norway he continued the work in the Gothic style, which he had
seen at Canterbury and elsewhere. The archbishop was also the
author of a Church lawbook (*Gulljaer*). A provincial council in
1218 declared Eystein to be a saint, and at the request of his
successor, Sigurd Endridesson (1231–52), King Hákon IV (1230–
52) applied to Rome for his official canonisation. The cause, however, never materialised: perhaps because the spectacular appeal
of martyrdom was lacking. The coronation of King Hákon was
performed at Bergen by Cardinal William of Sabina (Modena),
who had been dissuaded by the monks of Lynn from coming to
Norway on the ground that the inhabitants were 'wild men and
monkeys'! [4]

---

[1] Willson, *op. cit.*, chap. XI, pp. 146–7.
[2] *Ibid.* Eystein received the pallium from Alexander III in 1161.
[3] The sojourn of Eystein in the Abbey of Bury St. Edmunds (9 August 1181–16
February 1182) is mentioned in the celebrated *Chronicle of Jocelin of Brakelond* (edit.
H. E. Butler, p. 15. London, 1949).   [4] Stagg, *West Norway*, chap. III, p. 60.

As late as the 12th century, no Norwegian had actually settled in Finnmark (Lapland),[1] but an effort to spread Christianity among the Lapps was made by King Hákon Hákonsson in 1248. A church was built on Troms Island to serve as a missionary centre, and it was still known in the following century as *Maria-kirk juxta paganos*.[2] It became one of the fourteen royal chapels, to which the priests were nominated by the king. We hear also of the consecration by Archbishop Jorund of a church for the Lapps at Vardo in 1307. Six years later, King Hákon V issued a number of laws respecting the Lapps: Norwegians were instructed to take care of them, and not to practise extortion. A Lapp who became a Christian was exempt from taxation for the ensuing twenty years.[3]

A closer union between Norway and Iceland, both politically and ecclesiastically, was effected in the time of King Hákon Hákonsson (*ob.* 1263). Legend tells us that Iceland had been visited by Irish monks in *c.* 800, but the country nevertheless remained pagan until the arrival of the Norse missionaries. A bishop was appointed in 1056 with a see at Skalholt, and a second diocese was established at Holar in 1106.

The history of the Icelandic Church is found in the *Biskup-asögur* (Bishops' Sagas), recounting the lives of the early bishops.[4] We know that at least two of the bishops of Skalholt had studied in England: Thorlac (*c.* 1160) and his nephew Paul (*ob.* 1211). A Benedictine monastery had been founded by the missionary bishop Rudolf, who had worked in Iceland for nineteen years (*c* 1030–49), but it soon disappeared. The first house of which anything is known was Thingeyar in the diocese of Holar (1153), established by its first bishop (Jon Ögmundsson). A second abbey was founded by the third bishop of Holar (Bjorn Gilsson) at Thverá in 1155. Iceland's great clerical legislator, Thorlac Thorhallsson, bishop of Skalholt (1178–93), came to be reverenced as a saint (1198). An opportunity to bring the Icelandic bishops into more direct contact with Nidaros occurred in 1237, when the two sees were vacant, and it was possible to have two

---

[1] F. N. Stagg, *North Norway* (London, 1952), part 2, p. 61.
[2] *Ibid.*, p. 54.   [3] *Ibid.*, p. 58.
[4] *Stories of the Bishops of Iceland*, trans. from *Biskupasögur*. London, 1895.

Norwegian bishops consecrated. The last married bishop in Iceland is said to have been Magnus Gissursson, bishop of Skalholt (*ob.* 1237), but the question of clerical celibacy seems to have been a problem in Norway itself for a long time. We find priests maintaining that Nicholas Breakspear, during his legatine visit to the country, had specifically granted permission for priests to marry. The alleged concession was hotly denied by Pope Gregory IX in a letter to Archbishop Sigurd (May 1237). The Pope affirmed that his 'predecessor of blessed memory' could not have sanctioned such an 'enormity', and the plea of 'ancient custom' made matters worse instead of better: *peccatum non minuat sed augmentet.* Celibacy, however, continued to be a matter of some concern to the Norwegian bishops, and 'concubinage' among the clergy was condemned at synods of Bergen in 1307 (diocesan) and 1320 (provincial). Bergen in the 14th century would seem to have caused considerable worry to the ecclesiastical authorities in respect to its morals. Jacob Jensson, who became bishop in 1372, says in a letter of 1390: '. . . frequency of promiscuity—which is greater in this little city than anywhere else of the same size in all Christendom . . . if they will not abandon this sinful life, we by this letter forbid them and their mistresses to receive Christ's Body'.[1]

Communication with Iceland was all but broken after the Black Death (1349).

The 13th century witnessed the termination of the nominal rule of the Norwegian kings over the Hebrides (*Syderøer*) and the Isle of Man.[2] Scotland agreed, in return for these islands, to pay an annual tribute, in addition to a lump sum of money. The Treaty of Perth (1266), however, in no way affected the authority of Nidaros over the dioceses concerned, inserting a clause: 'saving the right, jurisdiction and liberty of the Church of Nidaros, which it has in respect to the bishop and Church of Man, and saving also the Orkneys and Shetland'.[3] The Isle of Man thus remained under

---

[1] Stagg, *West Norway*, chap. IV, p. 85.

[2] Before the suzerainty of Norway, the Church of Man appears to have depended on Dublin.

[3] P. A. Munch, *Chronicle of Man and the Sudreys*, vol. II, append., no. 27, p. 325. *Manx Society*, Douglas, 1874.

the jurisdiction of Nidaros until 1458, when Calixtus III (1455–85) transferred it to York.[1] Orkney became subject to the metropolitan see of St. Andrews on the erection of the province in 1472.

The last bishop of Sodor and Man to visit Norway officially seems to have been Magnus, who attended the coronation of King Eric in 1280. Bishops understandably fought shy of the dangerous crossing to Norway, preferring either the shorter journey to England or the more colourful one to Avignon.

Before the establishment of a metropolitan see at Nidaros (1154), the bishops of Man and, perhaps, also those of the Isles had been consecrated by the archbishops of York, although such a consecration did not necessarily infer ecclesiastical jurisdiction over the Island, despite claims to the contrary.[2] A letter of Pope Innocent IV (1243–54) refers to a claim on the part of the Cistercian monks of Furness to elect a bishop for Man from among their own community, but there is evidence that neither the king nor the people had any intention of thus ceding their rights.[3] The reason for the transference of the diocese of Man to the province of Nidaros (1154) can be accounted for by the presence in Norway of Godred, king of Man, in the previous year (1153), when, in return for assistance, he submitted himself to the Norwegian crown.[4] Pope Innocent III (1198–1216), in a brief addressed to Eric, archbishop of Nidaros, in 1205, stated categorically that all the bishops of the province were to be consecrated by him and his successors, and that in a case of *sede vacante* the consent of the chapter of Nidaros must be obtained.[5] Such a proceeding, however, was by no means always followed, and in 1244 Pope Innocent IV arranged for the archbishop of York to consecrate the bishops of Man, albeit with the consent of the archbishop of

---

[1] Politically, the Isle of Man depended on Scotland from 1290, but, after a period of disputed title, it was finally brought under English suzerainty in 1333.

[2] The diocese of Sodor and Man included the Isle of Man and the Western Isles of Scotland or Southern Hebrides.

[3] The alleged privilege of Furness was based on an agreement recorded in a letter of King Olaf I to Thurstan, archbishop of York (1134), in which the prelate was invited to consecrate the bishop-elect. Munch, *op. cit.*, vol. II, pp. 269–71. Furness was in fact the heir of Savigny, after the foundation of the Lancashire house in 1126.

[4] *Ibid.*, vol. I, p. 239.

[5] *Ibid.*, vol I, p. 241.

Nidaros, 'because the Church of Nidaros is very remote, and the Church of Man is separated from it by a most dangerous sea'.[1]

Diocesan synods were held in Man in 1229 under Bishop Simon, 1291 under Bishop Mark and 1351 under William Russell, but none of them make any reference to any provincial authority, except that in 1291 the ruling on one point is declared to be 'according to the custom of the English Church and ours'.[2] This is the more surprising because Bishop Mark was a Scot, and the nominee of the king of Scotland, who had over-ruled the choice of Furness and of the clergy and people of Man. The bishop, moreover, had himself assisted at a provincial synod in Norway.

William Russell, who had been Cistercian abbot of Rushen, was consecrated bishop of Man at Avignon by the cardinal bishop of Ostia in 1348. The reason for this departure from precedent was explained by Pope Clement VI (1342–52) in a letter to the archbishop of Nidaros, dated April 1349, in which it was said that it was 'by no means to be ascribed to any intention of the Pope to detach the Sudreyan see from the *Provincia Nidrosiensis*, or to give any prejudice to his metropolitan rights, but only to the circumstance that this episcopate, as all others, or in general all ecclesiastical benefices, had been reserved by the Pope for his own provision'.[3] It is noteworthy, however, that from this time no bishop of Man ever went to Nidaros for consecration, although the diocese remained in the Norwegian province until 1458.

So late as 1374, a letter of Pope Gregory XI (1370–78) to the archbishop of Nidaros says in reference to the bishopric: *suffraganea tua*.[4] The bull of Calixtus III (1455–58) in 1458 definitely established Man in the province of York, but by this time its connections with Nidaros had become so tenuous that it was doubtful whether Rome made a conscious and precise transfer of the see from one province to another or whether it merely acknowledged

---

[1] *Op. cit.*, vol. II, append. XIX, pp. 309–10. The Icelandic Annals omit the names of all those bishops who had not received consecration at the hands of the archbishop of Nidaros.

[2] *Secundum consuetudinem ecclesiae Anglicani et nostrae. Manx Society*, vol. IX, *Synodal Statutes of Bishop Mark*, p. 194.

[3] Munch, *op. cit.*, vol. I, p. 147; Vol. II, append., nos. 17, 18.

[4] *Ibid.*, vol. I, pp. 255–6; Vol. II, append., no. 47, pp. 399–400.

what it accepted as the by then *de facto* position.[1] In 1542, when England was already severed from Catholic unity, a statute of Henry VIII 'annexed, joined, and united (Man) to the said province and metropolitan jurisdiction of York'.[2]

A first-hand picture of Nidaros early in the 13th century has been left to us in the recorded personal observations of Snorre Sturlasson. The residence of the king had been removed from Nidaros to Bergen by King Hákon IV (1217–63) in 1223, and finally to Oslo in 1286. Northern Norway now became more remote, and as early as 1272 we read that 'the northern districts are now less populous'.[3] The most prosperous period of the Norwegian Church was probably attained in the reign of Hákon V (1299–1319), but from the time of the Black Death (*Sorte Dod*) in 1349, when a third of the population are said to have died, we find a gradual declension in the spiritual life of the Church: all the bishops, with the exception of Solomon of Oslo, perished; while at Nidaros only a single member of the chapter survived.[4] Whole villages were deserted, and, in some cases, their very existence was forgotten. Thus the *stav kirke* at Gol, now in the *Norsk Folkemuseum* near Oslo, was discovered by accident in a forest in the centre of Norway. The church, which dated from *c.* 1200, was the sole evidence that a village had once existed there. Further outbreaks of plague occurred in 1359 and 1371, and, on the accession of Thrond to the primacy, no more than forty old and feeble priests were to be found in the diocese, in place of the former three hundred. 'The clergy', says Commander Stagg, 'were the greatest sufferers, as they caught infection when administering the last rites, and with them dwindled such culture as there was in the North in the 14th century.'[5] As a result of the mortality, a priest could now be ordained at the age of eighteen instead of the normal twenty-five.[6] Such a departure from customary practice could not but have a deleterious effect on clerical culture. Archbishop Thrond (1373–81) would seem to have been the last primate of Nidaros to visit Avignon. Nicholas Finkenov, his successor (1382–6), was a Danish noble who plundered his

---

[1] *Manx Society*, vol. IX, pp. 21–3.   [2] 33 Henry VIII, cap. XXXI.

[3] Stagg, *North Norway*, part 2, p. 58.   [4] Albertsen, *op. cit.*, p. 19.

[5] Stagg, *North Norway*, part 3, p. 66.   [6] Stagg, *Heart of Norway*, part 3, p. 59.

cathedral of all its moveables, and never performed an ecclesiastical office or even confirmed a child. The archiepiscopal library was carried off to Vordingborg in Denmark, although this was retrieved by his successor, a Swede of the name of Vinalde (1386–1402).[1] Theodore of Niem, who was bishop of Verdun and, later, archbishop of Cambrai (*ob.* 1417) says of the Norwegian priests of his day: 'The clergy are, as a rule, poor in dress and adornments, and perform the Divine Service with few ceremonies and no solemnity.' [2] A certain revival was noticeable in the time of Archbishop Aslak Harniktsson Bolt (1428–50), the second primate to hold the position of papal legate. It would seem, however, that the prelate was more of a lawyer and canonist than a pastor, and one writer suggests that 'his main activities combined those of an estate agent and chartered accountant rather than a primate of the Norwegian Church'.[3] An inventory of church property in the diocese was compiled in 1440: known as the *Jordebog* or 'Doomsday book'. The compilation is a mine of information on the enforcement of Church discipline, and we read of one farmer who had to surrender a share of his farm because he had eaten meat before receiving Holy Communion.[4] Provincial councils, which had been abandoned since the days of Archbishop Olaf (1349–71), were revived in this episcopate, but at the council held at Bergen in 1435 not one of the suffragans put in an appearance; while at a similar gathering at Oslo in the following year (1436) the bishop of the diocese was himself absent. It is interesting to record the impressions of a Captain Quirini, who was shipwrecked with his crew on the Island of Rost at the extreme tip of the Lofoton Archipelago in 1432. The Italian commander seems to have been most edified by the inhabitants, all of whom, he says, attended Mass on Sundays and Saint's days; while at Easter 72 out of a total of 120 received Holy Communion. 'They never quarrelled or used bad language.' [5]

---

[1] Stagg, *Heart of Norway*, part 3, p. 60.

[2] Willson, *op. cit.*, chap. XVII, pp. 262–3. Theodore had been *abbreviator et scriptor* in the Curia under Urban VI (1378–89).

[3] *Stagg, op. cit.*, p. 61. An inventory, known as the 'Red Book', was compiled for the diocese of Oslo by its bishop, Eystein Aslaksson (1386–1407).

[4] *Ibid.*, part 3, p. 62.

[5] Stagg, *North Norway*, part 3, pp. 70–1.

Church reform received a setback from the union of Norway with Denmark, consequent upon the death of the Norwegian king in 1448. It was in this year that Pope Nicholas V (1447–55) nominated an ecclesiastical adventurer to the see of Skalholt, appointing him collector of Peter's Pence and nuncio. This Marcellus was in fact a runaway Franciscan, who had been several times imprisoned, and even sentenced to death. He crowned King Christian I (1449–81), but his misdemeanours finally came to the ears of the Pope, and he was excommunicated and imprisoned at Cologne.[1]

The times were evil, and we read of a sacrilegious tragedy in the abbey church of Munkeliv in Bergen. The year was 1455, and Bishop Torleiv stood before the altar with the sacred Host in his hands in a vain effort to save the small son of Olaf Nilsson, whom the Hansa Germans were seeking to kill. The assailants, caring nothing for either God or man, thereupon hacked off the hands of the bishop, and murdered him, together with those whom he was trying to protect, the chaplain and two Brigittine canons. The buildings of the abbey were burned to the ground.[2]

In 1469, King Christian waived the tribute which the Scottish kings were accustomed to pay for the Hebrides: first Orkney and then Shetland were pledged. The islands, however, had not been under the direct jurisdiction of the kings of Norway, but ruled by virtually independent earls. The patron saint of Orkney was in fact one of these earls: St. Magnus (16 April), who had been murdered by his cousin, King Hákon, in 1116. He was canonised in 1136.[3] A Latin hymn to St. Magnus, believed to have been written in Orkney in the 13th century, is preserved in the library of Upsala University. The music is described as 'a remarkable example of a composition of two parts dating from the middle ages'.[4] St. Rognvald, a secondary patron of Orkney, who was also an earl, was canonised in 1192.

---

[1] Stagg, *Heart of Norway*, part 3, pp. 63–4. Marcellus escaped from prison, and took refuge at the court of King Christian, where he exercised an influence on Church policy.

[2] The Benedictines had given place to the Brigittines.

[3] J. A. Storer Clouston, *A History of Orkney*, chap. VIII, p. 144. Kirkwall, 1932.

[4] Cf. John Mooney, *St. Magnus, Earl of Orkney*, Kirkwall, 1935; *Proceedings of the Society of Antiquaries* of Scotland vol. LXXIII, pp. 276–88.

The residence of the bishop was fixed at Kirkwall, but for about a century after the Isles' conversion there seems to have been no fixed episcopal see. The Shetlands became an archdeaconry. Kirkwall remained in the province of Nidaros until 1472, when it is expressly mentioned in the bull of Sixtus IV (1471–84) as a suffragan see in the newly constituted province of St. Andrews. The bishops were at first prevailingly Norse, but they had been of Scottish extraction for some considerable time before the change of metropolitan. If we may judge from two examples, the general episcopal standard in the 13th and 14th centuries would seem to have been far from satisfactory. In 1222, Bishop Adam of Caithness[1] was burned alive by his people for raising the scale of taxation to increase the revenues of his see; [2] while in 1320 the conduct of Bishop William of Orkney had been so scandalous that the archbishop of Nidaros (Eilif Arneson) was forced to send two commissaries—Cormac, archdeacon of Man and Grim Ormson, prebendary of Nidaros—to undertake an inquiry.[3]

The metropolitan see of Nidaros changed its name to Trondheim a little before 1483.

The province included also the Faröe Islands and Greenland. The Faröe Islands had been discovered by Irish monks in the early part of the 9th century,[4] but their settlements seem to have had little or no influence on the later Church, which owed its inception to missionaries sent by King Olaf Tryggvason (*ob.* 1002). A see was established at Kirkebo, and the bishops were usually chosen from among the canons of Bergen.

Christianity came to Greenland about the same time, and an organised Church came into existence, with sixteen parishes and an episcopal residence at Gardar. Continued disturbances in the Scandinavian countries, however, caused this remote colony to be forgotten, and eventually all relations between the Norse

---

[1] Caithness was never in the province of Nidaros. It was specifically named as a Scottish see in the bull of 13 May 1192, which was confirmed by Innocent III (1198–1216) and Honorius III (1216–27).

[2] *Ibid.*, cap. XIX, p. 217.

[3] *Ibid.*, cap. XX, pp. 237–8. In addition to personal misconduct, the bishop was accused of alienating church lands, neglecting the cathedral and failing to fill vacant canonries.

[4] Dicuil, *De mensura orbis terrae*, edit. Parthey, Berlin, 1872.

settlers and the mother country ceased. No bishop appears to
have visited Greenland after the beginning of the 15th century,
although a succession of titular bishops was maintained until
1537. In 1492, a bull of Alexander VI (1492–1503) had said that
no ship is believed to have made the voyage there for eighty
years. The inhabitants had nothing left to remind them of the
Christian religion, but a corporal which was exhibited once a
year, upon which, one hundred years ago, the Body of Christ was
consecrated by the last remaining priest there. The archbishop of
Nidaros, Eric Walkendorf (1510–22), planned a resumption of
communications with Greenland, but the attempt failed, as King
Christian refused to co-operate in the scheme.[1] The inhabitants
were thus lost to Christianity until the introduction of Lutheran-
ism by the Danes in the 18th century.

The Reformation in Norway was almost exclusively the work
of Denmark. 'Never', says Mr. Willson, a non-Catholic historian, 'was there a more wanton spoliation than that which befel
the Church of Norway, and never had religion less to do with it.
. . . But the fact remains that in Norway there was no reformation
movement whatever.' [2] On the other hand, the Norwegians can
hardly be said to have shown very much zeal for Catholicism.
The majority of the peasants seem to have been more or less indifferent to religion, and the impoverished nobility were not
averse to enriching themselves from the property of the Church.[3]
The Norwegian episcopate was too feeble to resist the Danish
attack, and a wholesale spoliation and destruction of ecclesiastical
buildings and property went on from 1528: 'a few years after,
with one ignoble exception,[4] . . . we find the historic episcopate
of Norway a thing of the past'. On the death of King Frederick I
in 1533, civil war raged, and for four years the crown of Norway
was vacant, with the government of the country carried on by a
council under the presidency of Archbishop Olaf Engelbrektsson
(1523–38). Unfortunately, at the most critical moments, the

---

[1] Willson, *op. cit.*, cap. XX, pp. 297–8.

[2] *Ibid.*, cap. XX, p. 310.

[3] Pius Wittmann, *Norway, Catholic Encyclopedia*, vol. XI, p. 119.

[4] The 'ignoble exception' was Hans Reff, bishop of Oslo, who apostatised to Luther-
anism.

archbishop failed to act decisively, with the result that Norway became wholly subjugated to Denmark (Christian III, 1537–59), where Protestantism was strong, and the ancient Church was swept away.[1] Events moved with great rapidity after 1536. In June of that year Archbishop Olaf fled to the Netherlands, and the rest of the episcopate, with the exception of the renegade of Oslo, were dispossessed and imprisoned. The old priests were for the most part left undisturbed in their parishes, and, when they died, Lutheran pastors took their place.[2]

A like fate overtook the dioceses of what one may call the *diaspora* of the province of Nidaros.

The Church in Greenland, as we have seen, died out from lack of communication with Norway in the 15th century; while in the other dioceses Protestantism in one form or another was forcibly introduced at the Reformation.

The rite of Nidaros ceased to exist.

ARCHITECTURE

St. Olaf, on the advice of the *hird* bishop Grimkell, enjoined, at a *ting* in Moster, that churches should be built by the people on sites selected by the bishop. The present church at Moster, however, dates from about 1150. It has a large bell with a figure of St. Olaf (impression) and an inscription: *Ave Maria gracia plena, Dominus tecum.*

Olaf Tryggvason (*ob.* 1002), to whom the permanent establishment of Christianity in Norway was largely due, erected a timber church dedicated to St. Clement in his capital of Nidaros. The earliest churches in the country were everywhere built of wood, and in the Olands and on the fjords they so continued throughout the Middle Ages. Stone, however, came to be the customary medium in the towns and on the weather-beaten coast and islands.

The wooden churches or *stavkirker*, as they are called, are unique in their way and deserving of special mention. It is estimated that there were at one time some seven hundred and fifty, but of these no more than twenty-four have survived. An ex-

---

[1] Willson, *op. cit.*, chap. XXI, p. 328.
[2] *Ibid.*, chap. XXII, p. 350.

Bangor Cathedral, North Wales

Carved Bench, Stave Church, Heddal, Norway

Above: Greenstead Church,
Essex (tenth century)

Right: Trondheim Cathedral

haustive study of these churches has been made recently by Anders Bugge.[1]

The term *stav* is derived from a word meaning 'rounded post' or 'pillar'. The origin of these buildings has been much disputed. Dietrichson [2] (1834–1917) proposes England, from whence Norway received the Faith, suggesting that Greensted near Ongar in Essex may well have provided a model.[3] In addition to this he maintains that the wooden belfry at Brookland in Kent has many similar features.[4] It may be that the method of constructing the walls came from the *Opus Scoticum* of the British Isles, and that the later form taken by the *stavkirker* was the result of modifications introduced to suit the Norwegian climate and local circumstances. Nicolaysen maintains that these churches are, and always have been, unique, and in no way connected with others, except perhaps those in Great Britain and Ireland. He discounts an Eastern origin, pointing out that the Norwegian churches are *langkirker*, that is long and rectangular, whereas those in Russia are many sided and sometimes nearly round. No old wooden churches now exist in Denmark, but as that country received the Faith from Germany the building would probably have been of a German pattern. The *Reisvaerk* German churches are the nearest of the Eastern group to the *stavkirker*, but they differ in that their sides are made of planks nailed to the cross-beams, and not mortised into them. On the other hand, J. C. C. Dahl says that their shape suggests a Byzantine origin, by way of Russia and the Slav countries, and he does not think that the English churches had any influence on Norway. A further suggestion as to the original inspiration for these churches is offered by Strzygowski, who would see their basic construction in the buried Viking ships at

---

[1] Anders Bugge, *Norwegian Stave Churches*, trans. Ragner Christopherson, Oslo, 1953.

[2] L. Dietrichson, *De Norske Stavkirker*, p. 165. Kristiania, 1892.

[3] Greensted church seems to have been built originally some time in the 10th century and in 1013 to have received the body of St. Edmund on its journey from London back to Bury. A part of the existing nave belongs to the original building: trunks of large oaks split and roughly hewn on both sides, which were set upright and close to each other. These were let into a sill at the bottom and a plate at the top, where they were fastened with wooden pins. The original church was probably 29 feet 9 inches in length: 17 feet in width.

[4] Bugge, *op. cit.*, p. 38.

C C

Oseberg and Gokstad: the shape of the church being the up-ended boat, with the mast pointing down.[2] The *stav* church, says Mr. Willson, is 'the crowning point of the mediaeval art of church building'.[1]

Probably one of the earliest of its kind, serving as a prototype for others, was Urnes, built on a nobleman's estate about 1130. It appears to have been an intentional imitation of a stone basilica, with animal ornamentation of lions and dragons.[2] The church may be said to offer a reflection of the reign of Magnus Barefoot (1093–1103), displaying a concentration of the new values with which Norwegian art was infused.[3] The golden age of the *stav-kirker* was from the time of the sons of King Magnus until the civil war which ensued on the arrival of the priest Sverre (1177): a sound economic background had been laid by the introduction of tithes under King Sigurd I Jorsalfer (1103–30), and the Church had come to be a power in the land under a native Norwegian archbishop.[4] The building of such churches inevitably slackened with the centuries, but it did not cease until the change of religion in the 16th century.

The staves or pillars in these buildings form a framework of upright timbers, which are joined to horizontal groundsills below, and transverse beams above, on a square plan to form frames, which are wholly or partially filled in with planks, thus providing complete or partial walls.[4] Ornamental detail underlines the structure of the nave. Light is obtained from a window in the west gable and from small apertures placed high above in the walls of the raised middle section.[5] The chancel, which is similar to the nave in construction, was originally rectangular, but a semicircular apse was often substituted at a relatively early date.[6] An ambulatory or cloister (*svalgang*, *omgang*) frequently, as at Borgund, surrounds the building, for the purpose of protecting the walls against snow and other sources of damp.[7] It was used also as a shelter in inclement weather. A truncated conical roof with small cylindrical tower was sometimes surmounted by a

---

[1] Willson, *op. cit.*, append. 2, p. 364.
[2] Bugge, *op. cit.*, p. 22.
[3] *Ibid.*, p. 21.   [4] *Ibid.*, p. 8.   [5] *Ibid.*, p. 10.   [6] *Ibid.*, p. 12.
[7] Cf. Exterior cloister in the Mozarabic churches of Wamba and Escalada.

conical room. The entrances to the church were small porches
with saddle roofs and pointed gables, with a richly decorated
west door.[1]

The *stave* churches, however, varied both in size and construction with three main types: Urnes, Borgund and Torpo.

Ornamentation was not merely adornment, but also a form of
poetic expression, and throughout the 11th and 12th centuries we
may trace a continuous 'pagan iconography', or rather decorative
poetic language. To this belonged the transformation of the
foreign description of the Day of Judgement to a *Ragnorak*, where
the powers of evil appear in the guise of dragons, and are to be
found decorating the west doorways of practically every *stave*
church, as well as being found in a host of other places.[2] One of
the portals of the church at Hylestad (*c.* 1200) is decorated with
scenes from the saga of Sigurd the Dragon Slayer (Siegfried) and
from Gunnar in the Serpents' pit: events invested with Christian
significance.[3] In the 13th century, when there was no longer any
recollection of paganism, we find, for the most part, biblical subjects depicted on doorways. It is interesting to note that a Scandinavian character of decoration is found in Ireland: on the doorway from Trinity Island, Lake Oughter (Co. Cavan);[4] Killeshin
(Co. Leix); and the west doorway of the Nuns' Church at
Clonmacnoise.[5]

Hoprekstad and Borgund provide a basic pattern for the ornamentation of doorways in *stave* churches in the latter part of the
12th century.[6] Borgund (*c.* 1150), which is one of the best preserved of the churches, probably gives a better picture than any
other of what an ordinary parish church looked like in the years
when Norwegian architecture enjoyed its greatest period.[7] The
prototype of the church at Holtalen in South Trondelag was probably from England, and it follows the customary Anglo-Saxon
plan. A sermon for the feast of the Dedication in an old Norwegian book of homilies takes a *stave* church as its subject, and

---

[1] Bugge, *op. cit.*, p. 12.   [2] *Ibid.*, p. 41.   [3] *Ibid.*, p. 46.
[4] The doorway is now used as the vestry door of the Protestant cathedral at Kilmore.
[5] Harold G. Leask, *Irish Churches and Monastic Buildings*, I (Dundalk, 1955), chap.
VIII, 7, pp. 146, 147.
[6] Bugge, *op. cit.*, pp. 41-2.   [7] *Ibid.*, p. 8.

shows that the Holtalen type, in respect to its inventory and decoration, must have been the normal type of church in those days.[1] Hitterdals, the largest of the existing *stavkirker*, dates from the 13th century, although its architecture and ornamentation belong to the 12th. Unfortunately, however, the insertion of windows in 1850 has somewhat spoilt its original character.

By the end of the 12th century, such churches as were still needed in country districts were often built of stone, as we find in the Trondelag district, shortly after the beginning of the 13th century.[2]

The cathedral churches of the three original sees in Norway— Nidaros, Bergen, Oslo[3]—as well as that of Stavanger, were dedicated in the first place to the Holy Trinity. Two of them, however, came to be known as Christ Church, 'because', says Mr. Willson, 'Christ was, to the mind of the people at that time, the most prominent of the three Persons of the Godhead.'[4]

The wooden church, erected by Harald Blaatand (Bluetooth), the first Christian king of Denmark, at Roskilde, had a similar dedication, although this was changed to St. Lucius, Pope and martyr, when the stone cathedral was built (*c.* 1080), as the church had acquired what purported to be the head of this Pope (*ob.* 254).[5]

A dedication in honour of the Holy Trinity is almost certainly due to English influence, and the cathedral church of Christ Church at Canterbury is styled in Domesday Book: *Ecclesia Sanctae Trinitatis*. It is known also that Christ Church in Dublin, which had been founded by Sitric, the Danish king of Dublin (1038), was consecrated to the Holy Trinity.

The stone church (Christ Church) at Nidaros, erected by King Olaf Kyrre over the relics of his saintly namesake in about 1077,

---

[1] Bugge, *op. cit.*, p. 16.

[2] *Ibid.*, p. 47.

[3] The cathedral church of Oslo came later to be known as *Halvard Kirke*, by reason of the relics of this Saint which were venerated there.

[4] Willson, *op. cit.*, chap. X, p. 120.

[5] St. Lucius was honoured as the chief patron of Roskilde. Fr. Thurston suggests that the relic belonged to some other saint of the name of Lucius, who was commemorated on the same day (4 March). *Lives of the Saints*, edit. Herbert Thurston, vol. III (March), p. 50. London, 1931.

was incorporated in the more splendid building envisaged by Archbishop Eystein Erlandsson after the establishment of the Norwegian province (1154). The site of the primitive church of St. Clement seems to have been occupied later by the chapter house; while a third church, St. Mary, was demolished to make room for the new choir (1231–48). The primate, as we have seen, began the work on the cathedral in the Romanesque style, but changed to Gothic, which was then coming into favour, after his exile in England. The octogan, dating from the first twenty years of the 14th century, probably served as a lady chapel, and may have been built in imitation of 'Becket's Crown' at Canterbury. It is difficult to gauge how much of the old building has survived. There have been no less than five destructive fires—1328, 1432, 1531, 1708, 1719—and the conflagration of 5 May 1531 left the church in a ruinous condition, which was not attended to for about three hundred years. The cathedral of Nidaros or Trondheim, as it came to be called after the closing years of the 15th century, served as a burial place for the kings in the 11th and 12th centuries, and three of the monarchs were crowned there—the Swedish king, Karl Knutsson, in 1449; Christian I in 1450; his son John (Hans) in 1483.

In mediaeval times, Nidaros could boast of nine churches and five religious houses.

At Bergen, King Olaf Kyrre (1066–93) constructed two churches: Great Christ Church and Little Christ Church: the latter of wood. It was in this reign that the episcopal see was moved from Selje to Bergen, while retaining Selje as the title.[1] Eystein I transferred the royal residence from Aarstad to Bergen in 1110.[2] It was here that the Norwegian kings came to be crowned. The cathedral church of Bergen was wantonly destroyed at the Reformation. It had possessed twelve canons and twelve altars.

The cathedral church of Stavanger is estimated to be the finest extant church in Norway after Nidaros. It was founded by Bishop

---

[1] The title of the see was changed from Selje to Bergen in 1170, when the relics of St. Sunniva were translated from Selje to the cathedral church of Bergen.

[2] Bergen remained the capital of Norway until 1299.

Reinald, a Benedictine monk from Winchester, at the end of the 11th century, and rebuilt after a disastrous fire in 1272.[1]

Many of the churches in the country districts originated as private chapels of great landowners, and a similar state of things existed in Iceland and Orkney. The church at Dønnes in North Norway was probably built in the 13th century to serve as the chapel of Paul Vaagaskelm.[2] The *Ursland* chapel system, as it was called in Orkney, was found in nearly every parish in the 11th century. In four or five parishes or parts of parishes there were 'head kirks', the sole representative of the universal parish system. It is possible also that the pagan community (*fylke*), with its own small sacrificial temple and officiating priest, gave place to the Christian parish.[3] Trøndenes near Harstad, one of the finest stone churches in North Norway, was probably built in the prosperous days of King Hákon Hákonsson (1217–63). A certain priest of the parish, Audun Raude, who was later nominated to the see of Holar in Iceland, is said to have shown a great interest in church building.[4]

Fourteen royal chapels were established in Norway at the beginning of the 14th century, some of which were collegiate. The churches were united under a single superior, holding quasi-episcopal authority, thus forming an 'exempt jurisdiction' or 'royal peculiar'. The privilege was obtained by King Hákon V from Pope Clement V at Avignon in February 1308. The provost of the Apostolic Church in Bergen became the superior and visitor of all the royal chapels, with the title of *Magister Capellarum Regis*. On the death of the king, the authority of the clergy of the royal chapels was restricted to the care of the souls of the royal family, the household guards and those 'who sit in the King's House'.[5]

The architecture of the churches of the *diaspora* in the Nidaros province are on the whole disappointing.

Man. The cathedral church of St. German, which was built in 1245 on the site of an earlier building, is now in ruins.

---

[1] St. Swithin, the patron saint of Winchester, was given to the cathedral church of Stavanger as its patron.

[2] Dønnes is one of the very few private chapels in North Norway that is still standing. Stagg, *North Norway*, part 2, p. 55.　　　[3] Stagg, *Heart of Norway*, part I, p. 5.

[4] Stagg, *North Norway*, part 2, pp. 53–4.　　　[5] Stagg, *West Norway*, chap. III, p. 76.

Orkney. Kirkwall cathedral (St. Magnus), which had been begun by St. Ragnvald in 1137, was completed by Robert Reid,
the last Catholic bishop, only in 1540.[1] It is perhaps the finest of
the existing churches in the Nidaros province outside Norway.
Considerable remains of the church of Broch of Birsay on Mainland are still standing, and there are traces of the church of St.
Magnus at Egilsay and of the round apsidal church on Ophir.

Iceland. The island has no more than seven stone churches,
most of which date from mediaeval times.

Faröe Islands. The ruins of the unfinished cathedral of
Kirkebö, with its thick basaltic walls broken by high, massive
windows, are evidence that its builders intended to erect a fine
Gothic church. A small stone church of the 12th century now
serves for Lutheran worship.

Greenland. Several stone monuments and ruins survive to recall the early Norse–Christian period. The most important ruin
is that of a comparatively small Romanesque church at Kakortok.
Tombstones with Runic inscriptions have also been discovered.

LITURGICAL BOOKS

A full appreciation of the rite of Nidaros, with its modifications
and embellishments, culminating in the printed missal of 1519, is
difficult to obtain, as Norwegian liturgical books are scarce. It
would seem that no more than four MSS. have survived the Reformation; while of printed books we have but a single edition of
the missal and breviary, both of which were printed in 1519. It
must not, however, be left out of account that a very considerable
number of fragments of liturgical MSS. from the bindings of
church accounts are to be found in the Arne Magnusson's collection in the University Library of Copenhagen.

The three MSS., now (1956) on loan at Oslo University
Library, form part of the valuable collection in the Royal Library
at Copenhagen. They were looted by the Danes at the change of
religion in the 16th century.

The MSS. in question are manuals or rituals, each containing

---

[1] The last of the bishops would appear to have been a very worthy pastor: *Vir omni
literatura cultus et in rebus gerendis peritissimus.*

the *Ordo Missae* or, at least, a substantial part of it. These *Ordines Missae* have been studied of late years by Dr. Helge Faehn, a professor at Oslo University, who in his book, *Fire Norske Messeordninger fra Middelalderen*, has numbered the three MSS. B, C and D respectively: A being reserved for the printed missal of 1519.[1] They have been similarly described here.

MS. B, on palaeographical grounds, is considered to date from about the year 1300.[2] It is difficult to determine the exact provenance of these MSS., as there are no calendars, and the six litanies of the saints contribute but little to the settling of the question.[3]

In the case of B, however, Dr. Faehn says that 'much goes to show that it belonged originally to a parish in the city of Nidaros', which is thought to have been that of St. Gregory.[4] There was in fact a church of that name in the city about the year 1100, which was a parish church in 1296 and still existing in 1381. The following reasons are given for the choice of city and church: (1) the distinctive way in which the name of Gregory has been transcribed: *GreGorius*; (2) the absence of St. Halvard from the litany, which would be unlikely if the manuscript had come from the neighbourhood of Oslo, and more understandable if its provenance had been some northern or western district; (3) the MS. is the only one of the three to include the statutes of Archbishop Eystein; (4) the details of the *Ordo Missae* would seem to suggest that the MS. had been written for use in one of the smaller parish churches; (5) the text of the *Ordo Missae* bears a closer resemblance to the printed missal of 1519 than either C or D; and (6) the formula for the blessing of a ship, which we find in B, would be a likely addition, if the book had been for use in a coastal town such as Nidaros.[5] The saints in the litany of MS. B include Olaf, Swithin, Vedast, Amand, Magnus, Sunniva, Columba, Faith, Hope and Charity.[6]

---

[1] H. Faehn, *Fire Norske Messeordninger fra Middelalderen*. Oslo, 1953.

[2] MS. NY. kgl. 133f, Roy. Lib., Copenhagen.

[3] On the other hand, a calendar is by no means always a reliable guide to the provenance of a MS.: liturgical books were often sent from one country to another, in which case either a new calendar was inserted or, at least, local saints added to the existing one.

[4] Faehn, *op. cit.*, pp. 19–20, 129.   [5] *Ibid.*, p. 19.

[6] Fols. 32v–33r. The position of the name of Columba seems to suggest that the reference is to St. Columba of Sens, rather than to the Saint of Iona.

MS. C probably dates from the beginning of the 13th century.[1] The first of the two litanies of the saints includes the names of George, Olaf, Thomas, Magnus, Halvard and Edmund as representing the martyrs; Cuthbert, Benedict, Botulph, Giles and Leonard for the confessors; and Sunniva for the virgins.[2] The MS. contains an Order for the Visitation of the Sick; a number of votive Masses and Masses for the dead; the formula for blessing water, followed by the *Ordo Missae* and Masses for certain days in the year, including four of the Blessed Virgin. The *Missa de reliquiis* gives three prayers in which help is asked *per intercessionem sancti olavi regis et martiris nec non et aliorum omnium quorum reliquie in presenti requiescunt ecclesia.*[3] The MS. concludes with the Order of Baptism, a second litany of the saints and the blessing of the font. It is noteworthy that the name of Olaf in the litany heads the list of martyrs, before that of Stephen, whereas in MS. D, written about a century earlier, we find the more normal arrangement: first the Protomartyr and then Olaf. The martyrs commemorated include Halvard, Magnus and Eric; Willibrord among the confessors; Walburga and Bridget among the virgins. Dr. Faehn has suggested that the MS. came from Bergen or the neighbourhood, possibly from a religious house such as Munkeliv or the Bridgettine cloister, although we have no evidence of any relic of St. Olaf preserved there to account for the exceptional prominence given to his name.[4] The inclusion of the name of St. Walburga, says Mr. Christopher Hohler, is 'decisive for German influence in some form'.[5] Willibrord also, the Apostle of the Frisians, may perhaps point to Teutonic connections.

The third MS., D, is the oldest of the three, and, says Dr. Faehn, 'must be assigned to the 12th century'.[6] The Order of Baptism, with which the MS. begins, is followed by a litany of the saints in which the names of Oswald, Olaf, Halvard, Swithin,

---

[1] MS. Thott 110, Roy. Lib., Copenhagen.
[2] Fol. 2r.
[3] Fol. 98.
[4] Faehn, *op. cit.*, p. 19.
[5] St. Walburga, a kinswoman of St. Boniface, came to Germany to help in the evangelisation of the country.
[6] Faehn, *op. cit.*, p. 130. MS. NY. kgl. S. 32, Roy. Lib., Copenhagen.

Bridget and Sunniva occur.[1] A number of English and Irish saints appear in a second and more prolix litany: Olaf, Kilian, Magnus, Dunstan, Brendan, Amand, Columba, Columban, Cuthbert, Cunibert, Willibrord, Arnulf, Botulph and Bridget.[2] Here again German influence is almost certain: Cunibert was bishop of Cologne and Arnulf bishop of Metz; while Kilian, although Irish by birth, is honoured as the apostle of Thuringia. It is unfortunate that the *Ordo Missae* of the most ancient of these MSS. only begins with the canon. The second litany is followed by Orders for the Visitation of the Sick, Extreme Unction and the Burial of the Dead. The MS. concludes with a number of votive Masses and the Mass for the Dedication of a Church.

An *Ordo Nidrosiensis Ecclesiae*, probably dating from the first half of the 13th century, is found as an appendix to Codex 679 in Arne Magnusson's collection of MSS. in the University Library in Copenhagen. The book was obtained in Iceland, where it had been used and possibly also written. General directions are given in respect to ceremonial, chant and the various duties of cathedral dignitaries and others.[3]

The Norwegian province had no more than two printed liturgical books: missal and breviary. They both appeared in 1519: the one published in Copenhagen, the other in Paris. The archbishop of Nidaros, Eric Walkendorf, although a Dane, was a very real friend to the Church in Norway. The liturgical diversity in the province was abhorrent to him, and, in order to obtain uniformity, the archbishop proposed an *editio typica* for both Mass and Office. The preface of the new missal explained the necessity for its publication: many of the manuscripts had become more or less illegible; while Mass was being celebrated in a 'singular way' by Cistercians, Dominicans and Friars Minor, as well as by the secular clergy. At first sight, this reference to religious orders would seem to imply an abolition of distinctive 'monastic' uses, but it was improbable that anything so drastic was intended, and

---

[1] Fo. 8.

[2] Fols. 52v–54v.

[3] A valuable and detailed account of the MS. is given by Oluf Kolsrud in an article entitled: *Korsongen i Nidarosdomen*; ap *Festskrift* til O. M. Sandvik (Oslo, 1945), pp. 83–121.

merely concerned those secular priests who had adopted the books of the religious. A study of the 1519 missal, however, shows clearly that, despite the insistence of the primate on the use of the 'said book and none other', it would, on certain days in the year, have been quite impossible for a priest to celebrate the liturgy without the aid of some other book.

The missal is exceptionally meagre in respect to rubrics; while the ceremonies of Holy Week, as well as for those of Candlemas and Ash Wednesday, are for the most part wanting. On the other hand, unlike the majority of missals, the *graduale* has been included. The corrections, additions and revisions were supervised by the dean, Olaf Engelbrektsson (subsequently archbishop), and the cantor, Peter Sigurdson; while a canon of Copenhagen, Paul Reff, saw the book through the press.[1] Paul Reff had also been responsible for the *Missale Hafniense*. His brother, Hans Reff, was a canon of Nidaros. The missal was intended for use throughout the kingdom of Norway (and province of Nidaros), as the title page indicates: *Missale pro usu totius regni Norvegie secundum ritum sancte Metropolitane Nidrosiensis ecclesie*. The use of a title page would seem to have been a novelty at the time. As a rule, books of this period began directly with the actual text, the first words being: '*Incipit*'. The whole issue was bound by one and the same bookbinder in Nidaros in 1520, using exactly the same binding and decorations on all copies. This happened very rarely anywhere at this time. A facsimile edition of the missal is in the press (1957).

The preface of the breviary, which appeared in the same year, was equally insistent on provincial uniformity. Visitations had revealed a serious dearth of liturgical books, as well as a considerable number of defective MSS., with the result that many priests were unable to perform their duties correctly. Special attention, says the preface, was to be paid to the due celebration of Mass: *non sincopando vel aliquid omittendo*. Visitors were directed to make inquiries as to the manner in which the clergy

---

[1] A colophon at the bottom of the last page of the missal says: 'The missal according to the use of the Church of Nidaros is happily ended. Printed in Copenhagen by Master Paul Reff, Canon of the said town, and accorded by our Holy Lord the Pope the title of Acolyte at the Church of Nidaros in the year of Our Lord 1519 on the 25th day of May'.

said Mass and recited the canonical hours. Diversity of rite within the province was deplored: some priests were found to follow Rome, Cologne, Lund, Upsala, Utrecht or Sarum; while others again had adopted the usages of the Preachers or Friars Minor. Different uses are thus found in the recitation of Divine Office: *quod dolentes referimus*.

This foreword, which had been undertaken by a certain John Reff, is dated the Kalends of April 1516.

The breviary appeared 'with the consent and mature counsel of the venerable chapter', but in less than twenty years the Danes succeeded in extirpating the Catholic religion, and Protestant handbooks took the place of the missal and breviary of 1519.

No more than four copies of the breviary are known to exist, some of which are incomplete. The University of Oslo is at the present time (1956) collating the four extant MSS., with the intention of producing a facsimile of the complete breviary.

In all, there are nine existing printed Scandinavian missals: one Norwegian (Nidaros, 1519), four Danish (Schleswig, 1486; Copenhagen or Hafnia, 1510; Lund, 1514; Dominican), and four Swedish (Straengness, 1487; Åbo, 1488; Upsala, 1513; and Linköping, of which no more than a few leaves are known to exist).[1]

An inventory of the bishop's private chapel at Bergen, attributed to the bishop, Nicholas Paschius, in the first years of the 15th century, is found in the *Registrum Praediorum et Redituum ad Ecclesias Diocesis Bergensis saeculo P.C.XIV pertinentium vulgo dictum Bergens Kalvskind*, edited by P. A. Munch. The books

---

[1] Lund, although incorporated in Sweden in 1658, must be reckoned as Danish in respect of its liturgical books. It was in fact the metropolitan see of Denmark. In addition to the printed missal and breviary of Lund, we have the canon of Roskilde (1522) and the missals of *Hafniense Vetus* (?1484), *Hafniense Novum* (1510) and Schleswig (1486). The British Museum (MS. C. 110.1.4) has a single folio of *Hafniense Novum*, containing parts of the Masses for Christmas and St. Stephen.

Swedish liturgical books include the missals of Upsala *Vetus* (1484), Upsala *Novum* (1513), Straengness (1487) and Åbo (1488). Breviaries of Linköping (1493), Straengness (1495), Upsala (1496), Skara (1498), Brigittines (1512) and Vesterås (1513).

Manuals of Åbo (1522) and Linköping (1525): gradual (1440), *psalterium Davidicum* (1510) and *Horae B. M. V.* (1525).

The sources, it will be seen, are scanty, and for some dioceses we have no information at all. War has taken its toll of liturgical books, as in the case of the missal of Viborg, but the main reason for their rarity was the destruction at the change of religion in the 16th century.

listed are by no means numerous, and seemingly the worse for wear: *Item jn. libris, jn. primis twa gradualia, badhen vnwnden cum nota. Item twa maessu boger cum nota badhae jllafaren* [1] . . . *Item aein canonn. Item aein sequencionarius.* [2]

LITURGICAL YEAR

It was decreed by St. Olaf at a *ting* in Moster that fourteen holy days were to be strictly observed in the year. Each of these days, whether feast or fast, was to last for thirty-six hours.

The three existing MS. rituals have no calendars, and it is therefore impossible to find much help from them in respect to the liturgical year, although the lists of saints in the litanies give some idea of those held in veneration at the time. We have, however, an *Ordo Nidrosiensis Ecclesiae* of the early years of the 13th century, from which we learn that feasts were divided into three main groups, and that the third group was subdivided into two grades: semidoubles and simple feasts of nine lessons. The directions are not so detailed that it is always possible to distinguish between the grades. On smaller feasts the choir was led by a single cantor (*singulariter tenetur*) in a cope. On some days all the hours were festal; while on others we find the use of lights and incense, but copes were worn only at Mass.

The grading of feasts was more explicit in the printed books of 1519: *summum, duplex majus, duplex, semiduplex, novem lectionum.* It is possible to refer for purposes of comparison to the printed calendars of Upsala (1513) and Lund (1514), although Nidaros would not seem to have been very beholden to either Sweden or Denmark.

The 13th-century *Ordo* gives a list of fifteen feasts of the highest grade, among which we find the Invention of the Holy Cross, Assumption and Nativity of our Lady and the Passion and Translation of St. Olaf. The feasts of martyrs are prefixed with the words *In Passione.* The number of saints commemorated is small, and of the Apostles there are no more than SS. Peter and Paul, St. John the Evangelist and St. Andrew. In addition to St. Olaf,

---

[1] 'Both of them unbound and in bad condition'.
[2] *Registrum Praediorum et Redituum* . . ., edit. P. A. Munch, p. 6. Christiania, 1843.

the martyrs include Stephen, Holy Innocents, Thomas of Canterbury, Laurence, Cecilia and Katherine. Martin and Nicholas represent the confessors; while outside the foregoing we find no more than Michael the Archangel and Mary Magdalene. Finally, it may be noted that feasts are provided for the Exaltation of the Cross, Transfiguration, Purification, Annunciation, the 'Reception of the Blood of the Lord' and All Saints.

A much extended calendar, as we should expect, is supplied in the printed books of 1519.

Sundays after Trinity and Sundays after the Octave of the Epiphany are found at Nidaros, as well as at Upsala (1513) and Lund (1514).[1]

The Nidaros missal is said to have a number of parallels to the late Sarum use,[2] but, as we shall see later, the secrets, which are distinctive of the Sarum rite, are not found in the Norwegian book.

No sequences appear in the text of the missal: they have been relegated to an appendix. Each of the three Masses of Christmas is provided with its own sequence.

Despite the claim of the 1519 missal to be the *editio typica* for all the churches of the province, some other book(s), since disappeared, must have been in general use. The forms for the blessings of candles (2 February), ashes (Ash Wednesday) and palms (Palm Sunday), together with many of the rites of Holy Week, are not found in the book. The ceremonies for Candlemas and Ash Wednesday are found, however, in the missal of Upsala (1513): three prayers, dialogue, preface and four more prayers are prescribed for 2 February; while on Ash Wednesday there was a versicle and response, followed by five prayers and the imposition of ashes.

The Nidaros missal prescribes the three tones for the singing of the Passion on Palm Sunday and the other days: *Alta voce* for the Jews, etc.; *tonaliter* for the *Christus*; and *media voce* for the narrator, *quia verba sunt evangeliste*.

---

[1] At Upsala, the Sunday after Easter was the 'Sunday in the Octave', and the other Sundays, 'the Sundays after the Octave'.

[2] Faehn, *op. cit.*, p. 130.

On Holy Thursday, *miserere nobis* is prescribed for the third *Agnus*, and vespers are sung after the Communion. There is no rubric respecting the reservation of the Host for the rite of the Presanctified.

The liturgy of Good Friday is more or less complete in the missal, with the exception of the Adoration of the Cross. The first lesson (*In tribulatione*) is followed by a tract (*Domine audivi auditum tuum*), versicles and collect (*Deus qui peccati veteris hereditariam mortem*). The second lesson (*Dixit Dominus ad Moysen*) by another tract (*Eripe me, Domine*). The Passion according to St. John, Solemn Prayers and Adoration of the Cross follow. Although there are no directions for the rite of Adoration, a rubric says: when the adoration is finished, the celebrant resumes his vestments, washes his hands, and 'goes to the place where the Body of the Lord has been laid on the previous day'. A procession is made to the altar, where the *Confiteor* is said as usual. The priest then pours wine and water into the chalice, censes the *oblata* and again washes his hands. The *Pater noster*, with its introduction and embolism, follow, and the celebrant breaks the Host into three parts: one of which he lets fall into the chalice. A rubric says: *sanctificatur autem vinum non consecratum per Corpus Domini*. The Communion is followed by vespers, and the liturgy ends with the prayer *Refecti vitalibus*.

The ceremonies of Holy Saturday are far from complete in the missal. The rubric gives no indication as to what is to take place before the reading of the lessons: 'The blessing of the candle being finished, a lesson is read without a title.' The four lessons which follow are similar to those in the Gregorian sacramentary: *In principio, Factum est in vigilia matutina, Apprehendent, Haec est hereditas*. At the conclusion of the last lesson, we find the tract *Attende, coelum*,[1] versicles and the prayer *Deus qui diversitatem gentium*. Then, after the blessing of the font, for which no directions are given, the tract *Sicut cervus* and another prayer: *Concede . . . ut qui festa paschalia agimus*. There is no reference

---

[1] *Attende, coelum* was sung after the eleventh lesson in the Roman rite before the revision of the Holy Week liturgy (1955): today after the fourth and last lesson, as at Nidaros.

to a litany before Mass, and a rubric says: *Deinde incipiatur missa cum Kyrie eleison.*

A similar ceremony is found on the Vigil of Pentecost, but on this day *Sicut cervus* seems to have been sung after the fourth lesson, and *Kyrie eleison* during the procession to the font. This *Kyrie* was in fact probably the litany of the saints. The rubric continues: *Cum ceteris omnibus sicut in vigilia Pasche prenotantur. Quibus per ordinem finitis: inchoetur missa cum Kyrie eleison.*

The Trinity preface is prescribed for the feast of the Transfiguration on 6 August.

We know that the feast of Corpus Christi was introduced into the Church of Iceland in 1236, and we may be certain therefore that it had been previously observed in Norway.

The two feasts of the Holy Cross (3 May; 14 September) were known in the Norwegian Church as 'Holy Cross in Spring' and 'Holy Cross in Autumn' respectively, although the titles are not found in the missal (1519). A relic of the true cross had been presented by King Baldwin of Jerusalem to Sigurd Jorsalfarer (1103–30), and a church was erected at the royal castle of Kongehalle in 1127, in order to house it worthily. The *stave* church of Nore in Numendal, which is cruciform and dating from 1170 to 1190, may well be the successor of the original church which was burned by the Wends in 1135.[1]

A feast of the Crown of Thorns appears in the missals of Upsala (1513) and Lund (1514) on 4 May, but it is not found in the Nidaros missal (1519).

There is, however, a commemoration of simple rite in the Norwegian book entitled *Susceptio sanguinis Domini* on 12 September. A relic of the precious Blood would seem to have been taken to Norway in the 12th century, and was probably venerated there from 1165. It is mentioned in the *Kristenrett* of Archbishop John in 1273.[2]

Blessed Virgin

The introit *Gaudeamus* was prescribed in the missal of 1519 for the feasts of the Visitation (2 July), Assumption (15 August),

---

[1] Bugge, *op. cit.*, pp. 35–6. [2] *Norges gamle Lover*, II, p. 358.

Nativity (8 September) and Conception (8 December) as well as for St. Agatha (5 February), All Saints (1 November) and St. Anne (9 December).

We know that the feast of the Visitation (2 July) was introduced into Iceland in 1472, and that of the Presentation (21 November) in 1479, so that, taking into consideration the close connection of Iceland with the mother country, we may assume that the two feasts were already observed at Nidaros.

The feast of the Conception (8 December) was celebrated with a rite similar to that of the Assumption: *summum*. The legend of the angelic messenger announcing to St. Anne that she would be no longer barren is recalled in the collect: *Deus, qui beate Virginis Marie Conceptionem parentibus angelico vaticinio predixisti.* A feast of St. Anne was observed on the following day (9 December) as a semidouble.[1]

The collect for the feast of the Assumption, at both Nidaros and Upsala, was *Veneranda*.

The oldest of the three MS. rituals, D, dates from about 1200 and records the usages of the latter part of the 12th century. It is therefore all the more remarkable that one of the litanies should have the invocation: *Sancta Regina mundi*, recalling the feast recently appointed for the Universal Church on 31 May.[2]

Votive Masses of our Lady in Advent, Christmastide and Eastertide, in addition to a common votive Mass, are found in MS. C, written some time in the 13th century.[3]

A list of the days on which a votive Mass of the Blessed Virgin is permissible is found in the printed missal. The same missal provides also two texts of a farced *Gloria in excelsis* for Masses of the Virgin. The first, which was said on feasts, was well-nigh universal in mediaeval and later missals. The other, for use on ferias, was less common: . . . *Domine Deus rex celestis Deus Pater omnipotens. Domine fili Marie unigenite Jesu Christe . . . Qui tollis peccata mundi miserere nobis per preces piissime tue matris Marie virginis . . . suscipe deprecationem nostram, ut nos tibi placeamus*

---

[1] A commemoration of the Compassion of the Blessed Virgin is found in the Upsala missal (1513) on 5 May.

[2] Roy. Lib., Copenhagen, MS. NY. kgl. S. 32, fo. 52v.

[3] Roy. Lib., Copenhagen, MS. Thott. 110.

D D

jugiter sacrosancte tue matri Marie virgini. Qui sedes ad dexteram Patris miserere nobis per Marie suffragia que mater sue piis filii.[1] *Quia tu solus sanctus Maria sola mater innupta. Tu solus Dominus, Mater sola domina. Tu solus altissimus, Pater Marie et Fili Jesu Christi. Cum sancto Spiritu in gloria Dei Patris. Amen.*

A number of Marial sequences are found in an appendix at the end of the missal.[2]

Saints

There is no calendar in any of the three MS. rituals, but the names in the litanies give some slight indication of the saints held in veneration in the Church of Norway from the 12th to the 14th century. A complete calendar for the province of Nidaros is found only in the missal of 1519.

The usual Gregorian feasts and 'Gelasian' feasts for the Apostles are found in both calendar and text.

The Division of the Apostles, which is commemorated on 15 July, together with St. Swithin, is a further proof of German influence somewhere.

Norwegian Saints

St. Halvard, patron saint of Oslo, to whom the cathedral church was dedicated, was accorded a feast (double) in the missal on 15 May.[3] His name is found in MSS. C and D.

St. Sunniva, patroness of Bergen and West Norway since 1170, when her alleged relics were translated from the Island of Selje to Bergen. A semidouble feast on 8 July is given in the missal of 1519: *Sanctos in Selio* ('Saints of the Island of Selje'). 'It seems probable that the whole story was invented by the clergy, who contrived to date the occurrence during the reign of the great missionary king, Olav Tryggvason.'[4] Adam of Bremen (*c.* 1070) gives a vague account of 'the holy ones of Selje', and puts the number of virgins as high as 11,000, who found their way into a cave, and were entombed with boats and attendants.[4] This legend

---

[1] *Sui pii filii* would make sense.

[2] The missal of Upsala (1513) has no less than twenty-three sequences for the Mass of our Lady on Saturday.

[3] The feast was accorded the rank of *duplex* by the provincial council of Oslo in 1436.

[4] Stagg, *West Norway*, chap. I, p. 34.

of Sunniva and her virgins bears a strong resemblance to the
story of St. Ursula. The name—Synneve—is not Nordic but
Frankish, and it is possible that the Sunniva legend is no more
than a Nordic version of that of Ursula. Be that as it may, the
cult of St. Sunniva was very popular in the Middle Ages. Her
name is recorded in the litanies of all three MSS.: B, C and D.
Regular annual payments, known as *Sunnivamel*, were contri-
buted by the Shetlands to Bergen until the 14th century.[1]

St. Olaf, patron saint of Nidaros (Trondheim) and protector of
the Kingdom of Norway, was accorded two feasts: 29 July (with
octave) and 3 August (Translation). His name is found in all
three of the MS. rituals, and in C (13th century) Olaf heads the
list of martyrs, even before that of Stephen the Protomartyr.[2]

St. Thorlac (*ob.* 1193), the great reforming bishop of the
Church in Iceland. His feast was officially introduced in Iceland
in 1199, but it would not seem to have been observed in Norway.[3]
His name is not recorded in any of the MS. litanies, although we
find a commemoration in the printed missal of 1519 on 23 December (simple). A complete Mass and Office of St. Thorlac exists in
the Arne Magnusson collection in the University Library in
Copenhagen, and is to be published by Mr. Offosson of Rejk-
javik. It is interesting to note that both Mass and Office have been
taken from those of St. Dominic. A Dominican friar of Bergen,
John Halldorsson, was in fact nominated bishop of Skalholt in
1332, and it seems very probable that he was responsible for this
Mass and Office.

Scandinavian Saints other than Norwegian

St. Magnus, earl of Orkney, despite the fact that he was murdered for political rather than for religious reasons, is venerated
as a martyr, and the cathedral church of Kirkwall was dedicated
in his honour.[4] The name of Magnus is recorded in all three of

---

[1] Stagg, *West Norway*, chap. I, p. 38.
[2] St. Olaf is commemorated also in the missals of Upsala (1513) and Lund (1514) on
29 July.
[3] *Dipl. Isl.* V, nr. 362 and L. Daae, *Norges helgener*, Chra. 1879, pp. 207–10.
[4] A church dedicated in honour of St. Magnus the Martyr may be seen today near
London Bridge.

the MS. litanies. The 1519 missal gives a feast on 16 April (double), and a commemoration on 13 December (Translation).[1]

St. Canute IV, king of Denmark, was the patron of a church at Tilven on Brønnøy in North Norway, of which the ruins are visible today, but neither he nor his more famous namesake, *St. Canute, duke of Schleswig*, find a place in the Nidaros missal.[2] The martyred duke was one of the patrons of Denmark, and the Lund missal (1514) gives three feasts: 7 January, 25 June (Translation) and 10 July (with octave). The Hafnia (Copenhagen) missal (1510) has a sequence for the January feast:

> *Preciosa mors sanctorum*
> *In conspectu Domini.*

Schleswig (1486) provides an altogether different text:

> *Diem festum veneremur Martyris:*
> *Ut nos ejus adjuvemur meritis.*

St. Henry, bishop of Upsala and patron saint of Finland, in which country he was martyred, has a feast on 19 January (simple).[3]

St. Anskar does not appear in the Nidaros missal, but his feast was celebrated at both Upsala and Lund on 3 February.

St. Eric, principal patron of Sweden, had a semidouble feast at Nidaros on 18 May: *totum duplex* at Upsala, with a further commemoration on 24 January (Translation). His name is found in a litany in MS. C (12th century).

St. Eskil, a missionary bishop in Sweden, was commemorated with St. Faith in the Nidaros missal on 6 October.[4]

St. Sigfrid, monk of Glastonbury and a companion of St. Eskil, had a feast on 15 February. The Hafnia missal gives two sequences: *Salve, gemma confessorum* and *Clara laude turma plaude dulci voce. Alleluia.*

St. Bridget, the Swedish founder of the Order of nuns and canons called after her name (Brigittines), was commemorated

---

[1] Upsala and Lund observed the feast on 19 August.
[2] No Danish saints are to be found in the Nidaros missal (1519).
[3] Double at Upsala.
[4] At Upsala on 12 June.

with a semidouble feast on 7 October. The feast had been reduced in rank, and the provincial council held in Oslo in 1436
prescribed St. Bridget as a double feast.

English Saints

Norway, as we have seen, had not only received Christianity
from England, but also had maintained a close intercourse with
this country for several centuries.

St. Cuthbert had two feasts in the Nidaros missal: 20 March
(simple) and 4 September (Translation; three lessons). The
secret (*Haec tibi, Domine*) and postcommunion (*Deus qui nos
sanctorum tuorum*) are identical with those in the York missal, but
the collect is different. The name of Cuthbert is found also in the
MS. rituals C and D. The Office of the Saint was derived, directly
or indirectly, from Durham, since it shared with the Durham
version the omission of the word *probis* in the responsary. This
omission is demonstrably due to a scribal error in King Athelstan's book, on which it must therefore depend.[1] It may be recalled that Turgot, to whom in the reign of Olaf III Kyrre (1066–
93) the Norwegian Church 'owed much of its early organization',
was himself a monk of Durham, and the shrine of the Saint was a
treasured possession of the cathedral priory church.

St. John of Beverley appears in the missal as a feast of three
lessons on 7 May, but his name does not figure in any of the MS.
rituals.

St. Dunstan, archbishop of Canterbury, is accorded a similar
rite on 19 May, and is found in a litany of MS. D.

St. Botulph, a saint popular in Scandinavia, was the founder of
a monastery at Ikanhoe, which is generally identified with Boston
(Botulph's town) in Lincolnshire. A feast of simple rite was
provided in the missal on 17 June, and his name appears in the
litanies of MSS. C and D.

---

[1] Christopher Hohler, *The Durham Services in honour of St. Cuthbert, The Relics of St.
Cuthbert*, p. 157. Oxford, 1956. The Office was written for the court chapel of King
Athelstan or his father, probably by a clerk from the Low Countries, and had a certain
diffusion in Wessex. It cannot be proved to have been used in the North before the
Conquest, but King Athelstan's book appears to have been rescued from obscurity and
its services tried out by the first Norman bishop, Walcher. *Ibid.*

St. Alban, protomartyr of England, has a feast of three lessons on 22 June. An abbey was founded in his honour by King Eystein I (*ob.* 1123) on the Island of Selje.

St. Etheldreda, abbess of Ely, is found in the missal on 23 June.

St. Swithin, patron saint of Winchester, figures in the missal as a semidouble on 15 July, and his name is found in the litanies of MSS. B and D. The cathedral church of Stavanger adopted St. Swithin as its patron after it had been rebuilt by Bishop Reinald, a Benedictine from Winchester. The printed breviary gives the feast a day later than the missal: 16 July. The Office in the Nidaros breviary was taken from Winchester. The English MS. is unfortunately incomplete, so it is not possible to give the antiphon to the *Magnificat* at the first vespers of the feast at Winchester. At Nidaros we find: *Letare plebs Wentonia: gaude gens Stavangaria.*[1]

St. Oswald, king of Northumbria and martyr, was commemorated in the Mass of the Octave day of St. Olaf on 5 August.[2] He figures in a litany of MS. D.

St. Edmund, archbishop of Canterbury, is in the missal on 16 November.

St. Edmund, king and martyr, appears in a litany in MS. C, and is provided with a feast (*simplex*) in the missal on 20 November. The Mass is the usual one which originated at Bury: collect, *Deus ineffabilis misericordie*; secret, *Hoc sacrificium devotionis*; postcommunion (*complenda*), *Sint tibi, omnipotens Deus*. Archbishop Eystein, during his exile, took refuge in the abbey of Bury from 9 August 1181 until 16 February 1182. The church of Stadtkirken in Vannylven Fjord (West Norway) is dedicated to St. Jetmund (Edmund), and we find one of the mediaeval guilds in Bergen which had St. Edmund, King and Martyr, as its patron.[3]

St. Thomas of Canterbury, the friend of Eystein, whose name is in the litany of MS. C, has two feasts in the missal: 29 December with an octave and 7 July (Translation), a simple commemoration.

---

[1] *Analecta Hymnica* XIII, p. 91.
[2] The feast is observed in the Nottingham diocese on 5 August: elsewhere on 9 August.
[3] Stagg, *West Norway*, part 2, chap. XII, p. 231.

Irish Saints

No Irish saint, other than St. Patrick (17 March), appears in the printed missal of 1519, but the name of Columba is found in MSS. B and D; while D has also Kilian, Brendan, Columban and Bridget.[1]

French and Flemish Saints

A number of the saints commemorated in the Nidaros missal were associated in some way or other with Rouen and its neighbourhood, where, according to the *Passio et Miracula Beati Olavi* of Archbishop Eystein, St. Olaf himself received the grace of Baptism. *SS. Medard and Gildard*, according to an untrustworthy legend, are reputed to have been twin brothers. It is possible that Medard may have been a bishop of the Vermandois: Gildard, bishop of Rouen. A joint feast (three lessons) was observed on 7 June.

St. Leutfrid (Leofrid), founder of an abbey near Evreux (7th century), had a feast of three lessons: 21 June.

The names of Medard and Gildard are found in a great many English books: Leutfrid in some, and it may be, as Mr. Hohler suggests, that these names were taken straight from some such book 'because they were in it', without any direct French influence. On the other hand, it would be hard not to see some such influence in the names of several of the other saints.

St. Bertinus, abbot in Artois, had a feast of three lessons on 5 September.

St. Audoenus (Ouen), bishop of Rouen, was commemorated in the Mass of St. Gorgonius on 9 September. His name appeared also in the first of the litanies in MS. D.[2]

St. Fermin, a missionary bishop in Gaul and said to have been the first bishop of Amiens, had a feast of three lessons on 25 September.

St. Ledger (Leodegard), a 7th-century bishop of Amiens, was honoured with three lessons on 2 October.

---

[1] Roy. Lib. Copenhagen, MS. NY. kgl. S. 32, fols. 53r–54r.
[2] Fo. 8.

St. Faith, a reputed martyr of Agen, also had a feast of three lessons, with a commemoration of St. Eskil, on 6 October.

St. Quentin, a 3rd-century martyr from the town on the Somme which now bears his name, was commemorated on 31 October.

St. Martin of Tours was honoured in the missal with two feasts: 4 July (Translation) and 11 November.

SS. Victoricus and Fuscian are said to have been put to death near Amiens in the 3rd century: 11 December.

In addition to the saints whose names found a place in the printed missal of 1519, the following names appeared in the litanies of the MS. rituals: Vedast and Amand in B; Giles, Leonard, Willibrord and Walburga in C; and Amand, Cunibert, Willibrord, Arnulf, Aldegund, Oda, Odila and Cordula in D. The names in the litany of MS. D, the oldest of the three rituals, show conclusively that there was some German influence somewhere.

Italian Saints

St. Juliana, who is said to have been put to death near Naples at the beginning of the 4th century: 16 February.

St. Erasmus, who is reputed to have been bishop of Formiae and a martyr in the early 4th century: 2 June. He was widely venerated as the patron of sailors.

St. Demetrius the great warrior-saint of the East, also finds a place in the missal with a feast of three lessons: 8 October.

The *Feast of Relics* was observed as a greater double in the province of Nidaros on 13 October. Upsala celebrated it on the first Sunday in September, and Lund on 11 July.

Upsala had also a Mass of the Holy Trinity *pro statu regni* on 20 June, and a feast of the Patron of the Kingdom on a Sunday in July.

Feast of Dedication. The anniversary of the consecration of the cathedral church of Nidaros is not given in the calendar, but from other sources we know that it was probably 29 or 30 April. The missal refers to the dedication of the high altar on 27 July.[1]

---

[1] Faehn, *Gudstjenestelivet I Nidaros Domkirke . . .*, p. 626.

ORNAMENTS OF THE CHURCH AND MINISTERS

The churches of Norway in respect to their architectual features and furnishings seldom attained to the magnificence of the cathedral and monastic churches in England and France. Nevertheless, the 13th century, with its liturgical codification, brought in its train a more elaborate form of worship necessitating a greater variety of both furniture and ornaments. Even so, how- ever, we read of Theodore of Niem, bishop of Verdun and later archbishop of Cambrai (*ob.* 1417), saying, after a visit to the country, that 'the clergy are, as a rule, poor in dress and adorn- ments, and perform the Divine Service with few ceremonies and no solemnity'.[1] It is possible that the simplicity and poverty were due in part to the Black Death, the ill effects of which must have been still apparent, but it would be a mistake to ascribe all the lack of pomp to that cause. The province of Nidaros would seem to have largely restricted itself to those ornaments which were essential for the due ordering of Divine Worship.

The Reformation, which was effected in 1536, was, as we have seen, a purely political affair and not a matter of conscience. The people themselves had not changed their faith. Iconoclasm was no part of the Protestantising of the country, save at Bergen, where the Hansa Germans were all powerful. At a meeting held here in 1569, it was decided to root out 'idolatrous images in God's house': all waxen figures were to be removed forthwith, and all statues, except those on the high altars, would quietly disappear.[2] The comparatively late date of the order, thirty-three years after the enforced change of religion, would seem to in- dicate a certain reluctance on the part of the people to abandon their traditional beliefs. We know that pilgrimages continued for many decades after the Reformation, and notably to Brune in Sunnmøre, St. Thomas' Church on Filefjell and Rødals. At the last named we find an annual service in commemoration of a miraculous crucifix so late as 1840.

The Lutheran clergy[3] retained the crucifix on their Communion

---

[1] Willson, *op. cit.*, chap. XVII, pp. 262–3.   [2] Stagg, *West Norway*, chap. V, p. iii.
[3] The first Lutheran pastors in Norway would seem to have been either Danes or Germans.

tables and wore vestments for 'High Mass', even in some cases elevating the bread. The authorities appear to have wished to make as few changes as possible in ornaments and ceremonial, in order not to arouse the suspicions of simple-minded people unduly.

In spite of this, however, the surviving ornaments would seem to be neither numerous nor remarkable.

The *Musée de Cluny* in Paris has some 13th-century Icelandic embroidery, depicting the life of St. Martin of Tours.

The paucity of old vestments may possibly be due to a statute passed at the provincial council which met at Bergen under Archbishop Eilif in 1320, at which the bishops of Orkney and the Faröes were present. The council directed that all discarded vestments should be burned in the church, and the ashes placed under the altar.

A somewhat late mediaeval chasuble, taken from Veøy church, Romsdal, is preserved in the Historical Museum at Bergen; and a vestment bearing the arms of Archbishop Walkendorf (1510–22) is to be found in the church of Kolding in Denmark, probably part of the loot removed at the Reformation. A facsimile of the Kolding chasuble has been made for the cathedral church at Trondheim. An earlier vestment, dating from about 1250, formerly in use in the church at Röldal, has also survived the passing of the years and the change of religion.[1]

The *Ordo Nidrosiensis Ecclesiae* of the first half of the 13th century has prescribed the correct choir dress, but without any reference to the vestments of the Mass.

Members of the choir are directed to wear surplices: while canons have in addition an almuce or *cappa nigra*, according to the season of the year. On great solemnities, four cantors in coloured copes led the choir (*quatuor cantores cappis induti cum coloribus tenent chorum*), and on second-class feasts two cantors (*chorus a duobus cantoribus tenetur*). These copes (*korkapa, kantarakapa*) were often richly embroidered. The canonical statutes of Lund (*c.* 1130) say that the cantor wore a *cappa purpurea*, and held a staff and *tabulae*: an instrument to give the correct key. In 1145,

---

[1] *Nordisk Kultur*, vol. XXIII, p. 251.

cantors in the cathedral church of Lund were permitted by Archbishop Eskil to carry *ornati baculi*.[1] It was customary on an appointment to a canonry in Denmark for the new canon to present
a cope to his church. Thus we find it at Roskilde in 1310,
Schleswig in 1352, Aarhus in 1388 and Viborg in 1440.[2]

Pontificalia in the shape of mitre and crozier were accorded to
the Provost of the Apostolic Church of Bergen in his capacity of
Superior of the Royal Chapels. The privilege was obtained from
Pope Clement V at Avignon by King Hákon in February 1308.
It is possible also that the designation of cantors by the title of
praelatar implied the use of a mitre, at least on more solemn
occasions. The head of a pastoral staff of walrus ivory with
traces of gilding and restored with bone, dating from the late 14th
or early 15th century, is preserved in the Victoria and Albert
Museum in London. It is believed to be of Norwegian workmanship, as on one side we find King Olaf and on the other a bishop
who may well be St. Thorlac, bishop of Skalholt in Iceland.[3]

The 13th-century *Ordo* of the cathedral church of Nidaros prescribed the uncovering of the *altaris tabula* on first- and second-
class feasts. A frontal or antependium of some rich material
(*preciosissimo velamine operitur*) was substituted on certain
octaves. This *altaris tabula* may have been something in the
nature of a frontal of copper and silver-gilt, and a somewhat
similar ornament was given by King Sigurd Jorsalfarer (1103–30)
to the church of the Holy Cross at Kongehelle.[4] On the other

---

[1] Kolsrud, *op. cit.*, III, p. 109.

[2] *Ibid.*, IV, p. 117.

[3] The figure of St. Olaf would seem to point to Norwegian or Icelandic workmanship,
but it has been suggested that the bishop might be either St. Eskil of Straengness, St.
Henry of Upsala or St. Willehad of Bremen. The restoration in bone was probably of
later date than the ivory work.

[4] The *Paliotto* in the basilica of S. Ambrogio at Milan (*c.* 835), consisting of reliefs on
a silver and gold ground, enriched with enamel and gems, is just such a frontal. Something similar—40 raised silver panels—encircled the altar of the cathedral church of
Torcello in the 11th century, probably contemporary with Orso Orseolo, the bishop who
reconstructed the church in 1008. Thirteen of these panels may be seen today in the local
museum. A frontal of ivory, with numerous figures in relief, depicting biblical scenes, and
dating from the 11th century, is preserved in the museum of the cathedral church of
Salerno. It would seem to have been based on earlier Byzantine originals. The *Pala
d'Oro* in S. Marco at Venice, which was executed at Constantinople in 1105, now forms
the reredos, but it was used as a frontal before its Gothic additions. It is uncovered at
Easter and on the feast of St. Mark.

hand, as Mr. Christopher Hohler says, it might have been a
'reredos', such as is found in the picture of the 'Mass of St. Giles'
(*c.* 1480) in the National Gallery (London).[1]

A number of altar stones have survived: some in museums and
others *in situ*, as at Maere, some miles north of Trondheim, and
at Trøndenes in North Norway. The museum in Trondheim has
a *mensa* from the church at Logtu which has retained its relics,
together with the seal of the consecrating prelate, Archbishop
Gaute. Altar stones with relics and seals intact, taken from the
churches of Orkdal (Trondheim diocese) and Bergen (*Maria
kirke*) have also been preserved.

A mediaeval paten, with a representation of the *Agnus Dei* in
the centre, formerly in use at Logtu, is to be seen in the museum
at Trondheim. A silver parcel-gilt chalice of the 13th century,
taken from the church of Grundt in Iceland, is found in the Victoria and Albert Museum in London. An inscription round the
lip says: *Summitur (sumitur) Hinc Nunda (munda) Divini Sanguinis Unda.* The accompanying paten is of later date.

The use of incense at Mass, lauds and vespers in the cathedral
church of Nidaros was regulated in the 13th-century *Ordo Nidrosiensis Ecclesiae.* The altar was to be censed with three thuri-
bles on first-class feasts, two on those of the second class, and one
only on days of an inferior grade.[2]

Such church furniture as has survived is not very remarkable,
but a carved pew in the *stave* church at Torpo is worthy of note.
The pew may have served as a confessional, and a carving on it
depicts what purports to be the sinner's fate: a man between the
jaws of a beast, while being bitten in the leg by a snake.

REGULATIONS REGARDING THE SACRAMENTS

Several of the provincial councils at the end of the 13th and the
beginning of the 14th century passed decrees respecting the due
administration of the Sacraments. In 1290, a council at Nidaros
under Archbishop Jorund directed parish priests to instruct their

[1] A chased silver reredos, executed *c.* 1290, is found in the church of S. Salvatore at
Venice.
[2] *Ibid.*, I, p. 86.

people concerning Baptism and Confirmation.[1] The *Pater, Ave* and *Gloria* must be taught to all the parishioners, both young and old: those who failed to learn them were to be punished. The same council also ordered due reverence to be paid to the Blessed Sacrament, not only in church, but also when it was being taken to the sick and dying. In the case of the viaticum, the priest was advised to carry the Eucharist in a little bag hung round his neck. Bination, or the saying of two Masses on the same day, was forbidden, except on great feasts or if a priest was compelled to serve two churches.[2]

Similar regulations in respect to the Blessed Sacrament were laid down at the council held in Bergen in 1320. Priests were directed also to see that the font was kept clean, and every year they were advised to get the oil of the sick from the bishop.[3] A strange request was made to Pope Innocent III by the archbishop of Nidaros in 1205. It was asked whether beer could be substituted for water in the sacrament of Baptism! One would certainly have thought that whatever else was wanting in Norway, water was plentiful enough! However, as one might suppose, the Pope replied in no uncertain terms: Water and nothing but water might be used.[4] It would seem, however, that the Norwegian archbishop declined to take no for an answer, and later in the century we find him making a similar request to Gregory IX, who, in a letter to Archbishop Sigurd in 1241, repeated the refusal of his predecessor.[5]

BREAD AND WINE

Wine was scarce and difficult to obtain in the province, especially in Greenland and Iceland. Thus in 1203 we hear of John, bishop of Gardar, while on a visit to Paul, bishop of Skalholt, instructing his host in the art of making wine from a species of berry called *kraekiberjum*. We do not know how popular such a concoction might have been, but it was forbidden by Pope Gregory

---

[1] Provincial synods were held at Nidaros in 1229, 1290, 1313, 1334 and 1351.
[2] Willson, *op. cit.*, chap. XIV, p. 222.
[3] *Ibid.*, chap. XVI, pp. 237–8.
[4] *Ibid.*, chap. XIII, p. 206.
[5] *Ibid.*, chap. XIII, pp. 206–7.

IX in 1237.[1] The same Pope was approached also by the arch-bishop of Nidaros, who asked if, when the Eucharist was wanting (*deficiente eucharistia*), they might communicate the people with any other sort of bread, along with beer or any other drink. The Pope replied that neither the one nor the other could be permitted under any circumstances (*quod neutrum est penitus faciendum*), and the matter of the sacrament must be *visibilis panis de frumento et vini de uvis*. In conclusion, the Pontiff said that *panis simpliciter benedictus* may be given to the people, 'as had become the custom in other places'.[2] Still, however, the shortage of wine in the country remained a very real problem, and the provincial council, held in Bergen in 1320, directed that there should be more water than wine in the chalice at Mass, so as to economise wine, which was sometimes difficult to procure. The celebrant, not the server, was ordered to add the water.[3]

CATHEDRAL DIGNITARIES AND OTHERS

The following account of the personnel of the cathedral church of Nidaros in the Middle Ages has been taken from *Korsongen I Nidarosdomen* by Oluf Kolsrud.[4] The translation has been made, for the most part, without comment, but one wonders whether it exactly represents a pre-Reformation cathedral staff, as we know it. A cathedral chapter was formally established in 1152, when Nidaros was accorded metropolitan status. A dean was appointed, and three archdeaconries were formed.[5] A hundred years later (1253–65), the chapter seems to have been presided over by an archpresbyter.[6] Later, until the reorganisation of the deanery in 1419, Nidaros was without a 'chairman'. Shortly before the Reformation, in the time of Archbishop Eric Walkendorf (1511–22), we find the cantor reckoned among the 'prelates' (*praelatar*), whatever may be implied by the term.[7]

---

[1] *Diplom. Island.* B I, pp. 513 seq.
[2] *Diplom. Norveg.*, vol. I, no. 16.
[3] Willson, *op. cit.*, chap. XVI, pp. 237-8.
[4] Oluf Kolsrud, *Korsongen I Nidarosdomen*, ap. *Festskrift til O. M. Sandvik.* Oslo, 1945.
[5] Kolsrud, *op. cit.*, III, p. 104.
[6] *Ibid.* A similar arrangement existed also at Oslo.
[7] *Ibid.* The office of cantor received a like 'elevation' at Oslo.

In 1523, the duties of the dean entailed the due ordering of the cathedral services, officiating himself on great feasts, and preaching in the parish churches of the city on certain days in the year. It was the dean also who in 1519 edited the breviary in conjunction with the archdeacon, and the missal with the assistance of the cantor.[1]

Canons in old Norwegian were known as *korsbraedr* or 'cross brethren'. The cathedral churches of Norway normally had a complement of 12 canons,[2] but in 1253 we find 15 at Nidaros,[3] and in 1540 the number had risen to 20, although by that time the change of religion had taken place.[4] In Denmark, most of the cathedrals had more than 12 canons: Aarhus and Viborg, 15; Ribe, 24 in 1291 and 15 in 1495; Schleswig, 24; Roskilde and Lund, more than 30. The number seems to have been restricted to 12 in Sweden, with the single exception of Upsala, where we find 20 in 1470.

In the 14th century, three out of the five collegiate churches in Norway were supplied with canons: the Apostolic Church in Bergen,[5] St. Mary in Oslo [6] and St. Michael in Tønsberg.[7] The superior at Oslo and Tønsberg was the provost.[8]

The vicars in the Norwegian cathedral churches were divided into two classes: *vicarii perpetui* and *vicarii chorales*. The former grade, which supplied the celebrants for the side altars, gave rise to the term *altaristi* or *capellani*. Some also had a prebendal stall or benefice, and were known as prebendaries or *beneficiati*. In some of the larger cathedrals these *vicarii perpetui* formed a college of their own, as at Aarhus and Roskilde in Denmark, but this was never the case in Norway. The number of vicars in Norwegian churches is not known for certain, although they may well have been the same as that of the canons. In 1430, Nidaros cathedral had fourteen altars, in addition to the high altar.[9]

---

[1] Kolsrud, *op. cit.*, III, pp. 104–5.   [2] *Dipl. Norv.* VI, nr. 72.

[3] *Ibid.* III, nr. 4. In 1303, we find that ten of the canons were normally in residence: in 1307, eight (Kolsrud, *op. cit.*, II, p. 98).

[4] *Ibid.* XII, nr. 597.

[5] *Ibid.* I, nr. 113; Bishop Eystein's *Jordebog*, s. 181.

[6] *Ibid.* XVIII, nr. 130.   [7] *Ibid.* III, nr. 110.

[8] St. Mary's Copenhagen had twelve canons and Haderslev, nine.

[9] Kolsrud, *op. cit.*, II, pp. 98–9.

The *vicarii chorales* or *chorales*, as they were called, included, among their number, deacons and subdeacons. Nidaros in 1281 would have had some twelve of the three grades.[1] The institution of *vicarii in choro* is important in respect to the instruction of priests, as vicars choral were for the most part newly ordained men, who had been appointed to 'stand in choir' in the cathedral church for a certain time, in order that they might obtain a practical knowledge of Church worship before they were permitted to do independent work as parish priests.[1] In imitation of the custom at Lund and Roskilde, Archbishop Laurence of Upsala in 1261 decreed that the newly ordained should 'stand in choir' for a year, but that if they stayed longer they might expect a better post. The time of probation varied with the cathedral: Linköping (1272), two years; Aarhus, two years in 1306 and three years in 1310; Haderslev (1309), two years; Schleswig (1352), two years; Ribe, two years; and Viborg (1440), three years.

The *Scholares* or *pueri*, as they are called in the *Ordo Nidrosiensis*, were the most junior of the cathedral choir. They would seem to have been the older pupils from the school, but some of them would probably have been in minor orders: *skolaklerkar*[2] or *smadjaknar*.[3] Surplices were worn for both Mass and Office. We read of Hákon Hákonsson, when heir apparent, attending just such a school at the age of seven or eight. His foster father, Earl Hákon, asked what he was being taught, and, on the reply of 'Song, sir', the Earl acidly commented: 'You are not going to be taught song, for you will become neither bishop nor priest.' The boy was removed from the school at the age of thirteen, and was made king in 1217. He may easily have been one of the *pueri* in the cathedral church of Nidaros.[4]

Cantors in many—but not all—of the Scandinavian churches would seem, in the course of the Middle Ages, to have become 'prelates' (*praelatar*), but it is difficult to know just how much or just how little the title implied.[5] Perhaps no more than the right to wear, on occasions, a linen mitre. 'Prelatical' rank for cantors

---

[1] Kolsrud, *op. cit.*, II, p. 101.　　　　[2] *Dipl. Norv.* III, nr. 39.

[3] i.e. Little deacon. *Dipl. Islan.* IV, nr. 463. The name 'little deacon' is employed today in the Coptic Church.

[4] Kolsrud, *op. cit.*, II, p. 103.　　　　[5] *Ibid.*, III, p. 105.

was achieved at Ribe in 1240; Aarhus in 1260; Roskilde in 1315; Linköping in 1370; and Upsala in 1415. The privilege obtained at Nidaros sometime during the Middle Ages, and subsequent to 1290, as the dispute in that year between Archbishop Jorund and his chapter, respecting the appointment of certain cathedral officials, makes it clear that cantors were not at that time reckoned as 'prelates'.[1]

The list of officials at the cathedral church of Nidaros, which we find in Kolsrud, is not always very clear: seneschall, *scholasticus*, treasurer, penitentiary and sacristan: sometimes also a 'clerk of works' and an official appointed specifically for the 'upper church', in addition to *vm ordinem*. [2]

The expression 'upper church' is perhaps misleading, as, in point of fact, its floor was lower than the rest of the building. The 'height', however, was spiritual rather than material: the choir was of greater importance than the nave. In 1323, Archbishop Eilif had stipulated that laymen might not be admitted to the choir (*song-hus*), unless they were themselves singers.[3] The official appointed for the supervision of this 'upper church' would seem to have been unique to Nidaros.[4] The office *vm ordinem* for the regulation of the Divine Office with its many complicated rules may have developed later into the *officium cantoris*: a term unknown to Nidaros in the 13th century. The *Ordo Nidrosiensis* made no more than a passing reference to cantors in the rubric '*tenent chorum*' (on feasts), and no cantor '*regere chorum*' is mentioned. It was otherwise in Denmark, where the canonical constitutions of 1130 had a special chapter (XX) entitled *De officio cantoris*.[5]

At Linköping in 1272, the bishop defined the authority of the *scholasticus: auctoritatem ordinandi et imponendi officium*, and directed all to obey him: *cuicunque legendi vel psallendi officium imposuerit*.[6] A similar leader of the choir was in all probability

---

[1] The duties of cantors were defined in the Statutes of Oslo (1410–1501).
[2] Kolsrud, *op. cit.*, III, p. 105.
[3] *Ibid.*, p. 106.
[4] *Ibid.*, pp. 106–7.
[5] The offices of both cantor and *cantoria* are found at Ribe, and a prebendal stall was set aside for the cantor at Aarhus in 1260. Kolsrud, *op. cit.*, III, p. 107.
[6] *Dipl. Svec.*, nr. 561.

E E

appointed also at Nidaros, as we hear of Laurence Kalvsson, on his appointment to the Icelandic see of Holar in 1324, organising the offices on the model of the metropolitan church, and nominating a priest as *rector chori*. He had himself officiated in Nidaros from 1294 to 1307.

Nidaros had employed an *Ordo usus ecclesiastici* long before the appearance of the printed books in 1519 and it was followed in Iceland from 1318.[1]

In 1430, we learn that the choir in the cathedral church of Holar consisted of a pentitentiary, two resident priests (*heimaprestar*), two *messedjaknar*, two *subdjaknar*, four *smadjaknar in choro* and one *formesseklerk*—twelve persons in all.[2]

Many of the Scandinavian cathedral churches had a *tabula* hung up in the choir as a weekly duty roster for the various dignitaries and officials. Such a roster board, dating from the 12th century, may be seen today in the treasury of the cathedral church of Chur (Coire) in Switzerland.

The duties of the hebdomadary (*vikuheld*), according to the statutes of Ribe (*c.* 1290), included the cutting of the hair and tonsure of the cantor.[3]

Two, four or six cantors were employed at Mass and Office, and a lectern was provided for their use in the middle of the choir.

Two *pueri de schola* in white shifts (*serker*) took the place of the cantors at Nidaros on third class feasts. This was customary also at Lund on feasts of virgins.[4]

Absence from duty in choir was punished by a fine, and Roskilde listed these duties as *officium in choro*, epistle, gospel, *inceptio*, *rectura*, verse, *alleluia*, *Venite*, and lesson.[5]

In some churches, we find a *notarius chori*, who was appointed to note down absentees and generally supervise the behaviour of the choir.[6]

---

[1] Kolsrud, *op. cit.*, IV, p. 110.
[2] *Ibid.* *Smadjaknar* ('little deacon'): the *scholares* or members of the choir. *Formesseklerk* was the supervisor of the choir.
[3] *Ibid.*, IV, p. 113.
[4] *Ibid.*, p. 116.
[5] *Ibid.*, pp. 117–18.
[6] *Ibid.*, p. 118.

CHANT

The chant in the Norwegian Church was at first in unison, but *c.* 1000 diaphony was introduced in some places, and a century later we find 'three voices'.[1] Diaphony infers a melody sung in fifths or octaves, and to this day some of the Icelandic folk songs are of this character. The term *organum* can be taken as synonymous with diaphony. This method of singing was followed at Upsala from 1298: *cum organum dicitur, cantores illius unam oram levent de oblacione*.[2] It was, however, still novel in Scandinavian chant some quarter of a century later, and we find it frowned on by the bishop of Holar, Laurence Kalvsson (1324–31). The bishop had been a priest in Nidaros for many years, and his devotion to plain chant was doubtless the result of what he had heard in Norway.

Faulty singing of the chant was punished by a fine at Upsala, and probably elsewhere.[3] A strictly accurate rendering was of the greatest importance: attention must be paid to the *punctum* in the Psalm verses, and there must be no question of sincopating (*sincopando*) or mutilating by omission (*apocopando*).[4]

In 1434, we find King Eric advocating perpetual psalmody in the cathedral church, as was the custom at Lund, Roskilde and Copenhagen. A ceaseless praise of God was proposed, and psalms were to be sung continuously outside the times of Office and Mass. Unfortunately we do not know whether this practice of *laus perennis* was ever adopted at Nidaros.[5]

The use of an organ in the first half of the 14th century is attested by an anecdote relating to Arngrim Brandsson, an Icelandic priest who came to Nidaros for a law suit in 1327. He stayed two years, but as his errand to the archbishop was distasteful to him, the priest went daily to an organ builder, who taught him his trade. When in 1329 the rival disputants returned to Iceland, Brandsson, who had lost the case, took an organ back with him: the first in the island. It is clear from the story that an organ

---

[1] Kolsrud, *op. cit.*, IV, p. 119. [2] *Dipl. Suev.*, nr. 1235, p. 262.
[3] *Ibid.*, nr. 1236. [4] *Scr. rer. Dan.* VI, p. 409.
[5] Faehn, *Gudstjenestelivet I Nidaros Domkirke . . .*, p. 624.

must have been already installed in the cathedral church of Nidaros.[1]

ORIGIN AND HISTORY OF THE RITE

Christianity, as we have seen, was introduced into Norway from England, and consequently the first service-books would have been those in use among the Anglo-Saxons and Normans.

The Chronicle of Symeon of Durham tells of a monk of the name of Turgot, who came to Norway about the year 1069. The King, Olaf Kyrre (1066–99), received him well and, 'having heard that a clerk had come from England, took him for his master in psalmody'.[2] Later, Turgot returned to his own country, where he became a monk of Durham and, finally, bishop of St. Andrews.

It is possible also that German liturgical books were to be found in some Norwegian churches, as Bremen was the metropolitan see for Scandinavia before Lund (1103), although there is no evidence on the point.

A Nidaros use, specifically for the country and province, would in all probability have been compiled after the erection of a primatial see for Norway in 1154, and the oldest of the three MS. *Ordines Missae* extant (MS. D) 'must be assigned to the 12th century'.[3]

Liturgical unity, however, if we may judge from the prefaces to the missal and breviary of 1519, was never achieved in all the churches of the province.

Any consideration of the origins of the rite of Nidaros is hampered by the shortage of books. Three MS. manuals (rituals), an *Ordo* of the first half of the 13th century and a printed missal and breviary (1519) are all that seem to have survived the change of religion in the 16th century.

The rituals include the Ordinary of the Mass, but for the propers it is necessary to wait until 1519, and it is therefore impossible to say whether earlier missals had different texts in respect to collects, secrets and postcommunions.

---

[1] Kolsrud, *op. cit.*, IV, pp. 120–1. The cathedral church of Ribe in Denmark had an organ in 1290.

[2] Rolls, *Chron. Sym. of Durham*, II, pp. 202–4.

[3] Faehn, *op. cit.*, p. 130.

The *Ordo Nidrosiensis Ecclesiae* is no more than a guide to the choir in the 13th century, with directions as to the chant and duties of the various officers of the cathedral church.

The following summary of suggested origins for the existing liturgical books of Nidaros has been supplied by Dr. Faehn in *Fire Norske Messeordninger fra Middelalderen:* [1]

A (1519), he says, 'seems to have been influenced mainly from Normandy and England, and shows several parallels to late mediaeval Sarum use. There is nothing which decisively indicates Dominican influence. Belonging to the 16th century, A may be characterised as rather conservative'.

B (1300) is 'especially influenced from France—in parts particularly from the leading Séez group. Some details in B—mostly in the rubrics—are obviously dependent on the explanation of the Mass in *Micrologus.* . . . We may perhaps say that B, taken as a whole, belongs to the second part of the 12th century'.

C (13th century) is 'without doubt dependent on French and Italian tradition. The canon is evidently influenced by the specific Roman missal of the 11th–13th century, and, on the whole, C may be ascribed to the beginning of the 13th century'.

In D (c. 1200) 'everything before the canon is lacking, but, in return, this part exhibits close relationship to Irish and especially old Roman tradition: the last is undoubtedly due to the fact that D evidently is influenced by the order of the Mass in *Micrologus.*[2] D on palaeographical grounds is believed to have been written in *c.* 1200, and must be assigned to the 12th century'. It is consequently the oldest of the four *Ordines Missae* in the Norwegian rituals.

'If we make a comparison of these four Orders of the Mass, A and B seem to have most in common. If this can be taken as a further indication that B gives the substance of the rite of Nidaros in the 13th century, then we have got a basis from which to determine the most important alterations in the rite of this diocese in the last 250 years before the Reformation.' [3]

Commenting on the foregoing summary of Dr. Faehn, we may

---

[1] Oslo, 1953.

[2] Faehn, as we shall see later, fails to take into account the German saints in the litany.

[3] Faehn, *op. cit.*, English Summary, pp. 130–1.

note that, among the Scandinavian countries, Norway would seem to have been the least influenced by the Dominican liturgy, although Erik Segelberg thinks it possible that the rite of Nidaros was at one time as beholden to the use of the Preachers as elsewhere.[1] In the diocese of Åbo (Finland), for example, we find the Dominican use integrally adopted, in spite of the fact that another tradition flourished in the country simultaneously.[1] The influence of the Black Friars seems to have been far-reaching throughout the whole Swedish province, although a reform was gradually introduced in the course of the 14th century, which explains how, towards the end of the Middle Ages, we find a certain similarity and harmony between the offertory and communion prayers.[1]

In 1240, the Order had houses in Nidaros, Bergen and Oslo, but in the time of King Magnus (*ob.* 1299) the Preachers in Bergen were engaged in an acrimonious dispute with the cathedral clergy which persisted for a generation. Feelings ran so high that a synod, held in the city in 1290, proposed that no one in the diocese should give house-room, food or alms to a member of the Order. The protest of Bishop Narve called forth the foulest accusations against the friars. The canons, at a meeting *in camera*, resolved that a priest having anything to do with a Dominican should be *ipso facto* deprived of his living; while he who betrayed the existence of such a resolution would be excommunicated.[2] Dominican influence in the national liturgy was hardly likely in the circumstances, and yet we find a friar of the house at Bergen, John Halldorsson, who in his youth had studied in Paris and Bologna, nominated bishop of Skalholt in Iceland in 1332.[3] A comparison between the Nidaros missal of 1519 and that of the Dominicans shows but little similarity, although, as one would expect, a few of the prayers afford a certain resemblance.

A somewhat closer connection is found with the Sarum use, but it would be unwise to over-emphasise the influence, and in

---

[1] Segelberg, *De Ordine Missae secundum Ritum Scandinavicum Medii Aevi*, *Ephem. Liturg.*, vol. LXV (1951), fasc. IV, p. 260.

[2] Stagg, *West Norway*, chap. III, p. 68.

[3] H. G. Leach, *Relations between England and Scandinavia from 1066 until 1399 in History and Literature*, Proceedings of the American Academy of Arts and Sciences (1909), p. 558.

fact there is no direct evidence of any association between the two rites. The *Confiteor* at Nidaros is similar but not identical, as also are the blessing of the deacon before the gospel, *Orate fratres* and the prayer at the commixture. The prayer *Domine sancte Pater omnipotens aeterne Deus* is found in both liturgies, but in Sarum before the *pax* and at Nidaros after it. Finally, it may be noted that the last gospel is prescribed in the two rites, but the Scandinavian missal has no rubric to say whether it was to be recited at the altar or on the way to the sacristy.

A more detailed comparison between Nidaros and Sarum is given in the section dealing with the text of the Nidaros rite.

In respect to the propers of the Mass, it must suffice to compare four of the secrets in the printed missal of 1519 with those for the corresponding days in the Dominican, Sarum, Upsala (1513) and Lund (1514) books.

1. *Ember Saturday in Advent*

Ecclesiae tuae, Domine, munera sanctifica . . . appears to be derived from a prayer in the Leonine sacramentary.[1] It is found at Hereford, Durham, Whitby, Rouen, Coutances, Bayeux, St. Augustine's Canterbury and in the Gelasian. Dominican, York, Upsala and Lund give: *Sacrificiis praesentibus;* Sarum: *Super has hostias fidelium.*

2. *Holy Innocents*

Sanctorum tuorum nobis, Domine, non desit . . . is Roman, and is found as the *super oblata* prayer in the Gregorian sacramentary.

It is given in the Dominican and two Scandinavian books, but Sarum has: *Adesto, Domine, muneribus Innocentium festivitate sacrandis . . .*

3. *Second Sunday after the Octave of the Epiphany*

Oblata, Domine, munera sanctifica, which is found also in the York and Dominican missals.[2] A fairly conclusive proof of direct

---

[1] *In Jejunio Mensis Decimi I, Sacram. Leon.,* edit. C. L. Feltoe, p. 168. Cambridge, 1896.

[2] It is found also in the 9th century sacramentary of St. Alban's, Mainz, now in the seminary of Mainz.

Sarum influence in the rite of Nidaros would have been forthcoming if the secret for this Sunday had been *Ut tibi grata sint*,[1]
as we find in the majority of Sarum books, although, even here,
there are exceptions, as in the case of the British Museum MS.,
Egerton 2677 and the printed missal of 1498, where we have
Placare, Domine.

4. *Third Sunday after Pentecost (Second Sunday after the Octave of the Trinity)*

Oblatio nos, Domine is a standard text. We find it at Upsala and
Lund, as well as at Salisbury and York.[2] *Oblationibus nostris, quaesumus Domine* in the Dominican missal is a variant.

The postcommunion for the same day: *Sacris muneribus* is
something of an oddity. It is both Sarum and St. Amand, while
disagreeing with all the standard books.

When we come to consider the sources for the *Ordo Missae* in
the three MS. rituals, summarised by Dr. Faehn, we see how much
the compilers of MS. B (1300) were beholden to the *Micrologus
de Ecclesiasticis Observationibus (c. 1100). This is especially true
of the rubrics, some of which we find taken almost verbatim from
the symbolic explanation of the Mass.[3] To a lesser degree, also,
the *Micrologus* may have afforded some assistance as to the text:
embolism, formula of Communion, ablution prayer and devotions
after Mass.[4]

MS. B, says Dr. Faehn, is 'especially influenced from France—
in parts from the leading Séez group'. The basic form of this
group is believed by Jungmann to have originated in France or
Germany some time before the year 1000, and has been so named
because the most characteristic example is considered to be the
Ordinary of Séez.[5] Distinctive indications of service-books of
the group include a psalm before vesting (missing in B), *Judica
me, Confiteor, Aufer a nobis, Suscipe sancta Trinitas, Deus qui

---

[1] *Ut tibi grata sint, Domine, munera populi tui supplicantis, ab omni, quaesumus, eum
contagione perversitatis emunda.*

[2] *Oblatio nos* is the secret for the Second Sunday after Pentecost in the 9th century
Mainz (St. Alban's) sacramentary.

[3] *Microl.*, cap. XVII; Hittorp, *op. cit.*, col. 741; *Pat. Lat.*, t. CLI, cols. 979 seq.

[4] *Ibid.*, cap. XXIII; Hittorp, *op. cit.*, col. 746; *Pat. Lat.*, t. CLI, cols. 994–5.

[5] Jungmann, *Missarum Sollemnia*, t. I. (Paris, 1950), part I, 10, p. 127.

humanae substantiae (missing in B), and the Canticle of the Three Children with Psalm L (said while unvesting).[1]

The *Ordo* of MS. C (13th century) is also thought to depend from French tradition, but a study of it would not seem to add very much to our knowledge of the origins of the rite. The prayer *ad incensum* recalls, in its references to the offerings and sacrifices of the Old Testament, a corresponding prayer in three of the Eastern liturgies: Maronite, Ethiopic and Chaldean.[2]

The oldest of the three rituals, MS. D (*c.* 1200), is unfortunately fragmentary, and only begins with the canon. 'This part', says Dr. Faehn, 'exhibits close relationship to Irish . . . tradition.' This 'Irish tradition' must refer to the canon in the so-called Missal of Stowe, which, however, is a Roman rather than a Celtic compilation. Even so, Stowe is without rubrics, and there does not seem very much with which to identify it as a source for MS. D beyond a certain similarity in the spelling of a few words. Thus the Nidaros MS. has *circum astantium* in the memento of the living: Stowe, *circum adstantium*; Nidaros and Stowe, *posteaquam* in the consecration of the chalice; and *tui servi*, in place of *servi tui* in the *Unde et memores*.

On the other hand, D reveals a marked borrowing from the *Micrologus* in the order and text of the prayers, and more especially in the wording of the rubrics. An examination of Chapter XXIII shows clearly to what extent MS. D has been beholden to it. The specific points of similarity will be noted later in the section devoted to the text of the rite.

It is strange that Dr. Faehn makes no reference to the very obvious German influence in the litany of MS. D and, to a lesser extent, in MS. C. The name of St. Walburga in the second of these would certainly seem to point to German influence in some form or other; while the litany in D bristles with saints derived from a Teutonic source: Cunibert, Willibrord, Arnulf, Aldegund, Oda, Odila and Cordula.

There would not seem to have been a great deal of borrowing from other Scandinavian missals, Lund or Upsala, for example,

---

[1] Jungmann, *op. cit.*, p. 128.
[2] Archdale King, *Rites of Eastern Christendom*, vol. I, chap. III, p. 262; vol. I, chap. VI, pp. 581–2; vol. II, chap. VIII, pp. 332–3.

but it is possible that certain features of the pontifical Mass at Lund were introduced into the cathedral church at Nidaros. The *Consuetudines canonice*, drawn up at Lund in 1130, directed that seven deacons, seven subdeacons, seven acolytes with torches and three thurifers should assist at a Mass celebrated solemnly by the Primate.[1] Now we know that the archbishop of Nidaros, Eric, by reason of his quarrel with King Sverre, spent twelve years of exile with Archbishop Absalom at Lund, returning to his diocese in 1202. It has therefore been suggested that Eric might well have introduced this more elaborate ceremonial in his own cathedral church, although we have no positive proof of this.[2]

If we may judge from the prefaces in the printed missal and breviary, it would seem clear that right down to the time of the change of religion there was a lack of liturgical uniformity in the province of Nidaros. A different tradition prevailed at Bergen, at least as regards the Divine Office, in the early part of the 15th century, for we read that when the bishop, Aslak Bolt, was translated to the metropolitan see in 1425 he took with him *unum breviarium per totum annum secundum modum Bergis*.[3] We learn also that by 1464 the breviary in use in the diocese of Skalholt was, with some exceptions, uniform with that of Nidaros. There is in fact evidence which suggests that a like uniformity existed in Iceland from 1318.[4]

The Isle of Man, as we have seen, reverted to the jurisdiction of the province of York in 1458, and the Orkneys and Shetlands to that of St. Andrews in 1472. We do not know, however, whether on that account Man adopted the use of York, but Orkney appears to have followed Sarum, in at least some of the churches.

It is possible that shortly before the Reformation the bishop of the Orkneys, Robert Reid, proposed to introduce the Roman rite in place of that of either Nidaros or Sarum. The existence of three books dating from his episcopate would seem to suggest this. The first is a copy of the Quignonian revision of the Roman

---

[1] Cf. *Ordo Romanus I*; Rite of Lyons.
[2] Kolsrud, *op. cit.*, I, pp. 86–7.
[3] Faehn, *Gudstjenestelivet I Nidaros Domkirke . . .*, p. 603.
[4] Faehn, *ibid.*, pp. 603–4.

missal, now in the Library of the University of St. Andrews. The book was printed at Lyons in 1550 (Gul. Rovillius and Ph. Rolletius), and a contemporary binding is inscribed: *M.A.S. Cancellarius Orcadensis.* Master Alexander Scott was chancellor of the Orkneys during the time of Bishop Reid.[1] The second book is a Roman breviary, also of the Quignonian revision, and now in the Preshome Library. It was published at Lyons in 1546, and has the word *Orchaden* stamped on the surviving part of the binding.[2] The third is a Roman ritual belonging to Bishop Reid, and now in the Library of Blairs College. The book appeared from the press in Cologne in 1557. It has an armorial book-stamp of the bishop on its binding, and contains the signature of William Forsyth, a Cistercian monk of Kinloss.[2]

An attempt was made towards the end of the Middle Ages to achieve liturgical unity in the province of Nidaros, and, as we have seen, the printed missal and breviary of 1519 were intended to effect this.

So early as 1464, however, we find John Stephen, bishop of Skalholt, insisting upon a following of the use of the metropolitan church for all the churches of his diocese, which probably went also for the other Icelandic diocese, Holar.[3] Many interesting details are brought to light by a study of the wills of the 13th, 14th and 15th centuries.

Mass for the soul of Earl Skule (1225) was to be accompanied by a ringing of the church bells throughout the city of Nidaros. Thirty Masses were to be said in 1430 for Arvid Ingeldsson and his wife, who were to be buried before the altar of Christ's Body. In 1307 the cathedral clergy pledged themselves to say Mass in perpetuity for the souls of King Hákon Magnusson and his wife Eufemia. A certain canon of the name of John promised in 1333 that the anniversary of Sigurd Jodgeirssons should be kept with 'two lights', and that prayers should be said for him every day in *Maria-stuken*. The knight Bjarne Erlingsson, who in 1308 was buried near the last altar in the south-west corner of the new

---

[1] D. McRoberts, *Catalogue of Scottish Mediaeval Books and Fragments*, p. 22. Glasgow, 1953.
[2] *Ibid.*, p. 20. The book has been described in the *Innes Review*, vol. III, pp. 39–41.
[3] Segelberg, *op. cit.*, p. 261.

building, directed that Mass and Office were to be celebrated for fifteen months at this altar, together with a gift of clothing to the priests and deacons. Every day Mass was to be said for all Christian souls, with candles and ringing of bells, and alms, food and drink were to be given to ten poor people. A remarkably detailed will was made by a knight of the name of Hendrik Jensson in 1454: Mass was to be said in perpetuity on the Tuesday before the feast of All Saints, with two pounds of wax, six Lubeck shillings and four of the same. In the evening, a catafalque with a gold pall was to be set up before the altar of St. Anne. The Office for the dead was to be sung with lights, and, at the sung Mass on the following morning, six shillings were to be offered, and alms given to the poor. The largest bell was to be rung after the dirge and Mass.[1]

Mass According to the Use of Nidaros

The Mass in the printed missal of 1519 has been collated with the Ordinaries found in MSS. B, C and D.

B may be said to depict the Norwegian Mass as it was celebrated in 1300, C in the 13th century and D about 1200.

At the same time also, similarities with the Sarum, Upsala (1513) and Lund (1514) missals, as well as with the use of the Friars Preachers, will be noted.

The Ordinary of the Mass in the missal is found between the temporal and the sanctoral. After the proper of the saints, a list of those days on which the creed is to be recited is given, and the occasions on which votive Masses of our Lady are permitted. A number of votive Masses and an appendix of sequences are found at the end of the book. The volume ends with the *accidentia circa missam.*

The paucity of rubrics, considering the late date of the missal, is remarkable.

Preparatory and Vesting Prayers

Preparatory prayers are found in MS. C, as well as in the missal. MS. B is defective and the first prayer is that for the stole. The

---

[1] Faehn, *Gudstjenestelivet I Nidaros Domkirke . . .*, pp. 621–2.

missal first directs the celebrant to say a prayer for the 'gift of tears': *Da mihi, Domine, lachrimas internas.* This is followed by a recitation of the hymn *Veni Creator Spiritus*;[1] psalms, two of which are concluded with *Ave Maria; Kyrie eleison; Pater noster;* versicles; and the prayer *Fac me quaeso Omnipotens Deus.* The *Kyrie* and *Pater*, as a transition to versicles, are already indicated in the *Micrologus*,[2] as well as in the missals of St. Vincent al Volturno (*c.* 1100) and Seckau (*c.* 1174), and the sacramentary of Modena (before 1174).

The 11th-century Séez group of missals habitually conclude these prayers before Mass with one or other of the formulas *Fac me quaeso* or *Aures tuas*, and sometimes with both of them, as at Séez.[3]

MS. C gives a different formula for the first prayer of preparation: *Exue me, Domine, veterem hominem,* followed by a washing of hands with the prayer *Largire sensibus nostris.* Upsala (from 1484) has a similar arrangement, but in the Swedish missal they are preceded, not followed, by the *Kyrie*, versicles and prayers. At Lund (1514) we find *Exue me*, together with a prayer to be said while combing the hair (*pectendo caput*): *Corripe me, Domine, in misericordia tua.*

Examples of the use of *Exue me* may be seen in many of the missals from the 12th to the 15th century, as well as in the missal of Augsburg (1555). It is found also as the prayer before a religious is clothed with the habit.

Largire sensibus nostris: the prayer for the washing of the hands, occurs also in the 14th-century Sarum ordinary and the York missal.

The preparation before vesting, as given in MS. C, ends with psalms, *Kyrie eleison, Pater noster* and the prayer *Aures tuae pietatis.*

The formula *Fac me quaeso* came finally to be attached to the chasuble,[4] but, at a time before prayers were said for each specific vestment, we find it recited as a general vesting prayer. Was it

---

[1] Cf. Sarum use, Maskell, *op. cit.*, pp. 3–4.
[2] *Microl.*, cap. I, XXIII; Hittorp, *op. cit.*, cols. 697, 744; *Pat. Lat.*, t. CLI, cols. 979, 992.
[3] Jungmann, *op. cit.*, t. II, chap. I, 2, p. 20, n. 14.
[4] e.g. *Alia oratio* in Upsala missal (1513).

possible that Nidaros had adopted it for this purpose, since the missal does not provide individual vesting prayers? On the other hand, the missal is not altogether comprehensive, and, as we have seen, it has omitted the blessings of palms, ashes and candles. Prayers for each vestment are found in MSS. C and B. Vesting prayers appear also in the breviaries of Linköping (1493) and Skara (1498), possibly because the chapter Mass in the cathedral churches normally followed the Divine Office.[1]

Fac me quaeso is found in the Supplement of Alcuin as a collect in a *Missa specialis sacerdotis*, which may indeed have been its original use.[2] It occurs in MS. C as the prayer for the alb.

Amice. *Indue me, Domine*, a very general prayer for the alb, is employed for the amice in MS. C. It was attached to both alb and amice in the Sacramentary of Amiens.

Alb. MS. C, which represents the use of Nidaros in the 13th century, gives *Fac me quaeso*, as we have seen, as the prayer on assuming the alb.

Girdle. MS. C has *Praecinge me, Domine, zona justitiae* for the girdle, as we find in a missal of Seckau (*c.* 1170) and in several later Styrian missals.[3]

Stole. *Stola justitiae circumda* is given in MSS. C and B, with a somewhat longer formula in B. It occurs in the Sacramentary of Gatian (Tours) and the missals of Upsala (1484) and Lund (1514).

Maniple. The prayer for the maniple is given after that for the chasuble in MS. B, whereas MS. C has the inverse order. The formula in C: *Da, Domine, virtutem manibus meis*, dates at latest from the 11th century, and is found in the so-called Missal of Illyricus [4] and the *Ordinarium* of Ratisbon.

It is in fact a formula for use at the washing of hands, and its employment for the maniple is a reminder of the original homely origin of the vestment. MS. B provides a different prayer: *In-nectione hujus manipuli*, of which variants are found in 'Illyricus' and the *Liber Ordinarius* of Liège.

Chasuble. *Indue me, Domine, ornamento humilitatis et caritatis*

---

[1] The council of Bergen (1320) directed Mass to be said after prime.
[2] Jungmann, *op. cit.*, chap. I, 3, p. 35, n. 70.
[3] *Ibid.*, chap. I, 3, p. 31, n. 44.
[4] Bona, *op. cit.*, p. 474.

is given in the missal, as well as in the two MSS. We find it also in 'Illyricus' and the missals of Upsala (1513) and Lund (1514).

Preparatory Prayers of the Mass

The psalm *Judica me*, followed by *Kyrie eleison*, *Pater noster* and *Introibo*, are found in the missal, but without any indication as to where they should be said.[1] MSS. B and C, on the other hand, direct *Judica me*, together with *Introibo* as a form of versicle, to be recited on the way to the altar, as in the *Micrologus* and the use of Sarum. Upsala (1513) followed a similar arrangement. The psalm in MS. C concludes with the prayer *Educ me, Domine, in via tua*. The missal and the MSS. then give the versicle *Confitemini Domino quoniam bonus*, as we find in the Dominican use. MS. C has also the following, but they have been crossed out: *Sine peccato, fiat misericordia tua, Domine, super nos; Quemadmodum; Domine exaudi; Et clamor meus*.

The three extant Nidaros ordinaries have each a variant for the *Confiteor*, if we may assume that the formula in the Mass of 1519 was the same as we find in the breviary (1519) for prime, as the text in the missal is not printed in full.

Missal: *Confiteor Deo celi, beate Marie virgini, omnibus sanctis et vobis: quia ego peccator peccavi nimis in vita mea, cogitatione, locutione, opere et omissione, mea culpa. Ideo precor Dei Genitricem virginem Mariam, omnes sanctos et electos Dei, et vos orare pro me peccatore ad Dominum Jesum Christum ut misereatur mei.*

MS. B: *Ego reus et fragilis confiteor Domino Deo celi et beate Marie virgini, quia ego peccator peccavi nimis cogitatione, locutione et opere: ideo precor te piissima semper virgo Maria et omnes sanctos Dei et te frater orare pro me peccatore apud Dominum Deum nostrum omnipotentem.*

MS. C: *Confiteor Deo celi et sancte Marie et omnibus sanctis ejus; quia peccavi mea culpa, cogitatione, locutione, consensu et opere; propterea precor te, ora pro me.*

The *Confiteor* in the *Micrologus* resembles the form in MS. C, rather than that in MS. B.[2]

---

[1] In the Sarum use, the *Kyrie* and *Pater* come after *Introibo*. Maskell, *op. cit.*, p. 8.
[2] *Microl.*, cap. XXIII; Hittorp, *op. cit.*, col. 744.

The Åbo (Finland) missal of 1488 is interesting as affording evidence of very strong affinities with the Dominican use:

Confiteor Deo et beate Marie et beato Dominico et omnibus sanctis et vobis fratres, quia peccavi nimis cogitatione, locutione, opere et omissione: mea culpa, precor vos orate pro me.

The Sarum formula is somewhat similar to that found in the Nidaros missal, although not identical. The second half of the Sarum is entirely different from the Dominican.

The three Norwegian texts of the *Misereatur* are not in entire agreement:

Missal: *Misereatur vestri omnipotens Deus dimissis (omnibus peccatis vestris perducat vos in vitam eternam. Amen).*[1]

MS. B: *Misereatur tui omnipotens Deus et dimissis omnibus peccatis tuis perducat te Deus ad vitam eternam. Amen.*

MS. C: *Misereatur tui omnipotens Deus et dimittat tibi Dominus omnia peccata tua, preterita, presentia, et futura: liberet te Deus ab omni malo, et perducat te Ihesus Xristus ad vitam eternam. Amen.*

Two versicles precede the absolution in the missal and MS. B: *Dominus custodiat nos ab omni malo* and *Custodiat animam tuam Dominus.*

Missal: *Indulgentiam et remissionem omnium peccatorum nostrorum spacium vere pentitentie, emendationem vite: gratiam et consolationem sancti Spiritus contribuat nobis omnipotens Pater pius et misericors Dominus. Amen.*

MS. B: The same as in the printed missal, with the exception of the second person instead of the first.

MS. C: *Absolutionem et remissionem peccatorum nostrorum, et spatium vere pentitentie, et emendationem vite, et gratiam sancti Spiritus tribuat nobis pius et misericors Dominus. Amen.*

The rubric: *In ascensu altaris*, before the versicles which follow, is found in MS. C.

The three ordinaries give: *Deus tu conversus vivificabis nos. Et plebs tua laetabitur in te; Ostende nobis, Domine, misericordiam tuam. Et salutem . . .; Domine Deus virtutum converte nos. Et ostende . . . ; Domine exaudi orationem meam. Et clamor meus ad te veniat; Dominus vobiscum. Et cum spiritu tuo.*

---

[1] The words in brackets are not in the missal: they have been taken from the breviary.

In addition to these we find in the missal: *Ab occultis meis munda me, Domine. Et ab alienis, Domine, Deus virtutum converte nos;* MS. C: *Sacerdotes tui induantur justiciam.*

The prayer *Aufer a nobis* is said at the conclusion of the versicles, with a second prayer in MS. B: *Actiones nostras.* The *Micrologus*, to which, as we have seen, MS. B was beholden, gives the two prayers before the vesting of the priest.[1] *Actiones nostras* occurs again in B: the last of the thanksgiving prayers after Mass.

The missal now provides further versicles, after the rubric: *Et osculato altari: Adjutorium nostrum (Qui fecit)* and *Sit nomen (Ex hoc nunc).* Then, *Benedicite Dominus. In nomine Patris,* etc. The Lund missal (1514) has a similar arrangement, with a third prayer: *Conscientias nostras.*

The MSS. are not identical in text.

After a rubric directing the altar to be kissed (*Dum osculat altare*), MS. B gives an *apologia: Omnipotens sempiterne Deus qui me peccatorem sacris altaribus adstare voluisti.* This is followed by the same two versicles as in the missal.

MS. C is different again: A prayer is given at the kissing of the gospel-book (*Quando osculatur textus*): *Pax Xristi quam nobis per evangelium suum tradidit, conservet corda et corpora nostra in vitam eternam. Amen.* A similar formula, at the kissing of the cross and altar, is found in the Lund missal.

The preparatory part of the Mass is concluded in MS. C by the well known *apologia: Ante conspectum divine majestatis.*

Oramus te, Domine is not met with in the Scandinavian missals.

Kyrie and Gloria in Excelsis

This beginning of the Mass of the catechumens is prefaced in the missal by the rubric: *Hic inchoatur officium misse,* and in MS. B: *Intonetur missa.*

The missal directs the *Kyrie* and *Gloria in excelsis* to be said, but they are not mentioned in either of the MSS.

The farced *Glorias* for Masses of the Blessed Virgin have been mentioned earlier in the chapter. At Lund (1514), on Sundays, the words *Salus nostra Jesu Christe* were interpolated after *Domine*

---

[1] *Microl.,* cap. XXIII; Hittorp, *op. cit.,* col. 744. Cf. York and Hereford.

Fili Unigenite; while in Masses of the Holy Spirit we find: *et sancte Spiritus.*[1]

Chants between Epistle and Gospel

The gradual at Nidaros, according to the 13th-century *ordo*, was sung by four cantors on solemnities and by two on second-class feasts. The alleluia admitted six for the former occasions and four for the latter.[2] The singers of the gradual and alleluia at Aarhus (Denmark) were known as *gradalarii.* The gradual is referred to in the *Consuetudines canonici* of Lund (1130): *Qui ad hoc notatus fuerit, graduale incipiat, quod dum percantaverit chorus, ille versum finiet, usque ad ultimum membrum melodie.*[3]

Sequences (proses) are not found in the text of the missal: they have been collected in an appendix at the end of the book. They would seem, for the most part, to be of a very indifferent quality.

Gospel

MSS. B and C give prayers for the blessing of incense in preparation for the gospel.

MS. B: *Odore celestis inspirationis sue Dominus accendat et impleat corda nostra. In nomine Patris, et Filii, et Spiritus Sancti benedicatur incensum istud et acceptabile fiat Deo in odorem suavitatis ad audienda et ad implenda evangelii sui precepta. Per Christum Dominum nostrum.*

MS. C: *Odore celestis inspirationis sue accendat et impleat Dominus corda vestra ad audienda et ad implenda evangelii sui precepta. Qui vivit.*

The formulas contain a reference to the gospel, distinguishing this censing from others. A prayer similar to that in MS. C is found in a missal of Troyes (*c.* 1050), as well as in one from Central Italy (11th century).[4]

The absence of any such blessing—or indeed of any other—in the printed missal would seem to be another case of failing to give the full text in a book which purported to be the *typica* for the whole province.

---

[1] The Lund missal provided also for farced *Glorias* in Masses of the Blessed Virgin.
[2] Kolsrud, *op. cit.*, p. 91. [3] *Ibid.*, pp. 114–15.
[4] The form of prayer would seem to have originated in the 11th century.

The blessing of the deacon is given in all three ordinaries.

Missal: *Dominus sit in corde tuo et in labiis tuis ut competenter pronuncies evangelium pacis omnibus nobis. In nomine Patris, + et Filii, et Spiritus Sancti. Amen.*[1]

MS. B: *Dominus sit in corde meo et in labiis meis ut annunciem competenter evangelium pacis omnibus audientibus.*[2]

MS. C: *Dominus sit in ore tuo, et in corde tuo, ad annuntiandum sanctum evangelium et avertat spiritum elationis a te.*

The response of the deacon, *Da mihi Domine*, is found in the missal, but not in the MSS., although similar texts were in use at York, Lund, Roskilde, Linköping (*c.* 1500), and in a 15th-century codex from the province of Prague.[3]

Missal: *Da mihi, Domine, sermonem rectum et benesonantem in os meum ut placeant tibi verba mea et omnibus audientibus et credentibus verbum Dei propter nomen sanctum tuum in vitam eternam. Amen.*

The missal gives the following prayer at the conclusion of the gospel: *Per istos sermones sancti evangelii pacis indulgeat nobis Dominus universa nostra delicta: et sit pax omnibus audientibus et credentibus verbum Dei. Amen.*

A formula at kissing the gospel-book is found in both missal and MS. B: *Pax Christi, quam nobis per evangelium suum tradidit, conservet et confirmet corda vestra in vitam eternam. Amen.* At Lund, we find: *Per haec sancta evangelia dicta deleantur universa nostra delicta. Amen.*

Creed

There is no reference to the creed in either of the MSS. It was introduced into the diocese of Skalholt in Iceland by the synod held under Magnus Gissurasson in 1224. Its use was diffused throughout the island by Arno Thorlac (1292) and John Sigurd (1395).[3] As we have seen, the days on which the creed was directed to be said are given in the missal (1519).

---

[1] Cf. Sarum and Dominican uses, which are somewhat similar, but not identical.

[2] Cf. Lund (1514).

[3] Eric Segelberg, *De Ordine Missae secundum Ritum Scandinavicum Medii Aevi*, ap. *Ephem. Liturg.*, vol. LXV (1951), fasc. IV, p. 254.

Sermon

The importance of a sermon in the parish Mass is stressed in the provincial statutes of 1290 and 1320, and two later councils (1351; 1436) say much the same thing. An old Norwegian homiliary of the 12th century gives a number of specimen addresses. About the year 1300 we read of a priest from Flanders who wanted to be on the staff at St. Mary's church in Nidaros. He was subjected to a trial sermon on Lenten duties, with a view to seeing whether he could speak Norwegian fluently. The result was not encouraging, and his hearers laughed heartily at his linguistic blunders. The priest was not appointed to the church.[1]

It is recorded that Archbishop Eystein (1161–88) preached a very long sermon at a procession in honour of St. Olaf, although, only three days before, he had fallen from some scaffolding and seriously hurt himself.[1] In 1336, a council decided that the canons should sing an annual Mass and preach; while in 1523, only a few years before the change of religion, the dean of the cathedral church was directed to preach the gospel in the city of Nidaros on certain days of the year.[2]

Offertory

The paucity of rubrics makes it difficult to say at what precise point in the Mass the *oblata* were prepared, but the most likely place would have been between the epistle and gospel.

MS. C gives a prayer *Ad incensum* at the very beginning of the offertory, but it is possible that the text is out of place in the MS., and that the gifts were censed after the offering of the elements, as elsewhere. On the other hand, Segelberg, probably on the strength of the position of this prayer in the MS., says that in 13th-century Norway the censing took place at the commencement of the offertory.[3] The prayer recalls the gifts offered to God by Abel, Noe, Aaron, Zacharias and Samuel: *Domine Deus meus, qui suscepisti munera Abel, Noe, Aaron, Zacharie et Samuelis, omniumque sanctorum tuorum, suscipe incensum istud, de manu mea,*

---

[1] Faehn, *Gudstjenestelivet I Nidaros Domkirke . . .*, p. 611.
[2] *Ibid.*, p. 612.   [3] Segelberg, *op. cit.*, p. 255.

in conspectu tuo in odorem suavitatis tue, in remissionem omnium peccatorum nostrorum per Christum Dominum nostrum. It is found in Swedish MSS. of the 15th century, as well as in the sacramentaries of Amiens, Ratold and Moissac, missal of Troyes (*c.* 1050), two Benedictine missals of the 11th or 12th century in Central Italy, another of the 13th–14th century at Fonte Avellana, and in a ritual of Soissons. The most recent example would seem to be in the missal of Châlons sur Marne, printed in 1543.[1] It occurs in the offertory itself in an 11th-century sacramentary of Besançon.[2]

The origin of the prayer must be sought in the East, where we find variants in the preparatory part of the liturgies of the Maronites,[3] Ethiopians [4] and Chaldeans.[5]

Sacramentaries and missals provide a large selection of offertory prayers, although, about the end of the Middle Ages, a certain uniformity is noticeable in the Swedish province, despite additional prayers in individual dioceses. Another type persisted in the Lund province, similar to the older Swedish tradition.

The offertory prayers at Nidaros vary in the three known ordinaries.

Missal: The deacon offers the chalice to the celebrant at the south side of the altar: the paten with the host resting on the chalice. The priest meanwhile says *Sancti + fica, quesumus Domine, hanc oblationem, ut nobis Unigeniti tui corpus et sanguis efficiatur. In nomine Patris, et Filii, et Spiritus Sancti. Amen.* The prayer is not found in any Scandinavian book other than at Nidaros, where it appears also in MS. C. There is, however, something almost identical in the so-called Mass of Illyricus.[6]

Then, having received the sacred vessels, the celebrant goes to the middle of the altar, where, elevating the chalice and paten together, he recites the prayer *Suscipe sancta Trinitas: Suscipe sancta Trinitas hanc oblationem quam tibi offerimus: in memoriam passionis, resurrectionis et ascensionis Domini nostri Jesu Christi. Et*

---

[1] Jungmann, *op. cit.*, t. II, p. 351, n. 23.

[2] Leroquais, *Les Sacram. et les missels . . .* (Paris, 1924), t. I, p. 139.

[3] King, *op. cit.*, vol. I, chap. III, p. 262.

[4] *Ibid.*, vol. I, chap. VI, pp. 581–2.

[5] *Ibid.*, vol. II, chap. VIII, pp. 332–3.

[6] *Sanctifica, Domine, hanc oblationem, ut nobis Unigeniti Filii tui Domini nostri Jesu Christi corpus fiat. Qui tecum vivit*, etc. Bona, *op. cit.*, append., p. 496.

in honorem sanctissime et perpetue Virginis Marie. Et beatorum apostolorum Petri et Pauli atque Andree: et omnium sanctorum tuorum. Ut illis proficiat ad honorem, nobis autem ad salutem. Et illi pro nobis intercedere dignentur in celis: quorum memoriam agimus in terris. Per eundem Christum Dominum nostrum. The missal of Upsala (1513), after the words *ad salutem*, interpolate: *et omnibus fidelibus defunctis ad requiem*.[1] The formula *Suscipe sancta Trinitas* appears to have originated in North France in the 9th century. Its use as the sole offertory prayer was advocated by Bernold of Constance (*ob.* 1100).[2] The province of Lund was unique in employing the prayer: *Tibi, Domine, Creatori meo*: At Lund and Schleswig in offering the host, and at Roskilde (Hafnia), where the chalice was offered together with the paten. It is found also in a Prague missal (1479).[3]

The double offering of host and chalice is envisaged in MS. B (1300), with the rubric *Dum tenet calicem in manibus*, but in MS. C (13th century) we find two prayers described *Ad oblatam* and *Ad calicem* respectively, indicating a separate offering of the host and chalice. The chalice and host were offered together in the Upsala province, whereas in that of Lund both practices obtained: first both together, and then each separately.[4] This duplicated offering is found also in missals of Mainz (1613) and Magdeburg (1515).

A Sarum ordinary of the 13th century directs the host and chalice to be offered together,[5] while one of the 14th century gives two prayers and two offerings.[6] The Dominicans have retained the double offering.

At the conclusion of the prayer of offering, the chalice is placed in the form of a cross on the altar, with the paten partially under the corporal to the right, after which the chalice is covered with a fold of the corporal. The priest says: *Acceptum sit omnipotenti Deo sacrificium nostrum. In nomine Patris, et Filii, et Spiritus*

---

[1] Yelverton, *Mass in Sweden*, p. 15.
[2] Jungmann, *op. cit.*, t. II, part IV, chap. I, 4, p. 324.
[3] Cf. Illyricus, Bona, *op. cit.*, append., p. 492.
[4] Hafnia, Roskilde, Lund, Schleswig.
[5] Wickham Legg, *Tracts on the Mass*, H.B.S., vol. XXVII (1904), p. 220.
[6] *Ibid.*, pp. 4-5.

Sancti. An almost identical prayer is found in the *Micrologus*,[1] and the missals of Linköping and Straengness have formulas of a similar type.[2] The prayer in 'Illyricus' is directed to be said by the deacon, as he receives the *oblata* from the subdeacon.[3]

The Nidaros missal then gives a prayer in which the priest blesses the bread and wine: *Veni sanctificator omnipotens eterne Deus ac bene + dic hoc sacrificium ad laudem et gloriam tuo nomini preparatum. In nomine Patris, et Filii, et Spiritus Sancti. Amen.* There is a similar prayer in the Lund and Roman missals.

The censing of the 'sacrifice' (*Deinde incenset sacrificium*) follows.

The formula of blessing the incense: *In nomine Patris, et Filii, et Spiritus Sancti Benedi + catur hoc incensum et acceptabile fiat Domino in odorem suavitatis. Amen.*

Three other formulas are found in Scandinavian missals, but the Roman form: *Per intercessionem* is found nowhere.[4]

The missal provides a number of prayers to be recited at the censing: *Incensum istud a te benedictum ascendat ad te Domine et descendat super nos misericordia tua; Domine clamavi ad te exaudi me; Intende voci mee dum clamavero ad te; Dirigatur oratio mea sicut incensum in conspectu tuo.*[5] *Elevatio manuum mearum sacrificium vespertinum.*

The psalm *Lavabo* is directed to be said at the washing of hands, as at Upsala and Lund. More ancient sources have other prayers, as, for example, *Largire* at Lund, Roskilde, Skara and Linköping; *Concedo mihi quaeso* at Nidaros (MS. B); *Munda me, Domine* at Linköping.

The missal concludes the offertory act with a prayer said profoundly inclined before the altar: *In spiritu humilitatis et in animo contrito suscipiamur a te et sic fiat sacrificium nostrum ut a te*

---

[1] *Microl.*, cap. XXIII; Hittorp, *op. cit.*, col. 744.

[2] Cf. York use at the offering of the chalice: *Acceptum sit omnipotenti Deo, sacrificium istud; in nomine*, etc. Maskell, *op. cit.*, p. 56.

[3] *Acceptum sit omnipotenti Deo, et omnibus sanctis ejus sacrificium tuum.* Bona, *op. cit.*, append., p. 493.

[4] Lund: *Ab illo sanctificeris*; Roskilde: *Incensum istud sit benedictum*; Upsala: *In nomine*, etc, *sit benedictum hoc incensum in odorem suavitatis, in remissionem peccatorum nostrorum.*

[5] The prayer *Dirigatur* in the Roskilde missal has the additional words: *Immolo Deo sacrificium.*

suscipiatur hodie et placeat tibi, Domine Deus omnipotens Pater. In nomine Patris, et Filii, et Spiritus Sancti. Amen. The prayer is found in the same position in the missal of Upsala (1513).

The missals of Lund, Roskilde and Straengness have *Hostias et preces* in place of the customary offertory prayers in Masses for the dead.

The order of the prayers in the two MSS. is different from that in the printed missal (1519).

MS. B: The prayer *Sanctifica* is wanting, and the rubric *Dum tenet calicem in manibus* is the first indication of the offertory. This is followed by a short prayer: *Suscipe sancta Trinitas hanc oblationem quam tibi offert populus tuus et presta ut in conspectum tuum tibi placens ascendat.*

There is no reference to incense, and the next formula is *Ad manus lavandas: Concede me queso omnipotens Deus, ita manus lavare ut possim dominicum corpus et sanguinem digne tractare. Per.*

Then, inclined before the altar, the priest says: *In spiritu humilitatis*, in a slightly shorter form than in the missal, and omitting *In nomine Patris*, etc.

This is followed by a prayer, which is a variant of the one in the missal: said when the celebrant covers the chalice with the corporal: *Acceptum sit omnipotenti Deo sacrificium istud et be + nedicatur ab ipso Domino nostro Jhesu Christo.* An almost identical prayer is found in the Lund missal (1514): when the priest offers the chalice.

The offertory prayers in MS.B conclude with a variant of *Suscipe sancta Trinitas: Suscipe sancta Trinitas et inseparabilis unitas hanc oblationem, quam ego peccator et indignus tibi offero in memoriam passionis et resurrectionis et ascensionis Domini nostri Jhesu Christi et in honorem sancte Dei genitricis Marie et omnium sanctorum tuorum qui tibi placuerunt ab initio mundi ut illis proficiat ad honorem nobis autem ad salutem et remissionem peccatorum, ut illi pro nobis intercedere dignentur in celis quorum memoriam agimus in terris per Christum.*

MS. C: The prayer *Item ad incensum*, with which the offertory section in this MS. begins, has been already considered.

It is followed by a prayer *Quando accipitur sacrificium*, which, as we have seen, appears in the missal in a slightly longer form: *Sanctifica, Domine, hanc oblationem, ut nobis Unigeniti tui corpus et sanguis efficiatur.*

Two separate formulas, *ad oblatam* and *ad calicem*, are given in this MS., which seem to indicate two distinct offerings:

Acceptum sit hoc sacrificium omnipotenti Deo.

Offerimus tibi, Domine, calicem salutaris tuam deprecantes clementiam, ut in conspectu divine majestatis tue cum odore suavitatis ascendat. The second prayer is found at the offering of the chalice in the Roman rite.

Then, inclined before the altar, the priest says: *In spiritu humilitatis* in a form similar to that in MS. B.

The blessing of the elements, which follows, gives the same text as the missal, with the omission of the words *ad laudem et gloriam: Veni sanctificator.* An identical prayer is given in the *Micrologus.*[1]

Suscipe sancta Trinitas, which ends the offertory in MS. C, is almost the same as in the missal, apart from the absence of the name of St. Andrew. A special form of the prayer for use in Masses for the dead is found in the missal of Lund (1514).

Orate Fratres and Secret

The *Orate fratres* in the Nidaros missal is very similar to the Sarum[2] and Dominican formulas, but the latter omits *sorores*: *Orate pro me fratres et sorores, ut meum pariter et vestrum in conspectu Domini acceptum sit sacrificium.*

There is no response, which is the more strange, since we find it in MSS. B and C.

MS. B: *Orate pro me peccatore fratres et sorores, ut meum pariter et vestrum coram Deo acceptabile fiat sacrificium.*

Responsio populi: Suscipiat Dominus sacrificium de manibus tuis ad tuam et ad nostram salutem, et omnium circumastantium, et omnium fidelium vivorum et defunctorum.

MS. C: *Orate pro me fratres, ut meum pariter vestrumque sacrificium sit acceptabile Domino Deo nostro.*

---

[1] *Microl.,* cap. XXIII; Hittorp, *op. cit.,* col. 744.
[2] Maskell, *op. cit.,* p. 68.

*Responsio: Sancti Spiritus gratia illuminet cor tuum et labia tua,
et accipiat Dominus hoc sacrificium de manibus tuis digne pro
peccatis et offensionibus nostris.*

A response of the people is found no more than five times in
Scandinavian liturgical books, with several variants. In addition
to the two Nidaros MSS., it appears about 1198 in Sweden:
Spiritus Sanctus superveniet. The words form the response in the
old missal of Fécamp, and they are found also at Beauvais and in
the Sarum MSS. of the 14th century.[1] The missal of Straengness
has a form which seems to have been previously unknown:
Acceptare dignetur Dominus sacrificium tuum et nostrum.

A number of versicles are found in the books of the province
of Upsala, but they appear to have been adopted late.

The salutation before the secret was admitted by the bishop of
Skalholt, John Sigurd, in the synod of 1345: *crastino Jacobi
apostoli i Scalhollti—ante secretam in missa cum nulla voce.*

Preface

A statute, prescribed by Magnus Gissurasson, bishop of Skalholt, on the occasion of a liturgical reform in 1224, directed that
no more than ten prefaces should be admitted in the missal, which
seems to suggest that a larger number had existed at one time in
the Icelandic Church. An additional preface, *alia de Apostolis*, is
found in MS. B.[2]

Canon

As we have seen, the third of the Nidaros MS. ordinaries is defective until the *Sanctus.* This MS.D. as it is called, is probably
the earliest of the three, dating from about 1200, and depicting
the liturgy of the second half of the 12th century.

The silent canon is attributed in an Icelandic document of
1500 to our Lord's injunction: 'Pray to thy Father in secret.'[3]

The T initial of *Te igitur* in the printed missal takes the form
of a crucifix, with the Blessed Virgin and St. John in attendance.
The canon in the Church of Norway, apart from a short inser-

---

[1] Jungmann, *op. cit.*, t. II, pp. 366–7, n. 37.
[2] MS. NY. kgl. S. 133f, fo. 5r.   [3] *Matt.* VI, 6.

tion in the *Communicantes* and a divergence of rubrics, is virtually identical with the canon in our Roman missal.

The insertion in question is found in the missal and, in a variant form, in MS. B.

Missal: *Et eorum quorum hodie gloriosus celebratur triumphus, et omnium sanctorum.* The form in the missal, as Mr. Hohler says, is 'quite evidently French in origin'. It is found at Chartres, Rouen (St. Ouen), Chezal-Benoît, Langres (?) and St. Stephen's Caen.

MS. B: *nec non et illorum quorum hodie sollempnis in conspectu glorie tue celebratur triumphus, et omnium sanctorum.* This form is found in many missals in the Middle Ages, e.g. York, and is the more usual one. It may well also have originally come from France.

The purpose of such an insertion was to satisfy the local desire to include the commemoration of saints unspecified in the official text of the canon without any further extension of the list. Such a device had been approved by Pope Gregory III (731–41) for the monks of an oratory, dedicated to All Saints, adjoining the basilica of St. Peter, which was exceptionally rich in relics.[1]

In the *Communicantes* also, the Nidaros missal has a seemingly inexplicable alteration in the text. The name of St. Sylvester has been substituted for that of St. Xystus. Why? We can do no more than suggest with Dr. Faehn that the change was occasioned by a faulty reading of the *De Sacro Altaris Mysterio* of Pope Innocent III (1198–1216).[2] The passage is entitled: 'Why confessors are not commemorated in the canon.' 'A probable answer to this question', says the Pope, 'lies in the fact that the canon was edited at a time before it was customary for the Church to celebrate the memory of confessors. Nearly all the saints commemorated in the canon preceded Sylvester, with the exception of John and Paul, Marcellinus and Peter, who followed him very closely. The Church, however, after the time of blessed Sylvester

---

[1] The Pope approved the additional words: *sed et diem natalitium celebrantes sanctorum tuorum martyrum ac confessorum, perfectorum justorum, quorum sollemnitas hodie in conspectu gloriae tuae celebratur, quorum meritis precibusque.* . . . Duchesne, *Lib. Pont.*, t. I, p. 422. Walafrid Strabo (*De exord. et increm.*, cap. XXII) cites this, with the amplification: . . . *celebratur, Domine, Deus noster, toto in orbe terrarum.* Hittorp, *op. cit.*, col. 684; *Pat. Lat.*, t. CXIV, col. 950. Cf. *Ord. Rom.* IV; *Pat. Lat.*, t. LXXVIII, col. 1380.

[2] Faehn, *Fire Norske Messeordninger fra Middelalderen*, pp. 83–4.

began to venerate the memory of holy confessors. . . . There is a tradition, moreover, that Pope Gelasius was the principal editor of the canon.' [1] Is it possible that the cathedral church of Nidaros had a relic of St. Sylvester? We know that the eastern chapel of the south transept was consecrated in honour of SS. John the Baptist, Vincent and Sylvester by Archbishop Eystein in 1161. The consecration is recorded in a Latin inscription on a moulding under the window.

It is interesting to note that a statue of Magnus Gissurasson, bishop of Skalholt (1224), says *skal syngia communicantes (debet canere Communicantes)*, which seems to suggest that in 13th-century Iceland the canon, or at least a part of it, was said in a somewhat louder voice than elsewhere. The direction was omitted in the later MS. copies of the statutes.[2]

The same statutes, also, lay down the number of variants permissible for the *Communicantes* and *Hanc igitur*: they are the same as we find in the missal today. The injunction, as in the case of the prefaces, leads one to suppose that a larger number had been customary, at any rate in some churches.

A study of the rubrics of the canon in MSS. B and D makes it clear that the compilers were greatly beholden to the *Micrologus*. In B, for example, we find the fanciful symbolism for the raising of the voice at *Nobis quoque peccatoribus* reproduced *verbatim: Hic exaltat vocem centurionem illum designat, qui visa morte Christi filius Dei erat iste.*[3] Similarly, imaginary reasons are given for the five crosses made with the Host over the Chalice,[4] and also for the taking up and putting down of the *oblata.*[5] A further agreement between the Nidaros MS. (B) and the *Micrologus* is to be found in the embolism after the *Pater noster*, in which the priest is permitted to insert the names of saints other than those in the text: *Hic quantalibet sanctorum nomina internumerare potest.*[6]

---

[1] Innoc. III, *De Sac. Alt. Myst.*, lib. III, cap. X; *Pat. Lat.*, t. CCXVII, col. 849.

[2] *Diplom. Islandicum*, 2, n. 1.

[3] *Microl.*, cap. XVII; Hittorp, *op. cit.*, col. 741.

[4] *Hic vero cum corpore dominico quatuor cruces super calicem faciat et quinta crux in latere calicis vulnus dominici lateris significat.* Cf. *Microl., Ibid.*

[5] *Corpus cum calice levamus et statim in altari posita. Cooperimus quia Joseph corpus dominicum de cruce levavit, et in sepulchro operuit.* Cf. *Microl., Ibid.*

[6] *Hic nominat quotquot sanctos voluerit. Microl.*, cap. XXIII; Hittorp, *op. cit.*, col. 746.

MS. D is also beholden to the *Micrologus*, as is evident from an examination of the two documents.

It has been suggested by Dr. Faehn that MS. D 'exhibits close relationship to Irish and especially old Roman tradition'.[1] It is, however, difficult to see wherein the Irish relationship lies, as the Missal of Stowe is without rubrics. There are certain affinities in spelling, although these would hardly seem to prove very much: *Et omnium circum astantium;* [2] *Simile modo posteaquam;* [3] *nos tui servi.*[3]

The canon in MS. C has no rubrics.

Distinctive rubrics, directing the priest to remember the living and the dead in his prayers, are found in the missal and also in MSS. B and D.

Missal: Before the memento of the living: *Petitio secunda pro fratribus spiritualibus.* Before the words *et omnium circumstantium: Hic faciat memoriam recommendatorum, sed non longam quia periculosa forte erit.* Before the *Communicantes: Petitio tertia pro sacerdotibus et ministris.* At the memento of the dead: *Petitio quarta pro universis fidelibus defunctis in qua due orationes dicuntur* and *Hic meditandum est pro familiaribus amicis defunctis.*

MS. B: For the living—*Hic commemorationem faciat fidelium vivorum sed non die dominica.* For the dead—*Hic recitentur nomina. . . . Hic agenda est commemoratio mortuorum qui in morte Christi redempti sunt.*

MS. D: For the living—*Oratio pro animabus vivorum quorum* (?). For the dead—*Hic recitantur nomina defunctorum quibus recita (ndum est).*

At *Hanc igitur,* the missal and MSS. B and D direct the priest to 'incline before the altar'. There is no reference to a spreading of the hands over the *oblata.*

A rubric in the missal, before the consecration in the recital of the Institution, says: *Hic accipiat panem in manus: et sursum erigat visum absque mora.*

---

[1] Faehn, *op. cit.,* p. 130.
[2] Stowe, *H.B.S.,* vol. XXXII, p. 11. Cf. Nidaros missal and MS. B.
[3] *Ibid.,* p. 13.

It is uncertain when the elevation of the Host was first pre-scribed in the Norwegian Church. We know, however, that the custom existed in Iceland in 1269, and that it was received from Nidaros.[1] It would seem probable that it was then a comparatively new custom in Norway. The provincial council, held at Nidaros under Archbishop Jørund in 1290, ordered priests to give in-struction to the people that they should adore the Body and Blood of Christ at the elevation, and also when it was being carried to the sick in their homes. If it was out of doors, the faithful were bidden to uncover, kneel and raise their hands.[1]

There is no evidence in Norway of that extra-liturgical cultus of the Blessed Sacrament, with adoration of the Host in the monstrance, that was customary in North Germany in the latter part of the Middle Ages.

A short rubric prescribes the elevation of the Host and Chalice, but there is no injunction respecting adoration, such as we find in the missal of Upsala [2] (1513): *Hic Hostia levetur et reponatur; Hic Calicem levat et postmodum reponat et cooperiat.*

At *Unde et memores: Hic extendat brachia in modum crucis sur-sum elevata.*

The size and the manner of tracing the signs of the cross in the final doxology of the canon are influenced by the somewhat fanciful Christological and Trinitarian interpretations. We may see this clearly enough from the lengthy rubrics in the Nidaros and Upsala missals.

The ceremonies prescribed in the embolism following the *Pater noster* were slightly different from present day usage: The paten was kissed at *propitius*; a sign of the cross made with the paten above the head (*supra caput*) at *pacem in diebus nostris*; the breast touched with the paten in the form of a cross at *adjuti*; and the eyes touched with the paten at *liberi*. Finally, after the word *securi*, the paten was laid at the foot of the chalice, which was then uncovered.

---

[1] *Diplom. Island.*, 2 nr. 7, p. 24; Faehn, *Gudstjenestelivet I Nidaros Domkirke . . .*, p. 615.

[2] Upsala (1513): *Hic levet Corpus Christi in altum ad adorandum; Hic levetur Calix cum Sanguine ad adorandum.*

Pax Domini, Agnus Dei and Commixture

The embolism is followed by *Pax + Domini sit + semper vobi + scum, Agnus Dei* and commixture.

The pontifical blessing before Communion would seem to have been customary at Lund and Åbo, but we have no evidence in respect to Nidaros.[1]

Various traditions are found in Scandinavia regarding the *Agnus* and commixture. In the provinces of Nidaros and Upsala, the *Agnus Dei* preceded *Haec sacrosancta*; while in the province of Lund the contrary obtained. The former custom was usual in England and France: the latter throughout the Continent, with the exception of France, and with the variant reading: *Fiat haec.*[1] Arno Thorlac, bishop of Skalholt, in 1292 directed that the *Agnus* should be said or sung three times after *Pax Domini*, 'as is now said in the archiepiscopal Church of Nidaros' (*sicut nunc dicitur in ecclesia archiepiscopali Nidrosiensi*). It is clear from this that some sort of liturgical reform had taken place at Nidaros, the results of which are known, but it is not possible to say what rites and ceremonies had existed previously. The reform seems to have begun about the year 1290, the year in which the bishop of Skalholt had visited Norway.

The formula for the commixture: *Haec sacrosancta commixtio*, is found in the missal, as well as in MSS. B and C. The form in the 1519 book is similar to what we find in the Dominican, Sarum and York uses:[2] the texts in the MSS. are variants.

It dates from at least the 9th century, and occurs in the Sacramentary of Amiens.

Missal: *Hec sacrosancta commixtio et consecratio corporis et sanguinis Domini nostri Jesu Christi fiat mihi et omnibus sumentibus salus mentis et corporis et ad vitam eternam promerendam et capescendam sit preparatio salutaris. Amen.*[3]

MS. B: *Hec sacrosancta commixtio corporis et sanguinis Domini Jhesu Christi prosit mihi ad remedium sempiternum in vitam eternam. Amen.*

---

[1] Segelberg, *op. cit.*, p. 257.   [2] Maskell, *op. cit.*, p. 114.
[3] Cf. Upsala (1513) and Lund (1514), omitting *et consecratio*.

MS. C: The formula is identical with the one in the missal, except for the omission of *et capescendam*. The MS. has also an alternative formula, which is found in the *Ordines Romani*[1] and the *Micrologus:*[2] *Fiat commixtio et consecratio corporis et sanguinis Domini nostri Jhesu Christi accipientibus nobis in vitam eternam. Amen.*

MS. D: *Fiat commixtio* only.

Kiss of Peace

The idea of a kiss of peace has a definitely Oriental flavour. The introduction to the confession of faith in the Byzantine rite says: Ἀγαπήσωμεν ἀλλήλους.[3] The idea is made clear in the *Interpretatio Officiorum* of the 8th-century Nestorian writer, Abraham bar Lipheh, edited by Hugh Connolly: 'Give the pax one to the other in the love of Christ', that is 'show your mutual peace in deed, and eradicate enmity from your hearts, that you may be worthy to receive the life-giving mysteries.'[4]

Before the kiss of peace, the missal gives the prayer: *Domine Jesu Christe qui dixisti apostolis tuis*. A slight variation is found between the missal and MS. C, on the one hand, and MS. B, on the other. In the former: *peccata mea sed fidem sancte ecclesie tue catholice;* in the latter: *peccata mea sed fidem ecclesie tue*. The prayer is said to have originated in Germany about the beginning of the 11th century.[5] It was omitted in Masses for the dead and on Holy Thursday (*in die cene Domini*), when the kiss of peace was not given.

About the year 1500, especially in Northern countries, we find it customary for the priest to kiss both missal and paten before giving the *pax*. A contract between the archbishop of Upsala and the printer, dated 23 February 1508, stipulated that the missal should have *una crux in margine por osculo circa Agnus Dei*.[6] Thus we find a rubric in the Upsala missal of 1513: *Hic osculetur librum*

---

[1] *Ord. Rom.* I, 19 (*Pat. Lat.*, t. LXXVIII, col. 946); *Ord. Rom.* II, 13 (*Pat. Lat.*, t. LXXVIII, col. 975).

[2] *Microl.*, cap. XXIII; Hittorp, *op. cit.*, col. 746.

[3] Brightman, *Lit. East. and West.*, p. 382.

[4] Hanssens, *Liturg. de Rit. Orient.*, t. III, part 2, cap. XI, p. 328.

[5] Jungmann, *op. cit.*, t. III, chap. III, 6, p. 258.

[6] J. Freisen, *Man. Lincop.* (Paderborn, 1904), p. xlvi.

et patenam, et det pacem ministro. At Nidaros, the book and the altar, but not the paten, are kissed at the conclusion of the prayer (*Domine Jesu Christe*), as the priest says: *Pax Christi et sancte matris ecclesie abundet semper in cordibus nostris.* Then, having kissed the 'sacrament of the Body and Blood', he continues: *per Spiritum Sanctum qui datus est nobis.* The *pax* was given with the formula: *Pax tecum,* to which the minister responded. The priest added: *Habete vinculum pacis et caritatis ut apti sitis misteriis sacrosanctis: per Christum Dominum nostrum. Amen.* This is the form in the missal of 1519.[1]

MS. B. says: When the pax is given, the priest says: '*Habete vinculum pacis*', etc., with the 'reply of the recipient': *Pax Christi et ecclesie habundet (sic) in cordibus vestris. Amen. Pax Christi,* however, is not strictly speaking a response to *Habete vinculum.*

MS. C begins the ceremony of the *pax* with this formula, substituting *nostris* for *vestris. Pax tecum* and *Habete vinculum* follow.

MS. D merely directs the altar to be kissed, with the formula: *Pax tecum,* and its response: *Et cum spiritu tuo.*

Habete vinculum pacis et caritatis was not only in use throughout Scandinavia, but we find it also in the Eastern parts of Germany, the Rhenish provinces and France.[2] It occurs in the uses of York and Hereford,[3] as well as in the Sarum ordinary of the 13th century.[4]

Archbishops of Nidaros in 1346 and 1395 alluded to the kiss of peace in their pastoral letters, and warned the faithful against imitating the 'kiss of Judas'.

Communion Prayers

The first of the Communion prayers in the missal is found also in MSS. B and C: *Domine sancte Pater omnipotens eterne Deus: da mihi hoc corpus et sanguinem Filii tui Domini nostri Jesu Christi ita digne sumere, ut merear per hoc remissionem omnium peccatorum*

---

[1] Cf. Upsala (1513) and Lund (1514).
[2] Segelberg, *op. cit.*, p. 257.
[3] Maskell, *op. cit.*, pp. 116, 117.
[4] Crawford MS.; *Tracts on the Mass*, edit. Wickham Legg. *Henry Bradshaw Society*, vol. XXVII (London, 1904), p. 226.

G G

meorum accipere, et tuo sancto Spiritu repleri, quia tu es Deus solus et praeter te non est alius, cujus regnum et imperium sine fine permanet in secula seculorum. Amen. The text in MS. C is identical with that of the missal, except for the absence of *solus* after *Deus*, and the additional word *gloriosum* after *regnum et imperium sine fine*. The variant in MS. B has the single word *tuum* in place of *Filii tui Domini nostri Jesu Christi*, and a somewhat shorter ending: *Deus benedictus in secula seculorum.* A similar prayer is found in the Upsala (1513) and Lund (1514) missals. We find it also in the Sarum missal, where it was directed to be said *before* the kiss of peace. The prayer seems to have appeared first in the sacramentaries of Fulda and Tours. MS. B has a second Communion prayer, unknown to the other Norwegian ordinaries: *Concede, Domine Ihesu Christe, ut sicut hec sacramenta corporis et sanguinis tui, tuis fidelibus contulisti, ita mihi indigno famulo tuo et omnibus per me sumentibus hec ipsa misteria obsint ad reatum, sed prosint ad veniam omnium peccatorum meorum. Per Christum.* It is found in the rite of the fraction in a Gregorian sacramentary of about the middle of the 11th century (1050–90), probably written for the Benedictine church of S. Abbondio outside the walls of Como, but in the possession of the church of S. Antonio, similarly situated, in the 13th century.[1]

The prayer *Domine Jesu Christe Fili Dei vivi*, the most general of the Communion prayers, and appearing today in our missal, is found in the Nidaros missal and in all three MSS. The variations in the several ordinaries are slight. In MS. D it is the sole Communion prayer. We find it in the sacramentaries of Amiens and Mans, both of the 9th century.

Communion

Salutations to the Blessed Sacrament before Communion do not appear to have been in use in the province of Nidaros, but they were common in the Swedish province of Upsala at the beginning of the 15th century, and they are found in the diocese of

---

[1] Bodleian Library, Oxford, MS. Lat. Liturg. d. 4 (J. C. 31535). The Keeper of Western MSS. in the Library tells me that an inscription explicitly states that the MS. came to the church of S. Antonio in the 13th century.

Åbo (Finland) at the end of the 14th century. They were, however, absent from the cathedral church of Upsala, which maintained the ancient tradition. The salutations in Swedish missals
included: *Ave, caro Christi sanctissima; Ave in aeternum, sanctissima caro Christi; Ave, coelestis potus.*[1]

Additional prayers for Communion are found in the printed
Nidaros missal: *Panem celestem accipiam et nomen Domini in-
vocabo*, which is preceded by a rubric: *Accipiat patenam inter
manus in qua locatum est Corpus Domini. Domine non sum dignus*
is said three times, after which the priest signs himself with the
paten, and says: *Corpus Domini nostri Jesu Christi custodiat animam
meam in vitam eternam. Amen.* Segelberg suggests that *Domine
non sum dignus* was first introduced into Scandinavia about the
year 1400: often in an elaborated form. *Et propitius esto* only
appears in the Church of Linköping.[2] An example of the elaborated form is found in the missal of Lund (1514): *Domine Jesu
Christe non sum dignus propter multitudinem peccatorum meorum ut
intres sub tectum meum, sed tantum dic verbo et sanabitur anima mea.*
The prayer is repeated before receiving the chalice.

At the conclusion of the prayer *Corpus Domini nostri*, the priest
receives the Host. Then, raising the chalice, he says: *Quid retri-
buam*, and signing himself with the chalice: *Sanguis Domini nostri
Jesu Christi custodiat animam meam in vitam eternam. Amen.*

The three MSS. date from a time before the introduction of
these additional prayers before Communion.

MS. B: *Corpus et sanguis Domini nostri Jhesu Christi prosit mihi
in vitam eternam. Amen.*

MS. C: *Corpus Domini nostri Jhesu Christi prosit mihi in remissionem peccatorum meorum et vitam eternam. Amen.*

*Corpus et sanguis Domini nostri Jhesu Christi prosit mihi in re-
missionem peccatorum meorum et in vitam eternam. Amen.*

MS. D: *Cum distribuit eucharistiam d(icit): Corpus et sanguis
Domini nostri Jhesu Christi custodiat me vel te in vitam eternam.
Amen. Postquam omnes communica(nt).* This is the sole ordinary
that mentions the Communion of the faithful.

---

[1] Segelberg, *op. cit.*, p. 258. A saluation of a somewhat similar character is found in the
Sarum missal. Maskell, *op. cit.*, p. 122.   [2] Segelberg, *ibid.*

A single formula, combining a reference to both species, was the more ancient tradition. Åbo (Finland) adopted the Dominican formula, as for the greater part of the texts of the Mass, although another tradition existed in the diocese. An almost similar form obtained at Straengness, where it served as the first prayer *after* Communion: *Corpus et sanguis Domini nostri Jesu Christi custodiant corpus et animam meam in vitam eternam. Amen.* The two formulas for the administration at Straengness are not found in any other Scandinavian missal, but something similar is to be met with in the uses of York and Hereford: [1] *Corpus Domini nostri Jesu Christi sit mihi ad remedium salutare in vitam eternam. Amen.*

Sanguis Domini nostri Jesu Christi prosit mihi ad remissionem omnium peccatorum et perducat me ad vitam eternam. Amen.

MS. C supplies the form for administering Holy Communion to the sick in the 13th century: The priest, taking the Host from the paten, says: *Ecce, frater, Corpus Domini nostri Jesu Christi, quoad tibi deferimus credis hoc esse in quo est salus, vita et resurrectio nostra.* The sick man answers: *Credo.* The *Confiteor, Misereatur,* and *Indulgentiam* follow. The Blessed Sacrament is given with the formula: *Corpus Domini nostri Jesu Christi prosit tibi in remissionem omnium peccatorum et in vitam eternam. Amen.* [2]

Ablutions and Prayers after Communion

The missal (1519) prescribes two prayers after Communion: the same as in the Roman missal today, but in the reverse order. *Corpus tuum, Domine, quod sumpsi et sanguis quem potavi adhereat semper in visceribus meis: et presta ut in me non remaneat scelerum macula quem pura et sancta refecerunt sacramenta. Qui vivis et regnas cum Deo Patri in unitate Spiritus Sancti. Per omnia secula seculorum. Amen.*

The second prayer is said after the priest has rinsed his fingers and consumed the ablution: *Quod ore sumpsimus, Domine, pura mente capiamus et de munere temporali fiat nobis remedium sempi-*

---

[1] Maskell, *op. cit.*, pp. 122, 123, 124, 125.
[2] Royal Library, Copenhagen, MS. Thott 110, fols. 11r, v.

ternum. Amen. A washing of the hands follows, during which the celebrant recites the *Nunc dimittis.*

No further reference to the ablutions is forthcoming from the missal, and the MSS. make no mention of them.

The missal of Linköping prescribes the psalm *Lavabo* to be said at the ablutions, not at the offertory. The custom would seem to have been introduced there towards the end of the 14th century.[1] A seemingly unique prayer is found in the Schleswig missal: *Ablutio corporis et sanguinis Domini nostri Jesu Christi proficiat mihi in vitam aeternam. Amen.*[1]

The three Nidaros MSS. give the prayer *Quod ore sumpsimus,* and MS. C has in addition *Corpus tuum, Domine,* in very nearly the same text as we find in the missal. Upsala (1513) has a variant of *Quod ore sumpsimus: ut de corpore et sanguine Domini nostri Jesu Christi,* in place of *de munere temporali.*[2] The two prayers appear in the missal of Lund (1514): *Quod ore sumpsimus* is said as the priest rinses his fingers over the chalice.

The same missal gives also *O sacrum convivium,* a versicle and response,[3] and two further prayers: *Deus qui nobis sub sacramento mirabili* and *Purificent nos, quaesumus.*[4] The second of these prayers is found in this place in the missal of Roskilde, and as a prayer at the conclusion of Mass in the *ordinarius* of Constance (1557). In the Gelasian and Gregorian sacramentaries the prayer has rather the character of a postcommunion.

The canticle or versicle *Benedicta tu a Domino* seems peculiar to the missal of Schleswig. A Sarum ordinary of the 13th century (Crawford missal) has, however, something similar, directed to be said at the ablutions: *Benedicta a filio tuo Domina quia per te fructum vite communicavimus.*[5]

A third prayer after Communion is prescribed in the missal

---

[1] Segelberg, *op. cit.,* p. 259.

[2] Yelverton, *Mass in Sweden,* p. 21; Jungmann, *op. cit.,* t. III, p. 336, n. 2.

[3] *Panem celi dedit eis. Panem angelorum manducavit homo.*

[4] *Purificent nos, quaesumus omnipotens et misericors Deus, sacramenta quae sumpsimus et presta ut hoc tuum sacramentum non sit nobis reatus ad penam sed intercessio salutaris ad veniam, sit ablutio scelerum, sit fortitudo fragilium, sit contra mundi pericula firmamentum, sit vivorum atque mortuorum fidelium remissio omnium delictorum. Per Christum.*

[5] *Tracts on the Mass,* edit. Wickham Legg, *Henry Bradshaw Society,* vol. XXVII (London, 1904), p. 228.

of Straengness: *Conservent*. It has been taken from a Gregorian
sacramentary, in which we find *Quod ore* as the first prayer, and
Conservent as the second.

Antiphons and hymns, which were said in a low voice by the
priest after Communion, are found in seven Scandinavian missals,
but not in that of Nidaros. They would seem to have been introduced into the Mass some time before the last period of the Middle
Ages. The more usual type appears in the Lund missal, which
has been already considered.

At Straengness (1487) and Skara (1498), *O sacrum convivium*
was preceded by twenty strophes of the hymn *Jesu nostra redemptio*.

O salutaris hostia was introduced into the Mass at Linköping
about the year 1450. *Jesu nostra refectio*, a more ancient usage
than *O sacrum convivium*, appeared in the diocese of Åbo about
1400. Outside the confines of Scandinavia, *O sacrum convivium*
is found in a missal of Lubeck, and *Jesu nostra redemptio vel Deus
qui nobis* in a missal of Trier: *dum corporale et calicem componit*.

Conclusion of the Mass

The ordinary of the Mass in MS. D gives the texts of a communion and postcommunion, which are, in fact, those given for
Trinity Sunday in our missal: *Benedicimus Deum celi et coram
omnibus viventibus confitebimur ei quia fecit nobiscum misericordiam
suam. Proficiat nobis ad salutem corporis et anime, Domine Deus,
hujus sacramenti susceptio, et sempiterna sancte Trinitatis ejusdem-
que individue unitatis confessio. Per.*

Scandinavian missals speak of postcommunions as *complenda*.

In these Northern countries, the diaconal monition before the
oratio super populum was *Inclinate capita vestra Deo*, in place of
the formula customary today: *Humiliate capita vestra Deo*. It was
used throughout Scandinavia, except in the diocese of Upsala and
the missal of Åbo, where we find the form employed on the Continent—Germany, Hungary, etc. In the Latin Church, *Humiliate*
appears first in *Ordo Romanus I*,[1] and it was very general in France
and England. The difference in the word may be due to two

---

[1] *O.R.I*, 24: *Pat. Lat.*, t. LXXVIII, col. 949.

mutually independent translations from the Greek: τὰς κεφαλάς ὑμῶν τῷ κυρίῳ κλίνατε. The Greek formula is found also in the Coptic liturgy of St. Mark.[1] *Inclinate* is the literal translation, whereas *Humiliate* gives rather its metaphorical significance. It is possible that *Inclinate* was the original Roman form, and it is certainly the more ancient in Latin. We find it in Commodianus, pseudo-Augustine (sermons), and the Passion of Firmus and Rusticus.[2]

The dismissal—*Ite missa est*—is noted in the missal, but the MSS. make no reference to it.

The rubrics of the three MSS. make it clear that the *Placeat*, which follows, was originally a prayer said *after* Mass, rather than a final prayer *of* the Mass. MS. B: *Finita missa inclinet se ante altare et dicat;* MS. C: *Post missam oratio;*[3] MS. D: *Finit(ur).* *Placeat tibi, sancta Trinitas, obsequium servitutis mee: et presta, ut hoc sacrificium quod oculis tue majestatis ego indignus obtuli tibi sit acceptabile mihique et omnibus pro quibus illud obtuli sit te miser-- ante propiciabile: hic et in vitam eternam. In qua vivis et regnas Deus. Per omnia secula seculorum. Amen.* The variations in the four texts are slight and of little importance.

Versicles precede the final blessing in the missals of Lund, Hafnia and Linköping. At Lund, they appear, together with the rest of the Mass, in a different type: *Adjutorium nostrum (Qui fecit); Sit nomen Domini (Ex hoc nunc).*

The formula of blessing in the Nidaros missal is not found elsewhere in Scandinavia, although the form at Upsala (1513) was somewhat similar:[4] *Benedicat vos divina majestas, Pa+ ter et Fi+ lius et Spiritus + Sanctus. Amen.*

The three signs of the cross, which today are reserved to prelates, were common to all priests in Scandinavia in the later Middle Ages.[5] Lund and Roskilde had as many as four signs of the cross. A rubric in the missal of Roskilde says: *Signat pectus cum pollice dexterae manus per modum crucis, et dat benedictionem dicens.*

The most general formula of blessing in the Scandinavian

---

[1] Brightman, *op. cit.*, p. 186.   [2] Segelberg, *op. cit.*, pp. 259–60.

[3] Cf. Upsala (1513).

[4] *Benedicat vos omnipotens Deus Pater, + Fi + lius, Spiritus + Sanctus. Amen.*

[5] The practice was not confined to Scandinavia.

liturgical books, which we find at Lund, Roskilde, Upsala, Straengness and Linköping, was apparently unknown before 1400, and was probably introduced from Germany: *Oremus. Celesti benedictione: Bene+ dicat vos divina majestas Pa+ ter et Fi+ lius et Spiritus+ Sanctus. Amen.*[1] Outside Scandinavia, a similar formula was in use at Magdeburg, Trier (1607) and, about 1450, the abbey of Cismar in the province of Holstein.

The last gospel (*In principio*) would seem to have been rather of an exception in Scandinavia, but it is found in the missal of Nidaros (1519) as an integral part of the Mass. The priest, at its conclusion, says: *Per evangelica dicta deleantur nostra delicta. Amen.* This gospel occurs also in the breviary of Skara, *manuale Lincopense* and the missal of Lund (1514). At Lund it appears among the prayers *post missam.*[2]

Thanksgiving Prayers after Mass

The missal of Nidaros has three prayers after the last gospel, which appear to be included in the Mass itself, as after the third prayer we find the rubric: *Finita missa cum se sacerdos sacris vestibus exuit dicat hos psalmos sequentes cum Antiphona Trium puerorum.*

The first of these prayers, which is taken from the Leonine sacramentary for the feast of Christmas, is found in our Roman missal at the blessing of the water: *Deus qui humane substantie dignitatem mirabiliter condidisti mirabilius reformasti: da nobis quesumus ejus divinitatis esse consortes: qui humanitatis nostre dignatus est fieri particeps Jesus Christus Dominus noster. Amen.*

The second prayer is the collect for the Third Sunday after Pentecost in our missal: *Protector noster in te sperantium Deus sine quo nihil est validum: nihil sanctum; multiplica super nos misericordiam tuam, ut te rectore: te duce: sic transeamus per bona temporalia, ut non amittamus eterna.*

The third is the collect for St. John the Evangelist (27 December): *Ecclesiam tuam, quesumus Domine, benignus illustra: ut beati*

---

[1] This form is found in the Lund missal of 1514.

[2] The following formulas are given after the blessing in the Lund missal: *Salve Regina, Da Pacem*, versicles, three prayers, the gospel *In principio*, four more prayers, and an additional form of blessing: *Jhesus Marie+ Filius sit clemens et propicietur.* Amen.

Joannis apostoli tui et evangeliste illuminata doctrinis ad dona per-veniat sempiterna. Per Dominum.

The rubric directs the priest to recite canticles, psalms, versicles and prayers while he unvests: *Trium puerorum, Benedicite sacer-dotes Domini Domino, Laudate Dominum in sanctis, Nunc dimittis, Ave Maria, Trium puerorum, Kyrie eleison, Pater noster*, versicles and two collects.

The first of these collects is a variant of a thanksgiving prayer in our missal: *Deus qui tribus pueris flammas ignium mitigasti: concede propicius ut per internos famulos tuos non exurat flamma viventum (sic) eorum et merita omnium sanctorum tuorum.*

The second has been said already at the conclusion of the pre-paratory prayers of the Mass, with the addition here of a com-memoration of the faithful departed: *Actiones nostras, quesumus Domine, aspirando preveni, et adjuvando prosequere, ut cuncta nostra operatio et oratio a te semper incipiat et per te incepta finiatur, et pacem tuam nostris concede temporibus. Et anime famulorum famu-larumque tuarum requiescant in perpetua pace. Per Dominum.* The form of thanksgiving in the missal ends with the salutation *Dominus vobiscum, Benedicamus Domino, Deo Gratias*, and a somewhat lengthy prayer: *Gratias ago immense majestati.* The prayer is similar to the one ascribed to St. Thomas Aquinas in our missal.

All three of the Nidaros MSS. give the hymn of the Three Children at the unvesting: B and C have also the psalm *Laudate Dominum, Kyrie, Pater* and versicles. The prayer *Deus qui tribus pueris* is found in all the MSS.: *Actiones nostras* in B and C, but not D. MS. C concludes, as in the missal, with the salutation, *Bene-dicamus Domino* and *Deo gratias*.

BIBLIOGRAPHY

1. *Breviarium Nidrosiense.* Paris, 1519.
2. *Cathedrals and Churches of Norway, Sweden and Denmark.* T. F. *Bumpus.* London, 1908.
3. *Cathedral of Nidaros*, A Guide to, Augustine *Albertsen.* Trondheim, 1946.
4. *Catholic Encyclopedia. Faröe Islands*, Pius *Wittmann*, vol. V. *Greenland*, Pius *Wittmann*, vol VI. *Iceland*, Pius *Wittmann*, vol. VII. *Norway*, Pius *Wittmann*, vol. XI. *Orkneys*, Pius *Wittmann*, vol. XI. *Sodor and Man*, Edwin *Burton*, vol. XIV. *Trondjhem*, Gustaf *Armfelt*, vol. XV.

5. *Chronica regum Manniae et Insularum* (2 vols.). P. A. *Munch. Manx Society.* Douglas, 1874.
6. *Faröe Islands.* J. *Russell-Jeaffreson.* London, 1898.
7. *Fire Norske Messeordninger fra Middelalderen.* Helge *Faehn.* Oslo, 1953.
8. *Gesta Hamburgensis Ecclesiae Pontificum. Adam of Bremen.* Hamburg, 1876.
9. *Gudstjenestelivet I Nidaros Domkirke I Middelalderen.* Helge *Faehn,* ap *Saertrykk av Nidaros Erkebispestol og Bispesete.* Oslo, 1953
10. *Heart of Norway* Frank Noel *Stagg.* London, 1952
11. *Heroic Age of Scandinavia.* G. *Turville-Petre.* London, 1951.
12. *History of the Church and State in Norway.* Thomas B. *Willson.*
13. *History of Orkney.* J. A. *Storer Clouston.* Kirkwall, 1932.
14. *History of St. Andrews* (2 vols.). C. J. *Lyon.* Edinburgh, 1843.
15. *Korsongen I Nidarosdomen.* Oluf *Kolsrud. Festskrift til O.M. Sandvik.* Oslo, 1945.
16. *Mass in Sweden.* E. E. *Yelverton. Henry Bradshaw Society,* vol. LVII. London, 1920.
17. *Micrologus* de Ecclesiasticis Observationibus. *De Divin. Cath. Eccles. Offic.* Melchior *Hittorp.* Cols. 733–66. Paris, 1610.
18. *Missal of Copenhagen Use (Hafniense Novum,* 1510). Four leaves. Brit. Mus., MS. C 110.1.4.
19. *Missale Lundense* (1514). Facsimile, Malmö, 1946.
20. *Missale Nidrosiense* (1519). Copenhagen.
21. *Missale Upsala* (1513). Basle.
22. *Missarum Sollemnia.* J. A. *Jungmann.* Tt. I (1950), II (1952), III (1954). Paris.
23. *North Norway.* F. N. *Stagg.* London, 1952.
24. *Norwegian Stave Churches.* Anders *Bugge* (trans. Ragner *Christopherson).* Oslo, 1953.
25. *Olav the King and Olav, King and Martyr.* J. F. *Vicary.* London, 1886.
26. *Olav, St. Butler's Lives of the Saints (Thurston),* vol. VII. July.
27. De *Ordine Missae secundum ritum Scandinavicum Medii Aevi.* Eric *Segelberg. Ephem. Liturg.,* vol. LXV (1951), fasc. IV.
28. *Passio et Miracula Beati Olavi.* Edit. F. *Metcalfe.* Oxford, 1881.
29. *Registrum Praediorum et Redituum ad Ecclesias Dioecesis Bergensis saeculo P.C. XIV pertinentium. Vulgo dictum 'Bergens Kalvskind.'* Edit. P. A. *Munch.* Christiania (Oslo), 1843.
30. *Relations between England and Scandinavia from 1066 until 1399 in History and Literature.* Henry Goddard *Leach. Proceedings of the American Academy of Arts and Sciences,* 1909.
31. The *Relics of St. Cuthbert.* Christopher *Hohler* and Others. Oxford, 1956.
32. *Saga of Saints.* Sigfrid *Unset.* London, 1934.
33. *St. Olafs Kirke 1000 Ar. Helligdomsarmen.* J. J. *Duin.* Oslo, 1956.
34. *Scottish Mediaeval Liturgical Books and Fragments.* David *McRoberts.* Glasgow, 1953.

INDEX

Aachen, 338
Aarhus, 419, 423, 424, 425, 442
Aarstad, 397
Aberdeen, use, 288–9; missal, 299, 300, 304, 306; brev., 236–7, 287, 289; St. Nicholas, 311
Ablutions, Sar. 323–4; York, 347; Heref., 369; Trond., 460–1
Åbo, 378; lit. 404, 430, 440, 454, 458–9, 460, 462
Abraham bar Lipheh, 456
Abruzzi, 52, 58
Absolom, abp. Lund, 434
Abundius, bp. Como, 24
Accendite, Heref. 357–8
Achad Fobuir, community, 234
Acoemetae, see Sleepless Ones
Adalwald, 20
Adam and Eve, book of, 229
Adam of Bremen, 376–7, 378, 410
Adam of Caithness, bp. Kirkwall, 390
Adamnan, ab Iona, 201, 202, 209, 236, 240, 243, 247, 248, 262, 265, 267, 270–1
Adelchis, 54
Admonitio Generalis, Charlemagne (789), 102, 104, 170
Adoptionism, 7, 9, 255–6, 259
Adrian I, Pope, 53, 103, 104
Adrian IV, Pope, *see* Nicholas Breakspear
Adso, ab. Montier en Der, 196
Advent, Aquil., 28; Gallic., 133–4
Aeduald, bp. Lichfield, 218–19
Aeduald, bp. Lindisfarne, 218
Africa, North, lit.,180
Agatho, Pope, 53
Agaunum, *see* St. Maurice
Agde, counc., (506), 95, 115, 150, 153, 183
Aghaboe, 247
Aghabulloge, 229
Agilulf, Lomb. k., 20
Agnello, ab. Blachernae, 30
Agnus Dei, Celt., 271, 272; Sar., 322 Trond., 455
Agrestius, Celt., monk, 197, 138, 252
Aghenny, cross, 214
Aidan, St., 193, 201, 327
Aidus, Celt., bp. 211
Aiguebelle, St. Cath., Savoy, 352–4
Aion, Benev. prince, 54
Aius, see Ajus
Aix en Provence, 111
Ajus, Gallic., 96, 153–4

Alaric, 95
Alban, St., 187, 228, 240, 280, 414
Albans, St., abbey, 187; missal, 299, 300, 303, 304–5, 306, 307, 352; scriptoria, 308
Alcuin, 103, 104, 116–17, 158, 159, 172, 236, 255–6, 259, 328, 438
Aldfrith, k. Northumb., 202
Aldhelm, bp. Sherborne, 186, 193, 239, 245
Alexander I, Pope, 345
Alexander II, Pope, 7
Alexander III, Pope, 12
Alexander IV, Pope, 22
Alexander VI, Pope, 391
Alexandria, I, 28, 29, 78, 108, 113, 134
Aljubarrota, 285
Alleluia, Gallic., 156, 167; Sar., 313, 319; York, 333; Heref., 351, 364; Trond., 442
Alleluia Victory, 188
Altar, Gallic., 114–15; Celt., 211; portable, Gallic., 195
Althing, Icel. parl., 376
Altinum, *see* Torcello
Amalarius of Metz, 147
Amalarius, pr. Tours, 149
Amalfi, 58
Amand, St., ordo; 249; liturg. family, 303, 304, 306, 326; missal, 304, 432
Amator, St., bp. Auxerre, 108
Amator, bp. Cividale, 8
Ambo, 17, 58–9, 112, 160
Ambrose, St., 4, 16, 24, 29, 34, 83, 121, 175; prayer of, 250–51, 264
Ambrosian rite, 24, 27, 28, 31, 32, 34, 35, 58, 63–5, 66, 159, 162, 170, 174, 179, 253, 262, 267, 272, 303, 311
Amelli, 27
Amelperge, abbess, 30
Amesbury, psalter, 295–96
Amiens, sacram., 438, 445, 455, 458
Analoen, pilgrim, 212
Anastasius IV, Pope, 381
Anastasius V, Jacob, pat., 138
Anatolius of Laodicea, 200
Andrews, St., 385, 390, 428, 434; register, 237; Univ. lib., 434–5
Angelo in Formis, S., 58
Angilbert, bp. Paris, 113
Anglia Sacra, Wharton, 350
Angus, Soliloquies, 242
Ani, Armenia, 212; St. Greg.,110
Anian, bp. Bangor, 326, 370, 371
Annadown, Ireland, bp., 349

467